# Managing Your School Counseling Program: K-12 Developmental Strategies Third Edition

by

**Joe Wittmer and Mary Ann Clark**

## With Original Contributions by:

| | | |
|---|---|---|
| Gail Adorno | Ellen Amatea | Bonnie Baker |
| Judy Bowers | Chari Campbell | Tom Clawson |
| Doris Coy | Marjorie Cuthbert | Harry Daniels |
| Susan Eubanks | Marie Faubert | Mary Flynt |
| Emiliano Gonzalez | William Goodman | Tom Harrison |
| Mary Hermann | Carlos Hernandez | Shifa Podikunju Hussain |
| Linda Kobylarz | Courtland Lee | Larry Loesch |
| Kristi McCaskill | Beverly O'Bryant | Laura Pedersen |
| Nancy Perry | James Pitts | Theodore Remley |
| Russell Sabella | Jennifer Sager | John Schmidt |
| Pat Schwallie-Giddis | Susan Sears | Sondra Smith-Adcock |
| Beverly Snyder | Rex Stockton | Carolyn Stone |
| Paul Toth | Angela Wagner | Cirecie West-Olatunji |
| JoAnna White | | |

Copyright ©2007
**Joe Wittmer and Mary Ann Clark**

Library of Congress Control Number 2006933146

ISBN 13:    978-1-930572-48-5
ISBN 10:    1-930572-48-4

Printing (Last Digit)

10    9    8    7    6    5    4    3    2

Publisher—

**Educational Media Corporation®**
PO Box 21311
Minneapolis, MN 55421-0311
(763) 781-0088 or (800)-966-3382

http://www.**educationalmedia**.com


*Production editor—*
**Don L. Sorenson, Ph.D.**


*Graphic design—*
**Earl R. Sorenson**

# Dedication

*This book is dedicated to the two very important women in my life; my wife Sue, a retired high school counselor, and to our daughter Diane, a high school counselor and counselor educator.*

*Joe Wittmer*

*This book is dedicated to my husband, John, whose support for my work has been so important, and for my son, Chris, who inspires me and reminds me every day of the importance of caring and dedicated educators.*

*Mary Ann Clark*

# References and Acknowledgments:

A very special thanks to each of the writers who contributed to this book. A special thanks also to the American School Counselor Association (ASCA) for permission to quote from, and/or reprint, several of their publications. In addition, our appreciation and special thanks is extended to Carolyn Skinner and Erin Oakley for their editoral assistance.

Every effort has been made to give proper acknowledgment to all those who have contributed to this book. Any omissions or errors are regretted and, upon notification, will be corrected in subsequent editions.

# The Authors

**Joe Wittmer, Ph.D.**, Distinguished Professor Emeritus of Counselor Education at the University of Florida, Gainesville, has been a teacher and a school counselor. He has often served as a consultant to school systems desiring to implement comprehensive, developmental school counseling programs. Dr. Wittmer has written more than 75 professional journal articles and has authored or co-authored 14 books.

**Mary Ann Clark, Ph.D.**, is an Associate Professor and School Counseling Program Coordinator in the Department of Counselor Education at the University of Florida. She has been a school counselor and administrator in stateside and overseas school settings.

Dr. Clark has published numerous journal articles and book chapters, and co-authored *Teaching Children to Respect and Care for Others* with Joe Wittmer.

# Preface

Although six new chapters have been added to update this book, the objectives of the third edition remain the same as that of the first two editions—to provide the reader an overview and a general understanding of (a) the historical perspectives and current activities of K-12 developmental school counselors, (b) their role and function, (c) techniques and strategies utilized by effective developmental school counselors, (d) the organization and management of developmental counseling programs, (e) current issues and trends in the field, and (f) additional topics of interest to school counselors and school counselors-to-be.

Additionally, we examine the numerous issues that have produced major changes in American life in general, and schools specifically, since the last edition was published. Consider the impact of the following on the school counseling field:

- The development of the National Model: A Framework for School Counseling Programs

- The influence of the Education Trust's *Transforming School Counseling*

- Legislation such as *No Child Left Behind* (2001) and *Individuals with Disabilities Education Improvement Act* (2004)

- The impact of mandated high stakes testing

- The academic achievement gap and providing access and opportunities to all students

- An increased emphasis on accountability and the use of data in program planning

- Revised ethical standards

- An increased emphasis on partnerships and outreach between universities and schools

- The changing role and influence of technology

- An evolving vision of the role of school counselors to include leadership, advocacy and systemic change efforts

- An increased threat of terrorism since September 11, 2001

- Castastrophic events such as the hurricanes that have devastated the southeast

This book is intended as a basic graduate level text for counselor education students training to become school counselors. Additionally, practicing school counselors will find the book helpful since it aims at the implementation and the management of the major concepts and practices of contemporary, comprehensive K-12 developmental school counselors.

Interest in the developmental approach to school counseling has stood the test of time and is perceived as being an essential part of a total school program. Thus, this book will also be useful in acquainting administrators, curriculum directors, teachers, and others with the scope of developmental, comprehensive counseling. Guidance supervisors who are interested in new approaches and strategies for implementing and managing a K-12 developmental school counseling program will also find the book helpful.

The book is divided into seven (7) sections. In the first section, we begin with a brief history of school counseling followed by the reconceptionalization of the school counseling movement. The training and the competencies needed by the developmental K-12 school counselor are also presented, including a description of the CACREP standards of training as related to school counselor preparation. In addition, guidelines for beginning the implementation of a comprehensive, developmental guidance program are given along with a model for changing an existing program into a comprehensive, developmental one, using the American School Counselor Association's National Model: A Framework for School Counseling Programs. Section I includes the examination of the role and function of a K-12 developmental school counselor as viewed by various school systems, state departments of education, practicing counselors, and experts in the counseling field.

Section II, written by school counseling practitioners and/or counselor educators, is concerned with managing a developmental counseling program. More specifically, the roles and the functions of the contemporary elementary, middle, and high school counselor are presented.

Section III is a continuation of the role of the developmental school counselor as it concerns individual and small group counseling, and large group guidance.

Educational Media Corporation®, Box 21311, Minneapolis, MN 55421-0311

Section IV concerns the counselor's role in working with diversity issues, including sexual orientation, counseling with special needs students, and student victims of abuse.

Section V focuses on the developmental counselor as consultant and as coordinator of the career, appraisal, and educational aspects of the counseling program. In addition, a chapter addressing the school counselor/consultant and the family is included in this section.

Section VI is devoted to strategies for involving peers, parents, teachers, and other professionals in the developmental school counseling program, including character education. A chapter on the Transformed School Counselor describes the evolving role of the counselor. Section VII, the final section of the book, focuses on special topics that are of concern to today's developmental school counselors. More specifically, original chapters concerning school counselor credentialing, ethical and legal issues, accountability, technology, public relations, and the counselor's professional image are presented. The culminating chapter looks to the future of school counseling.

In the introduction to each section, we have attempted to briefly present the background for, and the theme of, that particular section. Each contributor to the book wrote his/her chapter(s) *specifically* for this book. This is to acknowledge our heartfelt thanks to all of the authors for revising and updating their respective contributions. Without them this book would not have been possible.

*Joe Wittmer and Mary Ann Clark*
January 2007

# Contents

# Section I

# Developmental School Counseling: History, Reconceptionalization, and Implementation Strategies

In the first section of this book, we begin with a brief history of school counseling followed by a description of the dramatic reconceptionalization movement that has occurred in school counseling during the past three decades. Next, the training and competencies needed by the developmental K-12 school counselor are presented along with a description of the CACREP standards that apply to school counselor training and preparation. In chapter 2, guidelines for implementing a comprehensive, developmental K-12 school counseling program are presented. Section I also includes the suggested role and function of a K-12 developmental school counselor as viewed by experts in the field. Chapter three introduces the American School Counselor Association (ASCA) National Model: A Framework for School Counseling Programs by one of its co-authors, Dr. Judy Bowers, who is the Past President of ASCA.

*Joe Wittmer and Mary Ann Clark*

# Chapter 1

# Developmental School Guidance and Counseling: Its History and Reconceptionalization

by
Joe Wittmer and Mary Ann Clark

## A Brief History

Instructors teaching *Introduction to Counseling* courses usually cite Frank Parsons as the father of guidance. However, in actuality, the systematized approach to *school* guidance appeared first in 1889 when Jesse Davis made "guidance" a part of the school curriculum in a Detroit high school (Brewer, 1942). As school principal, Davis introduced "vocational and moral guidance" as a curricular component of each English course within his school.

Frank Parsons did found the Vocational Bureau of Boston in 1908 and also authored a text titled, *Choosing a Vocation* (1909). The Parsonian "counseling" method consisted of matching an individual's personal characteristics to the requirements of the occupation. However, his impact on the school guidance movement came much later. That is, his emphasis on testing and on stressing the measurement of individual aptitude and personality traits later influenced the role of the school counselor to a significant degree.

World War I and the Great Depression of the 1930s gave an even greater impetus to the testing of individuals. And, the term "counselor," rarely heard prior to the depression, was now in the vocabulary of all educators. Prior to this time, "guidance" was the term used by educators.

World War II and its aftermath created an even greater emphasis on "psychological testing" that directly affected school guidance (i.e., the use of the SAT and other tests to determine a student's admission to colleges and universities). During the 1950s, America's rapidly changing society created a need for more counseling and related services as crime, divorce, and so forth increased. Traditional values were being challenged. "Mental health" became important outside the school setting and "guidance counseling" became popular within the school, especially at the junior high and high school levels. The move was away from the technique of "testing" to one of "trait and factor," which later became known as "directive counseling."

Although his concepts did not "catch on" at that time, the first time that *developmental* guidance was written about, with schools in mind, can be credited to Robert Mathewson in 1949. Mathewson (1949) indicated that the school guidance process should move with the individual student in a "developmental sequence" up to the age of maturity. Mathewson (1962) later expanded and refined his notion of guidance as a process that aided student development. One book, *The Counselor in a Changing World,* by Gilbert Wrenn (1962) probably impacted school guidance more than any other publication. The central theme of Wrenn's book was that the primary emphasis in counseling students should be placed on their individual, developmental needs in contrast to the remedial needs and the crisis times in their lives. However, Wrenn's ideas were not incorporated in school counselor preparation until sometime later.

Both the American Psychological Association (APA) and the American Personnel and Guidance Association (APGA, later AACD, and now ACA) were formed during the 1950s. And, the client centered approach espoused by Carl Rogers made its impact on the counseling profession. His theoretical approach dominated the manner in which most counselors, including school counselors, were trained during the fifties, followed by more "directive" approaches in the early 1960s and back again to the "Rogerian" approach during the 1970s. The Rogerian approach to training school counselors is very much used today as a building block for establishing relationships with students today, but has given ground to more solution-focused, brief counseling approaches.

# The Impact of Rogerian Theory: On or Off Track for School Counselor Preparation?

As noted, Carl Rogers had a significant, positive impact on the counseling profession and his theoretical approach dominated counselor preparation programs. However, it is our opinion that Rogers' total focus on the individual somehow took us off-track in school counselor preparation and may have contributed to the inappropriate training of many school counselors, especially during the late 1960s and '70s. That is, in too many training programs, the focus was too narrow as it was almost entirely on small group and individual counseling. Very little attention was being given to the co-equal emphasis on prevention and on environmental intervention techniques so desperately needed in schools. Little attention was being placed (in counselor education programs) on the consulting and the coordination roles needed by effective developmental school counselors to reach all of their students.

School counselors did turn more toward the "directive" approach during the early sixties; an indirect result of Sputnik and of the passage of the National Defense Education Act (NDEA). However, this was a brief respite as the Rogerian model was the training approach of choice for counselor trainers from the mid-sixties through the seventies and into the eighties.

## The Impact of Sputnik

Sputnik, the Russian spaceship, launched in 1957, also launched the rapid development of school counseling and guidance in America, especially at the middle and high school levels. Federal legislation, in particular the National Defense Education Act (NDEA) of 1958, brought middle and high school counselors to the forefront as huge amounts of funds for their training were provided with the passage of this law. And, school guidance definitely headed in a different direction as a result. In essence, the U.S. government, highly concerned, concluded that Russian students were obviously superior to America's students in math and science since Russia was able to launch a rocket first. It was decreed that this was directly related to the fact that there were too few school guidance counselors as well as other shortcomings in American education. The race to the moon was on and government funds specifically earmarked toward the training of school counselors poured into counselor education training programs. For a short time following the NDEA Act, school counselors turned away from the Rogerian approach in favor of the more "directive" approach. This most likely occurred because it was assumed that being more "directive" would somehow help recruit bright youth for college and head them toward math and science. Somehow, as if by magic, more rocket scientists would emerge as a result. Unfortunately, school counselors were neglecting non-college bound youth during these times.

While the NDEA Act brought about the tripling of secondary school counselors between 1958 and 1967 (Shertzer & Stone, 1980), appropriate school guidance and counseling services were actually diminishing. Between 15,000 and 20,000 secondary school counselor trainees were funded by the government and graduated from counselor training institutes between 1958 and 1965. According to Gibson and Mitchell (2002), their numbers increased from only 12,000 in 1958 to more than 30,000 in 1964. Yet, as Audrey (1982) indicated, the profession of school counseling was close to becoming anachronistic as too much emphasis was being placed on non-guidance activities such as "clerical and administrative duties." And, Drawer (1984) wrote that school counselors were an endangered species and were contributing to their own destruction. Some experts believe that high school counseling, as we know it, is still in serious jeopardy unless drastic changes are made as many school counselors are still conducting inappropriate duties. While conducting an in-service training program for a large southern city's system-wide school counseling program, the superintendent of schools bluntly lamented that school counselors, as a group, were the "most over-qualified but least effective" staff members in his schools. It is our opinion that this is still the direct result of the inappropriate, too brief training, which occurred during the 1960s and '70s. That is, a school counselor not adequately trained in small group counseling, for example, probably won't make small group counseling a part of his or her counseling program. Fortunately, time (retirements) will take care of this problem. However, the training of school counselors must stay "on track," toward the "developmental" approach if school counseling is to survive.

It is our opinion that counselor education programs were not prepared for the onslaught brought about by the NDEA passage. As noted, school counselors were trained too quickly and in a sub-par fashion. The training was simply too brief and inadequate; and school counselors were ineffective in the "real world"—the school. In addition, training models not conducive to counselor effectiveness in the schools were being followed. The result of this too brief and inappropriate training of school counselors set the profession back several years as school counselors turned toward mostly clerical and administrative duties. The impact is still being felt today, especially at the high school level. The reconceptionalization of school guidance—the developmental movement—was timely and much needed.

# The Reconceptionalization of School Counseling

Fortunately, the guidance and counseling reform movement brought about the reconceptionalization of school counseling programs. That is, although still very important skills for the school counselor to possess, school counseling has moved from an ancillary, individual, small group, reactive, crisis oriented service to a more comprehensive, preventative, developmental approach. This reconceptionalization has resulted in a rather dramatic shift in training as well as in the role and function of today's school counselor. Not only are counselors being trained to provide crisis counseling, as well as to provide effective individual and small group services, they are also being trained as consultants, coordinators, and so forth. Further, with the impetus of the Education Trust's (1997) Transforming School Counseling, leadership and advocacy have become an essential part of a comprehensive school counseling model. The focus in the schools prior to the reform movement was almost totally "position" oriented. Somehow it was expected that the school counselor would simply "fix kids" or counsel them into the right university or into the right job, and then everything would be fine. School counselors possessed a "magic wand." Reconceptionalization toward the comprehensive, developmental approach has changed school counseling dramatically, and, for the betterment of students and society as a whole.

## Other Players in the Reconceptionalization of School Counseling: ACES, CACREP, and NBCC

Various professional groups and organizations played major roles in the "paradigm shift" that occurred in school guidance over the past 35 years. However, changes have occurred slowly. For example, the Association of Counselor Education and Supervision (ACES) began pushing for the development of school counselor training standards in the late 1950s and developed and approved the first standards for the training of secondary school counselors in 1964. However, the first counselor preparation programs (four) were not accredited by the ACES Commission on Accreditation until 1979!

The ACES Commission on Accreditation subsequently became the Council for the Accreditation of Counseling and Related Education Programs (CACREP) in 1981 and began the regular accreditation of counselor education programs. CACREP further revised and upgraded the standards of training in school counseling. One such example concerned the CACREP minimum conditions for a program to qualify for an accreditation visit. Among several others, one of CACREP's "minimum conditions" required a two-year minimum training program (48 semester/72 quarter hours). Thus, the accreditation movement played a major role in the manner in which school counselors were trained, especially after the CACREP school counselor specialty standards were developed and adopted. These specialty standards moved the training programs more toward the "program approach" and away from the "position" of "counselor as counselor." In addition, and most importantly, school counselors began carrying out the roles for which they were trained.

In the early 1980s, the National Board for Certified Counselors (NBCC) began certifying individuals as National Certified Counselors (NCC's). Although the statistics are not clear, it is estimated that more than half of the original 17,000 National Certified Counselors (in 1982) were school counselors. Becoming a National Certified Counselor indicated to the public that these individuals (at least) met minimum standards that added immensely to their credibility. In addition, such a credential added to their own self-esteem and resulted in school counselors "carrying their heads a little higher" that ultimately added to their professionalization. Then, in 1990, NBCC created the National Certified School Counselor (NCSC) specialty, the first such ever national credential for *any* professional educational group. Several other educational professions have initiated a national credential for their membership (i.e., school administrators). However, school counselors were the first. This activity has given, and continues to give, a tremendous boost to the "professionalization" of school counseling.

In sum, the basic reform in the school guidance movement was away from that of the counselor as simply a one-to-one, small group mental health service provider (as an individual in a counseling position), to that of becoming a coordinator, a consultant, a leader, an advocate, and a programmer—an overall catalyst in the school counseling program.

Someone once described the new developmental school counselor as one who is upstream giving swimming lessons instead of downstream rescuing people that are drowning. However, as noted, this is only partially true. School counselors are also being trained and are effective in "rescuing" drowning individuals, those students in crisis, and should continue to be so trained. The question becomes, who does the most good? The school counselor who works with 25 children (using a large group guidance approach) in a six-week, one hour per week unit on improving self-concept, or the school counselor who spends six hours with one child in crisis? Although the latter is important, it is obvious that the school counselor using the former approach meets the needs of more students and does much more good in the long run. The No Child Left Behind Act (NCLB) of 2001 has also shifted the emphasis to working with all students.

## The Emergence of the Elementary School Counselor

Historically, elementary teachers in their self-contained classrooms had been responsible for "counseling and guidance." Elementary counselors only appeared in schools some 30 years ago. Those professionals interested in training elementary school counselors worked at not repeating the mistakes incurred in training middle and high school counselors. One of the early leaders in the movement was Don Dinkmeyer, Sr. Also, Verne Faust (1968), a prime mover in the emergence of elementary school counselors, and one of his students, Robert D. Myrick, focused their approach on the developmental needs of the child and the use of the teacher and others in the school guidance process.

Don Dinkmeyer, Sr. was the first editor of the *Elementary School Guidance and Counseling Journal*, 1965 to 1972, and Robert D. Myrick was the second editor, 1972 to 1978. Both were pioneers in the training and research on elementary school counseling and remain so today. It should be acknowledged that Dinkmeyer's and Myrick's emphasis on the school counselor's competence and on accountability played a major role in school guidance reconceptionalization toward the developmental focus, not just at the elementary level, but at all levels. Both stressed that guidance programs be organized around the concept of a comprehensive guidance delivery system with a "true" guidance curriculum at its center. As noted, Wrenn (1962) also played a major role in this movement. In general, elementary school counselors tend to be much more involved in "guidance" and less in "non-guidance" activity than are their middle and high school counterparts.

At first, the value of placing counselors in the elementary schools was debated and questioned by educators and parents alike. For many, the words "school counselor" brought to mind someone they had seen a few times in high school to help them with their class schedules, testing, college applications, and discipline. This perception resulted in the debate concerning the need for elementary school counselors back in the seventies when the movement to place them in schools first began (ASCA, 1997). However, as we begin this new century, more elementary counselors are being employed across America and there is a large "push" to add these specially trained professionals to school staffs. Educators and others seem to agree that more developmentally oriented elementary school counselors are necessary if we are to respond adequately and effectively to the needs of children today. Unfortunately, however, when there are budget crises in school systems, elementary counselors can sometimes be more vulnerable to position cuts than secondary counselors.

## The New Approach: Developmental in Nature

As noted, the profession of school counseling has moved away from the individual, position-oriented, one-to-one, small group counseling approach to a more preventive, wellness oriented, pro-active one. The image of the school counselor sitting in his or her office waiting for a student client to drop by is passe. And, in those schools where a counselor simply manages a "miniature mental health clinic," priorities are out of sync and students fall "between the cracks."

The contemporary developmental school counselor is curriculum and program oriented, is available to all, embraces diversity, and is knowledgeable and competent to teach life skills to every student in the school.

The developmental professional school counselor has four basic publics: students, teachers/staff, administrators, and the parents/community. In an effective program, everyone in the school knows that "guidance" is everyone's business. Additionally, in an efficient counseling program, everyone in the school understands the needs of the students and how the counseling department is organized to meet these needs. In those schools where teachers, administrators, and staff appreciate and understand the role of the counselor, the more successful the school's counseling program will be. When teachers and administrators understand the counseling department's plan, they support the counselor(s), and appreciate a collaborative approach in working with their students.

For those interested, excellent accounts of school guidance history and its reconceptionalization are available elsewhere (Audrey, 1982; Gibson & Mitchell, 2002; Myrick, 2003; and Gysbers & Henderson, 2006).

# Developmental School Counseling Defined and Delineated

Many definitions of a comprehensive developmental school guidance program have emerged. One of the most quoted authorities in the field of school counseling today is Robert D. Myrick. A highly respected professional, his 2003 book, *Developmental Guidance and Counseling: A Practical Approach,* is among the most used textbooks in school counselor preparation programs today. Myrick (2003) defined the developmental approach as follows:

*The developmental approach is an attempt to identify certain skills and experiences that students need to have as part of their going to school and being successful. Learning behaviors and tasks are identified and clarified for students. Then, a guidance curriculum is planned which complements the academic curriculum. In addition, life skills are identified and these are emphasized as part of preparing students for adulthood.*

In the developmental approach, students have an opportunity to learn more about themselves and others in advance of problem moments in their lives. They learn interpersonal skills before they have an interpersonal crisis. If a crisis situation does happen, they can draw upon their skills to work themselves out of the problem.

Myrick (2003) also postulated the following seven Principles of Developmental Guidance Programs:

1. Developmental guidance is for all students.

2. Developmental guidance has an organized and planned curriculum.

3. Developmental guidance is sequential and flexible.

4. Developmental guidance is an integrated part of the total educational process.

5. Developmental guidance involves all school personnel.

6. Developmental guidance helps students learn more effectively and efficiently.

7. Developmental guidance includes counselors who provide specialized counseling services and interventions.

Norman Gysbers has also been a pioneer in school counseling reconceptionalization. His model is being used in many school districts. He and his co-writer indicated that the major focus of a developmental program is to provide all students with experiences to help them grow and develop. School counseling programs are comprehensive in that a full range of activities and services such as assessment, information, consultation, counseling, referral, placement, follow-up, and follow-through are provided (Gysbers & Henderson, 2006).

Gysbers and Henderson further indicated that such a program is based on the assumption that *all* school staff are involved in the guidance program. It is understood in their model that the highly trained and professionally certified school counselor remains "central" to the program. In the model espoused by Gysbers and Henderson (2006), school counselors provide direct services to students as well as work in consultative and collaborative relations with other members of the guidance team—the total school staff. That is, the guidance team consists of members of the total school staff, parents, and the community.

A developmental school counselor cannot be effective standing alone; everyone's involvement in the school is needed, sought, and appreciated. Involving the administration, school staff, parents, and teachers provides needed support and backing. Interested, involved individuals will defend the program (and the counselor) and will play a vital role within the program.

The historical approaches to school counseling included crisis intervention (waiting and reacting to critical situations), the remedial approach, preventive guidance, and a combination of the three. The remedial approach assumes a proactive counselor role of anticipating problems prior to their occurrence. The comprehensive developmental approach of today is an attempt to identify certain skills and experiences that students need, both in school and across the life span, and to *incorporate* the remedial, crisis, and preventive approaches. As written and implied throughout this book, a majority of the developmental school counselor's time is spent on the "program" and "guidance curriculum" portion of the overall guidance program.

Today's effective developmental school counselor is pro-active and strives for a flexible delivery system within his or her program. There are planned daily activities aimed at meeting the development needs of all students, not just those with problems. And, the program has a written philosophy statement, a written rationale, goals, objectives, and strategies and techniques for implementing the goals and objectives with the latter being targeted specifically for different grade levels (see Snyder, chapter 4). A comprehensive program has its beginning on the first day of school and ends on the last day of the academic year.

The program's curriculum implemented and conducted by the counselor consists of structured experiences presented in a systematic way to meet the developmental needs of all students. These are delivered via the classroom through large group activities, regular classroom structure, smaller groups, and so forth. The purpose of the curriculum is to provide students with competencies that they need for their personal, social, academic, and career development, and to assist them in gaining and using life skills (Dahir, Sheldon, & Valiga, 1998).

Developmental program priorities are set for the different services needed and there is always an accountability component. The administrative and clerical tasks will have been de-emphasized, and, although important, one-to-one counseling has also been de-emphasized. The developmental counselor knows when and how to refer a student to an outside the school agency counselor as needed.

Gysbers (1997), in his book, *Comprehensive Guidance Programs That Work,* indicated that the comprehensive school counseling program consists of structured developmental experiences presented through classroom and group activities Pre-K through Post-Secondary. The purpose of the program, according to Gysbers, is to provide all students at all grade levels with knowledge and assistance in acquiring and using life skills. Gysbers (1997) discussed the following as the main components of a comprehensive program:

**Individual Planning:** Consists of planned and counselor directed activities that help all students plan, monitor, and manage their own learning as well as their personal and career development.

**Individual Appraisal:** Counselors assist students in analyzing and evaluating students' abilities, interests, skills, and achievement.

**Individual Advisement:** Counselors assist students in establishing personal-social, educational and occupational goals, involving parents, students, and school.

**Placement:** Counselors assist students in making the transition from school to school, school to work and/or additional post secondary educational training.

**Responsive Services:** Consists of Activities to meet the immediate needs and concerns of students.

**Consultation:** Counselors consult with parents, teachers, other educators, and community agencies regarding strategies to help students.

**Personal Counseling:** Counseling is provided on a small group or individual basis for students.

**Crisis Counseling:** Counseling and support are provided to students and their families facing emergency situations.

**Referral:** Counselors use referral sources to deal with crises such as suicide, violence, abuse, and terminal illness.

**System Support:** Consists of management activities that establish, maintain, and enhance the total guidance program.

**Staff and Community Relations:** Counselors orient staff and the community to the comprehensive, developmental, standards based school counseling program.

**Consultation with teachers:** Counselors need to consult with teachers and other staff members to provide information, to support staff, and to receive feedback on the emerging needs of students.

**Advisory Councils:** Counselors support other programs through service on departmental curriculum committees, community committees, and so forth.

**Community Outreach:** Counselors participate in activities designed to help counselors become knowledgeable about community resources and referral agencies.

**Program Management and Operations:** Counselors coordinate planning and management tasks which support the activities of a comprehensive guidance and counseling program.

**Research and Development:** Counselors engage in and provide for program evaluation, data analysis, follow-up studies, and the continued development of updating learning activities and resources (Gysbers, 1997).

Gysbers (1997) indicated further that school counselors should continually monitor their professional development and be actively involved regularly in updating their professional knowledge and skills. And, in addition, counselors should support other school programs through service on school advisory councils, departmental curriculum committees, community committees, and so forth.

The American School Counselor Association's literature clearly indicated that a comprehensive school counseling program is developmental and systematic in nature, sequential, clearly defined, and accountable (ASCA, 1999). It is jointly founded upon developmental psychology, educational philosophy, and counseling methodology. The school counseling program is integral to the educational enterprise. The program is proactive and preventive in its focus. It assists students in acquiring and using lifelong learning skills. More specifically, effective school counseling programs employ strategies to enhance the academic, career, and personal/social development of all students. Writing on behalf of ASCA, Dahir, Sheldon and Valiga (1998) stated the differences between the "Traditional" and "Comprehensive/Developmental School Counseling" programs as follows:

| Traditional Guidance | Comprehensive/Developmental |
|---|---|
| Reactive | Proactive |
| Process | Outcome |
| Deductive | Inductive |
| Services | Program |
| Subjective Evaluation | Objective Evaluation |
| Individual Counseling | Individual and Group |
| Students initiate | Counselors initiate |
| Generalists | Specialists |

ASCA leaders believe that it is important to ensure that the school's "stakeholders," including the entire community in which the school is located, understand the important role school counseling programs play in the educational system. Professional school counselors therefore must become:

*Facilitators of change, leaders in school improvement, partners in educational excellence, coordinators of collaborative community efforts, advocates for equity and excellence, and managers of student achievement of school counseling competencies (Dahir, Sheldon, & Valiga, 1998).*

Dahir, Sheldon, and Valiga (1998), in their book concerning the implementation of the ASCA National Standards for School Counseling Programs (see chapter two), published by ASCA, indicated that if school counselors are going to change the perceptions and attitudes of school administrators, faculty, parents, and community members, they must get across the message that the school counseling program at all levels:

*Helps students develop knowledge and skills that are needed in today's and tomorrow's world; is an integral component of the academic mission of the school; supports student success and assists in students' academic, career, and personal/social development; use for all students—not just those in crisis or those going to college, and is effective and accountable. (Dahir, Sheldon, & Valiga, 1998).*

No doubt about it, much is expected from the "new millennium" developmental, K-12 school counselor. And, as in other helping professions, a school counselor's continued professional development is extremely important and expected by his or her "publics." *That is, your "publics" should have the confidence that you are indeed "up-dated" in your field.* As indicated elsewhere in this book, we believe that a developmental school counselor's professional development will be enhanced tremendously by becoming a National Certified Counselor (NCC) and subsequently, a National Certified School Counselor (NCSC).

# Changing Times, Changing Demographics, Changing Counselor Priorities

To follow up the ASCA National Standards (1997) in 2003, the ASCA National Model: A Framework for School Counseling Programs was published (ASCA, 2003). The model embellishes the National Standards and offers a foundation, a delivery system, management systems, and an accountability system for professional school counselors. The National Standards (1997) were included as part of the model. The four main themes of the National Model include leadership, advocacy, collaboration and teaming and systemic change. The model addresses the extremely important issue of school counselors working with and reaching all students. The ASCA National Model will be discussed in detail in chapter 3, by one of its co-authors, Judy Bowers, a past president of ASCA.

Additionally, the Transforming School Counseling movement put forth by the Education Trust (1997) has had much input and influence on the development of the ASCA Model. This movement has placed much emphasis on the role of school counselors in reaching out to all students, helping them have access and opportunities to higher education, and making systemic changes to reduce the achievement gap between Caucasian students and those of color, particularly African American and Hispanic students (Education Trust, 2003)

As we enter the 21st century, it is clear that our society and our schools continue to evolve and change at a rapid pace. Our increasingly diverse student bodies throughout the country reflect a myriad of needs in the interrelated areas of educational achievement, social-behavioral adjustment, and career development. The demographics of our population are shifting with an increase in the numbers of school age children, as well as increases in racial and ethnic diversity. Public school enrollment is up to an estimated 48.7 million pre-kindergarten through twelfth grade enrollment and is projected to grow to 51.2 million by 2015. The percentage of Caucasian students dropped from 78% to 57% from 1972 to 2004, while the proportion of Hispanic students during that period jumped from six percent to 19 percent (National Center for Education Statistics, 2006) and accounted for 50% of the population growth in the United States from July 1, 2004-July 1, 2005 (U.S. Census Bureau, 2006).

There has been an increase of students identified with disabilities and an estimated 6.6 million children received special education services in 2004 under federal law, up from 3.7 million in 1977. The number of children 5 to 17 who speak a language other than English at home more than doubled between 1979 and 2004 increasing from 3.8 million to 9.9 million (National Center for Education Statistics, 2006).

Statistics indicate that the poverty level in the United States has risen for the fourth year in a row, with 18%, or 13.5 million children, under the age of 18 living below the federal poverty level. Although black and Hispanic children are disproportionately likely to be poor, white children comprise the largest group of children living in poor families: Thirty five percent of all poor children are white (National Center for Children in Poverty, 2006). Poverty is associated with negative outcomes for children. It can impede children's cognitive development and their ability to learn and can contribute to behavioral, social, and emotional problems (National Center for Children in Poverty, 2006). Urban schools which often have large poor and minority student populations have significant and unique issues that need to be addressed by educators in general, and school counselors specifically (Lee, 2005).

The "achievement gap" between Caucasian and poor and minority students, specifically African American and Hispanic students, continues to be an important and controversial educational issue with the gap continuing to widen (Education Trust, 2003). Recent educational statistics also show a "gender gap" with girls as a group achieving at a higher level than boys, and fewer males than females enrolling in and completing college (Clark, Oakley & Adams, 2006; National Center for Education Statistics, 2006).

The school counseling profession has gone through a major transformation in the past decade as reflected in the American School Counselor Association (ASCA) National Standards (Campbell & Dahir, 1997), the ASCA National Model (2003, 2005), and the Education Trust's Transforming School Counseling movement (Education Trust, 1997), all of which emphasize the essential principle of working to help *all students* be successful in school. Furthermore, recent legislation such as the No Child Left Behind Act (2001), a re-authorization of the Elementary and Secondary Education Act, and the Individuals with Disabilities Improvement Act (IDEAI) (2004) have provided the legal foundation for schools to improve educational outcomes for *all* students (Yell, Katsiyannas, & Shiner, 2006).

Additionally, Section 504 of the Rehabilitation Act of 1973, is a civil rights piece of legislation that has supported accommodations for students with disabilities that have not been covered under IDEA (Council of Administrators of Special Education, Inc., 1999). For example, students who may be diagnosed with Attention Deficit Hyperactivity Disorder (ADHD) or specific mental or physical health issues, may receive classroom accommodations such as extended time on assignments or specific classroom seating. The application and implementation of this piece of legislation has increased greatly in recent years resulting in more students receiving classroom accommodations.

No Child Left Behind (NCLB) requires that all schools demonstrably improve achievement so that all public school students are proficient by the end of the 2013-2014 school year. An accountability system of measurable milestones called Adequate Yearly Progress (AYP) requires states and schools to use numerical data to provide evidence of improved student outcomes for all subgroups to include students who are economically disadvantaged, those from racial and ethnic subgroups, those with disabilities, and those students with limited English proficiency (Yell, Katsiyannas, & Shiner, 2006).

As the pressure to meet higher academic standards for all students has increased, the corresponding pressure on educators to produce results has also increased. The ASCA National Model (2003, 2005) recommends that counselors spend 80% of their time in direct services with students. Large group classroom guidance, small group work, and individual counseling are the traditional interventions that counselors have used to directly impact students in a developmental, comprehensive school counseling program (Gysbers & Henderson, 2006; Myrick, 2003). The Transforming School Counseling movement (Education Trust, 1997) and the implementation of the ASCA National Model (2003, 2005), has increased the emphasis on the role of consultation and collaboration among school counselors and important stakeholders: the students, their parents, teachers and administrators. Serving as educational leaders and advocates for student success have created new and important roles for school counselors to be involved at systemic levels of change and reform to promote access to opportunities for all students (Clark and Stone, 2000; Devoss & Andrews, 2006; House & Martin, 1998; Stone & Dahir, 2006).

The new millennium also coincides with an unprecedented opportunity for the school counseling profession. .Along with the federal government, many related professions and organizations have "jumped" on our bandwagon and support school counseling currently as never before. Among these are the National Association of Secondary School Principals and the National Association of Elementary School Principals (Dahir, Sheldon, & Valiga, 1998). Another such organization is the National Education Association (NEA). The NEA passed a resolution in 1999 urging strongly that the school counselor/student ratio never be more than 1:250. The support is there and now is the time to implement developmental counseling programs in every pre K-12 school in America. And, we must ensure that these programs are staffed by qualified and competent school counselors holding the appropriate professional credentials. As we go to press, the California Association of School Counselors announced that a state budget agreement had been reached to allocate $200 million to provide more school counselors to the middle and high schools of California. The funding will enable schools to hire an additional 3000 professional credentialed school counselors across the state.

## Summary

In this chapter we began with a brief history of school counseling followed by the reconceptionalization movement. The chapter concluded with a section describing the most recent demographic trends and corresponding school counseling needs with corresponding school counselor roles. Two figures concerning a description of the ASCA and CACREP standards of training as related to school counselor preparation are presented at the end of the chapter.

# Figure 1.1
# The Preparation of School Counselors: ASCA

## Position Statement: Credentialing and Licensure

### The Professional School Counselor And Credentialing And Licensure

(Adopted 1990; revised 1993, 1999, 2003)

### The American School Counselor Association (ASCA) Position

ASCA strongly supports passage of a professional school counselor credentialing law in each state providing legal definition of the counseling profession and of qualified practitioners and establishing standards for entry and role definition in school settings, including a privileged communication clause. ASCA strongly endorses and supports the school counselor standards developed by the Council for Accreditation of Counseling and Related Educational Programs (CACREP) and encourages all state education certification and/or licensure agencies to adopt these professional standards for school counselor credentialing. Further, ASCA supports the credentialing and employment of those who hold a master's degree in counseling-related fields with training in all areas specified by the CACREP standards. Any school internship shall be under the supervision of a credentialed and/or licensed school counselor and a university supervisor.

### The Rationale

Professional school counselor licensure legislation protects the public and its right to select which mental health specialty would best serve its needs. ASCA encourages legislation including a legal definition of the counseling profession, setting minimum standards for entry into the counseling profession and defining the role of professional school counseling. ASCA encourages insertion of a privileged communication clause for counselors in all settings and the inclusion of the ASCA Ethical Standards as part of said legislation. ASCA strongly supports the nationwide use of CACREP standards in establishing state certification guidelines for professional school counselors to ensure sound academic practicum and internship experience. This preparation and experience enhances the development of proactive and comprehensive school counseling programs.

### The Professional School Counselor's Role

The changing needs of students, families and schools require professional school counselors who are skilled in current counseling techniques focusing on students' academic, career and personal/social needs. School counselors must also possess skills in the development, implementation and evaluation of professional school counseling programs, as well as an ability to work in collaboration and consultation with others in the school and community.

### Summary

ASCA, recognizing the ever-changing needs of students, families, schools and communities, strongly supports sound academic preparation and the use of CACREP standards in establishing state certification guidelines for professional school counselors (ASCA, 2003)

## Figure 1.2
## The Preparation of School Counselors: CACREP

### CACREP Standards of Training

The Council for the Accreditation of Counseling and Related Educational Programs (CACREP) developed and implemented the first specialty standards for the training of school counselors in 1985.

In essence, the most recent CACREP standards call for school counselors in training to experience certain curricular and supervised experiences. In addition, several curricular experiences and necessary, demonstrated knowledge domains specific to school counselors are given in the standards.

All counselor trainees in a CACREP accredited training program must have curricular experiences and demonstrated knowledge in each of the eight common-core areas that follow:

1. **Human Growth and Development**—studies that provide an understanding of the nature and needs of individuals at all developmental levels.

2. **Social and Cultural Foundations**—studies that provide an understanding of issues and trends in a multicultural and diverse society.

3. **Helping Relationships**—studies that provide an understanding of counseling and consultation processes.

4. **Groups**—studies that provide an understanding of group development, dynamics, counseling theories, and group counseling methods and skills.

5. **Career and Lifestyle Development**—studies that provide an understanding of career development and the interrelationships among work, family, and other life factors.

6. **Appraisal**—studies that provide an understanding of individual and group approaches to assessment and evaluation.

7. **Research and Program Evaluation**—studies that provide an understanding of types of research methods, basic statistics, and ethical and legal considerations in research.

8. **Professional Orientation**—studies that provide an understanding of all aspects of professional functioning including history, roles, organizational structures, ethics, standards, and credentialing (CACREP, 1994).

Each of the above **core** required curricular experiences are described in detail within the CACREP standards (CACREP, 2001). As we go to press, CACREP is revising their standards to be published in 2008.

As noted, the CACREP Standards also require certain supervised experiences including an on-campus clinical (laboratory) experience followed by a supervised practicum and an internship. The latter two are briefly described below:

*An accredited CACREP program requires students to complete supervised practicum experiences that total a minimum of 100 clock hours. The practicum provides for the development of individual and group counseling skills under supervision.*

*An accredited CACREP program also requires students to complete a supervised internship of 600 clock hours that is begun after successful completion of the student's practicum. Consideration is given to selecting internship sites (must be in a school setting) that offer opportunities for students to engage in both individual and group counseling. The internship provides an opportunity for the student to perform under the supervision of a certified school counselor, all the activities that a regularly employed staff member in the setting would be expected to perform. A regularly employed staff member is defined as a person occupying the professional role to which the student is aspiring (CACREP, 2001).*

### Specialized Curricular Experiences for Accredited CACREP Programs in School Counseling

In addition to the common core curricular and supervised experiences listed above, specialized curricular experiences and demonstrated knowledge and skill competence in each of the areas below are required of all students in an accredited CACREP school program.

A. FOUNDATIONS OF SCHOOL COUNSELING

1. history, philosophy, and current trends in school counseling and educational systems;

2. relationship of the school counseling program to the academic and student services program in the school;

3. role, function, and professional identity of the school counselor in relation to the roles of other professional and support personnel in the school;

4. strategies of leadership designed to enhance the learning environment of schools;

5. knowledge of the school setting, environment, and pre-K–12 curriculum;

6. current issues, policies, laws, and legislation relevant to school counseling;

7. the role of racial, ethnic, and cultural heritage, nationality, socioeconomic status, family structure, age, gender, sexual orientation, religious and spiritual beliefs, occupation, physical and mental status, and equity issues in school counseling;

8. knowledge and understanding of community, environmental, and institutional opportunities that enhance, as well as barriers that impede student academic, career, and personal/social success and overall development;

9. knowledge and application of current and emerging technology in education and school counseling to assist students, families, and educators in using resources that promote informed academic, career, and personal/social choices; and

10. ethical and legal considerations related specifically to the practice of school counseling (e.g., the *ACA Code of Ethics* and the *ASCA Ethical Standards for School Counselors*).

B. CONTEXTUAL DIMENSIONS OF SCHOOL COUNSELING

Studies that provide an understanding of the coordination of counseling program components as they relate to the total school community, including all of the following:

1. advocacy for all students and for effective school counseling programs;

2. coordination, collaboration, referral, and team-building efforts with teachers, parents, support personnel, and community resources to promote program objectives and facilitate successful student development and achievement of all students;

3. integration of the school counseling program into the total school curriculum by systematically providing information and skills training to assist pre-K–12 students in maximizing their academic, career, and personal/social development;

4. promotion of the use of counseling and guidance activities and programs by the total school community to enhance a positive school climate;

5. methods of planning for and presenting school counseling-related educational programs to administrators, teachers, parents, and the community;

6. methods of planning, developing, implementing, monitoring, and evaluating comprehensive developmental counseling programs; and

7. knowledge of prevention and crisis intervention strategies.

C. KNOWLEDGE AND SKILL REQUIREMENTS FOR SCHOOL COUNSELORS

1. Program Development, Implementation, and Evaluation

a. use, management, analysis, and presentation of data from school-based information (e.g., standardized testing, grades, enrollment, attendance, retention, placement), surveys, interviews, focus groups, and needs assessments to improve student outcomes;

b. design, implementation, monitoring, and evaluation of comprehensive developmental school counseling programs (e.g., the *ASCA National Standards for School Counseling Programs*) including an awareness of various systems that affect students, school, and home;

c. implementation and evaluation of specific strategies that meet program goals and objectives;

d. identification of student academic, career, and personal/social competencies and the implementation of processes and activities to assist students in achieving these competencies;

e. preparation of an action plan and school counseling calendar that reflect appropriate time commitments and priorities in a comprehensive developmental school counseling program;

f. strategies for seeking and securing alternative funding for program expansion; and

g. use of technology in the design, implementation, monitoring and evaluation of a comprehensive school counseling program.

2. Counseling and Guidance

a. individual and small-group counseling approaches that promote school success, through academic, career, and personal/social development for all;

b. individual, group, and classroom guidance approaches systematically designed to assist all students with academic, career and personal/social development;

c. approaches to peer facilitation, including peer helper, peer tutor, and peer mediation programs;

d. issues that may affect the development and functioning of students (e.g., abuse, violence, eating disorders, attention deficit hyperactivity disorder, childhood depression and suicide)

e. developmental approaches to assist all students and parents at points of educational transition (e.g., home to elementary school, elementary to middle to high school, high school to postsecondary education and career options);

f. constructive partnerships with parents, guardians, families, and communities in order to promote each student's academic, career, and personal/social success;

g. systems theories and relationships among and between community systems, family systems, and school systems, and how they interact to influence the students and affect each system; and

h. approaches to recognizing and assisting children and adolescents who may use alcohol or other drugs or who may reside in a home where substance abuse occurs.

3. Consultation

a. strategies to promote, develop, and enhance effective teamwork within the school and larger community;

b. theories, models, and processes of consultation and change with teachers, administrators, other school personnel, parents, community groups, agencies, and students as appropriate;

c. strategies and methods of working with parents, guardians, families, and communities to empower them to act on behalf of their children; and

d. knowledge and skills in conducting programs that are designed to enhance students' academic, social, emotional, career, and other developmental needs.

As of this writing, 174 counselor education school counselor preparation programs are CACREP accredited. Many more programs are expected to seek accreditation during the next several years.

The above brief descriptions of the CACREP Standards were taken from the CACREP Manual (2001) and will remain in force until 2008. For a thorough description of the Standards, write:

CACREP
American Counseling Association
5999 Stevenson Avenue
Alexandria, VA 22304

Website: http://www.cacrep.org

# References

American School Counselor Association. (2003, 2005). *The ASCA national model: A framework for school counseling programs.* Alexandria, VA: Author.

Audrey, R.F. (1982). A house divided: Guidance and counseling in 20th century America. *Personnel and Guidance Journal, 61,* 198-204.

Brewer, J.M. (1942). *Education as guidance.* New York: Macmillan.

CACREP. (2001). *Accreditation procedures manual.* Alexandria, VA: Author.

Campbell, C.A., & Dahir, C.A. (1997). *Sharing the vision: The national standards for school counseling programs.* Alexandra, VA: American School Counselor Association.

Clark, M.A., Oakley, E., & Adams, H. (2006). The gender achievement gap challenge. *ASCA School Counselor, 43* (3), 20-27.

Clark, M.A., & Stone, C. (2000). The developmental school counselor as educational leader. In J. Wittmer, *Managing your school counseling program: K-12 developmental strategies* (2nd ed.) pp. 75-82. Minneapolis, MN: Educational Media Corporation.

Council of Administrators of Special Education, Inc. (1999). *Section 504 and the ADA: Promoting student access* (2nd ed.). Author.

DeVoss, J.A., & Andrews, M.F. (2006). *School counselors as educational leaders.* Boston: Lahaska Press.

Education Trust. (1997). *Working definition of school counseling:* Washington, DC: Author.

Education Trust. (2003). *School counselors working for social justice.* Retrieved June 14, 2006 at http://www2.edtrust.org/EdTrust/Transforming+School+Counseling/Social+Justice.htm

Dahir, C., Sheldon, B., & Valiga, M. (1998). *Vision into action: Implementing the national standards for school counseling programs.* Alexandria, VA., American School Counselor Association.

Drawer, S.S. (1984). Counselor survival in the 1980s. *School Counselor, 31,* 234-240.

Faust, V. (1968). *The counselor-consultant in the elementary school.* Boston, MA: Houghton Mifflin.

Gibson, L.G., & Mitchell, M.H. (2002). *Introduction to counseling and guidance* (6th ed.). New York: Macmillan.

Gysbers, N.C. (1997). *Comprehensive guidance programs that work.* Greensboro, NC: ERIC Counseling and Personnel Services Clearinghouse.

Gysbers, N.C., & Henderson, P. (2006). *Developing and managing your school guidance program* (4th ed). Washington, DC: ACA.

House, R.M., & Martin, P.J. (1998). Advocating for better futures for all students: A new vision for school counselors. *Education, 119,* 284-291.

Lee, C.C. (2005). Urban school counseling: Context, characteristics, and competencies. *Professional School Counseling, 8,* 184-188.

Mathewson, R.H. (1949). *Guidance policy practice* (1st ed.). New York: Harper & Bros.

Mathewson, R.H. (1962). *Guidance policy and practice.* New York: Harper & Bros.

Myrick, R.D. (2003). *Developmental guidance and counseling: A practical approach* (4th ed.). Minneapolis, MN: Educational Media Corporation.

National Center for Children in Poverty. (2006). Retrieved June 19, 2006 from http://nccp.org/pub_cpt.html.

National Center for Education Statistics. (2006). *Condition of education.* Washington, DC: Author.

No Child Left Behind Act of 2001. (H.R. 1). Retrieved May 20, 2006 from http://www.ed.gov/nclb/

Parsons, F. (1909). *Choosing a vocation.* Boston: Houghton Mifflin.

Shertzer, B., & Stone, S.C. (1980). *Fundamentals of counseling* (3rd ed.). Boston, MA: Houghton Mifflin.

Stone, C. & Dahir, C. (2006). *The transformed school counselor.* Boston & New York: Houghton Mifflin.

U.S. Census Bureau. (2006, May 10). *U.S. Census Bureau News.* Retrieved June 27, 2006 at http://www.census.gov/Press-Release/www/releases/archives/population/006808.html

Wrenn, C.G. (1962). *The counselor in a changing world.* Alexandria, VA: ACA Press.

Yell, M.L., Katsiyannas, A., & Shiner, J.G. (2006). The No Child Left Behind Act, adequate yearly progress and students with disabilities. *Teaching exceptional children,* 38(4), pp. 32-39.

# Chapter 2

# Implementing a Comprehensive Developmental School Counseling Program

**by**
**Mary Ann Clark and Joe Wittmer**

## Implementation Strategies

### Administrative Understanding and Support

It is important that the school administration understand and support a developmental school counseling program—its priorities, its demands on the staff and the counselors' time, the cost of an effective program, the facilities and materials needed, and so forth. The place to begin, then, is with the school principal. It is important that the principal has an *in-depth* understanding of a comprehensive program and that you as the school counselor, have his or her support for such a program prior to initiating one. Otherwise, it is much less likely to succeed.

School administrators will make decisions and establish policies and procedures in light of their understanding (or lack of it) of developmental counseling. For example, since access to students is necessary for an effective developmental program to be initiated, an administrator who understands and supports such a program will develop student schedules that allow maximum flexibility in students' accessibility. It is vitally important that the school principal understand the developmental counselor's role in the overall program (i.e., what such a program *does* and *does not* entail). And, it is the school counselor who can best bring about this understanding on the part of the principal.

It is suggested that the counselor's role and function be placed in writing, shared, and discussed with the principal, and his or her approval and support gained. When possible, also have the statement approved by the central administration and/or school board. Discussion and understanding of the time commitment needed from teachers, staff, the administration, and others to the program should be made clear. Overall, it is important for the principal to understand and support the conditions required for effective program implementation, including the proper facilities needed, overall work environment,

and an adequate budget. When your school principal truly understands, he or she will realize that a developmental counseling program will make your school a better place for all, contribute to a more productive staff, and a school more conducive to overall student learning. In our opinion, the most effective school counseling programs occur when counselors and principals work as a team to plan and implement them.

### Selecting a School Guidance Advisory Committee

In Section II, the focus is on managing a comprehensive program and on the roles played by the effective developmental school counselor at the elementary, middle, and secondary levels, respectively. Each of the writers emphasizes the selection and the utilization of a School Counseling Advisory Committee as a necessary prerequisite to initiating any effective developmental school counseling program. Members of the school guidance committee almost always include teachers, administrators, parents, and when appropriate, students. Some school counseling departments also have a school board member on their advisory committees while others also have a well-known local business leader as a member. An advisory committee's membership should depict and provide a link with the schools' various publics (Wittmer & Thompson, 2006).

The effective developmental K-12 school counselor coordinates the advisory committee meetings, its functions, and keeps the school administration informed of all deliberations, of meetings, and of the plans of the committee. One high school counselor has organized his advisory committee by electing a chair, a vice-chair, and a secretary. The secretary records the minutes of each meeting that are subsequently shared with the school's administrators, staff, and teachers. No doubt about it, an effective advisory committee is essential if a developmental counseling program is to be effective (Wittmer, Thompson, & Loesch, 1997).

## Developing and Writing a Philosophy Statement

One of the advisory committee's first duties should be to develop and to write a program philosophy statement that is locally appropriate for the school in question and developmental in nature. This does not need to be an elaborate, lengthy, or scholarly statement, but simply written along the lines of, "This we believe..." where students, education, learning, and so forth are concerned. The written philosophy statement, sometimes referred to as a "mission" statement, should lead directly into the development of goals and objectives based on the identified needs gathered from students, teachers, staff, parents, and other publics most appropriately reflecting the local school. As noted, it should be written simply and in a straight forward manner.

Developing and writing a philosophical statement is extremely important. A strong, well-written, philosophy statement will become the corner stone upon which the total counseling program is developed and built. It should be written in clear terms to coincide and be compatible with the overall school philosophy, and where appropriate, with the National Model, the state and district-wide philosophies as well. It is advantageous for the counselor to have the school's overall written philosophy statement available (and, if it is in writing, also have available the one from the district-wide school system) prior to having the advisory committee initiating the development and the writing of the specific school's counseling program's philosophical statement. As mentioned before, a school counseling program is an indisputable, integral part of the overall instructional program. Thus, the philosophy statement should reflect the values and beliefs of the total school faculty and staff, the local publics, and provide the basis from which this contribution will be made.

## Needs Surveys

Experts differ on which should occur first—the appointment of the advisory committee or a needs survey of the school's publics. However, we suggest the selection of the advisory committee first. Then, the committee, coordinated by the counselor, writes the philosophy statement and develops and administers specific needs surveys to the entire student population, the staff, the faculty, and parents. Some needs assessments may be administered by the school district as part of their school improvement plan. Others may be administered periodically as part of the school's accreditation procedure. The results of such assessments can be valuable information for school counselors in program planning and rationale. For example, if the school's results from a district wide survey showed that students and parents did not believe that students were feeling safe at the school, this data could be used to devise a plan to address the issue.

Analyzing the survey results should next occur. This will clarify the guidance and the counseling needs of the students, teachers, parents, and so forth from their viewpoints—the needs of *your* consumers! Accurately assessing and identifying the needs of the various publics the counselor serves is one of the most important components within a developmental counselor's role. For students and for parents, this should be done with a formal written needs assessment survey. Surveys can be developed quite easily. Simply ask questions or give checklists that you believe will help you obtain the most accurate and viable data. In addition to paper and pencil surveys, a simple, structured interview of the administration and the faculty may provide similar results. You may use the results of the district or accreditation bodies and can also develop your own surveys to meet the specific needs of the school. Aside from the two sample needs surveys given at the conclusion of this chapter, excellent sample school guidance philosophy statements, rationale statements, and sample needs surveys are available elsewhere. For example, Rye and Sparks (1999) provided several ideal school philosophy statements and needs surveys. Rye and Sparks permit the copying of their surveys by any school counselor desiring to use them in the development and/or strengthening of their specific school's counseling program.

## Developing and Writing a Program Rationale

Following the writing of the philosophy statement and the development, administering, and analyses of the needs surveys, it is important for the Counseling Program Advisory Committee to develop and write a program rationale statement. Such a rationale statement clearly states the societally based reasons for having a comprehensive, developmental counseling program in place and is based on the results of the needs surveys. Each school district is unique and the rationale (the reasons for having a developmental program) should "fit" with the specific "needs" of your school; it should be "locally appropriate." That is, the rationale statement should specifically state the rationale and how the developmental guidance program benefits the students, the faculty, the parents, and the specific community being served. The rationale statement should clearly imply and support the notion that school counseling services are a vital part of the overall educational process—an integral part of the overall school curriculum. Such a rationale statement (the most significant reasons for having a developmental program) should also emphasize how the developmental counseling program coincides and is coordinated with the philosophy and overall curricular aspects of the school. Many professional school counselors now include the ASCA National Model as a basis for writing their school philosophy statement.

# Current Trends in Youth Related Issues

Current trends in youth related issues are cause for deep concern and give impetus to the need for developmentally oriented school counselors at all grade levels. In addition to youth violence, *The Center for 4th and 5th R's* (1999) has provided the following as "troubling trends" among our youth:

1. Increasing dishonesty (lying, cheating, and stealing)

2. Growing disrespect for parents, teachers, and other legitimate authority figures

3. Increasing peer cruelty

4. A rise in prejudice and hate crimes

5. A decline in the work ethic

6. Declining personal and civic responsibility

7. Increasing self-destructive behaviors such as premature sexual activity, substance abuse, and suicide

8. Growing ethical illiteracy, including ignorance of moral knowledge as basic as the Golden Rule and the tendency to engage in destructive behavior without thinking it wrong (The Center for 4th and 5th R's, 1999)

The Center for 4th and 5th R's (1999) provided the following statistical examples representative of the above trends:

• According to FBI statistics, arrests of 13- and 14-year-olds for rape nearly doubled during the past decade.

• In a study of more than 6,000 college students by Rutgers University professor Douglas McCabe, more than 2/3 said they had cheated on a test or major assignment during college. The increase of technology such as cell phones and laptops has made information more accessible and cheating easier.

• Almost six of ten high school students say they have used illegal drugs, not counting alcohol, according to a federal study.

• According to a Centers for Disease Control study, 40% of American ninth-graders say they have already had sexual intercourse; a United Nations report finds that U.S. teens have the highest abortion rate in the developed world.

• Rising levels of hate-inspired youth violence promoted the organization Research for Better Schools to publish a handbook on dealing with hate crime in schools (Center for 4th and 5th R's, 1999).

We also know that between 5,000 and 6,000 adolescents take their lives each year and another 500,000 teens make unsuccessful attempts. Today, suicide ranks as the second or third leading cause of death among adolescents. According to a recent study, there has been a 300% increase in teen suicide since the 1960s and a 1000% increase in depression among children since the 1960s (Cloud, 1999). We also know that daily, approximately 3000 children witness the divorce of their parents. And, about every 50 seconds a child is abused or neglected in America.

According to the Children's Defense Fund's "Everyday in America," (2006), every day in the United States: 5 children and youths under 20 commit suicide., 8 children and teens are killed by firearms, 181 children under 18 are arrested for violent crimes, 380 youth are arrested for drug abuse, 1154 babies are born to teen mothers, 2,447 babies are born into poverty, 3,756 high school students drop out each school day, 4356 children under 18 are arrested, and 16,964 public school students are suspended each school day.

The types of youth issues mentioned above can be found across socioeconomic status, race and ethnicity, rural and suburban locations, and various geographical locations (Erford, Newsome, & Rock, 2007). These problems can seem overwhelming and they can certainly affect students' academic performance as well as their behavior at school. Classroom teachers often express that students need help with personal and family issues that they cannot provide and many welcome any support available from school counselors (Clark & Amatea, 2004).

The results of a national teacher opinion poll raised doubts about the progress being made with the above listed problems and concerns. The 1,007 public school teachers in the survey were questioned twice: in July, prior to beginning their first school year as a teacher, and again in the spring upon completing their first academic year.

*Sixty-five* percent of the teachers initially agreed that (in their opinion) many children appear in school with so many personal problems that it's very difficult for them to be effective learners. Unfortunately, following a year of teaching, *89%* held that view! In addition, *58%* responded (after a year of classroom teaching) that even the best teachers will find it difficult to educate more than two-thirds of their pupils, compared with 45 percent who said so before their first classroom jobs.

An identical *89%* replied both times that their students would benefit "If I do my job well." These teachers felt strongly that they would need assistance from other professionals in the school in order to "Do my job well." The surveyors concluded that school counselors are obviously among these "professionals" sought out by teachers for assistance with troubled students incapable of learning because of "personal" situations that impede learning.

More and more teachers are calling on school counselors for assistance with all their students. They have come to realize that a child bringing a problem to school that "gets in the way of learning" needs special professional help. Dr. Smith-Adcock in a later chapter writes of the need for collaboration between community agencies and schools to provide help for troubled students. At the same time, professional school counselors have large caseloads that make it difficult to carry out individual counseling on anything other than a short term basis.

It is our opinion that, in our "heart of hearts" we all know that the most viable "answers" to the above problems are "prevention" programs for all children beginning in preschool. Of course, such programs should involve parents and/or guardians as needed. And, yes, we also all know that prevention programs are expensive and a "hard sell." The results of the time, effort and money we put into prevention programs are long term and not immediately evident. Thus, we tend to continue to focus on the "problem" after it occurs, to respond to a crisis, instead of being proactive and trying to prevent it from occurring. We know that real prevention is much harder. It means addressing the underlying causes of the problem. These disturbing trends among our youth clearly reflect the need for highly trained counselors working in comprehensive, developmental school counseling programs that focus on prevention at all school levels (Wittmer, Thompson and Loesch, 1997).

Children affected by problems who are unable to achieve their academic potential may drop out of school and out of society. The school counselor's primary task is to assist each in becoming better, more effective learners by providing the appropriate programs and services to enhance current educational endeavors and learning across the life span. This is where a developmental school counselor enters the picture; a counselor who strives to help all students be successful at school. It is our opinion that if we can help students be productive, achieve to their highest potential and assist them in citizenship skills that their education can be a key to a satisfying and productive life.

Developmental school counselors know that intensive one-on-one counseling is important, is needed by some, and can be effective; but the counselor also realizes that it is the least satisfactory school counseling model to use as we are striving to help all students be successful in school. Thus, the basic rationale for having a comprehensive developmental counseling program is because

- All students need school counseling related services.

- Classroom and school climate can positively affect academic achievement (Zins, J.E., Bloodworth, M.R., Weissberg, R.P. & Walberg, H.J., 2004).

- Important aspects of child and adolescent development can be effectively addressed through a structured, developmentally oriented counseling curriculum.

- Most schools are large and complex and services can be best delivered to large groups of students with common needs.

- Most students, K-12, as they progress through developmental stages, are in need of assistance in corresponding developmental tasks (i.e., assistance with their everyday concerns so that effective classroom "learning" can occur).

You may wish to incorporate some, or all, of the above concerns into your program rationale statement. However, every attempt should be made to incorporate specific, locally appropriate concerns into the statement based on your own needs survey results.

## Setting Goals, Objectives, and Developing Strategies for Implementation

Developing a plan as to how the program can best, and most efficiently, meet the needs (gathered through needs surveys) is the next step in implementing a developmental school counseling program. This is best accomplished by developing a set of goals and objectives, followed by strategies and techniques for achieving each. Of course, these should coincide, and be representative of, the philosophy and rationale statements previously discussed.

Where appropriate, such goals and objectives should be the goals of the entire district, or even stateside system, and be similar for preschool through twelfth grade levels. There is obvious strength inherent in having common program goals and objectives across schools (district-wide and/or statewide) where possible. This permits counselors to work together as a unit; to pool "targeted" student and other evaluation data, and so forth. For example, one school system has written counseling program *goals* for grades K-12 that are in place in each elementary, middle, and secondary school within the district as follows:

**To assist *all* students in:**

1. community pride and involvement
2. career development and educational planning
3. school success skills
4. interpersonal communication skills development
5. decision-making and problem-solving skills
6. understanding attitudes and behaviors
7. understanding of self and others, and
8. understanding the school environment

Following the development of written goals for its particular school publics, the next task of the advisory committee is to develop and to write *objectives* revealing specifically how each goal will be reached. For example, again referring to the above mentioned school system, under goal number 8 above *(Understanding the school environment),* the district-wide *objectives* for grade six in *every* elementary school are:

1. Students will demonstrate knowledge of the physical layout of their school.
2. Students will demonstrate knowledge of the school code of conduct.
3. Students will demonstrate knowledge of extracurricular activities, special programs, and services.
4. Students will demonstrate knowledge of school personnel and their roles.

This large system has developed a set of objectives for *each* of the *eight* goals (listed above) for *each* specific *grade* level across the entire school system. These were developed with the different levels of student developmental stages in mind and differ from grade to grade.

After the goals and objectives have been written, the next step is to develop and to place into writing, those strategies and techniques to be utilized by the guidance department in carrying out and in fulfilling each of the objectives. A more detailed description of this process is given in chapter three.

## Accountability: A Continuous Process

The effective professional school counselor is accountable. Counselors simply "doing their job" without documentation of their effectiveness is passe. School counselors cannot simply believe and verbally contend that what they are doing "is good;" they must prove it with *hard* data through continuous evaluation. That is, the entire program should be evaluated in an ongoing, continuous process. Each aspect, each phase of the program should be evaluated for its effectiveness as well as each activity used to carry out the structure of the program. An ongoing evaluation process will reveal the strengths and limitations of the program, thereby permitting appropriate adjustments where and when they are called for. For detailed strategies on program evaluation and school counselor accountability, see John Schmidt's chapter. The ASCA National Model (2005) states that the question has changed from "What do school counselors do?" to "How are students different because of what school counselors do?" Thus, by implementing a school counseling program based on this premise, schools and districts can:

- Establish the school counseling program as an integral component of the academic mission of the school.
- Ensure every student has equitable access to the school counseling program.
- Identify and deliver the knowledge and skills all students should acquire.
- Ensure that the school counseling program is comprehensive in design and is delivered systematically to all students ASCA, 2005).

# The Developmental School Counselor: Appropriate Role and Function

As indicated throughout the first two chapters, most experts agree that to be effective, a developmental school counselor needs a written role and function statement approved by their respective principal, system-wide guidance supervisor, and so forth. We have studied many such role and function statements and have found them to be highly similar from school to school and even from state to state where effective developmental programs exist.

Many experts, counseling organizations, state departments of education, and various others have developed appropriate role and function statements for counselors. ASCA leaders indicate that a school counselor is a certified professional educator who assists students, teachers, parents, and administrators. According to the ASCA National Model (2005), the delivery system of a comprehensive program includes the school guidance curriculum, individual student planning, responsive services and system support. The responsive services component consists of activities which meet students' immediate needs. These needs require consultation, individual and small group counseling, crisis counseling, referrals and peer facilitation (ASCA, 2005). The following chapter will describe these services and their delivery system.

The developmental school counselor's work is differentiated by attention to age-specific developmental stages of student growth and the needs, tasks, and student interests related to those stages. And further, ASCA indicates that school counselors work with all students, including those who are considered "at-risk" and those with special needs.

According to ASCA, school counselors are experts in student learning and motivation and are responsible for developing comprehensive school counseling programs that promote and enhance student learning at all levels.

By providing direct interventions within a comprehensive program, ASCA states that school counselors focus their skills, time, and energies on direct services to students, staff, and families.

ASCA recommends that professional school counselors spend at least 80% of their time in direct services to students as described above. ASCA considers a realistic counselor student ratio for effective program delivery to be a maximum of 1:250.

Above all, according to ASCA:

*School counselors are student advocates who work cooperatively with other individuals and organizations to promote the development of children, youth, and families in their communities. School counselors, as members of the educational team, consult and collaborate with teachers, administrators, and families to assist students to be successful academically, vocationally, and personally. They work on behalf of students and their families to insure that all school programs facilitate the educational process and offer the opportunity for school success for each student. School counselors are an integral part of all school efforts to insure a safe learning environment for all members of the school community (ASCA, 1999).*

ASCA indicates that professional school counselors must meet the state certification/licensure standards and abide by the laws of the states in which they are employed. To assure high quality practice, school counselors are committed to continued professional growth and personal development. They are proactively involved in professional organizations which foster and promote school counseling at the local, state, and national levels. They uphold the ethical and professional standards of these associations and promote the development of the school counseling profession (ASCA, 2004).

## American School Counselor Association (ASCA) National Standards for School Counseling Programs

In the fall of 1997, the American School Counselor Association (ASCA) published the *National Standards for School Counseling Programs*. ASCA's National Standards provide the organizational basis for developing quality comprehensive, developmental school counseling programs that promote educational success and meet the developmental needs *of all students*. By creating this document, ASCA not only provided a framework for school based school counseling programs, but a comprehensive outline of the developmental needs of school children of all ages.

## Development of the National Standards for School Counseling Programs

Standards and credentialing in the counseling profession are not a new concept. For example, standards for ethical practices for school counselors were developed by ASCA a number of years ago and a national specialty certification for school counselors (NCSC) was developed by the National Board for Certified Counselors (NBCC) in 1986. Preparation standards for school counselor training programs were developed by CACREP in 1981. The 1997 ASCA National Standards for School Counseling Programs were established to advocate quality professional school counseling practice and training.

In July 1994, ASCA accepted the challenge of the national standards movement within education and began the process of developing the voluntary national standards for school counseling programs. This process required an examination of theory, research and practice to ensure that all aspects of school counseling were considered. The American College Testing Program (ACT) personnel served as research consultants. In addition, ACT served as the coordinator for the collection of survey information and donated personnel and resources to ensure that the survey design, distribution, and analyses followed universally accepted research practices. Three distinct but integrated components were the basis of the foundation for developing the National Standards: (a) ASCA membership survey data; (b) school counseling research and literature; and (c) field reviews of a draft document by ASCA members. These research components played an important role in designing the comprehensive National Standards for School Counseling Programs that have contributed to designing a K-12 school counseling program focusing on the developmental needs of all students (Campbell & Dahir, 1997).

## Organization of the National Standards for School Counseling Programs: Academic, Career and Personal/Social Development

The National School Standards for School Counseling Programs, now part of the ASCA National Model (2005) are divided into three broad areas: (1) Academic Development, (2) Career Development, and (3) Personal/Social Development. The standards for each content area are designed to furnish guidance and direction for states, school systems and individual schools to develop effective school counseling programs that encourage academic, personal/social and career success for all students. There are three standards found within each of the three content areas followed by several student competencies suggested as guidelines that enumerate desired student learning

outcomes. The student competencies define the specific knowledge, attitudes and skills that students should obtain or demonstrate as a result of participating in a comprehensive school counseling program. In other words, the student competencies list the developmental needs of kindergarten through twelfth grade students. The competencies offer a foundation for that which a comprehensive developmental school counseling program should address and deliver, as well as a basis to develop measurable indicators of student performance and success (Campbell & Dahir, 1997). However, ASCA has clearly indicated that the student competencies given under the nine standards described below are suggested as "guidelines" only. That is, the student competencies for each standard *must be adapted to reflect the particular needs of the student population and the academic mission of the school using the ASCA Standards for School Counseling Programs.*

The content standards for academic development found in the ASCA National Standards for School Counseling Programs are to be used as a guide for implementing strategies and activities to support and maximize student learning within the school counseling program. Academic development pertains to obtaining the skills, attitudes, and knowledge necessary for effective learning in school and across the lifespan; employing strategies to achieve success in school; and understanding the relationship of academics to vocational choice, and to life at home and in the community. ASCA leaders believe that when students' academic developmental needs are met, they are more likely to achieve in school (Campbell & Dahir, 1997).

Standards found in the career development section of the ASCA Standards provide the foundation for skill, attitude and knowledge acquisition that enable students (K-12) to make a successful transition from school to the world of work, and from job to job across the life career span. Career development includes using strategies that enhance future career success and job satisfaction as well as assisting understanding of the association between personal qualities, education and training, and a career choice. The recommendations of the Secretary's Commission on Achieving Necessary Skills (SCANS) and the content of the National Career Development Guidelines are also reflected in the career content area standards and competencies listed below (Campbell & Dahir, 1997).

As students progress through school and into adulthood, ASCA believes they need to acquire a firm foundation for personal and social growth. Implementing activities and strategies related to the content standards for personal/social development provide students with this foundation and contribute to academic and career success. Personal/social development includes skills, attitudes and knowledge which assist students in respecting and understanding others, acquiring effective interpersonal skills, understanding safety and survival skills and developing into contributing members of society. A chart of the three domains included in the National Standards is included as an appendix for Chapter 3 on the ASCA National Model: A Framework for School Counseling Programs which has incorporated the National Standards into the model.

## Why National Standards?

As a school counselor, or as a school counselor to be, you realize that schools and students have changed and will continue to change and it up to you to remain abreast of these changes. The ASCA Standards provide school counselors with the frame work with which to plan their school programs to keep up with the fast paced changes taking place in our society today. Therefore as noted, every school counselor should begin the process of implementing ASCA's National Standards for School Counseling Programs. These Standards provide developmental school counselors with a direction and a pathway to respond to the needs of students, at all levels (Dahir, Sheldon, & Valiga, 1998).

The National Standards support involvement in and commitment to increasing student achievement. The standards clearly connect school counseling to the current educational reform initiatives and to the educational mission of schools. A National Standards-based program requires school counselors to work collaboratively with classroom teachers to improve student learning and to document success. The standards provide a focal point and offer organizational structure to school counseling programs. They define a quality school counseling program and offer methods to be used to measure its effectiveness once put in place (Dahir, Sheldon, & Valiga, 1998).

Implementing a National Standards-based program requires school counselors to challenge their belief systems and to provide the advocacy and leadership to improve school success for all students. As educators who are student advocates, school counselors support equity in educational opportunities for all students and nurture dreams and aspirations (Dahir, Sheldon, & Valiga, 1998).

The National Standards began to define the vision and goals for 21st century school counseling programs and shift the focus from the school counselor to the school counseling program. As noted above, the standards:

1. Create a framework for a national model for school counseling programs;
2. Establish school counseling as an integral component of the academic mission of school;
3. Encourage equitable access to school counseling services for all students;
4. Identify the key components of a developmental school counseling program;
5. Identify the attitude, knowledge and skills that all students should acquire as a result of the K-12 school counseling program; and
6. Ensure that school counseling programs are comprehensive in design and delivered in a systematic fashion for all students (Dahir, Sheldon, & Valiga, 1998).

## Implementation of the National Standards

Within the booklet describing the National Standards for School Counseling Programs, ASCA addresses the need for a systematic method for implementing the National Standards (Dahir, Sheldon, & Valiga, 1998). ASCA indicates that implementation does not "just happen" because the school system has adopted a model program with standards, but that in-depth discussions, planning, designing, implementation and evaluation must occur. During the discussion and planning stages of implementation, ASCA stresses the importance of understanding students' needs and how they relate to the mission of the school. ASCA suggests that a student need assessment be conducted to acquire information regarding the skills students in each school need as they progress through school. Then designing and implementing a school counseling program that encompasses the needed skills outlined in the National Standards that ensure a successful transition throughout the school experience and on to life after high school should follow (Dahir, Sheldon, & Valiga, 1998).

## Development of the ASCA National Model: A Framework for School Counseling Programs

The ASCA National Model: A Framework for School Counseling Programs (2003, 2005) was developed to take the National Standards, which describe student competencies in the academic, career, and personal-social domains, several steps farther. The Model has provided a framework for the implementation of comprehensive school counseling programs by offering a philosophy, mission statement, and themes to be represented in each program. It offers a delivery system, a management system and an accountability system for professional school counselors. The ASCA National Standards, competencies, and indicators, discussed earlier, have been included as part of the National Model. Dr. Judy Bowers, one of the co-authors of the Model, describes the history, rationale, and the components of the National Model in chapter three, and an appendix in that chapter includes the components of the National Standards.

## More on the School Counselor's Role

Robert Myrick (2003) listed the following as the developmental school counselor's role:

- to assume leadership of organizing and developing a comprehensive developmental guidance and counseling program.
- to provide individual counseling services to students.
- to provide small group counseling services to students.
- to organize and lead large group guidance units, sessions, and activities.
- to train and coordinate peer facilitators.
- to consult with parents, teachers, and administrators regarding special concerns and needs of students.
- to consult with teachers and administrators about guidance and counseling interventions for students.
- to develop guidance units that evolve from students needs.

- to help develop and coordinate a teachers as advisors program (TAP).
- to co-lead, on occasion, a guidance unit or session with a teacher, perhaps during Teachers as Advisors Program (TAP).
- to serve as a professional resource to teacher-advisors about brief counseling and behavior change.
- to help identify students who have special needs or problems and to help find alternative education or guidance services for them.
- to coordinate faculty and staff development programs related to guidance.
- to coordinate other guidance related services (student assessment, advisement, community resources, special education, and placement). (Myrick 2003)

In addition to the above five interventions suggested by ASCA, Myrick (2003) added a sixth under the "indirect services" category; as *trainer/coordinator* of peer facilitator programs and projects. Myrick (2003) provided the following *weekly* time commitment scheduling plan for K-12 counselors: four to six individual counseling sessions with high priority students *(2 to 6 hours per week);* 4 to 5 small groups *(4 to 10 hours per week);* 2 to 3 large groups *(2 to 3 hours per week);* peer facilitator training/coordination *(1 to 5 hours per week);* consultation and coordination activities *(variable as needed)* (Myrick, 2003).

# Summary

In this chapter, the following guidelines for beginning the implementation of a comprehensive developmental guidance program were suggested:

1. Gain the support and approval of the school's administration for an appropriate role and function statement.

2. Appoint a School Counseling Advisory Committee.

3. Develop and place into writing a philosophy and/or mission statement for the guidance program.

4. Develop, administer, and analyze the needs surveys of students, parents, and other appropriate school counselor publics.

5. Write a locally appropriate program rationale statement—why a comprehensive program is needed in the school.. Use of a state model and the National Model can be used as a broad base, but it is also essential to delineate specific local needs.

6. Write realistic goals and objectives for the program.

7. Develop strategies for implementation and for delivery of the goals.

8. Develop an accountability system that is ongoing and continuous.

The chapter concluded with the role and function of a developmental school counselor as written by ASCA and others. Of the three figures given, two are examples of needs surveys and one is the ASCA position statement of comprehensive school counseling programs.

As noted throughout the first two chapters, students need specific information and counseling to address the societal problems they bring to school. Early exposure to a comprehensive school counseling program builds an emotionally healthy foundation for children and results in improved academic achievement.

Also, as noted, we must all take responsibility for our children as their future is our future. Teachers and parents look to counselors to respond to the academic, social, emotional, and career development needs of all students. Counselors should be prepared for their challenge.

In developing policies and programs to address the problems our young people face, we must make the best use of all our resources. School counselors are often the only mental health professionals to whom students will have access and they are the professionals who bridge the academic, career, and affective domain in students' lives.

Together, counselors, teachers, parents, and policy makers create a powerful force in the fight to enhance the lives of our young people. Through their collaborative efforts, children will achieve their maximum potential.

## Figure 2.1
## Sample High School Student Needs Assessment

### Instruction to Students:

Please read the following items CAREFULLY and CHECK any category that applies to you. Please answer this survey seriously!! Checking a category will NOT automatically place you in a group—this is just a survey, not a sign up sheet. At the end of each area there is a *blank line* which can be used to make suggestions as to activities you'd like to see offered, but are not listed here. The purpose of this survey is to help the Guidance Office determine what type of activities/groups students want offered during the next school year. We will review the categories most often checked by students and will try to offer those activities for you. Thanks for your cooperation.

### Educational Concerns

❏ I'd like to improve my study skills; I'd like to make better grades; I wish I could do better on standardized tests.

❏ I need help in choosing a college; I need to know more about financial aid; how do I apply to a college; what tests (SAT/ACT) do I need to take to go to college and what are those tests like; what classes should I take in high school to prepare for college.

(COLLEGE WORKSHOP)

### Other Educational Concerns: _____

### Career Concerns

❏ I need help in choosing a career; I don't know what I want to do after I graduate; I'm confused as to what type of work would really suit my personality, abilities, and interests.

(CAREER VALUES)

❏ I know what I want to do but need more specific information on a particular career; I'd really like to talk with someone in the career field I've chosen.

(CAREER CLUSTER EXPLORATION)

❏ I would like more information on the right way to apply for a job; I'm somewhat nervous about going on a job interview.

(JOB INTERVIEW SKILLS)

❏ I need someone to help me find a job; I'd like to or need to work part-time and don't know where to apply.

(JOB PLACEMENT SERVICES)

### Other Career Concerns: _____

## Health Concerns

❏ I'd like to know more about healthy lifestyle choices.
(GENERAL HEALTH CONCERNS)

❏ I'd like to learn more about drug/alcohol use and abuse; I have a friend who is really into drugs and I'm worried; what drugs are really dangerous; someone in my family is an alcoholic and I don't know how to handle it.
(SUBSTANCE ABUSE)

❏ I would like to talk to someone individually about a health-related problem (nurse, counselor, etc.).
(INDIVIDUAL CONFERENCES)

## Other Health Concerns: _____

## Home/Family Concerns

❏ I'd like to learn how to cope with my parents' separation or divorce; I'm having difficulty accepting a new stepparent, stepsister, or stepbrother.
(DIVORCE/SEPARATION)

❏ I'd like to learn how to communicate more easily with family/friends.
(RELATIONSHIPS)

## Other Home/Family Concerns: _____

## Personal/Social Concerns

❏ I lose my temper easily. I seem to feel nervous in the classroom and/or with other people. I need to learn to relax.
(STRESS/ANXIETY MANAGEMENT)

❏ I'd like to discover more about myself and others, better understanding of my feelings and personality; I'd like to be able to discuss my values, fears, and needs with other people my age; learn how to get along better with others.
(SELF-AWARENESS ACTIVITIES)

❏ I'd like to be able to talk to a counselor privately about a personal problem.
(INDIVIDUAL CONFERENCES)

## Other Personal/Social Concerns: _____

Adapted from Zephyrhills High School Guidance Department, Zephyrhills, Florida

# Figure 2.2
# Sample Middle School Student Needs Assessment

**Student directions:**

This survey is anonymous. PLEASE DO NOT WRITE YOUR NAME ON THIS PAGE OR ON THE ANSWER SHEET. Read the list slowly. After reading, please rank order the five (5) concerns important to you (in order of importance to you). Number one (1) is the greatest concern you have, number 2 is the second greatest concern, and so forth, down to number 5 in descending order. Place your ranking in the blank to the left of the items. Thanks.

_____ Physical Appearance

_____ Want more information about alcohol/drug issue

_____ Healthy Lifestyle Considerations

_____ Concerned about moodiness

_____ Stress

_____ Study Skills

_____ Grades and test scores

_____ Getting along with a teacher

_____ Speaking up in class

_____ Family changes

_____ Communicating with parents

_____ Deciding what courses to take in high school

_____ Want to know more about careers/career options

_____ Friendships/relationships

_____ Anger management

_____ Peer pressure

_____ Gaining self-confidence

## Other Concerns I Have (not listed above):

1. _____

2. _____

3. _____

4. _____

Adapted from Gulf Middle School Guidance Department, Pasco County, Florida

*Joe Wittmer, Ph.D. and Mary Ann Clark, Ph.D.*

# Figure 2.3
# ASCA Position Statement: Comprehensive School Counseling Programs

## The Professional School Counselor and Comprehensive School Counseling Programs

(Adopted 1988; revised 1993, 1997, 2005)

## The American School Counselor Association (ASCA) Position

Professional school counselors design and deliver comprehensive school counseling programs that promote student achievement. These programs are comprehensive in scope, preventative in design and developmental in nature. The ASCA National Model: A Framework for School Counseling Programs (ASCA, 2005) outlines the components of a comprehensive school counseling program. The ASCA National Model brings professional school counselors together with one vision and one voice, which creates unity and focus toward improving student achievement.

## The Rationale

A comprehensive school counseling program is an integral component of the school's academic mission. Comprehensive school counseling programs, driven by student data and based on standards in academic, career and personal/social development, promote and enhance the learning process for all students. The ASCA National Model:

- ensures equitable access to a rigorous education for all students
- identifies the knowledge and skills all students will acquire as a result of the K-12 comprehensive school counseling program
- is delivered to all students in a systematic fashion
- is based on data-driven decision making
- is provided by a state-credentialed professional school counselor

Effective school counseling programs are a collaborative effort between the professional school counselor, parents and other educators to create an environment that promotes student achievement. Staff and professional school counselors value and respond to the diversity and individual differences in our societies and communities. Comprehensive school counseling programs ensure equitable access for all students to participate fully in the educational process.

## The Professional School Counselor's Role

Professional school counselors focus their skills, time and energy on direct service to students and families. To achieve maximum program effectiveness, the American School Counselor Association recommends a professional school-counselor-to-student ratio of 1:250 and that professional school counselors spend 80 percent of their time in direct service to students. Professional school counselors participate as members of the educational team and use the skills of leadership, advocacy and collaboration to promote systemic change as appropriate.

The framework of a comprehensive school counseling program consists of the following four components: foundation, delivery system, management system and accountability.

## PROGRAM FOUNDATION

Professional school counselors identify personal beliefs and philosophies to address how all students will benefit from the school counseling program. These beliefs and philosophies guide the development, implementation and evaluation of the comprehensive school counseling program. Professional school counselors create a mission statement aligned with their school's mission and collaborate with others to promote academic, career and personal/social development of all students.

## DELIVERY OF SERVICES

Professional school counselors provide services to students, parents, school staff and the community in the following areas:

- School Guidance Curriculum – This curriculum consists of structured lessons designed to assist students in achieving the desired competencies and to provide all students with the knowledge and skills appropriate for their developmental level. The school guidance curriculum is delivered throughout the school's overall curriculum and is systematically presented by professional school counselors in collaboration with other professional educators in K-12 classroom and group activities.

- Individual Student Planning – Professional school counselors coordinate ongoing systemic activities designed to assist students in establishing personal goals and developing future plans.

- Responsive Services – Responsive services are preventative and/or interventive activities that meet students' immediate and future needs. These needs can be necessitated by events and conditions in the students' lives and may require any of the following:

- individual or group counseling
- consultation with parents, teachers and other educators
- referrals to other school support services or community resources
- peer helping
- information

  Professional school counselors develop confidential relationships with students to help them resolve or cope with problems and developmental concerns.

• System Support – System support consists of management activities that establish, maintain and enhance the total school counseling program and include professional development, consultation, collaboration, program management and operations. Professional school counselors are committed to continual personal and professional development and are proactively involved in professional organizations that promote school counseling at the local, state and national levels.

## PROGRAM MANAGEMENT

Professional school counselors incorporate organizational processes and tools that are concrete, clearly delineated and reflective of the school's needs. Tools and processes include:

- agreements developed with and approved by administrators at the beginning of the school year addressing how the school counseling program is organized and what goals will be accomplished
- advisory councils made up of students, parents, teachers, counselors, administrators and community members to review school counseling program results and to make recommendations
- use of student data to measure the results of the program as well as effect systemic change within the school system so every student receives the benefit of the school counseling program
- action plans for prevention and intervention programs and services that define the desired student competencies and measure achievement result.
- Allotment of 80 percent of the professional school counselor's time to direct service with students
- use of master and weekly calendars to keep students, parents, teachers and administrators informed and to encourage active participation in the school counseling program

## ACCOUNTABILITY

To demonstrate the effectiveness of the school counseling program in measurable terms, professional school counselors report on immediate, intermediate and long-range results showing how students are different as a result of the school counseling program. Professional school counselors use data to show the impact of the school counseling program on school improvement and student achievement. Professional school counselors conduct school counseling program audits that guide future action and improve future results for all students. The performance of the professional school counselor is evaluated on basic standards of practice expected of professional school counselors implementing a school counseling program.

## Summary

Professional school counselors develop and deliver comprehensive school counseling programs that support and promote student achievement. As outlined in the ASCA National Model, these programs include a systematic and planned program delivery involving all students and enhancing the learning process. The comprehensive school counseling program is supported by appropriate resources and implemented by a credentialed professional school counselor. The ASCA National Model brings professional school counselors together with one vision and one voice, which creates unity and focus towards improving student achievement.

# References

American School Counselor Association. (2003, 2005). *The ASCA national model: A framework for school counseling programs.* Alexandria, VA: Author.

American School Counselor Association. (2005). *Position statement: Comprehensive school counseling programs.* Alexandria, VA: Author.

Campbell, C.A., & Dahir, C. (1997). *Sharing the vision: The national standards for school counseling programs.* Alexandria, VA: ASCA Press.

Center for the 4th and 5th R's (1999). *Character education.* www.character.org.

Clark, M.A., & Amatea, E. (2004). Teacher perceptions and expectations of school counselor contributions: Implications for program planning and training. *Professional School Counseling (8)* 2, 32-40.

Cloud, J. (1999). What can schools do? *Time Magazine.* May 3, 1999. Author.

Dahir C., Sheldon, B., & Valiga, M. (1998). *Vision into action: Implementing the national standards for school counseling programs.* Alexandria, VA: ASCA Press.

Erford, B.T., Newsome, D.W., & Rock, E. (2007). Counseling youth at risk. In Bradley T. Erford's *Transforming the school counseling profession.* Upper Saddle River, NJ: Pearson Education.

Gysbers, N.C. (1997). *Comprehensive guidance programs that work.* Greensboro, NC: ERIC Counseling and Personnel Services Clearinghouse.

Myrick, R.D. (2003). *Developmental guidance and counseling: A practical approach* (4th ed.). Minneapolis, MN: Education Media Corporation.

Rye, D.R., & Sparks, R. (1999). *Strengthening K-12 school counseling programs: A support system approach* (2nd ed.). Muncie, IN: Accelerated Development.

Wittmer, J., & Thompson, D. (2006). *Large group counseling: A k-12 sourcebook* (2nd ed.). Minneapolis, MN: Educational Media Corporation.

Wittmer, J., Thompson, D., & Loesch, L. (1997). *Classroom guidance activities: A sourcebook for elementary school counselors.* Minneapolis, MN: Educational Media Corporation.

Zins, J.E., Bloodworth, M.R., Weissberg, R.P., & Walberg, H.J. (2004). The scientific base linking social and emotional learning to school success. In *Building academic success on social and emotional learning: What does the research say?* New York: Teacher's College, Columbia University.

# Chapter 3

## The American School Counselor Association National Model:
## A Framework for School Counseling Programs

**by Judy Bowers**

*Judy Bowers, Ed.D., retired as Guidance Coordinator in the Tucson, Arizona, Unified School District and is an adjunct professor at Northern Arizona University and at the University of Arizona. Dr. Bowers was a high school counselor for 16 years and a teacher for six years. She served as ASCA (American School Counselor Association) President in 2004-2005 and is a co-author of the ASCA National Model and of the ASCA National Model Workbook.*

## Introduction

In March, 2001, ASCA's Governing Board passed a motion to develop a model framework for school counseling programs to incorporate the best practices that have been developed over the last fifty years. This model emphasizes the importance of school counseling programs nationwide using the same framework and same language to bring counselors together following ASCA's theme of "One Vision, One Voice."

The two documents that have been published to meet this motion are *The American School Counselor Association National Model: A Framework for School Counseling Programs* (2003, 2005), and *The ASCA National Model Workbook* (2004). The philosophy of an ASCA National Model school counseling program is that it be comprehensive in scope, preventative in design and developmental in nature.

## Development of the ASCA National Model

The first step in creating a national model was to gather national leaders in school counseling along with practicing school counselors, school counseling educators, state guidance coordinators, school district guidance coordinators, and representatives from The Education Trust with the leadership of the American School Counselor Association. A two and a half day summit convened in June, 2001 where a framework for school counseling programs was established. Summit participants agreed on the following assumptions and criteria.

- A national model must provide a framework that allows flexibility for states and school districts to create a program based on their districts' individual needs and accountability.

- Comprehensive school counseling program must be integral to student academic achievement and must help set higher standards for student achievement.

- School counselors must be the leaders of site school counseling programs.

- School counselors must use the framework of the American School Counselor Association National Model: A Framework for School Counseling Programs, (2005) to deliver their program, and they must develop the four skills to effectively implement their program.

- School counselors in the 21$^{st}$ century are professionals who work as change agents within the educational system to advocate for student needs and student results.

- School counseling programs must be data-driven and result based.

- School counseling programs should be developed and implemented district wide to serve all students.

- Activities must be provided to close the achievement gap among under-performing students.

- School counselors and administrators must be a collaborative team working to have a positive impact on student achievement.

- School counselors must be licensed or credentialed professional school counselors to implement a school counseling program. (requirements are based on the individual state's criteria)

- School counselors utilize technology to implement the program, to advocate for the program, and to collect, analyze and interpret data.

Many states and districts contributed their written program materials to the committee to review. The editors took the best work from these samples and incorporated it within the framework developed by the committee. Many samples showed the work previously done by Drs. Norm Gysbers, C.D. Johnson, Sharon Johnson, and Robert Myrick.

Two other summits were held in May and November, 2002. Draft copies of the National Model were reviewed at these summits as well as the responses gathered during the public comment time. Final copies of the ASCA National Model: A Framework for School Counseling Programs was released in February 2003 during National School Counseling Week. The ASCA National Model Workbook was released in June, 2004, and "The Theory Behind the ASCA National Model" was included in the second edition in June, 2005. A CD with charts and worksheets is included with both of the books.

# New Vision for School Counseling

Now school counselors and principals have the ASCA National Model (ASCA, 2003, 2005) and ASCA National Model Workbook (ASCA, 2004) to use in designing and implementing their school counseling programs. The model represents what a school counseling program should include, providing organizational tools for implementation. Four elements provide the framework that is adaptable to all school counseling programs and can be modified to meet district needs. These areas are foundation, delivery system, management system, and accountability. In the ASCA model graphic, there are elements under each of the four areas that are part of the total school program. Four themes are repeated around the framework of the ASCA model representing skills and attitudes school counselors will need to develop as they implement the Comprehensive Competency Based Guidance (CCBG) program in their schools. The skills are leadership, advocacy, collaboration, and systemic change. The new model recommends that counselors spend 80% of their time in direct services for students. A recommended time allocation for elementary, middle, and high school counselors is found in the delivery system of the model.

The Education Trust (2002) is an independent, nonprofit organization whose mission is to shape educational policy and bring about educational change. In 2001, this organization received a grant from Metropolitan Life Insurance Company to prepare trainers to offer professional development to school district counselors and administrators. The professional development has provided workshops for counselors to develop their skills in the areas of leadership, advocacy, collaboration, and systemic change. The leaders in ASCA and The Education Trust collaborated to combined ASCA's counseling program framework and The Education Trust's four themes or skills for counselors in the ASCA National Model. The Education Trust has provided a major impetus to transform the role of school counselors in K-12 schools and to change the university and college training programs from a therapy based preparation to an education-based preparation (House & Martin, 1998). Collaboration between college educators and practicing school counselors is vital to providing the training program for future counselors that will put them at the center of educational reform.

As the No Child Left Behind (2001) legislation continues to be implemented in schools across the nation, school counselors are expected to take a more active role in academic achievement. National leaders in school counseling purport that it is imperative for school counselors in the 21st Century to know how to successfully implement the ASCA model and work for education reform. They support the idea that when counselors are in the role of being advocates for higher achievement, they are also at the center of the school mission and educational reform (Kuranz 2002; House & Sears, 2002). All students benefit when school counselors collaborate with teachers and principals in an effort to ensure student academic success. School counselors play a critical role in the academic success of all students through collaboration with teachers, parents, and principals (House & Sears 2002).

The ASCA National Model provides a framework to incorporate the three domains of academic achievement, career development, and personal/social development in a school-counseling program. This model encourages counselors to use student data in developing their school-counseling program and to show the results of their program. The biggest change in the future will be that counselors will be expected to spend a larger percent of their time working with all students using developmental guidance lessons and working in the classrooms to support academic achievement. Educational reform issues demand that a priority of school counselors is to promote academic achievement. Martin (2002) states:

*Measurable performance in terms of increased academic achievement for all students is the driving force of educational reform. Professionals who do not add to this bottom line are considered superfluous to our schools. Making school counselors integral players in educational reform requires a new vision, new ways of looking at helping (p. 151).*

House and Hayes (2002) discuss the new vision for school counselors in school reform that encourages them to work as advocates, leaders, and collaborators to help all students achieve by removing systemic barriers. They believe that school counselors are key players in educational reform who must relate their work to the mission of the school and to the student's academic achievement. They point out: "In fact, if school counselors do not relate their work and programs to the mission of schools and document success, they are at risk of extinction" (p. 255).

A variety of forces will affect the future of school counselors and school counseling programs. Counselors will need to be knowledgeable program implementers who successfully collaborate in schools to serve all students by using the ASCA National Model as a framework. School counselors will have the support of the American School Counselor Association as well as their state associations to provide training for counselors. Many state school counseling associations, state guidance directors, and school districts currently provide academies, workshops, and classes to train school counselors in the elements of the National Model. Governing board members, superintendents, principals, and counseling directors are looking for how students are "different as a result of a school counseling program."

# Components of the ASCA National Model

As the ASCA Summit Committee discussed the eighteen elements that needed to be in a school counseling program, the elements were organized into the four areas of foundation, delivery system, management system, and accountability based on similar successful models (Arizona Department of Education, 1997, 2003).

## Foundation

The framework of the National Model is built on the foundation component. The foundation defines the beliefs, philosophy, mission, domains, and standards and aligns with the school's vision, mission and goals. The elements of the foundation are:

- *Mission Statement*: A statement of the purpose of the school counseling program that provides the vision for all students in a school. The school counseling department mission statements aligns with district, state, and national missions for school counseling programs. It also shows linkages with the statement of purpose or mission of the administration and the board of education and reflects school data.

- *Beliefs*: Although beliefs are personal, department and district counselors must come together to discuss their beliefs in the process of developing a school counseling philosophy. What we believe about students, teachers, families, and our educational system is critical in supporting the academic achievement of all students. Beliefs have no right or wrong answers but our beliefs determine our behaviors as we advocate for students.

- *Philosophy*: The philosophy is an agreed-upon set of principles which guide the development, implementation and evaluation of a school counseling program. The principles address all students, focus on prevention, specify the management system, indicate how counselors will maintain their professional competencies, and indicate the ethical guidelines.

- *Domains:* The domains are broad developmental areas that include standards and competencies to promote student behavior and academic achievement.

Each of these areas of student development includes a variety of learning competencies consisting of specific knowledge, attitude, and skills for students to develop. School counseling programs are developed to emphasize age appropriate competencies to be taught to all students through the "guidance curriculum". School counseling programs that are using the ASCA National Model will deliver selected competencies to all students through regular classroom guidance lessons.

The *ASCA National Standards: The National Standards for School Counseling Programs* (Campbell & Dahir, 1997) preceded the development of the National Model and helped form a foundation for the principles of the Model. There are three major standards which correspond to the three domains of the National Model; academic, career, and personal/social development (See Appendix A).

The complete list of all the ASCA competencies and indicators are found in the ASCA National Model. When counselors are deciding on the competencies and indicators to use for the elementary school level, the middle school level, and the high school level, it is suggested that the ASCA National Standards for Students: Developmental Cross Walking Tool (ASCA, 2005) be used. This tool has four columns for each competency and counselors will be able to easily check the competencies they feel are appropriate for a particular grade. The Curriculum Cross Walking Tool includes standards, competencies and indicators that can be used to write the curriculum counselors will be using to implement each competency. Ideally, a K-12 core team of counselors in a district would plan a comprehensive program together.

## Delivery System

All activities that a school counselor performs to deliver the ASCA National Model program are framed within the delivery system.

- *Guidance curriculum:* This element consists of structured developmental lessons presented systemically through classroom and group activities for students in kindergarten through twelfth grade. The purpose of the guidance curriculum is to provide preventative, proactive lessons to promote positive mental health and academic achievement to succeed in the future. Guidance curriculum is provided to all students while closing the gap curriculum is provided to students who need extra help based on school data.

- *Individual Planning with Students:* This element consists of activities that help all students plan, monitor and manage their own learning as well as their personal career development. Within this component, students evaluate their education, career and personal goals. School counselors help students make transitions to the next level generally delivering these activities on an individual basis.

- *Responsive Services:* This element consists of activities to meet the immediate needs and concerns of students. This component is available to all students and is often student initiated and delivered through strategies such as consultation, personal counseling, crisis counseling, and referrals.

- *Systems Support:* Management activities that support the school counseling program such as professional development, staff and community relations, consultation with teachers, advisory council, program management, and research and development are contained in this element.

Elementary, middle, and high school counselors each devote varying amounts of time to the four areas of the delivery system. Gysbers and Henderson (2006) provide suggested time allocations for counselors in each of the three levels of school counseling (see Appendix B). Individual counselors and districts have adjusted these recommended time allocations to meet the needs of their schools. For example, in some elementary schools, school counselors spend 50% of their time in guidance curriculum and less time in responsive services (TUSD, 2005).

## Management System

Intertwined with the delivery system is the management system, which is a systematic way of delineating resources and staff responsibilities and defining accountability in terms of accomplished results. As managers of their program, it is vital that school counselors assume the responsibility to develop a school counseling program that is based on student data and reaches all students. Elements in this area are essential to successful program implementation and sustainability. Elements include:

- *Management/Counselor Principal Agreements:* This yearly agreement between the counselor and the site administrator is the most powerful tool of the ASCA Model. Included are the responsibilities of individual counselors for students, staff, and community as well as an indication of the amount of time the counselor will devote to each of the four areas of the delivery system.

- *Advisory Council:* A school counseling program advisory committee is an appointed group of people who are charged with the objectives of reviewing the school counseling goals and recommending changes to reflect community needs. Membership includes school and community representatives from a diverse background. Two meetings are held each year.

- *Use of Data:* Comprehensive school counseling programs are data driven, and school counselors are proficient in analyzing, interpreting, and displaying data. School counselors use student-achievement data, standards and competency-related data, and program evaluation data in developing their school counseling programs each year. Impact of the school counseling program is shown through process data, perception data, and results data.

- *Action Plans:* These are plans detailing how the competencies and results will be achieved. Similar to a lesson plan, the action plan details the competencies addressed, the description of the activity, curriculum used, students addressed, and evaluation method. Action plans are used with guidance curriculum and with closing the gap curriculum. After the lesson, school counselors evaluate the lesson delivered and they note suggested changes for the next time a lesson is delivered.

- *Use of Time:* The ASCA National Model recommends that school counselors spend 80% of their time in direct service with students. Recommended amounts of time for elementary, middle and high school counselors are shown in the chart under the delivery system.

- *Calendars:* Once counselors have decided the amount of time they will spend in each area of the delivery system, a master calendar and a weekly calendar should be developed to keep administrators, students, parents, and teachers informed. It is recommended that counselors put the weekly calendar on the office door indicating the teacher's classroom they will be in and the class period. Yearly calendars can be distributed to all teachers in the school and a list of major activities and dates could be put in the school's newsletter.

## Accountability System

Counselors, administrators, and school board members are continually challenged to demonstrate the value of school counseling programs. Accountability and evaluation of school counseling programs are absolute necessities and it is imperative that school counselors collect and analyze data to show their impact on student achievement.

Using a **results report**, counselors are provided with a simple form to show the results of their guidance curriculum using process, perception, and results data. In addition, immediate, intermediate, and long-range results are collected and analyzed for program improvement.

Thirteen **School Counselor Performance Standards**, basic standards of practice expected of school counselors implementing a school counseling program, are included in the National Model. These performance standards can be used as a self evaluation for school counselors and/or as a counselor evaluation tool by administrators.

**The Program Audit** is an organizational tool that can be used in two ways. School counselors can complete the audit evaluating the degree to which each National Model element is implemented in their school. It can also be used as a measure of excellence for each element.

# Implementation of the ASCA National Model

Implementing an ASCA National Model program does not mean throwing out what school counselors are doing and adding a completely new program, but rather, school counselors can look at what they are currently doing and analyze how their current program fits into an ASCA National Model. One of the activities that has been successfully used with school counselors and with administrators is to identify 5-10 types of work that school counselors do and write each on a sticky note. Examples could include groups, registration, attending meetings, and working on 4-year student plans. Each sticky note is placed in one of the four areas of the delivery system (guidance curriculum, individual student planning, responsive services, and systems support) on a large piece of paper. After all types of work are placed on the paper, counselors and administrators discuss how the counselor's work does fit into these four areas. Often there are tasks that do not fit in one of the areas, and some may be considered non-guidance work that school counselors should not be performing. When these areas are identified, it is suggested that school counselors and administrators discuss how some of these tasks might be assigned to other school staff members. By completing the process, school counselors and administrators come to acknowledge that the current school counseling program needs some modification to meet the criteria of the National Model.

In addition to working with school counselors regarding a change in school counseling programs, it is also important to work with administrators and governing board members to help them understand the changes necessary to improve the school counseling program. A survey may be given to gauge community support, leadership, school counselor beliefs and attitudes, school counselors' skills and district resources. School district leaders find such a survey valuable in looking at all the stakeholders and the requirements necessary to implement change.

## Successful Districts

In 1990, the state of Arizona combined the works of national leaders in school counseling (Gysbers & Henderson; Johnson & Johnson) in a model that was a precedent for the ASCA National Model. The work of Robert Myrick was added to the Arizona model in the mid 90s. It was the vision of Dr. Tina Ammon, Arizona Director of School Counseling Programs, to develop a model for school counselors that would serve all students in Arizona. That Arizona school counseling program is called the Comprehensive Competency Based Guidance (CCBG) program. Today Arizona school counselors use the ASCA National Model interchangeably with the Arizona CCBG program (see Appendix C). Several major state and national grants were written that provided for a large increase in school counselors who were involved in implementing CCBG programs. Evaluations of the programs resulted in the expansion of the programs.

Several conclusions have been identified through the work of these grants related to the implementation of the CCBG/ASCA National Model School Counseling programs. First, schools must have full time elementary counselors to fully implement the CCBG/ASCA National Model framework. Second, the ratio of 1 counselor to 350 elementary students provides the best opportunities to fully implement the programs. Third, school counselors implementing a CCBG/ASCA National Model School Counseling program do make a difference in academic achievement, in closing the gap between groups of students, in parent involvement, and in working with teachers to implement better systems of discipline. Such results have provided accountability data for these districts and have also provided an impetus for the implementation of the model across the country.

## Steps to Implement an ASCA National Model Program

As school counselors, administrators, and school district leaders begin the steps to implement an ASCA National Model School counseling program, consider following these steps as outlined in the ASCA National Model (2005) and the ASCA National Model Workbook (2004).

1. **Planning**
   - Establish leadership
   - Develop a commitment to action
   - Establish an advisory council
   - Gain administrative and board support
   - Assess what is currently working

2. **Building the foundation**
   - Analyze school and student data
   - Identify current strengths and areas for improvement
   - Discuss beliefs about students and learning
   - Write philosophy and mission statement
   - Select standards, competencies and indictors and assign to grade levels
   - Determine program priorities

3. **Designing the Delivery system**
   - Determine time allotments for each component
   - Develop action plans
   - Identify the guidance curriculum to be used

- Determine the data that will be collected
- Decide which counselors will perform which activities
- Rally administrative support

4. **Setting up the School Counseling Program (Management)**
   - Establish a program budget
   - Ensure the following preconditions are met: equal access, adequate budget/resources, collaborative efforts, administrative support, state leadership/technical support
   - Complete management agreement forms

5. **Working the School counseling Program (Management)**
   - Develop a master planning calendar
   - Set time allocations
   - Develop weekly and monthly planning calendars
   - Implement curriculum activities at each grade level
   - Develop at least one closing-the-gap activity

6. **Promoting the School Counseling Program (Advocacy)**
   - Develop a program brochure
   - Present the program to school staff
   - Prevent the program to the school board for official approval
   - Develop a website

7. **Monitoring Program Results (Accountability)**
   - Produce program results reports
   - Develop evaluation standards and indicators
   - Review audit results for improvement ideas
   - Use results for programmatic decisions
   - Assess the school counseling team

8. **Monitoring Students' Progress (Accountability)**
   - Assess student mastery of selected competencies
   - Track program impact on action plan goals
   - Track program impact on school wide goals, such as achievement and attendance

## Summary

As school counseling departments and districts move to implement an ASCA National Model program, it is important to remember to start slowly, celebrate accomplishments, expand the leadership base, brainstorm potential obstacles and develop strategies to overcome barriers. The ASCA National Model was written to be a framework for school counseling programs and each school and district is encouraged to personalize the model to fit their needs. The ASCA National Model workbook will take school counselor teams through the development of the model step by step. The audit at the end of each chapter will serve as a check list to ensure that all important point have been included. Schools are encouraged to modify forms to meet their school needs. School counselors working as leaders, advocates, and collaborators will create systemic change through the implementation of an ASCA Model school counseling program that serves all students and closes achievement gaps.

## References

American School Counselor Association. (2003, 2005). *American school counselor association national model: A framework for school counseling programs.* Alexandria, VA: Author.

American School Counselor Association. (2004). *The ASCA national model workbook.* Alexandria, VA: Author.

Arizona Department of Education. (2003). *Arizona counselors' academy: Hooked on results.* Author.

Arizona Department of Education. (1997). *Arizona comprehensive competency based guidance (CCBG program) Academy edition.* Author

Campbell, C.A., & Dahir, C.A. (1997). *Sharing the vision: The national standards for school counseling programs.* Alexandria, VA: American School Counselor Association.

Gysbers, N., & Henderson, P. (1997). *Comprehensive Guidance Programs that work—II.* Greensboro, NC: ERIC/CASS.

Gysbers, N., & Henderson, P. (2006). *Developing and managing your school guidance program* (4th ed.). Alexandria, VA: American School Counselor Association.

House, R.M., & Hayes, R.L. (2002). *School counselors: Becoming key players in school reform. Professional School Counseling, 5*(4), 249-256.

House, R.M., & Martin, P.J. (1998). *Advocating for better futures for all students: A new vision for school counselors. Education, 119,* 284-291.

House, R.M., & Sears, S.J. (2002). *Preparing school counselors to be leaders and advocates: A critical need in the new millennium. Theory Into Practice, 41*(3), 154-162.

Johnson, C.D., & Johnson, S.K. (2001). *Results-based student support programs: Leadership academy workbook.* San Juan Capistrano, CA: Professional Update.

Kuranz, M. (2002). *Cultivating student potential. Professional School Counseling, 5*(3), 172-179.

Martin, P.J. (2002). *Transforming school counseling: A national perspective. Theory into practice. 41*(3), 148-153.

Montano, R. (2004). *Sunnyside school district comprehensive competency based guidance program.* Sunnyside School District.

The Education Trust (2002). *Achievement in America: 2001.* Washington DC: Author.

Tucson Unified School District (1993, 1995, 1998, 2000, 2002, 2005). *Guidance and counseling program handbook K-12.* Tucson, AZ: Tucson Unified School District.

# Appendix A
## ASCA National Standards for Student Academic, Career and Personal/Social Development (Campbell & Dahir, 1997)

### Academic Standards:

A. Students will acquire the attitudes, knowledge and skills contributing to effective learning in school and across the life-span.

B. Students will complete school with the academic preparation essential to choose from a wide range of substantial post-secondary options, including college.

C. Students will understand the relationship of academics to the world of work and to life at home and in the community.

### Career Development

A. Students will acquire the skills to investigate the world of work in relation to knowledge of self and to make informed career decisions.

B. Students will employ strategies to achieve future career goals with success and satisfaction.

C. Students will understand the relationship between personal qualities, education, training and the world of work.

### Personal/Social Development

A. Students will acquire the knowledge, attitudes and interpersonal skills to help them understand and respect self and others.

B. Students will make decisions, set goals and take necessary action to achieve goals.

C. Students will understand safety and survival skills

# Appendix B
## Time And Task Distribution
## ASCA National Model Program Time Percentages

| Delivery System Component | Elementary Level % of Time | Middle School % of Time | High School % of Time |
|---|---|---|---|
| Guidance Curriculum | 35% - 45% | 25% - 35% | 15% - 25% |
| Individual Student Planning | 5% - 10% | 15% - 25% | 25% - 35% |
| Responsive Services | 30% - 40% | 30% - 40% | 25% - 35% |
| System Support | 10% - 15% | 10% - 15% | 15% - 20% |

# Appendix C
# Tucson Unified School District K-12 Guidance and Counseling Comprehensive Competency Based Guidance Program Model

The counselors in Tucson Unified School District implement a comprehensive competency based guidance program (CCBG). This approach consists of a system of elements that are interrelated in interdependent. CCBG provides a framework for the program, clearly defines the role of the school counselor, and is measured by student competency attainment. The following is the TUSD Guidance and Counseling conceptual model.

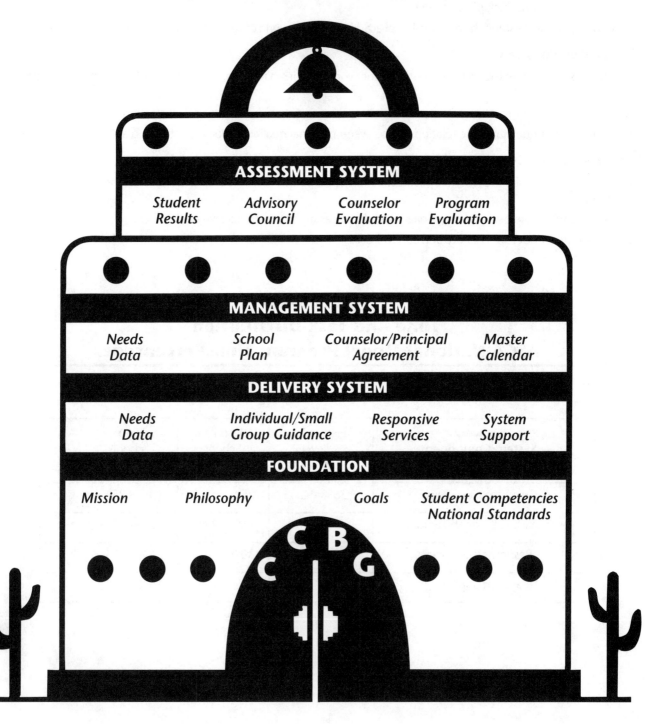

**ASSESSMENT SYSTEM**

| Student Results | Advisory Council | Counselor Evaluation | Program Evaluation |

**MANAGEMENT SYSTEM**

| Needs Data | School Plan | Counselor/Principal Agreement | Master Calendar |

**DELIVERY SYSTEM**

| Needs Data | Individual/Small Group Guidance | Responsive Services | System Support |

**FOUNDATION**

| Mission | Philosophy | Goals | Student Competencies National Standards |

CCBG

# Section II

# The Counselor's Role in Managing the Program

As noted in Chapter 2, school developmental guidance and counseling programs are designed to help *all* students (K-12) develop their educational, social, career, and personal strengths. In addition, effective developmental professional school counselors assist students to become responsible and productive individuals. What is the role of developmental school counselors and how do they effectively manage comprehensive counseling programs? That is the focus of this section.

The appropriate roles of developmentally oriented elementary, middle, and high school counselors, along with management strategies, are described and delineated. The writers of the chapters concerning the three school levels (elementary, middle, and high school) clearly indicate that the developmental approach focuses on the *normal* processes students encounter while growing up in our complex society. And, as noted several times throughout these next three chapters, the school counselor's function includes *creating*, *organizing*, and *managing* comprehensive developmental guidance and counseling programs which includes providing appropriate counselor interventions as needed. Developmental counseling programs, at all three school levels, are integral parts of a school's total educational program.

In Chapter 4, Dr. Beverly Snyder writes: *In an effective program, the school administration, faculty, students, parents, and community combine efforts to provide an all-encompassing, comprehensive guidance program for all students.*

Dr. Snyder does an excellent job of providing the organizational structure needed for a successful developmentally oriented counseling program at the elementary level. In addition, she discusses implementation strategies and describes the role and function of an effective elementary school counselor. Management strategies needed to succeed as an elementary counselor are also presented.

In discussing the role and function of a developmental middle school counselor (Chapter 5), Dr. Bonnie Baker writes: *The often used phrase 'caught in the middle' could easily serve as a motto for the middle school counselor of the new millennium for several reasons. First, the unique population of middle school students are 'caught in the middle' between childhood and adolescence in a developmental stage known as 'transescence.' This difficult developmental period accounts for many of the counseling issues middle school counselors must address each and every school day.* Dr. Baker does an excellent job in delineating workable strategies for today's developmentally oriented middle school counselor. Her section on effective "time management" strategies is especially appropriate for the busy middle school counselor.

Drs. Doris Coy and Susan Sears (Chapter 6) have written an excellent chapter concerning the developmentally oriented high school counselor's role and function. They state that the effective high school developmental counseling program is *driven by student needs and results in student outcomes for which counselors are accountable.* Coy and Sears also remind us that high school counselors must carefully choose how they spend their time and energy, particularly with the increased emphasis on success for all students.. In addition, they've provided (Figure 6.1) a crisis management policy that applies to schools at all levels.

Chapter 7 by Dr. Smith-Adcock discusses the important debate about meeting the mental health needs of students during an era when school counselors are expected to assist all students to be academically successful. She reviews the literature on this topic and makes recommendations for the coordination of such services and the importance of collaborative efforts with community agencies. Drs. Mary Ann Clark and Carolyn Stone write concerning the developmental school counselor as educational leader in the final chapter of Section II. The ASCA National Model emphasizes this important role for school counselors, and the authors urge counselors to look for opportunities to develop and implement their special leadership skills in their respective schools.

School counselors must be able to effectively and succinctly articulate their role and function to "self" and "others." If not (and unfortunately this is too often the case) someone else, usually the school principal, may do it for them.

*Mary Ann Clark and Joe Wittmer*

# Chapter 4

# Managing an Elementary School Developmental Counseling Program: The Role of the Counselor

by
**Beverly A. Snyder**

*Beverly Snyder, Ed.D., NCC, is a Professor at the University of Colorado at Colorado Springs, School of Education, Counseling and Human Services Program. She held the position of district Instructional Support Counselor in Orange County, Florida during the time the elementary counseling program described here was being developed and when this chapter first was written.*

## Introduction

Many researchers and school counseling experts (Gysbers, 1997; Myrick, 2003) believe that the learning, personal/social, and career development needs of students can be more effectively met with a kindergarten through twelfth grade guidance program that systematically and comprehensively addresses developmental stages that students experience as they progress through the school. Such developmentally-based school counseling programs are structured so as to systematically parallel the identifiable developmental stages through which children progress. Modern day developmental programs, such as the one described in this chapter, have advanced from a reactive, crisis model to a proactive approach.

As stated by Wittmer and Clark in Chapter 1, the concept that guidance and counseling services should be for all students is a fundamental tenet of the developmental approach described in this chapter. This approach also embraces several other ideas that found their beginnings in the school restructuring/reform movement. They include the following: (1) The elementary school developmental guidance and counseling program should have a curriculum-based approach responsive to the needs of the population it serves; (2) Activities conducted through classroom guidance, small groups, and so forth should be based on overall goals and objectives that are applicable to this age level (Gysbers & Henderson, 2006; Myrick, 2003; Wittmer & Thompson, 2006); (3) Developmental guidance and counseling programs are proactive and based on

educating today's youngsters rather than simply being reactive to the multiple concerns that invariably appear in their lives (Myrick, 2003); and (4) The unique and diverse needs of the school's student body should be included in program development.

## Program Description

A comprehensive elementary level developmental guidance program should be founded on the belief that each student is unique and singular, possessing intrinsic and specific rights. Developmental school counselors should attempt to identify certain skills and experiences that elementary age students need to experience as part of their being successful in school and in other aspects of their lives. As noted, the skill building component in the developmental approach is related directly to children's developmental stages, tasks, and learning conditions. The comprehensive developmental approach to elementary school counseling described in this chapter focuses on the needs common to all students and is based, in large part, on the often quoted and still relevant Havighurst (1972) model given below:

## Developmental Stages/Tasks

### Infancy and Early Childhood (Ages 0-5)

1. Learning to walk

2. Learning to take solid foods

3. Learning to talk

4. Learning to control elimination of body wastes

5. Learning sex differences and sexual modesty

6. Forming concepts and learning language to describe social and physical reality

7. Learning to relate emotionally to parents and siblings; identifying relationships

8. Getting ready to read

9. Learning to distinguish right and wrong and beginning to develop a conscience

## Middle Childhood (Ages 6-11)

1. Learning physical skills necessary for ordinary games

2. Building wholesome attitudes toward oneself and sense of self-concept

3. Learning to get along with age mates—moving from the circle to groups outside the home

4. Learning the skills of tolerance and patience

5. Learning appropriate masculine or feminine social roles

6. Developing fundamental skills in reading, writing, and calculating

7. Developing concepts necessary for everyday living

8. Developing conscience, morality, and a scale of values

9. Achieving personal independence

10. Developing attitudes toward social groups and institutions, through experiences and imitation

A comprehensive developmental guidance program is an integral part of the total elementary school program with the *counselor* being responsible for providing the leadership for its success. In an effective program, the school administration, faculty, students, parents, and community combine their efforts to provide an all-encompassing, comprehensive guidance program. Such a team approach to guidance and counseling is crucial to the success of any elementary school counseling.

I believe that the comprehensive, developmental counseling and guidance program described here results in the academic, career, and personal social development of elementary aged children as given in the ASCA National Model (ASCA, 2005). And, I urge all elementary schools to begin the implementation of these very important standards in their respective schools as Wittmer and Clark discuss in chapter two of this book.

## Program Overview

In order to conceptualize a typical elementary guidance and counseling program more easily, a chart should be developed showing the basis of the program, the structure used to achieve goals, and the functions assumed in implementing the program's components. Acknowledgment is given to the work of Norman Gysbers and Robert D. Myrick, pioneers in the field. A program overview is presented in Figure 4.1.

## Basis of the Program

Student goals and Myrick's (2003) principles of developmental counseling can provide the basis of an elementary guidance program. The structure of the program includes outlines of the system-wide philosophy and identifies the expected student outcomes. In addition, this structure provides an objective method for evaluating the effectiveness of the comprehensive developmental approach by measuring parent and student perceptions according to the goals. Further, administrators', counselors', and teachers' perceptions of the program's effectiveness can be measured by correlating their perceptions with the *principles* of the program. In order to be effective, the foundation of an elementary guidance program must also provide the means by which it can be evaluated. This is the age of counselor "accountability," regardless of the school level (Schmidt, 2003).

Myrick (2003) identified eight goals for school guidance programs can be adopted for use with its K-12 programs. These goals, the same for each grade level, are:

1. understanding the school environment

2. understanding self and others

3. understanding attitudes and behavior

4. decision making and problem solving

5. interpersonal and communication skills

6. school success skills

7. career awareness and educational planning

8. community pride and involvement

Objectives for each of the above goals can be implemented. These objectives are developmentally appropriate for each grade level and the activities to achieve the objectives are age specific.

Knowing your objectives, and having them approved by your administration and adhered to by the rest of your school's staff is essential to an effective elementary school guidance program. Place your goals and objectives in writing, have them approved by the school's administration, and then share them with all school faculty and staff members.

As Wittmer and Clark stated in Chapter 1, "A developmental counseling program serves all students." This is the main foundation of an elementary guidance and counseling program. In addition, developmental school counseling includes counselors who provide specialized counseling services and interventions. These specialized components are described next.

# Program Components

An elementary counseling program's structure provides the means to achieve student goals and is referred to as "Program Components." The program components are divided into the two categories of *direct* and *indirect* services. The direct category includes all activities conducted with students in order to provide necessary and needed services. This category includes, for example, large and small group guidance, counseling individuals, setting up and working with the peer helpers' program, consultation, parenting classes, and so forth. The indirect category includes those activities required to support the provision of the above direct services to students and others, and includes the coordination and administrative functions, facilitation of the career education program, professional development activities, and consultation.

## Large Group Guidance

The large group guidance component in an elementary program can provide delivery of services to the largest number of students possible (at one time) and is based on their age level and developmental needs. The large group guidance lessons are arranged by goal (listed previously) with lessons for both primary and intermediate objectives for each goal.

In addition to the lessons written by local educators, elementary counselors use commercially developed programs which can be led by counselors or teachers. Some programs may include communication skills, character education, cooperative discipline, conflict resolution, drug and alcohol prevention, study skills, and test preparation. However, all such activities are coordinated by the counselor. Various groups and members of the community also may provide large group guidance lessons on a variety of topics. Such groups' efforts are coordinated by the counselor to best meet the previously described goals of the counseling program. Conducting effective classroom guidance presentations must be a team effort and cannot rest with the counselor alone. It is best to incorporate *all* who work with children in your school. The team approach is the best and most effective approach in achieving the goals and objectives of a developmental program (Wittmer & Thompson, 2006).

## Small Group Guidance

Small group guidance is defined by Myrick (2003) as "a unique educational experience in which students can work together to explore their ideas, attitudes, feelings, and behaviors, especially as related to personal development and progress in school" (p. 187).

An Orange County writing team developed a "Curriculum for Small Group Counseling" by focusing on problem-centered, growth-centered, and crisis-centered groups as described by Myrick (2003). The curriculum was revised to include additional sessions for groups on "Divorce" and "Appreciating Cultural Differences."

As mentioned previously, accountability is vital for the elementary school counselor. Thus, elementary counselors should conduct regular evaluations of their small and large group counseling units.

## Counseling Individual Students

Professional elementary school counselors can guide students toward more productive actions at school and home and can assist students in solving problems that often occur unexpectedly.

Individual counseling has been popular in schools for many reasons. Individual counseling is easier to schedule than other interventions and may seem more practical (Myrick, 2003) to a counselor's non-counseling colleagues. While it is the most frequently used counselor intervention (Schmidt, 2003), elementary counselors are gradually reducing the time spent with individuals because it is less efficient than working with large numbers of children (Wittmer, Thompson, & Loesch, 1997).

Counselors are realizing that in order to reach all students there is a limit to the amount of time that can be spent in individual counseling.

Too much time with individual students may cause you to be perceived as a "therapist" and will probably shortchange most of the student body. You simply do not have the time; know when to refer a troubled student!

Problems appropriately addressed by individual counseling include peer-related difficulties, academic problems, and assistance in dealing with parents or community agencies. Individual counseling priorities can include facilitating behavior change, increasing coping skills, improving decision making and problem solving, improving peer relationships, and facilitating client potential. An additional goal, targeted for exceptional education students, is normalization. This is a process in which exceptional students are helped to acquire skills that allow for integration into the *regular* classroom.

With the advent of the Student Assistance Program (SAP), more help is available to children and families in crisis. The Student Assistance Program is an outgrowth of the national effort to reduce the number of children who are at risk for drug and/or other substance abuse and is funded with *"Drug Free Schools"* money available through the Federal government. This program provides each school counselor involved with the project with a SAP team who can be of immediate assistance when crisis intervention is needed. The SAP team members are considered to exist under the "umbrella of services" offered by the school counselor. This allows the counselor to continue implementing the regularly scheduled program (i.e., classroom guidance, small groups, consultation, peer helpers) while the individuals requiring crisis intervention also receive needed services from the SAP team personnel. Again, these services are coordinated by the school counselor.

Individual counseling is a respected and valued intervention; it is a luxury in elementary schools where the student/counselor ratio may be 1,000 to 1. Counseling students in groups provides more services to more students more efficiently. Thus, as indicated in Figure 4.2, elementary counselors are encouraged to do *no* more than *5 hours* of individual counseling with students each week.

## Peer Helpers

Several terms are used interchangeably to describe peer helpers. They include Peer Facilitators, Peer Counselors, Pals, and Helping Hands.

The process of peer helping refers to students who use helping skills and concepts to assist other students—and sometimes adults—to think about ideas and feelings, to explore alternatives to situations, to lead the conflict mediation program, and to help others make responsible decisions.

Many peer programs have become successful because of their well developed and well organized systematic procedures for teaching interpersonal skills and preparing facilitators for different roles. Elementary counselors can identify helping projects in which the peers can put their skills to use while being supervised.

Systematic training programs for peer helpers makes a positive difference, not the least of which is the professional and personal reward experienced by the peer trainer. Peer helping programs have enhanced the developmental guidance program by extending more services to more students, developing leadership skills among students, and empowering students to learn more about themselves and each other. Peers can be excellent helpers for the elementary counselor in various important areas and topics of interest to elementary level students. One of these very important and current, timely areas is in violence prevention programs where specially trained fifth grade peer mediators give invaluable assistance to the elementary school counselor (Wittmer, Thompson, & Sheperis, 1999).

## Consultation

The counselor's consultant role includes working with teachers, parents, administrators, and other educational specialists on matters that involve student understanding and management. The America School Counselor Association (ASCA) defines consultation as a cooperative process in which the school counselor/consultant assists others to think through problems and to develop skills that make them more effective in working with students (ASCA, 1999). Noting that consulting is a relatively new function for school counselors, Schmidt (2003) stated that "consulting is a relationship in which two or more people identify a purpose, establish a goal, plan strategies to meet that goal, and assign responsibilities to carry out these strategies."

There is a distinct difference between consultation and collaboration, which counselors may also engage in periodically. Collaboration occurs when the consultant agrees to be part of the plan. In doing so, the consultant loses some objectivity and increases the personal investment in seeing that the plan works. In collaboration, planning and implementing are a joint effort. It is an important distinction for elementary level counselors to be aware of when making professional judgments about entering counseling, consultation, or collaboration with a person who has requested their assistance. Each function requires a different perspective and involves the counselor in varying degrees.

## Parenting Classes

During the past decade we have witnessed the advent of inexpensive personal computers and the internet, an increase in convenience foods, electronic games, and cell phones, among other things. It appears that many families' life-styles revolve around a chase for better jobs, different housing, and the latest sports equipment, while others deal with the impact of abuse, neglect, poverty, and many varieties of dysfunctionalities. Each of these changes has its impact on the lives of our children and families. The changing face of the American life-style has affected all ages of children from preschoolers who lack security and stability to latchkey elementary aged students who have little supervision or little quality time with parents. These children, with their high energy levels, often lack guidance from the adults in their lives to cope with the fast-paced change surrounding them. Chaos often prevails in neighborhoods where little direction is provided on how to get through the growing years. Elementary school counselors play a major role in assisting both students and their families to effectively manage this fast pace.

Based on the work of Capuzzi and Gross (2003) involving at-risk children and youth, many counselors recognize they must involve the parents in a proactive guidance program. Rather than a psychotherapeutic approach, it is important to focus on a psycho-educational model entailing instruction for parents and families on a problem-solving method of handling stress and children's inappropriate behaviors. Elementary school counselors *teach* parents that interventions should be responsive to the factors that put children and families at risk, rather than just focusing on the behaviors themselves.

Experience indicates that if parents don't know how to be effective models for their children, they can and need to be taught. I believe this is the best (and maybe only) way to interrupt the cycle of unmet needs. To meet this goal, counselor-led parenting programs have been established in a number of elementary schools.

Many counselors use the *Systematic Training for Effective Parenting (STEP)* materials or have developed their own sessions based on their personal experience of "what works." The Student Assistance Program (SAP described previously) also offers parenting classes at adult education school settings. This program can provide child-care at the same location with certified teachers and with aides who work with the children, while their parents attend parenting classes. Some school districts have a Parent Resource Center. Personnel work closely with school counselors and others in community agencies to provide multiple programs in an attempt to meet the diverse needs of a multicultural population.

## Coordination: An Indirect Service

While coordinating is not always highly visible as one of the indirect services offered to students, it is a routine part of an elementary counselor's role and function. Coordination as a counselor intervention is the process of managing *indirect* guidance services to students, including special events and general procedures. It often involves collecting data and information, allocating materials and resources, arranging and organizing meetings, developing and operating special programs, supervising and monitoring others, and providing leadership (Myrick, 2003).

As we move further into the new millennium, more and more coordinating challenges will arise that need to be managed by the school-based elementary level counselor. These include the Peer Helper Program, Student Assistance Program, the rise of full-service schools that house a comprehensive battery of services provided by many agencies in the community, the various Partners-in-Education businesses that most schools have, parent volunteers, and the many community groups who have programs designed to meet students' *affective* needs. I visualize the counselor as the hub of this wheel, holding together (by coordination) the many spokes that complete the team effort required of a comprehensive developmental guidance and counseling program.

## Administrative Functions: Indirect Services

This component of indirect services includes the behind-the-scenes activities that need to occur to support the direct services of any effective school guidance program. Coordinating administrative functions includes records management, supervision of clerical support, high-stakes testing and other guidance-related administrative duties. Since many schools have a very high transient ratio, it is an important part of the counselor's function to monitor the incoming and outgoing student records to assure as smooth a transition as possible for the students. Counselors frequently have the guidance paraprofessionals (whom they have trained) check student folders for the necessary documentation to enter school. And then, the paraprofessionals pass them on to the counselor for perusal and subsequent action. This is especially so for exceptional student education records and any court ordered documents.

Other guidance related administrative functions include assisting the district-wide assessment coordinator with the process of arranging the achievement test schedule, occasionally monitoring the test-taking rooms, and most importantly, interpreting the test results to students and their parents. Most often, test results are conveyed to students and parents in group settings. However, counselors do consult with parents individually if they have specific concerns or make a special request for further interpretation or follow-up concerning their child.

## Career Education

Career Education includes coordinating the exploration and the acquisition of skills and attitudes necessary for students to be successful in a high-tech world. It is important to have an articulated plan for all grade levels. Its aim is to help students acquire and utilize the knowledge, skills, and attitudes necessary to make work meaningful, productive, and satisfying. The plan begins in kindergarten and extends throughout school, and hopefully, throughout one's working life, linking basic subjects together and relating them to the contemporary "real" world.

The elementary career education program assists children by developing career awareness. It helps them to know themselves, their interests, talents, and abilities; to know about available careers; to develop wholesome attitudes toward work and society; and to develop awareness of the decision-making process. The program also assists parents in becoming more involved in their child's decision-making process and to become more knowledgeable of occupations and labor trends.

# Professional Development

A counselor's continued professional development is imperative. This includes attending the monthly meetings held for all counselors district-wide, local ACA and ASCA meetings if available, state counseling association conventions, making presentations, being aware of which legislation affects counselors, and in general, staying abreast of the latest developments in the counseling field. The elementary school counselor's role will continue to change rapidly. The best way to "stay abreast" is through professional development activities. The non-involved counselor often "burns out."

# Program Implementation Strategies

Figure 4.3 depicts the process of implementing a developmental guidance and counseling program. Beginning with a needs assessment, the process then moves to the selection of specific goals and objectives by the school based guidance committee. Following the selection of annual priorities, the plan is developed and made available to the principal, faculty, and the county-level program specialist for guidance. As can be seen (and described throughout this chapter), the delivery of specific activities is conducted by teachers, administrators, counselors, and other specialists and parents. The plan is evaluated near the end of the school year to determine program effectiveness and to demonstrate accountability for having met student needs.

## The Guidance Committee

As Wittmer and Clark mentioned previously, it is important to establish, early on, a guidance and counseling committee. The committee helps identify student needs and recommends different kinds of guidance programs and activities throughout the year. It serves as a funnel through which information can be processed by counselors, teachers, and administrators. The committee meets regularly to search for ways that all school personnel can work together more efficiently in the delivery of guidance services.

The guidance committee may elicit support from faculty before initiating certain guidance and counseling procedures. A typical committee may be composed of the counselor and one teacher representative from each grade level, from exceptional education, an elective teacher, and parents, with input from the administration.

These committees can be initial sounding boards for new ideas and programs that are being considered. The committee might: (1) review guidance materials and activities; (2) recommend strategies and interventions; (3) examine student data to identify target populations that need guidance and counseling services; (4) help evaluate the guidance program; (5) discuss ideas before they are presented to the total faculty; and (6) serve as a resource group to the counselor.

In many districts, each elementary counselor develops an annual guidance plan; this is the guidance department's proposal for meeting the goals and objectives targeted by the guidance committee. The plan specifies the approximate dates for delivering the various guidance components such as classroom guidance sessions, small groups, and so forth, and includes activities provided by other resources beyond the counselor. The plan also contains procedures pertaining to program evaluation. It can be part of a school's "improvement" plan.

The Annual Guidance Plan is most effective if developed in coordination with the principal and the guidance committee. When completed, all school staff should be aware of, and have access to, the written plan. A copy of the plan should also be provided to the district administrator. The elementary level, comprehensive, developmental annual guidance plan is a team effort by administrators, teachers, counselors, other support personnel, the parents, and other community members representing the guidance committee.

## Principal's Role

The elementary school principal, as chief administrator, is ultimately responsible for the success of a developmental guidance and counseling program. He or she must *understand* and *appreciate* the counselor's role and function. Such support includes the provision of adequate facilities, materials, clerical help, and permitting the counselor to use his or her special training and competencies in an effective manner. Principals should also be encouraged by the counselor to provide input for program development. In addition, encouragement by the principal to support the participation of all school personnel in implementing the comprehensive developmental guidance program is needed. Of course, the school principal facilitates program improvement by providing a school climate conducive to innovation in guidance and counseling. A collaborative relationship between the administration and counselor is a vital part of a successful school counseling program.

## Teachers' Roles

Teachers play a vital role in the planning and implementation of an elementary level comprehensive developmental guidance program. As the professionals who have the most daily contact with students, teachers are in the best position to recognize and help provide for the developmental needs of students. Through appropriate communication and referrals, teachers facilitate the interaction between the students and the counselor. Teachers demonstrate their support for the program by providing adequate opportunities for counselor-student contact. Teachers can contribute directly by helping the counselor deliver programs that facilitate the emotional and social development and well being of students. With their support, input, and expertise, teachers make it possible for guidance and counseling to become an integral part of the elementary child's educational experience.

## The ASCA National Model

The original comprehensive guidance program evolved into what is known today as the *National Model* developed by The American School Counselor Association (ASCA, 2005). The actual model is the result of input from many experts in the field. The names are impressive and lend great credibility to this program that depended on the work of school counselors over several decades.

ASCA spearheaded the effort to organize the contributions made by many proponents of a comprehensive model. Through the efforts of many, ASCA was able to add to the growing body of school counseling literature into a cohesive whole and create a system that could be used throughout the country.

ASCA developed a cohesive list of assumptions, as follows: (ASCA, 2005)

A school counseling program:

- Reaches every student
- Is comprehensive in scope
- Is preventive in design
- Is developmental in nature
- Is an integral part of a total educational program for student success * Selects measurable student competencies based on local need in the areas of academic, career and personal/ social domains. * Has a delivery system that includes school guidance curriculum, individual planning, responsive services and system support
- Is implemented by a credentialed school counselor
- Is conducted in collaboration with all stakeholders
- Uses data to drive program decisions
- Monitors student progress
- Measures both process and outcome results and analyzes critical data elements
- Seeks improvement each year based on results data
- Shares successes with stakeholders

These assumptions describe the essence of The ASCA National Model and provide the philosophical parameters that undergird its implementation.

## Summary

When elementary level school personnel understand the purposes of a comprehensive developmental guidance and counseling program, they realize the goals of education and the goals of guidance and counseling are congruent. Principals, counselors, and teachers are most effective in promoting the cognitive, emotional, and social development of students when they are sensitive to both the distinct and the common elements of their roles. Mutual respect for and understanding of the professional competencies and contributions that each brings to the school setting will enable principals, counselors, and teachers to implement a comprehensive, elementary school, developmental guidance program that will become an essential element of the total school program.

The effectiveness of an elementary school counseling program in the new millennium clearly depends on the elementary school counselors' ability to deliver services as part of a team, with emphasis on learner outcomes and consideration for all aspects of a child's development.

# Figure 4.1
# Program Overview

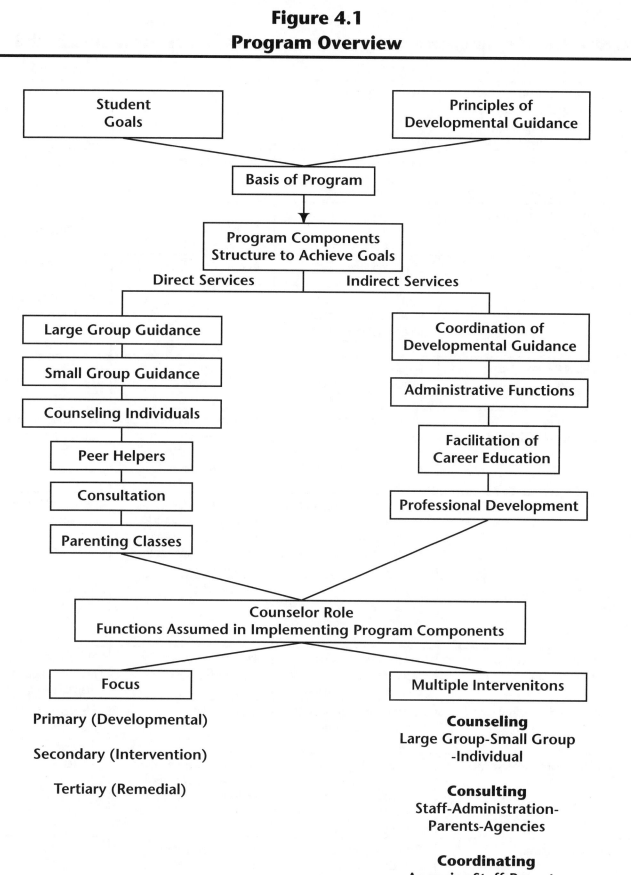

## Figure 4.2
# Elementary Comprehensive, Developmental Guidance Program Checklist

| | Ideal | Acceptable | Unacceptable |
|---|---|---|---|
| *1. **Classroom Guidance** career education, orientation, 8th grade development and coordination, involvement | 6-8 sessions/week | 4-6 sessions/week | 0-3 sessions/week |
| *2. **Group Counseling** by counselors (scheduled, ongoing) | 4-6 sessions/week | 2-3 sessions/week | 0-1 sessions/week |
| *3. **Counseling Individuals** Scheduled Unscheduled | 2-5 hours/week 2-3 hours/week | 2-5 hours/week 2-3 hours/week | > 5 hours/week > 5 hours/week |
| *4. **Consultation** (parents, faculty, etc.) | Scheduled time daily (1-2 hours) - Attends school administrative meetings. Responds to requests in timely and appropriate fashion. | Consultation occurs, but in an unplanned way. | No scheduled time for consultation. No school administrative meetings attended. |
| 5. **Teaching the Peer Helpers' Class** | Regular basis; either semester or year long. Both training and projects. | Training only; no projects (partial program). | No class. |
| *6. **Coordinating Developmental Guidance** | Written plan; all students have access; program planned, implemented and evaluated; community oriented. | Written plan; all students have access; program planned, implemented and evaluated. | No developmental guidance program. |
| *7. **Administrative Functions** | Counselors supervise clerical assistance; review incoming/outgoing records; responsive to student needs; attends cluster meetings. | Clerk not directly supervised by counselor; records reviewed and processed; responds to student needs. | Clerk used for non-guidance activities. |
| 8. **Career Education Program** | Provides classroom presentations, special career projects. Helps teachers to infuse curriculum. | Same as ideal. | No involvement with career education. |
| *9. **Coordinating Exceptional Education Program** | Timely and appropriate meetings conducted; clerk prepares letters and forms. | Program is managed with limited clerical support. | No program or only reactive program management evident. |
| *10. **Testing and Development** | Coordinates standardized testing; interprets test results. | Same as ideal. | Clerical aspects of managing the testing program evident. |
| 11. **Professional Development Activities** | Attends and is involved at all levels: local, state, and national associations; participates in all staff development activities. | Maintains memberships; attends district in-service activities. | No activities. |
| *12. **Advisory Program** | Participates regularly; provides materials; serves as consultant. | Participates in advisory, but on an irregular basis. | No participation. |

* Indicates a critical component

*Joe Wittmer, Ph.D. and Mary Ann Clark, Ph.D.*

# Figure 4.3
## Program Implementation

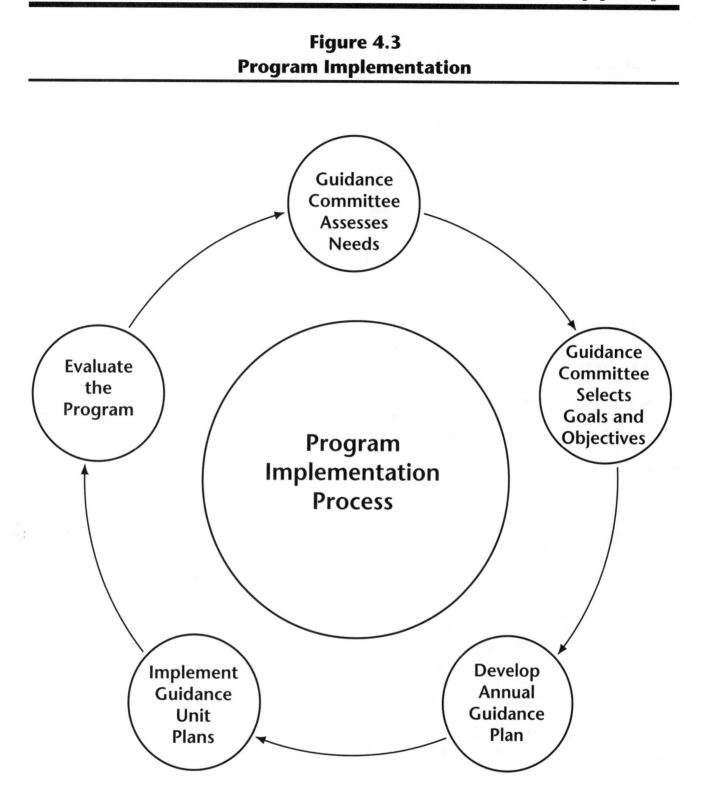

This diagram depicts the process of a developmental guidance program. Beginning with a needs assessment, the process moves to the selection of specific goals and objectives by the school based guidance committee; after selection of priorities, the annual plan is developed and made available to the principal, program consultant for guidance, and faculty. The delivery of specific activities is conducted by teachers, administrators, counselors, and other specialists and parents. The plan is evaluated near the end of the school year to determine program effectiveness and to demonstrate accountability for meeting student needs.

# References

American School Counselor Association. (2005). *The ASCA national model: A framework for school counseling programs*. Alexandria, VA: Author.

ASCA. (1999). *Role statement: The school counselor*. Alexandria, VA: ASCA Press.

Capuzzi, D., & Gross, D.R. (2003). *Youth at risk: A prevention resource for counselors, teachers, and parents* (4th ed.). Alexandria, VA: American Counseling Association.

Dahir, C., Sheldon, S., & Valiga, M. (1998). *Vision in action: Implementing the national standards for school counseling programs.*. Alexandria, VA: American School Counselor Association.

Gysbers, N.C. (Ed.). (1997). *Comprehensive guidance programs that work*. Ann Arbor, MI: ERIC Counseling and Personnel Services Clearinghouse.

Gysbers, N.C., & Henderson, P. (2006). *Developing and managing your school guidance and counseling program* (4th ed.). Alexandria, VA: American Counseling Association.

Havighurst, R.J. (1972). *Developmental tasks in education*. New York: Longmans.

Myrick, R.D. (2003). *Developmental guidance and counseling: A practical approach* (4th ed.). Minneapolis, MN: Educational Media Corporation.

Schmidt, J.J. (2003). *Counseling in schools: Essential services and comprehensive programs* (4th ed.). Needham Heights, MA: Allyn & Bacon.

Wittmer, J., & Thompson, D. (2006). *Large group counseling: A k-12 sourcebook* (2nd ed.). Minneapolis, MN: Educational Media Corporation.

Wittmer, J., Thompson, D., & Loesch, L. (1997). *Classroom guidance activities: A sourcebook for elementary school counselors*. Minneapolis, MN: Educational Media Corporation.

Wittmer, J., Thompson, D., & Sheperis, C. (1999). *The peace train: A school-wide violence prevention program*. Minneapolis, MN: Educational Media Corporation.

# Chapter 5

# Middle School Counseling in the New Millennium: A Practitioner's Perspective

**by Bonnie B. Baker**

*Dr. Bonnie B. Baker, Ph.D., LMHC, NCC is a Past - President of the Florida School Counselor Association and is a retired middle school counselor. She is currently working as a mental health counselor in private practice in Gainesville, Florida.*

## Introduction

The often used phrase "caught in the middle" could easily serve as a motto for the middle school counselor of the new millennium for several reasons. First, the unique population of middle school students are "caught in the middle" between childhood and adolescence in a developmental stage known as "transescence." This difficult developmental period accounts for many of the counseling issues a middle school counselor must address each and every school day.

Secondly, the middle school institution itself is "caught in the middle" between elementary and secondary school. As a result, middle school counselors must be knowledgeable of both elementary and secondary school programs and spend a considerable amount of time and energy in transition-related activities such as orientation, registration, and so forth.

Additionally, in performing their many roles and responsibilities, middle school counselors are frequently "caught in the middle" between various segments of their school communities, such as between students and parents, students and teachers, students and administrators, parents and teachers, and teachers and teacher. In short, middle school counselors may find themselves "caught in the middle" of most school-based relationships. This happens most often for those middle school counselors who view their "student advocacy role," as I do, as crucial. The goal of this chapter is to familiarize you with varied aspects of middle school counseling from the personal perspective of a middle school counselor who has been "caught in the middle" for over three decades, but who has, enjoyed each and every working day with this unique age group of students.

## Program Development

The trend toward creating comprehensive, developmental guidance and counseling programs that began in the '70s, '80s, and '90s continues in the new millennium.

With the mandate of high stakes testing in our country today, the emphasis on academic achievement has increased across the K-12 curriculum, and specifically at the middle school level. The ASCA National Model (2005) specifically recommends a guidance curriculum action plan for grades 6-8 which emphasizes organizational, study, and test-taking skills among other related personal-social, career, and educational issues. The achievement gap between Caucasian students and students of color has received much national publicity and there is an increased pressure on educators to assist in closing this gap. Thus, the variety of counseling interventions we design and implement should ideally relate to students' achievement and adjustment in these various arenas.

Middle school counselors play a key role in developing and coordinating the school guidance program. However, the entire school staff must participate in guidance-related activities in order to successfully implement a comprehensive, *developmental* guidance program.

An effective first step in developing a middle school guidance program is to form a school guidance committee. The function of this committee is to assist the counselor in developing and implementing the guidance program. The committee also serves as an ongoing advisory group and communication link between the guidance department and the school community. Committee members should include school counselors, teachers, parents, administrators, and students.

Initially, the school guidance committee is helpful in identifying and prioritizing student, teacher, and parent needs. An efficient method for collecting this type of information is the use of a needs assessment instrument. The committee then analyzes the collected data and assists the counselor in formulating a written program to meet the identified needs. Support for the program will increase because of the widespread participation in its development. Committee members, who served as program developers, will also be valuable in interpreting and promoting guidance program activities.

Ongoing school guidance committee meetings and projects should continue throughout the school year. A prepared agenda, minutes of meetings, and frequent reports to the entire school community about committee activities will produce a positive image for the guidance department. In addition to the development of the guidance program, suggested projects for the guidance committee include the following:

- Preview and selection of guidance material
- Research projects
- National School Counseling Week activities
- Career awareness programs
- Public relations project such as newsletter, bulletin boards, or newspaper articles
- Sponsorship of parent education programs

A year-end program evaluation is an appropriate concluding activity for the school guidance committee. And, showing your appreciation and recognition of individual committee member's participation at the end of the year is important. The benefits of an actively functioning school guidance committee are well worth the busy middle school counselor's time and effort.

# Counseling

The core of the middle school developmental guidance program is counseling. This unique function sets the school counselor apart from all other professional staff members. As societal problems grow in complexity, the need for social and emotional counseling increases. The middle school counselors of the future will need an extensive knowledge of counseling theory and methods. Expertise in counseling special populations will be required to assist students in understanding and resolving issues new to their generation. For instance, issues of the current generation of students include the threat of terrorism, fallout from catastrophes such as a hurricanes and earthquake, and changes in our country's demographics which will impact many students and their families during this decade. Beginning, as well as veteran, school counselors need to learn about the characteristics of these and other special populations and need to discover counseling strategies to respond to their unique needs.

The middle school counselor is increasingly viewed as the school-based mental health professional and is called upon to work collaboratively with community based mental health care providers to develop treatment plans and to provide therapeutic interventions for students with mental disorders. School counselor trainees would benefit by becoming familiar with diagnostic criteria to understand and facilitate the collaboration process.

## Crisis Counseling

Middle school counselors must be able to effectively intervene in crisis situations. Those who work in large schools face crises on a daily basis and need to develop skills for immediate intervention. The following is a sampling of the types of crisis situations encountered by this author in a single school year.

- Divorce
- Death of student
- Death of parents, grandparents, and siblings
- Peer rejection and conflict
- Family violence
- Homelessness
- Chronic transience
- Child abuse and neglect
- Abandonment
- Sexual molestation—familial and non-familial
- Runaways
- Drug and alcohol abuse—student and family
- Academic failure
- Teen pregnancy
- Miscarriage
- Truancy
- School phobia
- Discipline problems
- Incarceration of parents
- Incarceration of students
- Crime victimizations—assault and battery, larceny, rape
- Gang violence
- Poverty-related crisis—lack of food, clothing, and shelter
- Chronic medical problems and terminal illness of students and family

Due to the sudden onset of many crisis situations, individual counseling is the most immediate type of intervention. Group counseling can also be effective in assisting students experiencing crisis situations. Middle schoolers, in particular, desire peer group acceptance and support. Knowing that others are experiencing similar circumstances can provide needed support. Individual screening sessions *should* (required by ACA Ethical Standards) be held before placing students in a crisis-oriented group, or in any group for that matter.

In some instances, additional resources may be needed to assist large numbers of students in crisis. For example, a natural disaster or the death of a student or a faculty member may disrupt the entire school. Crisis management plans and personnel should be available on short notice for such emergency situations. District-wide crisis teams composed of school counselors, psychologists, district staff, and community mental health personnel frequently serve on emergency crisis teams. It is important to become familiar with the school system's plan (e.g., telephone networking, etc.) prior to a crisis situation occurring. Volunteering to become a part of the school crisis team can be a rewarding experience.

## Group Counseling

Group counseling is an efficient method of delivering counseling services in the middle school. Besides allowing middle school counselors to serve more students, group counseling is especially suited to peer-conscious middle school students. Group participation is preferable to individual counseling for many students. The camaraderie of group membership and of positive peer interaction assists the counselor in achieving group goals.

Developmental as well as problem-centered issues can be addressed in small group counseling sessions. Problem areas that can be treated in small group counseling include family issues such as divorce, academic failure, peer conflict, and behavioral problems. Developmental group topics that interest middle schoolers include study skills, friendship, career exploration, decision making, and interpersonal relationships.

Scheduling group counseling sessions can be tricky in a middle school. Scheduling problems can be avoided by informing classroom teachers about the purpose of the group, group membership, and group time schedules well in advance. Teacher referrals for group membership help to increase support for this activity. One method of scheduling recommended for middle schools is to schedule sessions on a rotating class basis throughout the school day. Teachers are more supportive if students miss their class only once or twice during the course of the group. Also, notifying the teachers of the group schedule helps them plan for student absences. Most teachers will require students to make up work missed while attending group sessions. And if this is the school policy, it should be supported.

## Classroom Guidance

Classroom guidance units provide school counselors with the greatest opportunity to impact large numbers of students. Topics selected for these units should have relevance for all students and, when possible, be infused into appropriate places in the regular school curriculum. For instance, a drug education unit might best be offered in a science class that is studying the human body. The affective guidance curriculum compliments the academic aspects of the same topic. Whenever possible, classroom guidance units should be inserted into related classes (Wittmer and Thompson, 2006).

# Consultation

Consultation is a process in which a human services professional assists a consultee with a work-related (or caretaking-related) problem within the client system, with the goal of helping both the consultee and the client system in some specified way.

A considerable amount of a middle school counselor's time is devoted to consulting with teachers, parents, administrators, and referral agency personnel. Through effective use of consultation, the counselor can impact greater numbers of students than would be possible through solitary efforts. Discussions and models of consultation appear frequently in the school counseling literature (e.g., Myrick, 2003; and Schmidt, 2003).

## Consultation with Administrators

Middle school administrators and school counselors must work together to develop appropriate and effective programs and services for students. Frequent communication, however, is often difficult due to the many demands placed on the administrator's and counselor's time. One technique to resolve this dilemma is to schedule a regular weekly counselor-administrator meeting. The agenda for this consultation and planning session might include the following components:

- Program planning, such as faculty in-service or parent workshops you are planning to conduct, or that the administrator might want done

- Curriculum planning, such as Advisor-Advisee program activities

- Discussions and intervention planning for students experiencing academic or behavioral difficulties

- Individual administrator or counselor work-related concerns

## Consultation with Teachers

Most middle schools have adopted a team approach to assigning teachers to work with particular groups of students. Discussions and decisions about student concerns are frequently made during regularly scheduled team meetings. By participating in these team meetings, the middle school counselor provides consultation services on an ongoing basis.

More formal methods of teacher consultation, such as in-service programs, are well-received when presented in a timely and succinct manner. Examples of topics that have been found to be of interest to middle school teachers include the following:

- child abuse identification and reporting procedures
- classroom management techniques
- affective classroom activities
- identification and interventions for exceptional education students
- career education activities
- standardized testing procedures and preparation activities
- sex education activities
- drug education activities

In addition to in-service programs, individual and small group consultation services are frequently requested of the middle school counselor. For instance, a teacher may be having a difficult time controlling a certain class and needs assistance in developing appropriate classroom management strategies. You might observe the class, make recommendations, or suggest resources that may help this particular teacher.

## Consultation with Parents

The "storm and stress" of the middle school years frequently results in equally distressing "storm and stress" for parents. An important role of the middle school counselor is that of consultant to parents who must guide their children through this difficult developmental stage. Talking to parents and providing information about "normal" middle school behavior will assist them in understanding and in responding appropriately to their children. Both individual and group consultation are needed. Program presentations at parent orientation and at organization meetings (PTA) are beneficial in meeting this need. Some counselors may choose to offer parenting classes or support groups to help prepare parents for the challenge of raising today's teenagers.

## Consultation with Referral Agency Personnel

Representatives from public and private agencies, such as mental health centers, commonly request consultation with middle school counselors. Either the agency personnel or the school counselor may initiate the discussion. Prior to any discussion or written communication, the school counselor must be certain that all ethical and legal guidelines regarding confidentiality have been observed. Occasionally subpoenas for court appearances will be issued to school counselors. When this occurs it is, generally, a good idea to consult with the principal and the school attorney in preparing for testimony. Depending on the type of hearing, the counselor's records could also be subpoenaed.

# Coordination

Program and services coordination is another major responsibility of the middle school counselor. Parents, teachers, and students rely on the counselor's leadership in planning and coordinating numerous special services and programs. The effectiveness of such programs and/or services often depends on the skills of the coordinator. In fact, poor coordination can ruin an otherwise excellent program. Some examples of coordinating activities a middle school counselor may be required to spearhead in a typical year are listed, here, in chronological order.

| | |
|---|---|
| September | New student orientation program (Students and parents) Child abuse awareness program (Faculty in-service) |
| October: | Drug awareness program (Students and parents) |
| November: | Sex education programs (Students and parents) |
| December: | Peer facilitator training program (Students) |
| January: | Career interest survey (Students) |
| February: | Career Day (Students) |
| March: | High school registration/orientation (Students and parents) |
| April: | Standardized testing program (Faculty in-service and students) |
| May: | Fifth grade registration/orientation (Students and parents) |
| June: | Student recognition programs (Students and parents) |

Additional coordination activities occur on an on going basis throughout the school year. They include the coordination of the following:

- referrals for community services
- referrals for psychological testing
- registration of new students
- peer facilitator program and special projects
- student records—maintenance and transfer

## Tips for Successful Coordination of Guidance Program Activities

1. Start planning early to allow ample time to thoroughly prepare for the program or activity.

2. Involve others in the planning stage of program development to offer suggestions for strengthening the program.

3. Attend to details in planning and coordinating activities. Written communication is helpful when coordinating a major activity such as a standardized testing program. All those involved should be kept well informed about program goals, objectives, and procedures for implementation. If necessary, a briefing session should be conducted to make certain that everyone involved understands what is being planned.

4. Evaluate the program immediately following its conclusion, prepare a written summary, and save it for future planning sessions.

## Time Management

Time is a precious commodity for today's middle school counselor. Finding ample time to develop and implement a comprehensive, developmental guidance program is difficult, particularly in schools with high counselor-to-student ratios. Counselors who are recognized as being helpful will soon find themselves inundated with requests for counseling, coordination, and consultation services. Not surprisingly, successfully responding to such requests generates even more. Quite often, the harder the counselor works, the more that is requested. A tee shirt purchased at a counselor convention proclaiming "I'M COUNSELING AS FAST AS I CAN!!" best sums up how many middle school counselors feel by the end of the first semester each year.

Effective time management is one of the greatest challenges facing the middle school counselor. The following are offered as ways to avert becoming overwhelmed by the myriad of roles and responsibilities assumed in the middle school setting.

1. **First, accept the reality that as a middle school counselor you cannot be all things to all people.** This is a difficult concept for school counselors because, by nature, we are helpers and dislike saying "NO" to requests for help.

2. **Your parameters for professional responsibilities should be clearly set.** This can be accomplished by developing and presenting a written guidance program and a role description to the administration, faculty, and parent community. Defining roles and responsibilities enables you to delineate essential activities and set limits on inappropriate requests. The program should be evaluated and revised annually to ensure that all functions are being performed as stipulated in your role and function statement.

3. **Develop good organizational skills.** A tremendous amount of your time can be saved by being well organized. Counseling material, counseling notes, calendars, and time schedules should be kept current and be maintained in an easily accessible system. Being able to quickly retrieve information can save you untold hours of searching for or recreating lost material.

4. **Avoid time wasters.** Unnecessarily lengthy telephone conversations, excessive socialization in the teacher's lounge, visitors, procrastination, lengthy meetings, and cluttered work spaces can reduce your efficiency and lessen the effectiveness of your guidance program.

5. **Be prepared for the unexpected.** Events that demand immediate attention will occur on a random basis throughout the school year. For example, crisis situations such as child abuse, death, accidents, and medical emergencies will inevitably occur. Prior to their happening, plans should be developed to allow you to quickly respond and resolve the situation with a minimal amount of disruption to scheduled activities.

6. **Differential staffing.** This technique saves time for middle school guidance departments with more than one counselor. Responsibilities are divided among department members in order to reduce the quantity of functions each counselor must assume. For instance, one counselor could be responsible for coordinating the standardized testing program and high school registration activities while another counselor organizes the fifth grade registration, career day, and the drug awareness program.

# Ingredients for Success

I am frequently asked how I successfully managed to survive working as a middle school counselor for thirty years. Reflecting on this question has turned up a "baker's dozen" of what I consider to be essential ingredients for success as a middle school counselor. In concluding this chapter, I offer these suggestions to colleagues and future colleagues:

1. **Genuine enjoyment in working with the middle school-aged student.** Genuinely liking and appreciating this age group is essential. Understanding and tolerance of the "storm and stress" experienced by the early adolescent is needed for survival in the middle school. Students quickly identify those adults who lack understanding of their behavior and turn away from their guidance. You can't play at being genuine with this age group.

2. **Tolerance for chaotic days.** Days rarely go as planned in the middle school, particularly in larger schools. Because of the high counselor-student ratios in most areas of the country, learn to anticipate some type of crisis or unexpected event to occur daily. The successful counselor must be able to adjust to change quickly. At times, multiple unexpected events happen simultaneously. Your ability to juggle activities will be put to a test on a daily basis.

3. **Flexibility.** The ability to change directions at a moment's notice is needed in middle school counseling. Within an hour's time, you may be called upon to participate in a parent-teacher conference, comfort a crying student, answer three phone calls, and consult with the school nurse. Successful counselors have developed skills in focusing on the task at hand and being able to quickly focus on completely different issues within a matter of minutes. This is a skill seldom taught in graduate school, but is one you can teach yourself "on the job."

4. **Crisis management skills.** Middle school counselors must have the ability to intervene quickly and competently in crisis situations. Middle school aged students are easily aroused emotionally during crisis events and require immediate counseling services. They are often inconsistent, but *you* must be consistent or their trust will be lost. Successful middle school counselors have crisis management plans in effect to handle unusual circumstances.

5. **Time management skills.** The many demands made on the middle school counselor's time makes this an essential ingredient for success. Specific suggestions for effective utilization of time have been previously discussed in this chapter.

6. **Communication skills.** The ability to effectively communicate with students, teachers, administrators, parents, and the public is vital to success as a middle school counselor. The use of active listening and appropriate feedback will assist in relating to such varied groups. Verbal as well as written communication skills are needed. Frequently middle school counselors are asked to speak or write about counseling issues or activities. You must be able to clearly articulate information about program objectives and strategies to students, parents, and professional colleagues.

7. **Organizational skills.** Middle school counselors are always coordinating or organizing something. Whether it be a standardized testing program, orientation program, or career education activity, the well organized counselor will achieve far greater success. The many details, time constraints, and paperwork associated with the middle school counselor's coordinator role makes this an essential skill. The well-organized middle school counselor will enjoy greater cooperation and support of the faculty and staff.

8. **Team player.** Cooperative relationships with school administrators and faculty members are essential for middle school counselors. Regular attendance and participation at team and faculty meetings will ensure colleagues that you are an integral member of the team. Demonstrations of support and appreciation for the efforts of other staff members and participation in non-counseling school activities, such as the science fair or band concert, will remind others that you are concerned about the entire school program. Staff members will reciprocate when you request their participation in guidance-related activities and will make access to students much easier.

9. **Ability to manage stress.** Stress management skills are needed in most professional positions. The level of stress in a typical middle school counseling office is especially high. This is due to the characteristics of the population served and the demands placed upon the counselor in fulfilling the numerous roles and responsibilities of the job. Unless preventive measures are taken, the middle school counselor could begin to feel "burnt-out." By attending to their personal emotional, physical, and spiritual well-being, middle school counselors will strengthen their performance at work and longevity in the profession.

10. **Personal support system**. Middle school counselors spend much of their professional energy nurturing their students and others. Although this is quite fulfilling professionally and personally, you, as a counselor, have similar needs for nurturing that *must* be met in order to continue helping others. The successful middle school counselor is aware of this need and receives such nurturing from family and/or friends on a regular basis. Allowing time for personally supportive relationships is needed for your personal growth as a school counselor.

11. **Professional support system**. Strong professional support systems help middle school counselors achieve success. The support of the school principal is essential and is best gained by frequent communication. The quality of this relationship can "make or break" the guidance program. Frequently you will need the principal's support and encouragement in handling difficult cases.

    Support of the faculty can be gained by implementing the previously discussed school guidance committee and staying involved in school activities. Once you are viewed as a team player, you will discover tremendous support from teachers.

    Joining a support group of other middle school counselors can also be beneficial. Processing difficult cases, planning district-wide programs, and sharing materials and strategies are ways that professional support group members can assist each other.

12. **Continued professional development**. Successful middle school counselors keep informed of the latest developments in the counseling field and continuously strive to improve their professional skills. The best way to accomplish this is by becoming involved in professional development activities. Joining professional organizations, reading journals, and attending conferences are ways to revitalize your counseling practices. Professional development activities help to strengthen weak areas and allow counselors to benefit from successful ideas shared by their peers.

13. **Sense of humor**. Last, but certainly not least in importance, is the ability to maintain a sense of humor. Students as well as co-workers appreciate school counselors who can laugh and enjoy their work. Using humor in your counseling sessions and classroom presentations often relieves tension and allows students to work on counseling issues with greater comfort.

# References

American School Counselor Association (2005). *The ASCA national model: A framework for school counseling programs*. Alexandria, VA: Author.

Myrick, R.D. (2003). *Developmental guidance and counseling: A practical approach* (4th ed.). Minneapolis, MN: Educational Media Corporation.

Schmidt, J. (2003). *Counseling in schools: Essential services and comprehensive programs* (4th ed.). Nedham, MA: Allyn & Bacon.

Wittmer, J., & Thompson, D. (2006). *Large group guidance activities: A k-12 sourcebook* (2nd ed.). Minneapolis, MN: Educational Media Corporation.

# Chapter 6

# The Scope of Practice of the High School Counselor

by
**Doris Coy and Susan Sears**

*Doris Rhea Coy is an Associate Professor and School Counseling Coordinator at Northern Kentucky University. Dr. Coy has served as President of the American School Counselor Association (ASCA) and has been a teacher and school counselor. She is a National Certified Counselor, National Certified School Counselor and a Licensed Professional Counselor.*

*Susan Jones Sears, Ph.D., is Associate Professor Emeritus in Counselor Education at The Ohio State University, Columbus. She is a former high school, junior high, and elementary school counselor and is a Licensed Professional Clinical Counselor. Dr. Sears has written extensively in the areas of school counseling and career development.*

## Introduction

Adolescents encounter many very real dangers as they grow up in our complex and ever changing society. The possibility of school violence, of contracting sexually transmitted diseases, the availability of alcohol and other drugs, growing economic pressures on them and their families, and lack of clear family and community values to guide them make young people's adolescence years both confusing and challenging. As indicated by the data presented in Chapter 2 of this book, there are many personal and social problems confronting our high school age youth today.

High school age youth are living in an exciting time within an increasingly diverse and mobile society. They are exposed to many new technologies and expanding opportunities and appropriate decision making in their daily lives becomes highly important. The American School Counselor Association (ASCA) has taken the position that to help ensure that high school students make the correct decisions in life and be better prepared to become the next generation of parents, workers, leaders, and citizens, they

need the assistance of a professional school counselor. According to ASCA (2006), high school students in today's confusing world would benefit greatly from the services of a professional counselor's support and guidance during this time of personal rapid growth and change. (ASCA, 2006).

The following found in the 2006 ASCA position statement on high school counseling, best summarizes the above:

*High school is the final transition into adulthood and the world of work as students begin separating from parents and exploring and defining their independence. Students are deciding who they are, what they do well, and what they will do when they graduate. During these adolescent years, students are evaluating their strengths, skills and abilities. The biggest influence is their peer group. They are searching for a place to belong and rely on peer acceptance and feedback. They face increased pressures regarding risk behaviors involving sex, alcohol and drugs while exploring the boundaries of more acceptable behavior and mature, meaningful relationships. They need guidance in making concrete and compounded decisions. They must deal with academic pressures as they face high-stakes testing, the challenges of college admissions, the scholarship and financial aid application process and entrance into a competitive job market (ASCA, 2006).*

A look at the past and current role of the professional secondary school counselor is the focus of this chapter.

# Secondary School Counseling: The Past

As noted in Chapter 1 of this book, secondary school counseling and guidance really began in the early 1900s when the primary emphasis of counseling was on guidance activities. An early distinction was made between guidance and counseling in which *guidance* focused on helping students make important choices, whereas *counseling* focused more on helping individuals make behavioral changes (Gladding, 2003). Early guidance work often occurred in schools with adults helping students make vocational decisions. The spread of public education, the advancement in testing and psychometrics and increasing diversity in the student population influenced the growth of guidance in schools. As guidance theory and practice became more clinically oriented, the focus shifted to counseling for personal and social adjustment. As stated previously in this book, in the late 1970s and 1980s, experts in school counseling encouraged counselors to develop "comprehensive programs" organized around student needs rather than simply offering a series of guidance services (Gysbers & Henderson, 2006). The information and advice-giving that is called "guidance" is still a component of most high school counseling programs. However, it should be acknowledged that other components such as individual and group counseling, parent consultation, staff consultation, community consultation, and coordination have taken on much greater importance.

Secondary school counselors, more so than counselors at either the elementary or middle school level, have performed (and too many continue to do so) clerical and quasi-administrative duties. These duties include such tasks as entering scheduling data into computers, checking the number of credits students have accumulated, pasting test scores into cumulative folders, organizing the senior prom, and so forth. In fact, to a large extent, the role of the high school counselor has been defined by the specific administrators supervising their work. Most counselors help students schedule; some counsel individually and in groups; while others complete clerical or administrative tasks their respective principals view as needing to be done. Thus, the tasks high school counselors perform in one school might have little similarity to those performed in another school. The lack of clearly defined roles is a result of several circumstances. First, since guidance was more process than content and counselor qualifications were not described as unique competencies, counselors have been, and still are, vulnerable both to criticism and to the assignment of inappropriate duties and tasks (Gibson & Mitchell, 2002). Secondly, early guidance began in secondary schools. And, since the organization of secondary schools is departmentalized and rather rigid, counselors tended to form departments similarly to the way secondary teachers are organized. Departmental organization resulted in an isolation that only seemed to heighten the confusion about what high school counselors did and continue to do. In addition, it was difficult to evaluate the effectiveness of the counselor. Evaluation became a numbers game (how many students were seen, how many parents were contacted, i.e., a head count) and a laundry list (what activities had been completed, how many letters of recommendation had been written, etc.). Without an appropriately defined content, without the appropriate professional qualifications, and without effective evaluation, it is not surprising that many high school counselors were, and still are, viewed as autonomous professionals without a road map.

During the last 20 years or so, the accountability movement has gained greater and greater strength in education, and especially in school counseling. National studies criticize schools and teachers for graduating students unprepared for the "information age" and the increasingly technological workplace. Schools and educators are being forced to reconsider outdated techniques and curricula. Legislative mandates dealing with curricula and assessment of student progress are common. Education and schools are changing. School counselors, especially high school counselors, must also change.

Past roles played by counselors in schools have been characterized by diversity and sometimes confusion. During the last fifty years, secondary school guidance programs have reflected different educational trends. Vocational guidance, educational guidance, testing, pupil mental health, group guidance, guidance for the gifted, guidance for the disadvantaged and cultural minorities, and career guidance have all been emphasized at one time or another (Gibson & Mitchell, 2002).

# The Role of the Professional Secondary School Counselor

ASCA (2006) sums up the role of the modern high school counselor as follows:

*Secondary school counselors are professional educators with a mental health perspective who understand and respond to the challenges presented by today's diverse student population. Secondary school counselors do not work in isolation; rather they are integral to the total educational program. They provide proactive leadership that engages all stakeholders in the delivery of programs and services to help the student achieve success in school. Professional school counselors align and work with the school's mission to support the academic achievement of all students as they prepare for the ever-changing world of the 21st century. This mission is accomplished through the design, development, implementation and evaluation of a comprehensive, developmental and systematic school-counseling program (ASCA, 2006).*

As so aptly stated in the above ASCA role statement, one of the goals of all school counselors should be to assist **all** students with their academic, career and personal/social development. In emphasizing this point, Stone and Dahir (2006) wrote that the emphasis in school counseling has shifted to reaching all students in their academic, career, and personal-social development (Stone and Dahir, 2006). Although it has been more in "theory" than in "practice," developing and implementing counseling programs with all students in mind has long been the stated goal of secondary school counselors (Myrick, 2003).

According to ASCA's (2006) position statement on high school counseling, professional secondary school counselors implement the counseling program described above via four major services or delivery components. The first such service listed in the position statement is **classroom guidance**. This component includes activities that focus on students' study and test taking skills, post-secondary planning, career planning, understanding self and others, peer relationships, substance abuse education, diversity awareness and coping strategies. **Individual student planning,** given next in the role statement, is a service whereby counselors focus on student goal setting, academic plans, career plans, problem solving and education in understanding of self. ASCA lists **responsive services**, which includes individual and small-group counseling, peer facilitation, consultation, collaboration and referrals, third in their list of vital service components making up the compre-

hensive high school counseling program. **System support**, which includes professional development, consultation, collaboration and teaming and program management and operation is listed as the final service component in the ASCA position statement. ASCA emphasizes the fact that successful high school counselors involve parents, students, teachers, administrators and members of the community in implementing the above described service components in their high school counseling program (ASCA, 2006).

Of the various emphases given above, by ASCA and others, several important services that should be performed by secondary school counselors today have emerged. In our opinion, they are: *individual counseling, group guidance, group counseling, career development and information services, placement, coordination of testing services, and consultation.* These seven service components should be central to any comprehensive, developmentally oriented high school counseling program. They are briefly described below:

## 1. Individual Counseling

With so many students experiencing serious social and emotional concerns, counselors at all levels find themselves dealing with more and more complex problems. Substance abuse, teen pregnancy, threats of suicide, and physical and sexual abuse are common concerns of too many of today's youth. Because of the seriousness of these problems, more time is required to deal with them. Consequently, in individual counseling, counselors actually work only with a minority, rather than a majority, of students. Individual counseling is really more remedial than preventative. And most high school counselors are using brief approaches (because of the lack of time) and making referrals when long term counseling is needed by a student.

## 2. Group Guidance

Providing educational and career information to classroom size groups is an important function of school counselors. In high school, students need accurate educational information to assist them in scheduling appropriate courses. Other important educational information includes post-secondary and financial aid options. Relationship building and conflict resolutions skills can also be taught to students using a group guidance format. Many high schools have even added "guidance periods" to the curriculum to ensure that counselors have time to provide these services.

## 3. Small Group Counseling

Small group counseling gives the secondary school counselor the opportunity to work with more students who may have similar or related problems. Small groups can focus on a range of topics from adjusting to a new school (new students) to dealing with social and behavioral issues that may be affecting school performance. Groups can be offered during lunch hours, before and after school, and during study halls. It is becoming increasingly difficult to pull students out of classes for counseling services, particularly if they are having academic problems.

## 4. Career Development and Information Services

Helping students make appropriate career choices has long been a function of high school counselors. This function includes providing opportunities for students to have interest inventories and achievement tests interpreted to them as they attempt to develop post-secondary career options. With both career inventories and information on computers, counselors can drastically improve their career services.

## 5. Placement

The traditional concept of placement (placement in an occupation) has been broadened in high schools to include placement of students in colleges, technical schools, jobs, and even in appropriate high school classes (scheduling) or extracurricular activities. While placement is important, most high school counselors maintain that far too much attention is given to scheduling students into classes. However, new technologies have helped streamline the process.

## 6. Consultation

Over the years, high school counselors have increased the amount of time spent in consultation with others. This service enables school counselors to share their knowledge and skills with others such as teachers, administrators, parents, and community agencies. The consultative role was formally acknowledged for the first time in 1966 when the American School Counselor Association (ASCA) and the Association for Counselor Education and Supervision (ACES) specified that counseling, coordination, and consultation should be the three primary role responsibilities of elementary school counselors. As indicated, this function is an increasingly important one for high school counselors as well. Collaborating with important stakeholders in the lives of students helps ensure that students are supported by the significant adults in their lives.

## 7. Coordination

Coordination is the process of managing various indirect services which benefit students and may include being a liaison between school and community agencies. Coordinating the testing program or the substance abuse program would be examples of instances in which counselors would perform this function. Coordinating gives counselors many opportunities to demonstrate leadership within and outside their school setting. The above described services or functions are used by effective high school counselors. However, more importantly, how do these services reflect student needs?

The American School Counselor Association provided an important framework for school counselors to follow when implementing the above described services by publishing the *ASCA National Model: A Framework For School Counseling Programs* (ASCA 2003, 2005). This model provides the organizational basis for developing quality comprehensive, developmental school counseling programs that promote the academic, personal/social and career development for all students at all levels. By creating this national model, ASCA has not only provided a framework for the development of excellent school counseling programs, but a comprehensive outline of the developmental needs of school children of all ages.

# Developmental High School Counseling Reflects Student Needs

Developmental-oriented high school counselors are not merely "doing more of the same" but rather they are "charting new courses." The major "new course," developmental in nature, is driven by student needs and results in student outcomes for which counselors are accountable (Myrick, 2003).

As mentioned in previous chapters of this book, the work of developmental school counselors at the various levels (elementary, middle/junior high, and senior high) is largely differentiated by attention to age-specific developmental stages of student growth (ASCA, 2006). Today's "new" secondary school counselors realize that they work with young persons who are experiencing adolescence—a unique developmental stage which includes biological, cognitive, and social-emotional aspects. They also realize that "special approaches" are needed to be effective as counselors with this age group. Biologically, adolescence is characterized by significant amounts of physical growth. Height and weight increase dramatically, especially during a growth spurt that takes place in early adolescence for girls and mid-adolescence for boys. This is accompanied by greater strength and stamina. The release of hormones is responsible for the physical changes as well as for the emergence of primary and secondary sexual characteristics. Effective high school counselors are cognizant of these changes and reflect them in their approach to working with high school students.

Using adolescent developmental tasks as a foundation for building school counseling programs and giving direction to the role of school counselors makes good sense and is not a new idea. Employing this approach, today's developmental school counselors spend much of their time helping students develop skills in understanding themselves, developing effective relationships with others, resolving conflicts, setting educational and career goals, managing stress, valuing diversity, and making effective decisions. Thus, the role of the developmental school counselor, rather than vague and administrator-driven, is *student-driven and measurable.* Student needs become the content of a proactive and developmentally oriented high school counseling program. Moreover, these well-documented needs give direction to the day-to-day functions of school counselors (Wittmer and Thompson, 2006).

## A Skills-Based Approach

In order to focus on students' needs and facilitate the development of student skills, it is important that counselors move from a services-oriented approach only (career development and information services, group guidance services, counseling services, placement services, consultation, and coordination services) to a developmental, comprehensive skills-based program approach. We believe strongly that counselors must be clear about their "scope of practice"—the responsibilities for which they are trained—and *not* allow themselves to become assistant principals, attendance officers, substitute teachers, and clerks.

If student needs and student skills (understanding self, developing effective relationships, setting educational and career goals, etc.) are the content of the counseling program, what functions do high school counselors need to perform to carry out or implement this skills-based approach? The responsibilities and specific functions of a developmental school counselor (with examples of appropriate activities) are given below:

1. As suggested above, the successful high school counseling program is designed to help all students gain specific life skills that they will accomplish upon graduation from high school. Deciding which life skills will be emphasized in your counseling program is the first step. Using adolescent developmental tasks as a foundation, suggested earlier in the chapter, provides for a developmental counseling program based on solid human development theories and concepts. Examples of life skills that would be appropriate in a high school counseling program include the following:

   - Understand themselves.
   - Analyze their personal skills, interests, and strengths.
   - Set appropriate educational and career goals.
   - Develop effective relationships with others.
   - Control and direct their feelings/emotions.
   - Resolve conflicts effectively.
   - Value diversity.
   - Practice strategies for resisting alcohol and other drugs.
   - Manage stress effectively.
   - Value learning.
   - Make effective decisions.

If each high school counselor was responsible for roughly one hundred students, all of the life skills mentioned above could be included in the counseling program. However, in most high schools counselors are responsible for many more students (350 to 800). Therefore, it is more realistic to focus on three, four, or five skills per year, choosing those that reflect the greatest needs in the school at the present time

Once you've chosen the life skills upon which you plan to develop the content of the counseling program, then divide the life skills into manageable parts or tasks that students will need to master. By mastering these tasks (or sub-skills), students will accomplish the general skill. For example, if, as a high school counselor, you wanted to ensure that students learn how "to make effective decisions," then we suggest you divide that skill into the following:

**Students will:**

- Learn a decision-making process that includes generating alternatives and assessing the consequences of each before making decisions.

- Discuss how decisions made today affect decisions of tomorrow.

- Apply decision-making processes to their own educational planning and career choosing.

- Evaluate their skills in setting goals, gathering information, and assessing the consequences of decisions.

- Take responsibility for their own decisions.

    These tasks are simply the building blocks for the general skill of decision making. The tasks give counselors ideas for activities and experiences they can design to help their students achieve the skills. Such specific, locally appropriate tasks also make evaluation of the program easier. Another advantage of emphasizing the skills-based approach is that counselors are seen as contributing to the growth of all students and not just working with those "in trouble."

2. Counselors are directly involved in the *delivery* of the skills-based program content they have developed. Therefore, counselors will have to allocate significant amounts of time to facilitate or team-teach activities designed to help students master skills. Given the structure of schools, much of the counselor's time should be spent in individual classrooms (This represents a major change for many high school counselors; many of whom rarely conduct classroom guidance activities). In addition to facilitation of classroom activities, as noted, developmental counselors deliver their program content in small group sessions. Large group or classroom sessions may be appropriate for information about and discussion of post-secondary or vocational education options and financial aid while small groups may be more appropriate for interest or aptitude test interpretations. Also, a major role of the developmental counselor is to in-service teachers enabling them to assist in the facilitation of the activities. Clearly, counselors must convince administrators and teachers that what they want to do with students makes as much or more sense than the so-called academic curriculum does. While some will be less accepting than others, many administrators and teachers will be supportive of a life skills approach, particularly if they have been consulted and their input valued as the program is being designed and developed.

3. As noted previously, the role of the developmental high school counselor includes counseling students both individually and in small groups. Effective school counselors do not forget their unique training in counseling skills. While schools are not appropriate sites for large caseloads of "clients," counselors must always allot time for counseling students with personal-social problems. In addition, they should allow for time to engage in crisis counseling when needed. In order to be as effective as possible in a limited number of sessions, counselors should consider utilizing newer theoretical approaches such as brief therapy (a focused, structured approach with a limited number of sessions). It is extremely important that school counselors continue their professional development and gain skills in needed areas if they do not already have those skills.

High school counselors must be prepared to see students before school, during lunch hours, and after school. Finding enough time to talk to counselors is a problem for students. Thus, effective high school counselors are as flexible as possible. Obviously, counselors' caseloads do not allow for more than five or six sessions with a student. Students with more chronic problems should be referred to appropriately credentialed mental health care providers in the community.

4. As noted, consulting with parents and others is an important function of the developmental high school counselor. Consultation is a cooperative process in which the counselor-consultant assists others to think through problems and to develop skills that make them more effective in working with children/students (ASCA, 2006). As a result of the parent consultation function, counselors should be prepared to assist parents by:

- Disseminating educational information including information about courses offered.

- Providing periodic workshops on parenting skills needed to work with adolescents and workshops on post-secondary options and financial aid opportunities.

- Disseminating testing/appraisal information to help them better understand their adolescents.

- Facilitating parent/teacher conferences. Newsletters, websites, e-mail, snail mail, as well as radio and local television can be used effectively to disseminate information to as many parents as possible.

5. Consulting with various community agencies to help students deal with more serious personal and educational problems is another important aspect of the counselor/consultant role. Interventions may include (1) referral of students and families to community agencies, and (2) the development of collaborative programs designed to assist students and their families. While counselor referral of students to social agencies in the community is not new, high school counselors have not collaborated with mental health counselors or social workers as much as is needed to offer family counseling or parenting workshops. Developmental counselors create ongoing, not just occasional, links between the schools and the community's social agencies.

6. Training school staff to facilitate their personal and professional development is a primary function of today's high school counselor. School counselors possess many skills that teachers need such as skills in communication (e.g., listening, demonstrating empathy, being non-judgmental, problem solving, conflict management, stress management, and group processing). By conducting regular in-service sessions with staff, counselors can train staff, especially teachers, so they can master these communication and relationship building skills needed to work with students effectively. Not only will such training be helpful to teachers (and therefore students), but it will also enable counselors to be seen as leaders within the educational team.

7. Coordinating or collaborating with others who may be offering mental health-oriented assistance in the school (e.g., community substance abuse agencies working within the school) is a coordinating function developmental counselors play. High school counselors report that more and more community-based programs are operating in the schools. Effective school counselors coordinate the efforts of these programs and collaborate in their delivery. Separate and disparate efforts by outside agencies attempting to impact students in the school have little success if coordination with the school counselor is lacking.

In addition, counselors coordinate programs within schools such as the testing program. In these days of accountability, you will want to be careful not to permit this counselor responsibility to consume too much time. As a counselor you should understand thoroughly all relevant interest, aptitude, and achievement tests and should be able to in-service teachers on their interpretation and use. Spending time in direct administration of tests is not the most effective use of your valuable time.

8. Managing the school counseling program is a critical function of high school counselors. Many counselors find themselves supervised by individuals who have more responsibilities than they can handle and have little direct knowledge of counselors and the services they provide. Effective counselors take charge of their own programs and encourage interaction and regular meetings of the counselors in their district in order to assure program progress. If more than one counselor is employed in your high school, one of you should consider taking a lead role in the management process. Rotating leaders (on a yearly basis) is often an effective management technique. Managing a school counseling program includes developing an active *staff/community* public relations program. Counselors should orient staff and community to the counseling program through newsletters, local media, and school and community presentations. As mentioned in previous chapters, assembling advisory committees of parents and community members to provide input regarding the needs of students is another task that falls within the management function of the counselor.

9. Evaluating the counseling program including counselor efforts with students, staff, and community is an especially important function of today's high school counselor. The best and most effective way to evaluate a counseling program is to determine whether program activities are effective in achieving program outcomes. As suggested earlier in this chapter, adequate program outcomes describe desired changes in student behaviors. Also, a well designed program incorporates short-term, intermediate, and long-term objectives. As noted, in a skills-based approach to counseling the desired student outcome (i.e., students will make effective decisions) is divided into manageable parts called tasks or sub-skills. These tasks are the short-term and intermediate objectives of the program while the desired student outcome is the long-term objective. The more specific these tasks or sub-skills are the easier they are to evaluate.

Gathering good evaluation data takes time. Teacher and student rating scales and short surveys to determine what students gained from the guidance activities are two techniques that can be used to evaluate whether or not student outcomes are being achieved. Standardized tests and performance-based assessments can also be used when appropriate (again, the focus is on student outcomes).

Counselors may want to gather some general evaluation data also. Examples of "general evaluation" data includes (1) the number of students seen in individual or crisis counseling, (2) the number of small group counseling sessions held, (3) the number of large group information sessions conducted, (4) the number of conferences with parents, and (5) the number of phone calls to parents and community agencies. While this kind of general evaluation does not speak to student outcomes, it does provide the school board and administration information about the scope or breadth of the counseling program.

Evaluation of "counselors as professionals" is included in the "evaluating" function. Obviously counselors need to evaluate themselves. Effective professionals must be willing to closely scrutinize their practices. Unfortunately, counselors have been content to let administrators who know little about counseling evaluate them using "teacher" evaluation forms. Effective counselors take the lead in designing and gaining approval of evaluation instruments developed to evaluate counselors specifically. Even though administrators are designated as the school district evaluators, counselors should advocate for peer evaluations also. By involving peers (other counselors) in evaluation efforts, counselors can receive feedback relative to their unique counseling functions.

## Summary

We have presented several daunting challenges facing modern day, professional, secondary school counselors and how the challenges and demands on their time will continue to grow. We have also discussed how the profession of school counseling is changing rapidly and how very important it is for school counselors to stay abreast with these changes. There are many organizations such as the American School Counselor Association, The National Board for Certified Counselors and others that stand ready to assist high school counselors in keeping up with their fast changing profession.

If secondary school counselors are to chart a new course in the new millennium, they need to design and deliver a student-oriented, developmental-in-nature, counseling program with measurable student outcomes. This new century will either bring an "ending" or a "new beginning" for high school counselors. It is up to "the secondary school counselor to be" and to those now practicing, to ensure that it is a "beginning."

# Figure 6.1
# A Crisis Management Intervention School Policy and Program

## by Joe Wittmer

It is extremely difficult for an elementary, middle, or high school and its guidance department to respond in an effective manner to a crisis situation if a crisis management/intervention policy and program is not in place when the crisis occurs.

It is probably only a matter of time before your school will be confronted with a crisis. Any counselor who has been greeted with, *"A student in our school has died,"* for example, knows the value of having a crisis plan in place. Attempting to respond to such a traumatic event without a prior plan almost always exacerbates the problem. In addition to having a plan in place, school counselors will be expected to be experts in how the crisis will impact students initially, its long term effects, grieving behaviors, etc. How the counselor(s) responds to a crisis will have a significant influence on students, staff, and faculty grieving (if a death occurs), overall school togetherness, and so forth. Such a policy should be adopted and approved by the school principal and, if appropriate, by the local board of education.

We have designed herein a program to assist the school counselor, as coordinator of the crisis team, and the other members of the team in developing a policy and program that will best meet the needs of the school population in time of crisis.

The purpose of a policy and program is to aid the educational institution beset by trauma due to a crisis minimize disruption of educational activities. Preparation for a crisis mollifies the overall impact and disruption to the educational process. As noted, a school without a crisis policy in place will experience great difficulty coping and responding effectively when a crisis does occur.

An effective education and preventive program should include a proactive as well as reactive plan and approach to crises situations. The plan should have a broad base of community involvement and support. Information concerning various types of crises that might arise should be included as a part of the plan.

Crisis as used in this brief essay is defined as any sudden death or other traumatic event that directly impacts an entire school population.

The policy should be developed by those individuals who will implement the policy. The crisis team should include, but not be limited to, the school counselor(s), school nurse, school psychologist, school social worker, administrators, and other qualified mental health caregivers from the community who volunteer to be members of the team. The inclusion of non teaching school staff can also be beneficial. A secretary, cook, custodian, or bus driver is often more aware than others of the mood of the total school population, especially of the students, and their expertise should not be overlooked. As noted, it is our belief that one of the guidance department counselors should be the coordinator of such a team.

When developing a school crisis policy and/or action plan, the following questions should be addressed and answered specifically:

1. In the event of a crisis who is the first person to be contacted?

2. If the first person or organization is unavailable, who becomes the second and third main contact?

3. Who verifies what happened? How will the information be verified for accuracy and consistency?

4. How will the procedures the school will use to deal with the crisis be shared with the family, or families directly affected by the crisis?

5. Who notifies members of the crisis management/ intervention team?

6. How and when is the school staff informed and by whom?

7. How and when is the student body informed?

8. Is a phone tree in place?

9. When and where does the crisis management/intervention team meet?

10. What specific information will be shared with the teachers and staff concerning the tragedy? Suggested faculty guidelines (i.e., how to identify students in distress, appropriate classroom discussions regarding the crisis, dealing with student reactions regarding loss and death, etc.) should be in place.

11. What specific information concerning the tragedy will be shared with the students?

12. How will the involved family's privacy be protected by the school?

13. What information will be released by the media and who will be the spokesperson for the school?

14. If teachers/staff are contacted by the media, will they have been briefed or told what to say? Who will brief them?

15. If a student or school staff member is killed or dies unexpectedly, how will the personal possessions of the deceased be handled?

16. Who will follow the schedule of the individual and explain or answer questions concerning the tragedy?

17. Will a crisis center (safe room) be available for students, faculty, and non-instructional staff members?

18. Where will the crisis center be set up?

19. Who will be responsible for covering the crisis center? What hours?

20. How will individuals be identified to come to the crisis center? Will teachers have been given guidelines to assist them in identifying students in distress?

21. For what length of time will the crisis center exist?

22. How will qualified community resources be identified and utilized?

23. What action will be taken on the first day? How will those students directly involved with the incident be dealt with? By whom?

24. If a death occurs, what policy will be followed on the day of the funeral?

In sum, each school should have formulated a detailed disaster/crisis plan which includes plans for the immediate reaction to the crisis, immediate steps for crisis control, as well as ongoing and long-term intervention plans. As noted, such a plan should always include steps to help individuals, support for peer groups (teachers and students) and guidance for the entire student body.

It is extremely important to realize that a policy and program cannot cover every aspect of a crisis. Flexibility within a policy and program provides the ability to adjust to the unexpected needs created by the crisis. However, the policy and program should provide a clear directive to the crisis management/intervention team and present clear guidelines for delivering the crisis intervention service to the school's population.

Once the policy has been written, it should be reviewed by a school board attorney prior to school or school board adoption. In addition, the policy should be reviewed to ascertain that the policy follows and/or is not in conflict with any appropriate ethical standards (i.e., those of the American Counseling Association, state guidelines, others).

The individual counselor designated as responsible for the crisis management/intervention program should develop the team membership early in the school year. Team members should be educated concerning the adopted school policy and drills on implementing the crisis program should occur on a regular basis. Key players on the team should be identified and major responsibilities assigned and practiced. In-service opportunities in crisis intervention and management should be made available throughout the school year to team members as well as for faculty and staff. This provides the opportunity for individuals to be informed regarding the appropriate response to various crises and will assist in keeping their crisis management/intervention skills sharpened.

The policy and program should be evaluated on an annual basis. By reviewing the policy and program, additions, deletions, and modifications can be made and the policy and program strengthened. The counselor coordinator of the program should update the school board on the strengths and weaknesses of the revised policy and program.

# Figure 6.2
# Warning Signs of Adolescent Suicide

## Situational Clues

Recent loss of a loved one

Survivor of suicide attempt

Anniversary of death or loss—especially suicide

Loss of prestige, loss of face

Serious illness

Exhaustion of resources real or imagined

Family history of suicide

Close friend commits suicide

## Behavioral Clues

Talking or writing about suicide

Giving away personal possessions

Change in behaviors—eating and sleeping habits

Ending close relationships

Preparing for death—talking about funeral arrangements

Crying frequently

Buying weapons, pills, etc.

Reading a lot regarding suicide

## Emotional Clues

Sense of personal failure

Continual or constant sadness

General lack of interest

Expressing feelings of helplessness

Guilt

Withdrawal/isolation

Feels like a burden to others

Sudden lifting of depression

## Verbal Clues

"I can't go on."

"I have nothing to live for."

"No one cares."

"There's nothing left to do."

"What's the use."

"They won't have me to kick around anymore."

"I'm at my rope's end."

"They're better off without me."

"I just want to stop the pain once and for all."

# What to Do

## Listen:

Take feelings seriously

Avoid criticism or advice

Don't be judgmental or moralistic

Offer genuine concern, not sympathy or pity

Maintain contact

## Inquire About Suicidal Plan:

Is a specific plan formulated?

How lethal is the chosen method? Is it easily accessible?

What outcome is expected? Anticipated reaction of others?

Were previous attempts made?

If so, when, how serious, response of others?

Remove any lethal methods

## Explore Resources:

Personal strengths and abilities

Willingness to consider alternatives

Ability to ask for help

Significant others—friends, family, clergy, teacher, etc.

Community resources—local suicide prevention center, professional

Counseling, community mental health center

*Joe Wittmer, Ph.D. and Mary Ann Clark, Ph.D.*

# Figure 6.3
# Myths About Suicide

Myths and fallacies tend to arise and circulate about the subjects our society has deemed taboo. Suicide is one of those subjects. Present knowledge refutes the following myths.

**Suicidal adolescents just want to die.**

FACT: Most of the time suicidal people are torn between wanting to die and wanting to live. Most suicidal individuals don't want death: they just want the pain to stop.

**Adolescents who commit suicide do not warn others.**

FACT: Out of 10 people who kill themselves, eight give definite clues to their intentions. They leave numerous clues and warnings to others, although clues may be nonverbal or difficult to detect.

**Teens who talk about suicide are only trying to get attention. They won't really do it.**

FACT: WRONG! Few commit suicide without first letting someone else know how they feel Those who are considering suicide give clues and warnings as a cry for help. In fact, most seek out someone to rescue him or her. Over 70% who do threaten to commit suicide either make an attempt or complete the act

**After a person has attempted suicide, it is unlikely they will try again.**

FACT: People who have attempted suicide are very likely to try again: 80% of people who commit suicide have made **at least one previous attempt:**

**Suicide only happens to "crazy" people:**

FACT: Suicide among adolescents knows no boundaries. Gifted and homosexual teens are more likely to show suicidal behaviors and attempts but it can happen to any family anywhere.

**Don't mention suicide to someone who's showing signs of severe depression: It will plant the idea in their minds and they will act on it.**

FACT: Many depressed youth have already considered suicide as an option. Discussing it openly helps them sort through the problems and generally provides a sense of relief and understanding. It is one of the most helpful things you can do. However, the danger is still there.

**More males attempt suicide than females:**

FACT: Gender differences in the suicidal behavior of adolescents do exist. More adolescent females do attempt suicide than males. However, more males are successful. This may be that males tend to choose more violent and lethal methods.

**Sexual orientation does not play a role in adolescent suicide.**

FACT: Attempted suicide rates among both gay and lesbian adolescent populations are two to six times greater than suicide rates within the general population. Most experts attribute this to lack of support systems, societal homophobia, parental and peer rejection, feelings of isolation, etc.

**Race is not a factor in suicide:**

FACT: Suicide rates among African-American populations have been found to be somewhat lower than for White Euro-Americans. The evidence concerning other subpopulations is not available.

# References

American School Counselor Association. (2006). *Role statement: The school counselor.* Alexandria, VA: Author.

American School Counselor Association. (2003, 2005). *The ASCA national model: A framework for school counseling programs.* Alexandria, VA: Author.

Coy, D. (1999). *The role and training of the school counselor: Background and purpose. NASP Bulletin, 83, 2-8.*

Gibson, R.L., & Mitchell, M.H. (2002). *Introduction to counseling and guidance* (6th ed.). New York: Macmillan.

Gladding, S.T. (2003). *Counseling: A comprehensive profession* (5th ed.). Columbus, OH: Merrill.

Gysbers, N., & Henderson, P. (2006). *Developing and managing your school guidance program* (4th ed.). Alexandra, VA: American School Counselor Association.

Sears, S. (1999). Transforming school counseling: Making a difference for students. *NASP Bulletin, 83, 47-53.*

Wittmer, J., & Thompson, D. (2006). *Large group guidance activities: A k-12 sourcebook* (2nd ed.). Minneapolis, MN: Educational Media Corporation.

Myrick, R.C. (2003). *Developmental guidance and counseling: A practical approach* (4th ed). Minneapolis, MN: Educational Media Corporation.

Stone, C.B., & Dahir, C. A. (2006). *The transformed school counselor.* Boston, MA: Lahaska Press.

# Chapter 7

# The Developmental School Counselor and Mental Health Counseling

**by**
**Sondra Smith-Adcock**

---

*Sondra Smith-Adcock is an Associate Professor in the Department of Counselor Education at the University of Florida in Gainesville. Her research interests include delinquency prevention and counseling youth at-risk and their families. She has prior work experience teaching and counseling children and adolescents in schools, alternative schools, agencies, and residential treatment settings.*

*The author wishes to acknowledge important contributions made to this chapter by Kimberly Martin Donald, Ed.S., a doctoral student in the Department of Counselor Education at the University of Florida and full-time school counselor.*

## Introduction

In today's school age populations, serious emotional and behavioral problems are increasing dramatically, concomitant with the growth of such social problems as poverty, homelessness, violence, gangs, suicide, child abuse, and substance abuse (Carlson & Lewis, 1998; Heathfield & Clark, 2004). Before students can learn effectively, the personal and social challenges that interfere with their learning must be addressed. Schools throughout the United States have been faced with helping students navigate the challenges of today's complex and often troubled society. As a result of the increasing number of students with mental health needs and lack of community resources, schools have increasingly become providers of mental health care by default (Rones & Hoagwood, 2000; Rosenblatt & Rosenblatt, 1999). However, many authors have contended that current school-based mental health services are inadequate to meet the needs of students (Adelman & Taylor, 1998; American Academy of Pediatrics, 2004; Heathfield & Clark, 2004). According to

several recent reports, there is a growing population of students whose social-emotional needs are serious enough to interfere with the learning process (Adelman & Taylor; Repie, 2005).

- According to a recent Surgeon General's report on children's mental health, though up to 20% of children and adolescents have mental health problems in any given year; approximately 75% of these children did not receive needed mental health services. (U.S. Public Health Service, 2000).

- Up to 13% of children and adolescents have anxiety disorders, 6.2% have mood disorders, 10.3% have disruptive disorders, and 2% have substance abuse disorders (U.S. Public Health Service).

- The 2001 Risk Behavior Survey coordinated by the Centers for Disease Control and Prevention reported that 9% of youth attempted a suicide in a 12-month period (Centers for Disease Control and Prevention, 2000). Suicide is the third leading cause of death in children 10 to 19 years of age (Hoyert, Freedman, Strobino, & Guyer (2001).

- According to a recent study conducted by the Center for Mental Health Services, Substance Abuse and Mental Health Services Administration (SAMHSA), 73% of schools reported that *social, interpersonal, or family problems* were the most frequent problems for students. *Aggression or disruptive behavior and behavior problems associated with neurological disorders* were often cited problems for boys. For girls, *anxiety and adjustment issues* were common (Foster, Rollefson, Doksum, Noonan, Robinson, & Teich, 2005).

---

Because school counselors are often the designated personnel within schools who are trained to deal with the impact of students' social-emotional needs on the learning process (ASCA, 2005; Ballard & Murgatroyd, 1999; Brown, Dahlbeck, & Sparkman-Barnes, 2006), their role in the delivery of appropriate mental health care for students is a critical one. Since the inception of guidance counseling in the 1950s, the role of the school counselor has evolved from providing guidance and career information to addressing the development of students' personal, social, educational and career needs (Bailey, Henderson, Krueger, & Williams, 1998). The evolution of the school counselor's role has been said to be reflective of changing forces in society and place demands upon school personnel to meet the needs of increasingly diverse student populations and societal problems (Keys, Bemack, & Lockhart, 1998). Recently, discussion has emerged concerning the school counselor's role as either a developmental specialist or as a mental health provider in the schools. Central to this debate is the extent to which school counselors have time to provide direct mental health services to students and families given their already exhaustive list of tasks and responsibilities (Paisley & Borders, 1995).

In this chapter, it is recommended that school counselors should be both developmental specialists and mental health providers in the schools. Current models of mental health counseling in schools are reviewed and recent literature regarding the mental health role of school counselors will be summarized. The remainder of this chapter is organized into three parts. In part one, the status of school counselors as mental health providers is presented, as it has been articulated in school counseling literature, In part two, current models for providing school-based mental health services to schoolchildren are listed and described. Finally, in part three, recommendations for strengthening the mental health counseling role of school counselors to meet the needs of at-risk and special needs students, based on literature, are summarized.

# The Mental Health Counseling Role of School Counselors: The Current Debate

The primary role of the school counselor is to facilitate the mission of schools, that is, to help children to learn. Current models of school counseling emphasize programs that are comprehensive and developmental, including direct counseling as well as consultation and coordination (Paisley & Borders, 1995). While school counseling programs still offer certain types of responsive services related to mental health and crisis intervention, they now emphasize primary prevention and the promotion of healthy development for all students (Brown, et al., 2006; Paisley & Borders, 1995).

According to the framework proposed by the ASCA National Model, school counseling programs foster the school's overall mission by promoting academic achievement, career planning and personal/social development (ASCA, 2005). Furthermore, delivery of school counseling programs, as articulated in the National Model, includes traditional responsive counseling services "to meet individual students' immediate needs, usually necessitated by life events or situations and conditions in the students' lives (Executive Summary, p. 2)." However, a statement made in the National Model also discourages the school counselor from working with one student at a time in a "therapeutic, clinical mode" [as in a mental health model] and instead recommends that the school counselor should be "working with teachers to present proactive prevention-based guidance curriculum lessons (Executive Summary, p. 4)." These statements taken together seem to emphasize the importance of school counselors working with all students—those students with developmental concerns as well as those who have psychosocial and/or mental health needs. The final statement, however, seems to suggest that ASCA has adopted a stance that limits the school counselor from providing mental health counseling services in the schools. Thus, these statements do not clearly articulate the extent to which school counselors are expected to provide direct counseling services to students with special mental health needs. Therefore, the school counselor's role in making sure that schoolchildren receive help for psychosocial or mental health problems requires further clarification.

## Existing Models of Mental Health Intervention for Schools

Some prominent authors have advocated for strengthening the role school counselors play in meeting the needs of students who are at-risk (Keys, Bemack, & Lockhart, 1998). According to these authors, the primary prevention focus of traditional guidance and counseling programs may be too broad to meet the mental health needs of students in today's society because all students do not respond similarly to the same intervention. Many students require more focused and intensive counseling services to prevent the further development of an existing problem. Too often, unless the school counselor initiates intensive counseling services, schoolchildren often do not receive the mental health counseling that they need. Keys, Bemack, and Lockhart cited limitations of the developmental guidance and counseling model in meeting the mental health needs of students who are at-risk as follows:

1. Primary prevention may be too broad and not sensitive to the needs of at-risk youth.

2. Primary prevention efforts have not been shown to be effective in the long-term with at-risk students because they often are too limited, do not account for contextual factors, and are not integrated well with other school and community based programs.

3. Developmental guidance and counseling programs often emphasize individual change through school-based strategies rather than system-based interventions that include the broader environments (i.e., families and communities) in which students live,

4. Developmental guidance and counseling programs often are limited in their ability to meet the needs of students at-risk because they are linked only to a school's educational program, rather than to a broader system of community institutions and services.

5. Developmental guidance and counseling programs are too often based on expected student competencies without assessing the unique needs of students in the school community, especially students who are at-risk.

6. "Guidance" as a term diminishes the role and identity of the school counselor as a counseling professional, whereas "school counseling" is a term more descriptive of the variety of counseling and consultation services, not just remedial or one-to-one relationships services, that are provided by counselors (Schmidt, 1996).

According to Rones and Hoagwood (2000), schools have become the primary providers of mental health care to children. According to these authors, if children receive any mental health services at all, they receive them at school. Increasingly, community mental health services are isolated from schools, inaccessible to students and families, and declining in number (Lockhart & Keys, 1998). In order to eliminate the barriers to mental health care for students and families, many school personnel are discovering the importance of collaboration with other service providers in the community in meeting the mental health needs of their students (American Academy of Pediatrics, 2004; Repie, 2005). As a result, school-based mental health programs are growing in number (American Academy of Pediatrics, 2004; Brown, 2006; Foster, et al., 2005; Repie, 2005). Integration of mental health services into the school setting has improved recognition, assessment, and treatment of mental health problems (Advocates for Youth, 1998; Brown, et al., 2006; Foster et al.). Brown (2006) reports that students receiving school-based mental health services have an increase in academic achievement, reduced disciplinary problems, and fewer absences from school.

School-based mental health delivery models are varied in how they are organized, financed, and staffed (American Academy of Pediatrics, 2004; Foster et al., 2005). Models for providing mental health services in schools were summarized in 2001 by the Policy Leadership Cadre for Mental Health in Schools, a policy-oriented coalition coordinated by the Center for Mental Health in Schools at UCLA. The Policy Leadership Cadre has articulated five approaches for the delivery of school mental health services (Foster et al.). These types of programs are not mutually exclusive. Many schools offer more than one type of program (American Academy of Pediatrics, Foster et al.).

(1) *Classroom-based curricula* are primary prevention approaches that are designed to enhance social and emotional growth. (2) *School-financed student support services* are provided by local school districts in which professional counseling staff is hired to provide traditional mental health services. (3) *Formal connections with community mental health centers* are formal agreements between schools and school districts and one or more community agencies to provide mental health services and to enhance coordination of services. Services are either provided at the school, the community agency, or both. (4) *School-district mental health units or clinics* are operated and financed by a district and provide mental health services, training, and/or consultation to schools. These services are either provided

## The School Counselor and School-Based Mental Health Services: A "Transformed" Role

through a school-based mental health clinic or through a multidisciplinary team that provide a wide-range of psychosocial and mental health services. (5) *Comprehensive, multifaceted, and integrated models* are coordinated by school districts and include multiple community partners and a full spectrum of services. These programs often offer mental health and wraparound services for children and families through partnerships with several child-serving systems (Foster et al., 2005; Policy Leadership Cadre for Mental Health in Schools, 2001).

A recent study conducted by the Center for Mental Health Services, Substance Abuse and Mental Health Services Administration (SAMHSA), *School Mental Health Services in the United States, 2002-2003*, examined the prevalence and distribution of mental health services provided to all children in the school setting (Foster et al., 2005). In this study, school personnel reported that schools were responding to the mental health needs of their students. Most schools reported that students were assessed for mental health problems and schools provided behavior management consultations, crisis intervention, and referral to specialized programs. The school counselor was most often the designated professional in the school who provided psychosocial or mental health intervention. School personnel, however, also reported many barriers to providing needed services (e.g., financial constraints of families) and decreased funding for school mental health initiatives. Though this study surveyed the prevalence of programs to meet the psychosocial and mental health needs of students, it did not evaluate the intensity or quality of those services.

School-based mental health services require the school counselor to coordinate partnerships between schools and community mental health agencies, define their role within broader systems of psychosocial and mental health care networks, and sometimes to reorganize existing programs (Brown et al., 2006; Keys, 2000; Keys, Bemack, & Lockhart, 1998; Keys & Bemack, 1997). The key to successful school-based mental health partnerships depends on the quality of collaboration between partners (Brown et al., 2006; Keys, Bemack, & Lockhart; Weist, Lowie, Flaherty, & Pruitt, 2001). When collaboration among professionals and co-ordination of services, however, is lacking, access to needed services is restricted and the outcome of services becomes less effective (Dwyer, 2002; Foster et al., 2005).

The school counselor is in a unique position to take a leadership role in forming collaborative relationships between schools, families, and community agencies (Brown et al., 2006; Keys, 2000; Keys, Bemack, & Lockhart, 1998). Keys, Bemack, & Lockhart have proposed a model for reorganizing the role and function of school counselors to meet the challenge of managing school-based mental health partnerships with families and community agencies. In a "transformed" model of school counseling, "the school counselor provides leadership within the school for an alliance with school-based mental health professionals and helps to establish school-based mechanisms to support a variety of collaborative efforts (pp. 383-384)."

The "transformed" model proposed by Keys, Bemack, & Lockhart (1998) includes school-based, mental health collaborative networks, which school counselors will establish and coordinate. They recommend the following components: (1) *School-family-community mental health teams* join school personnel, family members, representatives from service institutions (i.e., social services, health and mental health agencies, juvenile justice, and law enforcement) and helping institutions (i.e., churches, parks and recreation, and libraries) (Keys & Bemak, 1997). This interdisciplinary team meets on a regular basis to ensure the quality and continuity of services provided throughout the community. (2) *Program development groups* are subcommittees of mental health teams and extend the goals of the school-family-community mental health team by developing new community outreach programs and activities for the larger team's consideration. Several program development groups may exist at the same time, focusing on different mental health needs (Adelman & Taylor, 1998). (3) *Case management teams* also are a subcommittee of the school-family-community mental health team. The goal of this committee is to provide multidisciplinary planning and intervention for individual students. School counselors and other mental health services professionals meet as often as weekly to discuss the referral process, interventions, and other process issues such as confidentiality and mandated reporting (Porter, Epp, & Sharone, 2000).

Keys, Bemack, & Lockhart (1998) further suggest that the traditional roles of the school counselor: coordination, consultation, and counseling should be extended in the following ways in a transformed model: (1) *Coordination* becomes the primary function of the school counselor, but this function is expanded to include integration of mental health services. (2) *Consultation* is extended to include collaborative consultation. "Collaborative consultation is an interactive, interdependent process in which all members of the interdisciplinary teams exchange expertise and roles, engage in joint problem-solving, and share responsibility for outcomes (Dettmer, Dyck, & Thurston 1996; Keys, Bemak, & Lockhart; Keys, Bemak, Carpenter, & King-Sears, 1998). (3) *Counseling* services in the "transformed model" prioritize group counseling, brief therapy models of intervention, crisis intervention teams, and family interventions. (4) *Classroom-based instruction* remains an integral part of the school counselor's program. However, primary prevention efforts are more intensive and ongoing, based on relevant issues students and teachers confront, based on real-life problem situations, and connected with other school- and community-based programs, than traditional classroom guidance models.

Transforming school counseling programs and expanding the role and function of the school counselor to provide mental health services to schoolchildren is complicated and difficult (Brown et al., 2006; Keys, 2000; Keys, Bemack, & Lockhart, 1998). Brown et al. found that there is confusion regarding the roles and responsibilities of school counselors in collaborative partnerships with community mental health agencies. To help ease this confusion of roles and responsibilities, representatives from schools and community mental health agencies should jointly develop collaborative agreements and engage in ongoing dialogue concerning role definition of professionals and delivery of services (Brown et al.). Though these partnerships seem to be a step in the right direction for providing mental health services for schoolchildren, further articulation of how interdisciplinary teams work together to provide the best possible mental health services is needed (Brown et al.; Weist et al., 2001).

## Conclusions and Directions for the Future of School Counseling

A number of key points emerge from this overview of the school counselor's role in providing school-based mental health services for students. First, recent reports of the prevalence of mental health issues underscore the need for counselors to stay in touch with students who have serious psychosocial and mental health problems. It is clear that a broad continuum of mental health services are needed in schools to address the entire range of mental health concerns of students, ranging from primary prevention to targeted mental health counseling interventions (American Academy of Pediatrics, 2004; Heathfield & Clark, 2004).

Second, in order to provide a wide range of mental health services, collaborative partnerships between schools and mental health agencies appears to be a step in the right direction (Brown et al., 2006). These partnerships expand existing school counseling programs to provide quality mental health as well as academic counseling (Brown et al.). It has been proposed that school counselors do not have the time to provide extensive mental health counseling for students, and as suggested by the ASCA National Model, they may not be able to provide one on one, therapeutic, clinical counseling to all students who need it. However, if the school counselor's role in providing intensive, targeted, mental health services is diminished in importance relative to primary prevention efforts, many students will not receive the help they need. For those students that cannot be adequately helped through primary prevention or targeted counseling interventions, the services provided by a mental health collaborative is critical. Though school-community agency partnerships are increasing and showing promise as an effective way to meet diverse mental health needs in school communities, many schools and school systems have not yet developed these important services. Much also remains to be done to understand how these collaborative partnerships function best and what the long-term academic and psychosocial benefits of school-based mental health care are for schoolchildren and their families (Brown et al., 2006; Foster et al., 2005).

Finally, the school counselor should play a key role in organizing and facilitating school-based mental health services (Brown et al., 2006; Keys, 2000; Keys, Bemack, & Lockhart, 1998). Increasingly, school counselors are called upon to facilitate and lead a team approach and to mental health services in collaboration with community agencies. Such a "transformed" model of school counseling does not contradict traditional school counseling and developmental guidance models. Recent models show that school counseling and school-based mental health counseling can be integrated. These new models also provide a clear direction toward enhancing the role of the school counselor as a mental health provider (Keys, Bemack, & Lockhart, 1998). The integration of developmental school counseling with mental health counseling is imminent. School counselors must continue to provide what has traditionally been called developmental guidance, focusing on the larger student body, the school environment and academic success, but they must also serve as mental health consultants and counselors for their schools if they are to fulfill ASCA's stated mission to facilitate the learning of all students (ASCA, 2005).

# References

Adelman, H.S., & Taylor, L. (1998). Reframing mental health in schools and expanding school reform. *Educational Psychologist, 33,* 135-152.

Advocates for Youth. (1998). The facts: School-based health centers. Available at www.advocatesforyouth.org/publications/factsheet/fssbhc.htm. Accessed June 15, 2006.

American Academy of Pediatrics. (2004). Policy statement, committee on school health, school-based mental health services. *Pediatrics, 113 (6),* 1839-1845.

American School Counselor Association. (2005). *Executive Summary, The ASCA national model: A framework for school counseling programs* (2nd ed.). Alexandria, VA: Author. Available at http://www.schoolcounselor.org/content.asp?pl=325&sl=133&contentid=240.

Bailey, M., Henderson, P., Krueger, D., & Williams, L.A. (1998). *A visit to a comprehensive guidance program that works.* Greensboro, NC: ERIC-CASS.

Ballard, M.B., & Murgatroyd, W. (1999). Defending a vital program: School counselors define their roles. *NASSP Bulletin, January,* 19-26.

Brown, C., Dahlbeck, D.T., & Sparkman-Barnes, L. (2006). Collaborative relationships: School counselors and non-school mental health professionals working together to improve the mental health needs of students. *Professional School Counseling, 9(4),* 332-335.

Brown, M.B. (2006). School-based health centers: Implications for counselors. *Journal of Counseling & Development, 84,* 187-191.

Carlson, J., & Lewis, J. (1998). *Counseling the adolescent: Individual, family, and school interventions* (3rd ed.). Denver, CO: Love Publishing.

Centers for Disease Control and Prevention. (2000). Youth risk behavior surveillance—United States, 1999. *MMWR CDC Surveillance Summary, 49(5),* 1-32. Available at http://www.cdc.gov/mmwr/indss_2000.html. Retrieved June 15, 2006.

Dwyer. K.P. (2000). Mental health in the schools. *Journal of Child and Family Studies, 11,* 101-111.

Foster, S., Rollefson, M., Doksum, T., Noonan, D., Robinson, G., & Teich, J. (2005). *School mental health service in the United States, 2002-2003.* DHHS Pub. No. (SMA) 05-4068. Rockville, MD: Center for mental Health Services, Substance Abuse and Mental Health Services Administration. Available at put hyperlink here. Accessed June 15, 2006.

Heathfield, L.T., & Clark, E. (2004). Shifting from categories to services: Comprehensive school-based mental health for children with emotional disturbance and social maladjustment. *Psychology in the Schools, 4(8),* 911-920.

Hoyert, D.L., Freedman, M.A., Strobino, D., & Guyer, B. (2001). Annual summary of vital statistics: 2000. *Pediatrics, 108,* 1241-1255.

Keys, S.G. (2000). Living the collaborative role: Voices from the field. *Professional School Counseling, 3(5),* 332-338.

Keys, S.G., Bemak, F., Carpenter, S., & King-Sears, M. (1998). Collaborative consultant: A new role for counselors serving at-risk youths. *Journal of Counseling and Development, 76,* 123-133.

Keys, S.G., Bemak, F., & Lockhart, E.J. (1998). Transforming school counseling to serve the mental health needs of at-risk youth. *Journal of Counseling and Development, 76,* 381-388.

Keys, S.G., & Bemak, F. (1997). School-family-community linked services: A school counseling role for changing times. *The School Counselor, 44,* 255-263.

Lockhart, E.J., & Keys, S.G. (1998). The mental health counseling role of school counselors. *Professional School Counseling, 1(4),* 3-6.

Paisley, P.O., & Borders, L.D. (1995). School counseling: An evolving specialty. *Journal of Counseling and Development, 74,* 150-153.

Policy Leadership Cadre for Mental Health in Schools. (2001). *Mental health in schools: Guidelines, models, resources, and policy considerations.* Department of Psychology, University of California, Los Angeles.

Repie. M.S. (2005). A school mental health issues survey from the perspective of regular and special education teachers, school counselors, and school psychologists. *Education and Treatment of Children, 28(3),* 279-298,

Rones, M., & Hoagwood, K. (2000). School-based mental health services: A research review. *Clinical Child and Family Psychology Review, 3(4),* 223-241.

Rosenblatt, J.A., & Rosenblatt, A. (1999). Youth functional status and academic achievement in collaborative mental health and education programs: Two California care systems. *Journal of Emotional and Behavioral Disorders, 7,* 21-30.

Schmidt, J. (1996). *Counseling in schools.* Needham Heights, MA: Allyn & Bacon.

U.S. Public Health Service. Report of the surgeon generals conference on children's mental health: A national action agenda. Washington, DC: US Department of Health and Human Services. Available at www.surgeon-general.gov/topics/cmh/childreport.htm. Accessed June 15, 2006.

# Chapter 8

# The Developmental School Counselor as Educational Leader

**by**
**Mary Ann Clark and Carolyn Stone**

*Mary Ann Clark, Ph.D., NCC, is an Associate Professor in the Department of Counselor Education at the University of Florida where she is the Coordinator of the School Counseling Program. Dr. Clark was a school counselor at the elementary, middle and high school levels as well as a school administrator for twenty years, working in both stateside and overseas school districts.*

*Carolyn B. Stone, Ed.D., is a Professor in Counselor Education at the University of North Florida in Jacksonville, Florida. Dr. Stone spent 22 years with the Duval County public school system in Jacksonvillle as teacher, counselor, and Supervisor of Guidance. As a counselor educator, she has written a number of articles and has conducted workshops in the areas of legal and ethical issues for student service personnel as well as school counseling program development. She is currently serving at the president of the American School Counselor Association.*

## Introduction

As we enter the twenty first century, many educators are taking stock of where we stand currently and where we are headed in the future with regard to student academic achievement. Statistics concerning at risk youth, increasing violence in the schools, and American students' underachievement academically have become urgent issues as cross-cultural comparisons have caused us to question our country's ability to compete on a global scale. Leadership is becoming an increasingly valued and shared phenomenon at the school level but for the school counselor until recently it has not been duly explored and emphasized in either practice or in school counseling preparation programs. Thus, even when counselors play leadership roles, they are not necessarily given credit for such professional activities. School counselors specifically, as part of an educational team in the schools, have a vital role to play as proactive leaders, social change agents, and advocates for student success (Devoss & Andrews, 2006; Lee & Walz, 1998; Capuzzi, 1998; House and Martin, 1998). The mission and climate of the school, student advocacy, school effectiveness in delivering academic success, staff development, the school change process, and institutional decision making are all areas that school counselors can, and should, positively impact through a leadership role. Further, by assuming the challenge of such a role, counselors can expand their services and increase their resources. In the process, counselors can empower themselves to do so by seeking new and creative ways to benefit students and schools. In this chapter we explore and highlight what we view as the evolving leadership role of the school counselor. In addition, we validate and promote the ongoing leadership efforts made by school counselors throughout the nation.

Educational reform efforts, learning, and student achievement are at the heart of every educator's job; each has an important contribution to make. Rather than becoming a quasi-administrator, the school counselor has many unique opportunities to assert leadership in his/her own right. The counselor's role is involving increased collaboration and consultation interventions with those significant people in the lives of students; teachers, administrators, family members and people in the community. Instead of being isolated in their offices, to increase their effectiveness, counselors need to play an integral role in the total educational process (Myrick, 2003; Kaplan & Evans, 1999; Tollerud & Nejedlo, 1999). The past model of school counselors serving in a passive role waiting for students and parents to come to them for assistance is no longer meeting the needs of the school population. Taking a stand on important educational issues and being perceived as a strong leader and an advocate for change and continuous improvement has become essential to the effectiveness of the school counselor. "Counselors need to be role models and change agents which is more easily accomplished when they are seen in a leadership role in the schools. The more they are in the classrooms and working with teachers, parents, and administrators, the more credible they become" (Guerra, 1998).

Voices in the profession have called for a shift in the role of the school counselor from service provider to that of leader and advocate for removing barriers which impede students' academic success, thus promoting optimal achievement for all students (Devoss & Andrews, 2006; The Educational Trust, 1997; Dedmond, 1998; House & Martin, 1998). As team builders, counselors can enlist the support of teachers, parents, administrators, and the community to help visions become reality. The American School Counselor Association (ASCA) has included in the National Model: A Framework for School Counseling Programs the important themes of leadership, advocacy, collaboratioin and teaming, and systemic change (ASCA, 2005). The emphasis is on making the school counseling program an integral part of the total school program with the school counselors as leaders who are engaged in systemwide change to ensure student success.

# Specific Ways Counselors Can Demonstrate Leadership

## Professional Image

Developing and maintaining a professional image is essential to the perception of the school counselor as an educational leader. A counselor who is perceived as assertive, credible, hardworking, dependable, responsible, open and honest about beliefs, and is a skilled facilitator and communicator will stand out in the eyes of many as a true leader. Moreover, heading up school groups/teams, and taking a stand on important issues will further a leadership image and will empower the counselor in the school. More general areas of leadership related to image and visibility also include involvement with extracurricular activities and student organizations, serving as guest speaker for parent and community organizations, and coaching sports which involve a cross section of the student body.

## Organizational Roles

Specific organizational roles that a counselor may choose to play can include participation and leadership in school and district committees on school improvement, student assessment, enrichment programs, management advisory committees, curriculum committees, and parent-teacher organizations. Such involvement can increase visibility and infuse counselor input into a number of vital school functions.

## Staff Development

Staff development is another avenue for demonstrating leadership potential among school counselors (Dedmond, 1998). Conducting inservice training for teachers and parents in such important areas as educational planning, motivation, student appraisal and achievement, identification of and interventions for special needs students, and issues of student diversity and related attitudes is an example of where counselors can play a unique role in fostering understanding and cooperation among the school community. Other examples of counselor facilitated staff development can include medical issues for school age children, learning styles and strategies, student leadership training, school improvement plans, cooperative discipline and classroom management, study skills, and college admissions procedures. Although school counselors are knowledgeable and skillful in many of these areas, their role in staff development may involve the organization and planning of such inservices to include obtaining outside resources as well as being presenters themselves. An ultimate goal is to provide support to teachers through information, intervention, modeling, and encouragement.

One middle school counselor decided to address some student behavioral issues that frequently frustrated parents and teachers by organizing a Parent/Teacher Forum in her school. She conducted a needs assessment and identified the most frequently occurring problems and concerns of educators and parents in her school such as Attention Deficit Hyperactivity Disorder (ADHD), lack of study skills, underachievement, aggressive/defiant behavior, and substance abuse. She then organized and hosted a one night fair at the school in which parents and teachers were able to choose three different presentations to attend. Speakers were obtained from various community agencies to provide information and facilitate discussions on the topics of interest. The physical education coaches assisted in the endeavor by providing clinics in the multi-purpose room for children ages 6 – 16 while the adults were attending the workshops.

Staff development took a different twist for the counselor of a large elementary school when she decided to address the stress level of her faculty following a particularly grueling spring testing schedule. During a teacher planning day she set up wellness workshops in which teachers could attend lectures on nutrition, receive a massage, listen to a chiropractor, and participate in a healthy, low-calorie lunch. Evaluations indicated that these workshops were well received and contributed to an increase in faculty morale during a difficult period of the school year.

## Large Group Guidance

A traditional school counselor intervention, that of large group guidance, can be updated to incorporate more direct advocacy for student success. Test preparation, study skills, educational and future planning, career development, and the use of specific data to further such topics can be used to encourage a positive "mindset" for achievement and success for all students. For example, sharing statistics with students for how education affects lifetime salaries is appropriate information for them to have and may encourage a higher degree of motivation and understanding of course relevancy than just presenting course sign up sheets to students to complete. Specific up to date information on what jobs and accompanying skills/training will be required in our future society is very important data for students as well as for their parents to possess. Additionally, the use of technology to access such information should be an integral part of the counselor-as-leader repertoire. As well as facilitating the large group

sessions themselves, counselors can serve as consultants and resources for Teacher Advisor Programs (Myrick, 2003) which can disseminate similar types of information to students in an organized program with a planned curriculum.

One large urban school district has implemented large group guidance using closed circuit television and teachers as the purveyors of guidance lessons. Just prior to the school district's career and college fair, counselors trained teachers in delivering a simple lesson to encourage high schoolers to attend the fair and to instruct the students in how to get the most from the experience. The lessons were easy to follow and took only 30 minutes of the teachers' time. Additionally, the counselors of the district delivered daily 10 minute messages on closed-circuit television for six days preceding the college and career fair resulting in a significant increase in attendance.

## Coordinating Counselor Leadership Roles

In schools where there is more than one counselor, counseling departments should coordinate their leadership efforts in order to utilize and maximize their various personalities, strengths and interests. Counselor leadership is a fluid role that involves ongoing growth and development. Emphases and participation on committees as well as topics for staff development can change from year to year. One person can not effectively carry out all of the mentioned functions by oneself all of the time. Sharing of such leadership roles can make them more workable for individual counselors and more effective for the department as a whole. Counselors should be encouraged to find a "niche" with regard to leadership which would capitalize not only on their personal strengths but on the specific needs of the school and system for which they work. Such strategies as initiating planning and problem solving groups, expanding the use of parent and community volunteers, delegating appropriate tasks, and building political connections can strengthen the guidance and counseling program as well as heighten its visibility. All of these aspects should be a part of a comprehensive, developmental counseling program (Stone & Dahir, 2006).

The partnership between the counselors and the school administration is particularly crucial. Although the two departments may have separate and specific roles and responsibilities to carry out, there is overlap with regard to accomplishing common goals for the school and its students. Close communication and the coordination of efforts to improve and ensure student success are vital. Ideally, school administrators and counselors should be seen as a partnership who work closely together. A collaborative management model where the principals' and counselors' roles are interchangeable can allow them to work together to improve instruction and provide support in the classroom. Although this model is not implemented in many school settings, the principle of collaboration between school administrators and counselors is being seen as increasingly necessary to the operation of an effective instructional program (Amatea & Clark, 2005).

# Advocacy as Leadership

The *Random House Dictionary* defines advocacy as "active espousal: recommending and supporting." Helping to create alternatives and opportunities for people is one of the action steps that counselors can take. All people, particularly those who have been marginalized in society need more life choices (Lee & Walz, 1998). Counselors can advocate in numerous ways for students, particularly with regard to motivation, achievement, and future planning. To be seen as an advocate for "all students" is particularly important with regard to the perception of the counselor as an educational leader (House & Hayes, 2002; House & Martin, 1998; Stone & Clark, 2001). There are a number of specific areas in which counselors can demonstrate such advocacy.

## School Reform

Developmentally oriented school counselors can play an advocacy role by forming partnerships with school staff and by promoting the change process in school reform. Although school counselors have traditionally been left out of the school reform literature (House & Martin, 1998; Stone & Clark, 2001), they are in a unique position to exert a powerful influence on reform. As part of leadership teams as well as being trained facilitators, counselors can provide technical and staff support to facilitate change efforts and team building within a school and community thus promoting ongoing school improvement (Sheldon, 1998). Further, with their specialized knowledge and skills in collaboration, coordination, cooperation, resource brokering, and assessment and evaluation, counselors can be leaders in policy and process changes that can affect education and student achievement (Dedmond, 1998). Institutions do not change unless leaders within them initiate and implement change. Counselors are in a strategic position to do so.

More specifically, the developmental school counselor as leader establishes a vision and belief in the development of high aspirations in every child (ASCA, 2005) The developmentally oriented school counselor who believes that all children should be supported to be successful in rigorous academic coursework, behaves in ways that demonstrate that belief. "The leader must live the vision. He or she must not only believe in it but must be seen to believe in it.... To be real it has to come from the deepest parts of you, from an inner system of belief" (Handy, 1987, p. 11). Further, school counselors as human relations experts can impact the beliefs and attitudes of teachers and administrators regarding educating all students to achieve high standards. Their training in communication, interpersonal relationships, problem solving and conflict resolution give them a vantage point in promoting collaboration among colleagues to promote such achievement (West & Idol, 1993).

An example of helping students develop high aspirations can be found in one large school district who has made a commitment to inform students earlier in their high school careers than in the past as to available financial aid and scholarship opportunities. The school counselors in this district annually train approximately 100 volunteers who then deliver individual advising sessions to high schoolers about how to access financial aid and scholarships for postsecondary education. Plans are underway to move this program to the middle schools.

A school district who recently implemented a policy in which all students must pass algebra to obtain a high school diploma has mobilized the counselors to help change the attitudes and beliefs of teachers about the policy. Armed with data about the success of similar programs in other school districts, these counselors were able to show how the percentage of students enrolling in and passing algebra had skyrocketed.

## Multicultural Awareness

Our public schools continue to reflect the increasingly diverse population that makes up our society. By most population projections, the changing demographics of the United States are transforming the country into one in which a majority of its citizens are members of a variety of minority groups. Because of their training, visibility and positions of leadership, it is essential that school counselors and administrators work as a team to embrace cultural diversity for students, teachers, parents, and members of the community (Harris, 1999; Lee, 2005).

Collaboration and consultation on the part of the counselor with teachers, administrators, and parents to help individual students and classroom groups communicate regarding gender and racial/ethnic equity, multicultural awareness and understanding, as well as prejudice reduction is an essential role in today's rapidly changing society. Specifically, being willing to champion such causes and confront and challenge intolerance are roles for the counselor as leader and advocate for all students. Action should also include promoting student interest in careers in which students of culturally diverse groups have been underrepresented (Lee, 2005). School counselors as educational leaders can promote the concept of equitable access to job opportunities and can work to keep potential employers and other personnel from restricting such access based on stereotypes (Herring, 1998). Career Fairs which include speakers and representatives of a variety of cultural groups can help promote the concept of equitable access to job opportunities as well as to help dispel stereotypes about ethnicity and gender with regard to

employment. One developmental school counselor we know held a Career Day for middle school students featuring the parents as guest speakers. The counselor made a point of inviting people who were in nontraditional occupations. For example, a male nurse and a female police officer were among the participants. A variety of ethnic and racial groups were involved in the presentations as well.

School counselors can play a central role in the multicultural training and development of other educators as well as students (Pedersen & Carey, 2003). Counselors can help others recognize what teaching a diverse population involves, encourage them to become more knowledgeable about other cultures, and assist them in examining their own beliefs, values and prejudices (Lee, 2005). Further, by teaching communication skills and emphasizing the valuing of differences, they can work with teachers to help children learn to convey caring and respect for one another. The school counselor, serving as a consultant and collaborator with teachers, parents, administrators and community members can be in a pivotal position to teach and promote such skills (Harris, 1999, Lee, 2005).

## Use of Data

School counselors are expected to illustrate the impact of their programs on student achievement through the use of data (ASCA, 2005, Education Trust, 1997; Stone & Dahir, 2006). Student databases that are updated daily or weekly can be used by counselors to track grades, test scores, discipline referrals and attendance. They can also be used to sort groups of students who may be in need of specific services. Using data in a leadership role can be a powerful way to help students access educational opportunities.

One school district supervisor of guidance disaggregated district student data using free/reduced lunch information to identify low income seniors who would need financial aid to attend college. Using a variety of communication strategies to inform these students and their parents, he set up financial aid workshops for low income families assisting them to fill out the required federal forms and explaining the necessary procedures and deadlines. School counselors and counselor interns from the local university were trained to implement these workshops at each of the area high schools. Attendance by low income families tripled from the previous year resulting in a large number of low income students applying to college and receiving financial aid.

## Child Study Committee

Leadership by the school counselor in the Child Study Committee, which is used for special education referrals, processing and placement, can be a means to advocate for needed services for special students. Additionally, counselors can be instrumental in modifying programs and ending special services for students when that option is most appropriate. They can help teachers, school psychologists, and other resource personnel collaborate to identify and resolve student problems by designing the most appropriate and innovative program or instructional modifications. Their collaboration and facilitative skills as well as their unique perspective of the total school program make them natural leaders in coordinating such team efforts.

Leadership in child study committee provides the school counselor the opportunity to help team members explore options for students with learning difficulties who may not qualify for special education services. A number of elementary schools in one school district initiated a prescreening team called "The Care Team" for the purpose of implementing alternative interventions to address learning problems. One Care Team established a reading lab using computers and organized the Rotary Club to man the lab. This lab became a very effective intervention for this school and even reduced the number of special education placements.

## Mentoring Programs

All students need the positive influence of a significant adult(s) in their lives. Unfortunately, with the many changes occurring in society and the family, many students miss out on these special relationships. The number of single parent families has increased as has the number of dual career families often limiting the amount of time that parents spend with their children. More students are spending their after-school hours alone or unsupervised (Myrick, 2003). Initiating mentoring programs in the community is an important way to link students with adults who can have an important impact on the outcome of their lives. There are a growing number of community projects springing up around the country to facilitate the education and development of our "at risk" youth (Campbell-Whatley, Algozzine, & Obiakor, 1997). These mentoring programs are being developed in order to establish relationships with young people and to offer assistance and incentives encouraging them to set and achieve short as well as long term goals (Schnurnberger, 1997). Educational literature cites the importance of resilience and the role of significant adults in the successful development of young people considered to be at risk (Barbarin, 1993; Clark, Brooks, Lee, Daley, & Crawford, 2006; Connell, Spencer & Aber, 1994, Lee & Cramond, 1999).

Counselors can play a vital role in helping create linkages between such programs and students who need them. Specific ways in which counselors can contribute to successful mentoring projects include: identifying the students who would most benefit from having a mentor, leading, designing and developing programs that would best meet the needs of students, clarifying the focus of mentoring relationships, helping define the role of mentors, and enhancing parent and community involvement. Critical to the successful mentoring of students in the schools is the leadership and facilitation skills of the professional school counselor.

## Student Leadership

Counselors are in an advantageous position to recognize and encourage leadership potential in students. They have student data as well as observations and individual and group interaction on which to base such opinions. Positive student leadership can be a very powerful force in a school and can facilitate a school climate conducive to personal and academic growth and achievement as well as perceived needed changes in the school environment.

Several school counselors in one school system along with high school administrators and district office personnel, combined talents to conduct leadership training for sophomores and juniors who had been referred by teachers as having leadership potential. A weekend retreat was held where 50 students participated in small and large group activities designed to teach and foster communication and leadership skills. Various community organizations contributed food and supplies as well as providing some speakers for the event.

## Political Involvement

Counselors can also exert leadership through political involvement, either at the school and district level regarding school policies and procedures or through professional organizations. The American Counseling Association (ACA), the American School Counselor Association (ASCA) as well as state and local branches of these organizations are involved at a political level to promote policies to support the well being of students and their positive growth and development. It is becoming increasingly clear that ongoing political action is necessary to obtain funding for vital programs and counseling positions in the schools.

## Accountability and Leadership

Counselors can increase their visibility and empower their positions as leaders by demonstrating accountability and sharing pertinent data with students, teachers, parents, administrators and the community (Myrick, 2003; Stone & Dahir, 2006). Keeping records of students' educational and career decisions after high school graduation, tracking drop out rates and enrollment and retention in higher education, and sharing such information with the current school population can enhance the counselors' position as a credible resource and leader. Other examples of data to be collected and shared are school climate information, needs assessments, outcomes from various guidance and counseling interventions, and case studies. Daniels and Goodman in chapter 29, discuss details of evidence based practice by school counselors.

Such information can be publicized through articles in local newspapers and school and community newsletters as well as speaking to student, parent and community groups. Further, messages can be placed on an automatic dialer of the school telephone system. Counselors in a school system can create a website with a number of informational links of interest to students, parents and citizens in the community or they can have a link to the homepage of the local school district. If counselors systematically gather and analyze results of their work, ask for ideas for program improvement, and use this information to modify their services as appropriate, they will gain support, understanding and advocacy for their work. Sabella, in chapter 33 of this book, offers many useful ideas using technology.

## Conclusion

The time has come for school counselors to assume and exert leadership within their schools and communities. Educational reform and numerous societal changes have both contributed to the need for a shift in the role of the school counselor as an educational leader who establishes a vision and belief in the development of high aspirations for every child. Opportunities for leadership through social action and collaboration through increased community involvement and improved communication are natural roles for the counselor serving at the hub of a wheel in a school. Many counselors are involved in a variety of the activities and strategies described in this chapter. What remains is for counselors to view themselves as natural educational leaders and to look for opportunities to develop and implement their special leadership skills in order to maximize their effectiveness in the promotion of success for all students.

*Joe Wittmer, Ph.D. and Mary Ann Clark, Ph.D.*

# References

Amatea, E., & Clark, M.A. (2005). Changing schools, changing counselors: A qualitative study of school administrators' conceptions of the school counselor role. *Professional School Counseling, (9)* 1, 16-27.

American School Counselor Association. (2005). *The ASCA national model: A framework for school counseling programs.* Alexandria, VA: Author.

Barbarin, O.A. (1993). Emotional and social development of African American children. *Journal of Black Psychology, 19,* (4), 381-390.

Campbell-Whately, G.D., Algozzine, B., & Obiakor, F. (1997). Using mentoring to improve academic programming for African American male youths with mild disabilities. *The School Counselor, 44,* (5), 362-367.

Capuzzi, D. (1998). Addressing the needs of at-risk youth: Early prevention and systemic intervention. In C.C. Lee & G.R. Walz (Eds.), *Social action: A mandate for counselors* (pp.99-116). Alexandria, VA: American Counseling Association.

Clark, M.A., Brooks, M., Lee, S., Daley, L.P., & Crawford, Y. (2006). Factors influencing the educational success of minority pre-service educators. *Journal of College Student Retention: Research, Theory & Practice, 8* (1), 121-135.

DeVoss, J.A., & Andrews, M.F. (2006). School *counselors as educational leaders.* Boston: Lahaska Press.

Connell, J.P., Spencer, M.B., & Aber, J.L. (1994). Educational risk and resilience in African-American youth: Context, self, action and outcomes in school. *Child Development, 65,* 493-506.

Dedmond, R.M. (1998). Total quality leadership and school counseling. In J.M. Allen (Ed.). *School counseling: new perspectives & practices.* (pp.133-137). Greensboro, NC: ERIC Clearinghouse on Counseling and Student Services.

Guerra, P. (1998, April). Reaction to DeWitt Wallace grant overwhelming. *Counseling Today, 40* (10).

Handy, C. (1987). The language of leadership. Paper presented to the Irish Management Institute, 34th National Management Conference.

Harris, H.L. (1999). School counselors and administrators: Collaboratively promoting cultural diversity. *NASSP Bulletin, 83,* (603), 54-61.

Herring, R.D. (1998). *Career counseling in schools: Multicultural and developmental perspectives.* Alexandria, VA: American Counseling Association.

House, R.M., & Hayes, R.L. (2002). School counselors: Becoming key players in school reform. *Professional School Counseling, 5,* 249-256.

House, R.M., & Martin, P.J. (1998). Advocating for better futures for all students: A new vision for school counselors. *Education, 119,* 284-291.

Kaplan, L.S. (1994). School-based assistance teams. In D.G. Burgess & R.M. Dedmond (Eds.), *Quality leadership and the professional school counselor* (pp. 193-216). Alexandria, VA: American Counseling Association.

Lee, C.C. (1998). Counselors as agents of social change. In C.C. Lee & G.R. Walz (Eds.), *Social action: A mandate for counselors* (pp. 3-14).

Lee, C.C. (2005). Urban school counseling: Context, characteristics, and competencies. *Professional School Counseling, 8,* 184-188.

Lee, J., & Cramond, B. (1999). The positive effects of mentoring economically disadvantaged students. *Professional School Counseling, 2* (3), 172-178.

Myrick, R.D. (2003). *Developmental guidance and counseling: A practical approach* (4th ed.). Minneapolis, MN: Educational Media Corporation.

Pedersen, P., & Carey, J. (Eds.). (2003). *Multicultural counseling in schools: a practical approach* (2nd ed.) Needham Heights, MA: Allyn & Bacon.

Schnurnberger, L. (1997). When donors become mentors. *The American Benefactor.* Summer, 1997, 48-53.

Sheldon, C.B. (1998). School counselor as change agent in education reform. In J.M. Allen (Ed.). *School counseling: New perspectives & practices.* (pp. 61-65). Greensboro, NC: ERIC Clearinghouse on Counseling and Student Services.

Stone, C., & Clark, M.A. (2001) School counselors and principals: Partners in support of academic achievement. *NASSP Bulletin 85 (624),* 46-53.

The Education Trust (1997, February). *The national guidance and counseling reform program.* Washington, DC: Author.

Tollerud, T.R., & Nejedlo, R. (2004). Designing a developmental counseling curriculum. In A. Vernon (Ed.). *Counseling children and adolescents* (3rd ed.), pp. 333-362). Denver, CO: Love Publishing Company.

West, J.F., & Idol, L. (1993). The counselor as consultant in the collaborative school. *Journal of Counseling and Development, 71,* 678-682.

# Section III

# Individual, Small, and Large Group Counseling

This section begins with a chapter by Dr. Tom Harrison focusing on brief counseling in the school setting. As noted throughout this book, the successful developmental school counselor's role includes one-on-one individual counseling. However, the counselor seldom has the time to conduct intensive, in-depth individual "therapy" with lots of students. In addition, the counselor knows when, and how, to refer students to outside agencies. However, individual counseling (responsive, crisis) is important (sometimes in-depth) and is an important role of school counselors. But, as Harrison states; *Due to a school counselor's numerous duties, individual counseling approaches used need to be flexible, and in many situations, brief.*

Dr. Harrison presents three brief individual counseling approaches; the *Systematic Problem-Solving Model,* the *Structured Problem-Solving Model,* and *Solution-Focused Counseling.* Each can be effectively used by school counselors in K-12 counseling programs. All three approaches focus upon specific student client behaviors, are action-oriented, and use step-by-step, easily applied procedures. The three approaches are discussed in detail and practical examples are included for each.

In Chapter ten we also write about the school counselor as "personal" counselor with individual student clients. Our approach is somewhat different than the one espoused by Dr. Harrison in Chapter 9.

In Chapter 11, Drs. Rex Stockton and Paul Toth focus on the counselor and small group counseling as a function in the school setting. They have written regarding the importance of pre-planning for the small group experience, the training of group leaders, making interventions appropriate to the developmental age of the group members, the stages of development through which the group can progress, and so forth. They also stress the importance of structure and goal setting in organizing counseling and support groups. However, Stockton and Toth state: *While structure is very important, it is critical not to be so set in your plans and notions about how to conduct the group that you lose sight of the desirability for flexibility and being able to respond to the needs of the moment.* Stockton and Toth also present several excellent strategies for "how to get started" in leading groups, setting the climate, confidentiality concerns, and guidelines for group participants.

Delivering large group developmental guidance is an important dimension of a K-12 developmental school counselor's role. As Dr. Marjorie Cuthbert states (Chapter 12): *The large group format allows counselors to interact with many students and to impact on their development in a preventative way. They can reach large groups of students with developmental issues or timely topics that need addressing, and, can create units to meet specific needs of their populations.*

Large group guidance is one aspect of the total curriculum which helps counselors know many students. Dr. Cuthbert indicates that while working with students in large groups, counselors are often able to identify those who might need more individualized attention, either through the small group format or through one-on-one counseling. Cuthbert also makes the point that presenting large group guidance units allows counselors to serve as "teaching" role models for classroom teachers and other professionals who see counselors managing large groups of students with successful classroom techniques and behavioral interventions. She presents several excellent strategies for the K-12 counselor desiring to deliver large group guidance and provides an excellent example of a planned, six week unit for elementary students concerning individual uniqueness.

*Joe Wittmer and Mary Ann Clark*

# Chapter 9

# Brief Counseling in the K-12 Developmental Counseling Program

**by**
**Tom Harrison**

*Tom Harrison, Professor and Chair of the Department of Counseling and Educational Psychology at the University of Nevada, Reno, also serves as a consultant to the Nevada School Counselors Association and the comprehensive school counseling program for Washoe County School District in Reno, Nevada. He has authored several articles on school counseling.*

## Introduction

According to the American School Counselor Association (ASCA, 2004), counseling, consultation, and making referrals constitutes the "Responsive Services" element of K-12 developmental guidance programs. Due to the numerous duties assigned to school counselors, time for responsive services is limited. However, in spite of the limited time available, a review of the literature on school counseling outcome research (Whiston & Sexton, 1998) reveals that there is a high interest in school counseling activities which are remedial rather than preventive or developmental in focus. Therefore, the counseling approaches used need to help counselors function effectively given time constraints. Individual counseling approaches also need to be flexible in order to address the variety of student client concerns.

The development of the ASCA National Model (2005) was, in part, aimed at addressing the federal No Child Left Behind Act (2001). According to The National Model, the primary mission of the school counselor is to enhance student academic achievement. Hence, school counselors have felt the pressure to enhance academic achievement while continuing to provide strategies for helping develop students' personal/social and career development needs. According to Brown and Trusty (2005), school counselors can help students improve achievement through the use of carefully planned and strategic interventions. And, school counselors recognize the effect of social/emotional issues on academic achievement.

Brief counseling approaches can help address both counselor time constraints and concerns regarding effectiveness. Moreover, brief approaches can be implemented in preventative, developmental, and crisis situations thus making them ideal for the K-12 school setting. A review of the literature on brief counseling indicated several characteristics of successful approaches: Brief approaches tend to be action-oriented and geared towards problem-solving. They are logical, structured and are usually step-wise. Most often they are structured while being flexible enough to allow for their application to a variety of student clients' concerns. Effective approaches usually emphasize specificity and detailed clarification of the problem or issue of concern. They structure steps for the development of action plans. Finally, brief approaches are interactive in that they require counselors to be active, quickly helpful, expert, but yet nonjudgmental and permitting the counselor's demonstration of the core conditions of warmth, empathy, respect, and genuineness.

As mentioned, there is increased attention placed upon school counselor intervention outcomes that help improve academic achievement (Issacs, 2003; Myrick, 2003). According to Webb, Brigman, and Campbell (2005), student success skills (SSS) have been widely suggested as helping with school achievement and social outcomes. These skill sets include: a) cognitive and metacognitive skills such as goal setting, progress monitoring, and memory skills; b) social skills such as interpersonal skills and problem solving; and c) self-management skills aimed at managing attention, motivation, and anger management.

In this chapter, I present three brief counseling approaches; the *Systematic Problem-Solving Model,* the *Structural Problem-Solving Model,* and *Solution-Focused Counseling.* Each can be effectively used by school counselors in K-12 guidance programs to help students develop cognitive and metacognitive skills, social and interpersonal skills, and better self-management skills. All three approaches focus upon specific student client behaviors, are action-oriented, and use step-wise procedures. Each approach is discussed in detail and examples are included for each approach.

# The Systematic Problem-Solving Model

The Systematic Problem-Solving Model is based upon the works of Myrick (2003). The approach is a logical sequence of questions designed to guide student clients through the thought processes involved in solving a personal problem. While helping student clients resolve current problems, the Systematic Model is also a teaching model enabling student clients to generalize their problem-solving successes to other problematic concerns. Responsibility for successful resolution rests with the student client. However, counselors may choose to increase their involvement, especially in the action phase of the model.

One can often hear school counselors lament how no two days are alike and how they need to be flexible in order to meet the needs of the students as well as the administration's demands placed on them. The Systematic Problem-Solving Model lends itself to this type of atmosphere. The model is flexible so that counselors can utilize the approach with a variety of counseling orientations. It is as useful for the 20-minute session as it is for those situations requiring more time.

Additionally, counselors will need to be flexible while relying upon their skill and judgment in assessing how long each question needs their and the student client's attention. For example, an emotionally charged situation might leave the student client needing more time to process his or her emotions than a situation carrying less emotional intensity. Counselors need to be attuned to this need and act appropriately. It is useful for school counselors to remember that even while exploring emotions, problems are being clarified and prioritized. Therefore, no time is lost. In fact, if emotions are ignored, just the opposite will occur: Valuable time can be lost.

The Systematic Problem-Solving Model is action-based and uses four open ended "trigger" questions to structure the process. The four questions are: **1)** *What is the problem or situation?* **2)** *What have you tried?* **3)** *What else could you do?* and **4)** *What is your next step?* Each question represents a distinct paradigm shift in the problem-solving process. The first two questions essentially serve to collapse the problem and clarify it. The third and fourth questions set the course of action. By asking these four open-ended questions, student clients can explore their personal situation in terms of their own emotions, cognitions, and behaviors.

## What is the problem or situation?

By asking the student client to describe the problem or situation and then using selective attention and high facilitative responses to clarify the problem, the counselor is really attempting to accomplish several goals. One, of course, is for the counselor to understand the student client's situation so that needed help can be given. Another goal is for student clients to gain a different understanding of the problem situation. In describing their personal situations to their counselors, student clients may have a chance to hear themselves describe the problem in ways they have not done heretofore. This new awareness can often lead to increased ownership of the problem and motivation to solve it. Another goal of clarifying at this stage of the process is to help identify exactly what is the problem. As any experienced counselor realizes, in many cases the presenting issue, while an appropriate starting place for counseling, is not really the student client's central concern.

For example, 10-year-old Aaron transferred schools in the middle of March because his mother took a new job which required her to be away from home frequently. Although the travel was temporary, Aaron's aunt and uncle were taking care of him for the remainder of the school year. Aaron's fourth grade teacher had referred him to the school counselor because it had come to the teacher's attention that Aaron had been lying to the teacher and classmates about his background and current situation. It was the teacher's belief that Aaron's poor academic achievement was due in part to his preoccupation with making friends instead of concentrating on school work. His exaggerations were seen as attempts at mediating the shame he felt about his situation.

At first, Aaron was unable to, or did not want to, tell the counselor what the problem was. So, the counselor, aware of the teacher's concern, asked Aaron to go over in detail the conversation he had with his teacher that had lead to Aaron's being sent to see the counselor. What did his teacher say? Where did this conversation take place? Who else was around? What did Aaron say back to the teacher? As the dialogue progressed, the counselor listened for themes and attended selectively to those areas of student client concern. The counselor's use of high facilitative responses (tuning in to feelings, clarifying content, etc.) prompted Aaron to continue talking, and soon it became apparent that much was happening in Aaron's life. His parents had just divorced and were fighting over custody of Aaron and his sixteen-year-old brother. Aaron had left a lot of friends and a good support system at his previous elementary school. Because both his aunt and uncle worked outside the home during the day, it was very difficult for Aaron to get a ride over to see his old friends. Alone, confused, and hurt, the "bottom line" was: *Aaron*

## What else can be done or tried?

After clarifying what has been tried, counselors can encourage student clients to explore alternative ways of behaving. It is important that student clients initially generate this list. Counselors can ask questions such as, "What can you try?" or "What else can you try?" and, "Does anything else come to mind?" This reinforces the student clients' abilities in solving their own problems. Counselors can then add to the list. Using brainstorming techniques to generate a list of alternatives is effective. When brainstorming with the student client, the goal is to generate a list first and then go through the list and evaluate each alternative. Thus, the model is most effective if the counselor keeps the student clients focused upon generating a list while at first ignoring the feasibility of each alternative. Additionally, it is important that alternatives be clarified. This process allows for a more clear understanding of how each alternative will impact the solution.

Once the counselor and student client have generated a list of alternatives (other things to try in solving the problem or situation), it is now time for the counselor to guide the process into the valuation stage. That is, it is now time to employ values clarification to see which behaviors would be most effective in achieving the goal for the individual student client. Which solution best fits the student client? Counselors can use open-ended questioning (what, how, when or where) and feeling-focused responses to aid in this process. For example, Aaron's goal was to make friends and his list included among other things sitting with classmates at lunch, calling one of his classmates after school, getting to the bus stop 10 or 15 minutes earlier each day so he would have more time to talk, calling one of his old friends to see if they could get together, and asking his aunt and uncle if he could have a friend over to spend the night. Aaron felt frightened to ask his aunt and uncle about a friend staying over. He felt hesitant to call anyone after school. The counselor helped Aaron see how his fears kept him from making friends. However, the next step in the problem-solving model was to deal effectively with his inability to make new friends.

*was finding it difficult to make new friends.* He believed that exaggerating the truth would make him more appealing to others and they would befriend him. Although his lying was of concern, the counselor, by using the model, helped Aaron clarify *his* concern as really "feeling afraid of making new friends." His home situation would need attention and warranted the need for consultation with his mother and perhaps father as well as a possible referral for family therapy. However, the immediate concern of the counselor ("What is the problem or situation?") was helping Aaron to take steps to make some new friends at school. The counselor believed that by helping Aaron make some new friends, Aaron could then turn his attention to the important matters of school achievement.

## What has been tried?

Once the problem was clarified by both the student client and the counselor, attention was turned to identifying what Aaron had tried to do to solve the problem. As with the first question, there are several goals in exploring, "What has been tried?" This line of inquiry allows the counselor to demonstrate respect and a non-judgmental attitude, thus strengthening the relationship. The counselor's exploration of what has been tried by the student client also helps set the stage for appropriate counselor suggestions for possible solutions to the problem. Mutual exploration of what has been tried also allows the counselor to focus upon the student client's feelings. Identifying pleasant and unpleasant feelings puts student clients more in touch with their own personal process while clearing the way for action. Continuing with the example of Aaron, it was found that Aaron felt anxious and scared a great deal of the time. Making friends was an unpleasant experience for him. Through the use of paraphrases and clarifications, both Aaron and the counselor found that his fears of rejection were impeding his desire to make new friends. Aaron soon understood how trying to solve the problem by lying to his teacher and friends had distanced others rather than bringing them closer. That is, what he had tried, simply had not worked to this point. He truly needed the counselor's help in learning how to make friends.

## What is the next step?

In this phase, a plan of action is specified and agreed upon. Counselors need to help student clients organize a step-by-step plan which should include what will be done, when will it be done, how will it be done, what are possible barriers that might come up and hinder the process, and ways to overcome potential barriers. The plan does not need to be elaborate. However, it needs to be specific, and the steps need to be organized in such a manner as to increase the probability of success. And, helping a student client to clarify, and agree to take, the next step is one of the more important parts of the process. Some counselors have found it most effective if the student client places "the next step" into writing.

Because of Aaron's fears and anxieties about calling or asking his aunt and uncle, the counselor helped Aaron develop an initial plan whereby he would get himself to the bus stop early. Getting there early posed no problem because Aaron's aunt and uncle were up early and would feed him breakfast in plenty of time for him to walk the two blocks to the bus stop. The favorite activity at the bus stop was throwing rocks to see who could come closest to a big tree that was growing in the ravine. The plan was for Aaron to become involved in throwing rocks at the tree but to not say anything to others. He would do that for three days. Then, on the fourth and fifth day while at the bus stop, he was to throw rocks at the tree, sit in a seat on the bus close to someone he liked but not say anything. The following Monday, he was to repeat this sequence and add a new behavior: He was to sit close to someone and ask them one or two questions. Any type question would be okay. After that, Aaron and the counselor were to meet again to review how things were going and to make additional plans.

The follow-up is important. It can be very brief and conducted in the halls if need be. Touching base serves to reinforce the relationship and to provide an opportunity to adjust plans.

Naturally, the counselor was confident that even though Aaron was shy, nervous, and frightened about making friends, the plan of action almost guaranteed that someone would talk to him in spite of his self-imposed silence. The "win-win" approach would be effective because if Aaron followed what had been agreed upon and not talk, then he would have successfully followed his plan. If he altered the plan and spoke, he would still be meeting his goal of making friends.

The counselor's use of the four "trigger" questions helped Aaron make significant headway in making new friends because the model follows the sequential process that individuals go through when solving problems. In this fashion, a counselor's work is established. A challenge for counselors is to refine their skills in determining *when* to move on to the next "trigger" question.

Effective use of high facilitative responses is another challenge for counselors using this model. When exploring the student client's issue and what has been tried previously, using high facilitative responses helps put "chips in the bank" in the relationship with the student client. (Wittmer & Myrick, 1989). Strengthening the relationship during the initial phase of problem exploration and what has been tried, allows the action phase, questions three and four, to move along quickly. Finally, a counselor's demonstration of respect, empathy, genuineness, and being non-judgmental helps ensure student client success.

Aaron's problem may seem to some as being insignificant in the scheme of things. However, it was very important to Aaron and was obviously causing him problems at school, impeding his learning. Regardless of how insignificant or trivial it may seem, a student client with this type problem will take much precious counselor time unless dealt with appropriately. The problem-solving model is a quick, effective, yet facilitative method for dealing with problems such as Aaron's.

One middle school counselor has effectively used the model in homework assignments, especially with those students who seem to have "chronic" problems or situations and "must see you" everyday. She has written the four steps on an 8 1/2 X 11 sheet of paper with appropriate space available for the student client to fill in under each trigger question. She reports that many students, using this homework approach, report back that they've "solved" their own problem. The benefits incurred to the student client solving his/her own problem is obvious.

# Structural Problem Solving

Another brief counseling approach found effective in school situations is called, *Structural Problem Solving*. It is based upon the social learning work of Bandura (1997). The structural approach borrows from the cognitive aspects of Bandura's ideas and works well with student clients because it follows the natural thinking sequence leading to increased awareness, increased motivation, and problem resolution. Focus is upon the identification of behaviors and student client beliefs surrounding the behaviors.

According to Bandura (1997) and Sutton and Fall (1995), self-efficacy beliefs are based on an individual's expectations that he or she possesses certain knowledge and skills and the ability to take the action necessary to solve problems. Self-efficacy expectations result from the individual reflecting on and appraising the strength of these three components. Student clients who *believe* they cannot perform the behaviors necessary to resolve a problem will exhibit less motivation toward problem resolution. When student clients increase their self-efficacy beliefs, motivation increases.

Beliefs also play an important role in student clients' understanding of how a specific behavior will impact the goal. This is known as the outcome expectancy (Bandura, 1997; Sutton & Fall, 1995). If one does not believe a behavior has a significant impact upon the outcome, motivation to perform that behavior will decrease. For example, a student who had received a poor test grade might "realize" that memorizing information for a test did not help, complaining that other students studied less and performed better. Hence, the student who did not do as well may not spend time memorizing for the next test because it is believed that memorization has little impact upon earning a good grade. The Structural Problem-Solving approach focuses on student clients' beliefs about the impact specific behaviors have upon a desired goal and on student clients' beliefs concerning their abilities to perform those specific behaviors.

The Structural Problem-Solving model utilizes a rating system to specify behaviors and one's beliefs regarding those behaviors. By assigning numbers indicating strength of beliefs, student clients actually operationalize their belief system. This method of specification allows student clients a more clear understanding of the problem, an increased understanding of the behaviors involved in problem resolution, insight into their motivation, and increased awareness of self-efficacy beliefs.

Structural Problem-Solving can be a paper-and-pencil exercise, can be strictly a verbal exchange between counselors and student clients, or a combination of mediums can be used. Additionally, the model is flexible in that, as in the Problem-Solving Model previously described, it can be used as homework for student clients. For example, student clients can be given written directions guiding them through the process and asked to complete the assignment before meeting with the counselor to go over the worksheet. In this manner, valuable face-to-face counseling time can be diminished.

The structural problem-solving approach also works well with student clients in a group setting. Moreover, it can be employed in classroom guidance activities where the counselor would lead the class through this process and make appointments for those students who need additional attention. This approach also works well both with clients who are self-referred and those who are referred by teachers or other school personnel. Finally, a structural approach is most effective with middle (sixth grade on) and high school students. While it could be adapted to K-5 students, their cognitive development might preclude their ability to use a rating system. Therefore, elementary school counselors might employ this strategy omitting the use of numbers.

The Structural Problem-Solving Model involves seven basic steps and the counselor's use of high facilitative responses. The steps are:

1. Identification and clarification of the goal or outcome.

2. Generating a written list of *all* behaviors that are involved in attaining the desired goal or outcome.

3. Rating the impact *each* behavior has upon the goal or outcome using a scale of 1 to 30 (1 being "low impact upon the goal").

4. Prioritizing the behaviors from "most impactful upon the goal" to "least impactful upon the goal."

5. Rating clients' beliefs about their ability to perform each of those behaviors on a scale of 1 to 30 (1 being the belief they have "little ability to perform the behavior").

6. Examining student client's beliefs about their abilities to perform the important behaviors.

7. Helping clients develop a plan of action.

## Identification of the Goal

Identification and clarification of the student client's goal is a natural and logical place to begin. Clarification ensures counselors that they are working on the correct problem. Asking the student client to become more specific also lays a solid foundation upon which action plans can be built. For example, Debbie was struggling in her geometry class and sought help from her counselor. Debbie was aware that she wanted to do well on the exam but was confused as to why she couldn't seem to motivate herself to study. Debbie's school record indicated she had the ability to accomplish her goal. However, her awareness of the problem and her recognition that she wanted to do well were not sufficient in motivating her to study. Debbie's procrastination compounded the problem since she now had to deal with increased feelings of pressure, inadequacy, and guilt.

The counselor hypothesized that a part of Debbie's problem was that she had not clearly identified her goal. The ambiguity would likely account for her apparent lack of motivation to study. The counselor spent time clarifying what Debbie meant by "doing well" on the exam. Did doing well mean she wanted a perfect score of 100? Did it mean getting 90%? If she was getting mostly C's and B's in her class, did doing well mean getting another B? Through the counselor's use of facilitative responses such as open-ended questions, clarifications, and summaries, Debbie revealed that doing well for her actually translated into a range of scores falling between a perfect score of 100 and a high B. This range of scores allowed her to have "wiggle room" and helped to decrease her anxiety.

## Generating a List of All Behaviors Involved

When the goal has been clearly identified, the next step is to focus upon identifying *all* the behaviors involved in accomplishing the goal. More often than not, counselors will find that student clients are aware of only a few of the more obvious and necessary behaviors. Therefore, once student clients have exhausted their list, counselors can add to it. It is crucial to generate the list prior to assessing the impact of each behavior upon the outcome. Premature assessment will defocus the process and will usually result in the development of an incomplete list.

Continuing with the example, Debbie and her counselor jointly developed a list of behaviors involved in getting an A or a high B on her geometry test. Her initial list included typical behaviors of reading, going over class notes, memorizing postulates and corollaries, and practicing proving theorems. The counselor helped Debbie add to the list by identifying other behaviors such as going to class, paying attention in class, asking questions in class when confused, each day going over the material covered in class, having a quiet place to study, having some time to just relax and watch her favorite television show or to be able to telephone a friend, getting other class assignments done in advance to afford time for studying, and rearranging her after school work schedule. Debbie was surprised at all of the behaviors involved, and her insight prompted her to remark, "Wow, I never realized how much went into one stupid test!" No wonder I'm not studying. I don't have time!"

## Rating the Impact of Each Behavior Upon the Goal

Once the goal has been clearly identified and a list is made of all the behaviors impacting the goal, the next step is to invite student clients to examine the specific impact of each behavior upon the goal. This can be done with the use of a Likert-type scale. For example, counselors might ask, "To what extent do you think each of these behaviors impact your goal?" Going over the list of behaviors, student clients are asked to assign a number from 1 to 30 (1 = very little; 30 = very much) reflecting the extent to which they believe the behavior impacts their goal. It is important that all of the behaviors be rated. The same rating can be assigned to different behaviors.

Debbie assigned high numbers, indicating a strong impact upon the goal, to asking questions when confused (27), rearranging her after school work schedule (29), going over material each day (27), practicing proving theorems (29), and spending time with a girlfriend (22). Lower numbers were assigned to such behaviors as relaxing watching television (7), getting other class assignments done in advance (12), reading (16), and having a quiet place to study (10).

## Prioritizing the Behaviors

Prioritizing the behaviors impacting the goal is now appropriate. Using the numbers indicating the impact upon the goal, behaviors are ranked beginning with "most impactful" to "least impactful." This can be accomplished verbally or by actually having the student client write them down. Debbie's prioritized list included "rearranging her work schedule" (29) at the top and finished with "finding a quiet place to study" (10) at the bottom.

## Rating Beliefs About Abilities to Perform Behaviors

Once the student clients have rated the impact of each behavior upon the outcome, they are asked to identify the extent to which they believe they can successfully *perform* each behavior. Similar to rating the impact of behaviors, student clients are asked to assign a number ranging from 1 to 30 (1 = low belief in ability) to *each* behavior. This number will reflect student clients' self-efficacy beliefs or specific beliefs regarding their abilities to perform the behavior. The counselor might ask, "Okay, we have looked at how each behavior impacts your goal. Now, to what extent do you think you can actually perform each of those behaviors?"

**A note of caution.** Student clients will have a tendency to assign self-efficacy numbers based upon how the behavior impacts the goal. Beliefs about the impact of behaviors upon a goal and beliefs about one's abilities to perform the behavior can be quite different! Therefore, counselors will need to help student clients remain focused upon rating their beliefs about their *abilities* to perform the behavior *regardless* of the impact of that behavior upon the stated goal or outcome. (If the Structured Problem-Solving Model is used for homework, counselors will need to remember and focus upon the validity of self-efficacy ratings).

When Debbie was asked to rate her beliefs about her abilities to perform each behavior, she became very surprised upon noticing that many of the behaviors which had a strong impact upon her goal (those having high numbers) were the same behaviors she believed were the most difficult for her to perform. "Rearranging the work schedule" was perceived as significantly impacting her test score (29), however, Debbie did not believe she could accomplish this and rated it a "2." She rated "Asking questions when confused" as having a high impact (27) upon her goal. Yet, she assigned a "6" indicating little belief in her ability to get her confusion clarified. Similar patterns were found throughout Debbie's list.

## Examining the Student Client's Beliefs

It is now appropriate to examine the student client's beliefs about their abilities in performing the tasks necessary to accomplish their goal. The use of high facilitative responses is important during this process. As noted, high facilitative responses include open ended questions, paraphrases, clarifications, summaries, and feeling-focused responses. Open-ended questions such as, "What do you mean when you say you believe you can't do anything about it?" and "How is it that you know you cannot do that (specific behavior)?" Frequent use of clarifications and summaries allows student clients greater insight, will often increase their self-efficacy beliefs, and will usually positively impact motivation to perform the behavior. Additionally, the use of feeling-focused responses can facilitate student client's understanding of the problem as well as point out their resistances to problem resolution.

In Debbie's case, the counselor noticed that she linked rearranging her work schedule to many of the other behaviors. Focusing upon Debbie's work schedule was thus seen as the key to resolving the problem and would act to clarify her self-efficacy beliefs surrounding the other problematic behaviors such as having time to practice proving theorems, having time to go over the material each day, and having free time to attend the teacher's special help periods.

Focusing upon her beliefs about her work schedule, the counselor soon discovered that Debbie was afraid to ask for a different work schedule fearing her boss would refuse and think of her as not caring about her work. The counselor spent time focusing upon Debbie's feelings of fear and rejection. This examination served to lessen her anxieties and increase her beliefs that she could solve the problem by asking her boss for a different schedule.

## Developing a Plan of Action

The stage is now set for action planning. A detailed plan of action would include what would be involved in the task, how student clients will go about accomplishing the task, when they will accomplish the task, and predicting personal resistances. The counselor might say, "You have identified some behaviors that are important in reaching your goal and some of your beliefs about your abilities to perform those behaviors. Let's now plan how you can begin to get started and carry out those behaviors."

How could Debbie go about asking her boss for a different schedule? What would she need to do in order to increase the probability of a favorable response from her boss? When would she take the risk and ask her boss? What might keep Debbie from asking him?

By working together, Debbie and her counselor agreed it would be good to arrange someone to switch shifts prior to asking her boss for a schedule change. She worked at a fast food chain, and there were times when business was fast. So, they agreed that Debbie would ask her boss during a slow time. For Debbie, the sooner she asked the better. Finally, the counselor remarked that Debbie might become nervous right before asking and that would be okay. She could feel nervous and ask anyway.

A follow-up meeting with the school counselor was scheduled with Debbie to see how the conversation went with her boss.

# Solution-Focused Counseling

The time constraints facing school counselors can be greatly compounded when faced with student clients who are referred by school personnel and who are reluctant or resistant to change. Working with referred and reluctant student clients is a "double-whammy" and likely a source of significant frustration for many school counselors. While counselors are trained to deal effectively with reluctant student clients, little has been done in training counselors to work quickly with reluctance. Based upon the works of de Shazer (1988, 1994) and Miller, Hubble, and Duncan (1996), the solution-focused counseling approach (Downing & Harrison, 1992) addressed both time constraints and resistant student clients and works well for K-12 students. Solution-focused counseling can be employed with a variety of student clients and a host of student client concerns. The model is especially effective in working with "reluctant" student clients.

Students who are referred by teachers and other school personnel for counseling likely see themselves as flawed or having something wrong with them as people. Often, the students believe they have been "wronged" or are totally blameless. The resulting reluctance to change can be a formidable challenge to counselors.

The reason this approach is effective with the reluctant/resistant student client is that the focus is upon minimizing student client resistance to the counselor and to the overall counseling process. This goal is accomplished by 1) focusing upon "what is right" as opposed to "what is wrong" with student clients; 2) accepting student clients' perceptions that "there is no problem;" 3) reframing student clients' experiences so they can accept that a problem does exist; 4) focusing upon the thoughts, feelings, and behaviors already employed by student clients, and 5) aiding student clients in the identification of their own strengths and past or current successes.

Solution-focused counseling is a step-wise process which emphasizes client strengths, helps to reinforce student clients' self-esteem, and focuses upon solutions. This approach involves five steps, and like the two approaches previously described in this chapter, requires the effective use of high facilitative responses such as open-ended questions, paraphrases, reframings, clarifications, summaries, and feeling-focused responses. The five steps include:

1. Helping the student clients identify the issue or problem to be addressed.

2. Helping the student clients identify the desired change or coping goals related to the problem.

3. Encouraging the student clients to actively search and recall times when they have been successful in solving similar or other problems. This is known as finding the "exception" to the problem.

4. Encouraging the student client to identify and focus upon their strengths or "what worked" in that situation.

5. Helping the student client develop and carry out a plan of action.

Key to using this approach is the concept of stability and change which is a central concept in many family and other type counseling approaches. Briefly, this concept accentuates the idea that in order to change, student clients must have a sense of control over their environment. Without that stabilizing feeling and perception, change becomes too chaotic, too threatening. The stabilizing effect of the student client's environment is achieved by the counselor focusing upon what student client is *already* doing. In essence, no new behaviors, thoughts, or feelings are introduced. Student client awareness that nothing (or very little) new will be required of them for change acts as a stabilizing force giving way to feelings of increased self-control. The stability created by requiring little or nothing new in the way of student client behaviors also increases the rapport between the student client and counselor while decreasing student client resistance.

Another central concept in solution-focused counseling is that of identifying "rules" and "exceptions to the rules." The "rule" is the student client's perception of the problem. Often, student clients will likely see the problem as unmanageable and see little hope for change. This rigidity of perceptions acts as a rule which serves to govern student client behaviors and can actually help reinforce the problem and will serve to limit student client perceptions of options available to them. "Exceptions to the rule" are essentially student client success stories in which they have had positive experiences in solving similar or other concerns. That is, the "exceptions" are those instances in which the rules were "broken" and success was experienced. With reluctant student clients, identifying previous successes may be challenging for the counselor. However, it is important for counselors to remember that everyone has experienced success. By believing this and behaving with resolve, counselors can help student clients recall times when problems seemed more manageable and times when student clients were effective in changing themselves and their environment. As a result, student client's strengths and self-concept will be positively reinforced thus giving way to positive change.

## Gary: A Reluctant Teenager

Gary was referred to the school counselor by his eighth grade social studies teacher because of a "poor attitude." Mrs. Fisher, the school counselor, made an effort to talk with Gary's social studies teacher during the teacher's planning period. Mr. D'Andrea told the counselor of his repeated attempts to reach Gary, but says he "had given up" on Gary when the behavior persisted following spring break. Although Mrs. Fisher had seen Gary for class scheduling, that was the extent of their interaction. Still, from observing Gary during the counselor's hall duty, Mrs. Fisher was aware that he got along with his peers.

When the counselor called Gary out of his third period class, he arrived sullen and withdrawn. An explanation of the reasons for the visit did little to warm him up. To deal with this resistance, the counselor reframed the problem by explaining that Mr. D'Andrea expected her to be able to "fix" Gary, and asked Gary to help her solve this problem. She told Gary that it would be difficult for her to "fix" him because Gary saw nothing wrong, but that still left her feeling the need to satisfy Mr. D'Andrea. How could Gary help? Gary then began suggesting ways to get Mr. D'Andrea "off her back" which included telling him to "cool it," saying nothing and letting Mr. D'Andrea deal with it, telling him nothing was wrong, and telling him it was his problem. The counselor used the high facilitative responses of open-ended questions and clarifications during this exchange which was aimed at building rapport and decreasing resistance. She acknowledged his suggestions and assisted Gary in agreeing that the problem was indeed a challenging one. The counselor asked Gary, "When have you had a similar problem to mine where someone expected you to do something that appeared quite impossible?" Gary responded, "All the time." This was followed by the counselor asking, "What do you mean?" Now the focus began shifting more toward Gary. He disclosed, "Life stinks."

The use of paraphrasing and clarifications along with feeling-focused responses allowed the counselor to help identify that Gary had found out two weeks prior to spring break that his girlfriend had begun going out with his best friend while still claiming to be in love with Gary. Gary said that his girlfriend did not know he knew, but that she had become confused and angry with him for his abrupt change in behavior. Gary said he had tried to forget about the incident and pretend that nothing was wrong, but that had not helped. He agreed he needed to talk to her about his concerns, but was afraid he would lose control. The counselor asked Gary which of the two problems would he like to discuss, the counselor's problem with Mr. D'Andrea or Gary's problem with his girlfriend? Gary said that if they could work on his first, he would be willing to help her figure out what to do with Mr. D'Andrea.

The counselor explored the ways in which Gary was dealing with his anger, hurt, and disappointment. She asked him how he would like things to be between him and his girlfriend, and Gary said that he would like things to be the way they were before she began going out with his best friend. The counselor clarified what Gary meant by this. He wanted things back to normal where they would talk, laugh, and go out. Gary was asked what would need to be different in order to achieve this goal. At first he said she would need to never mess up again but finally agreed that he had little control over what she did or did not do. He said he would need to talk with her without losing control. The "rule" or problem was defined as Gary's perception that he was unable to talk about his feelings of anger without exploding into a rage. The counselor inquired when there had been a time that Gary had been hurt and angry and had been able to talk it out. Together, the counselor and Gary identified occasions in the past where Gary had been successful. The counselor encouraged a detailed exploration of how Gary had managed to be successful in those situations. She focused her facilitative responses upon Gary's strengths. Finally, she asked him to identify how he could use his past successes to help him out now, and a plan of action was set.

## Summary

When used appropriately, brief counseling approaches have been shown to be quite successful in the schools. The three approaches described in this chapter are geared toward quick, yet empathic, problem resolution. Moreover, these three approaches can address many of the significant issues that challenge students' efforts to improve their academic achievement. However, this is not to be confused with their being superficial. While effective for use with a variety of student clients and student client concerns, it is important to remember that not all student clients or issues will lend themselves to brief approaches. Some student client concerns will require counselors to consult with parents, teachers and staff, or to refer out to community services.

A few reminders are helpful. Faced with severe time constraints, counselors can be tempted to rush through the counseling process in attempting to "fix" problems. It is important that counselors initially take time building rapport with the student client. The effectiveness of brief approaches relies upon a solid counselor/student client relationship. Moreover, the counselor must spend time getting specific about the issue of concern. The action phases of brief approaches are greatly expedited when the problem is sufficiently clarified. Another reminder concerns helping student clients own their own problems. Counselors, in attempting to resolve issues quickly, might assume too much responsibility for the problem thus forgetting the basic tenet of any counseling approach which is that student clients need to *own* their *own* problem. Regardless of which approach is utilized, counselors must remember to use high facilitative responses. Open-ended questions, paraphrases, summaries, clarifications, and feeling-focused responses are basic to the counseling process and to successful problem solving. It is up to the expertise of school counselors to determine the appropriateness of brief counseling. The approaches will not work for every student client. Some students need in-depth counseling. Finally, counselors need to ensure they follow-up with the student client even if it is for only a few minutes in the hall. A simple, "How are things going with the action plan?" may be all that is necessary. Not only will student clients greatly appreciate your efforts, but a follow-up helps counselors assess their effectiveness and make adjustments when and where needed.

# References

American School Counselor Association. (2004). *The role of the professional school counselor.* Alexandria, VA: Author.

American School Counselor Association. (2003). *The ASCA national model: A framework for comprehensive school counseling programs.* Alexandria, VA: Author.

Bandura, A. (1997). *The exercise of control.* New York: N.W. Norton.

Brown, D., & Trusty, J. (2005). School counselors, comprehensive school counseling programs, and academic achievement: Are school counselors promising more than they can deliver? *Professional School Counseling, 9(l),* 1-8.

de Shazer, S. (1988). *Clues: Investigating solutions in brief therapy.* New York: Norton.

de Shazer, S. (1994). *Words were originally magic.* New York: Norton.

Downing, C.J., & Harrison, T.C. (1992). Solutions and school counseling. *The School Counselor, 39*(5), 327-332.

Isaacs, M. (2003). Data-driven decision-making: The engine of accountability. Professional School Counseling, 6,288-295.

Miller, S., Hubble, M., & Duncan, B. (1996*). Handbook of solution-focused brief therapy.* San Francisco: Jossey-Bass.

Myrick, R.D. (2003). Accountability: Counselors count. *Professional School Counseling, 6,* 180-184.

Myrick, R.D. (2003). *Developmental guidance and counseling: A practical approach* (4th ed.). Minneapolis: Educational Media Corporation.

Sutton, J.M., & Fall, M. (1995). The relationship of school climate factors to counselor self-efficacy. *Journal of Counseling and Development, 73,* 331-336.

Webb, L.D., Brigman, G.A., & Campbell, C. (2005). Linking school counselors and student success: A replication of the student success skill approach targeting the academic social competence of students. *Professional School Counseling, 8*(5), 407-413.

Whiston, S.C., & Sexton, T.L. (1998). A review of school counseling outcome research: Implications for practice. *Journal of Counseling and Development, 76,* 412-426.

Wittmer, J., & Myrick, R.D. (1989). *Teacher as facilitator.* Minneapolis: Educational Media Corporation.

# Chapter 10

# Counseling the Individual Student Client

**by**
**Joe Wittmer**

## Introduction

This chapter is about the school counselor as "individual" counselor. As noted throughout this book, personal, individual counseling with students is just one of the several interventions used by the effective school counselor working in a developmental counseling program. That is, there are many roles played, and various student interventions used, by the effective school counselor working in a developmental school counseling program. Although counselors will not be doing in depth individual counseling with all of their students, being effective in working with individual students is a vital counselor intervention.

## The Counselor as a Person

Because it has been difficult to empirically identify "effective" or "ineffective" methods of counseling, some experts have suggested that the effective counselor is an "artist" who is uniquely skillful in bringing about the desired results through a personal helping relationship. That is, these experts believe that counselors who are effective in their individual counseling with clients find ways of using themselves, their talents, and their surroundings to assist their clients in making the changes in their lives as needed to be more mentally healthy and productive persons.

Considerable research has been conducted in an attempt to discover more about the counselor as a person and his/her impact upon the counseling process. Researchers have compared the beliefs held by effective and ineffective counselors about people in general. Studies indicate that effective counselors, regardless of the settings in which they work, possess an internal rather than external frame of reference. The effective counselor is also more concerned with perceptual experiences rather than objective events. Moreover, effective counselors perceive others as having the capacity to look at their own problems, and, in most cases, have the capacity to solve their own problems with direct and/or indirect assistance from the counselor.

Personally, I believe that, regardless of the settings in which they work, effective counselors view themselves as *catalysts* in helping others to change by *empowering* them to do so. Effective counselors are also "trusted *experts*" who have the ability to "help" those who come to them seeking their assistance. And, in general, students and others seek counseling because, at that time in their lives, they feel "helpless" and thus seek "help" from an expert! A "trusted expert" is a professional who is *predictable and consistent.* Predictable and consistent helpers quickly gain the trust of their clients and are more effective personal counselors.

Effective counselors in any setting also view others with dignity and worth and as non-threatening individuals capable of enhancing their own personal growth. The effective counselor also has the skill to understand another person's "worldview" without any evaluation or interpretation of that worldview. That is, they have the unique ability to "enter" the other person's frame of reference, the way they view their current reality, without evaluation or judgement. This does not mean that they condone inappropriate behavior on the part of their clients. Effective counselors work at accepting and understanding the person and his/her frame of reference regardless of the behavior shown. Effective counselors know that there are as many views of "reality" as there are persons. *They are not deluded into thinking that their "reality" is the only "reality." They also understand that they may expose, but never impose, their values on their student clients.*

Research further indicates that effective counselors are sensitive to others and see themselves as *adequate, trustworthy, and able to help others.* Finally, effective counselors tend to see their purpose in counseling as one *of freeing rather than of controlling* their clients. Effective counselors also tend to be personally involved in the counseling situation and are concerned with the process as much as they are in achieving goals and outcomes.

In my opinion, everything written above applies to those school counselors who are effective in their work with individual student clients.

# The School Counselor as an "Enhancer" of Personal Growth

Within the last few decades we have learned a great deal about human behavior, about the counselor as a person, and about effective counseling relationships in general. Much of what we now know has come through careful analysis of helping relationships found in counseling and related fields. We have learned that to be successful as a counselor takes more than being an expert in the field of psychology; it is more than providing information and helpful insights; and, it is more than being thoroughly trained in counseling theory, techniques and procedures.

There was a time when we thought that lack of progress in counseling was probably because of some deep-seated problem that a student client was unable to discuss. Often those type students are referred to by the counselor as "resistant." The term "resistant clients" may be a misnomer. That is, perhaps ineffective counselors have coined this term. One thing we do know, if you refer to a student client as "resistant" to your counseling efforts, he/she now has at least two problems!

In the past, if a student client didn't function any better personally or academically as a result of counseling, it was certainly a loss and a disappointment, but the student probably was no worse off than before. Unfortunately, it now appears that these naive assumptions can no longer be accepted. We now know that counseling can be for better or for worse! That is, our counseling efforts make a "difference;" one way or another; we are almost never neutral. In some cases student clients may actually deteriorate into a routine that is detrimental to their overall personal growth and development. *The idea is frightening, but clients actually can be harmed in situations that are theoretically designed to enhance their growth.*

Closer examination suggests that counselors can differ in approach, theoretical rationale, training, sex, personal values, and experience; but there seem to be some essential "conditions" or core dimensions present in all successful counseling situations. When student clients experience these conditions, they tend to solve their problems quicker and become more fully functioning individuals. In general, these conditions are; *understanding, nonpossessive warmth, interest in others, genuineness, respectfulness, unconditional positive regard, caring, and acceptance.* And, as mentioned above, the effective school counselor is also a trustworthy and knowledgeable individual. I discuss some of these in greater detail below.

By now, as reader, you probably have the impression that I believe that a student client must experience a relationship that reduces defensiveness and opens the avenues for communication in a warm, close, nonthreatening setting for personal counseling to be successful. Generally speaking, clients in any setting who show the most therapeutic change, as measured by various indices, perceive more of the helping conditions in their relationship with the counselor than those who show less change. Thus, regardless of the theoretical orientation of the counselor, his/her clients "get better" if the above "conditions" are present. That is, it doesn't seem to make much difference whether the effective counselor was trained as a "Rogerian" or an "Adlerian," or in any other type theoretical orientation for that matter; it is when these core conditions are present that effective outcomes result.

As noted, counseling can be for better or for worse. We can no longer assume that if a student client does not benefit from a counselor there will be a negligible effect. In reality, it is possible that some students can actually suffer and become worse when the helping conditions are not present.

Although there is more to effective counseling than just a personal relationship with the client, I believe that school counselors who are effective in individual counseling situations are those who have the above described characteristics and the ability to reflect or create the essential core dimensions given above. These highly functioning individuals have a positive effect on their student clients. A truly person-centered approach to counseling nourishes these conditions. They are at the center of the counselor's success.

How do effective counselors create these core conditions? What do they need to do when counseling with student clients to bring them about? What things must be considered when developing a treatment plan that leads to resolving a student client's personal problem?

In this brief overview, I attempt to address these issues. But first, let's look at some personal characteristics of effective counselors.

# Characteristics of an Effective Counselor

There are probably many school counselors who have one or more of the characteristics which describe effective counselors. "Now there is an effective personal counselor," people might say. Some people describe effective counselors as "outstanding," "empowering," and "wonderful." Yet, they may not be certain as to what characteristics they possess that make them so effective as counselors.

As mentioned above, there are several conditions necessary for effective counseling outcome to occur. In addition, there are various selected, personal characteristics frequently used to identify counselors who are high facilitators of personal growth and who are recognized as most effective by students, their colleagues and others. In general, effective counselors are:

1. **Attentive**
2. **Genuine**
3. **Understanding**
4. **Respectful**
5. **Knowledgeable of culture**
6. **Skilled in Counseling Techniques**

Let's look at each of these characteristics/skills in more detail.

## The Effective Counselor is Attentive

Problems in personal counseling often result from non-attentiveness and ineffective listening on the part of the counselor. Although it seems like a simple thing to do, and we often take it for granted, being attentive is an effort that requires skills and practice. Fortunately, those skills can be taught and learned.

Being truly "attended to" and having an opportunity to talk about a matter that is personal for us is usually a pleasurable and relieving experience. It makes us feel better about the problem or situation we are discussing. This is especially true when the "helper" has the listening skills and other characteristics discussed above. For instance, when you feel that an objective and trustworthy person has really taken time to listen to you, and that what you are saying has been received with understanding, you probably feel better than before sharing it. In addition, there is usually a sense of our feeling closer emotionally to the person who has truly been listening to us. Data indicates that your student clients have the same feelings regarding your "attending" to them during personal counseling.

Unfortunately, the vast majority of people are not effective listeners. Except from among your trained counseling colleagues, you may not encounter very many during your lifetime. Sometimes, people seek out counselors for the simple reason of having a chance to talk to an objective, caring listener who will hear them without judgment or evaluation. How often do people in your life really listen to your words and feelings? How do you know if they have really heard you?

The next time that you are with a group of people at a party, note how well each attends and responds to you and the others present. Unless it is an unusual group, the conversation will jump quickly from one person to another, with little communication (i.e. two-way) being exhibited.

One person might start by expressing a concern about resistant students. The usual response from someone who is "listening" is to relate that particular idea to their own experience, without responding directly to the speaker. For example, "You know, I've been thinking of the same thing.... And I've decided...." At this point the focus moves to a new talker leaving the original talker to wait another turn. We usually agree or disagree, almost immediately, with the talker as opposed to truly tuning into him/her and listening for understanding.

As we examine everyday listening experiences and habits, and perhaps take note of our own behaviors, we recognize that many times a listener is simply waiting for a speaker to stop talking so that person can say something. Subsequently, many listeners hear only the first few words spoken, and then their minds rush rapidly ahead to their own concerns and reactions. In most cases, the periods of silence while listeners are waiting a turn to speak, represents a period of tolerance more than a period of attentive listening.

Motivations and feelings affect listening. These change, of course, even as the conversation moves along because listening is a shifting process. Attentive counselors know how to stay focused on their student clients and to absorb what is being said before jumping to conclusions or offering a quick reaction or solution.

Effective school counselors want to know more about their student clients. They want to know what the student is thinking and feeling. They know how to "tune in" and to listen with the "third ear." They know how to be effective. Subsequently, they have a powerful influence on the way in which helping relationships, as well as the flow of the conversations, are formed with their student clients.

Effective counselors are also aware that when they are unable to focus their full attention on their student client, they may be reacting to some of their own hidden feelings or motives. This preoccupation with our own interests and thoughts can communicate that we do not care what is being said. Sadly, the student talking might feel rejected or dismissed as unimportant.

Attending might be described as the process of acknowledging particular stimuli from an environment. Thus, listening is a selective process in which we choose from the things around us that most fit our needs, purposes, and desires. Sometimes we select a stimulus because of its suddenness, intensity, or contrast to what we have been experiencing. At other times there might be sounds (stimuli) that we hear automatically because of habit. We focus upon things to which we have learned to attend. This is often referred to as "selective listening" or hearing what we want to, or expect to hear. That may be true in everyday conversation. However, the effective counselor has learned the skill of "attentiveness" and possesses true, active listening skills.

If a counselor prejudges and expects to hear some expressed anger from his/her student client, for example, there is a higher probability that that student will be perceived as being angry. That is, our presuppositions control our perceptions, which determine how we will behave in that situation. The effects of such "mind sets" are significant. They can be detrimental to effective counseling, especially if the counselor jumps to conclusions and is unwilling to hear the student tell all of the "story". Unfortunately, we are not always aware of our mindsets and they are at times difficult to control. Listening habits that help us go beyond what we expect in a situation can be valuable and are imperative as a skill for effective counselors.

Attentive and careful listening on the part of the effective counselor also involves hearing "deeper levels" of communication. Effective counselors not only attend literally to words, but they also make a special effort to understand the personal meanings of the client's words. They have the ability to make "hunches" or "hypotheses" about what is really "going on" with their student clients. Effective counselors tune in to the feelings, thoughts and attitudes that are "behind" the content of the words. In summary, the counselor who wants to be an effective facilitator of change hears the words of the student client, but more importantly, hears and understands the feelings that add special meaning to what is being said.

## Attentive, Active Listening Counselors:

1. Have the ability to understand another person's ideas, thoughts and feelings without evaluation or interpretation.

2. Accept that feelings are always legitimate ones; a student client's feelings are never right or wrong. However, acceptance does not mean letting the student continue to "pull the wool" over his/her eyes as well as yours! Effective counselors also know how to give effective, helpful feedback as needed.

3. Are sensitive to the student client's feelings and let him/her know they are sensitive and not denying or ignoring any of their feelings (Going well beyond the student client's expressed feelings provides the student with a major new view of the emotions he/she is experiencing).

4. Notice the attitudes and feelings involved in the message given and respond appropriately.

5. Hypothesize (stating a hunch without interpretation or advice) back to the student client as precisely as they can regarding what they are hearing them say in terms of the attitudes, ideas, thoughts and feelings.

6. Always use words different (fresh words) from what the student client is using without changing their meanings (Credit for being a good listener is given only for short, precise statements).

7. Do not add or subtract from the student client's message. They deal only with the feelings they are hearing instead of with the facts surrounding the event the student is discussing. That is, when responding, they always "go to the student as a person" first before the event. For example, if a student client is talking about the impending divorce of her best friend's parents, effective counselors first focus on her *feelings* regarding the divorce; not the friends or the divorce, per se.

8. Do not respond with their own message and do not immediately agree or disagree with the student client. Examples: evaluating, sympathizing, giving opinions, using logic or persuasion, analyzing, untimely advising, ordering, probing or closed questioning.

## How Does Active Listening Help?

1. Helps free student clients of troublesome feelings when permitted to express them openly in the presence of a trusting person (burdens are usually lighter when shared with an objective other).

2. Helps student clients become less afraid of their negative thoughts and feelings and to label and understand how they (negative feelings and thoughts) often lead to negative behavior with unwanted consequences.

3. Helps promote a feeling of understanding between the counselor and the student.

4. Helps to facilitate problem solving through personal insight and ownership of the problem.

## Some Guidelines for Effective Listening:

1. Look directly at the student client. Effective eye contact suggests that you are attending to what is being said.

2. Avoid being preoccupied with your own thoughts. Don't rush ahead with your own ideas; rather, give attention to the way things are being said, the tone of the voice, the particular words or expressions being used, and bodily gestures. *Listen with the intent to "hear" and to "understand" and not with the intent to reply!*

3. Listen for feelings. A student client's feelings are the most important part of counseling. Feelings precede the way they will perceive the event, their problem or situation, and usually determine how they will respond in that particular situation or to that problem.

4. Say something to the student client that shows that you are listening carefully. This encourages (facilitates) the student to talk more about the subject. It enhances and invites the student client to continue talking.

5. Always respond in a non-evaluative manner and be sensitive and aware of the student client as a person who possesses both personal dignity and worth.

## Some Attending Skills:

### 1. Bodily and squarely face the student client

Facing the student you are counseling squarely is the basic posture that will reveal your interest and involvement. This says, "I'm available to you." Turning to the side, for example, lessens your involvement and receptivity.

### 2. Maintain eye contact

This lets the student know that he or she has your attention. Don't stare, but do look directly into a student's eyes when possible.

### 3. Maintain "open" posture

Facing the student client is a sign that you are open to what the student has to say and interested in communicating in an open manner. It is a non-defensive position. Crossed arms and crossed legs are often at least minimal signs of lessened involvement.

### 4. Lean forward

When both of you are seated and you lean forward toward him/her, it says to the student that you are interested and/or involved.

### 5. Smile, with a relaxed, open expression

This is important in order for you to be perceived as a warm, open, receptive, caring and respectful person. Be aware of the impact of your facial expression as you listen to your student client.

### 6. Simple acknowledgment

Smile, nodding, and "uh-huhing," "thanks for sharing that," "OK," etc. encourages your student client to continue talking and shows that you are interested in him/her as a person and that you are following what is being said. Acknowledge all client responses.

## The Effective Counselor is Genuine

Effective listening and understanding in the counseling process inevitably depend upon a counselor's genuine interest. However, unlike listening and attentiveness, genuineness is not really a skill to be learned. Are you genuinely concerned about how your student client thinks and feels? One thing is certain; your own authenticity will bring out the authenticity in your student clients. You may wonder how you can be genuine and yet practice and work at learning all the things discussed above. There is considerable evidence that if one continues to "try out" a new or different technique, role or skill in a sincere manner, genuineness will follow. That is, it will become spontaneous, natural and a "way of life" for you as a counselor.

"Tell it like it is" is still a popular expression. Children are especially suspicious of adults who talk one way and live another. Young people deplore hypocrisy. They want people to be trustful, honest, and genuine with them. Genuineness implies authenticity. You cannot be genuine if you are playing a role. Rather, genuineness denotes being in tune with yourself and acting in a way that reveals congruence. It is extremely difficult to feel one thing and communicate another, as the truth will always win out. However, genuineness does not mean that we should say exactly what we think at all times; to let it "all hang out."

Counselors who "say what they think" often hurt their clients emotionally. Genuine counselors can be themselves, but they are their "polite" selves and do not hurt student clients in the name of genuineness!

The counselor's genuineness could be the most important characteristic in a helping relationship. It sometimes makes "helpers" out of certain people simply because student clients realize quickly that they can depend on them for honest responses. On the other hand, some counselors, even though they have studied under the best instructors and know many counseling techniques, still play at being a helper. If you play a role that is not characteristic of yourself, then your ability as a personal counselor may be limited.

There is no real alternative to genuineness in a counseling relationship. As noted, even if we are shrewd and very skilled counselors, it is still doubtful that we could hide our real feelings from student clients. When we pretend to care, pretend to respect, or pretend to be open to experiences, we fool only ourselves.

## The Effective Counselor is Understanding

Being genuine is important. However, it does not mean necessarily that a person will understand another. As we listen to and discover our student clients' perceptions of their world, we begin to understand those students. Being genuine and listening attentively helps us to be empathic. The effective counselor also has the ability to understand the "worldview" of their student clients without evaluation of that worldview; or telling them how they should be acting in, or toward their "world."

True empathy means fully understanding another person, at both cognitive and emotional levels. It involves going beyond the mere expression of words and intellectual ideas to a deeper level of communication. Empathy means coming to know, to value, and to respect another person from that person's own frame of reference.

You have probably heard the expression, "Put yourself in the other person's shoes." This does not mean you must try to be that other person. Rather, when you have empathic understanding with a student client, you have an awareness of that student's internal frame of reference. However, you do not need to abandon, or change your own frame of reference or give up your values. Counselors who abandoned their values in counseling are vulnerable to change in a direction in which they may not wish to go. Empathic understanding means that, for a few moments at least, you are united with the student and the two of you have an overlap of perceptions, a commonality of meaning. You're "reading" and are "with" that student client without your evaluation entering in to the picture.

Your attempts to perceive and respond to clients' feelings, more than anything else, tells them that you are trying to understand. Moreover, they respect and appreciate these attempts even when you are not always accurate. The more accurate the empathy, the more credit you get. However, even the attempt at being empathic puts a "chip in the bank" towards the development of a nonthreatening, effective relationship with the student client. A few "chips in the bank" statements can help create the counselor/student bond that is needed for effective individual counseling.

Student clients come to know themselves and their feelings better through empathic understanding on the part of the school counselor. Letting them know that we are trying to understand also provides opportunities for self-initiated change. There is, unfortunately, considerable evidence that empathic understanding is not a characteristic of the general population. However, it is an interpersonal skill which can be learned. "Tuning-in" to our student client's feelings in an empathic manner is a skill that can be acquired, but it takes practice.

## The Effective Counselor is Respectful and Accepting

Respect for, and acceptance of, student clients means recognizing and accepting their experiences as important influences on their lives, regardless of their ages. All people have the human potential for joy, depression, success, and failure. It is not easy to be perfect and few accomplish such a lofty goal. In addition, it is an illusive goal that is not easy to define. Yet, we often judge students by some mysterious set of standards that reflect a desire for perfection. This perception on the part of the counselor will always lead to ineffective counseling outcomes.

True counselor respect indicates a concern for the student client as a special person with unique feelings and experiences. This encourages counselors to search for the real person rather than rushing in to approve, disapprove or to "fix them" which takes time. A 12-year-old who has a problem with authority, for example, took 12 years "to get that way" and cannot be "fixed" overnight. We live in a microwave-like, fast changing, fast paced society and students may expect quick results from our counseling. However, effective counseling still takes time.

Respect does not mean agreement with student clients or to "choose up sides" with them. To respect another person as a human being implies that we value that person's feelings and worth. It does not mean that we must agree with or condone their actions or approve of their behaviors.

Respect goes beyond optimism or simple reassurance. It is the communication of deep interest and concern. A high positive regard for your student clients emphasizes that their dignity is valued, their feelings are accepted, and that they are not being judged as good or bad. The degree to which a counselor communicates respect for student clients helps define the counseling relationship. If we feel and show positive regard for students, then they feel more positive toward us and are more willing to explore ideas and behaviors with us during counseling. Mutual respect opens the doors to effective counseling outcome.

Some students may come to you for counseling because they have low self-respect and their every day functioning is impaired; they have little or no personal regard for themselves. In many cases it is because their feelings and behaviors were not (are not) accepted or valued by self or others. As these students begin to experience your unconditional respect, they may stop "defending" themselves long enough to examine new patterns of living and thinking.

## Knowledgeable of the Student Client's Culture

Thus far I have given primary attention to what some call the "affective domain" of counseling. Effective counselors are also thoroughly familiar with the theories on which their techniques are based and know how to be of "expert" assistance to students in need. Effective counselors know that love, caring, respect, empathy, etc. are very important in counseling, but never enough! They know when not to offer "untimely advice" and when to offer "timely advice" to their students. Effective school counselors are also knowledgeable regarding the different cultures represented by the students in their respective schools.

As noted above, effective counselors are viewed by those students needing personal help as "trusted experts." In general, students seek out a school counselor because they feel "helpless" and thus expect to be "helped" by the "trusted expert." This applies especially when counseling with a student dissimilar in culture from the school counselor. Effective counseling with a student client dissimilar in culture takes the entire above discussed counselor skills and characteristics along with a thorough knowledge of that particular culture.

Surveys of school counselors in the United States suggest that most represent "white, middle class" America. And, many believe that this fact gives "white middle class" students an unfair advantage. Several publications describe how school counselors have suffered when they were forced to work in a situation that calls for cognitive knowledge of the culturally different. That is, in addition to knowledge of theory and knowledge of communication skills, there is a need for school counselors to know the cultural background and environmental situations of their student clients. Culturally competent and informed school counselors are knowledgeable about the various cultures represented by the students in their respective schools. They also know that "mental health" and or "psychological wellness" is culturally defined and that knowledge of their student clients' culture is imperative.

In today's diverse world, school counselors will, most likely, have many students who represent many different cultural backgrounds, religious beliefs, race, etc. It would be foolhardy to ignore these differences and assume that all students approach personal counseling with the same values and attitudes. In addition, to ignore student backgrounds and experiences is to ignore valuable resources and opportunities for counseling.

A large percent of America's total population lives in cities of 100,000 or more today, or in areas which lead into these large cities. This concentration greatly intensifies social and economic problems that could conceivably destroy the structure of society. In addition, intercultural conflicts, which are discouragingly high, could increase.

*Joe Wittmer, Ph.D. and Mary Ann Clark, Ph.D.*

Effective school counselors are keenly aware of these issues and their affect on their roles as personal counselors.

A basic reason for the lack of such understanding of other cultures is the prescriptions concerning American behavior, standards of conduct, and morality. That is, middle and upper class college graduates determined these. A middle-class, Anglo European American may be caught up in the notion of *assumed similarity*. That is, they may feel that everyone is like them, or should be; therefore, communication is one-way and distorted. School counselors with a sound knowledge of a student client's culture and environment will more likely understand the source and reasons for some student behaviors that appear odd or peculiar. That is, they know that a student's thinking, dreams, feelings and behaviors are culturally based. A thorough knowledge regarding participants from a different culture also helps overcome the "negative assumptions" sometimes held regarding participants from a culture different from ours.

When counseling the culturally different, or those students from environmental situations of which you may not be familiar (i.e. poor children, children from violent homes), it is important to preserve the self-respect and dignity of the student. The best way to do this is to learn all you can about the cultures represented in your school. The salesman in Meredith Wilson's *Music Man* lamented the fact that the new salesman would be ineffective because he was not familiar with his clientele to whom he was supposed to sell a certain product. Thus, his advice to the new salesmen was; "You gotta know the territory." *School counselor, know your territory!* Take a field trip through the communities where your students live! Learn as much as you possibly can about their values, mores and methods they use to cope in "their world."

## Informed and Culturally Skilled School Counselors Know that:

1. Culture is the predominant force in shaping behaviors, values and institutions.

2. The dignity of the student client cannot be preserved unless the dignity of his/her culture is preserved.

3. When the student client and counselor come from different cultures, there is a strong likelihood that sooner or later they will miscommunicate by misinterpreting or misjudging the behavior of the other.

4. They, most likely, have been trained in the traditional theories and models that are European and male based.

5. Traditional psychological and counseling theories and approaches have limited applicability when working with diverse client populations.

6. Not taking into consideration the cultural backgrounds of the student clients with whom they work results in their failure with those students.

7. Western values may be in direct contrast to the non-western worldviews of the student clients with whom they work on a day to day basis.

8. The objectives for the culturally different student client cannot be a reflection of Western perspectives.

9. Most Western cultures strongly encourage looking out for number one, which may be in direct contrast to the values held by some of their minority student clients.

10. There are many psychological similarities among participants from different cultures, but, that,

11. Cultural factors do significantly affect a student's psychological development.

Can attitudes concerning other cultures be changed and new ones taught? Yes, but, as Milton Bennett stated, where intercultural sensitivity is concerned, it isn't easy!

*Intercultural sensitivity is not natural. It is not part of our primate past, nor has it characterized most of human history. Cross-cultural contact often has been accompanied by bloodshed, oppression, or genocide. Clearly this pattern cannot continue. Today, the failure to exercise intercultural sensitivity is not simply bad business or bad morality —it is self-destructive. So we face a choice: overcome the legacy of our history, or lose history itself for all time.*

*Milton Bennett*

## The School Counselor's Theoretical Orientation

As Harrison indicated in the previous chapter, time for long term counseling with individual student clients is limited for the busy school counselor. Thus, brief individual counseling approaches can help address both the counselor's time constraints and concerns regarding counseling effectiveness. Considering the setting, it is my opinion that using brief counseling approaches with individual student clients is the most appropriate.

One such approach being used by many school counselors today is the solution-focused approach. Not only is it a brief counseling approach, most agree that it may be the most "culture free" approach available today. It is viewed as "culture free" because the school counselor focuses on the solution, not the client or the problem presented.

The solution focused approach:

1. Begins with a collaborative versus authoritative role in setting goals with the student clients.

2. Collaborates with the student in a joint effort to explore areas of concern and interest. This strengthens the student client's sense of empowerment and ownership in the counseling process.

3. Does not impose his or her values when using this approach as it should be used.

4. Helps students solve their problems while not converting them to the counselor's worldview and/or culture.

5. Builds on the preexisting adaptive strengths of all students, including those who are ethnically diverse.

6. Looks at how student clients construct their world and act on it, not how the counselor thinks they should act on it!

7. Respects and accommodates what student clients bring to counseling. That is, the student client's culture and resources is central to the solution-focused approach.

8. De-emphasizes the past history and underlying pathology and moves away from focusing on problems to focusing on the solution.

9. Adapts the counseling process to student clients instead of expecting them to adapt to the counseling process.

10. Respects and utilizes that which the student client brings to the counseling session. This concept lies at the heart of the solution-focused approach.

The solution focused approach seems to be a good "fit" for today's developmental school counselor because it is practical and efficient, shifts the focus from what's wrong to what's working or will work, and works in a short period of time. Counselors skilled in this approach know that, instead of trying to push, pull or resist the student client, it is more effective and efficient to go "with the flow." That is, the counselor skilled in this approach to counseling works with, rather than against, a student client's position. Student clients become a consultant to the counselor in how to best solve their own problems. The emphasis is on looking at what has worked in the problem solving process in the past for the student and what might work in the future. It also tends to work well when even slight improvement is beginning to show. Again, as noted previously, using the solution focused approach, or any other for that matter, does not negate the importance of the core counseling conditions described above.

## Facilitative and Not-so-Facilitative Counselor Responses

This section is about various verbal responses used by the counselor in the counseling relationship. More specifically, it is about counselor "talk" and how it influences the counseling relationship as well as the perceptions and subsequent behaviors of student clients. And, ultimately, how certain responses affect counseling outcome.

Current research indicates that some verbal responses used by counselors and other helping professionals tend to be perceived by clients as more empathic, caring, warm, and person-centered than do other responses. These responses have a higher probability of creating a more effective counseling relationship than others create and, once learned, are essential keys toward becoming an effective counselor. It is my belief that such responses are more likely to enhance the degree of counseling effectiveness and bring about the desired outcome a school counselor is seeking. There is no doubt that their use will greatly assist the counselor in postulating the "core dimensions" of an effective counseling relationship described above.

These responses have emerged from studies of verbal behavior in counseling and are categorized below from the most to the least in the degree to which they enhance a counselor's effectiveness. These are:

1. **Focusing on feelings**

2. **Clarifying and summarizing**

3. **Questioning (open-ended)**

4. **Reassuring and supporting**

5. **Analyzing and interpreting**

6. **Advising and evaluating**

While all of the above responses might be used by an effective counselor at one time or another (i.e. timely advise can be effective with certain student clients), they are ranked as above because of their probable effect in building a more helping, enhancing and facilitative relationship with student clients. Again, the point being made here is that the higher ranked verbal responses above will lead to more positive counseling outcomes. And I believe this to be so regardless of the techniques used and/or the theoretical counseling orientation espoused by the counselor.

**Focusing on Feelings:** A feeling-focused response conveys to students with whom we are counseling that we are "reading" or attempting to read what they are experiencing. It is a reflection of understanding of their message, their "story." It communicates that we are working at becoming aware of how they are feeling about themselves at this time. For example:

> You're disappointed, Jane, with your father's behavior and confused about what's causing it.

The reflection or understanding of feeling statement can be a difficult response to learn. It demands that we be empathic listeners (listening beyond mere words) who are sensitive to not only the words and behaviors being expressed, but also the feelings behind them. It calls for us to reflect, to mirror, these feelings back to the student client in a nonthreatening and facilitative manner. An effective, aware, sensitive counselor knows that the feelings concerning a problem or situation affecting us almost always predetermine how we will behave in that situation and/or in respond to a particular problem.

Effective counselors often verbalize what they think their student clients are feeling. This involves more than a restatement of words and should not be confused with other responses that focus on the general ideas that are being expressed. Nor should it be confused with an interpretation, which tends to explain why a person might be doing something. Rather, it gives priority to feelings that go with the words and behaviors that are being seen and heard.

To begin a sentence with "You feel..." does not necessarily mean that you will focus on someone's feelings. For example, "I feel that you would make an effective teacher" is not a feeling-focused response. It is an opinion. Effective counselors go beyond the words to the feeling within the speaker. Sometimes it can be helpful to ask yourself: How would I feel if I were to say something like that? Or, how would I have to feel to do something like that? After answering these questions, you may have some insight into the student's feeling. If this seems to be accurate or compatible with what you are sensing from the student, then this feeling could be appropriately stated and would be helpful to the student.

Effective counselors are aware that they can easily distort what a student client is saying. That is, their own value systems and perceptions, at times, can prevent them from being sensitive and accurately empathic to their clients' feelings.

It is almost impossible for us to talk, or to be silent for that matter, without showing feelings of some sort. That is, we humans cannot, **not** communicate feelings. All of us feel something at all times. Both verbal and nonverbal cues tell us how a person feels.

For our purposes, feelings can be categorized into 1) *pleasant* feelings or 2) *unpleasant* feelings. Sometimes we hear *both* kinds of feelings when a student client is talking. When listening to a student talk, we might ask ourselves: Do I hear unpleasant feelings or pleasant feelings, or both, at the moment? Think about the feeling words that might best describe what is heard or sensed from a student. If we hear pleasant feelings, then we might say something like:

> You're excited about how your relationship is now changing.

> You were feeling confident before that happened.

> You're delighted with the idea that you might be switching math teachers soon.

On the other hand, if we hear some unpleasantness, we might say:

> It was a painful experience for you.

> You're really angry with him right now.

> The results disappointed you.

Maybe we are hearing both pleasant and unpleasant feelings. Or, perhaps some ambivalence. We might then say something like:

> Getting to know her better is challenging to you and it is awkward just starting.

> The first experience disappointed you, but you're encouraged now about the new possibilities.

> You're excited about the new baby brother, but a little bit afraid of what's going to happen to you.

> You're proud, yet skeptical.

> You are interested in taking that course, but afraid you'll fail.

After responding to feelings, try not to rush in with other statements. Let the responses you made to the student have its impact; its full effect. Let them "soak." Pause a little, giving the student client an opportunity to experience your interest and understanding. More often than not, if you are reasonably accurate, the student will unconsciously nod (as if to say, "Yes, that's right" or "Thanks for hearing me" or almost an "ah ha" experience.) and talk some more. It is a pleasant experience for both counselor and student. I referred to this previously as putting a chip in the bank. But, again, pause and let the response "soak in" with the client before moving on.

It should be noted that when you respond to a student client's feelings, your statement could be rejected. Sometimes it's difficult for students to acknowledge their feelings, especially negative ones. They may even deny them. However, it is important that your response be made because it says you are trying to understand what the student is experiencing. Feeling focused responses communicate that you are not only listening to words, but that you are listening to that special part of the student client which makes up those words. A reflection of feeling is almost always effective because the student will usually gently correct you if you have misunderstood. That is, even the attempt at understanding puts another "chip in the bank" toward building that necessary facilitative counseling relationship.

Counseling in an attempt to tune in on a person's feelings and reflect them accurately takes practice, practice, and more practice! It does not come easily to most of us because we have not had many adult models to learn from while we were children, or even now as adults.

## Clarifying and Summarizing Responses

Any counselor response that is an attempt to acknowledge the content of what a client has said, or to identify the most significant ideas that seem to have been stated, can be termed a clarifying or summarizing response. Such a statement is helpful when there is some doubt as to whether you're really following the student's thinking and feeling. In this case, a clarification statement is a simple way of checking out what has been heard. In other situations, the clarifying or summarizing response is deliberately used to help student clients "hear back" what they have just stated. It also lets them know you "heard" them. Students, and others for that matter, like to be "heard." It gives us a feeling of affirmation and often brings about personal insight.

When there is a lot of talk in a spontaneous and fast conversation, you cannot expect to understand or grasp everything the student client is saying. Yet, an attempt to let students know that you are interested in following what is being said can help facilitate the type of communication needed to facilitate effectively counseling outcome.

The clarification statement involves "fresh" (or new) words. That is, we should not "parrot" what the student is saying. That is of no value whatsoever and often turns students off. A true clarification response is an attempt to simplify, restate, reframe or refocus what has been said while using new words. Clarifying. reframing, restating, refocusing, repeating or summarizing statements focus on the ideas or content of the discussion. This emphasis tends to separate these responses from feeling-focused responses. Clarifying or summarizing responses can give you some "wiggle room" so that you do not appear interpretative or evaluative. Consider the following:

*If I hear you correctly, you are telling me that....*

*You seem to be saying that....*

*If I am following you, you're saying....*

The above responses could also be used in providing a student feedback as needed. For example, "Stop me if I'm wrong, but last session you were saying that your difficult relationship with your parents is causing you all this stress. However, today you seem to be saying something else. Help me to understand this difference." That type statement is much more effective and counseling appropriate (and won't cash in any chips!) than would be, "You're really inconsistent in what you're saying." Or worse yet, "You're a real phony." Yet, I believe the student will get the message just as quickly when you use the first, more facilitative response than the latter responses. Effective school counselors use clarifying or summarizing statements when they want to check out a student's thoughts and ideas. These statements have a way of reassuring students that they are being listened to and heard but not necessarily being agreed with. Notice that none of these responses imply a reason for the student's behavior or why they did what they did. A "why" or a "because" becomes an interpretative response. Other examples include:

*I think you're telling me that this has happened before.*

*Let me see now, you're saying that cheating on a test, as long as you don't get caught, is okay.*

*Let's see, you said... and... and....*

## Using "Wiggle Room" Responses to Avoid Interpretation

To understand the thoughts, feelings, emotions, and behaviors of their student clients, effective, facilitative counselors attempt to enter their phenomenal field. That is, their personal frame of reference. Effective counselors have the ability to let their clients know that they understand how they (student clients) interact with their world without judgment, evaluation or interpretation. Think of it as "wearing their shoes" and/or understanding "their worldview" without imposing your values in any way shape or form. Work at being "with" them and/or "reading" them. This is when appropriately worded clarification of content and/or reflection of feelings statements can be very helpful and facilitative. Such understanding statements on your part will, as mentioned above, put a "chip in the bank" with your student clients. Then, should you "miss" with your reflection or clarification response, the student will still be willing to fill you in on "how you missed" and another chip still goes in the bank! If you remember to go first to your student (as a person) with your reflection or clarification response, and then to the *"event"* about which he/she is speaking, you'll be on your way to effective counseling outcomes.

Counselors need not be concerned about stating their "hypotheses or guesses" at what is going on with a student client. However, effective counselors make their "guess" or "hypothesis" statements without any form of interpretation or analysis. That is, they do not tell him/her why they think, feel and or behave in a certain ways; they simply state their hypothesis. However, they do give the client room to disagree without being defensive by using "wiggle room" phrases.

Below are some "wiggle room" phrases that may be useful when you trust that your perceptions are accurate and that a student client will be receptive to your hypothesis or guess as to what is "going on" with him/her:

*Stop me if I'm wrong, but I sense a real...*

*From your point of view it almost seems that...*

*Your experience seems to be telling you...*

*I may be way off base here, but from where I stand...*

*If I'm with you on this...*

*It's almost as if you think she...*

*What about the possibility that...*

*I'm wondering if when...*

*I'm not sure if I'm with you, but...*

*What I guess I'm hearing is...*

*Correct me if I'm wrong, but...*

*From where I stand you seem...*

*This is what I think I hear you saying, you...*

*You appear to be...*

*It appears you...*

*Perhaps you're...*

*I somehow sense that maybe you...*

*Maybe I'm out to lunch with this one, but...*

*This may be a long shot, but*

*As I try to hear what you're saying, it seems...*

*I almost get the impression that.....*

*Let me see if I'm following you, you seem.....*

Some other phrases you may find helpful are:

*You seem to believe...*

*What I hear you saying...*

*You're... (identify the feeling; but you need not use the redundant word "feeling")*

*I'm picking up that you...*

*I hear you saying that...*

*Where you're coming from...*

*You figure...*

## Questioning Responses

The art and skill of questioning has often been thought of as the central part of the counseling process. A lot has been written about how to ask questions, how to probe, etc. Counseling textbooks almost always include chapters with a series of "good" questions for counselors to use with their clients.

There is no doubt that questions are a valuable tool in the counseling process. However, many times counselors tend to ask too many questions. A question can be used to obtain information, stimulate further discussion, or to query an individual student client regarding a particular matter. Counselors assume that clients will benefit by answering a question and developing a point of view. Questions may also open up new areas for discussion. Effective questions encourage the sharing of information by *inviting* the client to *share thoughts, ideas and feelings*. Open questions also reveal your *interest* in hearing more about what the student is saying, an invitation for the client to continue to share.

Some counselors see cross-examination procedures or probing as an essential part of their trade. It is assumed that questioning procedures will be productive and that probing questions lead to problem solving and in-depth counseling. However, clients are also led to believe, concurrently, that whoever is asking the questions also has the answers.

If a student has a problem and a school counselor asks a lot of questions there may be the expectation that, since the counselor now has the information, the counselor should solve the problem or make the decision for him/her. Students reason that if counselors cannot solve the problem then why do they ask all the questions? This may be perfectly acceptable in cases where cognitive counseling is based upon confirmed information and facts. But, it can lead to a dead end street when there is no easy answer or correct response.

The open-ended question encourages student clients to develop their answers and responses further. The closed question, on the other hand, is structured for only a shrug of the shoulders or a yes or no response. It tends not to elicit an in-depth response and certainly isn't inviting the student to continue with their current line of thought. Look at the following examples:

*Do you like school? (closed)*

**What do you like or not like about school? (open and inviting)**

*Did you like reading this section? (closed)*

**How did you feel about this section? (open and inviting)**

*Are you ready to try out this homework assignment? (closed)*

**What can I do to get you better prepared to carry out this homework assignment? (open and inviting)**

As you read the above questions, did you "feel" the difference between the open and the closed questions? Did you find the open questions more "inviting"?

Our research indicates that the open-ended question invites clients to answer from their own perceptual fields. That is, they feel as if the counselor is truly interested in hearing more from them; more about the problem or situation they are dealing with in counseling. A closed question is narrow and forces student clients to answer in terms of the counselor's perceptual field. The open question solicits a wide range of thoughts and feelings. The closed question tends to seek cold facts. Consider the following questions, some of which seem to be open but are not.

*You don't like this classroom activity, do you? (closed)*

**What is it that you don't like about this classroom activity? (open)**

*Is this the part that's confusing to you? (closed)*

**What part is confusing to you? (open)**

Of all possible questions a counselor could ask, I believe that open-ended ones are the most effective for client growth. While closed questions might be used at times to gain specific information that will help clarify a situation; open-ended questions give student clients the most room to discover their innermost feelings and thoughts about a matter. However, it should be acknowledged, the effective counselor realizes that if he/she can ask a student a question, they might make a more appropriate and effective, non-question type response instead. That is, instead of asking a question, the effective counselor works at making a verbal response that is even more facilitating for the client such as a feeling focused and/or clarification statement as described above.

The "why" question is a type of closed question that deserves special attention. Most students, or anyone else for that matter, really do not know why they do the things they do. Do people who are abusing drugs really know why they started? A "Why are you sick" question will seldom get you any relevant information. Do individuals know why they are sick? Do persons who tell dirty jokes know why it is fun to tell them? Do children know why they have the friends they have? Why questions often have a negative connotation in our society left over from childhood, i.e. "Why don't you cut your hair?" "Why don't you study harder?" "Why don't you date someone more suitable for you?"

While there is probably an explanation behind most behavior, it is doubtful that a "why" question will help discover it. These questions have a way of making students uneasy. They require student clients to explain themselves, to be accountable, to come up with a reasonable link or connection. Effective counselors have learned to be cautious in the use of "why" questions. When such questions are posed, individuals tend to become defensive and feel pressure to "explain away" their behaviors, without seeking changes. When we ask a why question, student clients often get the feeling that we have the answer before asking the question, or at least think we do. In addition, students feel that they have to give us a "reason" for their behaviors, feelings or thoughts.

## The Least Effective Counselor Responses

As stated several times above, some verbal responses tend to be perceived by student clients as more empathic, caring, warm, and person-centered than do certain others. They have a higher probability of facilitating students to think more about their ideas, thoughts and feelings and to be willing to share them with the counselor. They provide a tone, which fosters a helping relationship, eliciting the conditions of warmth, understanding, respect, regard, and so forth. As noted, regardless of the counselor's theoretical orientation or techniques being used, skill in the use of these responses is the key to becoming an effective counselor.

The talking that takes place in counseling is important since every response makes some kind of impact on clients. And, as stated previously, counseling, whether in school situations or in other settings is for better or worse! Our responses invariably affect general perceptions, attitudes, and degree of comfort. Impressions are formed which, in turn, influence other responses, choice of topics, and what the student client will share with the counselor.

Thus far we have examined three of the more facilitative counseling responses, now let's look briefly at some others that are not used, at least not used as frequently, by the effective school counselor. Unfortunately, if used at the **"wrong" time**, these responses are considered practically noneffective in the counseling process. That is, their use offers the counselor a lower probability of effectiveness in personal counseling situations. They are; *reassuring and supporting, analyzing and interpreting and advising and evaluating*

## Reassuring and Supporting

Reassurance or support involves statements which are intended to tell student clients that the counselor believes in them, in their ability to meet situations, and their potential for solving their own problems. Such statements are meant to instill confidence that they will be successful. It is supposed to be a pat on the back, intended to empower them to keep going. Unfortunately, instead of empowerment, reassuring or supporting responses imply that students need *not feel* as they do. That is, there is a tendency by the counselor to dismiss their feelings as being normal or common and the student client is told, in so many words, not to be concerned, or worse yet, not to talk any more about these feelings at this point in time. For example:

*Don't worry, everyone feels worthless on occasion.*

*You don't have to feel that way because everything's going to turn out okay. His behavior isn't that bad.*

*You know, in that respect you're not much different from other children I've worked with.*

*Oh, all good friends are like that.*

*Things always look bad at this time of the year, but it will turn out okay.*

Data indicates that the reassuring or supportive type statement is the second most popular response used by counselors. However, data also reveals that they are not very effective in bringing about positive change on the part of student clients. Only advice and evaluation are used more frequently. Many counselors believe that a support-ive statement can encourage a student with whom they are working to do better. "I am building the student's self-confidence," is a common rationalization for this statement. But, it doesn't usually strike the student client this way. Despite efforts to reduce the apparent anxiety or intense feelings, the message comes through telling the student not to feel as he/she does. It denies feelings. It does not communicate acceptance, respect, or understanding. As a matter of fact, as mentioned above, it will often keep students from continuing to talk about those feelings or the situation involved. The message they hear is..." The counselor really does not want to hear more about the feelings I'm talking about." In other words, the message the student client hears is; don't feel that way. In every day situations this is understandable. That is, as a society, we tend not to like or to facilitative the negative feelings of others and often use reassurance or support to make them "go away." However, the effective school counselor realizes that the facilitation of negative feelings on the part of the student client is a must for individual counseling to be effective.

Sometimes supporting and reassuring statements create a negative effect because they come from a seemingly superior position. When we give reassurance or support, it frequently implies that we can see into the future and that our positive estimations will be correct. They can depend on us. Creating dependency on the part of the student client is seldom effective.

## Analyzing and Interpreting

Some counselors think that they can be helpful by analyzing (and subsequently "explaining") a student's situation to the student. Perhaps this response gained its popularity from the theory that there is always a logical reason why people do things. Look at these responses:

*Don't you see, you see your teacher being like your father. They both are authority figures and both trigger rebellion in you.*

*Your unhappiness stems from all your problems at home.*

In each of these examples, the intent is to explain, analyze, or interpret the student's behavior. Sometimes an effort is made to connect one event to another in the hope that this will give the student client some insight. Analyzing or interpreting responses try to give meaning to a counseling situation but they usually end up telling clients what they might or ought to think, why they did what they did, etc.

Remind yourself of how you feel when someone tries to analyze or interpret your behavior, i.e. "Oh I know why you did that, its because...." or, "I know why you wore that dress, its because..." Chances are you don't like it, especially if the interpretation is correct. Most of us dislike the idea that another person seems to know more about ourselves than we do and we will often "avoid" that person when possible.

One danger in making an interpretation to a student client is that we may, inadvertently, project our own attitudes, values, and feelings onto him or her. Such a response often emphasizes our personal interpretation of the world rather than the student client's perception of their world. Fortunately, effective counselors no longer rely heavily on these types of statements in an attempt to facilitate personal growth

## Advising and Evaluating

School counselors are often viewed by students as the one adult in their school who has the answers to their problems. Since counselors have probably studied more human behavior, and usually have more experience than most of their students have in the mental health area, they are sometimes prone to think they are in a position to evaluate, make judgments, and give untimely advice to their students. When counselors dispense untimely advice to student clients, their probability of counseling success goes down. Moreover, if that is their usual method of counseling, they are prone to use more of the less facilitative responses given here, and in my opinion, will be less effective as counselors.

As noted above, effective counselors are more concerned with what the student client is thinking and feeling than simply giving information and advice. Advising or evaluating are responses that indicate a judgment of relative effectiveness, appropriateness or rightness within the counselor's own value structure. An advising or evaluating response somehow implies what the student might or ought to do. Here are some examples:

*Don't let him get to you like that. Stand up to him!*

*Instead of arguing, try to see your mother's point of view.*

*If you'd be better at getting your homework in, your teachers wouldn't be so upset with you.*

Unfortunately, while most counselors are trying to give helpful advice, there is the likelihood the advice is a projection of the counselor's needs, problems, or cultural values. This can be easily seen in the statement, "If I were you...." Students might even follow the advice and find that it was not valid for them. Students who experience this approach from their counselor seldom continue to see their problem (if they ever did) as one they "own." Instead, ownership of the problem being discussed has now shifted from the student to the counselor. The student becomes the "subject" and the counselor becomes the "expert" operator with all the answers! Giving untimely advice to a student client is sort of like moving a neighbor's furniture around without their permission. They move it back as soon as you leave their house! That is, students may smile and acknowledge your untimely advice, but will forget it as soon as the session if over!

When advice is relevant, timely, logical, and practical, it can be very helpful to a student client. This is particularly true if it is offered at an appropriate time; a time when it is viewed as a suggestion, or as leading their thinking, rather than as a command (i.e. "Have you given thought to maybe going to a community college or...").

School counselors can fall into the trap of giving advice when a student continually seeks their advice. However, students are often defensive once the advice is dispensed and may no longer be receptive to anything the counselor has to say. They might even argue more in order to maintain their individuality following untimely advice. They may begin to play "Yea, but..." games with the counselor (who may respond in kind) and "counseling" per se, is now nonexistent. That is, neither one is hearing the other!

The effective counselor doesn't get caught up in the societal concept that implies that everything must be done in a hurry. That is, they do not "rush in and fix" students with an evaluation and then give quick, untimely advice on what the student client should do to "get better."

# Using the High Facilitative Responses

In summary, three counseling responses that have a higher probability of resulting in success for the counselor have been emphasized in this chapter. These three responses (feeling-focused, clarifying and summarizing, and open-ended questions) can be effectively used with most any counseling orientation, technique or intervention the school counselor chooses to use. Most importantly, their use will result in better, more facilitative counseling relationships with student clients and more positive counseling outcomes.

If an open, facilitative counseling relationship is not present, then student clients will, most likely, pull back into their proverbial "shells." They behave like a tortoise who, when threatened, will not stick it's head out. That is, student clients in a non-facilitative counseling relationship will not take the "risks" that might result in positive changes for them. They stop sticking their "necks out" for fear of even more rejection. Words never penetrate their hard shells or enter into their perceptual fields. As student clients experience a relatively nonthreatening relationship with their counselor, they are more apt to "stick their necks out and risk more." They are more likely to consider the alternative suggestions and methods that the counselor offers in an attempt at helping them.

# Chapter 11

# Small Group Counseling in School Settings

by
**Rex Stockton and Paul Toth**

*Rex Stockton, Ed.D., is a Chancellor's Professor of Counseling and Educational Psychology at Indiana University. He is a former high school counselor and has long been active as a researcher, writer, and teacher in the area of group work. Recently he has been working extensively with the African Association of Guidance and Counseling.*

*Paul L. Toth, Ph.D., is a Psychologist in the Student Health Center at Indiana University, Bloomington. His doctoral studies focused on group counseling and the training of group leaders. He has had a career of active involvement in youth work through public school teaching and YMCA work.*

## Introduction

Take a minute or two and think about the influence of groups in your life. As you think about how groups have impacted your life, the prevalence of groups and human beings' attraction to groups, probably becomes quite clear. Most people live in some type of group, we work in groups and we play in groups. In many ways groups make life easier and there is no doubt that "groups" are an integral part of any society.

Groups are also an integral part of any type of educational institution, especially schools. The very organization of schools relies on the organization of groups. Task oriented group work is essential to both the administrative organization of the school and the educational experience of the students. Much of the day to day work of the institution is done through group work. Moreover, students are purposefully involved in groups in order to design yearbooks, plan a debate strategy, complete a class project, engage opponents in an athletic contest, and many other activities and undertakings.

Schools have employed the use of small groups indirectly for the purposes of social skills education for a very long while. One way our nation coped with the economic and social changes born of the turn of the last century industrial era was to teach a turn-of-the-century version of human and social relation skills to children. The schools saw as one of their duties, in the midst of radical social change, the transformation of naive children into socially astute adults who could make their way in a world of business. Perhaps even more importantly, schools took on the responsibility of teaching students skills which would help them get along in a world of strangers.

Of course, group work in these early years was not as we know it today. The first groups were clearly task-oriented; they were not the psycho-educational or counseling groups that school counselors employ today. Teachers worked with students, and students worked with one another on various projects and problems in order to, not only solve the problem, but also to gain experience in working with peers and strangers.

Since these early beginnings, the impact of small groups within the educational setting has continued to grow. As the decades progressed, educators began to gain a more clear understanding of the importance of the student's emotional health and well-being in the educational process and the role small groups could play in the construction of a healthy and well-functioning person. Over 35 years ago Clarence Mahler (1969) wrote:

*If young people are to have a real choice, both personally and professionally, in planning their futures, they must have help in learning how to better understand themselves, learning how to make wise decisions and solve problems, and integrating their own personal growth with the increasing complexity of present-day society... A good group experience provides strong support for people to clarify their attitudes and strengthen their individuality (pp. 5-7, italics added by the authors).*

Helping students clarify their attitudes and working with them to come to understand their sense of self continues to be the challenge for counselors in the schools today. Small group work continues to provide an important means to meet this challenge.

Students today are faced with many serious issues such as substance abuse, sexually transmitted diseases, school violence, family changes, gangs, and eating disorders to name a few. Myrick (2003) indicated that group counseling can be a very effective intervention with students facing any of these issues. Greenberg (2002) wrote that students at all levels can benefit from participating in a small group counseling experience (Greenberg, 2002). Having the support of peers who may be going through similar experiences, learning to give and receive feedback, and having the helpful assistance of a professional counselor who is also a broker of resources, can be a positive and powerful experience for students.

One of the goals of all school counselors should be to assist all students with their academic, career and personal/social development. Small group counseling can be a very effective vehicle for accomplishing this important goal. In emphasizing this point, Stone and Dahir (2006) wrote,

*Our continually evolving society with its multidimensional influences of societal values, technological developments, and changing demographics, impacts the way in which school counselors work in 21st century schools. The emphasis has shifted to reaching all students in their academic, career, and personal-social development (Stone and Dahir, 2006).*

Even though we can identify a shift from Mahler's long ago concerns about the student's self-awareness and actualization, to current problems with which school counselors are confronted, to the current reports of social issues that reflect problems concerning today's counselors, all of these problems can be effectively dealt with in a group setting. It should be remembered, however, that major social problems are not a necessary starting point for group work in schools. Many counseling groups are arranged around such topics as new student support groups, raising self-esteem, peer relationships, anger management, social skills, study skills, dealing with parents and other significant individuals, and assertiveness training.

The American School Counselor Association's (ASCA, 2002) position statement on group counseling and the school counselor makes the following point:

*Many components of a comprehensive school counseling program are best delivered by means of group counseling. Small- and large-group approaches are the preferred medium of delivery for developmental counseling program activities, in terms of efficiency as well as effectiveness. Professional school counselors facilitate many groups, as well as train others as group facilitators. Such groups might include the parent education group, the peer helpers group or in-school support groups for students. The counselor may be involved in groups specific to a particular community/school district (ASCA, 2002).*

## Groups: A Definition

Small groups are a microcosm of the larger society. They are made up of a variety of people from various backgrounds with differing values and points of view and pathologies. Each member brings his or her own agenda. Like social groups, counseling groups have a definite beginning, middle, and end. Groups are the place for the activities of life to be experienced and explored: people meet, they share their lives, they learn about rules for membership, they learn to trust and confront one another, they share a variety of feelings, and they are faced with saying good-bye. Groups provide the forum in which members are able to learn authentic ways of relating.

The Association for Specialists in Group Work (2002) defined group work as a

> ...broad professional practice that refers to the giving of help or the accomplishment of tasks in a group setting. It involves the application of group theory and process by a capable professional practitioner or to assist an interdependent collection of people to reach their mutual goals, which may be personal, interpersonal, or task-related in nature (ASGW, 2002).

School counselors have both the challenge and the opportunity to continue forward with various types of group interventions that assist people to clarify their attitudes and meet their personal goals.

> According to the ASCA, group counseling involves a small number of students working on shared tasks and developing supportive relationships in a group setting. ASCA views group counseling as an efficient and positive way of dealing with students' developmental problems and situational concerns. And further, group counseling makes it possible for more students to achieve a healthier personal adjustment, handle the stresses of a rapidly changing technological and complex environment and to learn to work and live with others more effectively (ASCA, 2002).

## Training Group Leaders

There are many models for training group workers which have been examined by leaders in the field. In our opinion, there are four general areas of competency called for: (a) didactic knowledge; (b) individual clinical skills; (c) knowledge of group dynamics; and (d) achieving a healthy personality oneself. Standards for training group leaders are provided by the Association for Specialists in Group Work (ASGW), a division of the American Counseling Association (ACA). Current ASGW training guidelines reflecting generic and specialty skills are specifically outlined, ranging from that expertise required for basic task oriented groups through various gradations of personal growth groups to psychotherapy groups concerned with the reconstruction of personality. The preamble of the ASGW professional training standards stated:

> All counselors should possess a set of core competencies in general group work. The Association for Specialists in Group Work advocates for the incorporation of core group work competencies as part of required entry level training in all counselor preparation programs. Mastery of the core competencies detailed in the ASGW training standards will prepare the counselor to understand group process phenomena and to function more effectively in groups in which the counselor is a member (ASGW, 2000).

Because some of the areas in which counselors find themselves leading groups these days require specialized skills, it may be necessary for those lacking training to further develop their knowledge and skill levels through additional professional development. It would be quite helpful, and perhaps necessary, to enroll in group counseling or group dynamics courses at a local university or take part in one of the many workshops offered by professional organizations such as ASGW and the National Board for Certified Counselors. Especially important is taking advantage of opportunities for supervised group leadership. Most counselor education programs require a course in group counseling.

# Leading Groups

Have you been a group leader? If yes, do you remember leading your first group? Think about how you felt before you began? What was your biggest fear? Perhaps you have not yet led a group; think, then, of how you might feel about leading your first group. Even counselors who are well read in the area of group theory and well trained in group intervention are usually anxious about the prospect of leading their first group. The senior author has found that beginning group leaders who have all the didactic knowledge and experiential training needed to begin a group, are still often frozen by anxiety and feelings of inefficacy at the prospect of beginning their own group. When asked what it is they fear most when embarking upon their first group leadership endeavor, school counselors at workshops led by the authors usually respond with a variety of fears. They indicate that they fear the group will confront them with silence and that one or more members will breach the contract of confidentiality. In addition, they fear that the teachers who referred the group members will expect the leader to share confidential material with them. They are also concerned that they might perform the wrong intervention and actually cause harm to group members. Other fears include an inability to keep the group on task, that the group will become confrontational and challenge their authority and/or that they will lose control of the group. In short, like many of us, group leaders are often individuals who fear failing. These fears are very real and common among, not only novice group leaders, but more experienced counselors as well.

Getting started brings out feelings of anxiety and uncertainty. Knowledge, training and practice, however, will lessen the counselor's fear. As one gains a sense of self-efficacy in his or her group counseling ability, anxiety dissipates and the counselor feels more at ease in the situation.

# Pre-group Planning: Involving Teachers and Administrators

Before a school counselor actually begins the first group session, a great deal of reflection and planning should take place. Proper understanding of what needs to occur before the group ever begins includes necessary approvals (of parents, administration, and teachers), recruitment and *screening* of members, contact with teachers and administration, and scheduling appropriate times and comfortable facilities. In the authors' experiences, without proper attention to detailed planning before the group begins, leaders are likely to find themselves caught up in a variety of problems that may well hinder the progress of the group.

It is important to involve teachers in the group planning process (i.e., how many times, and when, will students be called out of class?) Some counselors have found it effective, at the middle or high school level to schedule the group during different class periods each meeting time so as not to have a student miss the same class time over and over again. Figure 10.1 reveals how one elementary school counselor effectively involves teachers in the planning process. Figure 10.2 is a proven method employed by a high school counselor for "signing up" students for small group counseling.

When planning a group counseling intervention, it is important to consider the needs and characteristics of the population which you wish to serve. One of the early leaders in group counseling who focused on this area was George Gazda. And, although his guidelines for effective small group work were published in the late 1980s, we believe his ideas and concepts are still relevant today. Gazda (1989) presented a compelling case for the counselor's consideration of the developmental level of children. He outlined developmental tasks, or stages, and suggests appropriate coping behaviors for various areas of human development. This provides a useful perspective for those planning a group for children or youth. For example, knowing the developmental level of a preadolescent (9 to 13 years old) means understanding that they form natural groups of the same sex. Therefore, in keeping with their developmental stage it is usually better to have single sex groups in this age range. This would contrast with adolescent groups where mixed sex groups could be more appropriate, depending on the theme (Gazda, 1989). Grade level placement is the public school's way to maintain developmental homogeneity.

Carroll and Wiggins (2000) suggested that it is best to form groups according to grade level when working in a school setting. The child's developmental level is also a useful guide to help determine maximum group size. Generally, younger children profit from a smaller group. Carroll and Wiggins reminded us that young children, immature adolescents, and those with special needs usually have a short attention span. Thus, they suggested that when working with very young children, the size of the group should be no more than three or four members. Older elementary, middle and high school students could function in larger groups. The optimal number would be about 6-8 students. School counselors must balance the optimal group setting and size with the number of students they need to serve.

Corey and Corey (2001) suggested developing a proposal as a part of the group planning. They recommend that this proposal include five major areas: (1) rationale, (2) objectives, (3) practical considerations such as meeting time and duration of the group, (4) procedures, and (5) evaluation. Marianne Schneider Corey, in writing about her experiences in doing group work in the public schools, recommended building trust with the teachers and administration as a first step. She suggested meeting with them to describe the group's rationale and objectives prior to the involvement of children or adolescents in the group (Corey & Corey, 2001).

In his school counseling days, the senior author found it helpful to consult with central administration staff, as well as teachers and principals, who then became supportive of a group program for potential school dropouts he co-developed. It was also found helpful to have support for the program already in place before the program began in order to head off any questions or confusion on the part of an uninformed administration or faculty. With such support in place, any questions or concerns can be diverted away from the program and toward the proper administrators who understand and support the group counseling effort.

In addition to the authors' personal experiences and our review of literature in the area of group counseling in schools, we have had the opportunity to lead and interact with panels of school counselors who were either conducting their own groups or wished to learn more about group work. The panelists concurred with the authors' personal observations and understanding of the literature concerning the importance of continued contact with teachers and administrators in order to forestall potential problems. From time to time throughout the remainder of this chapter, the authors refer to this panel as a useful source of information from those counselors currently in practice in K-12 school settings.

# Beginning a Group: Establishing the Climate, Norms, Goal-Setting, and Feedback

The way one begins a group sets in motion the tone and tenor and begins to establish the ground rules which last the duration of the sessions. Perhaps most counselors have a sense for the importance of the first few sessions of the group and this is one reason why they experience anxiety at the start. There are some activities, however, in which you can engage the group members, and there are behaviors you can model for your members, which will serve to set a positive and productive tone as your group gets going.

It is important to have in mind a fairly concrete outline of activity for the first meeting. This outline can always be modified at the leader's discretion, but having such an outline in place will lessen the leader's opening session jitters. The outline can be very simple and can include things like the introduction of the leader(s), norms, and special considerations and activities that you choose to use to break the ice. Since silence is one of the fears mentioned most often by beginning group leaders, it is very helpful to have a couple of activities or ice breakers that can be effectively used to help get the group talking. It is also important to remember that you, as the group leader, are not the only person in the room feeling a little anxious.

The members have many questions and concerns as the group commences: "Will I be accepted by the others?" They are also asking: "Am I on the inside or the outside?" "Am I going to have to talk about something that embarrasses me?" "What's an appropriate level of self-disclosure?" "Can others be trusted?" "How am I supposed to act in here?" "What are the group norms and rules?" These are all common concerns of students in the group setting. Therefore, a planned, structured opening activity will serve to bring reticent members into the group's social interaction from its inception and set the stage to begin to answer the students' concerns as well as reduce the counselor's "opening night" anxiety.

The first stage in group development is the *beginning* stage. One of the developmental tasks of this stage is for the members to get to know one another. One way to accomplish this task is to simply go around the group asking each member to say his or her first name and whatever else they want the group to know about them. You may, or may not, give the members some guidelines or suggestions as to what they might talk about at this time. You might say, "Tell us something about what brought you to this group"; or, "Make sure to include in your statement what you hope to get out of this group"; or, "What is your greatest fear as you enter this group"

*Joe Wittmer, Ph.D. and Mary Ann Clark, Ph.D.*

(Corey, et al., 2003). One counselor uses music as an icebreaker. She might play familiar tunes or ask the children their favorite music in order to begin to get them talking together. Another activity, which works well with younger members, is to have them describe an animal which they imagine they are like and tell why they are like this animal. As each member introduces him or herself they repeat the first name of the people before them (this may be too difficult for younger children) and say anything about any of them that has especially captured their attention. This little exercise facilitates introductions, begins the process of group interaction and encourages the members to participate in giving feedback to one another which is a strategy vital to group work. Another recommendation is to break the group up into dyads and have them carry on an activity similar to those mentioned above with just one other person. After time in the dyads each member introduces the other to the group. Though this activity is probably more suitable for older teens, the dyad exercise offers the members the security of one-to-one communication when they might not be quite ready to speak before the entire group. The authors find that people are much less reluctant to speak when speaking to just one other person. We also recommend that the leader(s) gets involved in the dyad introduction activity.

The major point of structuring the group is to create a safe environment for the members where they feel free to interact with others and reveal information about themselves. The focus then, is not so much on the counseling techniques, but on the goal of providing a safe place for members to explore themselves.

One useful generalization is that the younger the group member, the more *concrete* the opening activity needs to be. Gazda (1989) advocated heavy use of play and action oriented techniques for young (ages 5 to 9) children. One counselor who attended our workshop and works with very young children suggested using various materials such as paper, crayons, scissors, glue, and such, to help the children express their initial thoughts and feelings about being in a group.

Adolescents are very peer-conscious and self-conscious. Beginning a group with adolescents offers unique challenges and opportunities. They are experiencing life in the "here-and-now." Relationships appear very immediate. A crucial question for the adolescent is; "Am I accepted by the group, *today*?" Tomorrow may seem one hundred years away. One workshop participant with extensive experience with junior and senior high school level youth reported that she begins her groups by demystifying the process. "I make it very clear to them what I am going to do. When they know that what we do is not some mysterious ritual, they are more apt to participate."

Every group requires social interaction and whenever there is social interaction in a new situation it is very important to know the "rules of the game." Norms are the rules by which the group operates. Group norms provide structure; they help members feel secure and comfortable. Influencing and helping to set positive norms is an essential leader behavior. Norms are not always acknowledged—but they are always there. What is sanctioned in terms of language, attendance, confidentiality, degree of self-disclosure, punctuality, are all examples of norms. The most important benefit of these norms is their capacity to empower members to be able to share their life situations with others and to learn from the experience.

Group counselors need to be clear about the norms that have the greatest impact upon the success or failure of their group, and be sure to discuss these norms early on. With this in mind, it is important to remember that norms are an expression of the group, not any single member (including the leader). However, group counselors can and do have an important influence upon norm development. One useful way to involve the members with norm development is to list on newsprint or a blackboard "what works..." in the group, and "what doesn't work...." This usually brings up enough discussion to involve everyone in the decision making. The younger the child, the more concrete and structured the counselor needs to be. One school counselor indicated that she begins all groups with the following, positively stated, simple guidelines: (1) "We are here to listen to one another" (as opposed to; "You should not interrupt one another"); (2) "We will be sharing our ideas, thoughts, and feelings"; and (3) "We may pass a turn when we want."

Confidentiality is universally seen as an essential group norm. One counselor explored this norm with her group by asking the members if they had ever told a secret to another who, in turn, has reported that secret to those for whom it was not intended. Feelings around secret telling are explored and members begin to understand the impact of this norm; members begin to discuss the importance of confidentiality (**Note:** It must be remembered that there are certain situations where confidentiality legally must be broken. For example, when child abuse is reported most jurisdictions require that the counselor notify the proper authorities.) Any exceptions to the confidentiality rule *must* be discussed at the very beginning of the group. Some counselors have reported using contracts with students in order to impress upon members the seriousness of confidentiality. Others have stated that teachers, who often wish to be kept abreast of a child's progress, should have the importance of confidentiality explained to them before the group begins so that they understand when you, the counselor, cannot talk to them in specifics about any given student. It is also important to remember that when the group is over the group members will, most likely, continue to see one another in the class rooms and around the halls of the school. Therefore, it is important to be clear from the beginning that when the group ends, the *rule of confidentiality continues.* However, as one school counselor indicated, maintaining confidentiality in a group, especially with younger children, is difficult. Thus, among his group guidelines he always states: *"If you feel you must share with another person regarding something that happened in any of our group meetings, it must concern **only** something that happened to you within our group. That is, you should not share **anything** about any other person in this group."* This counselor feels this provides younger children a little leeway on the important notion of group confidentiality.

Group members also have the opportunity to learn important information about themselves through interpersonal feedback. In order to be most effective it is important for feedback to be linked to member's experiences. Leaders have an important role in facilitating member's recognition that the feedback that they have received is relevant to their individual goals, how they behave in the group, and what they say about their actions outside the group. This connection can be important to insight into themselves and their personal growth within and outside the group.

Along with the social process of getting started— learning the norms and asking, "How do I behave?" It is also very important for group members to talk about why they are there and what they would like to have happen. A very helpful way to do this is to have the members set goals for themselves. It is important for leaders to help members clarify their goals and make them concrete and realistic. Even though this is a difficult exercise for some, it is a very useful thing to work on. As members are helped to set goals, they are also establishing norms; as the leaders model appropriate behaviors they help the group process move along. Paraphrasing the member's goal and narrowing its focus is a helpful way for the leader to operationalize the member's desired change. If the group member's goal is rambling and not focused (this can be quite common) the leader should say something like, "What you say, Rachel, is very important; could you say it again using fewer words?"

Establishing group norms, discussing individual goals, and facilitating feedback sets the tone for a successful group.

# Moving Through Conflict and Transition to the Working Stage

It is important to realize that conflict is a very normal part of a small group experience. How conflict is dealt with will determine the degree to which the group can become a trusting working entity where members are free to examine their values and concerns. It must be remembered that conflict does not have to be like a violent storm. Conflict is often manifested as relatively mild interpersonal disagreements. One does not have to be in a fight in order to be in conflict. In psycho-educational groups, conflict is usually not dramatic. However, if a group is not experiencing at least some conflict at some level, the leader needs to examine why this might be. Is the leader too authoritarian to allow dissension? Are the members not trusting one another to the point that they can risk sharing emotions such as anger or grief? If feelings of disappointment or differences of opinion are not openly aired the leader would want to examine why this might be.

For any kind of group, the ability to resolve troubling issues is quite liberating. Once group members are able to work through their differences in a way that honors each person, they are more willing to take risks and become vulnerable. This leads to a greater degree of trust and creativity among members.

Leaders are especially able to help resolve *conflict* in two ways: 1) When a member is in conflict with him or her, the leader can model conflict resolution for the group by accepting the member's feelings in a non-defensive and non-judgmental manner; and 2) When two members are in conflict with each other, the leader can help the two process (and facilitates) their disagreement utilizing a structure that allows for safety as well as honest feedback; members will learn much from watching conflict being resolved. These appropriate leader behaviors model for the members a process for such resolution. This permits the members to risk greater involvement in the group and, therefore, enhances the potential for positive change. There are many facilitative techniques a leader can use which help the group move through conflict.

One helpful technique in working through *conflict* is the "go-around." The go-around is a very simple, yet important, group work skill. It can be used for a variety of purposes, but essentially it works to bring every member into some (if modest) level of participation. The leader simply asks the group to do a go-around by saying something like: "I'm wondering how the rest of the group is feeling about Bill not wanting to talk to Casey? Let's go around the group and each of us respond briefly to Bill." The group then proceeds, one at a time, to give Bill appropriate feedback. Go-arounds can consist of brief comments, one word responses, phrases that come to mind around significant words or conflicts, or some other concern that will stimulate a response or elicit feedback from members. The go-around both defuses and objectifies the conflict which frees members to gain a broader perspective.

Another example of good *conflict* resolution is making use of "I-messages." I-messages express the feelings of the speaker very personally and concretely, directing the message directly to the recipient. I-messages begin with "I" statements. For example, "I really feel hurt when I hear you say...." Stating an I-message is a non threatening way to confront another with how the speaker is feeling. It helps the speaker to take responsibility for the feelings and the statement as well as inform the person to whom the message is intended as to how they are being perceived. The counselor can not only model I-messages for his or her group members, but he or she can also instruct the members in this form of communication with relative ease. The basic formula for an I message is to state the other person's behavior and how it makes the speaker feel. For example, "When you missed the group meeting, I felt disappointed, and I wanted to find out if you were okay."

When conflicts are successfully resolved it is possible for the group to move into the *working* stage. The working stage of the group is more difficult to explain theoretically, than it is to see in practice. One of our panelists pointed out that she knows when her groups are working; it's when the group members are telling their friends that they ought to be in a group.

The *working* stage of the group is characterized by a greater proportion of member to member communication and less member to leader communication. Members become less defensive and begin to self-disclose at more frequent intervals and at deeper levels. There is also an increased frequency of more appropriate member to member feed back. Interactions have much more personal depth and a wide range of emotions is seen. Leaders can take a less active role, using more process statements and fewer norm-setting statements.

A particular useful leader intervention during the group's *working* stage is the use of *process illumination* statements. Using this approach, the leader clarifies the group dynamics which are occurring at that particular moment, or have previously occurred. Process statements are often made about observed behavior, or what takes place in the group as a result of this behavior. One example of process illumination is a statement which ties (links) together past and present behavior: The counselor says, "It seems that the group has been working very hard and has been very helpful to Mary today. Having worked through much of our conflict over the past two weeks has allowed us to be more helpful to one another." *Process illumination* statements can be made at any time in the group's development and can encompass any kind of group behavior but are especially helpful in moving the group along in the working stage.

## Termination

In our experience we have found that beginning group leaders need to spend more time than they had anticipated in planning for the beginning and ending of their group, and less time than they had anticipated in planning for the actual working stage. Just as with other parts of the group experience, it is important to give serious thought as to how you are going to end your group. It is important to help people make sense out of the experience, to take what they learned about themselves in the group and transfer that learning to the wider world. This is fine for all group members, but especially so for elementary aged children.

An important leader behavior is to remind the group throughout the meetings as to how much *longer* the group will continue. This reminder works to help keep the group on task and focused. This is particularly important with younger children. One of our panelists who works with very young children reminds the children every week of the number of sessions until conclusion. She has the children hold up their fingers, concretely illustrating the number of weeks left.

It is hard for people to say good-bye. This is as true for groups terminating as it is in our social sphere. It is important for the members of a group to recognize the reality of termination and process related thoughts and feelings. Members may well hesitate to say good-bye and get sidetracked by less significant interaction. Again, proper use of structure on the leader's part can help the group accomplish its task. One useful approach is to have the group do a go-around where the members voice their appreciation for what they have taken from the group experience and regrets about what they were not able to accomplish.

The single most important task in termination is to help the members *transfer* their newly acquired understandings, skills and behaviors to the world outside the group. The process of evaluating the group experience can include a group discussion, and thoughtful probing on the leader's part, as to how the members might use what they have learned from the group in a different setting.

When members have had the chance to sum up experiences in a personally meaningful way, mourn the loss of the group, consider how to implement their new skills and attitudes in a wider context, they will then have successfully experienced termination.

## Summary

In this chapter we have written about the importance of planning, making interventions appropriate to the developmental age of the group members, and the stages of development through which the group can progress. We have stressed the use of structure in organizing counseling and support groups. While these are all very important, it is critical not to be so set in your plans and notions about how to conduct the group that you lose sight of the desirability for flexibility and being able to respond to the needs of the moment.

For those wanting to know more, there are many resources available. We have referenced a number of authors and books in the field and, of course, there are many others. Publishers also have begun to develop helpful materials which stimulate group discussion and interpersonal learning, particularly at the lower grade levels. We have found that State Departments of Education and state professional counseling associations often collect and circulate helpful ideas for group leaders.

We cannot, in one short chapter, include more than an introduction to group counseling with students. Small group counseling is a major component of the ASCA National Model's (2005) responsive services to meet the needs and concerns of students. We hope that you have been stimulated to learn more about this process through further reading, course work, attending workshops, and supervised practice in leading groups. More importantly, we hope that, if you currently aren't, that you will incorporate group work in your school counseling program.

# Figure 11.1
# Involving Elementary Teachers in the Small Group Process

## Memorandum

**To:**     Third, Fourth, and Fifth Grade Teachers
**From:**   (Counselor's Name)
**Re:**     SMALL GROUP COUNSELING (5 or 6 weekly sessions)

I need your input so we can begin small group counseling. Below are listed some suggested timely topics for student groups which I feel we need to offer this Fall semester. You may have other topics in mind. *Please share them with me.* The purpose of each group, and some suggestions as to the type of student you may want to include are:

| TITLE | PURPOSE | POSSIBLE TYPES OF STUDENTS |
| --- | --- | --- |
| RETENTION | To encourage retained students to utilize their retention in a positive way and to help them feel success rather than failure. | Student who repeated a grade this year. |
| SELF-CONCEPT | Encourage a better understanding of each individual's strengths and weaknesses. | Insecure, unrealistically confident, low self-esteem. |
| COMMUNICATION | Strengthening listening and communication skills. | Inappropriately verbal, non-verbal. Inappropriate affect. |
| DIVORCE | To help students deal with family situations involving divorce, separations, etc. | Students having difficulty adjusting to divorce situations. |
| SELF-CONTROL | Developing responsibility and an understanding of one's own behavior. | Combustible, lacking in self-discipline. |

Please list any of your students who you think would benefit from being in one of the above listed groups. I will then talk to you and to each student before I begin any of the groups.

**Retention**          **Self-Concept**          **Communication**          **Divorce**          **Self-Control**

# Figure 11.2
# High School Group Sign Up Sheet

**(In packet outside the guidance office with sign indicating: "Take One")**

Dear Student:

If you would like to participate in a small group experience, please indicate by checking the line next to the topic in which you are interested; also check your second choice. Groups will meet weekly for six weeks.

Groups will begin in about two weeks. Please complete your class schedule so we know where to find you as one of us will talk to you individually prior to the beginning of the group meetings. Each group will be limited to six-eight individuals. If you have questions, please stop in the Guidance Office.

_____1. Healthy Living-eating habits, exercise, sleep

_____2. Getting Along with Others-Friendships and relationships

_____3. Staying on Task: Paying attention and enjoying it

_____4. Temper-Temper - how to be in control and not lose your cool

_____5. Career and life span planning - your future

_____6. Divorce - how to cope with your changing family

_____7. Managing Stress - staying cool during stressful times

_____8. Study Skills - how to become a better student

_____9. Peer Pressure - how to manage it

_____10. Interpersonal skills - becoming a better communicator

Student Name_____ Date_____

## Schedule

| Period | Subject | Room Number | Teacher |
|--------|---------|-------------|---------|
| 1. | _____ | _____ | _____ |
| 2. | _____ | _____ | _____ |
| 3. | _____ | _____ | _____ |
| 4. | _____ | _____ | _____ |
| 5. | _____ | _____ | _____ |
| 6. | _____ | _____ | _____ |
| 7. | _____ | _____ | _____ |
| Homeroom | _____ | _____ | _____ |

*Joe Wittmer, Ph.D. and Mary Ann Clark, Ph.D.*

# Figure 11.3
# Small Group Counseling Considerations for
# Professional School Counselors by Mary Ann Clark

I. Stages of Groups

    A. Beginning

    B. Transition

    C. Working

    D. Ending

II. Factors to Consider

    A. Purpose of the group: What is the theme?

    B. Motivation of the students

    C. Peer Relations

    D. Abilities and Interests; do the students have some important things in common?

III. Other Considerations

    A. Who should be in the group?

    B. Size? How many students for this particular group? (age, maturity, theme of the group are all important considerations)

    C. Meeting Time: (How much time should be allotted for each meeting and how many meetings should be held?)

    D. Starting and Ending: Student preparation

IV. Leader Responsibilities

    A. Using Facilitative Responses (reflecting feelings, summarizing, clarifying, asking open-ended questions, acknowledging, offering feedback, linking students' contributions)

    B. Group Activities: Choose those that can be related to the main point of the group.

    C. Processing Responses: Be sure to tie back themes of activities to the main theme of the group

V. More Organizational Issues…

    A. Open vs. Closed (can members join at any time or does the membership stay the same?)

    B. Voluntary vs. Involuntary

    C. Group Guidelines

    D. Accountability (examining results of group intervention)

# References

Association for Specialists in Group Work. (2000). *Professional standards for the training of group workers.* Alexandria, VA: Author

American School Counselor Association. (2002). *Position statement: The professional school counselor and group counseling.* Alexandria, VA: Author.

Carroll, M.R., & Wiggins, J.D. (2000). *Elements of group counseling* (3rd ed.). Denver, CO: Love Publishing.

Corey, M.S., & Corey, G. (2001). *Groups: Process and practice* (6th ed.). Pacific Grove, CA: Brooks/Cole.

Corey, G., Corey, M.S., Callahan, P., & Russell, J.M. (2003). *Group techniques* (3rd ed.). Pacific Grove, CA: Brooks/Cole.

Gazda, G.M. (1989). *Group counseling: A developmental approach* (3rd ed.). Newton, MA: Allyn and Bacon.

Greenberg, K.R. (2002). *Group counseling in k-12 schools: A handbook for school counselors.* Newton, MA: Allyn and Bacon.

Mahler, C.A. (1969). *Group counseling in the schools.* Boston: Houghton Mifflin.

Myrick, R.D. (2003). *Developmental guidance and counseling: A practical approach* (4th. ed). Minneapolis, MN: Educational Media Corporation.

Stone, C.B., & Dahir, C. A. (2006). *The transformed school counselor.* Boston, MA: Lahaska Press.

# Chapter 12

# Large Group Developmental Guidance

by
**Marjorie I. Cuthbert**

*Marjorie Cuthbert, Ph.D., NCC, served as Principal of Murch Elementary School in the District of Columbia Schools for the past five years. She is the former Supervisor of Guidance and School Support Services for the School Board of Alachua County in Gainesville, Florida.*

## Introduction

Large group developmental guidance, often referred to as developmental classroom guidance, is the systematic delivery of age-appropriate preventative guidance concepts and units to groups of students which usually contain more than 10 to 15 members. Counselors would differ on what they define as a large group; however, most would certainly agree that a classroom size (25 to 30 students) fits the description of large group guidance. As with the management of any classroom-size group around chosen curriculum or a specific program, selected techniques to enhance the delivery are used to help facilitate discussion, processing and learning (Wittmer & Thompson, 2006).

Large Group Developmental Guidance sessions provide unlimited opportunities for counselors to get to know significant numbers of students at any age or grade level. In addition, it permits the counselor to capitalize on the energy that the larger group naturally provides by the diversities of the backgrounds and experiences of the group members. Even though all students may not get a chance to present their own thoughts or feelings about a topic each session, they are exposed to a broad array of others' ideas. The large grouping allows those students who are really shy and have not yet developed the skills to speak out in the groups, to be exposed to their peers' perceptions on various topics. The large group format also allows those who choose not to participate to be in a group setting which, by its design, allows them to be a part of a peer grouping without the pressure of having to perform.

From leading the large group, the counselor learns quickly which students have difficulties managing their behavior in large group settings. These students can later be considered for inclusion in small groups or individual counseling to address specific behavioral needs where skills can be introduced and practiced. When the students have practiced chosen skills in the smaller group, the real test comes when they return to the large group setting. Often this test comes for the regular classroom teachers, but it is particularly effective if the counselor can monitor the targeted behaviors in the classroom when delivering large group guidance lessons.

Not only do large groupings of students for guidance units allow the counselors to know many students, this delivery system also allows counselors to be seen as "teachers of curriculum" in the perceptions of their colleagues. This will improve your image with those who are in the classrooms every day managing large groups of students. It helps dispel the misconception that some educators have, that counselors are teachers who no longer can, or want to manage large groups of students. It helps also dispel the misconceptions that counselors, particularly at the high school level, do mostly paperwork and do not interact much with the students. It helps counselors be seen as persons to whom others can go for suggestions on classroom management, especially when the counselor demonstrates effective techniques for classroom management during the large group guidance sessions. It is beneficial for classroom teachers to remain in the room when units are being delivered so they can do follow-up exercises; and it is an optimum time for the counselor to utilize skills and model techniques that work effectively with all kinds of student populations. Because of this exposure, it becomes a major responsibility of counselors to develop sound units which are age-appropriate and to know how to deliver them using large group behavioral skills. Counselors in these settings are powerful agents of change for both teachers and students.

# Effectiveness of Large Group Guidance Lessons

Large group classroom guidance units continue to be a major part of the delivery system of services as recommended by the American School Counselor Association (ASCA) National Model (2005). They are an efficient vehicle to use with students of all ages and use the "law of parsimony" (Myrick, 2003) in order to reach all students. Many studies involving different age levels and varied content have shown positive changes in outcome variables as evaluated by both students and teachers. There are many methods and instruments available to evaluate units. It is useful to write parallel statements to which both the teacher and students respond so comparisons to each other can be made, as well as outcome measures rated.

For example, a study involving fourth-grade students indicated that there were positive changes and significant differences in school attitude for both low and high students after their participation in six classroom guidance units (Myrick, 2003). Cuthbert (1987) concluded that developmental guidance units designed for counselors to teach school success skills to third graders, using modeling and coaching techniques, can influence student attitudes about school situations. There is thus substantial support in the literature to show that developmental guidance units delivered to large groups of students are effective in teaching students ideas and skills (Wittmer, Thompson, & Loesch, 1997).

Many different topics can be delivered to large groups. School counselors at all levels create units to meet objectives which often include ideas of understanding one's self and others, getting along with peers, dealing with peer pressure, accepting limitations, capitalizing on strengths, recognizing differences, using conflict resolution techniques, learning communication and interpersonal skills, exploring careers, etc. Any of the topics could be easily put into systematic units for delivery, keeping in mind the age to which they would be delivered so that appropriate developmental concepts can be included and age appropriate activities chosen.

Counselors, in addition to creating units around general topics mentioned above, teach units to any or all levels on subjects which include:

- Emotional, physical, and sexual abuse
- Safety from strangers
- Assertive skills
- Conflict resolution skills
- School success skills
- Drug education awareness
- Human growth and development (puberty/changes)
- Career planning
- Grade level transitions
- Grief issues
- Crisis management techniques
- Choosing colleges and financial aid
- Sexual harassment
- Sexually transmitted diseases/AIDS
- Awareness of physical disabilities
- Multicultural Awareness

Once you establish a workable format for a guidance unit that feels comfortable for you, you can create a viable set of lessons around any topic area. For example, teachers might request that the counselor come in for several sessions and work with the students on name-calling, or handling student-to-student "put-downs." Even though the counselors might not have sessions and activities readily available on the exact topic being requested, they can develop specific objectives and fulfill them through activities adapted from any other units.

Counselors at all levels are often asked to create units around very serious issues. For example, in times of crisis such as the terrorist attacks of September 11, 2001, the devastation of life and property from hurricanes in the Gulf Coast and in Florida, and a number of school shootings, many school counselors in large group guidance sessions gave information, processed feelings, and responded to needs of students who were affected both directly and indirectly. They were able to reach large numbers of students. Certainly, some students needed more personalized attention when they were adversely affected personally, and were seen individually for further processing. The death of a teacher or classmate often affects the entire school. The counselor goes in perhaps only once to help students gain correct information and begin processing the tragedy, but may end up designing units for subsequent sessions as a tragedy often elicits other fears of death, separation, or world catastrophes.

High school counselors meet success with large group guidance units dealing with registration procedures and issues that arise when students are transitioning from grade level to grade level. The middle school counselors also deliver large group guidance lessons to their eighth graders as they move from middle school to high school. They address some specific procedures, but also attend to all the social, emotional and academic changes that accompany these level changes. Addressing similar developmental changes and concerns, developmentally oriented elementary counselors deliver large group units to fifth graders as part of the orientation process for middle school.

High school counselors also meet with large groups of students to discuss results from interest surveys and career counseling instruments. They group college bound students to counsel with them about writing resumes and application essays, and to make them aware of general ways to look at colleges to meet personal needs and financial realities.

Middle school counselors help large groups work on career plans that cut across all the high school years which might include college, vocational opportunities, or general areas of study. Along this same topic, elementary counselors deliver units on career awareness which serve as the starting points for the other levels to build upon. As can be observed from the flow of an effective K-12 career education program, counselors often deal with the same topic at different levels and adjust the information given and its processing to the developmental level of the students. They build upon the work done by counselors at earlier levels.

Elementary guidance counselors deliver classroom guidance lessons on most of the topics listed above. Most local, district, or county guidance programs list goals and objectives for the different grade levels. Elementary counselors can best realize these objectives through 20 to 30 minute sessions in individual classroom settings, usually conducted once or twice a week for a total of four to six sessions depending on the content of the unit being delivered.

# Designing a Large Group Developmental Guidance Unit

By now it should appear clear to you that any topic or subject can become the theme of large group guidance sessions and be effectively delivered to students. However, such units must be developed appropriately and delivered through activities which reflect developmental levels. Creating sessions that comprise a large group developmental guidance unit with developmental levels in mind is not always an easy task.

There are some excellent resources available from educational companies for counselors to use on many specific large group topic areas. Often times these materials contain activities which can be utilized to comprise a systematic series of lessons to make a unit. These materials can frequently be used just as they come from the companies. However, there are times when counselors want to design their own units to reflect timely local topics or to realize their goals differently from the way someone else has marketed the activities. Activities from commercial units can often be incorporated into individually designed units. A workable format helps organize materials and sharpen the focus. A well designed developmental guidance unit is one that has an identified *purpose; age-appropriate activities for students to experience; coordination over sessions* (usually 4 to 10, depending on the topic and available time); *a processing component;* and *closure* or *summary*.

Myrick (2003), in the Florida Classroom Guidance Project, presented a logical workable format that consisted of six thirty-minute sessions, each of which was divided into four sections of Introduction, Activity I, Activity II, and Closure. Vernon (1989) utilized a user friendly approach in designing the individual sessions in her K-12 emotional education curriculum based on Rational-Emotive Therapy. Each session lists an *Objective, Materials, Procedure,* and *Discussion.* Since the sessions are designed for others to use, another section, *"To the Leader,"* was also included. This would be helpful for all counselors to include when creating large group units, since so many effective units are passed between counselors informally within systems or at conventions.

I have found several different formats helpful in organizing material. The first begins with the stated Purpose of the session, followed by the *Introduction, Activity One, Activity Two, Processing, Summary,* and for certain topics, an *Assignment* due by the next session. Along the same basic progression, a somewhat simpler format, which includes the *Goal; Objectives; Activity and Processing;* and *Closure* is very logical and useful in designing developmental guidance units.

Perhaps it would help you most at this point to show briefly how an original unit is developed from an idea into a systematic set of activities which comprise a large group developmental guidance unit. Keep in mind that effective units can, and should, also be evaluated. In this day and age of tight budgets and emphasis on accountability, it becomes imperative that counselors be able to show that their units are making positive changes for the students who participate in them. There are many ways to evaluate the units (e.g., a decrease in behavioral referrals, increased participation in classroom discussions, changes in self-perception ratings and/or teacher ratings from pre and post administrations of instruments, etc.). The particulars of evaluation and specifics of research designs are beyond the scope of this chapter, but counselors need to be aware of sound research practices. There are excellent books available for further study on research procedures. Many straightforward methods are available and easily implemented even in busy, day-to-day counselor schedules.

For the purpose of example, I will present here the idea of building positive self-concepts or raising self-esteem for the theme of a developmental guidance unit. There are many references available that support the importance of students perceiving themselves positively for success in school and life, and many that show those who have low self-esteem to be achieving less and more likely to drop out of school. I like to find studies and ideas from other sources to add strength and support to the unit being created. It is important to keep in mind that counselors should assist students in discovering their strengths so that positive self esteem has a concrete basis.

A major emphasis of this unit became the use of activities which could foster the growth and identification of self-accomplishments. Additionally, the unit was developed in order to aid students in developing a belief system based on self-accomplishment and realistic self-assessment so that resulting beliefs could have corresponding values which were positive. This goal was then implemented through chosen activities. The activities were chosen so that each could be adapted for any level (K-12) based on the stated goals.

A second goal was incorporated into the unit to assist students in understanding, communicating, and appropriately responding to their own feelings; and, in understanding the feelings of others. Learning how to express feelings about one's self is a growth-producing experience which can raise self-perception. This goal then could be made operational through objectives that state what students will experience. These could include the following objectives: (1) Students will increase their awareness of personal feelings, (2) Students will develop a vocabulary to describe their feelings, (3) Students will become aware of how feelings can impact on behaviors, and (4) Students will learn appropriate ways of responding to personal feelings. All goals included could be similarly supported by statements or research findings from other professionals. All the objectives presented could be developed into sessions which include activities and comprise a unit for any age level.

To illustrate the process of writing a complete developmental guidance unit which moves from choosing a theme and documenting supporting findings (as illustrated above), to making goal statements which become operational through objectives, identifying the grade level to which it will be given, choosing age-appropriate activities to be included, and finally compiling all information into a usable format. The following unit is included (see Figure 12.1) as a completed model for your use. I chose to call the unit *"Each of Us is Special"* and designed it for delivery in the second grade. Remember, by changing the activities and method of processing, the unit could be adapted for any grade level.

As mentioned before, the effectiveness of any large group unit needs to be measured for outcome effectiveness. This unit was evaluated by students' self-perception on a pictorial rating scale which was given to them prior to experiencing the unit and again following the sixth (final) session. The results revealed that the guidance unit was effective in changing at least some aspects of children's ratings regarding several aspects of school and self.

The development of the large group unit was presented to illustrate how any developmental unit can be created to meet the needs of students, and modified if results of evaluation show that it is not making a positive difference for students. Once the unit is developed, the delivery becomes the next important stage.

# Implementing the
# Developmental Guidance Unit

When and how to deliver developmental guidance units is an important topic. Many counselors work closely with a guidance committee in their schools to plan out a yearly calendar which includes time for the counselors to work with large groups of students. In crowded curricula, it is very important for counselors to be included in master planning, so that time to work with students is given with everyone's knowledge of how guidance services enhance the school environment for students. Elementary counselors plan with the guidance committee or grade level chairpersons to schedule blocks of time which allow for delivery of classroom guidance units of about 30 minutes for six sessions in every classroom. Of course, with counselor to pupil ratios often exceeding 1:600, it becomes difficult to meet this standard and sessions are cut down in number, or several classes are grouped together for a very large group delivery. This latter method works well for some topics, but can become impersonal if used too much for topics that demand more individualized discussions.

Middle and high school counselors often arrange to deliver career planning or college planning guidance units during chosen classes (e.g., all English classes or all math classes). When they are able to do this, they know they have reached the majority of their students. Many middle and high schools have designated a block of time at the beginning of each day where teachers give out necessary information about scheduling and planning. They also help deliver chosen guidance objectives which are consistent with the goals and objectives of the developmental plan. These blocks of time where teachers are delivering guidance components are often referred to as Teacher Advisor Programs particularly at the middle school level. Guidance counselors often assist classroom teachers with information for these units and suggest ways to process with students. The counselors often rotate through these designated times to discuss timely topics that are part of the guidance and counseling curriculum. Such topics may change as priorities in schools and districts change. Using school wide data available from school advisory committees can help provide the impetus and support for large group work in schools.

It is crucial that all counselors work closely with their faculties to plan times when they can deliver their large group guidance units. Meet with teachers and find out timely issues they feel would be important to include in units. Knowing how to build a strong unit and creating it is exciting, but its actual delivery is the key to knowing how it really affects students. In crowded and limited daily schedules, it is imperative that counselors and their large group guidance units be seen as part of the total curriculum so that they (counselors) do not have to constantly fight for time. That is, your large group units are scheduled at the outset because of the recognized *importance* of what you do with and for students.

# Delivering the Large Group Guidance Unit

Actually, teaching the guidance lesson is an exciting and rewarding experience. It is so important to be enthusiastic about being there in the classroom and excited about what you have to teach, since you see the students in this setting perhaps only 4 to 6 times for unit delivery, or much less if presenting on a timely topic. Each lesson can begin with charged energy if you are there on time, have planned ahead and have your content well prepared.

Successful teachers are knowledgeable about their subject matter, understand it in depth, and are also able to deliver the ideas to students in ways that they can understand it, experience it, and process it. By the same token, successful, effective school counselors create theoretically sound large group guidance units with exciting age-appropriate activities and present them in ways that the students can understand and benefit from them. Knowledge of subject matter and effective planning cannot be over emphasized. Counselors at all levels need to be aware of large group dynamics and become excellent behavioral managers when they are delivering units. Counselors are often working with established groups or intact classrooms where teachers have already created certain learning climates. Teachers also have evaluative power over students which can help with classroom management. Counselors come into these existing environments and must adapt to them, but also must make them workable situations for their own curriculum delivery. Because counselors do not have to evaluate students when working in the classrooms, students may respond more freely. However, students may also realize that they can act out more since the counselor does not contribute to the grades given. This is why the counselor needs to be aware of large group dynamics and aware of behavioral techniques that are effective in working with large groups.

Over the years, I have been asked to help beginning counselors prepare for delivery of classroom guidance units and to help teachers know better how to manage large groups. From these requests, *"Cuthbert Cues"* evolved. It is a series of "c" words that help me remember different parameters to consider when ensuring all has been attended to in order to assure optimum success. The word "cues" is used as a signal to me or to the user to make certain all bases are covered when working with large groups of students or adults. The *"Cuthbert Cues"* include the following dimensions of large group management: (a) *Cohesion,* (b) *Cooperation* (c) *Communication,* (d) *Coaching,* (e) *Contribution,* (f) *Control,* (g) *Configuration,* (h) *Closure,* and depending on the topic being discussed, (i) *Confidentiality.* Let us look briefly at each category to trigger more thinking about how you might want to make yourself aware of all the parameters and dynamics that go into an effective large group guidance unit.

**Cohesion** can be built in any group, one that is already in existence or a new one you may be forming. Begin to establish it quickly by saying, *"We work together"* and *"We will plan how we will use our time,"* and so forth. Use go-arounds in early sessions, where everyone in the group will get to share something about himself or herself, even though it is a large group. Obviously, this cannot be done every time by everyone, because of time constraints. When you know you will be coming back to this particular classroom for more sessions, have a symbol to leave with the group that you can add onto each week (e.g., the school mascot cut out and laminated works well to post in each room so that a sticky dot can be added to it each week upon the successful completion of a guidance session). Brightly colored folders seem to work well for older students or adults. This reminds them that those who have these folders are all working on the same project. This helps to build group cohesion.

**Cooperation** is explained and modeled by the counselor in groups. You teach group skills to the group about taking turns; listening to others as they will be asked to listen to you; respecting risk-taking and knowing that you will not be laughed at by anyone; and learning skills for how to disagree, agreeably. These skills can be practiced and learned, if part of your large group guidance lesson includes a time when the group is divided into smaller groups. When the smaller groups are brought back to one large group, you can process how things went in terms of both the groupings and how well cooperation was achieved in both.

**Communication** is the key element to success for counselors and teachers. Choose a system of communication and practice the suggested skills so that delivering content and eliciting feelings from large groups becomes natural and very rewarding. Myrick (2003) and Wittmer, Thompson, & Sheperis (1999) suggested a continuum of skills that moves from least facilitative responses to those most successful in keeping good communication flowing. They would suggest using open-ended questions, clarification techniques, and responding with feeling-focused statements which let those to whom you are responding know that you have heard, not only the content of their words, but also have picked up on the underlying feelings. Other techniques suggested by Myrick (2003) are also very useful in maintaining communication flow in large groups. The *"simple acknowledgment"* statement guides you to say "Thanks" to a group member for giving out ideas by actually saying the word "Thanks" or something like, "Okay, that's a unique idea" or, "Thanks for sharing that," and then moving on to the next member. Counselors effective as large group leaders will also *"pair"* ideas and link them with other members' ideas. This communication skill contributes heavily to group cohesion.

**Coaching** is a technique for instilling new behavior by direct instruction and practice with shaping by observers. The group leader or group members help other students by encouraging them to "try out" the presented skills and reinforcing their performance. Large groups work well when counselors teach students that no one fails in the group because all other members "coach" each other for success. Students also learn how to give facilitative, helpful feedback to each other which makes participation valuable to members.

**Contribution** refers to everyone in the group feeling that they have valuable opinions, ideas or something to give the class. Everyone likes to feel that their presence in the lesson is important. You may need to teach volunteering skills to those who are not able to raise their hands, take risks about sharing ideas, and so forth. They may need some added work on deep breathing techniques, positive self-talk, to name a few. Invite students to help with handing out papers, choosing whether to write on the board or newsprint, or any kind of managerial skills that you as the counselor do not need to own.

**Control** refers to your leadership style in large groups. Are you autocratic, facilitative, permissive? Know yourself and what you can tolerate and what is acceptable to you in terms of the behaviors of the group members. When counselors go into all the different classrooms in their schools, they see all the extremes of leadership styles. It is very important for you to know what works for you and quickly let the group know your style, since they will be already have been members in the teachers' systems. Control has to do with not only leadership style, but with classroom techniques such as pacing, varying formats of activities, and being sensitive to ever changing individual behaviors and group behaviors. This permits control techniques to be applied which match the presenting situations. Counselors who present some ideas didactically and then have students role-play, break into smaller discussions, or demonstrate ideas with other students as models, etc. find that these varied activities help control the group and often alleviates the need for disciplinary procedures.

**Configuration** has to do with room arrangement. Many times because of time constraints of multiple groups using classrooms in the middle and high schools, or elementary teachers not wanting their own room design varied too much, counselors are asked to work in rooms where the placement of the students' desks, and so forth, may not be conducive to the most effective delivery of the guidance unit. Planning ahead with classroom teachers can sometimes help remedy the situation. Since the time the counselor is in the room is so limited, teachers ask their students to put the room into the configuration the counselor has requested just before the scheduled time for delivery of the unit. This is ideal as lesson time does not have to be devoted to moving desks, charts, and so forth. Time to put the room back for the classroom teacher should be built into each lesson so that the courtesy is reciprocated. There are many excellent books available on room configuration with attention given to placements for hard to manage students and how your configuration enhances learning. How the room is set up and where you place yourself as the group's leader is important to consider as you get ready to deliver large group guidance units (Wittmer, Thompson, & Loesch, 1997).

**Closure** means giving a summary of what you have learned within the lesson. This is particularly important in that counselors may not see the same group until the following week or even longer. The closure from a previous lesson serves as review in the next session and helps bring continuity to lessons that are often separated by long periods of time. In the closure section you give the summary and outline plans for next time. This helps insure that the students participating in the large groups look forward to your next lesson.

**Confidentiality** or keeping ideas contained within the group most often comes up in small groups. However, it helps the counselor in large group settings to be aware of the concept and the possibility that the issue might need to be discussed. When counselors create caring, comfortable atmospheres, and discuss issues that conjure up personal experiences, anything can happen in large groups. Students begin to self-disclose very personal perceptions and counselors must attend to the protection of students by addressing confidentiality issues with the other students. In peer counseling classes in the high schools and peer training classes in the middle schools, confidentiality issues are dealt with in large group sessions.

As you can observe from the above, working with students in large group guidance lessons demands a lot of thought about many concepts, and much energy goes into actual delivery of the units. Managing large group guidance involves not only attending to the content of the units but to the classroom dynamics which are there and ever-changing. Using effective managerial skills when working with large groups adds to the success of such units. There is nothing more exciting than presenting a good classroom guidance unit to students who feel the cohesiveness of the group, cooperate with each other, communicate freely as they coach each other, contribute without fear of being ostracized or repeated, and who are in working configurations where control is shared between leader and group. It is an exhilarating experience that is beneficial to the counselor, to many students and can be an excellent learning experience for the participating teacher as well.

## Summary

In summary, delivering large group developmental guidance is an important dimension of counselors' roles. This format allows counselors to interact with many students and to impact on their development in a preventative way. They can reach large groups of students with developmental issues or timely topics that need addressing. They can create units to meet specific needs of their populations. Large group guidance is one aspect of the total curriculum which helps counselors know many students. In working with them in large groups, counselors are often able to identify students who might need more individualized attention, either through the small group format or through one-on-one counseling. Presenting large group guidance units also allows counselors to serve as role models for teachers and other professionals who see them managing large groups of students with successful classroom techniques and behavioral interventions. This role strengthens the consultative aspect of the counselor's role, as teachers feel that the counselor is in touch with how to manage students with varying presenting behaviors and will seek consultation for strategies that will assist them in becoming more effective in their own teaching. In tight budget times, delivering developmental guidance units is also an efficient and effective way for students to receive direct services from their counselors and at the same time experience success while participating in a group of their peers. The ASCA National Model (2005) emphasizes the provision of services for all students, and large group work is the primary means by which to reach that goal.

# Figure 12.1
# Each of Us is Special:
# A Large Group Classroom Guidance Unit for Second Graders

## Session I
## We are Alike and Different

**Goal:**

To assist students in developing positive and realistic self-concepts.

**Objectives:**

1. Students will increase their understanding of the ways in which people are similar and different.

2. Students will become aware of personal strengths and limitations.

**Activity and Processing:**

Begin the session by having the students describe "Glenna Springs," the school doll. Have the students compare her to the counselor (likes and differences). Lead the group in generating ways in which people are alike and different by having a student volunteer to come up and stand with counselor for comparison. The list might reflect the following ways that people are alike or different in their (1) thinking, (2) feelings, (3) actions, (4) physical appearance, (5) family size, and (6) choice of sports, and so forth.

Discuss the fun of having differences and likenesses and the importance of respecting these uniqueness in each other.

**Closure:**

Summarize how people are alike and different. Tell how the class will make a *"This is Me"* poster in the next session.

## Session II
## The Real Me

**Goal:**

To assist students in developing positive and realistic self-concepts.

**Objectives:**

1. Students will increase their understanding of how being different is valuable.

2. Students will gain an appreciation for the unique qualities of each individual.

**Activity and Processing:**

Review ways people are alike and different (skills, bodies, ideas, etc.). Make a *"This is Me"* poster where the students will draw or list five positive unique things about themselves.

Each individual student will be asked to share one special thing about himself or herself. The counselor will encourage each, but students may pass if they cannot share. They will be reinforced for listening nicely to others so that all may have a positive experience.

**Closure:**

Summarize the session by restating that each of us is unique and important to school, home, and society.

# Session III
# My Feeling—Your Feelings

### Goal:

To assist students in understanding, communicating and appropriately responding to their own feelings and to understand and appropriately respond to the feelings of others.

### Objectives:

1. Students will increase their awareness of personal feelings.

2. Students will develop vocabulary to describe their feelings.

3. Students will become aware of how feelings can impact on behaviors.

### Activity and Processing:

Categorize feelings into *pleasant* and *unpleasant*. Generate a list on the board of feelings words. Demonstrate how feelings are affected by words, tones of voice, body language, and facial expressions. As time permits have the students share times that they felt certain ways.

### Closure:

Summarize about listening to see if someone's feelings are *pleasant* or *unpleasant*. Highlight the fact that we are all special and can feel all the ways that were listed.

# Session IV
# Dial-up a Feeling

### Goal:

To assist students in understanding, communicating and appropriately responding to their own feelings and to understand and appropriately respond to the feelings of others.

### Objectives:

1. Students will increase their awareness of personal feelings.

2. Students will learn appropriate ways of responding to personal feelings of others.

### Activity and Processing:

Review the feelings categories and list at least six *pleasant* and *unpleasant* feelings the board. Make feelings wheels. Have students choose three *pleasant* feelings and three *unpleasant* ways that they sometimes feel so that they can print these words on their wheels. Have them put their wheels together. With time permitting have volunteers dial-up a feeling on their wheels and share them with the class (self-disclosure).

### Closure:

We all have unique feelings. We can feel different from others but also understand and respect how they might feel because each of us is unique and special.

# Session V
# The Proud Clubs

## Goal:

To assist students in understanding personal values, attitudes, beliefs, and rights in understanding, recognizing and respecting these in others.

### Objectives:

1. Students will gain awareness of personal attitudes, values, and beliefs.

2. Students will become aware of similarities and differences in attitudes, values, and beliefs of self and others.

### Activity and Processing:

Use the *"Proud Whip"* activity (Canfield & Wells, 1995) for value clarification. The counselor "whips" around the room calling upon students in order. Students respond with 1) I am proud of , or 2) I'm proud that. The following questions could be used to begin the "whip": 1) What are you proud of that has to do with you in school?, 2) What are you proud of in relation to your family? and 3) What are you proud of about yourself?

The counselor records all who are able to share in the different categories by making a tally on the board. As each is tallied the students are told that they have joined the School Club, the Family Club, or the Self Club. The momentum is kept going by whipping around and asking who else would like to join one of the clubs.

### Closure:

Reiterate that we are all alike, yet uniquely different. We all have our own looks, feelings, and beliefs. We all learn to respect each other for our special qualities.

# Session VI
# Giving and Receiving

## Goal:

To assist students in developing positive and realistic self-concepts.

### Objectives:

1. Students will experience the "cool seat" or positive strength bombardment.

2. Students will experience giving and receiving positive statements to classmates.

### Activity and Processing:

Review how we learned that people are alike and different and unique in the ways they look, act, and feel inside. People have their own beliefs and values too. Today we will tell each other the things we admire in each other. (Only positive statements are allowed). Verbal praise is given to the sender of the message and to the receiver of the feedback.

### Closure:

Each of us is very special. We have all heard others tell us special things about ourselves today. We have also told others the things about them that make them special too. Let's remember to respect the special things about our classmates and about all others that we come into contact with in our activities at school and at home. (An award is given to every student at the conclusion of the session).

# References

American School Counselor Association. (2005). *The ASCA national model: A Framework for school counseling programs.* Alexandria, VA: Author.

Canfield, J., & Wells, H. (1995). *100 Ways to enhance self-esteem in the classroom.* Englewood Cliffs, NJ: Prentice-Hall.

Cuthbert, M.I. (1987). *Developmental guidance for school success skills: A comparison of modeling and coaching.* Unpublished doctoral dissertation, University of Florida, Gainesville.

Myrick, R.D. (2003). *Developmental guidance and counseling: A practical approach* (4th ed.). Minneapolis, MN: Educational Media Corporation.

Wittmer, J., & Thompson, D. (2006). *Large group counseling: A k-12 sourcebook* (2nd ed.). Minneapolis, MN: Educational Media Corporation.

Wittmer, J., Thompson, D., & Loesch, L. (1997). *Classroom guidance activities: A sourcebook for elementary school counselors.* Minneapolis, MN: Educational Media Corporation.

Wittmer, J., Thompson, D., & Sheperis, C. (1999). *The peace train: A school-wide violence prevention program.* Minneapolis, MN: Educational Media Corporation.

# Section IV

# The Counselor and Special Student Populations: The Culturally Different, Victims of Abuse, Gay and Lesbian, and Those with Special Needs

Section III concluded with a chapter which dealt with the "how-to" of large group guidance. Section IV begins with an excellent example incorporating the large group approach in teaching K-12 students about an important but often neglected concept—the valuing of cultural diversity, and specifically language. In Chapter 13, Drs. Emiliano Gonzalez and Marie Faubert present a structured model for teaching students to value cultural diversity and an appreciation of language difference via large group, classroom activities at the elementary, middle, and high school levels, respectively. They present developmentally appropriate, creative strategies for delivering large group guidance activities. The three, six-week long, large group guidance units presented by Gonzalez and Faubert, were written with the school counselor as coordinator/director of the activities and the classroom teacher as co-facilitator.

In Chapter 14, Dr. JoAnna White and Ms. Mary Flynt focus on K-12 counselors and their important work with student victims of abuse. As a school counselor, it is important to remember that each student you counsel may be the ongoing victim of abuse, or may be carrying the secret of abuse alone. Contemporary school counselors are currently grappling with the difficult issues abuse raises with their students. White and Flynt present several excellent workable strategies and programs for school counselors struggling with the tragedy of student victimization.

Next, Ms. Gail Adorno writes (Chapter 15) concerning counseling with students who are "victims" of a different kind—gay, lesbian, bisexual and transgender youth. These youth are the least "visible" of any minority group in the school and often need the assistance of a skilled counselor. Major issues relating to sexual orientation as well as strategies for working with these youth are provided by Adorno. Chapter 16, by Drs. Carlos Hernandez and Jennifer Sager, complements Adorno's chapter very well as they write about creating a safe environment for sexual minority youth. Times are changing and federal legislation and school board policies aim to protect students from harassment based on sexual orientation.

Federal and state legislation have changed the role of the school counselor where "exceptional" students are concerned. Dr. Beverly Snyder, in Chapter 17, posits that developmentally-oriented school counselors hold the keys which assure that special needs students in their schools will achieve and succeed. She writes: *Counselors, being child development specialists, play pivotal roles in their work with special needs students. No other educator is better equipped to assist the exceptional students, their families, or their teachers to reach greater understanding of the nature of being a special needs student. It is through using the skills of both counseling and consulting that counselors reach out to all who work with this unique population.* She provides many excellent strategies, program ideas, and tips that "work" with special needs students.

*Mary Ann Clark and Joe Wittmer*

# Chapter 13

# The Counselor's Role in Teaching Students to Value Cultural Diversity

**by**
**Emiliano Gonzalez and Marie Faubert**

*Emiliano Gonzalez, Ph.D. is Associate Professor in the School of Education at the University of Saint Thomas (UST) in Houston, Texas. He is an authority on language and language acquisition and collaborates with Sister Marie Faubert fostering appreciation for the place that language diversity and language acquisition have in effective counseling. His scholarly presentations and publications focus on multicultural populations, culture, diversity, and language related issues.*

*Marie Faubert, CSJ, Ed.D. is Professor and Director of the Counselor Education Program at UST in Houston, Texas. She teaches on-line courses, which provide the opportunity for her United States students to interact with students from the Middle East. Sister Faubert collaborates with Dr. Gonzalez fostering appreciation for the place that language diversity and language acquisition have in effective counseling. Her scholarly presentations and publications focus on the preparation of culturally competent professional counselors.*

## Introduction

The Latin-American population in Texas has reached 7.3 million, approximately 51% of the population (U.S. Census Bureau, September 8, 2004). This figure is indicative of the changing demographics taking place in the U.S. (U.S. Census Bureau, 2000). Schools as well as colleges and universities are showing an increase in the diversity of their students, reflecting a changing American culture in which a homogeneous majority is becoming less dominant (Saveri & Falcon, 2000). For example, since the 1990 U.S. Census, the Latin American population has increased more than 50% (U.S. Census Bureau, 2000). By 2050, this population is projected to reach 102.6 million, representing 24% of the total population, not counting Puerto Rico (U.S. Census Bureau, September 8, 2004). Other groups, such as African Americans and Asian Americans, are also growing rapidly in population. Our university, the University of Saint Thomas (UST), a liberal arts Catholic university, shows similar trends.

During the 2004 fall semester, there were 41 nations represented among UST's international students with the most coming from China, Columbia, Mexico, Taiwan, and Venezuela. Less than one-half the population of UST student body was white (46.8%); 32.8% were Latin Americans; 13.6% were Asian Americans, and 6.0% were African Americans. Other cultural groups represented less than 10% of the student body (Hester, C., Bychowski, S. R., Bosché, C. M., & Emmite, L. (2005).

In addition to cultural diversity, there is a great diversity of belief systems in the 2004 fall student body at UST: Buddhist 2.5%, Catholic Christian 66.7%, Jewish 0.7%, Muslim 2.3%, and Protestant Christian 23.6%. Other belief systems each represent less than one-half of one percent of the student population (Hester, C., Bychowski, S. R., Bosché, C. M., & Emmite, L. (2005).

Similar population trends are occurring around the country. Wherever professional school counselors find themselves working, they have the opportunity to participate in the development of educational systems, which will prepare students for a global village that includes instantaneous communication among very different points of view.

Additionally, a topic salient among professional counselors, is that of language diversity. The U.S. is becoming more multilingual than ever. There is a tension between U.S. citizens who are monolingual English-speaking, and U.S. citizens and immigrants who are bilingual or multilingual. At a time when global communication, mutual understanding, and national security are essential for survival, it is incumbent upon educators to foster bilingualism and multilingualism.

School counselors have an opportunity to nurture the speaking of more than one language and value the students and their families who are bilingual in their educational endeavors. Parents, other family members, and caregivers who are immigrants provide a wealth of information about their language and the culture that it represents. These stakeholders are valuable resources to enhance students' learning because they can contribute to providing a school culture where cultural and linguistic diversity is not only respected but valued. Additionally, when such diversity is valued, family members feel more welcome in the school environment and are more likely to participate and collaborate in their children's education.

Language is more than words. With language a person experiences the spiritual, affective and cognitive aspects of life. For students who are not first-language-English speaking, professional school counselors have the opportunity to infuse an appreciation of language difference into comprehensive, developmental curricula. Language is the expression of self that transmits who one is ethnically, culturally, spiritually, emotionally, intellectually, socially, and all the other possible variables, immutable and changeable, that make students part of their respective cultures. Language is the vessel of that given culture. Language transmits culture.

Language (L1) represents the culture (C1) of students by the way they act in accordance with their own culture as well as to other cultures and languages (L2C2). When students are bicultural/bilingual, a combination of L1C1 and L2C2, they negotiate how to act in the host culture/language. Such students first observe and assimilate the new culture/language and its influences. That language is an expression of culture is complex and confusing for some monolingual, U.S. English-speaking counselors and teachers. Although counselors cannot be fluent in every student's language, they can respect and value every student who comes speaking a first language other than U.S. English, and can role model that appreciation for other educators.

Instantaneous communication, mutual respect and understanding, and knowledge of points of view otherwise unfamiliar can become more nearly familiar realities with the use of technology. Hence, various aspects of technology will be incorporated into the activities presented in this chapter.

On the other hand, if school counselors do not have access to technology, the suggested activities can be adapted in order that they can be done without the use of technology. The activities are presented as series. Each series can be divided into activities according to the age of the student. For example, first grade students have a much shorter attention span and need much more assistance than third graders.

This chapter will present six series for each of three levels, namely, elementary, middle, and high school, that will begin to enhance the appreciation of language difference in particular and diversity in general. Various methods using technology will be suggested.

## Developmental Perspectives for Enhancing the Value of Difference

Have you ever observed a two-year-old who is being raised in a dual language home? Suppose Jonathan's father is first-language English, and his mother is first-language Spanish. If Jonathan's father always speaks to him in English, and his mother always speaks to him in Spanish, Jonathan will become biliterate/bicultural. He will take for granted that he can speak two languages. In this case, Jonathan is considered truly a biliterate/bicultural individual (L1C1 and L2C2).

By the time Jonathan is five, he will wonder why he hears adults talking about how difficult it is to learn English. He might ask his mother, "When did I learn English?"

By the time Jonathan reaches fifth grade, he will take for granted that his vocabulary is equally good in English and Spanish provided the dad continues to speak to him in English and his mother in Spanish. When he is 14, he might be asking if he can learn French.

This multilingual person is a real person known by the authors and there are many others like him. As Jonathan grows, he will be personally enriched and socially enhanced because he is multilingual. As the world village comes closer together, knowing more than one language will not only be essential but necessary for making significant contributions in the world of work, politics, commerce, government and education.

Similar stories can be told by the students of families of recent immigrants from Africa, Asia, and Europe. These students will share that they may speak three or four languages and that the language of the colonizer is their common language across traditional groups. A major fear among immigrants is that the traditional languages, which carry the culture, history, and traditions, will undergo a language loss according to socio-linguistics as they compete and strive to survive in a nation that has offered little support for maintaining traditional languages. However, a language which is becoming universal, is that of technology. Hence, the use of technology in this chapter is a major tool to be used in education and communication. Its use can help bring people closer together by offering a common means of communication.

It might surprise adults how easily elementary school children learn how to use Word and Power Point. The authors have seen kindergarten children write stories using Word with very little help from adults. One way to give children who do not have access to computers, equity with those students who do, is to offer them computer knowledge, abilities and skills. Equity is an important ethical principle that all counselors are required to practice (Schulte & Codhrane, 1995).

## Establishing the Environment

For most of the activities herein suggested principles of large group guidance are recommended. Where possible, it is suggested that the students be seated in a circle with the counselor and teacher sitting in the circle with the students. When students are asked to use a computer, they can move to the computers in the classroom. If students are going to write, then they can sit around a table. The purpose of the presence of the teacher is to involve the teacher in the activity in such a way that s/he is an effective partner with the counselor in the development of the students. In addition, presence and participation will facilitate the teacher's being successful in integrating the content and process of the guidance lesson into the other curricula.

It is imperative that appropriate space for large group activities to occur be provided. The large group sessions, which follow, are written with the school counselor as coordinator/facilitator of activities and with the classroom teacher as partner/co-facilitator. The teacher may be invited to collaborate in the activities planned by the school counselor. If the counselor or teacher is bilingual or multilingual these skills can enhance preparation and execution of the activities.

# Elementary School Students

## Introduction

During the elementary school years, students move from being spontaneous and magical to becoming more concrete and logical. With this principle of cognitive development in mind, the following guidance activities were designed. They will contribute to enhancing an understanding of language difference in age appropriate ways. Each series can be implemented over more than one guidance lesson and offer content for integration into the academic curriculum. Each series provides opportunity for research, challenge to cognition, and use of writing skills, as well as opportunities to integrate knowledge, abilities, and skills from the contents of academic subjects.

## Series One

Birthday anniversaries are special for many students. The way birthdays are celebrated is influenced by culture and family. This activity will give students the opportunity to share how their birthdays are celebrated. In addition, students will see one another as individuals with a traditional language and history, and as a community defined by being a member of the class.

This activity enhances understanding of *same* and *different*, part of an elementary curriculum. The celebration of birthday anniversaries helps students understand their own identities and those of others. They come to understand that each person is unique in many ways and, at the same time, all people are the same in other ways. All people share a birthday whether or not they celebrate its anniversary, and for those who do celebrate the anniversaries of their birth, different cultures and families celebrate them in different ways.

During the first session, the teacher and counselor have a conversation with the students in which the students share their experiences of celebrating the anniversaries of their birthdays. If some students do not celebrate birthdays, invite them to share what their families do celebrate that they like especially. They can share something to which they really look forward.

Students might be encouraged to share that they sing songs relevant to the celebrations. If these songs are sung in languages other than English, invite students to sing their song. Use this opportunity to tell students that the speaking of more than one language is valued. Students may be offered the opportunity to teach their songs to other members of the class, if they would like to.

After this conversation, talk with the students about what they will do during the school year:

The students, with the help of the counselor and teacher and, if possible, with the help of members of the family and community prepare a Power Point presentation illustrating their birthday anniversary celebrations. They might like to use pictures scanned into Power Point to illustrate the event. They might want to choose one special activity, ceremony, or custom that they would like to share with the counselor, teacher, and class. They can be invited to download pictures from www.altavista.com into their Power Point. The important thing is that the students grow in appreciating themselves and the other members of the class. The journey toward appreciating rather than fearing differences can be enhanced by this activity.

Tell the students that they will share their Power Point presentation on the anniversary of their births. If students have birthday anniversaries when school is not in session, let them pick any day that they would like to share their story. If students do not celebrate the anniversaries of their birthdays, invite them to share their special day on a day of their choosing. The important thing is that students have their special days when they and their culture will be highlighted.

This exercise can engage the students throughout the school year in experiences to which they can look forward. In addition, this exercise will introduce the students to technology. Finally, the students will begin to appreciate and embrace differences begin to realize that people are more the same than they are different.

## Series Two

Begin by inviting the students to comment about the experiences of preparing their Power Point presentations. Make a calendar noting the days that students will share their Power Point celebrations with the class. Place the calendar on a bulletin board, which the students have decorated. If students have pictures of their celebrations, they may include them among the decorations. Students will be invited to make a *Happy Birthday* sign in the language of their family and place these signs on the *Birthday Bulletin Board*. Help students understand how their Power Point presentations are the *same* and *different*. This conversation provides students with opportunity to think on their feet and develops their feelings of competence in speaking with their peers about their cultures.

First graders might need some help with words that mean *same* and words that mean *different* before this activity is introduced. Teachers or counselors can draw words from the students and put on the board or newsprint more words that are in the speaking vocabulary but not in the reading or writing vocabulary of the students. This activity can be a valuable vocabulary building and reading enhancing exercise.

Have a conversation with the students about family: What is family? Who is a member of my family? Help the students understand that family means something different to different people, and, at the same time, there are some things about families that are the same. List the ways that families are the *same* and ways that families are *different*. For example, some children live with their biological parents; some are adopted or live with foster parents. Some children live in extended families; some live in nuclear families, etc. The counselor and teacher will affirm all family types from which their students come. This activity is an opportunity for counselors to demonstrate the first principle of ethics, namely, absolute respect for persons (Schulte & Cochrane, 1995).

Place students in pairs. Choose students from different cultural backgrounds to work together if that is possible. Using a simple Word program, have the pairs work together finding pictures that remind them of their families on www.eduhound.com or www.altavista.com . Instruct the pair that no words are to be used, only pictures.

When the pairs of students finish, let them explain their pictures to one another. Finally, have students get in touch with how they feel about sharing their families with another person. Invite them to share on whatever level they feel comfortable with the entire class. Some students may choose not to share. They may say, "I pass," when it their turn to share. Some student may only want to share with their partner. Other students may want to tell their stories to the teacher or counselor

## Series Three

Review orally what has been learned so far about *same* and *different*. List ideas on newsprint and hang the newsprint on the wall. Invite students to share how they feel about learning the various ways others wish one another well with phrases like *Happy Birthday*. By this time the phrases in different languages are on the bulletin board.

Using a simple Word program, help students to write a grade-appropriate script about what they have learned about *same* and *different*. Invite the students to make up a story to illustrate the use of more than one language. Of course, the first graders will need much more help from counselors and teachers than older students. Additionally, the family members/caregivers can be invited to help their children to write their thoughts and feelings in various languages. If the class is monolingual English, the teacher or counselor can show students how different languages say, *Happy Birthday* or greet one another for a holiday to which children look forward.

When the students finish, invite them to read their stories to their partner, to the class, or to the teacher. Let the students print their stories, and place them in their portfolios.

## Series Four

Review orally what has been learned so far about *same* and *different*. Refer to the newsprint on the wall. Focus on individual and family. There are ways students are different from other students and the same as other students. There are ways the families of students are different from the families of other students and ways in which they are the same. Make sure language difference is mentioned. This gives the counselor and teacher the opportunity to again affirm that the ability to speak more than one language is valued.

Students will create their own *Name Acrostic* using Power Point. The counselor and teacher can illustrate using their first name, middle name, last name, or a combination of first, middle, or last names. Using Word, students will type their names vertically down the left margin. They fill each letter in the acrostic with verbs, adjectives, or phrases to describe, name, or say something special about themselves. When students finish, they will have a sentence. This activity is an opportunity and exercise to review the parts of speech. For example:

**A**lways looking

**U**nder the clouds

**D**edicated and daring

**R**ight of wrong

**E**xactly like

**Y**our little sister.

Some students might want to write two acrostics using US English and another language. After students complete their *Name Acrostic*, the counselor or teacher will project the Power Points onto the screen, and students will read them. They can be printed and placed on the bulletin board with student permission. Of course, students can say, "I pass," if they do not want to read their acrostics. Teachers or counselors will take these children aside, find out what their hesitancy is, and encourage them to share at another time or invite them to read it to the teacher or counselor.

Summarize by identifying themes of similarities and differences among the *Name Acrostics* and write these on newsprint in two columns. Remind students that they are more the same than they are different. Repeat that the speaking of different languages is valued.

## Series Five

This series of activities will continue to encourage students to interact with their partners and the class. Students will use Word to complete the activity that follows. Students will select someone who is different from them. This difference can be gender, race, ethnicity, hair color, first language, etc. Teachers and counselors ensure that every student has a partner. If there are odd numbers of students, one group can work in a group of three. Once the individual is selected students will make two columns. On the left, students will write how they are the same, and on the right, students will write how they are different:

## Figure 13.1
## Names of Collaborating Students

| Same | Different |
|------|-----------|
| 1. | |
| 2. | |
| 3. | |

Etc.

Students will talk with their partner as they work. Then they will share with the class. Students will generalize that they are more the same than they are different from their partner and other people. The counselor and teacher can point out that differences make life interesting and exciting. It would be very boring if all people were the same, yet finding similarities provides things people can share in common.

## Series Six

As a summary of the series of activities suggested for the enhancing of an appreciation of *same* and *different*, students are invited to create a Venn diagram using Word to distinguish characteristics of sameness and difference. Students will think of all the words that they have learned to describe same and different. Most of them will be hanging on the walls of the classroom. First graders might need some review of the words that are in their speaking vocabulary but not yet in their reading vocabulary. Students will put the sameness words in the overlap of the circles in the Venn diagram. They will write the difference words in the parts of the Venn diagram that do not overlap. The students might notice that the Venn diagrams overlap more than they do not.

Students can close this series of activities understanding that people are more alike than they are different, that the differences do matter and make life interesting, and that differences respected and nurtured are essential for personal, family, and community growth.

# Middle School Students

Teachers and school counselors have noticed that middle school students are different now than they were just a few years ago. Sometimes teachers and school counselors reminisce about when they were in middle school and find their students today to be much more mature. They seem to know so much more than their teachers and school counselors did at the same age, mature earlier physically, and have been exposed to more outside influences than in previous generations. There is much data reported in the literature to support the observations of teachers and school counselors (see Chodick, Huerta, Balicer, Davidovitch & Grotto, 2005). However, the range of maturity varies more for this age group than for any other, and middle school students are particularly interested in being accepted by their peers. Accepting and valuing differences as well as finding commonalities is an important developmental task for middle schoolers.

The following series of activities are designed to meet the needs of the changing population of middle school students. Their development includes assisting them in their journey toward adulthood. Since middle school students do not always exercise good judgment in the eyes of adults, school counselors working with teachers can be their beacon directing them toward the shores of adulthood in culturally appropriate ways.

## Series One

The school counselor and teacher explore the origins of their family names. They share this information with their students and explain what their family names tell them about their history, land base, traditions, and culture. If the school counselor or teacher is African American, this is an opportunity to let the students know how s/he feels about having a family name given by the slave master of the ancestors or the reasons that the family name was chosen from among traditional African names.

S/He might want to explain that some African Americans keep the name given to them by the slave master of their ancestors because it is a sign of strength, dignity, and survival in the face of great oppression. On the other hand, some African Americans have taken traditional African names to remind themselves and others that they come from a history, land base, tradition, and culture that flourished before Jamestown.

The school counselor will ask the students to share what they know about their family names. Counselors and teachers are ready to discuss the historical reality that African-American students might have family names given to them by the slave masters of their ancestors or they might have family names taken from the African land base.

European-American students might have had their names changed by accident or deliberately when their ancestors immigrated to the United States. Asian-American students might have an American name and an Asian name. There may be other variations of stories about how names were changed. All are significant and offer an opportunity to embrace the stories, sometimes painful, of all the students, if they are comfortable to share their stories. This activity may be an opportunity to discuss the socio-political issues in the United States concerning family names in the context of an academic class.

The students can begin exploring their family names using the website www.traceit.com. They might explore coats of arms and family name data bases. They might interview the elders in the family and ask them the story of their family name. Finally, they can share what they have learned with the other members of the class. The school counselor and teacher have the opportunity to show profound respect for the story of each student.

## Series Two

Students investigate their traditional foods in this series. They can record their research on Power Point. Desired pictures can be downloaded from www.edu-hound.com or www.altavista.com. They explore food from a specific country and download pictures of foods represented by a culture of that country. They are not to use words to describe the foods, just pictures. Students will share their Power Point with their classmates.

Students can be asked to interview elders of the family or a care giver. They might like to bring one special family recipe to class. The class can make a cook book from the recipe and some of the pictures that the students have downloaded.

These activities open students' awareness and appreciation for different foods around the world and how each culture/ethnic group is interconnected. Students can see how each group feeds self, family, and community. Students can come to understand that, although one's way of preparing food is unique, all peoples have a need for nourishment.

Brainstorm poverty, drought, famine, tsunamis, hurricanes, earthquakes, tornados, and other forms of natural and people-made disasters which can affect the food supply. Discuss how such events negatively impact people. Maybe some students have personal experiences they would like to share.

Have students problem-name and problem-solve. What are the problems and what are the methods available for transportation and funding? What types of food could be sent to affected areas: Grains, powder, canned or non-perishable? Are there foods that the people do not eat because of custom or religion? For example, traditional people of the tundra do not eat grains. They look upon them as food for the weak. Those who follow Islam or Judaism do not eat pork. Engage students in a socio-political discussion which might include some of the following points: It might be dangerous to enter affected areas; the problem might be caused by war, not weather. Invite the students to think of how food is power when there is not enough for everyone.

## Series Three

Students find pictures of food from around the world and investigate catastrophic events to see what types of foods could be sent to such areas. The school counselor asks the students to search the internet and find websites that explain different foods modified by science as well as foods that are sent to disaster areas. If there are industries in the area that prepare food for the military, astronauts, or disasters, arrange for a field trip for the students to see how these foods are researched and prepared. Invite students to share their findings of at least two different types of foods that are sent to countries when disaster strikes, and, if they had the opportunity to go on the field trip, have them write a reflection paper on the experience.

## Series Four

The school counselor and teacher divide the students into groups of five. Each group prepares a dramatization illustrating what they have learned in these large group counseling sessions, on their field trip, and from interviewing people in the community. Encourage the students to be creative. The students begin with a story board. Have the students videotape their session to illustrate their drama. Tell the students that in the next session, they will show their drama to the rest of the class and lead a discussion of the meaning of their drama.

## Series Five

Have each group show their drama to the class. Have them lead a discussion on the meaning of the movie. Develop appropriate processing questions to give them ahead of time which will help them shape a discussion on their drama.

## Series Six

The school counselor explains to the students that they have had many experiences during this time they were together. Explain to them the importance of being in touch with one's own feelings. Explain that silence affords the opportunity to get in touch with feelings. Have the students sit in silence for five minutes. Invite them to know how they are feeling, to give words to their feelings. After five minutes, invite the students to write an essay on their feelings in this moment. When they have finished, invite them to share if they wish. Collect the papers, make supporting comments on them, and return them to the students. Depending on technology available, the class may want to make contributions to a group website on their findings.

# High School Students

High school populations are complex, and schools and school systems are trying to develop environments to meet the unique needs of today's students. The physical, cognitive, and emotional changes that take place between the ages of 14-18 are vast as are the rights and responsibilities that accompany students' chronological ages. Schools vary in size and population as well as locale. In many urban schools, there are students from a variety of different cultural backgrounds. But some individual high schools may have a student body that is predominantly of one ethnic group, for example, African American, Latin American, Asian American, or European American. Rural schools may have a more homogeneous population of students than larger, urban or suburban schools. However, most schools nation-wide have seen an increase in the cultural diversity of their student bodies over the past generation, and most have their own unique needs.

Depending on the families and communities from which students come, some high school students will be free to study and will have their own computer with access to the internet. Others will have the responsibility to care for younger siblings or work a substantial amount of time to help support the family. Some students take on adult responsibilities practiced in their countries of origin where adolescence does not exist. Thus there are a wide range of maturity levels and expectations for responsibility that are represented in our high school students.

Professional school counselors are crucial to the development of the academic, social, emotional, and psychological health of students. Successful high school counselors are culturally competent and confident. They understand the families and communities from which students come. They have a difference model, not a deficiency model. They have a profound respect for students, the first and absolute principle of ethics (Schulte & Cochrane, 1995).

Fundamental to the high school journey is coming to understand one's identity. Who am I? On whose shoulders do I stand? What part did my ancestors play in making the world the way it is? Where am I going? How do I fit in the world? Often, high school students do not consciously ask these questions pertaining to who they are and how they fit, but, implicitly, they search for the answers in everything that they do.

High school students are searching for their collective memory. The restoration of the collective memory where historic oppression has erased it or the reconstruction of the collective memory where history has privileged it is essential to all high school students.

The following exercises are suggestions as to how high school counselors and teachers can restore the collective memory and reconstruct the collective memory. The exercises written here can act as stimulating suggestions to which counselors and teachers will bring their own creative gifts.

In Spanish there is an expression, "*Conosco a mis hermanos.*" It means "I know you so well that I can anticipate your needs and wants. You can trust me so completely that I can safely think of you as if you were my brother or sister." Effective high school counselors and teachers know their students so well that they can anticipate their needs and wants, and they can be trusted absolutely. Identity in the context of community is the most essential personal work of high school students. Knowing one's self is essential to develop trust, willingness to take the kind of risks necessary for success, and the ability to know one has a fruitful future. The development of such knowledge can be encouraged and facilitated by adults important in the lives of students. Particularly school counselors and teachers can elicit this essential process.

## Series One

The purpose of this exercise is to learn how to search for answers to one's history. Only when a person knows one's history can one develop an integrated identity. In this series, students will learn how to find out the answers to their questions.

Counselors and teachers draw from students, ways in which they can find out about their history. Some may have already begun to do that by means of genealogies, family stories, or interviewing elders in their family or community. Make a list of the suggestions of the students and put their list on Power Point. E-mail the list to each student.

Introduce the students to the story of how in the 1930s during the Great Depression the Federal Writers' Project workers interviewed people who had been held as slaves. Their stories were audio-taped and some photographs were taken. Technology such as computers, digital cameras, and camcorders were unknown. The records were placed in the Smithsonian. In 1998, a book and a collection of audio-tapes were published (Berlin, Favreau, & Miller, eds., 1998). Although this book and these tapes were not the first available source for the story of a people who survived slavery with dignity, purpose, and hope, it is the most easily available.

Invite students to use digital cameras, camcorders, audio tapes, or any other way they might choose to interview family members, the elders of the community, or others that they might think will have information about their past. Encourage students to search the web and libraries for information about their past. Students can visit community based organizations to find information that they may have. Be sure that students have access to the technology they need, or that they have an alternative for obtaining the information.

When students return for another guidance class, have them share their stories. Using Word, have them write a reflection paper about how they feel about what they found. Have the students prepare a record of their search and the results for their portfolios.

## Series Two

*Who am I?* The students now have some information to use in answering this question. Divide them into pairs, and have them share their personal answer to this question. Invite the students to write using Word a summary of what they heard from their partner. Bring the class together and have them discuss the statements: *We are more alike that we are different. The ways we are different bring many gifts to our lives.*

## Series Three

The high school counselor and the home room teacher ask the students to think of categories important to answering the question, **Who am I**? Invite students to think of what they thought and felt during the last two sessions.

- What rights, privileges, and responsibilities do I have because I am a person?

- Where is my country of origin? For African-American students this is a complex question that needs to be addressed in the context of history. Native American student might name their nation within the Western Hemisphere. Some students may be first generation American, or may identify as mixed race/ethnicity and have several ways in which they identify themselves.

- What contributions have my ancestors made to the making of the United States?

- What parts of United States history are most troubling?

- If my family or I are recent immigrants, what do we bring to the United States that will enhance it?

- What values have my family and community taught me?

- How are these values going to help me succeed in life?

- What does my family expect of me? What do I expect of myself?

It might be appropriate for the counselor and teacher to model responses to the categories. Students can prepare a Power Point presentation reflecting on their answers to the question *Who am I?* Students can be invited to present their Power Points to the class.

Some students might feel more comfortable doing this exercise in small groups. Students from some cultures might feel uncomfortable focusing on themselves. The choice can be offered to work alone or in a small group. Being sensitive to the view of the world of students from all over the world is one of the essential components of an effective, developmental, comprehensive, guidance and counseling program.

## Series Four

The facilitator divides students into small, convenient groups of three or five persons. Invite the students to discuss some major themes they have learned in traditional history classes with regard to culture. Ask them how what they learned in history classes has helped them investigate their collective memory. Ask them how they would suggest history classes could be different in order that they can see themselves in history in a more nearly accurate way. Invite each group to prepare a Power Point presentation to share with the other members of the class.

## Series Five

The facilitator divides students into small, convenient groups of three or five persons. Using a Word document invite students to prepare a curriculum for a United States history class including in it what they have learned in their own research. Have students share their curriculum with the class. Finally, have them e-mail their Word document to one another.

## Series Six:

Have students spend five minutes thinking about and being in touch with their feelings about what they learned about themselves while engaged in the activities. Playing music, not familiar to any one in the class, may offer a soothing background. Using a Word document, invite students to write an essay that answers the question *Who am I?* When they finish, the counselor collects the essays. S/he reads them with supporting comments and returns them to the students, who may, if they wish, put the essays into their portfolios. Depending on the availability of technological support, such tasks may be done via e-mail or on a class website

## Summary

The series of activities suggested in this chapter were written with creative, investigative, and committed professional counselors and teachers in mind. Both authors teach future professional school counselors and teachers, who are inspirations to the professions. They make commitments to earn a master's degree while they are teaching or counseling full time. They have families and bills to pay. Yet, they come to improve their professionalism. They are the hope of the students of the present and future.

Both authors supervise future teachers and counselors. In order to be effective educators, professional school counselors and teachers are in touch with their stakeholders: administrators, counselors, teachers, community, family, and student. Educators have knowledge, ability, and skills to demonstrate by their thinking, feeling, and behaving that **education is about relationships**.

When students feel nurtured, valued, and respected, when their families and communities see respect for their interests, their truth, their freedom, and when students, families and communities are treated with equity (Schulte & Cochrane, 1995), then education will be on the way to being about relationships and embracing cultural diversity.

## References

Berlin, I., Favreau, M., & Miller, S.F. (Eds.). (1998). *Remembering slavery: African Americans talk about their personal experiences of slavery and freedom.* NY and Washington, DC: Published by The New Press in Conjunction with the Library of Congress as a companion to Smithsonian Production's radio documentary.

Chodick, G., Huerta, M., Balicer, R. D., Davidovitch, N., & Grotto, I. (2005). Secular trends in age of menarche, smoking, and oral contraceptive use among Israeli girls. *Preventing Chronic Disease: Public Health Research*, 4. Retrieved from and Settings\\Computer-\\MyDocuments\\MyDocuments\\PUBLICATIONS onDecember 27, 2005." file://C:\Documents and Settings\Computer\My Documents\My Documents\PUBLICATIONS on December 27, 2005.

Hester, C., Bychowski, S.R., Bosché, C.M., & Emmite, L. (2005). *UST Fact Book 2004-2005.* Houston, TX: Office of Strategic Planning, Institutional Research and Evaluation (SPIRE).

Saveri, A., & Falcon, R. (2000). Planning for the 21st century workforce. Key trends that will shape the employment and career landscape. In J.M. Kummerow (Ed.). *New directions in career planning and the workplace.* (pp. 33-76). Palo Alto, CA: Davies-Black Publishing.

Schulte, J.M., & Cochrane, D.B. (1995). *Ethics in school counseling.* NY: Teachers College.

U.S. Census Bureau (2000). *The Hispanic population 2000.* Washington, DC: U.S. Department of Commerce Economics and Statistical Administration.

U.S. Census Bureau. (September 8, 2004). Retrieved from http://www.census.gov/PressRelease/www./releases/archives/facts_for_futures_special_editions/002270.html on December 25, 2005.

### Websites of Interest

www.altavista.com

www.eduhound.com

www.traceit.com

# Chapter 14

# The School Counselor's Role in Prevention and Remediation of Child Abuse

**by**
**JoAnna White and Mary Flynt**

*JoAnna White, Ed.D., Professor and Chair in the Department of Counseling and Psychological Services at Georgia State University, is a former school counselor. She is a leader in the field of play therapy. She has many years of experience in counseling abused children and consulting with their families.*

*Mary Flynt, Ed.S., a former school counselor and currently Coordinator of Safe and Drug Free Schools in Gwinnett County, Georgia, has worked extensively with students and school personnel in the areas of behavioral diagnosis and remediation.*

## Introduction

School counselors are called upon to provide a variety of services to students, teachers, parents, and administrators and have become their school's number one expert on affective education. In order to ensure that students are emotionally prepared to learn, the school counselor must assure that all students are provided a place where they feel safe and valued. Of the variety of children and adolescents seen by the school counselor, no student is more in need of an adult who will listen, understand, and advocate for them than the one who has been abused.

With the dramatic increase in the number of reported cases of child abuse in the United States and the increase of violence in the schools as well as in homes, school counselors are increasingly called upon to report cases of child abuse, coordinate counseling services for abused students, and develop child abuse prevention programs for the schools in which they are employed. In this chapter the writers describe types of abuse and the role of the school counselor in employing remediation and prevention efforts to deal with child abuse issues.

Child abuse and children's rights are relatively new concepts when one considers that legal rights for adults, and not children, are documented throughout history. In fact, the history of child rearing, until the mid-twentieth century, appears to be synonymous with the history of child abuse. Attitudes toward children have traditionally been ones of ownership and indifference in which child abuse of all kinds was the norm. Alice Miller (1990) called this attitude toward children "poisonous pedagogy." This attitude is driven by the mistaken belief that we must retaliate against children for their own good; in other words "spare the rod and spoil the child."

Throughout history one can read accounts where children have been wrapped in swaddling clothes, sexually molested, tortured, killed to fulfill religious rites, abandoned, sent away to monasteries, ignored, starved, and generally emotionally abused and neglected. Not until 1974 did Congress pass the Child Abuse and Prevention and Treatment Act (Paisley, 1987). This act required each state to develop a policy for reporting and investigating child abuse. Today, each state and the District of Columbia have passed this type of legislation (Paisley, 1987). It is legally mandated, as well as ethically correct, that school counselors *must report any and all cases of suspected child abuse.*

In spite of the fact that each state recognizes that child abuse is illegal and society is becoming more aware of the realities of child abuse, the National Child Abuse and Neglect Data System reports that in 2002 (National Clearinghouse on Child Abuse and Neglect Information, 2005) there were an estimated 1,400 children who died from child abuse in the United States. Experts believe that these data underestimate the actual number of fatalities, some believe by as much as 50-60 % (Crume, DiGuiseppi, Byers, Sirotnak, & Garrett, 2002). Even though 76 % of child abuse occurs with children under four years of age, school-age children are still experiencing abuse at an alarming rate. Perhaps the most important fact is that most abuse is perpetrated by a child's parent. It is estimated that in 2002 one or both parents were responsible for 70 % of the child abuse or neglect in the United States (National Clearinghouse on Child Abuse and Neglect Information, 2005).

Abusive detachment from children is evident in our society wherever one chooses to look. Adults are often obsessed with the attainment of wealth and status. They are stressed with their "getter" life-style and unavailable to their children. There is little time for play with their child. Even on vacations, many families plan to go to a place where they can engage in adult fun (golf, tennis) and their children are put in structured activities away from them.

On the other end of the continuum, parents are struggling with the inability to make a living, lack of adequate child care, and stress related issues such as drug or alcohol abuse. These societal stressors are precursors to abusive situations, ranging from emotional detachment to violence and sexual abuse.

## Ethical and Legal Issues

School personnel have learned to rely on their counselors when confronted with procedural and legal concerns regarding the subject of abuse. In order to fulfill the requirements of efficient crisis intervention, counselors must have a clear understanding of the existing legal parameters. School administrators are increasingly utilizing a counselor's expertise and special training as a source of leadership and responsibility for identifying and reporting cases of child abuse to the investigative agency, sometimes titled the Department of Family and Children Services (DFACS), Health and Rehabilitation Services (HRS) and so forth. Throughout this chapter the writers refer to this service as DFACS.

School districts are required to offer their support by providing a written policy for counselors and other employees of the district to follow when abuse is suspected. School personnel who fail to report their suspicions of child abuse to the designated school official may be prosecuted under state laws. School counselors are often that designated official. To ensure clear application of the law, school counselors should consider inviting DFACS representatives and a specialist in school law to serve as consultants at yearly staff development offerings for all teachers, administrators and other mandated reporters in the school building.

It is critical that school counselors cultivate a professional working relationship with the state appointed protective service workers in order to expedite the investigative process. Counselors' busy schedules should be interrupted if necessary to allow for visits and or calls from DFACS personnel. Communication with DFACS workers should facilitate the acquisition of helpful case related information and provide a supportive atmosphere in which the serious and painful reality of abuse can be treated. The child further benefits from this cooperative approach by the familiar and reassuring presence of the school counselor during the investigation conducted by the DFACS worker.

The existence of a school team composed of three or four school members to handle abuse cases enhances the accuracy of the abuse report by clarifying any discrepancies existing among other professional educators before the report is filed by the counselor (Howell-Nigrelli, 1988). The involvement of several school members necessitates the clear awareness on the part of the counselor of the issue of responsibility to the student as outlined in the Ethical Standards of the American Counseling Association (ACA) (American Counseling Association, 2005) and the 2004 Ethical Standards for School Counselors of the American School Counselor Association (ASCA) (American School Counselor Association, 2004).

Counselors will want to make the abused student aware of the steps and procedures to be followed prior to any action taken with his/her particular case (Ethical Standards for School Counselors, 2004). The distrust and sense of hopelessness associated with the experience of abuse are considerably lowered (toward the professionals involved in the reporting aspect of the case) when the child is cognizant of the future steps that will be taken on his or her behalf. The assurance of confidentiality and knowledge of the procedures encourages the victim to disclose in an accurate and confident manner. In reference to record keeping, counselors should note the dates of interventions in abbreviated form. This note taking is for the school counselor's knowledge rather than documentation for other agencies.

The ASCA Ethical Standards for School Counselors (2004) emphasize the importance of confidentiality and re-establishing the trust of the child after the report of abuse is made. It is the opinion of the writers that your relationship with the child must remain intact so that ongoing counseling services can continue after the crisis is over and/or referred to appropriate community agencies. The school counselor's role as a child advocate is at the heart of the issue of efficient and successful solutions to child abuse. Incorporating up-to-date information with skillful ethical practices will produce positive outcomes for children and parents involved in the tragedy of child abuse and neglect.

# Types of Child Abuse

## Neglect

Neglect has been defined as the failure by the parents to provide those things needed for the child's healthy growth and development. This concept implies that harm may come to the child as a result of the parent's unreliability as providers (Childhelp USA, 2005). Indicators include:

- Abandonment
- Lack of supervision
- Lack of adequate clothing and good hygiene
- Lack of medical or dental care
- Lack of adequate education
- Lack of adequate nutrition
- Lack of adequate shelter

Exploitation" and overworking of children are also characteristics of neglect. It is often extremely difficult to obtain decisive action from investigative agencies when cases of neglect are reported by the school counselor. This is usually because of the lack of concrete evidence. This sad state of affairs, however, should not be a deterrent to the reporting process. It is the legal responsibility of the school counselor to report suspected child abuse, not to be responsible for conducting the investigation.

Behavioral signs of neglect need to be constantly monitored by the school counselor in order to ensure affirmative action during the investigative process. They are as follows:

- The child begs or steals food.
- The child attends school in an erratic manner.
- The child is addicted to alcohol or other drugs.
- The child engages in delinquent acts such as vandalism or theft.
- The child states that there is no one to take care of or look after him or her.
- The child constantly falls asleep at school.
- The child comes to school very early and leaves very late (Crosson Tower, 1984).

When dealing with cases of suspected neglect the school counselor must actively work to have daily and/ or weekly involvement with the child. Even though the counselor's role only requires reporting the neglect, a substantial amount of information gathered (i.e., dates of absences, duration of illnesses, etc.) creates a much stronger case. Such counselor initiated documentation enables the DFACS worker to proceed in a more decisive and swift manner. Statistics from The Third National Incidence Study of Child and Abuse and Neglect (2005) show that child neglect has increased by 102% since 1986.

As counselors become involved with a child within the context of the family, it becomes important to be able to identify common characteristics of the neglectful caretaker. These parents/guardians may have a chaotic home life, may live in unsafe conditions, may be mentally retarded, may abuse drugs or alcohol, may be impulsive individuals, may be employed but unable to afford child care, have experienced little or no success in life, have little motivation or skill to create changes in their lives, and tend to be passive.

One important consideration to investigate is whether the resulting conditions of maltreatment are present because of poverty or neglectful parental behaviors. Through effective, non-judgmental parent consultation, the school counselor can obtain a clear assessment of the situation and offer referral sources, such as free medical services or mental health services that in many instances may improve the situation at home. These successful exchanges foster positive and open relations between home and school. In many instances the child's situation will improve as the parent becomes connected with a caring professional such as the school counselor.

Individual counseling and small group counseling are preferred interventions to use with the neglected child. Encouragement, problem solving skills, coping skills related to latchkey issues, the use of expressive play in counseling are all important components that address the low self-esteem and the sense of helplessness often felt by the neglected child.

## Emotional Abuse

Emotional abuse or neglect implies a consistent indifference to the child's needs and interfering with the child's mental health and social development. (Childhelp USA, 2005). It is an underlining consequence present in all forms of abuse and one of the hardest conditions to prove in court. It can be observed in the following examples:

- Parent who never speaks to the child
- Psychotic parent unable to acknowledge the reality of the child's world
- Parent who actively rejects the child through verbal abuse and excessive punishment (Childhelp USA, 2005).

School counselors' caseloads are flooded by emotional abuse and neglect. Garbarino, Guttrnan, and Seeley (1986) described five types of psychological maltreatment: rejecting, isolating, terrorizing, ignoring, and corrupting. They also accentuate the importance of prevention and intervention techniques utilized with families and the community at-large. The counseling channels suggested are marital counseling, family therapy, parent/child intervention methods for working with socially isolated families, and educating the public. The three latter suggestions can be included in the school counselor delivery systems such as PTA meetings, parent study groups, individual consultation and follow-up with parents. Efforts in emotional abuse prevention are especially important because it is difficult to show concrete evidence to the investigative agency. The difficulty in showing proof of abuse often leaves the school personnel as the only advocates for this child. Crosson Tower (1984) identified certain behavioral indicators as follows:

- Habit disorders (bed wetting, sucking, hitting, rocking)
- Conduct disorders (withdrawal and antisocial behavior; destructiveness, cruelty, stealing)
- Neurotic traits (sleep disorders, inhibited play)
- Psychoneurotic reactions (hysteria, obsession, phobias, hypochondria)
- Behavior extremes (passive-aggressive, very demanding or compliant)
- Overly adaptive behaviors (parenting other children or infantile behavior)
- Lags in emotional and intellectual behavior
- Attempted suicide

The lines that exist between faulty parenting skills and actually damaging interactions are difficult to define. School counselors must rely on their psycho-educational skills to provide a support system within the school setting. The appropriate school placement, taking into consideration the psychological as well as the developmental needs of this child, must be the result of counselor coordinated efforts that involves teacher consultation and staff development on psychological maltreatment. Healthy adult role models in the schools might be the only opportunity available to children to learn how to value themselves and others.

Sometimes school personnel themselves are perpetrators of emotional abuse of students. Krugman and Krugman (cited in Neese, 1989) found, after investigating third and fourth grade classrooms, psychologically abusive teacher behaviors that included labeling, screaming at children, allowing some children to harass others, and setting unrealistic academic goals. School counselors must be leaders in adjusting and changing the climate in schools where teachers and peers may be among the perpetrators of emotional abuse.

The counseling utilized in dealing with the emotionally maltreated child needs to allow the child to proceed at his or her own pace. That is, where the tools of communication are controlled by the child, whether they may be drawings, puppets, playing with a doll house, storytelling, and so forth. The sensitive counselor can sometimes break through the wall of secrecy created by parental threats or excessive loyalty to the family and bring a change to this child's life by reporting the pertinent information to the authorities and/or forming a bond of trust and respect with the child (White, Draper, & Jones, 2001).

## Physical Abuse

Physical abuse of children involves non-accidental physical injury (Childhelp USA, 2005). Indicators include:

- Unexplained bruises or welts
- Unexplained burns
- Unexplained fractures
- Unexplained lacerations or abrasions
- Unexplained death

Physical abuse may occur through hitting, beating, kicking, pinching, or falls that are a result of aggression from an adult. Even though accidents do happen to children, it is the counselor's duty to investigate thoroughly the incident, especially with children who have repeated injuries. In many instances children are threatened not to tell, so they cover up the incident by stating that it was an accident. It is important for counselors to be aware of the probability of this happening and continue to follow through (White, Draper & Jones, 2001).

School counselors will want to be aware of the behavioral indicators of physical abuse in order to identify and help these children. White and Allers (1994) conducted a literature review of the play behaviors of abused children. They found that these children are often developmentally immature, oppositional and aggressive, withdrawn and passive, self-deprecating/self-destructive, and hypervigilant. They further contended that abused children exhibit literal play themes that tend to be repetitive and compulsive in nature. Elementary school counselors should have a heightened awareness of these issues as they work with children in individual play counseling and in play groups.

Adolescent physical abuse does occur, but it is often incorrectly identified. Unfortunately, adults often have the attitude that adolescents can take care of themselves. Signs of adolescent abuse may be:

- Rebelliousness/problems with authority figures
- Drug and alcohol abuse
- Running away
- Change in grades and academic attitudes
- Withdrawing
- General lack of self esteem
- Unusual compliance toward adults

In addition, children's and adolescent's artwork will often serve as a metaphor for the child's and teen's abusive situation. Drawings may display violence, threatening figures, and large adult figures in relation to small child figures who appear powerless (Peterson & Hardin, 1997). The child's use of colors and the intensity with which they draw are also indicators of their emotionality related to the physical abuse. The use of blacks, brown, and other dark colors along with heavy strokes could possibly indicate anger and violence, while faint lines using pencils or other light colors could indicate evasiveness and low self-esteem.

## Sexual Abuse

Sexual abuse is the exploitation of a child for sexual gratification of an adult or an older child. Sexual abuse includes exhibitionism, the exposure of children to pornographic material, the use of children in pornographic materials, fondling, and intercourse. Often sexual abuse involves an incestuous relationship (Childhelp USA, 2005). Vanderbilt (1992) described incest as, "any sexual abuse of a child by a relative or other person in a position of authority over the child." Vanderbilt estimates that one in three persons is the victims of incest before the age of 18. Incest involves a second traumatizing dynamic for the child because he or she cannot run home for help. The abuser is usually in the home.

Because sexual abuse is not as evident as the signs of physical abuse, it is even more important that the school counselor be aware of the signs of sexual abuse. They are often subtle and more difficult to detect than are signs of physical abuse.

Signs of sexual abuse may include:

- Sleep disorders
- Enuresis or fecal retention
- Fear of being alone with an adult
- Low self-esteem
- Eating disorders
- Inappropriate sexual behaviors toward adults or other children
- Masturbation in public
- Poor peer relationships
- Withdrawal
- Dissociation
- Sudden drop in school performance
- Difficulty in walking or sitting
- Urinary tract infections, yeast infections, pain or itching in genital area
- Suicide attempts (especially in adolescents)
- Chronic runaway (adolescents)
- Anorexia (adolescents)
- Early pregnancies (adolescents)

In their literature review, White and Allers (1994) indicated that in addition to the typical play behaviors of physically abused children, sexually abused children often exhibit play behaviors that are sexually beyond their developmental age. They are often hypervigilant or protective of themselves from any perceived danger. In addition, they often exhibit a behavior known as dissociation in which they appear to go off to another place. For example, one child expressed that she was "in the wall" when her counselor asked what she was thinking. Dissociation is a way for the child to escape from the reality of sexual abuse. Homeyer and Landreth (1998) in their research of the play therapy behaviors of sexually abused children concluded that there are identifiable and highly-interrelated play behaviors of sexually abused children that can help counselors identify signs of abuse.

Experts also suggest that the use of art materials is an appropriate counseling technique for sexually abused victims (Whitney Peterson & Hardin, 1997). Drawing provides a safe way for these children and adolescents to ventilate their feelings and show the counselor what they are dealing with.

The artwork for sexually abused children and adolescents may include many of the themes described previously for physically abused children. In addition, there may be more themes of violence, sexuality, or aggression. Children and adolescents may draw people with no eyes or no mouth. If there are eyes present, they may be just dots that no one could see out of. There may also be people in the drawings that have a marked division between the upper body and the lower body such as emphasis on the waist or a line drawn across the neck. Further, the child or adolescent may draw people with just heads and no bodies.

# Abuse Prevention

The concept of prevention is an integral component of a developmental school guidance and counseling program. There are a variety of prevention programs in use at the present time. The most comprehensive plan for schools is the one that would include a variety of publics by targeting parents, school personnel, teachers, and students. School counselors who are involved with abuse cases in a direct manner need to continue to work towards the development of effective treatment programs as well as the implementation of promising programs of child abuse prevention. It is important to note that no one program can reach out to all the publics you have as a school counselor. A variety of program strategies can best address the multiple objectives of a comprehensive abuse prevention curriculum.

The Office on Child Abuse and Neglect (2003) studied demonstration projects aimed at prevention of child maltreatment. They found that parent and teacher education, direct services to at-risk children were all successful in helping the child improve school performance, attendance and appropriate behaviors. The following is a skeletal outline, developed by the authors, of abuse prevention programming.

# Preventive

| Target Population | Strategies | Outcomes |
|---|---|---|
| **Students** | Classroom guidance And Small Groups<br>1. Sequential<br>2. Age appropriate<br>3. Variety of techniques<br>   A. Role play<br>   B. Puppets<br>   C. Discussion<br>   D. Open-ended stories<br>   E. Information giving | 1. Develop assertive skills<br>2. Develop problem-solving skills<br>3. Increased self-esteem<br>4. Increased awareness of their rights |
| **Parents** | 1. Individual Consultation<br>2. PTA program<br>3. Material preview night<br>4. Parent education classes | 1. Parenting skills<br>2. Improved communication skills with their child<br>3. Increased knowledge of community resources<br>4. Increased trust in school personnel |
| **Teachers** | 1. Individual consultation<br>2. Staff development (faculty meetings, teacher groups, written handouts) | 1. Improved skills for Identification of abuses<br>2. Increased knowledge concerning reporting process<br>3. Ability to communicate more effectively with the abused student. |

Allsopp and Prosen (1988) and Thompson and Rudolph (1992) described certain educational objectives that must be present in order to ensure the effectiveness of sexual abuse prevention programs. The following are a list (not all inclusive) of such indicators:

- Sexual abuse may be inflicted by someone known by the child.
- Identify who can offer help.
- If the adult does not believe the child, try other adults until someone does.
- Sexual abuse occurs in many ways other than just touching.
- Differentiate between good touches, bad touches, and confusing touches.
- Sexual abuse is never the child's fault.
- The importance of verbalizing feelings connected with the abuse.
- Secrets are not OK unless they are about something positive.
- It is important to tell so the abuser can get help and no one else will be victimized.
- People can get into difficult situations but that does not mean that they are bad people.
- When to trust and when to be cautious.
- Not all adults are to be obeyed how to tell the difference.
- Teach the child to say "no" to inappropriate abuse behavior.

Thompson and Rudolph (1992) pointed out that because of children's developing cognition, and in order to soften the anxiety connected with sexual abuse, most programs utilize a variety of activities such as role play, coloring books, films, and puppets. Prevention programs are delivered to adolescents within the context of human sexuality programs, dating issues and communication skills training. Freeman and Hart-Rossi (cited in Hollander, 1989) summed up the concept of prevention by pointing out that children who are empowered by knowing what steps to take concerning the prevention and handling of abuse are less likely to be victimized.

## Abuse Remediation

Play counseling can be an effective technique for elementary school counselors to use with children who are suspected of being abused. Because children cannot engage in "talk therapy" due to their developmental level, play provides a comfortable environment in which they can express and explore interpersonal conflicts through the use of toys and art materials. Experts agree that children need play in order to learn and develop, yet abused children often do not or cannot play due to malnutrition, neglect, overwhelming anxieties, unrealistic adult expectations, or perfectionism (White, Draper, & Jones, 2001).

White and Allers (1994) stated that even though there is little empirical research on the relationship of play therapy to abuse issues of children, most of the anecdotal literature suggests that it is effective. In addition, this process affords the counselor the opportunity to observe patterns of play that may indicate abuse. As previously mentioned in this chapter, these patterns revolve around literal, compulsive, repetitive play in which the child has difficulty being creative or imaginative.

Through the use of individual play counseling or small group play, the school counselor can help children work through fears and anxieties learn how to play freely, and increase self-esteem. The school counselor can help children and adolescents create a safe distance from the abuse through age appropriate toys, artwork, puppetry, dramatic play, and movement play.

Remediation in the school should incorporate three major phases: identifying, reporting, and follow-up. This process cannot end after the physical signs have healed and the abuser has been relieved of the custody of the child. In many instances the child continues to live in the same abusive environment, which creates a mandate to remain involved with the child. Thompson and Rudolph (1992) pointed out that the violation of the victims' trust level influences their ability to verbalize and benefit from traditional counseling methods. It is important that the counselor provides a safe place and a safe relationship within which the child may experiment with new adaptation to a safer world. The awareness of the normal developmental process of children and ways in which this step by step process becomes altered are important concepts to consider in working with maltreated children.

The following is a remedial sequence for school counselors to follow and two case studies to illustrate the comprehensive nature of this process.

## Remedial

I. Identification

    A. Teacher referral

    B. Student self referral

    C. Family referral

    D. DFACS referral

II. Reporting process

    A. Referral to principal or principal designate (School Counselor)

    B. Student interview by School Counselor

    C. DFACS contacted by School Counselor

    D. School Counselor available for DFACS visitation to school (Ideally the school counselor should be present for child/DFACS interview) (In some states the professional first suspicious of abuse is required to make the phone call to DFACS).

III. Counseling

    A. Follow-up with child and teacher

    B. Further consultation may take place with DFACS and police officer in case of student removal from the home.

    C. Provide counseling (individual, small group)

    D. Possible parent consultation, parent volunteer, and peer helper

# Case Study 1: Elementary Child

## Identification Process

Danielle was a six-year-old kindergarten student who transferred to School X during the seventh month of the school year. She lived in an apartment housing complex with her mother and mother's boyfriend. There was a great-aunt who lived nearby and baby-sat with the child on a daily basis. Danielle exhibited a variety of characteristics that concerned the classroom teacher, such as: tardiness, excessive sleeping at school, unkempt appearance and daydreaming. The teacher, Mrs. B., consulted with the counselor describing Danielle as a compliant child who utilized her vivid imagination when asked about her family. The teacher added that she had been unable to establish contact with the mother. The counselor saw the child for play sessions twice and excellent rapport was established through play media.

## Reporting Process

One early morning Danielle's great-aunt, Rose, reported to the counselor that Danielle had been beaten and terrorized by the mother's boyfriend. After reassuring Rose and answering her questions concerning the reporting process, the counselor interviewed the child. She related that her "dad" had thrown her against the wall and hit her with his belt because she could not find her shoes. She was still very sore from the injuries on her back and leg.

After actively listening to Danielle's story, the counselor proceeded to tell her that what happened was not her fault and beating her in such a manner was wrong. The counselor also told her about the reporting process, as follows: "There are some people I know whose job it is to help children and their families. They also make sure that children are safe from harm." The counselor then asked:

"How would you feel more comfortable showing me the marks? Would you like to do it in my office or maybe in the office's bathroom?" She chose the office's bathroom. There were purple lacerations on the buttocks and on the back of both legs. The counselor clarified further the reporting process and reinforced the child for telling about the abuse.

The counselor called DFACS and the worker visited the school that afternoon. A report was filed and mother was contacted directly at work from the counselor's office. Danielle's mom tried to conceal the incident and to protect the boyfriend by saying he was out of town. As a result the DFACS worker decided to remove the child from her home. Danielle was allowed to spend the night with Rose and on the following day she was visited at school by a female police officer and the DFACS worker. That seemed to ease the tension. Danielle was taken from the school that afternoon by DFACS and the police.

## Counseling/Follow-Up

Danielle returned to school a week later. Aunt Rose brought her back and stopped by the counselor's office. She explained that the judge had given her unlimited access to the child, and mother's boyfriend had been ordered to obtain help for his drinking problem. Rose felt good about Danielle's safety at the present time.

The counselor began play sessions with the child. This time her storytelling was more closely related with the abuse and violence among family members. After four sessions she began to incorporate problem resolution to the hitting and fighting among family members. Danielle's appearance had greatly improved and her energy level was more in tune with other students in her class.

## Community and School Resources

The counselor coordinated with a parent volunteer to spend time with Danielle to help and support her with academic tasks. A fifth grader, a trained peer helper, came everyday at playground time to facilitate cooperative play between Danielle and her classmates.

# Case Study 2: Middle School Child

The following case study is one in which many school personnel were involved as opposed to just the school counselor. Jimmy was a sixth grader in a middle school in an upper-class neighborhood. He lived with both biological parents and his third grade sister. Jimmy exhibited a variety of aggressive behaviors such as: verbal arguing, name calling, physical outbursts towards other students, and refusal to do work and cooperate in the classroom (at times). His student record indicated that he was in a self-contained emotionally handicapped (E.H.) classroom prior to entering sixth grade at his new school. In sixth grade he was placed in a regular classroom due to parent pressure. He received some resource help in the area of E. H. Jimmy's academic potential was above average, but his performance was below his ability level. Often he appeared sullen and detached.

## Identification Process

Jimmy's special education teacher consulted with the school counselor relating his lack of progress in spite of a variety of interventions and classroom modifications. She was concerned about his despondency toward life in general and possible suicidal tendencies. She was also very concerned that he had violated school rules several times (fighting) resulting in disciplinary actions from the principal. It was agreed by the counselor, special education teacher, and assistant principal that parent consultation would be a helpful step to take.

At the parent conference all three professionals agreed that the parents were very much into denial concerning Jimmy's special needs. It was also noted that the family exhibited poor communication skills and some behaviors that led the counselor to the suspicion of alcoholism in the family.

Counseling began with Jimmy and the school counselor. About two weeks later, he came to school with a bruise on his eye and a cut on his cheek. That morning he shared with his special education teacher that his mother had hit him in anger and used a knife to cut him. The teacher immediately reported this to the school counselor.

The school counselor, the teacher, and Jimmy then talked about the abuse, and he confirmed it. The counselor explained to the child the procedure that she would be following in reporting this abuse. She then called the Department of Family and Children Services (DFACS) to report the incident. The DFACS worker related that they had a thick file already compiled on this family.

The DFACS worker called the school counselor back the next morning to tell her that the father had been given the choice of hospitalizing his wife for alcoholism or the children would be removed from the home. He further indicated that the father had hospitalized the mother, and that he (the DFACS worker) felt encouraged by the father's reaction and attitude toward the family's recovery. The school counselor then shared this information with the special education teacher, the principal, and Jimmy's other classroom teachers.

That same day the counselor met with Jimmy and plans were made for him to join the Children of Alcoholics group at school, and individual counseling was to be continued. Even though this may seem farfetched, the counselor found Jimmy smiling with friends in the lunchroom only two days later. As of this writing his progress continues, especially in the area of academics. Jimmy continues to struggle with activities that involve structured interactions with others since the trusting of others is so difficult for him at this time in his life.

## Summary

School counselors are responsible for a variety of functions related to the identification of abused students and for providing various services for them. In addition to reporting the abuse and working cooperatively with protective services, it is important that school counselors are prepared to provide counseling for the student on an individual basis, in small group, and through family consultation. Finally, counselors should be prepared to train teachers and other school personnel concerning the issues of abuse and how to help abused students at school.

With the ever increasing stressors of poverty, addiction, terrorism, catastrophic events, and marital discord, it is critical that school counselors provide leadership and serve as child advocates when their students are in danger from abuse and neglect. With the estimation that the cost of child abuse is 94 billion dollars a year in the United States (Fromm, 2001), it behooves the schools to take a vigilant approach to intervention and prevention.

This is best accomplished through classroom guidance, small targeted groups, parent education, and teacher workshops. Many times adults (even administrators and teachers) would rather not deal with the issues surrounding abuse. This fear may lead to denial of the problem even when a child is communicating the abuse clearly. The school counselor is the key to insuring that all abused children are heard and properly assisted.

# References

Allsopp, A., & Prosen, S. (1988). Teacher reactions to a child abuse training program. *Elementary School Guidance and Counseling, 22,* 299-305.

American Counseling Association. (2005). *ACA code of ethics.* Alexandria, VA: ACA.

American School Counselor Association. (2004). *Ethical standards for school counselors.* Alexandria, VA: ASCA.

Childhelp USA. (2005). *What is abuse?* Retrieved December 13, 2005, from http://www.childhelpusa.org.

Crosson Tower, C. (1984). *Child abuse and neglect: A teachers handbook for detection, reporting and classroom management.* Washington, DC: National Education Association.

Crume, T., DiGuiseppi, C., Byers, T., Sirotnak, A., & Garrett, C. (2002). *Underascertainment of child maltreatment fatalities by death certificates, 1990-1998.* Pediatrics (110) 2. Retrieved on December 16, 2005 from http:// www.nccanch.acf.hhs.gov/pubs/factsheets/fatality.cfm.

Fromm, S. (2001). *Total estimated cost of child abuse and neglect in the United States.* Prevent Child Abuse America. Retrieved December 13, 2005, from http://www.preventchildabuse.org/learn_more/research_docs/cost_analysis.pdf.

Garbarino, J., Guttman, E., & Seely, J. (1986). *The psychologically battered child.* San Francisco, CA: Josey-Bass.

Hollander, S.K. (1992). Making young children aware of sexual abuse. *Elementary School Guidance and Counseling, 26,* 305-316.

Homeyer, L.E., & Landreth, G.L. (1998). Play therapy behaviors of sexually abused children. *International Journal of Play Therapy, (7) 1,* 49-71.

Howell-Nigrelli, I. (1988). Shared responsibility for reporting child abuse cases: A reaction to Spiegel. *Elementary School Guidance & Counseling, 22,* 275-283.

Miller, A. (1990). *For your own good.* New York: The Noonday Press.

National Clearinghouse on Child Abuse and Neglect Information. (2005). Retrieved on December 1, 2005, from http://www.nccanch.acf.hhs.gov/pubs/focus/school based/index.cfm.

Nesse, L. (1989). Psychological maltreatment in schools: Emerging issues for counselors. *Elementary School Guidance and Counseling, 23,* 194-200.

Office on Child Abuse and Neglect, Children's Bureau. (2003). *School-based child maltreatment programs: Synthesis of lessons learned.* Retrieved December 13, 2005, from http://www.nccanch.acf.hhs.gov/pubs/focus/schoolbased/index.cfm.

Paisley, P.O. (1987). Prevention of child abuse and neglect: A legislative response. *The School Counselor, 34,* 226-228.

Peterson, L.W., & Hardin, M. E. (1997). *Children in distress: A guide for screening children's art.* New York: W.W. Norton & Company.

Third national incidence study of child abuse and neglect. (2005). Retrieved on December 13, 2005, from http://www.nccanch.act.hhs.gov/pubs/statsinfo/nix3.cfm.

Thompson, C.L., & Rudolph, L.B. (1992). *Counseling children.* Pacific Grove, CA: Brooks/Cole.

Vanderbilt, H. (1992, February). Incest: A chilling report. *Lear's,* pp. 49-77.

White, J., & Allers, C.T. (1994). Play therapy with abused children: A review of the literature. *Journal for Counseling and Development, 48,* 324-329.

White, J., Draper, K., & Jones, N.P. (2001). Play therapy behaviors of physically abused children. In G.L. Landreth (Ed.). *Innovations in play therapy* (pp. 99-118). Philadelphia: Brunner-Routledge.

Whitney Peterson, L., & Hardin, M.E. (1997). *Children in distress: A guide for screening children's art.* New York: W.W. Norton.

# Chapter 15

# Counseling Sexual Minority Students

by
Gail Adorno

*Gail Adorno, LCSW, ACSW, is employed at Shands Teaching Hospital at the University of Florida, Gainesville. Ms. Adorno has made presentations to different professional groups on various GLBTQ issues.*

In a previous chapter, Flynn and White discussed the serious social, ethical, and legal problems school counselors face when a student becomes a victim of abuse. In general, these are visible victims, and as a school counselor, you know when they need your assistance. Many students who self-identify as gay, lesbian, bisexual, transgender or who question their sexual orientation or gender identity (GLBTQ) are often invisible victims. And sadly, if they do bring this situation to the awareness of others, they may face discrimination and further victimization. Many school counselors may find it difficult to be of effective assistance to sexual minority students because of their own views and beliefs, or lack of training.

In 1973, after much heated discourse, the American Psychiatric Association eliminated "homosexuality" as a category within the Diagnostic and Statistic Manual widely used by mental health professionals in the diagnosis of mental illness. In addition, the gay and lesbian civil rights movement in the 1970s opened the door to dramatic, positive attitude changes, in general, by society, gays and lesbians themselves and helping professionals. Legislation both to protect the civil rights of sexual minorities as well as to punish those who commit violence against sexual minorities as having carried out "hate" crimes, has continued to be passed in this country. Although many gains have been made in the last 35 years resulting in GLBTQ youth "coming out" to their peers, teachers and families in growing numbers, polarization of attitudes about sexual minorities continues to exist. A deep and pervasive current of discrimination, prejudice and even hatred for sexual minorities persists, perhaps, even among some helping professionals. More commonly, counselors may be inexperienced and lack understanding and comfort with sexual minority issues, thus, making intervention ineffective or even harmful. As GLBTQ youth choose to "come out," they open themselves to visibility with a price that includes the potential for harassment, discrimination, bullying and even violence. As school counselors, you have a responsibility to explore ways you can increase your effectiveness with this population and make your school a safe place for them to grow and learn.

What role should school counselors take in eliminating the discrimination and violence against sexual minority students? Coursework addressing these issues is not required for most school counseling programs, and the issue may be perfunctorily addressed in a class on diversity issues. Lacking is a full exploration of the salient issues that led gay and lesbian youth to claim a spot in the 1999 U.S. Surgeon General's "Call to Action to Prevent Suicide" as a group defined by its increased risk for suicide, particularly for males. Counselors must be proactive in pursuing continuing education and research opportunities to learn the issues that concern GLBTQ youth and to become effective advocates for attitudinal change. Awareness of your own attitudes, beliefs and feelings is a beginning step for counselors towards understanding and helping this diverse group.

Do you have any GLBTQ friends? How do you feel about being seen alone in public with them? Do you feel discomfort or even revulsion? Does something inside your head say this is "wrong?" What do your religious beliefs tell you? These are but a few questions asked by inventories available for persons to gauge their level of homophobia, which is commonly defined as an irrational or abnormal fear of homosexuality. An honest exploration of your own attitudes, beliefs and feelings including ease with your own sexual orientation and gender identity is the basic foundation for learning more about sexual minority youth.

Although times are changing and scores of public and private institutions extend domestic partner benefits to their employees in same-sex relationships, the majority of adult gay and lesbian couples lack the legal safeguards taken for granted by the heterosexual population. A dominant heterosexual view is found in every aspect of our lives from how we communicate with each other to the assessment forms and interview questionnaires located in our offices. Same sex marriage and whether to condone it and legalize it is a major societal issue today.

The American Psychiatric Association (2006) stated:

*Public opinion polls in the United States show that in the past twenty years, feelings toward gay men, lesbians and bisexuals have moved in a significantly positive direction. Nevertheless, when compared to other social groups homosexuals are still among the most stigmatized groups in the nation. Hate crimes are prevalent. Gay men and lesbians are still banned from serving openly in the US military service. Child custody decisions still frequently view gay and lesbian people as unfit parents. Gay and lesbian adolescents are often taunted and humiliated in their school settings. Many professional persons and employees in all occupations are still fearful of identifying as gay or lesbians in their work settings (American Psychiatric Association, 2006).*

One simple but powerful way you, as a school counselor, can initiate an inclusive environment is a review of your counseling intake forms and other questionnaires to incorporate inclusive language. When speaking with a parent, do you ask "Are you married?" A better way to phrase this may be "Are you partnered?" or "Who do you include in your family?" These statements imply "acceptance and awareness" on the part of the speaker. GLBTQ youth pick up on this kind of language. They also watch you and know from your past behavior in situations with sexual minority issues whether or not you are trustworthy.

Keeping items in your office such as a rainbow flag or pink triangle symbolizing gay pride or advocating for curriculum inclusion of GLBTQ history may be other ways to signal to GLBTQ youth that you have done your homework in understanding their issues. And powerfully, you help validate their experience and begin to be identified as an ally in an often hostile environment. Rather than attempting to change an adolescent's identification as GLBTQ, the school counselor's focus should be on transforming the environment's negative impact on GLBTQ youth to one of safety, acceptance and empowerment in which GLBTQ youth develop skills to form positive identities and cope with societal attitudes.

Gay, lesbian, and bisexual youth are a varied heterogeneous group. Their commonality lies in their same-sex affectional orientation and coping with society's attitudes toward them including discrimination, hatred, and violence. They are often referred to as troubled kids with higher rates of drug abuse and truancy who frequently run away. Findings from the first nationally representative study of U. S. adolescents confirms with strong evidence earlier reports that sexual minority youth are more likely than their peers to think about and attempt suicide (Russell & Joyner 2005). Interestingly, these findings emphasize the commonalties among all adolescents that youth suicide risk factors in general such as hopelessness, depression, alcohol abuse, and recent suicide attempts by a peer or family member, are the mediating factors between sexual orientation and suicidal tendency in adolescents. And, indeed, many sexual minority youth may cope with confusion, stigma, rejection and isolation imposed by society through risk taking behaviors such as alcohol and drug abuse, multiple sexual partners, and unprotected sex, thus increasing their exposure to HIV. While this may be true for many sexual minority youth, often overlooked are the adolescents that don't fit a classic gay or lesbian stereotype, such as a class president who busies himself with activities to the exclusion of dating, or the high school quarterback, or a popular cheerleader. Some teens choose to engage in sex with multiple opposite-sex partners. Some lesbian teens may deliberately pursue pregnancy. These behaviors may be the result of efforts to change, to "fit" and conceal a budding awareness of a GLBTQ identity.

Highlighting again the heterogeneity of GLBTQ youth, you as a counselor must keep in mind the diversity and complexity within this group. Gender differences exist among gay, lesbian, and bisexual youth. Males may come to an awareness of their sexual identity partly through sexual experiences while females more so develop their awareness through affectional ties with other females prior to sexual contact. Gay males are particularly prone to violence and taunting from peers, especially other males, whether they have actually "come out' or if they simply do not adhere to traditional notions of masculinity. While lesbian teens experience prejudice and even violence as well, this point emphasizes our society's particular abhorrence of male-male affection.

Often overlooked are the unique challenges faced by gay, lesbian, and bisexual youth of color and ethnicity. Sexual minority youth of varying ethnicity and color must integrate their developing sexual identify within a context of other competing minority challenges. In addition, cultural pressures against homosexuality in certain racial/ethnic communities add external pressures to "coming out" and accessing support through social relationships. As such, it is suggested while cultural influences do not impede sexual identity formation, gay, lesbian, and bisexual minority youth may have delayed identity integration (Rosario, Schrimshaw & Hunter, 2004).

As counselors, it is important to be aware of the context in which GLBTQ adolescents live. Is your school located in a rural tradition-bound community or situated in a metropolitan or suburban area with progressive resources and outreach programs for sexual minority youth? Are the adolescent's parents religiously conservative? What other minority issues effect the adolescent (e.g. ethnicity, religion, disability)? Does this adolescent already live in a chaotic home situation? What coping skills, adaptive and maladaptive, has the adolescent already developed to navigate life's challenges? What is the particular climate in your school district surrounding GLBTQ issues? Are topics of sexuality allowed in the classroom? What are the risks and benefits within these contextual factors for the adolescent to begin the "coming out" process? Questions such as these will help frame the environment, both internally and externally, in which gay, lesbian, and bisexual youth "come out."

The Gay, Lesbian, and Straight Education Network (GLSEN), a national organization founded in 1994 is dedicated to assure that each member of every school community is valued and respected regardless of sexual orientation or gender identity/expression (GLSEN, 2006). GLSEN provides a wealth of resources for school professionals (e.g. teachers, counselors, administrators) and students to bring creative programs to school and community in efforts to address anti-GLBTQ attitudes and stereotypes, promote support and acceptance, and create a safe school environment for all sexual minority students. GLSEN also conducts relevant surveys regarding GLBTQ bias and threat in the daily school environment.

A national survey conducted in 2005 by GLSEN, "From Teasing to Torment: School Climate in America," provides some startling data about the daily climate in which our children attend school. The following findings suggest that GLBTQ youth clearly are at increased risk for harassment and abuse each day they attend school (GLSEN, 2006a):

- Two-thirds (65%) of teens report that they have been verbally or physically harassed or assaulted during the past year because of their perceived or actual appearance, gender, sexual orientation, gender expression, race/ethnicity, disability or religion.

- One-third (33%) of teens report that students are frequently harassed because they are perceived to be lesbian, gay or bisexual.

- GLBTQ students are three times more likely than non-GLBTQ students to say that they do not feel safe at school (22% vs. 7%).

- Two-thirds of GLBTQ students who have experienced harassment never report such incidents. Cited twice as often as non-GLBTQ students, GLBTQ students say that it is because school staff would not do anything or things will continue.

A harassment policy in place that specifically mentions sexual orientation and gender identity/expression is one measure associated with more students feeling safe. GLSEN recommends ten steps as a starting point to making your school a "Safe Space" (See Appendix A at the end of the chapter for a list of these important steps, GLSEN, 2006b).

According to GLSEN (2006a), results of interventions and support for GLBTQ students included a range of positive indicators including greater sense of safety, fewer reports of missing school, and a higher incidence of planning to attend college. Students also reported a lower incidence of verbal harassment.

The public schools have been viewed as the agency most essential in bringing about appreciation for diversity and respect for the rights of all. A growing number of school districts and communities have developed special schools specifically to meet the needs of GLBTQ students in safe, supportive environments (e. g. the Harvey Milk School in NYC, EAGLE Center in Los Angeles). In addition, programs within school districts which promote positive education and counseling about sexuality including sexual minority issues have proved successful resources for GLBTQ students (e.g. Project 10 in Los Angeles, Project 10 East in M.A., The Triangle Program in Toronto). These programs have been designed with the participation of parents, teachers and representatives of the GLBTQ community.

In the fall of 2004, a consortium of national organizations, with leadership from the National School Boards Association (NSBA), published a resource document to help schools address legal issues surrounding students' sexual orientation and gender identity. Aimed at school policy makers and administrators, *"Dealing with Legal Matters Surrounding Students' Sexual Orientation and Gender Identity"* provides practical guidance on schools' legal rights and responsibilities with respect to students, school programs, and curriculum. In addition to NSBA, participating organizations are: American Association of School Administrators, American Federation of Teachers, American School Counselor Association, Association for Supervision and Curriculum Development, National Association of Elementary School Principals, National Association of Independent Schools, National Association of School Psychologists, National Association of Secondary School Principals, National Education Association, National Student Assistance Association, School Social Work Association of America, and United Church of Christ Justice & Witness Ministries (GLSEN, 2005).

The American School Counselor Association's position statement on GLBTQ youth (ASCA, 2005) contains the following:

*Professional school counselors promote equal opportunity and respect for all individuals regardless of sexual orientation or gender identity. Professional school counselors work to eliminate barriers that impede student development and achievement and are committed to academic, personal/social and career development of all students (ASCA, 2005).*

The entire statement is found at the end of this chapter. Clearly, school counselors are expected to take a leading role in promoting a safe learning environment where barriers are impeded and opportunities are available for GLBTQ students.

In recognition of the need for understanding and appropriate services to all students, the National Education Association (NEA) Board of Directors approved in 2002 *"The Report of the NEA Task Force on Sexual Orientation"* (NEA, 2002). The Report includes an in-depth examination of the needs and issues confronting GLBTQ students and education employees. The Report also addresses students and education employees who in fact are heterosexual, but who may be perceived to be GLBTQ because they do not appear to fit gender stereotypes, and heterosexual students whose parents are acknowledged to be GLBTQ, who may to some degree have similar needs and confront the same or similar problems

The increased protection by professional organizations is a big step in the right direction. And school counselors and other educators committed to social justice and human rights need to continue to examine their own specific responsibilities concerning students who are struggling with their sexual orientation or gender identity/expression. There are children in every classroom that will at some time in their lives recognize themselves to be either gay, lesbian, bisexual or transgender. They need your counsel, your support and protection, along with the opportunity to mature into sensitive, confident productive adults. Every classroom also has children with a first-generation relative (e.g. mother, father, sibling) or extended family member (e.g. grandmother, aunt, cousin) who is gay, lesbian, bisexual or transgendered. For these reasons, it is timely and appropriate for educators including school counselors to introduce sexual minority issues into the school curricula.

In addition to creating a more positive environment for adolescents, counselors must become aware of the unique personal pressures facing GLBTQ students. As previously mentioned, it is often during early adolescence (a period of critical development) that gay, lesbian, and bisexual youth come into self-awareness regarding their same-sex attractions. While the majority of gay and lesbian adolescents eventually develop a positive and healthy self-identity into adulthood, many find living with a stigmatized sexual identity stressful and a significant number of gay and lesbian youth have difficulty coping with this stress without appropriate resources and support. Can you, if you are heterosexual, imagine the stress faced by a gay or lesbian adolescent who realizes his or her sense of being different? Counselors know that adolescence is a time of conforming. How do you conform, if gay or lesbian, when your environment lacks appropriate gay and lesbian role models to mirror development? Can you imagine, as a teenager, suddenly realizing that you are attracted to a member of the same sex and hearing from an early age that this is "forbidden" and "shameful" according to society? Since many gay and lesbian students fear being discovered, they may begin isolating themselves as much as possible. Some may become chronic school truants while others may drop out completely. They learn to hide their true feelings and behave in ways to "fit in" in order to protect themselves or risk physical harm and rejection. School can be a great source of stress for these youth, many of whom will choose to either suppress their sexual feelings or deny their true sexual orientation. However, there will still be many adolescents who decide to begin the process of accepting their same-sex orientation.

Those gay and lesbian youth who do decide to "come out" may face immediate rejection from their peers. Gay and lesbian youth who come out may be rejected by their own family as well as their faith organization. Sadly, such blatant, overt, non acceptance by family and peers can lead to alienation, abandonment and even physical abuse by family members. Counselors know that feelings of alienation among youth frequently plays a role in attempted or completed suicide. Few solid research studies on the relationship between sexual orientation among youth and suicide have been conducted (Russell & Joyner, 2005). Sampling difficulties and methodological limitations have impeded drawing accurate conclusions about suicide among sexual minority youth. However, what remains clear is the damaging impact that cultural attitudes, discrimination, and violence against sexual minorities has on sexual minority youth challenged with identity development in the context of limited visible support and information.

Can gay, lesbian, bisexual, and transgender youth get help in their schools? Does your school have a policy prohibiting discrimination on the basis of sexual orientation and gender identity/expression? While many schools have general anti-harassment policies, many still do not have a specific policy in place regarding sexual orientation. A counselor who decides to take a stand and advocate for change on behalf of sexual minority students will need much personal courage because the rejection faced by these students may also be experienced by those who try to help.

# Tips on Counseling Students Questioning Their Sexual Identity

The tips given below for school counselors were developed by a group of students in a graduate level counseling course taught by the senior author/editor of this book at the University of Florida. The 16 points/tips are summarized below with permission.

1. First, look to yourself as a person and understand your true feelings regarding homosexuality. This is the most important tip you can receive and incorporate when counseling anyone "different" from yourself. If you feel that homosexuality is "wrong," "wicked" or "immoral," the gay/lesbian student will immediately be aware of these biased feelings; and you will be ineffective. If you hold these beliefs, or you feel pity, repulsion, and so forth; you must refer the student to another counselor.

The graduate students mentioned above indicated that there are many ways you can tell if you are homophobic. For example, would you perform the following activities? And, yes, how would you feel while performing them?

   a. Consider doing a presentation on gay and lesbian issues at your school, in your community, at your state convention, and so forth.

   b. Go into a crowded bookstore and ask the person behind the counter for a book on "coming out."

   c. Read a book about being gay/lesbian in a public place where people can walk by and read the cover

   d. Join PFLAG (Parents and Friends of Lesbians and Gays).

If you would feel awkward performing these activities, you should ask yourself why? Most likely the answer is because others will assume you are gay or lesbian and you would find this embarrassing. Think about what you are saying and revealing about yourself by being afraid of being labeled gay/lesbian. What is it about being gay/lesbian that you find negative? How would these beliefs (if you hold them) affect the way you, as a school counselor, would deal with students questioning their sexual identity? It is important that you acknowledge and challenge these beliefs if you are to work effectively with these youth.

2. Understand that gays and lesbians are aware of their orientation at a young age, just as heterosexuals are, even if they have never had a sexual experience. Understand also that gay/lesbian students have very few (visible) positive role models, especially couples.

Unlike other minority students in your school, gay/lesbian role models simply are not readily available, at least publicly.

3. Become involved in local gay and lesbian organizations. This will help break down any stereotypes you might have and will help you develop friendships with gay and lesbian individuals. It will also help you learn about available resources for these students. It is also a great opportunity to ask questions and learn. Become familiar with those groups that are available in your community.

4. Know where your school administration and the school district stand on the issue of sexual orientation. Many districts now include protection of students from harassment concerning sexual orientation. Having such a policy in writing gives counselors the opportunity to take a leadership role in reaching out to sexual minority students.

5. When trying to help a student deal with their feelings regarding homosexuality, it is important that you not invalidate their family or religious beliefs. Instead, focus on their feelings.

6. Reduce the "us" and "them" in your speech and actions. One middle school counselor said, during a large group guidance session on AIDS, "Its not just homosexuals, it could happen to us too." This would immediately alienate any students in the audience facing the question of their own sexuality. Would you, if a student in that situation, open up to that counselor? Probably not.

7. Assume every student is somewhere along the continuum of sexual orientation. Don't immediately assume every student is "straight." This puts the student in the position of lying and causes them to feel uncomfortable, incongruent, and so forth. Asking a female student new to your school if she has met any boys she likes would make her feel very uncomfortable if she were a lesbian. Instead (if you feel the need to ask such a question), try to leave her sexual orientation neutral by asking if she has found anyone special.

8. Be aware of what the research says about changing one's sexual orientation. Most knowledgeable researchers consider it unethical and ineffective to make such an attempt. Also, learning some of the theories about the origins of homosexuality can be a help when you work with gay/lesbian students.

9. Have visible appropriate resources in your school counseling office concerning homosexuality. This gives students the idea that you can be trusted and that it is okay to come out to you.

10. Have empathy for your gay/lesbian student clients, not sympathy or pity. The latter emotions imply to students that there is something terribly "wrong" with being gay/lesbian, which is something they've most likely heard, overtly or covertly, over and over again.

11. If you don't understand the feelings of the student, don't be afraid to ask. Asking if you don't understand something is usually taken as a sign of interest and caring.

12. Seek consultation from an adult who is gay or lesbian. Friends or fellow counselors who are gay or lesbian will provide you with valuable insight and many helpful hints for counseling gay/lesbian youth. Do not rely on the gay or lesbian student as your sole source of information.

13. Do not personally label the student lesbian or gay. The research indicates that over 50% of the population have had some type of same-sex sexual experience. Labeling should be left to the individual student.

14. Coming out should be left entirely to the student. This is very important, and most likely, a risky step for them to take. They should decide when and who to come out to. No one else can do it for them. You can, and should, help them realize the possible personal "costs" and "benefits," but allow the student to maintain control over the coming out process.

15. Refer the gay/lesbian student to reputable community groups. Throughout their lives they may have felt different and alone. Referring them to groups with understanding students helps them discuss issues with others their age who are experiencing the same things they are currently experiencing. Most cities have resources available to gay and lesbian students. Your local information and referral hotline will also have these resources available for you

16. Parents feel a loss when they are told their offspring is gay/lesbian and often need counseling. They may also seek you out, especially if their child came out to you. Be prepared, some may blame themselves. Being aware of the current literature regarding the etiology of homosexuality can be very helpful when these parents come to your office.

## Summary

Schools can have a positive or negative impact on sexual minority youth. The school climate will influence GLBTQ students to repress and or/suppress their true feelings regarding their sexual orientation or gender identity, or, lead to a process of trust and true expression. Creating a safe climate for an authentic self should be our goal as school counselors. What is the climate in your school? Is it open to such free expression? Position statements and policies of school districts and national organizations are beginning to include sexual orientation in their language about harassment. School counselors have the opportunity and the responsibility to respond positively in a leadership position to the needs of sexual minority students in their respective schools

## References

American School Counselor Association (ASCA). (2005). *Role statement: The professional school counselor and sexual minority youth.* Alexandria, VA: Author.

American Psychiatric Association. (1998). *Position statement: Psychiatric treatment and sexual orientation.* Washington DC: Author.

American Psychiatric Association. (2006). *Healthy minds. Healthy lives.* Retrieved July 2, 2006 at http://www.healthyminds.org/glbissues.cfm

GLSEN. (2005). *Education organizations release groundbreaking legal guide regarding LGBT issues in schools.* Retrieved July 2, 2006 at http://www.glsen.org/cgi-bin/iowa/all/library/record/1742.html

GLSEN. (2005b). *Ten things educators can do to ensure their classrooms are safe spaces for ALL students.* Retrieved July 2, 2006 at http://www.glsen.org/cgi-bin/iowa/all/library/record/1796.html

GLSEN. (2006a). *National school climate survey sheds new light on experiences of lesbian, gay, bisexual, and transgender students.* Retrieved July 2, 2006 at http://www.glsen.org/cgi-bin/iowa/all/news/record/1927.html

National Education Association. (2002). *Report of the NEA task force on sexual orientation.* Retrieved July 2, 2006 at http://www.nea.org/nr/02taskforce.html

Rosario, M., Schrimshaw, E.W., & Hunter, J. (2004). Ethnic/racial differences in the coming-out process of lesbian, gay, and bisexual youths: A comparison of sexual identity development over time. *Cultural Diversity and Ethnic Minority Psychology, 10 (3),* 215-228.

Russell, S.T., & Joyner, K. (2005). Adolescent sexual orientation and suicide risk: Evidence from a national study. *American Journal of Public Health, 91(8),* 1276-1281.

# GLSEN's (2005b) Ten Steps for Making Your School a "Safe Space"

1. Do not assume heterosexuality. Remind yourself and others that GLBTQ people are found on every staff, in every classroom, and on every team.

2. Include the significance of LGBT people in lessons. "Out" the figures you study whose sexual orientation and gender identity/expression is not discussed. Just as race, class, sex, and ability affect the way people shape the world, sexual orientation and gender identity/expression impact people's experiences deeply.

3. Work with the librarian towards inclusive collections of literature. The library is frequently the first place to which students turn for accurate information on sexuality and gender.

4. Work with athletic staff/athletes to reduce bias on the field. Transphobia and homophobia are often the worst in the locker room or in the gym.

5. Work towards inclusive dances, proms, and social programming. These activities often set the tone for the community. Make them memorable for everyone.

6. Work with student or staff groups concerned with diversity and oppression. The same conditions that allow homophobia and transphobia to develop most likely promote other forms of prejudice. Collaborate to unite against all oppression.

7. Provide appropriate health education. Sex education should address the needs of GLBTQ youth, and should affirm the fact that they go through many of the same changes, and face many of same challenges during adolescence as their straight peers.

8. Celebrate GLBTQ History Month. Recognize the struggles, contributions, and victories of the LGTB community with special lesson plans, events, and displays.

9. Join or start a Gay-Straight Alliance (GSA). Creating a time and place to     talk about GLBTQ issues recognizes their value and opens up dialogues which can lead to healing.

10. Create inclusive anti-discrimination policies.

    GLBTQ members of the school community need to know their schools value equality and that they are protected against discrimination. In addition, sexual orientation and gender identity/expression should be included in multicultural and diversity statements as a way to communicate equal treatment to all. (*GLSEN Safe Space: A How-To Guide for Starting an Allies Program* (2005b).

# American School Counselor Association (ASCA, 2005) Position Statement on GLBTQ Youth

## The Professional School Counselor and Gay, Lesbian, Bisexual, Transgendered and Questioning (GLBTQ) Youth

Professional school counselors promote equal opportunity and respect for all individuals regardless of sexual orientation or gender identity. Professional school counselors work to eliminate barriers that impede student development and achievement and are committed to academic, personal/social and career development of all students.

### The Rationale

Gay, lesbian, bisexual, transgendered and questioning (GLBTQ) youth often begin to experience self-identification during their pre-adolescent or adolescent years, as do heterosexual youth. These developmental processes are essential cognitive activities, and although they may have an impact on student development and achievement, they are not a sign of illness, mental disorder or emotional problems nor do they necessarily signify sexual activity.

Some students face obstacles in school and society that inhibit them from understanding and accepting their sexual orientation/gender identity or the identity of others. Students may face bullying, harassment and name-calling based on real or perceived sexual orientation/gender identity. Professional school counselors realize these issues may infringe upon healthy student development and limit their opportunities in school and the community.

### The Professional School Counselor's Role

The professional school counselor works with all students through the stages of identity development and understands this development may be more difficult for sexual minority youth. It is not the role of the professional school counselor to attempt to change a student's sexual identity but instead to provide support to GLBTQ students to promote student achievement. Professional school counselors are:

- aware of their own beliefs about sexual orientation and gender identity
- knowledgeable of the negative effects that result from stereotyping individuals into rigid gender roles
- committed to the affirmation of youth of all sexual orientations and identities

Identity development is an important developmental process for all students, and to assist in this development, professional school counselors:

- assist all students as they clarify feelings about their own sexual orientation/gender identity and the identity of others in a nonjudgmental manner
- advocate for equitable educational opportunities for all students
- address inappropriate language from students and adults
- promote sensitivity and acceptance of diversity among all students and staff
- provide GLBTQ-inclusive and age-appropriate information on issues such as diverse family structures, dating and relationships and sexually transmitted diseases
- model language that is inclusive of sexual orientation/gender identity
- encourage policies that address discrimination against any student
- promote violence-prevention activities to create a safe school environment that is free of fear, bullying and hostility

Recognizing that sexual orientation is not an illness and does not require treatment, professional school counselors may provide individual student planning or responsive services to GLBTQ students to:

- promote self-acceptance.
- deal with social acceptance
- understand issues related to "coming out," including issues that families may face when a student goes through this process
- identify appropriate community resources

### Summary

Professional school counselors promote affirmation, respect and equal opportunity for all individuals regardless of sexual orientation or gender identity. Professional school counselors also promote awareness of issues related to sexual orientation/gender identity among students, teachers, administrators, parents and the community. Professional school counselors work to eliminate barriers that impede student development and achievement and are committed to the academic, career and personal/social development of all students.

# Chapter 16

# Creating a Safe School Environment for Sexual Minority Students:
# A Special Role for School Counselors

**by Carlos Hernandez and Jennifer Sager**

*Carlos Hernandez, Ph.D., is a Clinical Assistant Professor at the University of Florida Counseling Center. His clinical and research interests include multiculturalism, sexual orientation, and vocational issues. Dr. Hernandez has guest lectured for numerous graduate counseling courses and has presented at national conferences on topics of sexual orientation and career issues. He developed and taught a course entitled, "Counseling the Lesbian, Gay, Bisexual, and Transgender Client." Dr. Hernandez provides individual, group, and couples counseling to students with a variety of clinical, vocational, and interpersonal issues and concerns.*

*Jennifer Sager, Ph.D. is an associate staff member/ therapist at the University of Florida Counseling Center. She also maintains a private practice and serves as an assessment consultant with Intensive Therapy Modalities. Dr. Sager's interests include multiple identities, specifically the intersection of race, sex, and sexual orientation. She is a member of the Harry Benjamin International Gender Dysphoria Association, assists transgender individuals with change of life issues and has presented and published on lesbian, gay, bisexual, and transgendered issues. She is the author of The Psychology of Transgender, a book chapter featured in* The New Goddess: Transgender Women in the Twenty-First Century.

The current school environment is comprised of an ever-increasing diverse student population. According to estimates by the U.S. Census Bureau, minorities are increasing in such dramatic numbers that they will make up nearly half of the U.S. population by 2050 (U.S. Census Bureau, 2004), thus impacting all segments of our society. School systems nationwide need to be prepared to understand, support, and guide culturally different children and adolescents through the complexity of an academic curriculum which may not have been developed and implemented with the needs of these students in mind. The role of the school counselor is a unique one in that they must adapt their counseling programs to the needs placed upon them by the various stakeholders they serve: students, parents, and/or legal guardians. One culturally different population of students that is often overlooked in the school curriculum is the gay, lesbian, bisexual, transgender, or queer (GLBTQ) students.

It should be noted that the GLBTQ acronym is also used by such professional organizations as the American School Counselor Association (ASCA), among others, to represent lesbian, gay, bisexual, transgender, and "questioning" as opposed to "queer" youth (GLBTQ).

The GLBTQ population is marginalized in our society, yet each year an increasing number of GLBTQ students and their parents/legal guardians disclose their sexual orientation (i.e., coming out) and sexual/gender identity during the formative school years. Increasing numbers of GLBTQ and ally support groups and organizations are being formed to help support GLBTQ students and educate the general school population on GLBTQ issues and concerns. School counselors are often the first person to whom a GLBTQ student or parent/legal guardian discloses their sexual orientation and elicit their assistance in navigating through a (sometimes) harsh, homophobic environment or uninviting school system. The role of school counselors in supporting GLBTQ students is monumental, and yet many school counselors may feel unprepared to assist these students.

In this chapter we have presented the various issues school counselors may encounter when working with GLBTQ students and their parents/legal guardians. We present this information using a developmental approach by introducing vignettes, discussion, necessary knowledge, and counseling interventions (action items) that may be applied at the elementary, middle, and high school levels. We have tried to provide insights into the challenges and needs facing GLBTQ students in the school system as well increasing the understanding, sensitivity, and support of school counselors whom are tasked with taking care of the psychological, and sometimes physical needs, of the students in their respective schools. Another important element in counseling GLBTQ students is being aware of one's own personal challenges. To this end, we discuss personal biases, heterosexism, and self-care that can affect our work with GLBTQ students. We close the chapter with specific programs that school counselors may implement so as to create systematic changes to better assist those GLBTQ students who may be hesitant to overtly seek assistance from school counselors and would otherwise remain invisible.

# Elementary School

## Case Study

*Johnny is a second grade student. According to his teacher, he has been missing school and often gets into fights with other kids. When the teacher asked Johnny what was happening, he started to cry. He said he was afraid to come to school because some of the boys in the third grade teased him on the school bus, often calling him names like sissy, queer, and faggot. He reported that he did not know what all the words meant, but he has heard of the word "sissy." When Johnny told his parents about the older kids teasing him, his father told him he should learn to" fight back and be a man." The teacher informs you, as the school counselor, that she has noticed Johnny's preference to play and interact with girls rather than with boys and that he is often ridiculed by his classmates for this behavior. The teacher has asked that you speak to Johnny to see if you can be of assistance to him.*

This scenario is all too common as GLBTQ kids experience harassment in either a verbal or physical manner. According to Barret and Logan (2002) the Gay, Lesbian, Straight Educators Network (GLSEN) conducted the first national survey of sexual minority youth which revealed that 69% of the youth reported experiencing some type of verbal, physical, and sexual harassment and assault while attending school. Furthermore, 90% of the sexual minority youth surveyed reported being verbal harassed by hearing homophobic comments such as dyke, sissy, or queer. The youth reported that most of the negative comments came from other students, but 30 % reported hearing derogatory name-calling from school faculty and other staff members. A third of those surveyed reported that it was rare for anyone to intervene on their behalf. When someone did intervene, it was often other students. The students reported that rarely did a faculty or staff member intervene to try and stop the harassment.

Even in the primary and elementary levels derogatory comments are made by students and adults with regard to physical height, weight, ethnicity, disability, socioeconomic status, and sexual orientation. With the case of Johnny described above, the school counselor must create and ensure a safe environment for him to share his feelings, fears, and frustration. It is important for the school counselor to maintain a non-judgmental and bias free attitude and demeanor. This will allow Johnny and similiar children to feel accepted and better understood.

At his current developmental age, Johnny may not know how to define his sexual orientation, a distinction that is typically made after puberty. A child such as Johnny may express himself as being different or may indicate that it "feels more natural" for him to play with the girls. Often times GLBTQ individuals have expressed feeling "different" from a very young age, but unable to label the feeling until they were much older. School counselors should be aware of the following in regard to younger GLBTQ students:

- Young children may identify with or outside of traditional gender role expectations, regardless of sexual orientation or gender identity.

- Transgender children may present outside of socialization roles for boys and girls

- Heterosexual parents may not be aware of what it means to have a GLBTQ child.

- GLBTQ kids are usually picked on by other children or adults for being different thus creating an unsafe environment for him/her to learn or grow.

- Discipline issues and low academic performance may be a factor for a child trying to cope with their GLBTQ identity or expression.

- A GLBTQ child may exhibit psychosomatic illness due to the stress and anxiety brought about from having to endure homophobic comments and harassment. This may lead to higher rates of absenteeism.

- Parents of GLBTQ students or GLBTQ parents may disclose their child's or own (respectively) sexual orientation or identity as a way of identifying the type of family they have.

- As a result of a hostile, unsupportive environment, GLBTQ children may have a higher rate of depression. Left undetected or treated, this depression may lead to suicidal ideations, attempts, or completions. It is important that you monitor the child's psychological and physical well-being and assess for any possible suicidal ideations. When in doubt seek guidance from other counselors or administrators.

- Be aware that not all GLBTQ children may be dealing with a homophobic environment at school or at home. There are parents that are supportive of their GLBTQ children and children of their GLBTQ parents.

- Educate and serve as a consultant for your school on GLBTQ issues. You can provide in-house training to increase sensitivity and understanding, especially about name-calling.

- Be aware of your own biases and limitations in working with GLBTQ children or individuals. Your support, normalization and validation are critical. If you cannot be supportive, then please refer the student to someone else.

- It is important to identify allies in your school and community to serve as resources to you and your GLBTQ students or colleagues.

## Action Items: Combating Name Calling

It is not unusual to hear students insulting one another. Some students are creative in their insults and may be using new and innovative terms to tease their classmates. However, the racial, ethnic and sexual slurs tend to remain the same and are easily understood. We would rarely allow a racist slur to occur without commenting and correcting the student. However, slurs about GLBTQ students are often overlooked, creating an unsafe environment for these students. Terms such as "faggot or lezzie" should be corrected and be explained as socially unacceptable. Many students use the term "gay" as a general term meaning "not good" or "stupid," such as "This term paper is so gay." Even these statements should be challenged, whether students, staff, teachers or administrators make the statements. Allowing such language to exist in the school teaches all youth that hatred of GLBTQ individuals is condoned. As a school counselor, you have the opportunity to personally correct students' language, as well as encouraging teachers to create a cooperative learning environment that emphasizes the celebration of diversity (ASCA, 2005).

# Middle School Level

## Case Study

*April is in the eighth grade at your school. She usually presents herself as a "tomboy", dressing with baggy jeans, T-shirt, and short-spiked hair. She transferred to your school from a large Northeast city. April and her friend Nancy were sent to the school counselor's office after being caught kissing in the girls' bathroom by one of the teachers. The girls appear nervous and keep asking if their parents need to be called.*

While divisions among friend groups and name-calling are a mainstay of elementary school, puberty and identity development often begins in middle or junior high school. Sexual awareness often begins during this developmental age when children begin to notice changes in their bodies caused by hormonal changes. If not addressed, these drastic changes can frighten some students. Thus, we think it is important that an explanation of the physical changes that occur during this developmental stage be addressed and discussed in all middle school counseling programs. The middle school counselor can also play the role of a catalyst in assisting parent(s) or guardian(s) to play an active role in assisting their child's understanding of the complexity of puberty and sexuality.

In addition, gender appropriate behaviors are often strongly encouraged through peer pressure. For example, a boy who is interested in a home economics elective course is likely to be teased by his classmates, regardless of his sexual identity. Subtle reactions from school counselors about gender appropriate behaviors will have lasting effects. School counselors are in a powerful, key position to encourage students to explore new interests, while having a frank discussion about how classmates may respond to archaic gender role divisions. A discussion about the impact of challenging gender norms is appropriate, and necessary. Avoiding this discussion will leave the student facing this issue to be socially unprepared. Although this may appear to be a delicate conversation to hold with a middle school child, the "anti peer pressure" message has been used effectively in anti-drug and alcohol campaigns for decades and is easily adapted for gender norms.

A more complicated issue of gender norms is transgender identity. To better understand transgender, it should be understood that "sex" refers to the biological classification of an individual as either "male" or "female" based on morphology such as chromosomes, genitalia, or secondary sexual characteristics. On the other hand, "gender" refers to a personal psychological identification as either "man" or "woman," or what has been considered to be masculine or feminine (GLSEN, 2003). Thus, gender is not necessarily a dichotomous concept and may vary markedly, depending on the interpretation of the individual and society. Terminology used in the transgender community is constantly changing with new terms and concepts being created periodically. In our opinion, the terms appearing here are currently the most widely accepted in current literature and the transgender community. "Transgender identity" is a self-applied term, which a student may use to identify with the transgendered community as a whole, whereas "gender identity" refers to "an individual's innate sense of maleness (masculinity) or femaleness (femininity), or both. Therefore, individuals who identify with a transgendered identity are experiencing "gender incongruence," which emphasizes incongruence between gender and sex (Sager, Gustafson, & Byrd, 2006).

It is especially important to recognize that sexual orientation occurs separate from a transgendered identity (Sager, Gustafson, & Byrd, 2006). Sexual orientation terminology for transgendered individuals is based on what gender, not sex, the person ascribes to and the gender of their sexual attraction. Therefore, if April identifies as transgendered, "he" may be attracted to females (making "him" heterosexual), attracted to males (making "him" gay), or attracted to both females and males (making "him" bisexual). This is a complicated issue as terminology often challenges our basic assumptions about sex and gender.

GLBTQ youth may experience shame regarding their bodies, especially transgender students. For example a transgender boy (i.e., genetic female) may not want breast development or the menstrual cycle to begin. Physical education classes may be a source of frustration, pain and fear for GLBTQ students as they have to change and shower in front of other students and engage in physical activities that may not be appropriate for their gender identity. In addition, transgendered students may feel uncomfortable using a public restroom because (a) they do not feel comfortable using the "wrong" bathroom, (b) concerned that other students will make fun of them for using a bathroom that is incongruent with their gender expression, or (c) fear of violence in an isolated room often not supervised.

In sum, we would caution the school counselor to not make assumptions regarding an individual's gender presentation and/or expression. Not all students who eschew stereotypical gender presentation would consider themselves transgendered; gender nonconformity can represent any number of identities, values, cultures or popular trends.

Overall, middle school is when GLBTQ students become increasingly aware that they are different from their heterosexual counterparts. Students who believe they are different from their classmates may act out in a variety of ways. Some students may disconnect from the school experience, either throwing themselves into academics (i.e., focusing too much on studying) or withdrawing from academics (i.e., tardiness, behavior problems). Both sides of this spectrum may indicate social withdrawal and are cause for concern. Other students may find a counter culture social group which appears to challenge authority. This sub-culture allows the student to avoid isolation while retaining an "I'm different" identity. GLBTQ students may adopt a challenging self-presentation style to determine who is accepting of them. For instance, a GLBTQ student may think, "If this person cannot accept that I wear black all the time, then how will this person accept my sexual orientation." Efforts to include students in finding their identity should occur during the middle school years. A focus on identity during the high school years may be too late as group formation will usually have occurred in middle school.

School counselors need to be aware of the following where middle school students are concerned:

- Puberty and sexual awakening takes place during this developmental period.

- Middle school students may not be verbose about their sexual orientation or gender identity. Having something gay affirming (e.g., SAFE zone sticker, Gay-Straight Alliance poster) in your office may identify you as a safe person and encourage them to talk to you about sensitive issues.

- GLBTQ students may act out more then heterosexual kids in an attempt to be viewed differently or as a way to gain control of their environment; an environment that can appear scary, unfamiliar, threatening, and non-supportive.

- GLBTQ students, parents, and teachers may seek assistance and/or consult with you during this time.

- Honor students' privacy and guarantee confidentiality. If you cannot guarantee confidentiality for legal reasons, then ethically you should inform the student of this fact ahead of time.

## Action Items: Honoring Culturally Diverse People of History

As our student population becomes more culturally diverse, it is important for school counselors, teachers, and administrators to ensure that the school reflects this cultural diversity. Too often text books minimize cultural diversity and as such, it is important for school personnel to find creative ways to honor culturally diverse people and events. Without role models, lesbian, gay, bisexual, and transgender students may feel invisible, unsupported and isolated. Celebrating national coming out day, using a display case to celebrate PRIDE awareness month, putting up posters in classrooms/offices, diversifying the school library to include GLBTQ books, reports on famous GLBTQ individuals, and inviting an GLBTQ guest speaker are potential ways to raise cultural awareness with students and school personnel. In addition, the inclusion of sexual orientation/trans-identity of famous individuals (e.g., http://www.lambda.org/famous.htm) can help students understand that GLBTQ individuals have made/make important contributions to mainstream society, through the arts, scientific advancements, and leadership. These types of activities can make the "invisible visible" and will assist GLBTQ students to feel more viable and will help them develop more self confidence and personal dignity. Lastly, GLBTQ identity is not limited to Caucasian individuals. An effort should be made to show that GLBTQ involves all cultural groups. For example, Baynard Rustin was one of Martin Luther King's advisors during the Civil Rights Movement and a primary organizer for the 1963 March on Washington. However, because of his gay sexual orientation, his involvement was downplayed and few people are aware of his importance in the overall civil rights movement of the 60's (for more information, see *Out of the Past* documentary or the movie *Brother Outsider*).

# High School Level

## Case Study

*You are summoned by the Principal to her office where she has a group of boys who were caught fighting in the locker room. According to the P.E. teacher, three boys were beating and fighting with another boy whom they claim was staring at them while they were taking showers. The boy they were hitting was taken to the nurse's office due to cuts obtained in the fight. The police were called as the incident was severe and several students and coaches heard the boys making homophobic threatening comments. The boys claim the lone boy was "checking us out and we had to teach the faggot a lesson." The Principal asked you to assist her in investigating this matter and in notifying the parents of the students involved in the incident*

Overt heterosexism and homophobia often occurs during the high school years. Homophobia is the fear or hatred of the GLBTQ individual and may be manifested as prejudice, discrimination, harassment, or acts of violence. Heterosexism is a subtle form of oppression and involves the assumption that heterosexuality is the appropriate norm.

The above described scenario indirectly involves all students in the school, not just the boys involved in the specific incident described. While the boys directly involved have obviously engaged in homophobic behavior, and potentially a hate crime, the atmosphere that allowed such behavior must be examined. Has the coach made homophobic comments? Did the boys feel they would be positively rewarded/thanked for attacking the other boy? Were there prior incidences between these boys which were ignored by the coach or other school personnel? And most importantly, how will the school send a message to the student body that this behavior is unacceptable and will not be tolerated? A message to the student body not only protects the injured boy, but also protects every closeted or out GLBTQ student in the school. A school counselor is in the unique position of not only assisting with this particular violent act, but to also create systemic change to avoid subsequent anti-gay violence in his/her school.

There are many negative consequences to allowing an anti-gay atmosphere to continue in the school. For instance, depression strikes homosexual youth more often and more severely than their non-gay peers. In addition, GLBTQ students are more likely than their heterosexual counterparts to engage in alcohol, drug use, smoking and unprotected sex (Russell & Joyner, 2005). Furthermore, there can be serious legal ramifications and financial consequences for your specific school and the central administration by permitting an anti-gay atmosphere to continue. Some administrators may not be aware of the fact that on May 24, 1999, the U.S. Supreme Court in Davis vs. Monroe County Board of Education imposed a ruling that, when coupled with recent interpretations of legislation and court cases, can have far-reaching implications. The Davis case established that public schools can be forced to pay damages for failing to stop student-on-student sexual harassment. School counselors have long understood that a fair and inclusive education is not possible for a student whose physical and emotional safety is regularly compromised. The Davis ruling and other court cases strengthen school counselors' efforts to create a more humanistic school environment. With the court's backing, socially active school counselors are stepping forward and saying to school officials that the schools have to do more to eliminate bullying and harassment incidents within the schools or face the consequences.

## Coming Out

"Coming out" is a phrase used to indicate when someone has expressed or indicated their sexual orientation to another person or to themselves. It may be accomplished in a direct or indirect manner. For example, a student may approach you and say, "I have something to tell you... I think I may be gay." Other people may also "out" a student's sexual orientation. For instance, you might hear another student or staff member talking about a student whom they suspect might be gay. Too often these comments have a negative connotation (i.e., I saw those girls holding hands; he is a sissy; he acts like a girl). Coming out is a process that can happen during any time in a person's life.

# Career Development

In today's ever changing global economy, students are starting to explore and consider career opportunities at an earlier age. School counselors play a vital role in assisting students with exploring career interests and assist them with applying to post secondary institutions and vocational programs. As a school counselor you may have a GLBTQ student who is not only struggling with trying to fit in, but also may find him/herself anxious about a future career path. GLBTQ students may also be concerned about selecting a college or university that will support and encourage them to further explore and integrate their sexual orientation. GLBTQ individuals are found in all facets of work and at all levels (e.g., managerial, blue-collar). However, due to a lack of GLBTQ role models, GLBTQ youth may not know, or have come in contact with, teachers, lawyers, doctors, or construction workers who are GLBTQ, let alone publicly out in their professions. This lack of professional visibility may cause GLBTQ students to feel that they are limited to stereotypical career paths. The media has often portrayed GLBTQ individuals in the arts (e.g., actors), social sciences (e.g., counselors) and gender nonconforming service providers (e.g., hairdressers, florists, mechanics). Not only are these interpretations sexist, but also they are false. Despite the assumptions associated with these careers, not all of individuals holding such employment are lesbian or gay.

As a school counselor, your understanding and support in normalizing the career decision-making process for GLBTQ students is critical. Sexual orientation or gender identity should not limit an individual's vocational interests or pursuits. Provide the GLBTQ student with the same career exploration interventions and assessments as you would any student. Have them take interests and vocational inventories, attend career fairs, identify their likes and dislikes, have them conduct information interviews with individuals in careers they are considering, and encourage them to pursue internship opportunities. However, GLBTQ students will have some additional needs. You can assist your GLBTQ students by searching the Internet to identify what companies or firms have sexual orientation and gender expression in their non-discrimination policies or clauses. This will ensure that the company is legally supportive of their GLBTQ employees. This same exploratory process can be applied to looking for institutions of higher learning. Through colleges' and universities' websites, examine whether the campus has GLBTQ student and/or faculty and staff support groups (see Windmeyer's *The Advocate College Guide for LGBT Students*, 2006 for more information).

As a school counselor you can better prepare yourself to assist GLBTQ students by attending career workshops and contacting local businesses in your area asking them what policies or support they have for diverse groups of employees including GLBTQ individuals. Additional steps you can take are: (a) create a resource list to share with GLBTQ students; (b) contact GLBTQ professionals that would be willing to answer questions or serve on a panel to discuss GLBTQ issues in the work place; (c) partner with local colleges, universities or public libraries to tap into their GLBTQ resources; and, (d) explore how your school district can work together with other libraries to provide information and knowledge on career-related books and careers for GLBTQ individuals.

It is important is to remember that GLBTQ students are unaware of the career/job possibilities that are open to them. As a school counselor, your willingness to listen, support, guide, and encourage can make a significant difference in the way in which GLBTQ students will see their future and strive to achieve their dreams and potential.

Specific issues school counselors should be aware of during the high school years:

- Same sex attraction can become more prominent at this stage. Dating success or failures are experienced at this time.

- If a student identifies as or is perceived to be GLBTQ, they may be targeted for harassment (verbal or physical or both) from peers, teachers, administrators, and parents.

- "Coming out" may be achieved or attempted at this time- either voluntarily or involuntarily by others.

- Be aware of a possible change in behavior or academic performance including tardiness, distrust, emotional or physical distance, and possibly desiring to dropout of school.

- Empowered GLBTQ students, parents, and allies may challenge school policy and custom.

- Transgender students and individuals are often misunderstood and sometimes are discriminated against by heterosexuals as well as experiencing discrimination from lesbians, gays, and bisexual communities.

- Suicide is high among teens; estimates range from 20%-40% of all teen suicides are related to sexual orientation issues. Gay and lesbian youth are two to three times more likely to attempt suicide than heterosexual young people.

- Many gay and lesbian youth are forced to leave home because of conflicts with their families over their sexual orientation. Do not advise youth to come out to parents, family and friends. Coming out must be their decision and they may have a better understanding of how their family will react than you do.

## Action Items:
## Creating a Safe Zone

Many schools have initiated SAFE ZONE sticker campaigns to create a more accepting and positive environment. Stickers are distributed to school personnel to display in classrooms or offices to show support for GLBTQ students. The purpose of the stickers is to identify supportive adults in the school system available to discuss issues related to sexuality, gender identity and safety. An important element of the SAFE ZONE program is that all personnel who opt to participate in the program receive a packet of information with resources, referrals, and information on GLBTQ youth. School counselors can enhance this program by organizing workshops on how to best help GLBTQ youth or bringing in guest speakers to help educate school personnel. Safe Zone resource packet information can be obtained by contacting Youth Pride, Inc. (http://www.youthpride-ri.org/) or Gay Straight Alliance's Making Your School a Hate Free Zone (http://www.gsanetwork.org/resources/hatefree.htm).

## Personal Challenges

Working with GLBTQ students is different than learning a new counseling skill; it involves challenging your belief system and having a deep commitment to learn about, support and appreciate GLBTQ students. First be aware of your own bias and prejudices in working with GLBTQ issues and individuals as well as your personal view of GLBTQ families. Although students may identify as heterosexual, they may have parents or family members who identify as lesbian, gay, bisexual, or transgendered. Reducing your own heterosexism is a worldview change, which will involve considerable attentiveness to personal language. Always use gender natural language; such as avoid asking if a student has a boyfriend or girlfriend. Instead ask, "Is there a significant other in your life or who are you dating?" Ask, "Tell me about your family" instead of asking "what is your father's and mother's name?" Gender natural language shows sensitivity and openness for thinking outside the proverbial box.

Second, as a school counselor you may find yourself in a precarious situation of being an advocate for the GLBTQ students, parents, or legal guardians and having to uphold antiquated school board polices as they pertain to GLBTQ issues. Many non-GLBTQ individuals face having their sexual orientation in question for assisting or advocating for GLBTQ rights and privileges. You may experience strong opposition and resistance to your attempts to educate or advocate for GLBTQ individuals. You may also encounter a lack of school or community resources to assist your efforts in providing services to GLBTQ students and their parents. Graduate programs often do not provide adequate training for school counselors on GLBTQ issues.

Creating a safe environment and challenging homophobia can be a daunting task but it can be made easier with personal support and guidance from colleagues. To increase your awareness, you can attend workshops; identify schools with integrated GLBTQ policies and curriculum to increase your understanding of the issues confronting GLBTQ students, parents, and their families and how you may be able to bring about changes to your specific school.

## Strategies to working with GLBTQ Students, Parents, Legal Guardians, and Allies

Be aware of the ethical considerations and codes of conduct for your national and state organizations and licensing boards. For example, confidentiality is important when working with GLBTQ students and parents. Although a student or parent/guardian may appear comfortable having a private conversation about their sexual/gender identity, this openness does not mean they are "out" in the community or that they would want you to share their personal stories with others.

Provide a safe, accepting, and opening environment for all students, including those that are GLBTQ. Decorate your office to appear GLBTQ friendly and acceptance by having books, posters, or a safe zone card to indicate you and others are GLBTQ friendly. In addition, consider having posters or bulletin boards in the hallway that may send a message of being open and accepting towards diversity issues.

Be prepared to provide education and training to your teaching colleagues and parents about GLBTQ issues. Build and maintain community resources that may be helpful in assisting you with your GLBTQ work. It is important to identify allies such as students, parents, teachers, school administrators, mental and medical health care providers, and religious and spiritual leaders who may serve as partners in creating a safe and supportive environment for GLBTQ students and their families at your school. Work with your school PTA to provide a welcoming environment for GLBTQ families. Find or consider creating a state/national wide association for teachers, school counselors, and administrators dealing with GLBTQ issues in their schools.

Consider making a safe environment a legal aspect of your school environment. Review any school-based forms and identify and replace heterosexual language that may be considered insensitive to GLBTQ students and their families. Review and incorporate, if necessary, nondiscrimination clauses to include sexual orientation and gender expression. The implementation of non-discrimination policy guidelines in schools should reveal clear support for GLBTQ students and respect for all students. Many school districts have created non-discrimination policies that include sexual orientation and we would urge you to initiate such a policy for your school if one is not already in place. The following wording can be used as a model for such a policy to protect school employees and students from harassment on the basis of their sexual orientation:

> Harassment on the basis of an individual's sexual preferences or orientation is prohibited. Words, actions, or other verbal, written, or physical conduct which ridicules, scorns, mocks, intimidates, or otherwise threatens any individual because of his or her sexual orientation constitutes homophobic harassment when it has the purpose of effect of unreasonably interfering with the work performance or creating an intimidating, hostile, or offensive environment (The Gay, Lesbian, and Bisexual Speaker's Bureau, 1997).

The authors are aware that you may be working in an environment that may not allow you the flexibility and freedom to advocate or educate on GLBTQ issues. It is important to keep in mind that you may be the only person to whom a GLBTQ student or parent(s) has confided their sexual orientation or gender identity. Remember that the simple act of listening, showing empathy and caring may make a difference in a GLBTQ person's life. If this is all you are able to achieve in your school, then know that it is far better then doing nothing. Changes, both personal and institutional, may take time, but for the GLBTQ individual finding a caring and accepting person who values them as an individual with dignity and worth can make a tremendous difference in allowing them to achieve their full potential.

## Summary

It is important to remember that as a school counselor, your role is one that is visible to students, parents, fellow teachers, and administrators. You will be called upon to intervene in disputes, handle parent/teacher conferences, and educate others on the ethical protocol in providing a safe living and learning environment for all students in your school. As we stated previously, the first step in working with GLBTQ individuals is to assess your own level of comfort and knowledge with this population. We have attempted to provide you, the school counselor, with some of the issues and concerns in working with GLBTQ students and their parents/legal guardians. We have provided issues, suggestions, and interventions on how to understand and work more effectively with GLBTQ students and their legal guardians, parents and teachers. The authors are aware that the role we have described for the school counselor may be daunting and difficult but we urge you to take steps to improve your school's climate where GLBTQ and other minority students are concerned. You might begin by assessing how supportive your school culture is and who your allies are who are willing to assist you in making the school environment a safe place for GLBTQ students. Many school districts have previously gone through these challenges and can offer you guidelines in implementing policies that are supportive to GLBTQ students and families. Changes will take time, but the rewards far outweigh the challenges and setbacks. The GLBTQ student you are working with will benefit greatly from your understanding and efforts and will greatly appreciate your efforts on his/her behalf.

## Web Resources

- COLAGE: Children of Lesbians and Gays Everywhere. Tips for Making Classrooms Safer for Students with Lesbian, Gay, Bisexual, and Transgender Parents. http://www.colage.org/resources/safe_classrooms.htm

- GSA: GayStraight Alliance. Empowering youth activists to fight homophobia and transphobia. http://www.gsanetwork.org/

- LAMBDA is a non-profit, gay / lesbian / bisexual / transgender agency dedicated to reducing homophobia, inequality, hate crimes, and discrimination by encouraging self-acceptance, cooperation, and non-violence. Youth OUTreach program. http://www.lambda.org/

- PFLAG: Parents, Families and Friends of Lesbian and Gays. PFLAG promotes the health and well-being of gay, lesbian, bisexual and transgender persons, their families and friends http://www.pflag.org/

- Youth Pride. Youth Pride, Inc. (YPI) is a statewide nonprofit organization with programming dedicated to meeting the social, emotional and educational needs of youth and young adults impacted by sexual orientation and gender identity. http://www.youth-pride-ri.org/

## References

American School Counselor Association (ASCA). (2005). *Role statement: The professional school counselor and sexual minority youth.* Alexandria, VA, author.

Barret, B., & Logan, C. (2002). *Counseling gay men and lesbians: A practice primer.* Pacific Grove, CA: Brooks/Cole.

Gay, Lesbian, and Bisexual Speaker's Bureau. (1997). *Nondiscrimination policy.* As cited in Youth Pride, Inc. (1997). *Creating safe schools for lesbian and gay students: A resource guide for school staff.* Retrieved May 28, 2006 from http://members.tripod.com/~twood/guide.html

GLSEN. (2003). *Talking the talk: A glossary of LGBT terminology and match-up game.* Retrieved May 28, 2006 from http://www.glsen.org/cgi-bin/iowa/all/library/record/1278.html

Russell, S.T., & Joyner, K. (2005). Adolescent sexual orientation and suicide risk: Evidence from a national study. *American Journal of Public Health, 91(8),* 1276-1281.

Sager, J.B., Gustafson, L.M, & Byrd, C.E. (2006). The psychology of transgendered. In G. Teague (Ed.), *The new goddess: Transgendered women in the twenty first century.* Waterbury, CT: FineTooth Press.

U.S. Census Bureau. (2004). *Census bureau projects tripling of Hispanic and Asian populations in 50 years; Non-Hispanic Whites may drop to half of total population.* Retrieved May 28, 2006 from http://www.census.gov/PressRelease/www/releases/archives/population/001720.html

# Chapter 17

## School Counselors and Special Needs Students

by
Beverly Snyder

---

*Beverly Snyder, Ed.D., is a Professor of Counselor Education at the University of Colorado at Colorado Springs. She formerly served as Resource Counselor for Orange County Public Schools, Orlando, Florida.*

## Introduction

School counselors often feel overwhelmed by the many hats they find themselves wearing during the course of a school day. But, most likely, counselors find that working with exceptional education students is one of the most rewarding and enlightening parts of their busy day. School counselors can often be heard saying that working with Exceptional Student Education (ESE) provides them with more satisfaction than any other facet of their work as counselors. However, it must be acknowledged that, if working with special needs students becomes (or is) a part of your role as a school counselor, you will find yourself being a lawyer, a public relations expert, an advocate, a teacher, sometimes a lobbyist, and often a mediator.

While you are, or will become, a "counselor" in the true sense of the word for all your students, no where is it more important than with the exceptional student and his or her family. I believe that our role as school counselors is to promote these students' rights to have and to fulfill their dreams of a better education, and ultimately, a better life. School counselors hold the keys which assure that these special needs students will achieve and succeed "just like everyone else" in the school.

## Special Needs Students and the Law

*The Federal Education for All Handicapped Act of 1975* changed the role of the school counselor by providing equal opportunity for all students classified as "handicapped." Counselors had always provided services for the gifted and highly talented, but the 1975 act increased their participation in the lives of special needs children. This participation takes the form of coordinating the Exceptional Student Education (ESE) Program and managing the flow of paperwork required to document the various phases of placement.

The federal legislation, *Individuals with Disabilities Education Improvement Act of 2004* is the nation's law that works to improve results for toddlers, infants, children and youth with disabilities. It requires that anyone with a perceived handicapping condition (i.e., asthma, obesity, abnormally short for age) must receive accommodations in the learning environment to equalize his or her educational opportunities. These students are not necessarily staffed into an ESE program, but are eligible to receive appropriate interventions so that they may participate equally in learning experiences. In many school systems, counselors are involved with coordinating these specially designed interventions. The *Individuals with Disabilities Education Improvement Act* amended IDEA to bring the law into closer alignment with the *No Child Left Behind Act* (2001). The amendments focus on teaching students with disabilities to meet challenging general education standards to the maximum degree appropriate, and on accountability for academic success.

IDEA requires schools to develop an infrastructure to deliver appropriate services to students with disabilities focused on improving academic results. The 2004 amendments include changes and additions that directly affect delivery of instruction, including evaluation and identification of students, changes in IEP program provisions, and early intervention for at-risk students. The amendments also address systemic improvements, such as staff qualifications and training, use of instructional time, and communication between families and schools.

The Americans with Disabilities Act of 1990 (ADA) is a civil rights law to prohibit discrimination solely on the basis of disability in employment, public services and accommodations. Any individual with a disability who (1) has a physical or mental impairment that substantially limits one or more life activities; or (2) has a record of such an impairment; or (3) is regarded as having such an impairment is protected under this law (ERIC, 1992). The ADA does not specify evaluation and placement procedures; it does specify provision of reasonable accommodations for eligible students across educational activities and settings. Reasonable accommodations may include, but are not limited to, redesigning equipment, assigning aides, providing written communication in alternative formats, modifying tests, redesigning services to accessible locations, altering existing facilities, and building new facilities. Schools and local districts must find the needed funding to support these services and facilities as none is provided by the Act.

Students with "special needs" with whom school counselors work can either be described as "ESE" or as "regular" education students. In either case, documented interventions required by federal law must be noted in the student's permanent cumulative folder to establish that the school recognizes that a special need exists and has been, and is, being considered when planning that child's education.

The Exceptional Education program is regulated by Federal laws and guidelines as to documentation, procedures, processes, and approaches that must be followed when working with special students. An ESE student will have an easily recognizable folder inside his or her cumulative folder in which records are kept that relate to placement in an exceptional education program. "Regular" special needs students do not usually have such a special folder; therefore, documentation for their interventions are kept in chronological order with other records inside the cumulative folder.

Another important concept for educators and families alike is the notion of inclusion. Inclusion describes the process of placing students in a general education classroom for the entire school day. Students receive the supports and services necessary to ensure an appropriate education and the student is not "pulled out" into a special education classroom for instruction (Hardman, et al., 2006). The goal behind full inclusion is to educate students with disabling conditions with their non-disabled peer group as a way to increase their access to and participation in all school activities and learning experiences. However, while the goal is a worthy one, the reality is that specialized academic instruction can frequently be best provided in a pull-out setting (Hardman, et al., 2006). There are arguments on both sides of the inclusion issue and each school district must decide how it will be handled to best meet the needs of their district.

Federal and state statutes for exceptional education students require students to receive the *"least restrictive environment"* possible. This means that all school personnel must utilize the regular school facilities and adapt them to the needs of the exceptional student. This ensures that ESE students are not isolated from regular students any more than is absolutely necessary. The law further stated that no segregation should occur unless it is proven necessary by the student's behaviors which indicate an inability to benefit from a regular classroom. Thus, all students, including the ESE students, begin their school careers in the regular classroom. Placement in a more restrictive environment follows only after many interventions have been attempted, conferences with parents and teachers held, vision and hearing screenings conducted, and most often, after psycho-educational testing has been completed. Each district and state has its own approaches to Exceptional Student Education, and counselors are encouraged to become familiar with them. The process of placing a student in an exceptional program is a complicated one that requires constant referral to a policy and procedures manual.

# The Process of Exceptional Student Education

The ESE process usually begins with a teacher or parent raising a question regarding the special nature of a student (i.e., an inability to stay on task, to complete assignments, hyperactivity, sleeping in class, or a host of other concerns). An Educational Planning Team (EPT) meeting is scheduled (usually by a counselor, who also functions as staffing chairperson or staffing coordinator). This meeting is usually attended by whomever has insight as to the nature of the child's problem(s). This includes parents, classroom and elective teachers (especially a PE coach), administrators, the counselor, and a Curriculum Resource Teacher (CRT). Depending on the nature of the problem, the school psychologist and/or social worker might also be invited to attend.

This team may meet for 15 or 20 minutes prior to the parents' arrival to ensure that all information is available and meeting goals are understood by all school personnel. The counselor, who may serve as chairperson, keeps the team on task and creates a "safe" place for the entire team to be heard. The counselor also may have the responsibility for making sure the parents feel welcome and a vital part of the meeting. The teacher(s) discuss the specific *academic* issues and specific *behaviors* they have observed which have created their concerns. It is important that the child's *behaviors* and *problems* are discussed, not his or her *personality*. The chairperson documents the meeting on an EPT form, noting interventions, who is responsible for what, follow-up meetings to be held, and so forth. Everyone present signs the document and the parents receive a copy.

Parents have particular rights concerning their child. Thus, if the EPT recommends testing, parental permission must be obtained. All testing, regardless of the type, requires written permission from the parents. Since parents are the child's "case managers," they have the right to refuse any and all evaluations, and some do. (In extreme cases, when parents withhold permission to test, the School Board, acting "in loco parentis," can request the court order the tests be done.) Once permission is obtained, the evaluation process can begin.

Each exceptionality has its own procedures for placement and the paperwork varies from district to district. The typical range of programs usually includes: Specific Learning Disabilities (SLD), Emotionally Handicapped (EH), Educable Mentally Handicapped (EMH), Trainable Mentally Handicapped (TMH), Physically Impaired (PI), Visually Impaired (VI), Hearing Impaired, (HI), Speech and Language (S/L), Autistic or Profoundly Mentally Handicapped (PMH). There can be other classifications as well, such as Gifted, Highly Gifted, or Learning/Language Disabled. The list of acronyms grows longer each year. School counselors *must* remain abreast of the language so as to effectively manage the maze of program requirements and procedures.

In addition to the above noted acronyms, "mainstreaming" is a concept that counselors need to also be familiar with as they facilitate the appropriate placement of students. The process in which students are placed in regular classrooms with regular students "as much as possible" is called "mainstreaming." Research reveals that ESE students consistently achieve higher when they are with regular students in regular classrooms. The inclusion model mentioned earlier is a form of mainstreaming where the student receives special services within the regular classroom. In addition, every effort should be made to avoid placing "labels" on students by referring to them as "EH" or "LD." Labeling only restricts the view of a student's capabilities and does nothing to assist (it may cause harm) the learning process.

The process leading to placement continues with collecting evidence which suggests that the child needs an exceptional education program in order to achieve at his or her optimal level in school. As noted above, the process differs among the exceptionalities. As noted, counselors are encouraged to refer to the school district's *Staffing Handbook* or an *ESE Manual* for information relative to each program. Once documentation has been assembled, an Educational Planning Conference (EPC) is scheduled by the counselor or person designated to coordinate such activities.

Various members of the original EPT meeting group are invited to the EPC, and others, as dictated by the specific program under consideration, are also invited to participate. At the meeting, to which parents *must* be invited, the documentation is discussed and a team decision is made by those involved as to whether or not the student should be staffed into a particular special program.

Since parental permission must be obtained for placement to occur, it becomes apparent how important parental involvement is throughout the process. Their agreement with placement is much more likely if they understand the situation thoroughly and that their child is not a "problem," but rather a "student who has a learning problem." When an EPC results in a student being placed into an ESE program, it is referred to as a "staffing." At that time, an Individual Education Plan (IEP) is developed by the parents and the exceptional education teacher(s). Counselors' involvement in the IEP is crucial, and they are viewed as "learning experts."

It is important that all stakeholders realize that the IEP is a legal document, and that any goals and services that are stated must be implemented.

For the counselor, the process does not end here. An EPC can be held at any time a program modification on behalf of the student needs to be considered. There are annual reviews required to determine eligibility for continued placement in a program, and three year reevaluations as well. All meetings involve the counselor, who as chairperson, facilitates the smooth flow of interpersonal interactions and the appropriate paperwork. If, as counselor you are in charge of Exceptional Education at your school, you will be called upon to use all your counseling, consulting, coordinating, and mediation skills.

## Important Considerations

School counselors are encouraged to develop an intellectual framework in which they can operate as they facilitate the success of their special needs students. The conceptual framework begins with an understanding of what "exceptional" means. Webster defines it as "exclusive, extraordinary, important, particular, remarkable, and unusual." Reflecting on this definition provides an excellent basis on which to work. With this focus, it is possible to reframe your approach from working with "handicapped" students to working with students with "special needs."

I believe there are three major considerations which require understanding by counselors to be effective in working with the ESE population in their schools. These include: *1) working with the special needs students, 2) working with their families,* and, *3) working with the faculty.*

## Working with Special Needs Students

Once a student has been identified and labeled with an exceptionality, the basic role of the counselor is to assist with the adjustment process. Some students will be relieved to know they have been diagnosed in a specific way; others will feel that something is "wrong" with them. Many feel they must be "stupid." Some will be open and excited about the new path and eager to get started in their new environment, most often an exceptional education setting. Some will be extremely frightened about the change and will need your close attention and counsel. Others are so accustomed to failure and the frustration that coincides with their special condition, that to them, the new diagnosis, the new possibility, is just another road to personal disaster. Whatever the case, it is extremely important that counselors are sensitive to their individual needs, meet them where they are, and understand their unique worldview, their way of seeing things, without evaluation.

It is important to reinforce students who indicate that moving to exceptional education has given them new hope. They usually recognize that their "old" academic life just wasn't working for them. And now, after being placed in exceptional education programs, they have found a different educational approach that, hopefully, will work for them.

An effective way to explain this to just staffed ESE students is to sincerely inform them that they will be receiving the *same* information as any other child in school, just in a different way. They will experience the same information at a *different* pace—*their* pace—and it will be presented to them at *their* level. Above all, counselors should facilitate the school's personnel to remove the harmful labels where possible. These students know who they are (i.e., there is no need to have a room labeled "Special Education.")

When students are assigned to exceptional education, counselors should work hard at having them leave their offices to enter an ESE class, in the case of a pull out progam, feeling as positive and confident as possible. It may be best to go with them that first day in order to help them feel the support, safety and encouragement needed to succeed. The first few weeks are crucial and may require some close monitoring by the counselor. They will need and cherish the special attention only a professional counselor can provide.

ESE students have the same wants and needs as other children: to be successful, to experience some measure of control over their lives, to be liked, and so forth. Urge teachers to focus on their good habits and any strengths that emerge (all do have strengths!) and how these strengths can add to their ability to succeed at school and in life. That is, encourage teachers to use each child's special strengths to the advantage of both the student and the teacher. This tends to reinforce appropriate classroom behavior and raise self-esteem.

It is most effective to be calm and consistent when talking and working with these students. However, like any other students, some may misbehave to gain attention since it has worked for them in the past. However, it is best not to demand a rational explanation when they do misbehave (to do so requires an intellectual answer, and individuals who misbehave from an *emotional* point of view, as these students do, will be unable to supply cognitive reasons). Instead, try to understand what's happening *behind* the unacceptable behavior. Try to identify the emotion causing the behavior.

Counselors are encouraged to provide teachers with methods of dealing with the behavior instead of "labeling" the child because of acting out. Generally speaking, special needs students will have little trouble correcting their "misbehavior" if teachers are specific enough when attempting to help them change.

There are some behavioral issues that counselors and other educators should be aware of concerning some exceptional children. Many tend to give up easily, some withdraw quickly and others act out. Some complain about others and are quick to blame others for their own problems. Special needs children tend to seek out peers who will accept them, problems and all. Counselors will want to use their counseling skills to intervene in these cases.

# The Counselor's Role

Schmidt (2005) outlined specific services counselors can be expected to provide for special needs students; these services generally include the following:

1. Participating in school-based meetings to determine appropriate services and programs for exceptional students.

2. Assisting with the development of the Individual Education Plan (IEP) required for every student who has an identified exceptionally.

3. Providing direct counseling services for students.

4. Counseling and consulting with parents.

5. Consulting with classroom and special education teachers.

6. Planning, coordinating, and presenting in-service programs for teachers.

7. Planning extracurricular involvement for special education students.

8. Keeping appropriate records of services for students.

The American School Counselor Association (ASCA) developed position statements concerning various special needs students. For example, ASCA (2004) states the following regarding the school counselor's role in working with these students:

*ASCA encourages its members to participate in the implementation of the following counseling activities: (1) serve on the school's multidisciplinary team actively involved in the multimodal or multifaceted delivery of interventions or services to the special needs child/adolescent; (2) serve as a consultant and resource to the parents, staff, and other school personnel on the characteristics and problems of special needs students; (3) serve in the capacity of providing regular feedback on the social and academic performance of the special needs children to the members of the multidisciplinary treatment team; (4) help staff design appropriate programs for special needs children which include opportunities for special needs children to learn more appropriate social skills and self-management skills; (5) provide special needs children activities to improve their self-esteem, self-concept and encourage children to practice transferring the content of individual counseling sessions to external settings; (6) promote special needs workshops for staff and support groups for parents and families with a special needs child; and (7) serve as an advocate for special needs children in the community (ASCA, 2004).*

# A Note on Working with the Gifted

It may surprise some counselors to learn that gifted and talented students also need their services. As a matter of fact, oftentimes more than the "average" student as they have their own set of unique concerns and problems. Many gifted students have poor self-esteem and are "stressed" by the pressure, both real, and imagined, to succeed and excel academically. Hitchner and Tifft-Hitchner (1996) indicated that the gifted student and their parents need counseling services as much, or more, than others. They provide a list of unique and common problems faced by these youngsters. Their list, in part, includes:

- A loss in enthusiasm for learning.

- Doing poorly—or even failing—for the first time in their lives.

- Being shunned for life by family and friends if he or she doesn't go to a "good" college.

- A super-accelerated freshman's feelings about being kidded about his diminutive size as he sits with juniors in an honors math class.

- Being too focused on the academics, and not enough on the non-academics. Here you can warmly—but candidly—bring reality to bear, and share with your counselee the real world of college admission.

- Reaching out and leveling with parents who may have unrealistic expectations. Not only might a youngster be misplaced in a particular course, he or she might be misplaced in a particular school.

- Helping a student sort through his or her priorities to keep things in perspective.

- Counseling a high achiever who looks on cheating as a practical, not an ethical issue.

- Helping a counselee deal with the pressure to get into a "hot" college, which he or she views as a ticket to a "hot" career.

- Helping gifted and talented students through the bureaucracy as they search to satisfy a special objective.

- Counseling a gifted and talented youngster who feels he or she has dishonored the family name and is contemplating suicide.

Being gifted and talented isn't easy. Then again, being exceptional in any way isn't easy.

The American School Counselor Association (ASCA) believes that the counselor has a role to play in the gifted program and suggests the following:

1. To assist in the identification of gifted students through the use of a multiple criterion system that uses at least the following:

  A. General intellectual ability

  B. Specific academic ability

  C. Visual and performing arts ability

  D. Practical arts ability

  E. Psycho-social ability

  F. Creative thinking ability

2. To advocate that the personal, social, emotional and vocational needs of the gifted are included in the program.

3. To act as an advocate for gifted students in all matters involving the school.

4. To act as a consultant to the school administration in curricular concerns and the school's involvement with the parents.

5. To provide leadership in the establishment of training and sensitivity programs concerning the gifted to staff, parents, and administrators.

6. To recommend material and resources for gifted programs.

7. To provide group and individual guidance and counseling to all gifted students.

8. To continue to upgrade knowledge and skills in the area of the gifted and talented (ASCA, 2001).

# Working with the Families of Special Needs Students

Families with special needs children are like any other family. They are units connected emotionally, physically, intellectually and spiritually. When any part of the unit becomes disconnected, imbalance is created in the unit and disruption occurs. Therefore, when a child is classified by the educational system as needing "exceptional" services, the family is deeply affected.

There are various ways that a family might discover that their child is exceptional. Sometimes a neighbor, friend or family member raises the question. Sometimes it is the school, either through a teacher, administrator, or counselor. Occasionally a family is strong enough to bring their special child's needs to your attention. Regardless of how the exceptionality is discovered, you will find that it is important that consideration and nurturing be provided to the family. School counselors should be available to the family when it learns of its child's exceptionality as they most likely will need your assistance and counsel during this stressful time. You will learn that you, as counselor, will usually be the first one in the school to whom they turn.

## Various Family Styles

Families react differently when they learn their child has been diagnosed as having special needs. The *supportive* families accept what the school can do for their child. They are more aware of options and alternatives and are willing to embrace new methods which might enhance their special child's learning. These families are the school counselor's allies. They appreciate the services being offered to their child. If you approach them as team members, you can learn many things from them that will help you (and the school) be more successful with their special child.

The supportive type of family desires to learn all they can about the particular needs of their child. It is best to be open, honest, and as knowledgeable as possible about their child's special needs. This type of family will quickly inform you if there is something you or the school should become more familiar with concerning their child. Their expectations are high and they reveal an awareness of their child's interests and show the pleasure and pride in his or her achievements. No matter how small or trivial it may seem to others, they truly value the accomplishments of their special needs child. Most of all, the supportive family accepts and respects its child for what he or she "is" and "is not."

Within the supportive type families there are some who may be less well educated concerning exceptional students and available services. They are supportive in that they accept their special child and what "education" can and is doing. They have the same dreams as other parents have, but there is a difference in their knowledge and understanding of their child's exceptionality. They often do not understand the limitations their child has, sometimes creating unrealistic expectations. However, because of their supportive nature, they will be open to the counselor's suggestions. They are interested in working with the school counselor, but they need constant support, and above all, a counselor's expertise concerning the nature of their child's exceptionality.

A third family type is one that has intellectual ability but has very little to give to the special child emotionally. This family often finds it difficult to accept the fact that their child is "exceptional" or that they have the personal resources capable of coping with him or her. Such families have great difficulty in getting through the "denial stage" and will need the counselor's assistance to do so. Their own self-esteem becomes involved and they may attempt to cover up the special needs their child has, as well as the overall reality of the situation.

Fear is a big factor with this type of family—they are fearful that their child will never be successful in the "real world." They also fear rejection, discrimination and may have a defeatist attitude. They need patience and honest, open, facilitative feedback concerning their child. Provide them with information as factually as possible and make certain they understand their alternatives and rights. Be aware that the expectations they place on their child may create problems for the counselor and others in the school. Many counselors have found it most effective to provide family counseling in these situations.

# Working with the Faculty

Working with the faculty as they work with ESE students will test a counselor's facilitative skills, his or her public relations skills, and every other counseling skill he or she possesses! Remember that these are colleagues, educational peers, and that most have a strong desire "to fully educate" the students in their classroom. However, when working with ESE students, they often become frustrated and their patience grows thin.

These students can create overwhelming frustration, especially among untrained teachers. Most teachers are not adequately prepared to teach exceptional children and many say it is unfair that a special child is "mainstreamed" into their class. Others feel inadequate, helpless, and confused when encountering the various exceptionalities.

Sometimes it is difficult for a teacher to realize the difference they make in an exceptional child's life is not necessarily in the academic area. Often it is not. Your role as counselor is to care for, support, and give assistance to teachers who work with special needs students. Become as knowledgeable as possible about the many exceptionalities that teachers find in their classrooms, and be assertive about your availability to help. Counselors may consult with teachers at the beginning of each school year informing them of the special needs students in their respective classrooms. They can provide details of the special needs each student has and provide suggestions (when appropriate) on how best to teach this student. Teachers appreciate knowing these things and will value suggestions or tips on how best to work with such students.

You will find that teachers desire more strategies, techniques, and assistance when it comes to teaching these children than when working with non-special needs students. Find out what the teachers already know (perhaps a needs survey) and then assist them in learning more about the various exceptionalities. The school counselor can provide a real service to children by helping teachers become more skilled in understanding and applying how special needs students learn as well as how to motivate them.

One of the critical concepts counselors can help teachers develop is that special needs students must feel that "no student has more worth and dignity" than any other. If teachers understand that logic often tends to work best with certain special needs students, it makes it easier for them to understand how to apply discipline, and so forth. Some teachers need to be reminded that certain students require more time for written work and test taking. Some need special assignments, preferred seating, peer tutors and other types of assistance.

As a counselor, you can provide workshops for regular teachers on how to work effectively with ESE students who have been mainstreamed into their classes. And finally, gently inform teachers that to embarrass a special needs student in front of peers almost always fails to achieve the desired results. Encourage teachers to correct these students in private when needed.

## Summary

Counselors, being child development specialists, play pivotal roles in their work with special needs students. No other educator is better equipped to assist the exceptional students themselves, their families, or their teachers to reach greater understanding of the nature of being a special needs student. It is through using the skills of both counseling and consulting that counselors reach out to all who work with this unique population. The special needs students are some of the most challenging, and at the same time, the most rewarding students you will work with.

Finally, I offer the following ten "tips" to lessen your and their stress when working with special needs students:

1. Show genuine affection at all times.

2. Find opportunities to build their self esteem where and when possible.

3. Give them your undivided attention when working with them.

4. Be available to talk to them about their problems when they are ready to talk.

5. Use humor and empathy, not sympathy.

6. Try to understand their stressors—wear their shoes.

7. Provide them with safety and security.

8. Most enjoy having fun, so have fun with them.

9. Provide them with love, patience, and understanding.

10. Enjoy them!

## References

ASCA. (2004). *Role statement: Special needs students.* Alexandria, VA. American School Counselor Association. Author.

ASCA. (2001). *Role statement: The school counselor and the gifted student.* Alexandria, VA. American School Counselor Association. Author.

ERIC Clearinghouse on Disabilities and Gifted Education. (1992). *Legal foundations 1: Americans with Disabilities Act of 1990.* Reston, VA: Author.

Hardman, M.L., Drew, C.J., Egan, M.W. (2006). *Human exceptionality school, community, and family.* Boston, MA: Allyn & Bacon.

Hitchner, K., & Tifft-Hitchner, A. (1996). *Counseling today's secondary students: Practical strategies, techniques, and materials for the school counselor.* West Nyack, NY: The Center for Applied Research in Education.

Schmidt, J.J. (2005). *Counseling in schools: Essential services and comprehensive programs* (4th ed.). Needham Heights, MA: Allyn & Bacon.

# Section V

# The Counselor as Consultant and Coordinator: The Family, Appraisal, Career, and Educational Counseling Programs

This section begins with a chapter written by Dr. Tom Harrison concerning the developmental school counselor's role as consultant and coordinator. Dr. Harrison provides some excellent "real life" examples of consultative roles faced by the school counselor of the new millennium and presents an easy-to-follow model for effectively working through several consultative situations. In addition, several consultant models are presented that a school counselor will find extremely helpful. The counselor/coordinator function is also described in detail.

The school counselor and strategies for working with families as a counselor and consultant is a topic that has seldom appeared in school counseling books. However, it is a role that is becoming increasingly important to school counselors. In fact, the results of a counselor work behaviors study, conducted by the National Board for Certified Counselors (NBCC), revealed that randomly selected counselors, including school counselors, placed "working with families" as one of their five main functions. Drs. Ellen Amatea and Cirecie West-Olatunji (Chapter 19) indicate that an ecosystem orientation can be an effective approach for understanding the negative patterns of family-school interaction that can develop when students experience problems at school. They recommend that a positive approach be taken which reinforces home and school resources and the student's own ability to make changes. They present case illustrations that offer insight Into the application of this approach within school communities. Next, Dr. Larry Loesch and Mr. William Goodman detail the appraisal function K-12 school counselors fulfill in a developmentally oriented counseling program. They describe the coordination role the counselor plays in the appraisal program and emphasize the importance of appropriate consultation with teachers, parents, and others concerning results of appraisals given in schools. Concerning the latter Loesch and Goodman write: *When school counselors help other school personnel understand appraisal results effectively, these school personnel can then provide the best educational services to students.* Loesch and Goodman also offer some excellent strategies for interpreting appraisal results to students, teachers, parents and others.

Dr. Pat Schwallie-Giddis and Ms. Linda Kobylarz offer several innovative career development concepts and practices for the K-12 school counselor in Chapter 21. They write: *It is clear that the workplace of tomorrow will be very different from the workplace of today. The emphasis in the future will be on change, flexibility, multiple career paths and lifelong learning.* The writers also suggest various strategies for school counselors to use in implementing and managing a comprehensive K-12 career development program. They challenge K-12 school counselors to *reenergize our schools and help all our students succeed in a dynamic and demanding workplace.* Schwallie-Giddis and Kobylarz indicate that school counselors are uniquely positioned to promote movement toward a truly comprehensive approach to career development through their coordination activities.

In Chapter 22, Dr. Jim Pitts and Ms. Shifa Podikunju Hussain focus on the educational counseling and educational guidance roles of the developmental high school counselor. They define the two concepts as follows: *Educational counseling refers to counselors' efforts to help students develop self concepts which keep their educational options open. Educational guidance refers to counselors' interventions aimed at assisting students to make the best use of the options available.*

Helping students realize that they have educational and career options, helping them keep their options open, and assisting them to make the best use of those options are important school counselor tasks. School counselors can make a difference in students' lives by finding ways to do these things effectively. Pitts and Podikunju Hussain write: *Effective educational counseling and guidance is highly important and should be a high priority for all developmental high school counselors.*

*Joe Wittmer and Mary Ann Clark*

*Joe Wittmer, Ph.D. and Mary Ann Clark, Ph.D.*

# Chapter 18

# The School Counselor as Consultant/Coordinator

by
**Thomas C. Harrison**

*Tom Harrison, Ph.D., is Professor and Chair of the Department of Counseling and Educational Psychology at the University of Nevada, Reno. He is both the Director of Graduate Studies in Marriage and Family Therapy and Director of the Downing Counseling Clinic and teaches courses in consultation. Dr. Harrison is a consultant to the Nevada School Counselors Association as well as to other school and local organizations. He has written a book and several articles on consultation.*

## Introduction

The school counselor may have the toughest job in the educational profession. The student population itself is challenging enough, but what makes the counselor's job so challenging is the variety of roles assumed in their respective schools. As noted throughout this book, these roles include: counselor, advocate, confidant, leader, collaborator, human relations expert, teacher, administrator, consultant, and coordinator. The latter functions, consultant and coordinator, are two important roles for the counselor and are addressed in this chapter. When utilized effectively in a comprehensive guidance program, these two important counselor functions can help in shaping the direction of the entire school in different and exciting ways.

In this chapter the author addresses the role that consultation and coordination play in the comprehensive school guidance and counseling program. A definition and discussion of consultation is followed by several examples depicting consulting issues in the schools. The role of school counselor as coordinator is also presented. The goal of this chapter is to help those training to become school counselors better understand the implications of a consulting and coordinating role in the school setting. In addition, practicing school counselors hoping to do their job as consultant/coordinator more effectively, should find the chapter very helpful.

## Promoting the Guidance Program through a Consulting Role

### Consultation Defined

Consultation became a widely accepted form of service delivery for school personnel during the 1970s (Schmidt, 1999). Simply stated, consultation is a process whereby the first party (consultant) assists a second party (consultee) in finding a solution to a problem that concerns a third party (client) (Harrison, 2004). In schools, consultation is considered an *indirect* service to students through *direct involvement* with teachers, administrators, and parents. That is, students are the central focus and counselors working directly with teachers, administrators, and parents serve to benefit the student population. Consultation, when put into practice by professional educators, can be a key element in helping to design effective learning environments for the twenty-first century (Dettmer, Dyck, & Thurston, 1999).

Counselors can be consultants to individual professionals such as teachers, other counselors, administrators, and so forth. In addition, they often consult with parents as well as to groups and various systems throughout the community. The interventions can be *developmental, educational, preventative,* or *crisis-oriented*. For example, a developmental guidance program is designed to be proactive and preventative and counselors work with individual teachers, administrators, and parents in implementing the developmentally oriented program. Within the domains of the program itself, counselors can help individual students assess career goals which are developmental issues. Counselors can also help teachers and others deal with crises situations and may aim their efforts toward the prevention of similar crises in the future. In addition, counselors often work with groups of teachers on learning ways to better manage their respective classrooms, which is considered educational consultation.

In order to meet the challenges of a consulting role, school counselors-in-training, and those now employed as counselors, need to be equipped with *knowledge* and *skills*. Knowledge of the consulting process is requisite as is the knowledge of consultant characteristics, needed skills and behaviors. Moreover, knowledge of Schein's (1999) *process consultation model,* Caplan and Caplan's (1993) mental health consultation and collaboration model, and Myrick's (2003) *systematic consultation model* can be of help to the counselor assuming a consulting role.

In the following section, I describe pertinent stages for consulting in the schools and consultant characteristics and behaviors. Relevant information from the three consulting models mentioned above are presented briefly. For a detailed analysis of the consultation models, you are urged to refer to the works of Caplan and Caplan (1993) and Myrick (2003).

## Consultation Stages

In general, the stages of consulting include *entry, initiation of a relationship, assessment, problem definition and goal setting, strategy selection and implementation, evaluation,* and *termination* (Brown, Pryzwansky, & Schulte, 1998). These stages are of particular importance for an "outside" consultant (one who is hired for a specific purpose). However, when applied to the school setting, some consulting stages are seen as having unique implications for the counselor/consultant. In particular, the *entry stage* and *relationship initiation* stages are of special significance. And, it is important for a school counselor to understand the implications.

School counselors are considered "internal consultants" because they are employed members of the organization in which they consult. Thus, the school counselor's "entry" into the system is unique because administrators are likely to be familiar with the consultant (school counselor), although in another role. If you are a beginning school counselor, your entry into a school setting is even more unique and contains important issues needing to be addressed. For example, administrators will be familiar with the counselor(s) already practicing in their respective school. As a new "internal consultant," you may be cast into the same role(s) as is the established counselor(s), one which you may not desire. Therefore, it is to the beginning school counselor's advantage to discuss his or her anticipated role with the administrator (and new counseling colleagues) and have that role clarified and agreed upon as soon as possible.

A request for a formal introduction to the school faculty, parents, and others, describing the counselor's role as consultant can be very helpful. This introduction will serve to diminish "role ambiguity" which occurs when the counselor/consultant becomes unsure of his or her role. This uncertainty can lead to problems when implementing the guidance program's objective and goals. For example, a counselor unsure of the consulting role may perpetuate the perception that he or she will eventually take responsibility for someone else's problem(s) by providing counseling to a student who is having a personality conflict with a teacher. In a consulting role, the counselor would help the teacher and student solve *their* problem and never "owns" the problem, per se.

Also during the entry stage, the new school counselor will want to anticipate confidentiality issues involved in the consultant role and relate his or her concerns and orientations of confidentiality to the school administrators, faculty, and staff. Without this discussion and understanding, the counselor new to the school can be placed in uncomfortable situations or in situations where there is a possible conflict of interest. Attending to this concern early in the entry and relationship-building stage presents an opportunity to deal with confidentiality before critical situations arise (Brown, Pryzwansky, & Schulte, 1998).

Developing good relationships requires the school counselor to gather *informal or "working" knowledge* of how their respective school operates. Informal knowledge refers to having information about the particular idiosyncrasies of the school. Without this "working" knowledge, new counselors can likely find themselves quickly overwhelmed with resistances from administration and staff. For example, historically, many school personnel have considered counseling an ancillary service. Therefore, knowledge of how counseling and current counselors are viewed by the school's administration and staff can help the beginning counselor avoid pitfalls which may hinder the implementation of the guidance program's objectives.

In building relationships in a consulting role, effective school counselors understand that consultation is not a process whereby one person (consultant) *imposes* upon another individual (consultee or client). They do—and are expected to—*expose* their values and beliefs. However, consultation is always a *collaborative effort* and the importance of this cannot be understated. Collaboration is an approach in which one professional (consultant) is helping another professional (teacher, administrator, or parent) and requires the establishment of a "*coordinate relationship.*" Each "professional" has his or her own areas of expertise. A problem for the counselor can arise if he or she is remiss in demonstrating a collaborative approach. For example, it is not uncommon for the counselor to be asked by the principal to work with a particular teacher who is "unaware of any problem" or who has a history of reluctance to work through issues. Unless the counselor can focus efforts in a collaborative manner by demonstrating understanding of *both* sides (principal and teacher), the risk of alienating the teacher increases dramatically and may impede the consultative process.

Fortunately, counselors find collaboration and the "coordinate relationship" to be a familiar approach because it is also used in counseling situations. Moreover, the school administration and parents also understand and expect this approach. Both collaboration and the "coordinate relationship" is covered in greater detail later in this chapter.

According to Harrison (2004), a generic school-based consultation model can be conceptualized as occurring in several sequential stages or phases. Primarily, there needs to be *a request for help* that is communicated to the counselor/consultant. During this phase, the expectations of what the counselor/consultant can do needs to be outlined and understood by the consultee. In this phase, the consultee is also informed of the boundaries of the help that can be provided. It is important for consultants to help consultees determine what dimensions of the problem are owned by the consultee and which dimensions belong to some other entity. Moreover, consultants need to help consultees understand that consultees own both the problem and the solution.

This process leads directly into the second stage: *gathering information*. Gathering information can be formal or informal. Because the information that is gathered needs to be appropriate to the issue, this second phase also involves determining what information is to be gathered as well as how it is to be gathered. The third phase centers around *identifying effective strategies*. Again, consultants need to allow consultees to develop their own plans. The fourth phase and fifth stages are *implementation and evaluation* respectively. An evaluation of the effectiveness of any given intervention can lead to modifications of the intervention, if needed. Finally, the consultant and consultee need to agree upon *terminating* the relationship related to the given presenting issue.

With the knowledge of consulting stages and, in particular, the importance of the entry and relationship-building phases, the counselor is prepared to initiate a consulting role in the schools. When initiating this process, awareness of the characteristics of successful consultants can help.

## Consultant Verbal Skills

In his original work on school counselors acting as consultants, Myrick (1977) identified several facilitative responses that consultants can use to move issues through to resolution. Based upon the works of Wittmer and Myrick (1989), Myrick (2003) discusses six specific responses which, when used effectively, can guide the consultation process. These six responses vary from more directive and least facilitative to least directive and most facilitative.

According to these researchers, the *most directive and least facilitative response is advice.* Advice occurs when the consultant suggests directly or implies what the consultee a) should or should not be doing; b) must or must not do; and/or, c) needs to do or needs not to do. While helpful when timed accurately, reasons for the lack of effectiveness of advice vary. The authors believe that most of the time when consultees are asking for help, they receive advice, and the advice they receive is usually what they have already thought about or tried. Hence, advice creates distance in the relationship between consultants and consultees rather than closeness and helpfulness. (To see how ineffective advice can be, one needs to look no further than her or his own experience: Think of the last time that you received advice in the form of what you should do about something that is troubling you. Likely, you did not follow the advice. This may have been due to the fact that you had already tried what was suggested and/or had already determined that the particular course of action suggested would not work). In most cases, (not all cases, though) the person asking for advice needs help in accurately identifying the issue. Therefore, instead of giving advice at the outset, a more facilitative response would be to gather more information from the consultee. This can be accomplished by asking open questions.

*Open questions* are questions that usually begin with such words as *what, where, how, or when.* For example, asking consultees, "What have you tried?" or "How are you approaching this situation?" or *"When* did the problem first come to your attention?" are questions that allow consultees to reflect upon the issues more deeply. At the same time they are reflecting and responding, consultees have the opportunity to assess the consultant's non-verbal acceptance of the consultee's situation. Often, when giving advice, there is a non-verbal message (also referred to as a *meta-message)* of disapproval. That is, advice implies a course of action that, if not taken, would mean that the consultee would be behaving inappropriately. This exchange would limit or restrict the consultee's freedom to choose other courses of action that might be more efficacious. Open questions, as opposed to *closed or "why" questions,* also allow consultees to "fill-in-the-blanks". Closed questions are a class of questions that can usually be answered by a simple "yes" or "no". Examples of closed questions are, "Did you ask the students to sit down before you began explaining the problems with their behaviors?", or "Why did wait to talk to the students instead of talking to them right after the incident occurred?." As can be easily seen, these questions not only put consultees on the defensive, they also imply a course of action that is more appropriate than any action they have already taken. Thus, consultees can feel guilty of not behaving appropriately when consultees were originally only asking for help! One can see that using closed questions and/or "why" questions can quickly become nonhelpful: the opposite of the consultant's intention.

The second most directive and least effective response is *analyzing and interpreting* the consultee's situation. Clearly, consultants need to analyze and interpret consultee's situations. Yet, providing untimely analysis and interpretive responses can lead to consultee's becoming defensive while, at the same time, creating distance in the consulting relationship. These analyzing/interpretive responses can be identified most by the words, "The *reason you are* having difficulties *is because…*". Consultees are not often as interested in the reason they are doing or not doing something as they are in finding solutions. Moreover, when consultants use analysis and/or interpretive responses, they are forcing the personal dimensions of the consultee's experiences to become public. In addition, the reasons that someone does or does not do something are almost never that simple or direct. Any single behavior has a multitude of motivations. So, identifying one reason is at best incomplete and at worst, a personal violation of the consultee's experiences. It is almost like saying to the consultee, "I know better than you why (or why not) you are doing something." (On a more personal note, this is like saying to you, the reader, that the reason you are reading this chapter is because you are afraid that if you don't you will not pass the professor's test. Even though this may be partially true, chances are you feel a sense of violation).

Instead of providing untimely or inappropriate analysis, Wittmer and Myrick (1989) and Myrick (2003) suggest that consultants ask consultees to *clarify* the situation. This clarification process can include the use *paraphrasing* or *restating* in order to better understand exactly what the consultee is experiencing. Through the process of clarifying and paraphrasing, both consultants and consultees arrive at a more clear understanding of what is happening. At the same time, consultees have a chance to hear how the consultant understands the situation while becoming more collaborative in their efforts to solve problems effectively. Two heads are better than one is an apt phrase for this clarifying process.

The third directive and least facilitative response that consultants often use with consultees is to provide *untimely reassurance.* Untimely reassurance occurs when the consultants tell consultees or imply *not to worry about the situation.* Telling consultees not to worry often invalidates their experiences. Again, this dynamic would create distance in the consulting relationship. Wittmer and Myrick suggest that *reflecting consultee's feelings* augment the trust between consultees and consultants while allowing for a deeper exploration of the situation at hand. When consultants reflect consultee's feelings, they use the words or phrases, "You are feeling…" or "You seem to be feeling…". While personal, the process of identifying consultee's feelings often helps them crystallize the clarity of their experiences while tending to bring the relationship between consultant and consultee to a deeper, closer, and more personal level; a level at which meaningful change can occur.

The three responses, *advice, analyzing and interpreting, and untimely reassurance* are not categorically taboo. However, the authors suggest that these responses be used sparingly in consultant-consultee interactions. In other words, it is appropriate to provide advice, interpretation, and reassurance with consultees. The key is when to use such responses and how often to use them. The researchers believe that these responses are used too often and can be supplanted by the more facilitative responses of open questions, clarification, and feeling-focused responses. A general rule to follow is to ask open questions, clarify the consultee's responses and identify consultee's feelings before you provide advice, analysis, or reassurance.

## Consultant Characteristics

Counselors wishing to work in a consulting role in the comprehensive guidance program will likely find that the characteristics needed for a successful consulting experience are essentially the same characteristics as those needed for effective counseling. Core conditions so important to effective counseling outcomes need to be demonstrated as does an ability to 1) *assess problems*, 2) *explore alternatives*, and 3) *choose appropriate courses of action*. Likewise, the use of open questions, clarifications, restatements, and summaries can be especially enhancing to the consulting process.

It should be acknowledged, however, that consultation does require a need to focus upon specific attitudes, values, knowledge, and skills that are somewhat different than those of counseling. For example, in a consulting role, counselors will need "*structural integrity*." This refers to the counselor's abilities to maintain the *perception* of themselves as consultants in the face of adversity or other challenges within the system. A counselor taking on the role of consultant will also need to set *parameters* or *boundaries* upon his or her role and upon the activities undertaken. Establishing parameters or "boundaries" refers to a counselor's willingness to communicate to school personnel activities that are appropriate, and those inappropriate to her or his role. Coordinating an activity such as an intramural softball game between the school's seniors and sophomores, while sounding like fun, will consume valuable counselor time and might be more appropriately coordinated through the physical education department. Finally, counselors need to be *patient* and mindful that system change requires some discomfort, anxiety, preparation time, work up-front, and much attention to establishing collaborative relationships with teachers, administrators, and parents.

## Consultation Models

Equipped with informal knowledge, counselors can then utilize more formal knowledge of group leadership styles and group processes to assist them in consultative situations. Specifically, counselors need to be especially knowledgeable in *diagnosing* group dynamics and the ways in which groups arrive at solutions to problems. This is required in part because of the many people involved and the variety of decisions needing to be made.

Schein's (1999) *process consultation model* addressed the dynamics of group problem-solving and group decision-making styles (i.e., "plop method," authority rule, minority rule, majority rule, unanimity, and consensus). Awareness of how the decisions are made can help the counselor plan for teacher and administrator's resistances as well as helping the counselor see potential ways to reduce resistances. Consensus occurs when communication is open to the point that a formal vote does not need to be taken, yet all have a "sense of the meeting" and of the decision. For example, all meetings in which guidance issues are discussed will be regulated by the group's decision-making style. A decision on a course of action made by consensus is more difficult to achieve, but drastically increases the group's cohesion and performance (Schein, 1999). Cohesion can then enhance commitment to the guidance program and it's objectives since "all have a sense" of the program's goals. Subsequent behaviors by those in the group will likely reflect this supportive commitment to the program.

In addition to awareness of group process, knowledge of Caplan and Caplan's (1993) mental health consultation and collaboration model can be helpful to the counselor/consultant. Useful principles of Caplan and Caplan's model include the *consultant as collaborator* with an emphasis upon establishing a "*coordinate*

*relationship*" with consultees and clients, and his diagnostic categories identified in "consultee-centered" case consultation.

In the guidance program, *collaboration* occurs when the consultant (school counselor) engages one or more individuals in working upon the same problem. For example, the counselor has learned of a problem occurring in the classroom between a teacher and a student. Using a collaborative approach, the counselor works with the teacher (consultee) on learning new methods of interacting and reinforcing student behaviors while at the same time provides individual consultation (perhaps using specific counseling strategies) to the student (client) on how he or she can help themselves be more successful by controlling their behaviors in the classroom. To help the student, both teacher and counselor need to successfully execute their "part of the deal." In this case, the teacher benefits and can generalize his or her new knowledge to other situations involving students; the student benefits by learning new ways to feel more in control in the classroom; and the school system benefits as a result because the student's other teachers can now experience more classroom compliance with this student.

Caplan and Caplan's advocation of a "*coordinate relationship*" implies that school counselors will be most effective as consultants when they approach teachers, administrators, and parents "on the same level." That simply means that the counselor demonstrates *respect* for everyone's expertise and knowledge. Therefore, using a "coordinate relationship" approach when consulting through collaborating takes on the idea of two or more professionals working on the same problem together. The concepts of collaboration and "coordinate relationships" also help with the counselor's "mental set" or role orientation.

Collaboration and the establishment of "coordinate relationships" ought not to be problematic for the school counselor. Collaboration is a skill with which all counselors have some familiarity upon graduating from a counselor preparation program. However, ease in establishing "coordinate relationships" could prove more problematic and does require practice and experience. While most school personnel and parents will anticipate being respected for their knowledge, the school counselor just beginning the consultant role should move slowly and deliberately in assuring that this "coordinate relationship" is established and maintained.

Differentiating four diagnostic areas of consultee-centered case consultation into a *lack of knowledge, lack of skill, lack of confidence,* or *lack of objectivity* have also proven useful to Caplan in his professional work and can prove to be of equal value to the school counselor/consultant. Counselors using this perceptual framework can more effectively assess problems and determine appropriate courses of action to help teachers, administrators, and parents. For example, in working with a teacher having a problem communicating with an administrator, one counselor noted a close parallel between the teacher's problems with the administrator and the teacher's well-known problems with his spouse. The counselor determined that the problem was one of a *lack of objectivity* on the part of the teacher. This "diagnosis" guided the counselor's consultive intervention. Simply having told the teacher what to do or trying to educate him on how to behave differently (lack of skill or knowledge) would likely have been unsuccessful.

Effective diagnosis of problem areas through the use of Caplan and Caplan's (1993) categories require time and practice in which to become skillful. However, it can help the counselor to understand that these categories closely parallel the assessment processes used in normal counseling situations and therefore should present little challenge in the incorporation of these concepts.

## Myrick's Systematic Consultation Model

While the consulting models of Schein (1999) and Caplan and Caplan (1993) can help orient the counselor to the consulting role, Myrick's (2003) *systematic consultation* model is a "how to" model and puts consultation into action. When combined with the works of Schein and Caplan and Caplan, the systematic consultation model provides the counselor with an explicit consulting paradigm. The systematic consultation model is a step-wise model which includes: *1) identifying the issue, 2) clarifying the problem, 3) identifying the goal, 4) observing the behaviors (when indicated), 5) developing a plan, 6) initiating the plan,* and *7) following-up.* Emphasis is upon the consultant's facilitative skills and the willingness to become involved.

School counselors can readily use this model because it falls well within the range of what school personnel expect from a school counselor. The use of core conditions and facilitative responses such as those used in counseling have particular value in this consulting model.

In the first two phases, *identifying the problem and clarifying the issue,* school counselors need to help their consultees organize their experiences of the issue in a way that can be readily understood. Identifying the problem is more difficult than it may at first appear. This is true because problems in schools rarely lend themselves to simple cause and effect paradigms. Almost all problems are multifaceted and multileveled. For instance, a teacher who comes to the school counselor for advice on how to manage a particular child in a classroom seems simple and straightforward enough. However, managing a child's behavior in the classroom is not an isolated event because attending to one child has an effect upon all other children in the classroom. In addition, a child's behavior is also affected or partially caused by all other children's behaviors. So, from a systems perspective, all behaviors in a classroom are reciprocal in nature: Behaviors are both caused by other children and cause other children's behaviors at the same time. Hence, addressing a teacher's concerns about one child means that the school counselor/consultant probably needs to facilitate that teacher's understanding of a more complex system of causes and effects in the classroom.

In other situations, identifying the problem can be difficult because the consultee may or may not know exactly what the issue is. While consultees may have an idea about what the issue is, consultees may need help in organizing their narratives about the problem in a way that can propel action towards resolution. In still other situations, consultees may have identified the problem correctly, yet the issue lies in who owns the problem. Consultees may mistakenly assume that a problem is their issue when, in fact, the ownership of the problem may belong to some other entity such as a principal, parent, or the larger school system. Thus, during the problem identification phase, consultants need to not only help consultees determine the issue, consultants may need to help consultees clarify the appropriate venue of ownership. The more time that is spent on problem identification and ownership, the less time is needed to arrive at meaningful solutions.

In the process of identifying the issue and clarifying the problem, consultants will quite often need to help consultees identify their feelings about the situation. Sometimes, little effort is needed to accomplish this. For example, an exasperated teacher who comes to the school counselor/consultant for help immediately after an incident has occurred will probably present themselves in an emotionally charged state. In this case, consultants can easily reflect consultee's feelings of anger, irritation, frustration, powerlessness, and/or helplessness. In other situations, identifying consultee's feelings about the issue may be more problematic. This can be especially true if the incident in question has occurred a few days prior to seeking help or when seeking help comes after the consultee has already worked through their emotions. In these situations, consultants may not feel such a need to identify and work through consultee's feelings. Another difficult issue surrounding consultee's feelings can occur when consultees' are not "particularly emotional." While everyone is emotional, showing emotions to others may vary from consultee to consultee. In this case, identifying a "stoic" consultee's emotions would seem to have an adverse effect in that consultees could perceive consultant's help as an invasion or too "touchy-feely." Nonetheless, consultant's efforts at helping consultees work with their emotional content surrounding an issue should be measured and intentional rather than ignored. Consultants can employ self-disclosure to help "stoic" consultees identify and work through their feelings about the issue. From the previous discussion on facilitative responses, it can be seen that identifying feelings not only helps consultees view the issue more clearly, this process also helps bond the consultant and consultee while solidifying their effective working relationship.

Once the issue has been identified and clarified by using facilitative responses, consultees should be directed towards identifying an outcome or goal. It is important to note that the goal can be general or specific. This implies that consultees may consider a problem resolved even if they just "feel" like it is better. In this instance, a problem can be resolved when consultees have an opportunity to share their feelings about an issue and feel better about having shared it and/or when information is provided by the consultant that puts a hopeful perspective on a situation. For example, a teacher who comes to the school counselor/consultant for help about classroom morale may feel better when she or he finds out that they are not the only faculty member struggling with the issue. In turn, this information may increase the teacher's confidence to handle the problem with no further help. Another situation might be where a parent (consultee) of a child with low grades might feel relieved to find out that the missing homework can always be made up within two weeks for full credit. In most cases, though, goals will have some measurable outcome dimension such as a decrease in the number of times a child acts out, a decrease in the number of referrals to the dean of students, an increase in positive self-talk, an increase in a child's academic performance, or some other variation.

It is important for the goal or outcome to have some built-in system for determining success. A teacher who is seeking help in enhancing students' academic performance might need help in clarifying if "academic performance" means an increase in homework that is turned in, or higher quiz grades, or higher achievement scores, or higher test scores. Moreover, does "enhanced academic performance" mean the entire curriculum or just reading, or math, or social studies? Clearly, if a specific goal is desired, it is important to determine when and how their goal is met.

The fourth phase of Myrick's model is *observing* and *recording behaviors.* In some cases, counselor/consultants will be asked to observe or will actually need to observe the problematic situation in order to gain a better understanding of the issue and identifying an appropriate outcome. For instance, teachers may ask for the counselor to come in to their classroom and conduct a type of behavioral analysis. Teachers or other consultees may also engage in a type of self-observation or to conduct an informal behavioral analysis themselves. For instance, a teacher who is complaining about students not turning in their homework on time might be asked to determine if this occurs across the board with all subjects. This analysis might also include noting what particular days the students fail to turn in homework. Further detailed observation could also reveal if only particular students are being remiss. In any case, this analysis clearly provides a more incisive understanding of the issue at hand. A result could be that the goal or outcome can be adjusted based upon this new detailed data. Through this analysis, the consultant and consultee can then embark upon a plan that has a better chance of being effective.

*Developing* a plan, the fifth step, needs to be conducted conjointly with consultant and consultee. One of the more effective approaches is to brainstorm ideas. Brainstorming is a structured process in which the consultant invites the consultee to generate a list of possible ideas without regard to their efficacy. This means that the consultant helps consultees feign away from evaluating whether or not a particular idea or plan will actually work until the list has been exhausted. The goal here is to simply get a list of possibilities. One of the underlying assumptions of brainstorming is that some ideas will spawn other ideas which, in turn, lead to yet other ideas. Consultants can add ideas to the list once consultees have run out of their own ideas. Between the two lists, there is most often one idea or combination of ideas that will work.

Once the lists have been combined, consultants then help consultees evaluate the potential efficacy of each idea. Clearly, some ideas will cancel themselves out; others will have a low probability of success; and others will seem to rise to the top as potentially helpful. Consultants and consultees then choose a plan and begin to detail the procedures. During this evaluative process, the consultant's use of facilitative skills, especially open questions and clarifications, will keep the focus of the process upon consultees while helping them to commit to the plan.

Developing a plan not only involves the "what and how", it also involves the "when and where". This means that consultants and consultees detail the conditions for the plan of action that includes exactly what is to be done, how it is to be done, when, and under what conditions the intervention is to be implemented. For example, a teacher who has decided upon a plan to increase students' time-on-task (the "what to do and how to do it") will also need help in understanding the frequency and conditions under which the reinforcement will occur (when and where).

*Initiating the plan* is the sixth phase, while *following-up* is the last phase of Myrick's consulting model. Initiating the plan is self-evident. Follow-up can be formal or more informal. Because time is of the essence with school counselor/consultants and teachers alike, a formal follow-up where both go over in detail how the intervention went can be problematic. Hence, a mere "checking back" can suffice. In any case, the followup is critical for several reasons. Primarily, following-up has the advantage of seeing what did and did not work and can lead to further refinement of the plan of action. Second, follow-up demonstrates to the consultees that the consultant is also invested in the outcome. This show of allegiance often is a morale booster for teachers or other consultees. When consultees feel cared about and the work conducted with consultants has been fruitful, there is a greater likelihood that consultants will be called on in the future for other issues. In this way, school counselor/consultants can involve themselves deeper in the students' academic, social, and career-related concerns.

A variation of Myrick's Systematic Consultation Model is advanced by Vacc and Loesch (2000). These researchers maintain almost every important component of Myrick's work and condense the seven steps into four sequential questions. Step One has consultants asking the question, *"What is the problem situation?"* Critical to the efficacy of this step is consultant's use of empathy skills and allowing the consultee to vent. In Step Two, consultants ask the consultees, *"What have you tried?"* Using open-ended questions and clarifications are particularly effective in this phase. Step Three involves the consultant inquiring as to, *"What else can you do?"* Again, consultants are urged to employ facilitative responses including summaries and paraphrases. Finally, consultants ask consultees to determine *"What is the next step?"* While, Vacc and Loesch do not formally identify follow-up in their model, the researchers urge consultants to do some type of formal or informal follow-up.

# Promoting the Guidance Program through Coordinating Activities

Coordination is a counselor initiated leadership process in which the counselor helps organize and manage the comprehensive guidance program and related services. As noted throughout the previous, and later chapters in this book, it is an important counselor intervention aimed at managing various indirect services which benefit students. Some examples include coordinating career development programs, student appraisal, child study teams, peer helper programs, teacher-as-advisor programs, academic/educational guidance programs, and many others.

Theoretically, the central thrust of coordinating efforts is aimed at "*institutionalizing*" the comprehensive guidance program. In other words, the goal is to have the school personnel "own" the counseling program (the guidance curriculum) so that there is routine infusion of such important concepts as self-esteem and career development issues into regular classroom activities and in other activities throughout the school.

The coordinating role will likely be the least visible role played by counselors if the program/activity is successful, while paradoxically being their most far-reaching and broad-based function. However, this can lead to a pitfall. The "invisible" nature of coordinating the program can influence counselors not interested in providing direct counseling services to prefer this role. This is made possible by the sheer time that can be involved in coordinating inappropriate, non-counseling type activities. However, as Myrick (2003) pointed out, this preference for behind-the-scenes-work can be at the expense of performing other necessary counselor functions such as responsive services (counseling) individual student planning, and so forth. Therefore, awareness of this potential pitfall is crucial for school counselors. As noted in section two of this book, coordination is only one aspect of the role of the developmental school counselor.

Myrick (2003) also pointed out that, similar to a consulting role, effective coordination of the program requires good *leadership skills, expertise in individual and group process,* and *effective listening skills.* In addition to this list there are other behaviors such as: an ability to diagnose student and program needs, awareness of how system change takes time, willingness to thoroughly plan and prepare for the activity, patience, persistence, time-management, "structural integrity" as explained earlier in this chapter, a commitment to the coordinating role, and foresight and forethought.

## Summary

"Foresight and forethought" is a subtle skill, yet one that is most helpful. One's ability to attempt to "see into the future" allows the counselor to move from a *reactive stance* to a *proactive stance* and a more creative posture. A proactive stance helps the counselor maintain more control over his or her valuable time. Without this creative posture, the school counselor can quickly become absorbed into a coordinating role that becomes less productive to the overall counseling program goals and objectives.

Some school counselors take on the coordination of inappropriate activities because they believe the job will not get done unless they themselves do it. This tradition of over-extending serves some counselors well, but inappropriately, by providing them a non-counseling, "administrator driven" role and function. However, coordinating a comprehensive guidance program requires that counselors guard their time and determine which activities are appropriate to coordinate and which are not a function of the job. It is best to avoid inappropriate and untimely requests if possible.

Parents, teachers, and students rely on the counselor's leadership in planning and coordinating numerous special services and programs. And, as noted, the effectiveness of such programs and/or services often depends on the skills of the counselor/coordinator. In fact, poor coordination can ruin an otherwise excellent counseling program. In addition to those listed above, some other examples of appropriate coordinating activities a school counselor may be required to spearhead in a typical year are: a) new student orientation/registration; b) career interest surveys; c) Career Day; d) standardized testing program; e) student recognition programs; f) referrals for community services; g) referrals for psychological testing; h) peer facilitator program and special projects; and, i) student records-maintenance and transfer.

It is important to begin early in the school year when planning a program or activity under your coordination. Involve others in the planning. Get their input on how to make it better than "last year." Keep everyone, including parents, fully informed about the program goals, objectives, and procedures for implementation. And, always evaluate the activity or program immediately following its conclusion so that you can improve it "next year."

Schein (1999) summarizes ten principles that most consultants should follow in every consulting situation. Although aimed at organizational consulting, their applicability to schools is evident:

1. Always try to be helpful
2. Always stay in touch with the school's current reality
3. Work to understand things you are ignorant about
4. Remember that everything you do is an intervention
5. It is the client who owns the problem and solution
6. Go with the flow
7. Timing is crucial
8. Be constructively opportunistic with interventions
9. Remember that errors are inevitable
10. When in doubt, share the problem with consultees

Consulting and coordinating activities in the schools can be challenging and rewarding for school counselors. Both of these interventions require counselor knowledge and skill. The key to successful consulting/coordinating in the schools, however, lies in the counselor's ability to establish good working relationships with school personnel and parents. Through commitment, interpersonal skills, patience, and knowledge, the school counselor can address these challenges and find much reward through consulting and coordinating roles.

# References

Brown, D., Pryzwansky, W.B., & Schulte, A.C. (1998). *Psychological consultation.* Boston: Allyn & Bacon.

Caplan, G., & Caplan, R.B. (1993). *Mental health consultation and collaboration.* San Francisco: Jossey-Bass.

Dettmer, P., Dyck, N., & Thurston, L.P. (1999). *Consultation, collaboration, and teamwork for students with special needs.* Boston: Allyn & Bacon.

Harrison, T.C. (2004). *Consulting for contemporary helping professionals.* Boston: Allyn & Bacon.

Myrick, R.D. (2003). *Developmental guidance and counseling: A practical approach* (4th ed.). Minneapolis, MN: Educational Media Corporation.

Schein, E.H. (1999). *Process consultation revised.* Menlo Park, CA: Addison-Wesley.

Schmidt, J. (1999). *Counseling in schools* (2nd ed.). Boston: Allyn & Bacon.

Vacc, N., & Loesch, L.L. (2000). *Professional orientation to counseling* (3rd ed.). Philadelphia: Brunner-Routledge.

Wittmer, J., & Myrick, R.D. (1989); *Teacher as facilitator.* Minneapolis, MN: Educational Media Corporation.

# Chapter 19

# Rethinking How School Counselors Work with Families and Schools: An Ecosystemic Approach

by
**Ellen S. Amatea and Cirecie West-Olatunji**

*Ellen S. Amatea, Ph.D., is a Professor of Counselor Education at the University of Florida. Dr. Amatea has developed a practical approach for school counselor use in working with the families and teachers of students with behavior problems. This approach is described in her book, **Brief Strategic Intervention for School Behavior Problems**.*

*Cirecie West-Olatunji , Ph.D., is an Assistant Professor of Counselor Education at the University of Florida. Dr. West-Olatunji has consulted frequently with school staff from the pre-kindergarten to the high school level regarding the learning and development of children from diverse cultures.*

A fourth-grade teacher desperately consults the school counselor for help. One of her students, a little boy of nine, named Andrew, has been stealing items from his classmates and from her. Not only has Andrew stolen pencils and apparel belonging to other children, he had recently urinated on all the toilet paper rolls in the boys' bathrooms. The teacher reports that her efforts to resolve Andrew's problems by using questioning, behavioral rewards, punishments, or scolding have been fruitless. Her efforts to have Andrew's grandmother, with whom he lives, take action to correct the child have been equally unsuccessful as the grandmother has admitted that she is unable to make the child behave.

• • • • • • • • • • • • • • • • • • • • • • • •

An angry parent phones the school principal complaining that an eighth-grade teacher has been so critical and punitive with her daughter, Robin, that she vomits every day before school. The principal refers this case to the school counselor. When the counselor meets with the teacher and tells her of the parents' call, the teacher is indignant, refuses to decrease the girl's homework, and counters that the parents are too accommodating because they allow Robin to avoid work at school. When the

counselor calls the parents, they report that Robin has continued to vomit every day before school, and insist that she is too upset to attend school.

• • • • • • • • • • • • • • • • • • • • • • • •

Rosalinda, an eleventh grader, writes an essay describing an explosive argument she has had with her father. Her English teacher is concerned and consults with the school counselor. She reports to the counselor that Rosalinda is barely passing English, seems disinterested, rarely turns in work, and when she does so, she makes many careless errors. As a result the girl is getting D's and F's on most of her assignments. The teacher reports that she has suggested that she would be willing to work with Rosalinda after school and has encouraged her to use the after-school tutoring program. However Rosalinda has not followed through with any of these activities. The teacher has also sent a note home to Rosalinda's parents reporting her poor performance, but has not heard from them. She has recently called Rosalinda's home to discuss the argument, but Rosalinda's mother minimized the argument saying that the father just got mad at Rosalinda for being so "lazy" and that Rosalinda just needed to get down to work.

• • • • • • • • • • • • • • • • • • • • • • • •

The above vignettes are typical of the encounters that teachers have with students' families when students demonstrate problems at school. In these encounters, not only does the student demonstrate problems, significant difficulties are also evident in the interactions between the students' family and the school staff. As can be seen in these vignettes, the school counselor is often invited to participate only when teachers are unable to resolve a student's problem on their own or are unsuccessful in gaining the parents' backing in solving the student's problem. However, by this point, interaction between the adults at home and school has become laced with feelings of mutual blame and anxiety. As a result, the counselor is faced with the problem of mediating the conflicts between these adults as well as resolving the student's problems.

How can school counselors effectively intervene in such situations? What can they do to intervene at "the front end" rather than at the "back end" of such interactions?

To address these difficulties school counselors are rethinking their roles with families and with teachers and taking two very different courses of action. One course of action taken by counselors is to deal with the immediate crisis at hand by deliberately inserting themselves into and directly influencing the pattern of family school relations in which adults at school and at home are often embroiled (Amatea & Sherrard, 1997; Johnston & Zemitzsch, 1997). A second, more preventative and long-range course of action counselors are taking is that of assisting teachers and other school staff in developing a more collaborative mindset and skills for working with parents to facilitate children's learning (Amatea, Daniels, Brigman & Vandiver, 2004; Christenson & Sheridan, 2001).

Both of these ways of working with families and school staff address many of the challenges that beset contemporary school communities, and represent a radical departure from counseling practices focused exclusively on working with students. However, school counselors are often so beleaguered with their day-to-day demands that they can feel anxious and overwhelmed by the challenge of encountering new counseling approaches. Similarly, counselors frequently disclose feeling overwhelmed by the current demands and expectations made on them by students, their parents, as well as teachers, staff, and administrators (West-Olatunji & Behar-Horenstein, 2005). It is often difficult for them to conceive of a counseling approach that will alleviate these stressors. Yet, the model described in this chapter provides school counselors with both an opportunity and a choice. What is offered is the opportunity to discover an alternative approach for resolving the common conflicts counselors are often asked to resolve and the choice to begin applying new knowledge – today.

In this chapter we examine these two ways of working with families and school staff. First we describe common patterns characterizing the interaction between adults at school and at home which can either facilitate or impede student problem resolution. Second we describe an ecosystemic intervention model that a school counselor can use either to intervene immediately with adults at school and at home to resolve a student's problem or to facilitate school-wide change in the nature of family-staff interaction. We illustrate the use of this approach in intervening in a student problem and in teaching a school staff how to collaborate and problem solve effectively with students' families. Finally, we discuss the shifts in counselor role that these changes in thinking and practice entail.

# Patterns of Interaction in the School-Family-Community Ecosystem

Both schools and families can be defined as relationship systems in that each has its own distinctive memberships and activities, predictable ways of interacting, shared values and beliefs, coherent identity as separate units, and membership in larger community systems. When a student enters school these two distinctive human systems join forces to carry out the aims of educating and socializing the student and thus become an interconnected *ecosystem*. If a student develops difficulties in school, additional persons such as the school counselor as well as other professionals both in and outside the school may become members of this ecosystem as they join in the effort to assist the student or members of the school staff or student's family in resolving the student's difficulty. Thus a variety of persons at school (e.g. teachers, classmates, counselors, principals, etc.), at home, in the immediate community, and in related helping positions who communicate about a student and attempt to resolve the student's difficulties comprise the student's *ecosystem*. That is, that system of persons constructing meaning about the student's behavior.

For adults at home and at school to interact competently, it is important that a collaborative and mutually respectful relationship be developed between them with each party achieving coequal status (Christenson & Hirsch, 1998). In addition, clear agreements need to be developed between adults at home and at school in order for teachers and parents/caregivers to know which activities and responsibilities belong to whom. However, how responsibilities are defined depends on the beliefs and preferences of staff members of the particular school, the families whose children attend that school, and the community the school serves. For example, while one school (or teacher) may believe that a science project is exclusively the student's responsibility, another school or teacher may believe that the student's family should assist them in developing or getting needed resources to carry out the project. Furthermore, teacher's views may differ considerably from parents' beliefs regarding their appropriate role in a student's homework. Consequently, explicit agreements often need to be developed as to what role the family might have in a variety of student tasks. In addition, explicit agreements often need to be developed about how the family and school might work together to resolve a student's learning or behavior difficulties. Because there are often significant differences in beliefs and expectations held by adults at home and school concerning: (a) whether a particular student behavior is problematic, (b) who is responsible for causing the behavior and for resolving it, (c) what problem resolution methods are acceptable, and (d) how the family is to be involved in such problem resolution efforts; discussion and agreement about these expectations needs to be made explicit.

Regrettably, many times school staff and students' families come together without much conscious thought or discussion about how they expect to work together. Power and Bartholomew (1987) describe five common family-school interaction patterns that often result: avoidance, competition, merging, pursuer-distancer, or collaborative. The *avoidance* pattern is characterized by social distance and limited contact and communication between adults at home and at school. This is a common pattern characterized by adults at home and at school operating separately and independently from one another. There is usually little exchange of information about problem definition or problem resolution efforts concerning the children. Instead adults at school may expect to handle all student problems "in house" and hence make no effort to form collaborative or conjoint relationships with the home. Often this pattern is maintained on the part of teachers out of a desire to protect their professional status and autonomy, and by parents who fear someone else becoming expert or judge of their child's abilities. In addition, parents with lower levels of education or academic skills may feel inadequate and mistrustful in dealing with the school concerns for their child. As a result, they may choose not to offer observations and suggestions about their child. Because there is little opportunity to share information or develop trust, adults at home and at school do not share their concerns, aspirations or expectations for the child with each other or develop a common understanding of the child's difficulties. Thus, even when students' problems grow more serious, teachers may continue to attempt to handle the student problems completely on their own fearing that efforts to involve the family will create even more difficulties. Families may also avoid contact with the school staff and decide to handle student problems separately form the school and not to share relevant information about a student's past or current difficulties with school staff for fear their child might be stigmatized or their parenting judged negatively.

Often, however, when school staff are unsuccessful in resolving a child's difficulties and they decide that the responsibility for the child's school behavior should be returned to the parents, school staff may decide to shift from a pattern of avoidance to one of engagement with a student' family. Usually, at this point, parents may be brought into the conversation about the child's problematic school behavior with the expectation on the part of the school staff that the parents will follow the school's recommendations for getting the children to behave or perform at school. There may be notes and calls to parents about the problems at school, conferences at school, demands for increased homework supervision or tutoring by parents, formulation of behavior contracts about school behaviors with parents expected to dispense rewards and punishments, or monitor suspension to the home, or recommendation that parents seek outside medical or psychological consultation and treatment for their child.

If the school is successful in joining with parents, together they may solve the child's school problems. However, if the school is unable to gain the parents' backing either in carrying out their recommendations or in developing a joint agreement, three other problematic patterns of home-school relations may develop. One is a pattern of *competitive relations* between home and school in which both home and school try to exert influence over the other's domain. For example, in the case of Robin given above, both teacher and parent have strong ideas about how to respond to her with each attempting to dominate the other by having the other party act in accordance with their preferences. In such relations, conflicts often escalate to the point where the child is placed in a no-win position; neither party is willing to back down from their position and the relationships between home and school become increasingly competitive and hostile. Then the students' school problems begin to be defines as very serious and chronic by the school. Often the child is labeled and stigmatized as a "trouble-maker," an "emotionally disturbed student," or an "underachiever." Adults at home and at school are also labeled and stigmatized. A parent may be stigmatized as "irresponsible", "intrusive" or "dysfunctional" by the school staff; while the family may label a teacher as "rigid", "biased", or "uncaring". The interaction between adults at school and home often becomes laced with feelings of mutual blame and anxiety, as each party seeks to determine who is responsible for the problem and how best to solve it. Each adult blames the other for the child's problem and argues with the other regarding what should be the appropriate way to solve the child's difficulty. For example, in the case of Robin, the more the teacher feels attacked and dictated to, the more entrenched he or she becomes in her original position, triggering the parent to feel more strongly that if only the teacher would change, the child's problem would be resolved. The teacher in turn feels likewise. Thus these patterns of interaction often escalate in a "vicious circle," in that each side is prompted to elicit more of a particular behavior when they perceive the other as having elicited more of that behavior. Such competitive struggles can extend beyond the adults at home and at school, to include a bevy of other helpers (e.g. outside therapists, welfare workers) lined up on each side to continue the original battle. At this point, the child's problems at school are often exacerbated by the confused expectations and failures experienced by adults at home and at school and the overt conflict emerging between them.

In the dominant-submissive or *merged relationship* teacher and caregiver may agree that a problem exists and agree on a joint plan of action. However, such agreements are often a pseudo consensus made by one party "giving in" to the perspective of the other. Hence one party's view dominates, while the other submits to that view. For example, parents may find themselves attempting to carry out a teacher's expectations for a certain level of homework completion that is not appropriate for the child's level of comprehension. Rather than question the appropriateness of the assignments with the teacher, the parent may spend inordinate amounts of time and effort assisting their child in completing the assignments. One hazard of both systems merging is that the child can feel unheard and that an alliance against him or her has been created. As a result, the child can feel more isolated and frustrated and develop more problematic behavior.

The *pursuer-distancer relationship* occurs when the attempts of one individual in the system to direct the other person to act are ignored by individuals in the other system. For example in the first case given above of Andrew, the more the school attempted to call attention to the situation and demand the family take charge, the more the grandmother defines herself as helpless, triggering the school to push harder to have something be done by the grandmother, with the result that the grandmother feels even more discouraged and hopeless that she can be effective in her management of the child. Feeling overwhelmed with the care of three young children, the grandmother ignores the school's request that she manage Andrew or get outside help for him. The more the school pursues the grandmother to follow their recommendations, the more she avoids taking action. The above-mentioned case of Rosalinda reveals a similar pattern of relations—the mother seemed to avoid acknowledging the teacher's concern for Rosalinda's performance. The more that the teacher's worry is met by a minimizing response on the part of the girl's mother, the more the teacher escalates her concern by inviting the counselor in to further explore the girl's situation.

The fifth pattern of interaction, the *collaborative pattern*, involves adults at school and at home trusting each other and working together in a reciprocal and complementary fashion. The partners have regular contact and communication with each other, work toward similar goals, and develop some agreement as to what each party's role will be and how they will complement each other's efforts. For example, consider the case of Tyrone,

a fifth-grade student with a learning disability who had been in a full-day special education classroom since first grade. His teacher believed his math skills were strong enough to have him begin to attend a regular education math class. A team meeting was held that included Tyrone's parents. The school staff was in favor of Tyrone transitioning to the regular math class, but his parents were hesitant. They expressed their concern about Tyrone's ability to function in a less supportive setting and their fear that this action would set Tyrone up for failure because Tyrone, who was easily frustrated, would give up too easily in the new setting. After a long discussion, the parents and staff developed a plan together in which Tyrone would be supported at school with a teaching aide in the math class until he felt comfortable on his own, and would be supported at home by his parents who would discuss his concerns and fears with him and encourage him not to give up. The team decided they would try this plan on a trial basis; the plan would be discontinued if either the parent-school team or Tyrone did not consider it effective. In this case, teachers and parents held common goals for Tyrone and collaborated on a solution to the problem. Each party felt comfortable sharing concerns, and neither dictated what the other should/would do. Instead they came up with a joint plan of action that addressed each party's concerns.

# Applying the Ecosystemic Model to Resolve a Student Problem

Traditional approaches for working with students and their parents in the schools have assumed that either the parent's or the family's interaction is the exclusive target for one's intervention efforts. A variety of intervention approaches used by school counseling practitioners, such as family intervention (Steele & Raider, 1991), parent education (Fine & Carlson, 1992), or parent consultation and referral (Walsh & Williams, 1997) take this perspective by assuming there is some causal relation between problems at school and in the child's family or parenting (i.e. that some "flaw" or deficit in the family is causing a child's school difficulty.) What is often overlooked in these traditional ways of working, are the strengths and resources for change that exist in the family, the larger community, and the school. The ecosystemic approach assumes that because the school environment and the larger sociocultural environment influence the family, and the family and community influence the school, the target for intervention is this larger relationship system involving the student, his/her family, the school staff, and members of the larger community. By including these various persons in the child's world in addition to the family, the boundaries of the "system of interest" can be drawn differently and greater resources for change can be accessed.

By ecosystem we mean the social context for the presenting problem that evolves out of the recurrent exchanges of messages about the child and his/her problem among participating individuals in the child's ecosystem. In the school setting, this ecosystem may include: classmates, teachers, the school counselor, other support personnel or the school administrator. Outside the school, the ecosystem may include parents, siblings, extended family, outside helpers, neighbors, or community or church members. Second, it is assumed that while a child's problem can originate in any number of communication exchanges in a particular life arena (e.g. at school or at home) a student's problem behavior is often maintained by the responses to that behavior by other member of the ecosystem. Third, people often persist in their responses to a student's behavior because they feel their efforts are the only right and logical way to respond to the problem. In effect, then the student's problem is not the identified target for intervention, instead the solution efforts enacted around the problem (Amatea, 1989). Fourth, it is assumed that change can be affected by interrupting these problem-maintaining solution cycles. To alter these problem-maintaining patterns, a change in action quite different from the original solution efforts is usually required. A key to such a change in action is the use of language. Often different meanings must be attributed to a change in action in order for the persons involved to be moved to attempt it. These meanings much be close enough to fit "the facts" of the situation but different enough to provide an opportunity for different solution efforts to evolve. Thus the role of the school counselor in such a change effort becomes that of a co-participant who interjects new meanings and a new reality into the larger ecosystem to bring about change.

## Identifying and Assessing the Ecosystem

Deciding who in the ecosystem should be included in the change effort in order to interrupt the current solution efforts and how to involve them are the first steps. The counselor should concentrate his/her efforts on the persons who are most concerned about the problem and therefore most strongly motivated to take action toward change. This person may or may not be the child demonstrating problems. In addition, but secondarily, it is useful to consider who has the most power to change things. For example, in the case of Robin, the eighth grader vomiting before school each day, while the child is clearly suffering, it is the parents (specifically the mother), and secondarily, the child's teacher who seem most involved in the problem. Since these are warring parties (i.e., involved in a competitive struggle with one another), having several meetings in which they are both involved will probably only result in putting the counselor in the position of referee. An easier and more productive alternative would be to see one or both of the warring parties alone at which time the counselor can readily take a commiserating position of agreeing that the other party is indeed difficult. Such a position of alliance relaxes the teacher/parent's defensive posture and sets the stage for acceptance of suggestions for changes in behavior in dealing with the other party—which can be defined as necessary precisely because such a difficult person requires special handling.

A sampling of the types of questions that a counselor may use to elicit information as to the membership of the "ecosystem" and the nature of their solution efforts appears below. These questions can be phrased to include both family members, classroom members (i.e., teachers and students) or other school staff (e.g., the principal, special resource teachers or aides), outside helpers (e.g., therapists in private or public agencies, child welfare workers, probation officers, etc.), and friends. The questions can be addressed either to the individual identified as having the problem or individuals seeking help for the identified client.

1. **Who else has been involved in helping with this problem?** This question immediately expands the frame of the problem from one belonging to the student demonstrating the problem to one that has interactional connections. The resulting answers provide information for determining who talks to whom about this problem and how they talk about it.

2. **What is the nature of the problem and what solutions have been tried to solve this problem?** The counselor begins to gather data on the problem-maintaining interactional cycle. Each involved persons' responses need to be addressed separately to get clarity about the solution efforts they employ, the value positions these signify, the possible conflicts in advice given by the various persons involved, and the existence of escalating relationship patterns between adults at home and at school.

3. **If you were to bring in anyone to help with this problem whom would you invite?** The answer to this question can be used to identify how people may be aligned around the problem and problem person and what potential resources may be available. The answer may or may not be a reflection of whose solutions are actually most helpful, instead it often reveals who persons are closer to and more distant from. Phrasing this question as a hypothetical one, suggests in a non-threatening and non-demanding way that intervention for the child's problem may best be conducted by involving others beside the child.

4. **Who would be the last person(s) to bring in to help with this problem?** The answer to this question provides information about the pattern of interaction among adults at home and at school which has developed, possible secrets among members, marginalized members of the system-of-interest, or coalitions of protectiveness toward other members of the systems who have personal problems. Whether or not these identified individuals are worked with in the intervention is a secondary issue; what is important is that the answer to this question provides the counselor with clues as to whom to include in conceptualizing the membership of the ecosystem.

5. **If this present problem is solved, how would things be different? What, for example, would happen between (specific family member) and (specific school staff person/helper)?** Answers to these questions reveal the degree of hope that members of the system have for change, and the expectations various members hold for the change effort.

## Intervening in the Ecosystem

The following case illustration demonstrates how the relations between the school staff and the family around the resolution of a student's problem can be targeted for change. Andrew was one of the first cases referred to the new school counselor in the fall of the year. A third grader who lived with his 78-year-old grandmother and a younger brother and sister (ages 7 and 5), Andrew was a teacher's worse nightmare—he stole, he lied, and when provoked by his peers, he did the most outlandish things he could think of—like urinating on *all* the rolls of toilet paper in the boy's bathrooms at the school. He and his siblings had been placed with their paternal grandmother a year earlier due to the fact that their father, who struggled with chronic alcoholism, and their mother, who was addicted to cocaine, had physically and emotionally abused all three children. The family was considered "no-good" by members of the small community in which they lived with the father often returning to town between jail terms, becoming drunk, and beating up his wife in public. Andrew and his younger brother had already developed a negative reputation among the teaching staff that had little hope that the children would turn out any differently from their parents. In considering who was involved with Andrew and how were they defining and responding to his problem (Questions 1 & 2), the counselor learned from his teachers that despite his placement in a class for emotionally handicapped children, Andrew constantly created problems in this class as well as the larger school facility, had many confrontations with teachers and the other children, and exhibited considerable difficulty with learning. The teachers perceived that Andrew was "severely disturbed" and that he had not mastered even the most basic interpersonal skills. They had attempted to manage Andrew's outbursts by sending him to the principal's office (where he often spent the majority of the school day), calling his grandmother and insisting that she make him behave, or temporarily suspending him from school. It was quite evident that many of the teaching staff felt that Andrew was a "hopeless case" and that the family was at fault for his behavior.

Meeting with Andrew individually, the counselor observed that Andrew was quite guarded and had few skills for expressing how he felt. It took a great deal of gentle nudging for him to talk about himself. Over a few weeks, however, using play media, Andrew began to reveal how upset he was that his family, and his father, in particular, was made fun of by the other students. He described a number of situations in which he had initiated a number of serious fights after being teased by a group of boys about "his Daddy being a no-good drunk." He now seemed to go out of his way to keep his classmates and teachers in an uproar, and had managed to get himself completely ostracized by his peers because of his behavior.

Dropping by to chat with Andrew's grandmother (since she had no phone) to see how she was aligned with the other involved with Andrew (Questions 3 & 4), the counselor said, "I'm worried about your grandson, and I'll bet you are too. I am new to the school and I know you know your grandson better than I do. Would you help me understand what has happened and how we might be able to get him on track at school?" The counselor learned that the grandmother seemed overwhelmed as to where to start to deal with him. She complained angrily about Andrew's problems at schools, which she described as "his being bad", yet acknowledged that she felt completely helpless as to how to manage him. The school had called her numerous times and was now threatening to expel Andrew permanently, her health was fragile, and she was completely exhausted from trying to manage him and the other two children who were very much like him. Although outside therapy had been recommended by the school several earlier times, the grandmother had not sought it out since she felt that it was hopeless to attempt to change Andrew.

It was obvious that the school and home were caught in a *pursuer-distancer* pattern. The more desperate the school became that something be done with Andrew and the more they told his grandmother that he was seriously disturbed, the more powerless the grandmother felt at having any impact on his behavior, and the less she tried to control him, triggering the school to grow even more concerned, and press her harder. To alter this vicious cycle the counselor decided to frame Andrew's behavior differently so that the grandmother might be more hopeful that she could have some impact on him and the counselor could build an alliance with her in which the grandmother felt she had some power. In addition, it would be important to interdict the negative feedback cycle so that the grandmother would not constantly be told how hopeless things were. Volunteering to serve as a conduit for information about Andrew from the school to the grandmother could serve this purpose. Thus the counselor asked the grandmother if she knew exactly what the fights that Andrew had gotten into at school seemed to involve. The grandmother admitted that she did not. The counselor then indicated that she had learned from Andrew that most of his fighting seemed to involve protecting the family's, and particularly his father's, honor. The counselor stated that: "It was as if Andrew feels he has to be the "family's champion." As the counselor described a number of the situations in which Andrew had initiated serious fights after being teased about his family, the grandmother seemed to visibly soften. She admitted that although she often scolded him when he got into trouble, she did not question him about the circumstances of the

fights. The counselor acknowledged how difficult it was for her too to get Andrew to describe how he felt. She then proposed that she would like to drop by and chat with the grandmother every so often, since maybe between the two of them they could get some idea where Andrew was coming from and how they might work together to help him.

Over the next several weeks, the counselor met with Andrew on an individual basis several times. Andrew slowly began to develop some language for describing his feeling experience and shared more and more about his anger and disappointment with school. He began to see the counselor as someone who did not treat him like a "bad kid", but was nurturing and playful with him. At the same time, the counselor consulted with Andrew's teachers at school and indicated that she agreed with them that Andrew did not know how to behave in school and that she would be willing to work with him if and when he behaved disruptively. During this same time the counselor dropped by the grandmother's house on a regular basis, and rather than sharing Andrew's school mishaps with the grandmother, she shared things that Andrew had said that showed his soft, nurturing side and asked for the grandmother's help in trying to understand what he meant.

As the grandmother began to be treated like a coequal by the counselor, she became less defensive and discouraged and began to ask how to handle certain situations with the children. She disclosed in response to the counselor's inquiry as to what she would like to have be different (Question 5), that when her husband had died recently, each of the three children "went nuts, tearing up the house, and everything in it" rather than acting sad. She was confused and upset by their response and unsure what to do. The counselor suggested that the grandmother was probably the first person in these children's lives who cared about how they felt and would take time to talk to them about their feelings. She encouraged the grandmother to talk with the children about how they felt about the situation with their father and their mother. As the grandmother became more confident in being nurturing, she admitted that she probably needed to be firmer with the children. The counselor stated that she knew that these children had been through a lot, and that both she and the grandmother might need some help figuring out what to do. The counselor then suggested that one of the family counselors in the local mental health clinic might be able to help them. With the grandmother agreeing, the counselor then arranged a meeting with this family counselor. In this initial meeting which all the family and the school counselor attended, they decided together that the grandmother and the children would meet with the agency counselor and deal with family matters, and the school counselor would continue to drop by for a chat with the grandmother every so often and fill her in on school matters. In addition, the school counselor would continue to meet with Andrew on a regular basis. The grandmother and her family followed this arrangement conscientiously, meeting with the agency counselor regularly for the next several months. They experienced considerable success in developing a clearer routine and structure for the children at home, and in building in more opportunities to talk to the children about emotional issues. The counselor worked with Andrew and his teachers to reinforce his behavior in the classroom and with other students. By the spring, Andrew had developed a much more cooperative attitude with his teachers, was working up to grade level in all his subjects, and had begun to develop workable relationships with some of his peers.

# Applying the Ecosystemic Model to Resolve a School-Wide Problem

Traditionally, school counselors have been expected to work with individual children demonstrating difficulties or to consult with teachers and parents about these children, to meet with groups of children to develop skills or discuss problems, to develop and conduct the classroom guidance and testing programs for their schools, to oversee special education processes, and to mediate conflicts between students, or between teachers and parents. Most school counselors do not envision working with the "whole school" staff. However, in recent years, school counselors have begun to assume a leadership position in helping their school staffs develop a more collaborative mind-set and skills for problem solving with students' families (Amatea, Daniels, Bringman & Vandiver, 2004; Bryan & Holcomb-McCoy, 2004; Walsh, Howard & Buckley, 1999).

## Assessing the Ecosystem

The case of a particular student will often trigger a school counselor to begin noticing how the staff at their school think about and work with students and their families, to ascertain whether their might be a need for staff change by assessing these patterns more systematically, and to facilitate how their staff might plan to work differently with students and their families.

Such was the case with Rosalinda, the eleventh grader described in the opening case who had gotten in a violent argument with her father. As the counselor talked with Rosalinda's other teachers, some of them acknowledged that they had not attempted to communicate with her parents about her academic performance other than to send home the routine progress report. These teachers asserted that they believed that it was the student's responsibility to complete their assignments and neither the teacher nor parent should be "bird-dogging" them to get their work in. Other teachers, however, noted that they had tried to contact the parents to come in for a conference, but that the parents had been unresponsive. At a subsequent faculty meeting, several teachers disclosed their feelings of frustration and irritation at parents who seemed to be unresponsive to their telephone calls and requests to come in and discuss their children's progress or difficulties. One teacher suggested that there might be some cultural factors affecting parent's responses to these requests. Another teacher angrily dismissed this idea by stating that it would be a disservice to the students to give them or their parents any special treatment because of their ethnic background or social status. Other teachers expressed agreement with this opinion. Given the heated discussion, the principal validated the teachers for bringing up an important issue and recommended that the faculty look at this issue more closely by gathering additional information from the staff and parents. The principal then invited the Director of Guidance and a teacher from each grade level to form a study committee whose responsibility would be gathering information from different stakeholders about their perceptions of family-school relations at the school and their ideas and recommendations for change.

Members of this committee decided to gather feedback from parents from different economic and cultural backgrounds and from parents of children performing at different ability levels. They discovered that most of the contact that the students' families had with the school staff were either large scale, formalized contacts such as "back to school night," or brief, problem focused parent-teacher conferences that did not include the student. Typically, the goals of these conferences were for the school staff to explain to the parent the seriousness of the school's concerns, and what the school had decided to do to solve the complaint. Generating solutions for a complaint typically occurred before, rather than during the time that the staff met with a parent. Such a structure did not permit much opportunity for authentic dialogue or effective problem solving between school staff and students' families.

The committee discovered that the initial attitudes and practices held by the school staff were not designed to bring families into their children's learning process as equal partners. Interviews with teachers revealed that most of the school staff operated from a school-to-home "transmission" mindset (Swap, 1993) regarding how family-school relationships should be structured. In this mindset school staff routinely identified the values and practices outside the school (i.e., in the home) that contributed to school success and expected parents to take a supportive and subordinate role (i.e., "to do what they were told"). Teachers believed that desirable family-school involvement consisted of teachers clearly and consistently informing parents of the nature of the instructional program and of the child's progress in that program; and of parents cooperating by means of checking homework, reading notices, coming to school when called, taking an interest in their children's education, and supporting the instructional program in a myriad of ways. Neither students nor their parents were viewed as possible resources for enhancing student learning and educational planning or for solving student problems. Such tasks were the exclusive responsibility of the school staff. Two-way communication between adults at home and at school was not commonplace or sought out because the goal was for parents to understand and support the educator's objectives. There were no procedures for sharing information in a two-way dialogue between adults at home and school. Contacts with students' families were infrequent and uncoordinated. Those contacts that did occur usually followed incidents of children's inappropriate behavior or academic difficulty, or occurred informally when parents picked up their children from school, or when parents attended brief, highly ritualized encounters such as "back to school night". Students' families were viewed either as a cause of student problems or as the source of greater demands. Consequently, although teachers often had friendly, informal contacts with some of the parents of their students, these contacts were neither regular now systematic.

## Designing and Implementing a School Change Strategy

How might the school staff change their mind-set of operating separately from families and from each other? To accomplish the goal of fostering a mindset of partnership and collaboration among the school staff and students' families, the committee proposed a number of objectives concerning how current family-school interactions needed to change. First, *parents and students needed to have active, influential roles in participating in no fault family-school problem -solving*. Rather than have only a passive role, both parent and student needed to have active, influential roles, not as an audience but as full participants in family-school problem solving. Following the example of the staff of the Family-School Collaboration Project at the Ackerman Institute (Weiss, 1996), the committee proposed that family school problem solving meetings be redesigned to underscore the role of parent and students as co-decision-makers and illustrated the belief that everyone—parents, teachers and students—had a job to do to insure the student's educational success. To learn how to do this, the school counselor took on the responsibility for coaching individual teachers in how to: (a) focus on identifying a problem, (b) determine who might be available to help solve the problem, (c) search together for solutions rather than fixate on attempt to determine who caused the problem and why, and (d) develop action plans together with all the stakeholders. This process allowed the counselors to facilitate the implementation of culture-centered solutions developed by parents in collaboration with teachers. Thus, counselors need not feel anxious or hesitant when working with individuals of socio-cultural groups with which they have little familiarity or knowledge (West-Olatunji, 2001).

A second objective *was to build collaborative relationships with all parents whether the parents could come to school or not.* To do this, the committee suggested that the school staff needed to make clear to parents the relationship between their active participation in their child's educational experiences and the academic and developmental outcomes for their child. In addition, the committee recommended that the staff look for ways to communicate a genuine interest in connecting with the parents of all their students to insure these outcomes. Thus, if some parents were not able to come to the school because of work or family demands, the school staff continued demonstrating their belief that these parents still cared deeply about their child's learning by providing them with the means to understand and keep up with what is happening in school (e.g., through use of summary letters describing an event they missed, regular newsletters, and homework assignments).

Third, the committee recommended that the school increase opportunities for non-problematic family school interactions and that all these activities should be planned to maximize student learning. Rather than simply trying to "get parents involved," the committee suggested that the school staff use the family-school relationship to meet specific educational goals, solve problems, and celebrate the students and their achievements. Rather than be organized only around a discussion of problems, the committee proposed that the staff and families maintain a dialogue about learning and about our school's interest in each student. Consequently, the committee recommended that the staff look for opportunities for parents, students and school staff to interact with one another in ways which emphasize family involvement in children's planning, decision making, problem solving and learning. To do this, grade-level counselor-teacher teams were organized to examine the various aspects of the school experience (curriculum, administrative and communication procedures, special programs, assessment and evaluation of student progress, etc.) and design opportunities for families and school staff to experience each other differently. The school staff decided to embed a collaborative focus into student progress reports. Like most schools, this school staff had structured parent teacher conferences so that the teacher was central, parents had a passive role, and students were not included. Conferences only were scheduled when a student was experiencing problems. As a result, parents believed that while they needed to show up for these meetings there was little that they could do to influence their children's learning or achievement. The committee proposed to redesign the existing parent-teacher conference format by introducing a student-led parent conference format. They believed that by redesign-

ing this common school routine to create an opportunity for positive, non-problematic contact, they could enhance the sense of trust and increase the number of people involved in helping our students succeed in school. The conferences were designed to supplant the traditional parent-teacher conference in which the teacher was central and the child was usually not in attendance. In this new format the students would share their school progress (academic and behavioral) and develop a plan together with their parents for how to move forward. Not only did this approach create a structure for cooperative -planning and problem solving, but also students were taught ways of communicating with their parents in a respectful and cooperative manner (Amatea, Daniels, Bringman & Vandiver, 2004).

# Conclusion

This chapter has provided a detailed introduction to ecosystemic counseling in the school setting. The authors' experience indicates that an ecosystemic orientation can be an effective approach for understanding the negative patterns of family-school interaction that can develop when children experience problems at school. This approach can *help* the counselor assess the numerous pitfalls involved in working with adults at school and at home, not the least of which is the tendency for him/her to be drawn into a destructive cycle of blame and discouragement by which other members of the school staff are often organized. In addition, it can reinforce the fact that there are a broad array of resources at school and at home that can be called upon to effect change in the child's problem, including the usually well-intentioned attitudes of school staff, the ability of parents to increase their involvement with their child's school world if approached as coequals, the strength inherent in any given school system, and the child's own (often underestimated) abilities to change.

While this is only an introduction, the overview and case illustrations offer insight into the application of this approach within school communities. However, school communities vary in size and nature of their student body, faculty, and counseling staff, in their location (e.g., urban, suburban, and rural), and in their staff's readiness to change their educational practices. As a result, some counselors may find it possible to apply all of these ideas for working with families, while other counselors may find only parts of these ways of working with families are accepted by staff in their school. There is no definitive way to affect change. One small change can create a ripple effect throughout the school.

# References

Amatea, E. (1989). *Brief strategic intervention for school behavior problems.* San Francisco, CA: Jossey Bass.

Amatea, E., Daniels, H., Brigman, N., & Vandiver, F. (2004). Strengthening family-teacher-counselor connections: The family-school collaborative consultation project. *Professional School Counseling, 8 (1)* 47-55.

Amatea, E., & Sherrard, P. (1997). When students cannot or will not change their behavior. Using brief intervention in the schools. In W.W. Walsh & C. R. Williams (Eds.), *Schools and family therapy: Using systems theory and family therapy in the resolution of school problems* (pp 59-68). Springfield, IL: Charles C. Thomas.

Bryan, J., & Holcomb-McCoy, C. (2004). School counselors' perceptions of their involvement in school-family-community partnerships. *Professional School Counseling, 7*(3), 162-171.

Christenson, S., & Hirsch, J. (1998). Facilitating partnerships and conflict resolution between families and schools. In K.C. Staiber & T.R. Kratchowill (Eds.) *Handbook of group intervention for children and families* (pp. 307-344). Boston: Allyn & Bacon.

Christenson, S.L., & Sheridan, S. (2001*). Schools and families: Creating essential connections for learning.* New York: Guilford Press.

Fine, M.J., & Carlson, C.I. (Eds.) (1992). *The handbook of family-school intervention: A systems perspective* (pp 1-17). Boston, MA: Allyn & Bacon.

Johnston, J.C., & Zemitzsch, A. (1997). Family power: An intervention beyond the classroom. In W.W. Walsh & C.R. Williams (Eds.). *Schools and family therapy: Using systems theory and family therapy in the resolution of school problems* (pp. 23-37). Springfield, IL: Charles C. Thomas.

Power, T.J., & Bartholomew, K.L. (1987). Family-school relationship patterns: An ecological assessment. *School Psychology Review, 16(4),* 498-512.

Steele, W., & Raider, M. (1991). *Working with families in crisis: School-based intervention.* New York: Guilford.

Walsh, W.W., & Williams, C.R. (1997). *Schools and family therapy: Using systems theory and family therapy in the resolution of school problems.* Springfield, IL: Charles C. Thomas.

Walsh, M.E., Howard, K.A., & Buckley, M.A. (1999). School counselors in school-community partnerships: Opportunities and challenges. *Professional School Counseling, 2,* 349-356.

Weiss, H. (1996). Family-school collaboration: Consultation to achieve organizational and community change. *Human Systems: The Journal of Systemic Consultation and Management, 7,* 211-235.

West-Olatunji, C., & Behar-Horenstein, L. (2005). *Teaching and learning in fact-based pedagogy, (2).* Alexandria, VA: Association for Supervision and Curriculum Development (ASCD), pp. 7-14.

West-Olatunji, C. (2001). Counseling ethnic minority clients. In D. Capuzzi & D.R. Gross (Eds.). *Introduction to the counseling profession.* Boston, MA: Allyn and Bacon.

# Chapter 20

# The K-12 Developmental School Counselor and Appraisal

**by**
**Larry C. Loesch and William J. Goodman**

*Larry C. Loesch, Ph.D., NCC, is a Professor in the Department of Counselor Education at the University of Florida. Prior to receiving his doctorate he taught in a secondary school and later was a school counselor in a K-12 school in Kent, Ohio.*

*William J. Goodman, Ed.S., LMHC, is the Director of Guidance for the Alachua County Schools, Gainesville, Florida. He also is a licensed mental health counselor who specializes in counseling children and youth.*

## Introduction

Almost all school personnel receive some pre-service training in appraisal methods ("tests and measurements"), the primary focus usually being on construction of classroom tests. However, *only* school counselors and school psychologists *routinely* receive advanced, graduate-level training in appraisal. School psychologists typically use specialized appraisal techniques (e.g., individual intelligence, interest, or personality assessments), and therefore the scope of their appraisal activities is relatively small. In contrast, school counselors are involved with tests and other appraisal techniques applicable to and used by a wide variety of people. Thus school counselors in K-12 settings should, can, and do fulfill important appraisal functions in schools, a point emphasized within the American School Counselor Association *National Model*: (ASCA, 2005).

*School counselors work with students analyzing and evaluating students' abilities, interests, skills and achievement. Test information and other data are often used as the basis for helping students develop immediate and long-range plans. (p. 41)*

It is not possible to separate completely the appraisal functions school counselors fulfill because the natures of the activities as well as the persons affected by them are complex and interrelated. However, sets of roles can be clustered for discussion purposes. Shown in Figure 20.1 are three primary school counselor appraisal functions and some of the major focal points within them.

## Coordination

The coordination function capitalizes upon school counselors' training and expertise in appraisal techniques because it calls for use of relatively specialized knowledge and skills. The selection of appraisal techniques is a good example.

### Selection

The primary uses of appraisal techniques include: (a) gathering information not easily obtained through other methods (e.g., when students are hesitant to self disclose the information), (b) confirming subjective impressions of students (e.g., when a school counselor has a "hunch" about some characteristic of a student), (c) collecting large amounts of data (e.g., when information about an entire class or grade level is desired), and (d) evaluating change (e.g., when empirical evidence of the effectiveness of a counseling activity is needed). The information derived from appraisals is useful only to the extent that the appraisal methods from which the information is derived are *appropriate, reliable,* and *valid.* Indeed, the 2005 American Counseling Association (ACA) *Code of Ethics* stipulate in subsection E.6.a that, "Counselors carefully consider the validity, reliability, psychometric limitations, and appropriateness of instruments when selecting assessments." Although these terms are commonly used in casual conversation, they have specific meanings within the contest of appraisal. School counselors are aware of the technical meanings and use them appropriately in evaluating appraisal methods.

In selecting an appraisal potentially suitable for use with student, the school counselor first determines whether the appraisal is *appropriate.* For example, if the students have limited reading abilities, visual impairments, or physical disabilities, the use of "paper-and-pencil" appraisal instruments *may* be inappropriate. The psychosocial development levels of students also is an important consideration (i.e., some students may not be emotionally ready to respond to certain types of appraisals). Similarly, depending upon whether the school counselor wishes to use an appraisal on a single or two or more occasions, the appraisal's *reliability* information is an important consideration. *Validity* is the primary selection criterion because without it the other criteria are meaningless. Further, school counselors are aware that validity is a situation-specific construct. An appraisal technique (test) is not valid in general, but rather is valid only for use with particular person in specified situations. Much of the information needed for theses evaluations can be obtained from careful reading of the technical manuals for appraisal instruments. Additional information can be obtained from critiques in professional journals and books. Thus school counselors' specialized preparation in appraisal allows them to evaluate he evidence supporting use of an appraisal allows them to evaluate the evidence supporting use of an appraisal for the particular context in which the appraisal in which the appraisal is to be used.

Effective appraisal selection requires that school counselors have comprehensive and accurate knowledge of appraisal techniques, the students to whom appraisals will be applied, and the persons who will use the appraisal results. School counselors are uniquely suited for this task because of their specialized training in appraisal and their comprehensive understandings of students, teachers, parents, and other professionals.

## Administration

Effective administration of appraisal techniques also capitalizes on school counselors' specialized appraisal and counseling skills and knowledge. The conditions under which an appraisal is conducted must be conducive to students' responding and the students must be in "the right frame of mind" in order for the appraisal to yield meaningful and useful information, and for students to respond or perform effectively on appraisals. Excessive anxiety (including feelings of pressure to respond in the "right" ways) or excessive complacency (including not understanding the importance) invalidates the results of appraisals. Therefore, providing "orientation" to forthcoming appraisal is always professionally appropriate. It is also ethically appropriate. For example, the 2004 (ASCA) *Ethical Standards for School Counselors* stipulate in subsection A9.d that:

*The professional school counselor: Provides explanation of the nature, purposes, results, and potential impact of assessments/evaluation measures in a language the student(s) can understand.*

Similarly the 2005 ACA Code of Ethics stipulate in subsection E.7.d that:

*Prior to administration of assessments, conditions that produce most favorable assessment results are made known to the examinee.*

School counselors use large group, small group, and individual activities to facilitate students' appropriate responding to appraisals. For example, school counselors typically conduct classroom guidance activities to help students be prepared for participation in various state (e.g., academic competency) or national (e.g., Armed Services Vocational Aptitude Battery) tests. Other times, commercial materials (e.g., films, videotapes, or print media) and/or structured activities available from publishers and testing companies are used. In either case the purposes are to enable students to *understand* the purposes and uses of the appraisal and to *motivate* students to respond accurately, honestly, and to the best of their abilities.

Small group activities are used for similar purposes. However, often this modality is preferred when several students have a commonality (i.e., are a "target" group) that distinguishes them from a class-size group of students. For example, some school counselors conduct small-group counseling activities for groups of 10 or fewer students who are experiencing relatively high levels of test anxiety.

Individual, pre-appraisal counseling/orientation activities are appropriate when a student will benefit most from specific, individually-tailored activities. For example, some college-bound students experience relatively severe test anxiety and/or other performance inhibiting psychological states when confronted with having to take the Scholastic Aptitude Test (SAT) or the American College Test (ACT). For these students, the school counselor can use individual anxiety reduction and test-preparedness interventions to help them perform more effectively on such tests.

So-called "high stakes" tests are those for which student performance on them has significant, perhaps life altering, implications for the students. For example, performance on mandated statewide achievement (or competency) tests may determine students' placements in educational curricula, rate of progression in grade levels, eligibility for graduation, or advancement into a postsecondary educational program. Although many school counselors disdain the "busywork" involved in implementing such testing programs, ironically they are likely the school professionals best-suited to the task because of their advanced-level training in psychometrics, understandings of student psychosocial development and academic performance, and knowledge of ethical practices. Therefore, school counselors can and should take a leadership role in the successful administration of high stakes tests.

## Development

The development component of school counselors' appraisal functions involves creation of appraisal instruments and/or techniques for local (i.e., within the school or school district) purposes. Successful fulfillment of this function necessitates that school counselors directly *apply* their knowledge and skills to create appraisals which will yield information uniquely useful to their settings. In particular, it requires that school counselors have good skills in various appraisal techniques (e.g., gathering attitudinal or factual data), item writing, response format determination, and scoring procedure development and/or application. Applications of these skills differ for different school and/or grade levels, and therefore they must be applied within the context of good understanding of respondent groups. Appraisal development functions are closely related to evaluation functions because school counselors typically develop locally-appropriate instruments or techniques to fulfill their evaluation functions.

## Evaluation

Appraisal evaluation functions conducted by school counselors usually are implemented either before or after other school counseling activities. As a prelude to activities, a comprehensively useful function in which school counselors typically engage is "needs assessment." Many school counseling experts suggest that a needs assessment should serve as the foundation for a school counseling program. In general, a needs assessment is a process which identifies the counseling-program-related needs of any of a variety of persons who may benefit from the program, including students, parents, teachers and other school personnel, and even professionals in agencies associated with schools. Needs assessment is advocated in the ASCA National Standards (1997): Knowledge about your students and their needs is essential. This information can be obtained by conducting a needs assessment (p. 34). Similarly, the ASCA *National Model* stipulates that, "School counselors must show that each activity implemented as a part of the school counseling program was developed from a careful analysis of student needs, achievement and related data" (p. 49). In response, some school counselors routinely

administer (personally) developed needs assessment surveys to students, teachers and parents in the Fall of each academic year. Many of the items on the surveys are parallel across years to allow comparisons across respondent groups. The results then serve as the basis for the year's program planning as well as for program evaluation purposes.

The usual form of a needs assessment is a survey that includes items reflecting elements and/or services that could be included in a school counseling program and a response scale that allows respondents to indicate the extent to which they believe each element would be of particular use to them. Thompson, Loesch, and Seraphine (2003) provided an example of a needs assessment instrument for use in elementary schools. The results of a needs assessment survey can be prioritized by total respondent group mean per element and/or by element group mean for selected subgroups (e.g., males and females or parents, teachers, and students.) In either case, school counselors derive information from needs assessments that serves as the basis for establishing counseling program priorities and for subsequent program evaluation. These priorities are established most effectively when considered by school counselors in collaboration with others such as a Guidance Committee, an Educational Planning Team, teachers, parents, or administrators. Because programs can not encompass all potentially appropriate services all the time, needs assessments are the best way to develop school counseling program priorities.

Another important evaluation method being used with increasing frequency by school counselors is behavioral observation, which typically include use of a behavior checklist or rating scale. This technique involves a school counselor identifying specific, carefully defined behaviors and then observing and noting or rating the frequency with which a student engages in the "targeted" behaviors within a defined time period. The targeted behaviors observed usually are ones for which change is desired through a counseling intervention. Often the targeted behaviors are academic in nature and observed in classrooms. However, behavioral observations also may yield information about social behaviors. For example, a classroom observation record form may be used to assess students' social, assertiveness, learning, time management, decision making or relationship skills.

Appraisal methods are commonly used after counseling activities as a means of determining the effectiveness of those activities. One simple tactic useful in both large and small group and individual contexts is to re-administer the same appraisal instrument after the counseling as was administered before counseling to determine what, if anything, has changed in the dynamics or behaviors addressed. Even more common is the similar use of appraisals for program evaluation and/or personal accountability. For example, the junior author developed several surveys, based in part on items from needs assessment surveys, to obtain students', parents', and teachers' evaluations of various school counseling services provided throughout each academic year. Loesch and Ritchie (2005) provide numerous examples of how appraisal results can be used for personal school counselor accountability.

The four coordination functions within the context of appraisal evolve directly from the more technical aspects of the school counselor's appraisal expertise. However, effective completion of those functions is not possible unless the resultant information can be understood effectively, and that involves use of school counselors' interpersonal skills.

# Interpretation

Good professional practice, as well as legal standards, require that participants in appraisals (or their legal guardians) be informed of the results of the appraisals in ways that are understandable to them. For example, both the APA/AERA/NCME *Standards for Educational and Psychological Testing* and the laws derived from the *Family Educational Rights and Privacy Act of 1974* stipulate that it is the appraisal user's responsibility to insure that participants understand the results. This requirement necessitates skills beyond understanding item discrimination and difficulty indices, reliability coefficients, and the like. Rather, it necessitates appraisal users having good *communication* skills - what effective developmental school counselors already have!

For large scale appraisal programs, such as district wide achievement or aptitude testing, in which commercial tests are used, test publishers routinely provide extensive interpretive materials for respondent students and/or their parents or legal guardians. To the credit of the test publishers, most of these materials are very well-developed, nicely packaged, and most importantly, relatively self-explanatory. They do much to help people understand appraisal results and school counselors are well-advised to use them to supplement their own interpretations. However, rarely are they completely sufficient for fully effective interpretations because most people *simply do not understand* normal distributions, deviation scores, stanines, and so on by just reading about them or looking at even well conceived diagrams or graphs. Students, parents, teachers, and others who receive appraisal infor-

mation have all kinds of questions about appraisal results, and usually face-to face interactions are needed to provide effective answers to those questions.

## Students

School counselors often use *large-group* (i.e., classroom) appraisal interpretation activities for students in middle or secondary schools when the appraisals are in regard to "non-threatening" topics such as achievement, aptitudes, or vocational interests. For example, each December some counselors conduct classroom-group activities to help students understand the results of the Preliminary Scholastic Aptitude Test they took earlier in the year. Large-group interpretation activities also may be appropriate when an entire class has participated in a specific type of appraisal, such as of attitudes toward substance abuse or sexual harassment. Some of these activities are intended to supplement information provided in test publishers' interpretive materials. More importantly, however, even large-group interpretation activities allow students to ask questions about their results and what they mean in personal ways. Perhaps most importantly, they allow students opportunity to request further, perhaps individualized, interpretation assistance or for school counselors to identify students in need of such assistance.

*Small-group* (counseling) interpretation activities are particularly appropriate for use in elementary schools and/or when students can gain from learning about their similarities or dissimilarities to others. In the latter context, the primary benefit is most likely from the discussions which follow from the interpretations rather than from simply (cognitively) understanding the appraisal results. If students have been appraised in regard to social attitudes or behaviors, study habits, familial values, or career plans, the appraisal results may provide effective stimuli for discussions in which students can come to understand one another better. For example, a survey of family relationships conducted in conjunction with small-group counseling sessions for students experiencing difficulties in family life may serve to stimulate group discussions.

The small group context also provides a forum in which students can support one another so that appraisal results are not personalized in inappropriate ways. That is, students can encourage one another to "accept" the results as simply descriptive rather than as reflecting personal deficiencies. Again, the school counselor's expertise in both appraisal and counseling are essential to facilitate appropriate interpretations.

Students should be provided with *individual* interpretations when there is likelihood that they will personalize appraisals of personal characteristics such as self-concept, personality traits, or interpersonal behaviors. Appraisal results are almost always simply descriptive; typically there are no value judgments inherent in them. However, people make value judgments about the results, and therefore some students may interpret some appraisal results to mean there is something "wrong" with them. Through counseling in conjunction with interpretation, school counselors can help students individually to foster students' self understanding in way that will facilitate students' self, social, academic, and developmental improvement.

## Parents

Appraisal interpretations for parents usually are made through large group or individual activities. Large group sessions for parents are routinely conducted to explain the results of systemwide achievement, aptitude, or competency testing, particularly for "high stakes" testing. These sessions have essentially the same purposes and functions as those for students: to facilitate understanding of appraisal results and to allow for questions. However, parents usually have greater interest in the long-term implications of the results than do the student respondents themselves. For example, they often are interested in what the results mean in particular for their children's class placements, psychosocial developments, or vocational possibilities. They also may be interested in the overall curricular implications of the results -- how well are their children doing in comparison to other children in the area, state, or nation? School counselors can use information provided by testing companies, school districts, and/or their own surveys, tests, or questionnaires to respond effectively to their questions.

Individual meetings with parents to discuss appraisal results are appropriate when either the parents do not understand results as explained through other means or when they have particular concerns about specific implications for their child(ren). The former is simply a substitute for other means of explanation. However, the latter requires that school counselors use their counseling skills to present information so that the best interests of the child can be fostered. For example, a school counselor may have to explore family dynamics and behaviors to determine appropriate ways and means for a child to improve study practices, interpersonal relationships with peers or adults, or academic and career planning decisions.

## Teachers and Other Professionals

Some of the most valuable appraisal interpretation assistance school counselors provide is that for teachers and other professionals in schools. Given that the primary purpose of schools is to educate children, appraisal results frequently can be used to enhance educational processes, particularly instructional methods and academic advising. When school counselors help other school personnel understand appraisal results effectively, those school personnel can then provide the best educational services to students. For example, when a teacher understands the differences among a student's various abilities, the teacher can instruct the student in ways that capitalize on the student's strengths as well as improve on the student's limitations. In effect, school counselors can use appraisal results to individualize instruction even though they are not actually providing the instruction. Similarly, competent understanding of the results of appraisal of a student's non-academic characteristics can enhance all school professionals' abilities to interact with the student in ways that will improve the student's academic, personal, and social developments.

The school counselor's role in interpreting appraisal results is crucial to helping students and others gain maximum benefit from appraisals. However, there is yet another context in which school counselors can use their combined appraisal and counseling expertise to assist students without direct provision of interpretation services.

# Consultation

School counselors frequently serve in consultation roles as they work to help students help themselves or with other professionals to help students. Each person in any consultation scenario contributes information that can be useful. In such situations, school counselors do not necessarily need to provide technical interpretations of appraisal data; they need only be able to communicate the meanings and implications of those data pertinent to the purposes of the consultees' activities.

## Students

Innumerable "tests" and other "self-evaluation" methods are now available on the Internet/World Wide Web, and most students have access to them. Some (such as those provided through the Occupational Information Network (O*Net) Resource Center at www.onetcenter.org) are professionally developed and highly credible, and can be of valuable and substantive assistance to students. However, many (likely most) of the online measures lack psychometric credibility and therefore may actually be harmful to students by giving them inaccurate information about themselves. In what are essentially consulting relationships, school counselors can help students use online tests effectively by (a) identifying credible online measures, (b) guiding students toward online measures that will meet their needs, (c) helping students interpret information from online assessments (even though "self-interpretation" information is usually provided), and (d) suggesting follow-up activities that are in the students' best interests. In effect, school counselors can and should be the primary "online assessment resource" for students.

## Teachers

Most commonly, school counselors consult with teachers to help them work better with individual students so that the students can be more effective and successful in the teachers' respective classrooms. Sometimes this consultation involves the school counselor capitalizing upon appraisal data the school counselor has for the student. For example, in consulting with a student's teacher about how the teacher can modify a student's classroom behaviors, a school counselor who has appraisal information about the student's personality characteristics or social or familial situations does not need to provide extensive interpretation of the appraisal data. Rather, the school counselor may relate only the implications of the appraisal results for the teacher's future interactions with the student (e.g., appropriate "positive behavior" reinforcements). Conversely, the school counselor may determine from the consultation that an appraisal is appropriate, conduct it with the student, and then provide implications within a consultation relationship with the teacher.

## Parents

Similar procedures may be used by school counselors in consultation activities with parents. However, in this context, activities recommended should probably be more specific and instructive. That is, school counselors likely will have to provide direct, explicit, behavioral instruction to the parent(s). For example, if the goal is have parents help to improve a student's self-concept, the school counselor may have to provide detailed descriptions of desired parental behaviors such as when and how to reinforce a student's positive self-concept behaviors or what words to use to encourage positive self-concept. In so doing, school counselors capitalize on their knowledge of human development, individual psychology, familial interactions, and appraisal.

## Trainees

On-site supervision of school counselor trainees is an important professional function fulfilled by many school counselors. As aspiring school counselors, trainees need to become familiar with and adept at use of appraisals as they are a part of school counselors' professional roles and functions. It is *not* the school counselor's responsibility to teach trainees about the technical aspects of appraisal; that responsibility is inherent in counselor education programs. However, it *is* appropriate for practicing school counselors to engage trainees in various appraisal functions and to provide appraisal activity feedback, assistance, and consultation whenever trainees need them. Thus practicing school counselors should involve school counselor trainees in coordination, interpretation, and consultation appraisal functions in ways that reflect their own activities in fulfilling each of these functions.

## Other Professionals

An increasing number of students are receiving mental health counseling services from professionals not officially connected with schools (e.g., counselors in community agency or private practice settings). Those professionals usually are called upon to provide services not frequently available in schools (e.g., long-term counseling or family counseling), but their efforts can be enhanced by information from and consultation with school counselors. In particular, school counselors often have access to appraisal information which could be obtained by counselors in other settings only through great effort (and possibly expense). For example, a school counselor who obtains a measure of family cohesion to appraise a student's perceptions of their family dynamics can provide the results (with parent or legal guardian permission) to other counselors in a professional consultation context for students and their families who enter into family counseling. Thus school counselors can provide useful information and foster better interprofessional relationships through appraisal-related consultation activities.

School counselors' appraisal activities also may serve as the basis for initiating consultation activities with counseling professionals not in the schools. In consultation with other professionals, school counselors can rely to some extent on the other professional's expertise for determination of appropriate behaviors. For example, school counselors often use children's drawings as a form of appraisal with elementary-school-age school children. Sometimes revealed in those drawings are indicators of need for counseling services beyond those which can be provided effectively by school counselors. Children's drawings in which child abuse and/or neglect are indicated are good examples because school counselors are required by law to report those indicators to "outside" authorities. In such situations, school counselors' appraisal activities lead directly to consultation activities with professionals outside the schools.

## Summary

School counselors' successful fulfillment of their appraisal coordination, interpretation, and consultation functions is crucial to their effective provision of school counseling services. Fortunately, by virtue of their training, knowledge, and skills in both appraisal and counseling, they are well-suited to fulfill these functions effectively. The most effective school counselors are those who routinely integrate appraisal activities into their functioning, and who therefore derive the most benefit from appraisals.

## References

American Counseling Association. (2005). *Code of Ethics.* http://www.counseling.org. Retrieved August 26, 2005.

American School Counselor Association. (2005). *The ASCA national model: A framework for school counseling programs.* Alexandria, VA: Author.

Campbell, C.A., & Dahir, C.A. (1997). *The national standards for school counseling programs.* American School Counselor Association. Alexandria, VA: Author.

Thompson, D.W., Loesch, L.C., & Seraphine, A.E. (2003). Development of an instrument to assess the counseling needs of elementary school students. *Professional School Counseling, 6*(1), 35-39.

Loesch, L.C., & Ritchie, M.H. (2005). *The accountable school counselor.* Austin, TX: ProEd.

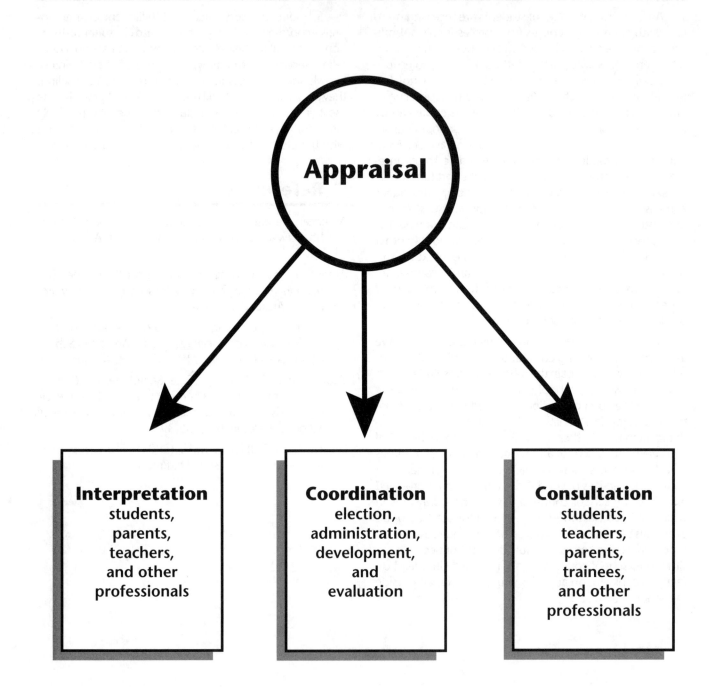

**Figure 20.1**
**School Counselor Appraisal Functions**

Appraisal

**Interpretation**
students,
parents,
teachers,
and other
professionals

**Coordination**
election,
administration,
development,
and
evaluation

**Consultation**
students,
teachers,
parents,
trainees,
and other
professionals

*Joe Wittmer, Ph.D. and Mary Ann Clark, Ph.D.*

# Chapter 21

# Career Development: The Counselor's Role in Preparing K-12 Students for the 21st Century

by
**Pat Schwallie-Giddis and Linda Kobylarz**

*Pat Schwallie-Giddis, Ph.D., is an Associate Professor at George Washington University in Counseling/Human and Organizational Studies. She also serves as a consultant to the Center for Occupational Research and Development (CORD). Dr. Schwallie-Giddis was formerly an elementary counselor, district-level administrator, school board member, and the program director for Career Education in the Florida Department of Education. Most recently she served on the executive staff at the American Counseling Association (ACA) and the Association for Career and Technical Education (formerly AVA).*

*Linda Koblylarz, M.Ed, is president of Kobylarz & Associates, a career development consulting group providing program design and implementation, staff development, program evaluation, and research services to K-12 schools, colleges, federal and state agencies, and business. Kobylarz has served as President of the Connecticut Counseling Association (CCA), on the Board of Directors for the National Career Development Association (NCDA), the National Employment Counselors Association (NECA), and the Association of Computer Systems for Career Information (ACSCI). She was recipient of CCA's Professional Development Award and NCDA's Outstanding Career Practitioner Award.*

## Introduction

During the past several decades, our nation has experienced extensive psychological, sociological, and economic changes. There have been many studies and reports about the state of American education and the American workforce. They suggest that education must continue to keep pace with the new and more demanding knowledge and skills required in the emerging workplace. Schools are expected to deliver a revised curriculum that is both more relevant and more rigorous for all students. National, state, and local initiatives seek to meet the challenge of preparing a high productivity workforce. The *No Child Left Behind* (NCLB) legislation sets imperatives for improving the quality of education. What role can schools play in dealing with this issue? More specifically, what role do K-12 school counselors play? A discussion of these questions, including effective counselor strategies, is the focus of this chapter.

To meet the challenges of the new millennium, all educators, but especially K-12 school counselors, need to seek to improve and extend existing career development programs and create new methods and strategies within the school's guidance programs. What is career development? Consider these comments from national experts. Dr. Edwin Herr (Herr, 2004) describes career development as a lifelong process comprised of many tasks that arise in conjunction with exploring, choosing and implementing decisions about educational, occupational and related life roles. It is that aspect of human development which includes how individuals incorporate their values about work, their beliefs about their own interests and abilities, their decisions about education, the ways they negotiate transitions into and out of work experiences and their unique interactions between work and other life roles. Dr. Donald Super (Super, 1976) defined career development as "the sequence of occupations and other life roles which combine to express one's commitment to work in his or her total pattern of self-development." It follows then that career development is the process by which we develop and refine our self-identity as it relates to many life and work roles including those involving occupations, education, social responsibility, and leisure. Herr and Cramer further comment that career development is a lifelong process in which individuals come to understand themselves and how they relate to the world of work. Through the career development process individuals gain self-knowledge, explore educational and occupational options, acquire work related skills, and develop decision making and planning skills. This process should be an essential component of any comprehensive k-12 guidance and counseling program (Herr & Cramer, 2003).

Experts agree that in today's workplace each of us must become our own career manager.

But, exactly what is a career? Put simply, it is the sum total of the work (both paid and unpaid) that a person does throughout life. Each person has one, lifelong career. It might include many jobs (positions, usually for pay), numerous occupations (the type of work we do such as nurse or diesel mechanic), volunteer work, schoolwork and work in the home. Even in our leisure time we are doing "work" when we produce goods or provide services for others or ourselves.

During a person's career, he/she must make many decisions about work—that is, manage his/her career. To do that successfully, requires much. Ongoing career development activities provide experiences for students that can help them gain valuable knowledge of themselves and the world of work and to learn the skills needed for effective career planning and preparation.

Generally speaking, experts have defined three broad competency areas involved in an individual's career development process; 1) personal/social development, 2) educational achievement and lifelong learning, and 3) career management. In the personal/social development area, individuals increase in awareness of their interests, aspirations, aptitudes, abilities, and values. They move toward becoming more self-directed individuals, accepting responsibility for their own behavior, and developing positive interpersonal skills.

As individuals become more skilled in the career development area of educational achievement and lifelong learning they acquire a deeper understanding of themselves as learners and the importance of academic and technical education to all career goals. In the career management area career planning and decision-making skills are honed. Students come to understand that career planning is a lifelong process and to accept responsibility for their own choices, for managing their own resources, and for directing their own lives.

Students also become more aware of the nature and structure of the world of work and the major trends impacting our economy. Information about self and the world of work are combined to focus on career options. Skills required for seeking, obtaining, keeping and advancing in a job are learned. The competency areas listed above should be at the center of any K-12 career development program.

## Who Needs a Career Development Program?

Career development programs are appropriate for all people and at all educational levels; kindergarten through adult. We are all in various stages of the career development process. Children in the elementary grades are gaining new awareness of themselves as they interact with others. They should be systematically introduced to workers in the community and begin to relate education and work. As a school counselor, your role is to help them come to know that good work habits and personal responsibility are expected of them and that decisions they make have consequences for themselves and others (Wittmer, Thompson, & Loesch, 1997).

Counselors help youth in middle/junior high school to fine tune the interpersonal and social skills required for positive interaction with others. Students should, as a result of your middle school counseling program, grow in self confidence and become aware of their interests and abilities. They need to see clearly the relationship between educational achievements and career opportunities and to express positive attitudes towards work and learning. The ability to locate and use information in their educational and career planning is also important. They must have knowledge of job seeking and survival skills and begin to develop competencies.

High school students are at a pivotal time in their lives where decisions about staying in school, entering work directly after graduation, joining the armed forces, or continuing with some form of post-secondary education will have a significant impact on their lives for years to come. School counselors must ensure that their career development programs respond to the individual needs of students while helping all students prepare for transition into the adult world. The following are keys to the successful career development of high school students: 1) Clarification of individual interests, 2) An understanding of personal strengths and skills, 3) Well developed interpersonal skills, 4) A wealth of knowledge about occupations and how the self relates to them, 5) Good work attitudes, and 6) Sound decision-making and planning skills.

## Who Delivers the Career Development Programs?

As noted, career development programs are essential to any quality K-12 developmental counseling program that seeks to offer comprehensive, systematic and sequential services to all students. The delivery of the career development programming is a team effort with counselors, career development facilitators, teachers, administrators, parents, and the community at large all playing a part. However, school counselors have a leadership role in designing the program and identifying student outcome standards; assuring coordination with other programs and articulation across levels; supporting the professional development of staff; and conducting ongoing program evaluation and improvement. School counselors must also be proactive in public relations and advocating the allocation of necessary resources and budget. School counselors should maintain a working relationship with post secondary institutions and community employers to facilitate smooth transitions for their students. Also many career development programs now utilize activities outside of the school site to promote student career maturity.

## Career Development Program Content

The American School Counselor Association (ASCA) has long been a strong advocate of K-12 career development programs and in 1997, the Association developed the National Standards for School Counseling Programs of which one-third concern K-12 career development standards. In Chapter 2 of this book, Clark and Wittmer presented an overview of ASCA National Standards for School Counseling Programs.

The ASCA Standards provide the foundation for skill attitude and knowledge acquisition that enables students (K-12) to make a successful transition from school to the world of work, and from job to job across the life career span. Career development, according to the ASCA Standards, includes using strategies that enhance future career success and job satisfaction as well as assisting, understanding of the connections among personal qualities, education and training, and a career choice. The recommendations of the Secretary's Commission On Achieving Necessary Skills (SCANS 1991) and the content of the National Career Development Guidelines are also reflected in the career content area standards and competencies found in the ASCA standards. As students progress through school and into adulthood, ASCA believes they need to acquire a firm foundation for career development. ASCA urges school counselors to implement activities and strategies related to the content standards for career development to provide K-12 students with the foundation for future career success (Dahir, Sheldon & Valiga, 1998). These National Standards are now part of the ASCA National Model: A Framework for School Counseling Programs (ASCA, 2005).

## National Career Development Guidelines

The National Career Development Guidelines (Guidelines) resource, developed for the U.S. Department of Education-OVAE through funding from Perkins, Section 118) offers a comprehensive framework for career development programs, K-Adult, that complements the ASCA standards. The Guidelines can help counselors:

- prepare students for the changing workplace by increasing their understanding of the need for lifelong learning and the relationship between education and employment;
- reduce student risks by promoting better understanding if self, improving social adjustment, and enhancing decision-making and planning skills;
- increase program accountability by evaluating program processes and outcomes through regular assessment based on the Guidelines indicators;
- promote program coordination and articulation by defining a sequence of delivery for program activities, reinforcing learning from previous levels and reducing duplication of services; and
- expand public awareness of the need for and benefits of career development.

The Guidelines content includes eleven goals that define broad areas of career development competency for Personal Social Development, Educational Achievement and Lifelong Learning, and Career Management as described below.

Personal Social Development

- Develop understanding of self to build and maintain a positive self-concept.
- Develop positive interpersonal skills including respect for diversity.
- Integrate growth and change into your career development.
- Balance personal, leisure, community, learner, family and work roles.

Educational Achievement and Lifelong Learning

- Attain educational achievement and performance levels needed to reach your personal and career goals.
- Participate in ongoing, lifelong learning experiences to enhance your ability to function effectively in a diverse and changing economy.

*Joe Wittmer, Ph.D. and Mary Ann Clark, Ph.D.*

Career Management

- Create and manage a career plan that meets your career goals.

- Use a process of decision-making as one component of career development.

- Use accurate, current, and unbiased career information during career planning and management.

- Master academic, occupational, and general employability skills to obtain, create, maintain, and/or advance your employment.

- Integrate changing employment trends, societal needs, and economic conditions into your career plans.

The goals are further detailed by indicators that define the specific career development skills and competencies students need. Visit the America's Career Resource Network web site (www.acrnetwork.org) or the National Career Development Association web site (www.ncda.org) for more information about the Guidelines and related online activities and resources.

## Program Delivery Methods

A variety of processes are used by K-12 counselors to deliver the career guidance and counseling program content to students (National Occupational Information Coordinating Committee, 2001). They include: *outreach, classroom instruction, counseling, assessment, career information, work experience, placement, consultation, referral, and follow-up.* These eleven processes are described below.

1. **Outreach.** A proactive approach to alerting students to the career guidance and counseling services available from the school helps ensure that the program reaches all students.

2. **Classroom Instruction.** Planned and sequential career-related curriculum activities delivered by teachers and counselors through classroom instruction or large group guidance activities can be used as one vehicle to reach all students in your school. The classroom instruction process couples academic curriculum objectives with career development competencies. For each subject the existing curriculum is reviewed and areas that can be used to deliver career development concepts are identified. Lesson plans are refocused to include both academic and career development objectives. For instance, a short story might be used to help students clarify their own goals, or math problems could be written to reinforce the use of math in various occupations. Integrating career development concepts into academic instruction helps make instruction meaningful to students and actively engages them in the learning process.

3. **Counseling.** Counseling focuses on helping students explore personal issues related to career development, examine how to apply information and skills learned to their personal plans, and develop individualized career plans. This includes both individual and small group counseling approaches.

4. **Assessment.** Assessment includes the administration and interpretation of a variety of formal and informal measures to provide students with a clearer understanding of their skills, abilities, interests, achievements, and needs.

5. **Career Information.** Resources are available to provide current and unbiased information to students about occupations, educational programs, post secondary training, the military, employment information, and financial aid.

6. **Career Information Delivery System (CIDS).** In many states a computer-based information delivery system brings comprehensive, accurate and up-to-date information about occupations and education/ training opportunities to students. Some CIDS target high school to adult audiences while others offer versions of the system suitable for upper elementary to middle/junior high school students. The Career Resource Network staff is usually affiliated with the CIDS and can answer any questions you might have as a counselor regarding the system in your state. The foundation of a CIDS is the quality of its data. Most CIDS provide descriptions of hundreds of occupations including duties, requirements, earnings, and employment outlook for the respective state. Some also contain national information. Information about related education and training in your state is generally part of the CIDS, as well as information about financial aid resources available. The information is easily accessed and printed. Most CIDS programs are available on PCs or via the Internet. Staff supporting the CIDS might offer state-wide training workshops for a hotline to assist counselors. We urge you to check into the CIDS in your state. You will find the system extremely helpful to your career development program.

7. **Work Experience.** Opportunities for students in actual work settings facilitate the testing of career decisions and develop effective work abilities and behaviors.

8. **Placement.** Placement resources and assistance help students make a successful transition from high school to employment, post-secondary education, military service, or other options.

9. **Consultation.** Through consultation, counselors provide direct assistance to teachers, administrators, parents, and others who interact with students that will help them to better understand the nature of career development and effective strategies for supporting career development.

10. **Referral.** For some students, physical or psychological problems may inhibit career development. Professional school counselors who coordinate career guidance and counseling programs will recognize such problems and make appropriate referrals.

11. **Follow-up.** Maintaining long-term contact with students as they progress through their school years and beyond through their school years and beyond has benefits for both the students and the career guidance and counseling program.

## School/Community Connections

It is evident from the above information that the array of career development competencies students must acquire cannot be addressed by schools alone. To be successful, the school's career development efforts require the involvement of the entire community (i.e., the home, business and industry, labor, and government). Very important resources are available close at hand; usually only one phone call away. Parents, senior citizens, employers and employees, civic organizations and youth groups can make major contributions to the development of students by offering a dimension not normally available in the classroom. Employers have a vested interest in the youth who will eventually staff their enterprises. Local employers realize they have a valuable resource that can extend the learning environment of students beyond the school walls. Public awareness and public relations are both keys to developing community connections. It is important to know what you want from the community and to be able to clearly articulate your needs and wishes. To maximize effectiveness, a school district's approach to the community should be coordinated throughout all of the schools. A school counselor's time spent developing concrete ways to coordinate the use of community resources is time well spent. Some ideas follow:

1. Local chambers of commerce might help in disseminating materials about your school's career development program: provide speakers, identify interesting field trip sites, work shadow sites, and/or work experience sites. The Chamber member may also serve as a point of general coordination with the business community.

2. The Boy Scouts, Girl Scouts, 4-H Clubs, and Junior Achievement offer a wealth of resources such as career-related booklets, career awareness programs, interest surveys, field visits, and even experience in running a small business. Contact them. They are usually "help" oriented people who will be invaluable to you and your career development program.

3. Parents and senior citizens, if asked, will willingly serve as volunteers in the guidance office and career resource center as well as serve the role models so critical to a youth's career development.

4. Local businesses have traditionally been supportive of field trips to their respective business, in providing career speakers, work-experience sites, and work shadowing experiences. They might also provide teachers and counselors with new insights by offering them summer employment. However, you will have to actively seek them involvement in your program.

5. Colleges, universities, and career-technical schools also make excellent field trip sites and will provide guest speakers as well if requested.

6. The military has a great deal of free career information available to schools and the ASVAB aptitude test is a resource used effectively by many high school counselors.

7. Many labor organizations have an educational unit that will be happy to work with schools in a variety of ways.

Remember, the resources are there, but you must ask for help. Be sure to coordinate (district-wide when possible) your efforts. Keep your community informed about what you and your school are doing to promote student career development and how they can participate.

# Career Resource Center

The school career resource center serves as a focal point for many different kinds of career development activities and is central to any developmental guidance program. Students at all levels can use the center's materials to research information about occupations, post secondary education/training options, and financial aid. The center is also a great place for high school counselors to hold meetings with college recruiters or local business people. Counselors might also use the center for meetings with small groups of students to discuss career development issues, to administer an interest inventory to student and/or to conduct a mini course on various career related topics.

School career resource centers, coordinated by counselors, come in all sizes and shapes. They fit into guidance areas, corners of the media center or library, sprout wheels and move into the cafeteria during study hall and lunch periods, take up temporary residence in classrooms for special projects, and/or spill over to bulletin boards in hallways. More than simply a place, the career resource center is a concept that fosters easy access to a variety of career information and related activities. Effective school counselors make full use of such a center.

Just as the location of a career resource center will vary from school to school, so do staffing arrangements. Many schools use community volunteers quite successfully in their career centers. Using student aids or peer helpers is a very important method of providing coverage in the resource center, especially if the center has a computer-based career information delivery system. You might also take advantage of existing staff such as career development facilitators, career specialists, media specialists, librarians, or teacher aides to oversee the operation of the center. However, as noted, the center should be under the coordination of the guidance department.

Career resource centers house a variety of information and are usually organized around interest areas. Typically, they contain information about occupations, post secondary education and training opportunities, financial aid, the military, job seeking and job survival skills, and perhaps part-time and full time jobs available in the local community. Information about occupations is delivered through print publications, media (DVDs, and video), the computer, and online. Numerous low cost career information materials are also available from government agencies. *The Occupational Outlook Handbook* and the *Guide for Occupational Exploration* are excellent resources available from the Federal Government. You can access these resources online at www.bls.gov/oco/home/htm. Your state Career Resource Network office probably produces a variety of materials such as a career information tabloid, a job hunter's guide, an apprenticeship directory, state employment outlook, wage rates, and more. Many of these resources are now online and school counselors can compile a list of websites to provide up to date access for their students.

Many commercial companies produce career information books, kits, DVDs, and videos for use by school counselors. There are several career magazines that provide timely and inexpensive career information. When selecting commercially produced materials the school counselor should ensure that they are bias free, accurate, and up-to-date. The *Occupational Outlook Handbook* has a section that provides addresses for more information about specific occupations. This is often a good source of free brochures. Technology adds another dimension to information delivery. Computer-based career information delivery systems (CIDS) and the Internet are examples. As noted, many states have a CIDS that contains state and national information regarding many occupations, post secondary educational opportunities, and financial aid. Many school districts have a web site and counselors have their own pages. This is a fantastic way to reach both students and parents.

Computers certainly provide an exciting vehicle for the dissemination of career information, but counselors are encouraged not to overlook some more traditional and very cost effective methods for sharing information. Career posters are a lively way to provide information and brighten the school's career center. Bulletin board displays scattered throughout the school and within the career center can be used to stimulate student thinking about the many decisions facing them and to present concepts such as career clustering and career ladders. In addition, using bulletin boards (and, do change them frequently) is good public relations for the counseling department. Some bulletin board ideas are:

1. "Math—Who Needs It:" (features occupations that require math skills).

2. Personal Values "Coat of Arms" (students draw a large shield and express on it personal values and priorities by completing sentences such as: A word that describes me__, I am so proud of __, Its important to __, Someone I admire is _____).

3. Life Style Collage (students express various aspects of a desired lifestyle through a collage which might include interests, hobbies, family, occupation, etc.).

4. Educational Level/Occupations (highlights post secondary education/training routes and shows sample occupations for each).

5. Interests Collage (nice follow-up to interest inventories and can be done as a student group project).

Many students are planning some sort of education/training following high school graduation. Catalogs from career/technical schools, community colleges, two and four-year colleges and universities should be included in the career resource center, although websites now seem to be the quickest and easiest way to pull up information. Students can even take "virtual" college tours online. Information about apprenticeships is available from the State Labor Department. A telephone call to your State Labor Department or Career Resource Network office can get you a wealth of free materials. Scholarship and financial aid information is also very important. Many college applications and financial aid applications can now be filled out online, as well.

As a high school counselor, you will find many students exploring the military as an option for additional education and training and/or as a career. Abundant free information is available from each of the branches of the armed services. The *Military Career Guide* contains descriptions of over 200 military occupations with related information about civilian occupations. The military will also provide, administer, and interpret an aptitude test for military occupations; the Armed Service Vocational Battery (ASVAB). The ASVAB also includes a popular interest inventory provided free to every student who takes the ASVAB. The ASVAB is a free test and there is no obligation to the military by students who elect to take the test battery.

Many school counselors have a section of the career center devoted to materials about job seeking skills; finding your first job, filling out applications, resumes, and interviewing. Others have "job boards" with part-time job openings in the community listed as well as full-time employment opportunities for graduating seniors.

# A Working Career Preparation Model

The Florida Department of Education's approach to career development in schools embraces the concepts presented in the ASCA National Model (ASCA, 2005) and the National Career Development Guidelines and uses many of the methods described above. The Florida K-12 state-wide plan, Florida's Career Resource Network (Florida Department of Education, 2006), addresses the need to prepare students for the global marketplace. Career development has been the backbone for this state-wide initiative that has impacted thousands of Florida's K-12 students. Florida's Career Resource Network provides the framework for educators to prepare youth and adults to successfully enter and remain in their chosen fields of work. Schools, through the coordination of their counselors, integrate academic and career/technical education making both meaningful for students' career development. The Network stresses that curriculum should relate to careers and vice versa. The integration of the two approaches means that students gain both career and academic training A series of activities and steps to be taken to carry them out are as follows (Florida Department of Education, 2006).

America's Career Resource Network funds each state through the Perkins Vocational and Applied Technology Act (Section 118: Occupational and Employment Information) to carry out activities outlined in the law. The Career Planning Section in the Division of Community Colleges and Workforce Development, Florida Department of Education, is the state entity that forms Florida's Career Resource Network. The activities include:

- Promoting improved career and educational decision making by individuals.

- Making available to students, parents, teachers, administrators, counselors, and career specialists information and planning resources that relate educational preparation to career goals.

- Equipping teachers, administrators, counselors, and career specialists with knowledge and skills needed to assist students and parents with career exploration, educational opportunities, and education financing.

- Tailoring resources for use by state entities.

- Improving coordination and communication among planners and administrators of programs.

## How Does The Career Planning Section Carry Out These Activities?

1. Provides a Career Information Delivery System (CIDS) to high schools, post-secondary schools and state agencies. The CIDS currently funded by the Department of Education is the CHOICES career exploration program.

2. Provides training on Florida CHOICES as well as other career development programs and products.

3. Conducts Career Resource Network Seminars throughout the state.

4. Promotes educational products through the Department of Education Products Catalog.

5. Provides Florida's School Counseling and Guidance Framework as a model for districts to use in developing their guidance plans.

6. Maintains the Career Planning and Product Distribution toll free phone number for technical assistance on career related issues, such as Florida CHOICES and to place orders for products listed in the Products Catalog.

7. Develops career resources. (Florida Department of Education, 2006).

## Summary

It is clear that the workplace of tomorrow will be very different from the workplace of today. The emphasis in the new millennium will continue to be on change, flexibility, multiple career paths, and lifelong learning. Numerous reports suggest strategies for school reform and challenge Americans to re-dedicate themselves to attaining new standards of quality and productivity.

The career development concepts and practices described above support the call to re-energize our schools and help our students succeed in a dynamic and demanding workplace. Research affirms that comprehensive career guidance and counseling programs, coupled with other interventions, can provide students with the means to develop the career survival competencies they need. School counselors are uniquely positioned to promote movement toward a truly comprehensive approach to career development. As a school counselor and/or future school counselor you have an exciting opportunity to make a difference, not only for your students, but also for the very future of our country.

## References

American School Counselor Association. (2005). *The national model: A framework for school counseling programs.* Alexandria, VA: Author.

Dahir, C., Sheldon, B., & Valiga, M. (1998). *Vision into action: Implementing the national standards for school counseling programs.* Alexandria, VA: ASCA Press.

Florida Department of Education. (2006). *Florida's career source network.* Retrieved July 7, 2006 at http://www.firn.edu/doe/programs/cd_info.htm

Herr, E., & Cramer, S. (2003) *Career guidance through the lifespan* (6th ed.). Boston, MA: Little Brown.

Herr, E.L. (2004). *Career development: Some perspectives.* Unpublished document: The National Training Support Center.

National Career Development Association. (2006). *National career development association guidelines.* Retrieved July 7, 2006 at http://www.ncda.org

National Occupational Information Coordinating Committee (NOICC). (2001). *The national career development guidelines handbook k-adult.* Washington, DC: Author.

National Training Support Center. (2004). *The national career development guidelines.* America's Career Resource Network website (www.acrnetwork.org). December 2004.

Osipow, S.J. (1996) *Theories of career development* (4th ed.). New York: Appleton-Century Crofts.

SCANS: Secretary's Commission on Achieving Necessary Skills. (1991). *What work requires of schools: A SCANS report.* Washington, DC: U.S. Department of Labor.

Super, D.E. (1976). Career education and the meaning of work. In *Monographs on career education.* Washington, DC: U.S. Department of Education.

Wittmer, J., & Thompson, D. (2006). *Large group counseling: A K-12 sourcebook* (2nd ed.). Minneapolis, MN: Educational Media Corporation.

Wittmer, J., Thompson, D., & Loesch, L. (1997). *Classroom guidance activities: A sourcebook for elementary school counselors.* Minneapolis, MN: Educational Media Corporation.

Zunker, G. (2001). *Career counseling: Applied concepts of life planning* (6th ed.). Pacific Grove, CA: Brooks/Cole.

# Chapter 22

# High School Educational Guidance and Counseling

**by**
**James H. Pitts and Shifa Podikunju Hussain**

*James H. Pitts, Ph.D., is a former counselor educator, retired from the University of Florida. His career in education included public school teaching, college counseling, and teaching both undergraduate and graduate students at the university level.*

*Shifa Podikunju Hussain, Ed.S., is a doctoral student in the school counseling program at the University of Florida. She has practiced as a high school counselor for eight years in Alachua County, Florida.*

## Introduction

The main goal of educational guidance and counseling, a vital function of a developmental school counselor's job, is to help students keep their educational options open. As with many situations encountered by school counselors, there is "good news" and "bad news" concerning this goal. The good news is that many young people have families that provide them with positive role models and encouragement to do their best in school and make the most of their abilities. The bad news is that many other young people are not so fortunate. In these cases counselors need to help students realize that they *do* have options, and that they have opportunities to become more productive and successful than they might imagine possible.

In this chapter, we focus on educational *counseling* and educational *guidance* as these activities relate to high school students' postsecondary educational plans. Educational counseling refers to counselors' efforts to help students develop self concepts which keep their educational options open. Educational guidance refers to counselors' interventions aimed at assisting students to make the best use of the options available.

High school students are at the threshold of transitioning from childhood to adulthood. During the four years in secondary school, the focus of students, their parents and the school counselor is to make a smooth transition from the expectations of secondary education to the expectations of postsecondary education or the workforce.

## ASCA National Model and High School Counseling

In accordance with the ASCA National Model (2005) for school counseling, high school counselors are focused on the three domains of student development: academic, career and personal/social. Nowhere else are these three domains of more crucial importance than at the high school level. Students' decisions in each of these domains will have an impact on their future goals and plans for careers and higher education. Academically, students have to choose the correct sequence of course work to be eligible for college admissions, special programs, and scholarship opportunities. Concerning career choices, students need to experience as many opportunities as possible to help inform decisions later on. Personally and socially, students can benefit from participation in activities that enhance interpersonal skills, which will stand them in good stead in the present as well as in the future. In today's changing world, oral and written communication skills are considered one of the most vital sets of skills required for success.

School counselors in high schools are charged with integrating the three domains of the ASCA model, as well as carrying out other duties as defined by their work settings. Following a developmental counseling program, school counselors can start the process of fulfilling the ASCA model in the academic arena by meeting with every student in the ninth grade and initiating a four-year plan for coursework. This plan gives students a clear idea of academic expectations for the next four years.

# Large Group Guidance for High School Educational Planning

Counselors can utilize large group guidance presentations to disseminate information about the four-year high school plan, graduation requirements, college admissions process and requirements, and the scholarship and financial aid procedures. The process of course selection is essential to offering students access and opportunity for postsecondary options. It is this same process that can promote or prevent students from taking the necessary courses for their next steps, particularly with regard to college admission. Large group guidance activities can be done at different times of the year. For example, at the beginning of the school year, counselors can talk to individual classes or the whole grade level in an assembly about the services offered by the student services office, the general features of the four-year plan, and graduation requirements. Towards the end of the school year, during registration of courses for the following year, counselors can revisit the four-year plan in a large group setting, and include information on postsecondary school options. In addition, presentations on college admissions and scholarship and financial aid can be offered in the classroom, especially in the spring semester of the junior year. Counselors can follow up with the students with individual meetings that address the needs of each student.

Students can also be encouraged to join clubs or organizations on campus to help develop their social and personal domains. Being a member of a club or organization can help the student make friends, take on leadership roles and responsibilities and improve other skills like public speaking, teamwork, and social awareness. All plans are made in the bigger context of future goals and ambitions but at the same time with the explicit understanding that these plans can change and be modified as needed in the ensuing four years.

For ninth graders, school counselors can provide career exploration activities such as Choices (Bridges Incorporated, 2005) and SIGI 3 (Valpar International Corporation, 2005); both are on-line career assessment programs that integrate self-assessment with in-depth and up-to-date career information. There are also pen and paper assessments like PLAN and DISCOVER (ACT, 2005) that can help students understand the extent of career choices that are available to them and the preparation starting in high school that is needed to achieve them.

Working with tenth graders, school counselors can "check in" with students on their academic plan and make any modifications that are needed. For the career domain, experiences like a career day and field trips to businesses (like the local utilities company or a local publishing company), or to community colleges to explore high demand and high wage technical jobs are appropriate. Students are also preparing for standardized state testing, college admissions testing and Advanced Placement (AP) exam testing during this year. With the increased pressures and stress of the high stakes testing that usually occur in tenth grade, school counselors can focus on test taking skills and issues related to self-concept and self-esteem to help students feel motivated and confident in the social and personal domain. Small and large group presentations by the school counselor can assist students in these important areas, as well as to inform them of calendars and deadlines for essential events.

Eleventh grade students should revisit their academic four-year plan and make sure they are taking the courses they need for graduation, college admission, and/or career choice. Students may have the option of taking courses while being dually enrolled at a local community college or university to help them achieve their goals. School counselors can guide students on appropriate coursework and AP exams that they may want to take at the end of this year. In the career domain, students can further explore their career interests by participating in job shadowing experiences. Some students may need a reassessment of their career interests and further counseling on the choices they will have available after high school, and counselors can offer individualized career counseling for these students. In the social and personal domain, students may be experiencing stress and anxiety over choices they have to make that will impact their future. Counselors can help make the steps towards graduation clear and attainable so that students don't feel overwhelmed with the pressures of schoolwork, extracurricular activities, social roles, and high stakes testing. Thinking ahead is clearly an important strategy for students at this stage.

Counselors should work with twelfth grade students to ensure that they are "on track" with coursework for the year, college choices and applications, scholarship and financial aid information and applications, and alternative career options for post-graduation. In the personal domain, students may be experiencing feelings of anxiety about the changes in their lives with the transition from high school to college and adulthood. Also, students may feel stress concerning the tasks they need to complete during their last year of high school and may feel uncertain that they can be successful. Counselors can be invaluable in this year of decisions and changes by providing students with a time line to complete application processes and graduation requirements. Counselors can make classroom visits and provide more individual time for the students. In these sessions, counselors can also address the feelings associated with the impending changes that are looming after high school graduation and offer tangible information about transition to college and/or the world of work. Focusing on the positive aspects of post graduation plans and celebrating the last four years of hard work and achievement is also helpful for the students.

Many high school students are interested in postsecondary educational options and information. The options available to students at this level include Tech Prep programs, which are two year technical degree programs, community colleges which offer certificate programs and associate degrees, and four year college and university programs that offer the Bachelors degree. It is also important that counselors reach out to parents to offer information necessary to help their children with these important decisions as well as knowledge of resources.

# Tech Prep Career Programs

Tech Prep is a nationwide program designed to give high school students a head start on a college degree or certificate by earning college credit in technical and or professional courses while in high school. In the Bureau of Labor Statistics' list of fastest growing occupations for 2002-2012, seventeen of the top 30 occupations fall into tech prep fields:

| Rank | Occupation |
|------|------------|
| 1. | Medical assistants |
| 4. | Social and human service assistants |
| 5. | Home health aides |
| 6. | Medical records and health information technicians |
| 7. | Physical therapist aides |
| 10. | Physical therapist assistants |
| 11. | Fitness trainers and aerobics instructors |
| 13. | Veterinary technologists and technicians |
| 14. | Hazardous materials removal workers |
| 15. | Dental hygienists |
| 16. | Occupational therapist aides |
| 17. | Dental assistants |
| 18. | Personal and home care aides |
| 19. | Self enrichment education teachers |
| 21. | Occupational therapist assistants |
| 25. | Environmental science and protection technicians, including health |
| 30. | Respiratory therapists |

[**Note.** From Table 3, Fastest growing occupations, 2002-2012, in "Occupational employment projections to 2012," published in the *February 2004 Monthly Labor Review Online.*]

Tech Prep programs offer motivation for students in high school to connect their academic courses with hands-on learning at a work site or in a simulated work setting. Students in Tech Prep programs are prepared for a high-wage, high-demand career and/or postsecondary education when they graduate from high school. Tech Prep is comprised of a planned sequence of courses in a career or technical field beginning as early as ninth grade. Students enroll in the specified courses that link their high school studies to two years of community college occupational education or an apprenticeship program. This path leads most often to an Associate of Science degree at a community college or vocational-technical school. Similar to AP courses, students take Tech Prep courses, followed by an exam that will grant college credit at those institutions that have a link to the Tech prep articulation (Fagan, Carol, & Lumley 1997).

## Community Colleges

Community colleges make up one of the largest sectors of American higher education. More than 6 million students attend approximately 1200 public and independent community colleges throughout the United States (College Board, 2006b). Community colleges offer a wide variety of courses and majors. Students can choose an immediate career or pursue the first two years of general academic course work required for a bachelor's degree. Community colleges prepare students for careers in both existing and emerging technologies such as training in high tech fields like telecommunications, digital systems, robotics, laser optics, Web design, and interactive media. They offer honors programs that allow students to take rigorous courses supplemented by special opportunities (College Board, 2006b).

Community colleges have two major purposes. The first is to serve as a bridge from high school to college by providing courses for transfer toward a bachelor's degree (B.A. or B.S.). Four out of 10 college-bound high-school graduates start their college education this way (College Board, 2006b).

The second function of community colleges is to prepare students for the job market by offering entry-level career training as well as courses for adult students who want to upgrade their skills for workforce reentry or advancement. Many community colleges have certificate options that provide intensive training in a specialized field such as computer-assisted drafting, food-service technology, or paralegal studies. These certificates usually take six months to a year to complete (College Board, 2006b).

Many four-year colleges and universities have selection criteria for attendance, such as a minimum required GPA, while community colleges have an open admissions policy. The average class size at most community colleges is significantly smaller than at public four-year universities. The main responsibility of the community college faculty is teaching, not research and publishing, which promote greater accessibility to students (College Board, 2006b).

Lower tuition is one of the major benefits of attending a community college. Community colleges cost significantly less (particularly for state residents) than state or private colleges and universities. The money that is saved by living at home the first two years of college and going to the local community college can help pay for the last two years at a four-year college or university (College Board, 2006b).

At four-year colleges, course schedules are geared mainly for full-time, traditional students who take classes during the day. At community colleges, the student population tends to be highly diverse with regard to age, experience, family background, socioeconomic level, and employment status. Course schedules are offered with attention to the variable needs of both part-time and full-time students, so classes are usually offered throughout the day and evening, and sometimes on weekends. Many of these colleges offer online courses (College Board, 2006b).

Community colleges are dedicated to student success. They offer a wide-ranging variety of support services that include counseling, tutoring, advising, and career planning. Through developmental courses students can improve skills in math, reading, and writing. Many people who began their higher educations at community colleges have achieved recognition in a variety of fields including business, science, entertainment, government, and communications (College Board, 2006b).

## Four-Year Colleges

Four year-colleges and universities vary in admissions requirements, size, and mission. An institution which is a "college," rather than a "university," is generally smaller than most universities and has a mission which emphasizes *teaching* more than *research* as a major responsibility of its faculty. Since college faculty are primarily responsible for teaching, students may find that individual attention in classes is more readily available than it may be at a university. While the quality of courses may be quite high, the quantity and variety of classes available at a college is not likely to be as great as at a larger university. A student's intended major will help dictate whether or not a college is a desirable choice. Many liberal arts majors are available at such institutions, as are a number of others, depending on the individual college. Opportunities for involvement in out of class activities are often readily available at colleges, and living in a residence hall provides many experiences that will be remembered fondly for years to come. Colleges vary widely in cost and admissions requirements; many are private, but a number of public colleges are also available.

## Universities

Universities have an appeal for many students. Some of the attraction is the wide range of academic offerings; some is associated with the appeal of "big time" football and other athletic events. As is the case with colleges, there is a wide range of cost and admissions requirements. Public universities are typically much less expensive than private ones, especially if the student attends a public university in his or her state of residence. Universities typically offer opportunities to live in residence halls with a diverse group of students and to participate in a large selection of out of class activities. Since a major responsibility of faculty is conducting research, classes are sometimes quite large and are sometimes taught by graduate assistants rather than regular faculty. Counselors may wish to advise students to find out who will be teaching the majority of the classes they will be taking, especially the first two years, and weigh this aspect of the universities they are considering. This is a fair question for a student applicant to ask university authorities before agreeing to enroll at a specific institution.

In general, if financial resources and academic ability permit, there are some real benefits to attending a college or university which provides an opportunity to live on campus and become involved in campus life. Organized student activities can add a dimension to the college experience that is difficult to achieve any other way. Research has shown that students who become involved in campus activities are more likely to persist in college and graduate than are those who do not become involved. It is, of course, quite possible for students to succeed in college without extensive involvement in campus life, but it is a desirable aspect of the college experience when conditions permit. School counselors have an obligation to share such information with their aspiring college or university clientele.

# Helping Students Select and Apply to Post Secondary Institutions

The college application and selection process has become more complicated than ever before. With the varying types of admissions deadlines and online applications, students truly need guidance and counseling in the choices they make for college application. School counselors need to be highly involved in this process for those students who know that attending college is a future goal.

Information about types of colleges and universities and information about costs related to attending them are important considerations. Students and their parents should be directed to reliable sources of information concerning the types of institutions that are available, admissions criteria, and costs involved. The following resources are useful:

*College Costs & Financial Aid Handbook 2004-2005.* The College Board Publications, Two College Way, Forrester Center, WV 25438.

*The College Handbook 2006.* College Board Publications, Two College Way, Forrester Center, WV 25438.

Online: www.collegeboard.com

The Best 361 Colleges 2006 Edition.

Online: www.review.com

*Fiske Guide to Colleges 2006.* Published by Sourcebooks, Inc. P.O. Box 4410 Naperville, Illinois, 60567. Online: www.sourcebooks.com

www.campustours.com (virtual tours of colleges as well as their websites are available at this site)

The increased use of the Internet makes college information more readily accessible. Comparing programs, costs, size of college and other factors important to the application process can be much quicker and more user friendly than plodding through books. Plugging in priorities for college selection can help students access a list of "matches" for their input. Taking "virtual" college tours online can help families get a "feel" for what is offered at a college as well as the appearance of the campus. However, the amount of information available from a variety of resources may also be overwhelming to students and their parents, and they welcome guidelines and recommendations about resources from knowledgeable school counselors.

College admissions preparation starts as early as ninth grade. Counselors can guide students to make the most of their academics *and* their extracurricular activities from day one. Furthermore, for highly selective college admissions, students should be counseled on summer programs and activities that will help develop and enhance their likelihood of success in this very competitive process.

Students intending to make college applications need to be aware of the admissions criteria that are in general use in selective institutions of higher education. The following is a list of what college admissions officers look for in order of importance as reported to the National Association of College Admissions Counselors (2004).

1. Grades in College Prep courses

   The quality of work a student has done in high school is the single most important record. Students need to know that freshman grades are part of the college admission record, as are poor grades and failures, even though they may have been made up later. Grades in academic subjects are of particular importance; also important is the level of difficulty of courses taken. Many colleges judge the "rigor" of a student's academic program.

2. Admission Test Scores

   SAT I and/or ACT scores should all indicate potential for college work.

   SAT Subject tests scores may be required. Advanced Placement and International Baccalaureate scores are generally used for placement rather than for admissions but can still indicate potential for college work.

3. Grades in all Subjects

4. Class Rank

5. Essay/Writing Sample

6. Counselor Recommendation

7. Teacher Recommendation

8. Interview

9. Community Service/Work/Extracurricular Activities

   Colleges are interested in knowing about the meaningful extracurricular school and community activities, travel, and work experiences of the student.

10. Student's Demonstrated Interest

    Special talents are taken into consideration. A "passion" in one area is viewed more worthy than a multitude of activities, which may appear to "pad" the resume. Colleges are looking for students who are mature, serious about their work, enjoy learning, show intellectual curiosity, and are willing to work hard. Colleges often ask secondary school personnel to evaluate the student on the basis of these qualities.

11. Ability to Pay

    81% of colleges state that ability to pay has no importance. Students and parents should be aware, however, that loans may comprise a significant part of financial aid, and that such loans must eventually be repaid. There may be a discrepancy between what financial aid formulas state that the family should contribute and what figure the family believes it can afford to contribute to their child's education.

Counselors can also help guide students on what actions they can take starting in ninth grade to enhance the activities in which they are involved.

- Take on a variety of roles within organizations
- Identify strengths and preferences
- Keep hard copies of materials from events or projects the student helps to organize
- Maintain a personal record of tasks, responsibilities and achievements
- Be a leader/active participant in a few organizations rather than simply showing up to many. Use those organizations as an opportunity to develop other leadership skills

## Talking to Parents About College Admissions

The role of the parent is very critical in the high school period. Parents can help both the student and the school in different ways. Often most parents need as much direction and information as the student. They feel anxious about whether they are providing all the opportunities available to their child. Due to the changes in high school graduation requirements and college admissions from year to year, parents may be confused and feel uninformed about the process especially as compared to when they were in high school. Counselors are the key source of information and expertise for the parents. They can help the parents navigate the different steps of the graduation and admissions process in a less stressful way by providing timely workshops and informational sessions.

Counselors should provide parents with the same information that their students are receiving in the large group or individual sessions helping to minimize communication problems and misinformation among the parent, child and the school. Parents greatly appreciate information on graduation requirements, college admissions and financial aid being offered as night programs, lunch meetings, or immediately after school.

Parents are resources to the counselors by motivating the child at home and keeping them on track with their goals and four-year plan. By encouraging parents to be involved with their child's goals, counselors are also building allies in ensuring the success of the student. Parents can also help by volunteering in the student services office, and preparing information packets for the programs and presentations. This helps the counselors utilize their time better with having contact with their students rather than being trapped in clerical tasks.

## Getting Started on the College Application Process

At the end of the junior year students should have their college application advisement meeting with the counselor. This gives the students the opportunity to work on the different parts of the process in a time-efficient manner. The preliminary individual sessions should explore students' expectations of where they would like to attend college. Questions like size of college, location and distance from home, public or private institutions, instate or out-of-state, and academic major or career interest are some of the guiding questions that will help formulate a list of possible colleges to explore. Using this list, students should be directed to the following steps:

- Obtain information about the colleges and universities: application deadlines, entrance test requirements (New SAT I, SAT Subject Tests, ACT), median test scores and GPA of current freshman class, etc. This information will help students gauge how competitive they will be in gaining admission to a given college.

  This information should be available from the college's homepage via the internet.

  Other good sources on the internet are www.college-board.com, and www.usnews.com, both of which have a college search and scholarship search component. Books that have the above information are *The College Handbook* (2006), *The Fiske Guide to Colleges* (2006) and *The Best 361 Colleges* (2006).

- Register to take the appropriate entrance tests as required by the colleges to which the student wishes to apply (New SAT I, SAT Subject Tests, and ACT). Register online at www.collegeboard.com for the SAT and www.act.org for the ACT. Students can also register by paper with registration booklets that are available from the school's guidance office. Fee waivers are available for students in financial need for both the SAT and the ACT. Obtain and use test practice

information. There are practice test booklets available that can help students prepare for the test. These materials contain critical test taking tips and a sample test. Commercial books are also available.

- Obtain, complete, and submit college applications in accordance with deadlines. The best source for applications is the college's website where students can download the application. Counselors can help with downloading these applications if students have problems accessing a computer. Call, email or write to the college to obtain paper applications if they are not available online. Fee waivers for college applications are available for students with documented financial need. Submit applications online if possible and especially if the college prefers online applications.

During the senior year, students should be encouraged and reminded to meet with the counselor as needed to discuss graduation requirements and the college application process. Meeting with the counselor in this way also helps the counselor get to know the students better for the critical counselor recommendation letter that has become a requirement for almost all private colleges and many public universities. Sometimes, depending on the students and the circumstances, the counselor's letter can make the difference in whether students will be admitted or not to certain colleges.

Students can assist counselors with the writing of recommendation letters by sharing their resumes and an essay about themselves. If they are required to submit a personal statement to a college, they can provide the counselor with a copy. Counselors can also ask teachers for feedback on the students. Some counselors even ask parents for their input. Parents' information can be helpful especially if there have been extenuating circumstances in the student's life.

College representatives who are trying to recruit students are also a very important resource for students. These representatives are advocates for the students and want to be connected with them. Counselors can help by arranging for students to meet with college representatives or giving the representative's contact information to students if they have questions concerning the application process. In some cases, especially if students are able, visiting college campuses is an excellent way for them to decide if they want to go to a particular college.

## Advanced Placement and Other College Level Coursework

Some students are interested in opportunities to receive college credit or to be placed in higher level courses through taking advanced placement (AP) courses in high school and taking an AP exam. Individual colleges vary in their policies concerning AP credit, so counselors should assist students in finding out whether an acceptable score (usually in the 3 to 5 range) will enable them to obtain credit for the course or will simply permit them to skip an introductory course and begin at a higher level.

Other advanced courses that also offer similar benefits as the AP are the International Baccalaureate (IB) and the Cambridge University Advanced International Certificate of Education (AICE) programs. These are newer programs offering advanced college level courses at the high school level and are recognized internationally. They emphasize writing and critical analytical thinking skills in their curriculum. Students also have to take IB and AICE tests at the end of the school year. With eligible scores on these tests, students can receive college credit or be advanced to the next level of the subject in college.

The use of AP, IB or AICE credit can be useful to some students, but it is sometimes a mixed blessing. If inexperienced college freshmen obtain AP credit to replace a number of introductory courses and begin college in a number of advanced courses, with "seasoned" college students as classmates, they may feel overwhelmed by the experience. Careful planning is advisable in the use of AP/IB; students may need guidance when making this important decision.

## Scholarships and Financial Aid Information

The term "financial aid" is a broad term generally used to indicate money provided by a third party to help students meet the costs of attending college. Financial aid can be provided by various agencies including federal, state and local governments; universities; community organizations; and, private corporations or individuals. The four types of financial aid are grants, scholarships, loans, and work-study. Grants refer to financial aid that does not have to be repaid. Generally, grants are for undergraduate students and the grant amount is based on need, school cost, and/or enrollment status.

- Scholarships are money awards that do not have to be repaid. Scholarships come from many different places including national, state, public and private sources. Scholarship money can be awarded based on a variety of different factors such as financial need, academic or athletic achievement, program of study, and background. Every scholarship has its own set of criteria and amount.

- Loans are borrowed money that must be repaid with interest. Both undergraduate and graduate students may borrow money. Parents may also borrow to pay education expenses for dependent undergraduate students. Maximum loan amounts increase with each year of completed study. Often times, repayment is deferred until after graduation, withdrawal, or termination of attendance.

- Work-study is money for education expenses paid by the school for on-campus or community-based employment.

During the winter of the twelfth grade, students and parents should file a Free Application for Federal Student Aid (FAFSA) form and all other financial aid forms required by the college(s) to which application(s) is/are being made. The FAFSA contains information about family finances and is used to determine financial aid eligibility, including eligibility for a Pell Grant or Federal Stafford Loan. The FAFSA should be submitted as soon after January 1 of the senior year as possible. After the FAFSA is processed, the Department of Education will send a Student Aid Report to the student. This report is also sent to the colleges that students have indicated in the FAFSA application as the colleges of choice for admission. The online FAFSA is faster and less error prone than the paper application. Students are highly encouraged to apply online at www.fafsa.ed.gov. Counselors can organize financial aid workshops for parents and students to help with completing this form either online or on paper.

## Some Administrative Considerations for Counselors

Many colleges and universities require the CSS/Financial Aid Profile for purposes of awarding private aid funds. This form is different from the FAFSA. It is a service provided by the College Board and requires the payment of a fee. It is also available online through www.collegeboard.com. Students should be advised not to confuse the FAFSA, required for all federal aid, with the Financial Aid Profile. When the FAFSA, and the Financial Aid Profile if it is used, have been processed by the college's financial aid office, that office will construct a financial aid package and send students an award letter describing the financial aid they have been awarded. Students must respond to the award letter, indicating acceptance of all, part, or none of the financial aid package that has been offered. The financial aid package may consist of a grant, a loan, and a work/study job. Additional information concerning the financial aid process may be obtained from the financial aid offices of colleges or universities or from their college's websites. Other websites that are trusted and offer up to date information on financial aid and scholarships are:

www.collegeboard.com

www.fastweb.com

www.finaid.com

www.ed.gov/prog_info/SFA/FYE

www.fafsa.ed.gov

The guidance office usually receives scholarship information from various sponsors throughout the school year. Having a monthly newsletter is a helpful resource for students and parents to apply for these scholarships. Students are also encouraged to sign up with a scholarship search site like Fastweb.com that will email eligible scholarship information to the student.

Counselors can offer workshops in December or January on financial aid and scholarship search for parents and students. These workshops can offer helpful information on filling out the FAFSA. The workshops can also serve to inform parents of the various options available in student financial aid at the college level. There may be financial aid officers at local community colleges who may be available to assist high school counselors with the delivery of these workshops.

High school counselors have a number of administrative responsibilities concerning educational counseling and guidance. Individual meetings with students and their parents may be indicated as the college selection process moves along. Hosting college representatives is a matter that is worthy of planning and preparation. If the representatives feel welcome, are given adequate facilities in which to meet with students, and have reasonable access to students who are genuinely interested in talking with them, they are likely to be cooperative with the high school in scheduling future visits. Counselors sitting in on group meetings conducted by college representatives can become informed about what is being discussed and, by their presence, communicate the counseling department's interest in the college selection process. Information gathered through this process will improve the counselors' educational counseling and guidance sessions with students.

*Joe Wittmer, Ph.D. and Mary Ann Clark, Ph.D.*

## Summary

Helping students realize that they have options, helping them keep their options open, and assisting them to make the best use of those options are important school counselor tasks. Counselors can make a difference in students' lives by finding ways to do these things effectively. Effective educational counseling and guidance is highly important and should be a high priority for all developmental high school counselors. This chapter, the other chapters in this book, and the additional materials cited can assist counselors in making a positive difference with their student clients as they navigate their way through high school and beyond.

## References

American School Counselor Association. (2005). *The ASCA national model: A framework for school counseling programs*. Alexandria, VA: Author.

Bureau of Labor Statisics. (2004). *Monthly labor review, (127)* 2. Retrieved March 1, 2006 at: http://www.bls.gov/opub/mlr/2004/02/contents.htm.

CHOICES [Computer software]. (2005). Oroville, WA: Bridges Transitions, Inc.

DISCOVER [Computer software]. (2005). Iowa City, IA: American College Testing.

Fagan, C., & Lumley, D. (1997). *Tech prep career programs: A practical guide to preparing students for high-tech, high-skill, high-wage opportunities*. Thousand Oaks, CA: Corwin Press.

Fiske, E.B., & Logue, R. (2006). *Fiske guide to colleges 2006*. Naperville, IL: Sourcebooks.

Florida Academic Counseling and Tracking for Students. (n.d.). *Types of financial aid*. Retrieved May 5, 2006, from http://www.facts.org/cgi-bin/eaglec?-MDASTRAN=SW-HMMNE00

Franek, R., Meltzer, T., Maier, C., Brown, C., Doherty, J., & Freidman, A. (2006). *The best 361 colleges*. New York: Random House.

Hecker, D.E. (2004). Occupational employment projections to 2012. *Monthly Labor Review Online, 127*(2), 81-105.

Hitchner, K.W., & Tifft-Hitchner, A. (1996). *Counseling today's secondary students*. Englewood Cliffs, NJ: Prentice Hall.

National Association for College Admissions Counseling (2004). *State of college admission report*. Alexandria, VA: Author.

PLAN (2005). Iowa City, IA: American College Testing.

SIGI3 [Computer software]. (2005). Tucson, AZ: Valpar International Corporation.

The College Board. (2004). *College costs & financial aid handbook 2004-2005*. New York: Author.

The College Board (2006a). *College h0andbook 2006*. New York: Author

The College Board (2006b). *Community Colleges: Places so near can take you so far...* Retrieved May 5, 2006, from http://www.collegeboard.com/student/csearch/where-to-start/48391.html

# Section VI

# Strategies for Involving Others in the School Counseling Program: Peer Helpers, Parents, Community Members, Teachers, and Other Professionals

The notion of using students to help other students is not a new idea. However, structured peer helper programs where school counselors specifically train student peers in helping techniques is a relatively recent idea in schools. And, as Dr. Chari Campbell indicates (Chapter 23): *Peer helper programs proliferated during the 1970s and '80s and has continued to grow in numbers as we begin the new century.* Dr. Campbell continues: *Everyone benefits from a peer helper program. Research reveals that the student helper benefits as much, if not more than does the student helpee. Teachers and parents benefit from the program because the guidance services in the school are expanded. The counselor also benefits in numerous ways.* She highlights these benefits and then presents some unique strategies for getting a peer helper program started, training the peer helpers, the needed supervision, peer projects (at all three school levels), and so forth. There are many other helpful suggestions and strategies given for the school counselor who wishes to initiate a peer helper program or who desires to improve an existing one.

In chapter 24, Dr. Courtland Lee and Ms. Angela Wagner write of the increasing diversity and the unique needs of students in urban schools. They cite examples and statistics that describe the challenges that school counselors must meet in working with these students, their families and communities. Collaboration is essential among stakeholders in the urban context.

In Chapter 25, Dr. Laura Pedersen writes of the collaboration and teaming specialist role played by the school counselor. She indicates that to assure that all students are provided with necessary services that encourage their personal, social, and educational development, counselors and other specialists, teachers, and administrators, must work together as a team to offer an effective educational delivery system. She examines the important role of advocacy and collaboration for the transformed school counselor. Dr. Pedersen offers steps for teaming and collaboration and describes how to identify and recruit team members.

In chapter 26, we present a character education program that involves school counselors collaborating with teachers to teach children to show caring and respect for themselves and others. If we can teach students to use the important communication skills in their daily interactions, that as counselors we all know are so important, we can have a profound impact of the classroom and school climate, and ultimately on academic achievement.

In the final chapter of this section, Ms. Nancy Perry, a longtime school counselor, State Supervisor of Guidance, and ASCA leader, addresses school counselor interactions with parents and families. She suggests management strategies to effectively involve the parents and community in the comprehensive, developmental school counseling program.

Ms. Perry writes: *The effective school counselor realizes that he/she must understand the entire system if the whole child is to be best served. Since developmental school counselors are dedicated to the development of the whole child, they must reach beyond the walls of the school building and actively involve and interact with the families and community.* She indicates that school counselors need to involve parents, educators, and community members in their developmental guidance program if it is to be truly responsive to the needs of all students. Several "hands on" ideas for such involvement are presented for K-12 counselors.

*Mary Ann Clark and Joe Wittmer*

# Chapter 23

# K-12 Peer Helper Programs

**by**
**Chari Campbell**

*Dr. Chari Campbell, Ph.D., NCC, retired as Professor of Counselor Education at Florida Atlantic University. Prior to her work in higher education, she was an elementary and middle school counselor. Dr. Campbell coordinated peer helper programs each of her 16 years as a school counselor.*

## History and Current Status of Peer Helping Programs

The notion of using students to help other students is not a new idea. Peer helping was a natural occurrence in the one-room schoolhouses during the 1930s. Teachers who were responsible for teaching basic academic skills to children in eight or more grade levels turned automatically to an older, more skilled student to assist with the learning of younger, less accomplished students. These early teaching pioneers were simply applying a common sense solution to the problem of the lack of enough teacher time for each student. They also realized how much the experience of teaching younger students reinforced skills in the older student. Wouldn't they have been surprised to discover that their practical solution would be considered an innovation in the late twentieth century?

In the 1960s peer helper programs once again became very popular. As drugs became more of a problem in our society, counselors and educators searched for ways for reaching students before they developed problems with drug addiction. Surveys from this decade revealed that students with problems turned to other kids first, then to their counselors, and to coaches last. Peer helper programs proliferated, especially at the high school level. However, many of these programs did not last due to lack of planning and commitment by the adults coordinating the programs. According to Myrick (2003), those peer programs which flourished concentrated on training the peer helpers in the areas of interpersonal and communication skills. The variety of projects expanded, and high school peer helpers were trained to lead preventive guidance with elementary students, to help with cancer projects in hospitals, and to work with incarcerated youth, and so forth.

Peer helping spread to elementary schools in the 1970s. Counselors trained fourth and fifth grade students to work with primary grade students in a variety of projects including: orientation programs for students new to the school ("Meeters and Greeters"), Study Buddies, small and large Group Leaders, Special Friends, and Teachers' Assistants.

### Current Status

As the peer helping movement grew, school counselors and other educators interested in peer helping began to network informally, sharing training techniques and successful projects. In 1983, Dr. Bob Bowman, an early contributor in this area became the first editor of the *Peer Facilitator Quarterly*, a journal devoted entirely to the interests and needs of student peer helpers and their trainers. The National Association of Peer Programs (NAPP), formerly the National Peer Helpers Association, grew from sixty members to over a thousand in a period of about four years. The Association has sponsored a national conference each summer since 1987 which is well attended by school counselors, school psychologists, teachers, and other mental health workers. These are professionals devoted to assisting others learn about and remain abreast of this rapidly growing, and unique, care delivery approach.

Hundreds of articles have been written in professional journals and popular magazines since the early 1970s describing successful programs and substantiating the effectiveness of peer programs aimed at reducing the school drop-out rate, increasing appropriate school behaviors and positive attitudes towards school. Today, numerous books are available outlining curriculum for K-12 school peer helper programs, the type of training required, who should be a peer facilitator, how to select the helpers, and so forth.

Many school counselors at both the elementary and secondary level, devoted to implementing a comprehensive, developmental guidance and counseling program, include peer helper coordination as one of the six major roles of today's developmentally oriented school counselor (Myrick, 2003).

# Rationale for a Peer Program

Everyone benefits from a peer helper program. Research reveals that the student helper benefits as much, as does the student helpee. Teachers and parents benefit from the program because the guidance services in the school are expanded. The counselor benefits in numerous ways. Some of the benefits occurring to the peer helpers, the counselor, and others are highlighted below.

## Benefits to Students

It is difficult to discern who benefits the most, the helper or the helpee. Ample research shows gains in productive behavior, attitudes towards school, self-esteem, and report card grades for both the helper and the helpee.

Students generally apply for and are selected into the peer helper program on the basis of their application and teacher recommendations. The position of peer helper appears to carry status among students and places considerable responsibility on the helpers selected. The students take pride in the trust that has been placed upon them by their teachers and counselors. Helping a younger student brings out the best in them. It is explained from the beginning that only students who are positive role models for other students are chosen for the program and that it is their responsibility to maintain their grades and to make up any assignment missed in their own class as a result of a peer project away from school, and so forth. Many peer helpers have discovered that having extra responsibilities in school fosters excellent time management skills. Many student helpers also indicate they are able to complete their own classroom and homework assignments more efficiently after they receive training in the peer helping preparation program.

The peer helper program essentially provides leadership training for students. Feedback given by business and industry about our public school graduates is that many of our "elite" students don't know how "to get along" or "relate to" those they work with, sell to, and so forth. Sometimes our "good kids" are so isolated in top academic classes that they lack the people skills required in many real life work positions. The training experience and helping projects that follow provide student peer helpers with excellent leadership training.

## Benefits to the Counselor

Why implement a peer helper program in your school? Many school counselors, whether their counselor-to-student ratio is 1 to 700 or whether they are one of the fortunate few who serve closer to 250 students, have learned that (as did the teachers in the one room schoolhouses of the 1930s) they don't have time to meet all of the (counseling) needs of all of their students. Many times a student simply needs someone who will listen and care as they solve minor social, family problems, and so forth. Counselors all across the nation—literally in all 50 states—have learned how to expand their counseling program through the use of well trained peer helpers. These skillful listeners "become the eyes and the ears" for the guidance department. Counselors report that their counseling load sometimes increases significantly due to referrals by teenage peer helpers of students who need professional help, but probably would not have turned to an adult on their own. Even elementary students will frequently "tell a secret" to a same aged friend before they would tell an adult. Frequently, kids don't turn to adults for help because they think the adults "wouldn't understand." Thus, counselors can spread their positive influence throughout the entire school with trained peer helpers.

Another part of the rationale for training students to help other students is that kids of all ages are influenced by peer pressure. This is particularly true of upper elementary, middle school and high school students, although there is evidence of peer pressure existing even in kindergarten. The pressure is so powerful that many parents cave in and purchase $100 to $150 athletic shoes for a middle schooler who will outgrow them in a few months. Peer pressure influences the way kids dress, wear their hair, carry their books, complete or don't complete homework assignments, experiment with drugs and sex, and so forth. While I was a practicing middle school counselor, a seventh grade girl told me that "everyone who is anyone in the seventh grade has French kissed." When asked if she had tried it and what did she think of the experience, it was apparent that it had not been very rewarding. However, in her relating her experience to me, it was obvious that she felt it was worth it to feel that she was part of the "in-crowd."

Many other examples of how peer pressure influences the behavior and attitudes of students in a negative way could be given. The challenge for counselors and teachers is to somehow harness this powerful peer pressure existing in the hallways and the school parking lot and turn it into a positive force within the school. This is what peer helper programs can do. Many counselors deliberately solicit volunteers for the program from different cliques and groups that reflect the population of the school (i.e., some "preppie", some student athletes, maybe a cheerleader, some "new-age" types, and students from differing racial and socioeconomic groups. In this manner, hopefully, every student in the school can find a trained peer helper that they can relate to and view as a positive model for themselves.

Another major reason, or part of the rationale for establishing a peer helper program, is that it serves as a good public relations campaign for the school counselor. The peer program enhances the reputation of the counselor in the eyes of the teachers as well as the students. Teachers are favorably impressed because it puts the counselor's skills on display. When teachers observe a well trained peer helper leading a small or large group discussion with obvious polish and self-confidence, they recognize that the counselor can teach as well as counsel. Students see that the counselor who has a peer program works with all kids, and there is no longer the stigma that attaches so quickly when the counselor is only seen with the kids "who have problems." Thus, the counselor's image in the school is greatly enhanced.

Another benefit of the peer helper program is what it will do for professional development and morale as a counselor. Both beginning and veteran counselors recognize that when they share their facilitative communication skills with students, they often refine and reinforce their own effective listening skills. In addition to polishing their own counseling skills, counselors benefit from the peer helpers through the enjoyment that comes from having the opportunity to work with delightful, happy, well-adjusted kids. Counselors must so often work with the students who drain and strain them. Suicidal, disruptive, alienated kids who are hurting are rewarding to work with when you can see some improvement in the coping skills of the youngster, but they will also drain your "emotional cup." The peer helpers will have the opposite effect on you. They will help to relieve the symptoms of burnout often felt by educators who work only with very troubled students.

# A Rose is a Rose, is a Rose, is a Rose...

Most counselors involved with peer helper programs today avoid the use of the term "peer counseling." The term "Counselor," in the school setting, is a professional role which requires extensive graduate level training. The title of "peer counselor" concerns some people who believe this title gives the impression that the students are doing more than they are capable of doing. Thus, terms such as *peer helpers, peer facilitators, peer mentors,* and *teen aiders* are preferred. Some students give their groups a catchy name which identifies them with their schools such as the "Bishop Buddies," or the "Fairfield Friends." Tee shirts with such names on them are the norm in schools where peer programs exist.

It is important for administrators, teachers and parents to understand that the guidance department does not view the peer helpers as low budget, junior counselors. On the other hand, kids are "counseling" kids in every school, at all grade levels, across the nation without any training in communication skills or, for that matter, referral skills. By giving at least some of the students in the school special training to enable them to be more effective listeners and to know when and how to refer friends for professional help results in more students (who are in need) actually finding their way to the counselor's door. Legal issues such as liability become a non-issue when peer helpers are students trained to be special friends. These are students who have explored with a professionally trained adult the difference between "squealing" on a friend, and making a referral or consulting with a mental health professional about a friend who is in trouble.

# How to Get Started

Getting started is easier than you might imagine, especially if you begin small and build on your success. There are four issues to consider when initiating a peer helper program: (1) building support, (2) selection, (3) training, and (4) projects.

## Building Support

Tailoring the program to the particular demands of the setting will help to ensure support for the program. It is helpful to solicit faculty and administrative input when developing the goals and objectives of the peer program.

Peer helper projects should reflect the guidance needs of the schools in which they are established. Hence, the needs, attitudes and values of the students, teachers and parents influence the types of projects in which the helpers will engage. After the needs of the school have been assessed, projects can be outlined which specifically address those needs. This process helps to build the teacher commitment essential to the program.

As noted, the best way to gain support for any program is to start small and then build on success. It seems trite, but in peer programs, success truly breeds more success. For example, if, as an elementary counselor you can identify just one fifth grade teacher who shows interest and enthusiasm in the program, then you can select six volunteers from that class for the peer program. If you train these six students for a highly visible role, such as assisting with classroom guidance activities with a second grade class, then the second grade teacher will have a chance to see the peer helpers perform. It's likely that the second grade teacher will say complimentary things about the fifth graders and their performance to other teachers and the "good word" spreads. Soon other teachers will want the peer helpers to work with their students and the fifth grade teachers will want their students to have an opportunity to be trained and to participate in a similar project, and on and on. Starting small, with a highly structured project which fits the needs of the school (with a high probability of success) helps to get the peer helper program off to a good start. In sum, start small, take your gains where you can, and build on your successes! It is easy and can be fun!

## Selecting Peer Helpers

There is no one best way to select peer helpers in a school. Some counselors, at both the elementary and secondary levels, have selected from the highest grade level in their school. Others have been successful by selecting from the two highest grade levels. This allows them to have some previously trained peer helpers always ready to help with orientation and with classroom guidance projects at the beginning of the following school year.

Peer helpers are generally drawn from the pool of students who have good study habits and earn good grades. They need not be the "straight A" student, or the brightest kid in the class to be successful as a peer helper. On the other hand, you will want students who are succeeding in school and who can afford to take some time away from their routine academic activities and who are responsible enough to make up any assignments missed as a result of being in the peer program.

A major point central to an effective peer program is to look for the student who is consistent and dependable. It's essential to have students who will show up for training sessions and for appointments with their helpers on time and who will be well prepared for any project assigned. Consistent kids also seem to be viewed as more trustworthy, a prerequisite for successful peer helpers.

A good peer helper is also someone who is well liked by their classmates and teachers. This need not be the "most popular" kid in the class because kids who are experiencing problems at home or in school frequently have difficulty relating to the "local stars." Also, sometimes the "local stars" lack compassion for a kid who is having difficulty "fitting-in." Therefore, *seek out a student that other students are likely to choose as someone in whom they would be able to confide, rather than the first person they would think of to invite to a party.* You are looking for the "natural helpers," the kids who possess the core helping qualities of empathy, genuineness, caring, compassion, and respect for others. And, above all, look for personal commitment. The peer helpers will occasionally be torn between competing activities (i.e., working with targeted younger students or free time with their own-aged friends). Thus, commitment to the peer program is essential.

There are a variety of ways of identifying the natural helpers. Some counselors use sociograms, others depend on a combination of teacher referral and volunteers. It is best to first advertise the program through class presentations conducted by you. The peer program may be an elective course (Peer Helping I) at the high school level, or a club (The "Bishop Buddies" Club) at any level.

By asking potential helpers to reflect on the causes of stress in their lives or in the lives of their friends, to look carefully at the large percentage of students who never complete high school, and so forth, helps students become aware of the need to try to help peers who are "at risk" for school failure, and so forth. After this awareness is developed, you might describe a specific peer helper project designed to reduce the risk for a particular group of students. Then, describe the training experience needed to be a peer helper and ask for volunteers. Generally, a structured approach such as this will help you "weed out" those who won't become good helpers.

There are numerous checklists available to the counselor to facilitate a quick screening by teachers of the qualities previously described as desirable in a good helper (see Figure 23.1).

In addition to positive recommendations by teachers, a student may be asked to complete an application form (Figures 23.2 and 23.3) and to turn it into the counselor's office by a certain date. This process serves two purposes. First, it gives the student a chance to reflect on their skills and aptitude for helping other students. Usually they are requested in the application to tell what qualities they possess which would be helpful to another student and why they want to be in the program. You will learn a lot about the student and the student's insight about self and relationships through this structured selection process.

Secondly, the process of filling out the application form correctly and turning it in by a certain date is a good way to assess commitment and dependability. Students who care enough to get the application turned in on time, tend to be conscientious about the responsibility of showing up for training and project appointments later.

One counselor designed a creative approach to the application process with lower elementary students by requesting that a picture be drawn to represent friendship. Students were requested to put their pictures in a box by a certain date if they wanted to be a helper. Then the counselor interviewed the children as each explained their pictures and described their thoughts about friendship.

Other elementary and middle school counselors have incorporated peer helping into a career education program. The counselor serves in the role of a personnel specialist who screens and trains the helper for a given job. The teacher of the helpees "hires" the applicant, a contract is signed, and the teacher can "fire" the student for not fulfilling the contract. Students very seldom need to be fired from the program. The opportunity to help another student is usually so rewarding that it serves as a "carrot" for the peer helper to get his/her own work done and to stay out of trouble that might result in dismissal from the peer program.

# Training

The most critical variable in a peer helper program appears to be systematic training . It is important to define the training program in detail and to select peer projects carefully tailored to the skills of your student helpers (Myrick, 2003).

The training naturally will reflect the theoretical orientation of the counselor/coordinator. The professional literature on peer helper programs provides examples of training programs which vary in theoretical basis from person centered, to Adlerian, to behavioral. In addition, the training usually reflects the professional strengths and personality of the trainer.

Wittmer, Thompson, and Sheperis (1999) suggested a training model that has two phases. Phase one focuses on basic relationship and communication skills, phase two concerns more advanced skills. Students are prepared to carry out some structured beginning projects following their initial training. Peer helpers are best trained in groups, even if their project involves working with students individually.

The emphasis in phase one is on experiential learning and skill development, rather than on didactic training. Therefore, the training of elementary peer helpers does not differ greatly from the training of secondary peer helpers. In fact, some young children seem to possess a natural empathy and easily pick up the active listening skills that graduate students in counseling sometimes labor to acquire.

The length and number of training sessions varies according to the nature and sophistication level of the peer project as well as the availability of counselor and student helper time. It is possible to train students successfully to handle some beginning projects (i.e., welcoming newcomers to the campus, in a few half hour sessions). A more advanced project, such as serving as a small group leader may require over twenty 45-minute training sessions. Some school counselors have found weekend marathon training sessions to be successful with all ages of students. In some school districts where peer helper programs are widespread throughout the district, senior high peer helpers are used to assist in training middle school and elementary peer helpers in phase one skills.

Following the initial training, focusing on interpersonal and communication skills, specific skills needed for the particular project are taught and practiced. As a general rule, the younger the peer helpers, the more structured the project should be. Regardless of the age of the helpers, however, care should be taken to break down the project into manageable steps and to be certain that the helpers have the necessary skills or can acquire them in the training sessions. Peer helpers have been trained to serve in various helping roles. Myrick (2003) categorized the helping roles as follows: (1) student assistants, (2) tutors, (3) special friends, and (4) small group leaders.

Student assistants require the least amount of training. They assist teachers, librarians, or office staff with clerical assignments such as answering the phone, checking books in or out, or putting up bulletin board materials. Tutors assist students to acquire or review academic skills. They are trained to clarify the speaker's content, to reflect feelings, and to use encouragement to motivate students who are reluctant to "try on their own" to succeed in school. A special friend is trained in interpersonal skills and is paired with a younger student needing extra personal attention. The special friend serves in a big brother or big sister role, taking interest in the younger child and their progress in school. Small or large group leaders usually receive extensive training on how to facilitate group discussions on topics such as friendship and safety at the elementary level, college applications, substance abuse prevention, or career exploration at the secondary level.

# Peer Helper Projects

Projects can be viewed as beginning, intermediate, or advanced according to the amount of training required for the task and the degree of structure with characterizes the project (Myrick 2003). The following description of projects may help to illustrate the variety of activities at which peer helpers can excel and the extent to which they can add to your developmental school guidance program.

## Elementary School Projects

An example of a beginning project at the *elementary* level is the Meeters and Greeters Club. These are usually children from the intermediate grade levels who have been taught how to ask open ended questions, summarize content, and to reflect feelings. They are given some suggestions of comments and questions they can use to help draw out a new student and make them feel welcome in their new school. For example, while taking a newcomer and perhaps their parents, on a tour to show them the cafeteria, the library, and the location of various classrooms, the peer helper might ask "where are you from?" After paraphrasing, the peer helper might share where they are from or how long they have been in the school, and then say "tell me about your previous school," or "what was something you liked about your previous school." They might also ask "was

there something you didn't like about your old school" and share a gripe they have about school. They could end the conversation by saying "I bet you miss your friends from (Name of City, State), but we are glad to have you here. I think you're going to like it here. I'll look for you tomorrow." This is an example of a structured beginning project because, although the students can ad lib and just be their genuine selves, they also will want to try to use the facilitative skills practiced in the training sessions.

Another use of peers in elementary schools is that of mediators. Peer mediators have shown to be very effective at solving student conflicts (Wittmer, Thompson, & Sheperis, 1999).

## Intermediate Projects

An example of an *intermediate* project with elementary students which requires more training is a small group leader for the primary grades. In my school, six fifth grade students who had made the commitment to learn the skills and become group leaders for a unit on friendship, first participated in a small group on the same topic, led by myself, the counselor/trainer. I modeled the skills needed to lead a group discussion and stopped (froze) the conversation from time to time to talk about each skill as it is used so that the students could learn the skills of summarization and reflection of feelings. Gradually, I turned over control of the group, allowing students to share in the responsibility of leading or co-leading the group. Following sufficient practice, the group topics were put on cue cards and the students entered a primary grade classroom, each with their own small group to lead. The peer helpers returned to the same small group for six visits, until the unit was completed. Sometimes it is best to pair a strong, effective group leader with one who is less skilled and allow the peer helpers to co-lead the discussions. This is especially good when peers are "leading" their first group. This type of intermediate project can also be implemented in the middle schools.

## High School Projects

High school peer helper projects are frequently less structured than projects for younger helpers. An example, however, of a fairly structured *secondary* project is using peer helpers to lead college preparation seminars. Giving information about what tests to take, where to take them, how much they cost, how to find information about particular colleges, their specific admission requirements, costs, financial aid information, and how and when to apply for admission, are covered in such student led seminars. Such things generally take up a lot of a high school counselor's time, and, if properly coordinated, can be done by peer helpers. It is possible to give peer helpers enough preparation to not only help them find their own way through this maze of information, but to prepare them to answer most of the general questions that student colleagues have concerning this subject; plus orienting other students regarding how to find out more information. By using peer helpers to give college prep seminars to their own age-mates, as well as to interested freshman and sophomores, counselors have more time to work with potential drop-outs and students with personal problems.

Another example of a *high school* project is having the peers work with students at-risk for school drop-out. The counselor identifies freshman who have two or more failing grades (D or F) on the first report card of the year and arranges to pull out all such "targeted" freshman at a time when the peer helpers are available. The junior and senior helpers offer support during the "rough" times and invite the freshman to participate in motivational activities such as goal setting, values clarification, career education, and so forth. Research has shown that programs of this kind result in improved academic grades for student helpees.

The possibilities for high school projects are endless. In one high school peers are trained to use puppets to communicate with kindergarten children about safety issues, and, in another to coordinate orientation programs for entering freshman and to welcome new students during the year. One counselor trained her peers to lead large and small group discussions on a variety of topics ranging from college and career exploration, to reducing test anxiety. They also assisted the counselor in leading small groups of students (five or six each) during large group guidance activities within classroom settings.

## Supervision

Most peer projects require on-going supervision by the counselor. It is imperative that time for the supervision be scheduled into the program as this can become an ethical and legal issue. Supervision of peer helper projects is also a practical concern, because without proper supervision, peer helper programs will fail. Even the seemingly simply role of tutor needs timely supervision (weekly) to help the peer facilitator reflect on how things are going and solve small problems as they occur.

At the elementary level it is best to reserve the last 5 to 10 minutes of each "session" with a student, or group of students, for "de-briefing." This could occur informally in the hallway to save time. For example, you may want to ask each peer helper to share something fun or positive about their experience with the younger children that day. Then each child can describe an unexpected problem that came up that they didn't know how to solve or deal with. The fifth graders will occasionally be frustrated by a youngster's misbehavior and are ready and able to learn how to use positive reinforcement tactics to gain co-operation from their group.

At the high school level where more individual peer helping sessions occur, students need formal, confidential supervision sessions. In these sessions they can discuss concerns they might have about a friend's personal safety without breaking confidentiality, when its not necessary, or help decide when it is time to break confidentiality and to seek professional help for their friend. Sometimes, supervision simply focuses on a review of basic listening skills. Counselors realize that these basic, important counseling skills can atrophy when not monitored carefully.

# Evaluation of the Peer Program

Everything that can be and has been said or written (in this book and others) concerning accountability for a developmental school counseling program applies equally as well to a peer helper program. Accountability can become a counselor's best friend. Administrators, parents, teachers, and others who influence the guidance program, and hence the peer helper program, have a right to know how it's working. Collecting written feedback from students and teachers served by the program is helpful. Taking the time to do a pre and a post test using a control group technique occasionally is helpful and productive. If several schools in the same district have peer programs it is helpful to plan a project together (perhaps a "targeted" group of disruptive students) and pool the data. Presenting such effective outcomes data to the school board at the end of the year will bring about positive results.

# Cautions and Problem Moments

At the *high school* level, perhaps the most controversial issue in peer helper programs is the notion of having teenagers "counseling" other teens who may have deeper problems than the teen aider is prepared or trained to deal with. The issue becomes even more controversial when the "counseling" takes place on school time. School counselors agree that peer helpers should not be involved in issues where professional counseling help is needed. Group projects are most appropriate for peers, and if they hear of deeper issues, they can refer students to the school counselor.

Most counselors prefer to only schedule structured group projects and to allow the individual counseling to occur naturally (i.e., in the locker room, on the school bus, and/or after school). Most counselors have regular peer supervision on school time so that the teen aiders can review cases and obtain advice from their peer group or the counselor on how to proceed.

At the *elementary* level, one of the most controversial issues is whether or not parent permission is needed for a student to become a peer helper. Some counselors feel that to request parent permission insinuates that there is something potentially dangerous about the program. Of course, parent permission is required before a student goes off-campus (for any reason due to potential liability issues) and this includes off-campus peer projects. If permission is requested for training their child as a peer helper, the parents may wonder why, and question whether the program may be potentially harmful. Some counselors prefer to notify parents that their child has been *selected* to become a peer helper as opposed to requesting permission. The written notification implies clearly that it is an honor to have been chosen and that their child has been selected for a position of leadership in the school; they have earned the trust and respect of their peers, the teachers, and especially the counselor(s) (see Figure 23.4).

Most elementary counselors schedule a parent meeting to orient the parents about the goals and benefits of the peer program and to answer questions and address any concerns a parent might have. It is rare for a parent to ask that their child not participate in the peer program if it is appropriately explained.

Another problem that seems to be especially troublesome for elementary counselors is the issue of helping young children understand and respect confidentiality. Some counselors are concerned that its a mixed message to tell children to be wary of people who ask them to "keep secrets" and then ask them to keep confidential personal information that was shared in a group session. Experience working with younger children usually proves to counselors that children are frequently very wise. Fourth and fifth grade students are able to understand the difference between respecting a friend's privacy and withholding important safety information from adults. Confidentiality issues, and when and how to break it, are an important part of peer helper training.

A problem that sometimes occurs at the elementary and secondary level is that occasionally a peer helper will engage in behavior that is "unbecoming" of a peer helper (i.e., embarrassing to the school and reflects negatively on the counselor). The guidelines concerning peer helper behavior should always be made clear at the beginning of the program. Students are generally asked to sign a contract to formalize the agreement they are making with the other peer helpers and the counselor to serve as a "model student" (see Figure 23.5). These guidelines generally reflect "good citizenship" at both the elementary and secondary levels.

## Materials and Resources

Many counselors have trained peer helpers and have supervised very successful projects by teaching students the communication skills they learned while seeking their degrees in counselor education. It is not essential to have a large budget to initiate a peer helper program in your school. There are many helpful inexpensive books available to the school counselor that outline in detail excellent peer training programs. Most have been found successful and easy to use. You need not re-invent the wheel; simply purchase at least one of the numerous books available and get started! Commercial kits and packages on peer helping are also available and are helpful. Most counselors discover that just as in parent education, it is advantageous to have a book or a kit to lead your first group, but following an exposure to a sampling of materials, most professionals pick and choose what they like best from various programs and add some ideas of their own to meet the specific needs of their school.

## Summary

A word of warning to the school counselor implementing a peer helper program for the first time: be careful, peer helping programs may be addictive! Most school counselors who are involved in peer facilitation report that this is their favorite part of their entire school counseling program. The school counselors look forward to the training sessions and the project supervision as enthusiastically as do the student helpers. So, what may begin as an experiment in your school could easily turn into a career-long habit.

# Figure 23.1
# Teacher Recommendation: Teen-Aiders

Dear (Teacher),

_____ has applied to the Peer Facilitator/Teen-Aiders Class. Please take a few minutes to evaluate this student (your rating will remain confidential) according to the following qualities:

|  | Poor | Fair | Good | Excellent | Unknown |
|---|---|---|---|---|---|
| Respectful | ❏ | ❏ | ❏ | ❏ | ❏ |
| Friendliness | ❏ | ❏ | ❏ | ❏ | ❏ |
| Sense of Responsibility | ❏ | ❏ | ❏ | ❏ | ❏ |
| Reliability | ❏ | ❏ | ❏ | ❏ | ❏ |
| Self-Confidence | ❏ | ❏ | ❏ | ❏ | ❏ |
| Trustworthiness | ❏ | ❏ | ❏ | ❏ | ❏ |
| Concern for Others | ❏ | ❏ | ❏ | ❏ | ❏ |
| Leadership Potential | ❏ | ❏ | ❏ | ❏ | ❏ |
| Emotional Stability | ❏ | ❏ | ❏ | ❏ | ❏ |
| Sense of Humor | ❏ | ❏ | ❏ | ❏ | ❏ |
| Accepts Criticism | ❏ | ❏ | ❏ | ❏ | ❏ |
| Sense of Judgment | ❏ | ❏ | ❏ | ❏ | ❏ |
| Politeness | ❏ | ❏ | ❏ | ❏ | ❏ |
| Personal Energy | ❏ | ❏ | ❏ | ❏ | ❏ |
| Sensitivity | ❏ | ❏ | ❏ | ❏ | ❏ |
| Adaptability | ❏ | ❏ | ❏ | ❏ | ❏ |

Comments: _____

Signed: _____

Please Return To: _____

# Figure 23.2
# Peer Helper Job Application (Elementary School Level)

Job Applied For:_____ Date: _____

Last Name_____ First _____ Middle_____

Male ❑  Female ❑  Age _____ Grade _____

1. Write a short paragraph giving reasons for wanting this job.

   _____

   _____

   _____

   _____

2. What are your qualifications for this job?

   _____

   _____

   _____

   _____

3. If your best friend were recommending you for the job of Peer Helper, what would they write about your qualifications?

   _____

   _____

   _____

   _____

4. Write, in one sentence, why you should be "hired" as a peer helper.

   _____

   _____

   _____

   _____

# Figure 23.3
# Peer Facilitator Application (High School Level)

Last Name: _____    First Name _____

Date: _____    Grade: _____

1. List the names of 5 teachers who would recommend you for a Peer Facilitator Program.

   _____

   _____

   _____

2. Write a short paragraph telling why you would like to be a Peer Facilitator.

   _____

   _____

   _____

3. What personal qualifications do you have that would enable you to be a good Peer Facilitator?

   _____

   _____

   _____

4. What else would you like us to know about you as it concerns your being a Peer Facilitator?

   _____

   _____

   _____

# Figure 23.4
# Parent Notification
# (Name of your school, address and phone number)

Dear :

Your child, _____ , has been selected by the counselor(s) to be trained as a Peer Facilitator. Your child was chosen because he/she is perceived by teachers and others as someone who:

1. Is easy to get along with and is capable of helping others.
2. Has the personal traits of: acceptance, patience, consistency, a sense of humor, and caring about others.
3. Has positive attitudes towards peers, school, and adults.
4. Is a good student and overall good citizen.

Peer Facilitators work with other students. They are guidance assistants. They are trained by the school counselor to be effective listeners. In addition, they are given systematic training in interpersonal skills, which they use to help other students talk about their ideas and feelings. They work through carefully organized and supervised guidance activities. As they help others learn, they learn about themselves.

Peer Facilitators are regarded as positive leaders in our school. They are expected to keep up with their school work and their behavior should set a good example for others. Your child has made the commitment to make up any academic assignments missed while working on a guidance project. Please feel free to call me if you have any questions regarding this program.

Sincerely,

(School Counselor)

cc:

# Figure 23.5
# A Student Facilitator Contract

_____ has been selected to participate in the student facilitator program. Training sessions to become a Friendly Helper will begin shortly and upon completion of training, helping projects around the school will take place. It is understood that Friendly Helpers:

1. Attend school regularly

2. Complete class assignments

3. Serve as model students

4. Assist other students

5. Follow school rules

I, _____ hereby agree to conduct myself as a Friendly Helper and to take an active part in the student facilitator program.

_____

Reference Person #1

_____

Reference Person #2

_____

Student Signature

_____

Trainer or Coordinator Signature

_____

Parent Signature

## References and Resources

Foster, E.S. (1992). *Tutoring: Learning by helping.* Minneapolis, MN: Educational Media Corporation.

Hazouri, S.P., & Smith, M.F. (1991). *Peer listening in the middle school: Training activities for students.* Minneapolis, MN: Educational Media Corporation.

Myrick, R.D. (2003) *Developmental guidance and counseling: A practical approach* (4th ed.). Minneapolis, MN: Educational Media Corporation.

Myrick, R.D., & Bowman, R.P. (2004). *Becoming a friendly helper: A handbook for student facilitators* (rev. ed.). Minneapolis, MN: Educational Media Corporation.

Myrick, R.D., & Bowman, R.P. (1991). *Children helping children: Teaching students to become friendly helpers* (rev. ed.). Minneapolis, MN: Educational Media Corporation.

Myrick, R.D., & Folk, B.E. (1991). *Peervention: Training peer facilitators for prevention education.* Minneapolis, MN: Educational Media Corporation.

Myrick, R.D., & Sorenson, D.L. (1997). *Peer helping: A practical guide* (2nd ed.). Minneapolis, MN: Educational Media Corporation.

Myrick, R.D., & Sorenson, D.L. (1992). *Teaching helping skills to middle school students: Program leaders guide.* Minneapolis, MN: Educational Media Corporation.

National Association of Peer Programs (NAPP). http://www.peerprograms.org.

Sorenson, D.L. (1992). *Conflict resolution and mediation for peer helpers.* Minneapolis, MN: Educational Media Corporation.

Stone, D.J., & Keefauver, L. (1990). *Friend to friend: Helping your friends through problems.* Minneapolis, MN: Educational Media Corporation.

Sturkie, J., & Gibson, V. (1992). *The peer helper's pocketbook.* San Jose, CA: Resource Publications.

Tindall, J. (1994). *An in-depth look at peer helping* (4th ed.). Muncie, IN: Accelerated Development.

Tindall, J.A., & Salmon, S. (1991). *Peers helping peers.* Muncie, IN: Accelerated Development.

Wittmer, J., Thompson, D., & Sheperis, C. (1999). *The peace train: A school-wide violence prevention program.* Minneapolis, MN: Educational Media Corporation.

# Chapter 24

# Counseling in Urban Schools: Context, Challenges, Characteristics, and Competencies

**by Courtland C. Lee and Angela M. Wagner**

---

*Courtland C. Lee is a Professor and Director of the School Counseling Program at the University of Maryland, College Park. He is the author of numerous journal articles and books and has held a variety of national and international leadership positions in the counseling profession.*

*Angela M. Wagner is a master's degree student in the School Counseling Program at the University of Maryland, College Park.*

- *Students at one local high school in a metropolitan area must pass through metal detectors upon entering the building. Once inside they encounter armed security guards. These precautions have been precipitated by a rash of gang-related student stabbings on school grounds and in the neighboring community.*

- *At the start of the school year in one major city, scores of children are sent home because they do not have the immunizations required to begin school.*

- *In one urban community, a student was recently attacked on his way to school by a group of youth who wanted his expensive and popular brand of ski jacket.*

- *Students in several schools in a big city school system have been hurt by falling plaster in their old, physically deteriorating classrooms.*

- *In one big city high school almost an entire school year passes before students receive their required textbooks in several classes.*

- *Recently, parents in a large city staged a protest against plans by the state government to take over of their city's failing public school system.*

- *The superintendent of a large city school system notified 1,100 uncertified teachers –about 25 percent of the system's teaching force – that they will lose their jobs if they do not obtain proper credentials.*

Vignettes such as these have come to increasingly characterize education in urban America. Scores of young people in urban school systems are confronted daily with challenges that often appear to be unique to this educational setting. Complex issues that characterize life in cities and their immediate metropolitan areas often confound effective learning in urban schools. Within such an environment, professional school counselors must promote academic, career and personal-social development against the backdrop of issues and challenges that, by degree, are often more profound than they are in suburban or rural educational settings (Lee, 2005).

The purpose of this chapter is to explore the nature of professional school counseling in contemporary urban settings. The chapter begins with an overview of key characteristics that describe the urban context. The urban context of schools is explored next. The chapter continues with an examination of specific challenges that generally confront school counselors in an urban environment. It concludes with a discussion of competencies considered important for successful counseling in urban schools.

## The Urban Context

In order to fully appreciate the issues confronting urban school counselors it is important to examine the context for those issues. It is necessary, therefore, to define what is meant by *urban* and examine crucial characteristics of such an environment.

The U.S. Census Bureau (2002) classifies as *urban* all territory, population, and housing units located within an urbanized area or an urban cluster. It delineates urban area and urban cluster boundaries to encompass densely settled territory, which consists of: 1) core census block groups that have a population density of at least 1,000 people per square mile and 2) surrounding census blocks that have an overall density of at least 500 people per square mile. According to the Census Bureau an urbanized area consists

---

of densely settled territory that contains 50,000 or more people. An urban cluster consists of closely settled territory that has at least 2,500 people but fewer than 50,000 people. The Census Bureau introduced the urban cluster for the 2000 census to provide a more consistent and accurate measure of the population concentration in and around places.

Concomitant with the operational definition of *urban,* the Census Bureau also defines the general concept of *metropolitan area.* This is an area with a large population nucleus, together with adjacent communities that have a high degree of economic and social interaction with that nucleus. Each metropolitan area must contain either a place with a minimum population of 50,000 and a total metropolitan area of at least 100,000. A metropolitan area contains one or more central counties. It may also include one or more outlying counties that have close economic and social relationships with the central county.

Given these Census Bureau definitions the term *urban* can be conceived of as referring to cities, and in most instances, the municipalities or counties in close proximity to them. While there are many examples of urban configurations throughout the United States, one in particular can be used to demonstrate the concept – Washington, D.C., the nation's capital. Metropolitan Washington, D.C. consists of the city of Washington at its core which is surrounded by the heavily populated urban counties of Prince George's and Montgomery in the state of Maryland, and Fairfax County, Arlington County, and the city of Alexandria in the state of Virginia. According to the 2000 U.S. Census, the population for this metropolitan area is approximately four million residents, which makes it a major urban center (U.S. Census Bureau, 2005).

Conceptualizing an urban area in this manner suggests a number of important characteristics that may help to define the nature of such places. The following is list of characteristics that help to define the urban context. The list is by no means exhaustive, but it does represent many of the aspects that have come to characterize urban settings:

- Population density
- Structural density
- High concentration of people of color
- High concentration of recent immigrants
- High rates of reported crimes
- Per capita higher rates of poverty
- Complex transportation patterns
- High concentration of airborne pollutants
- Strong cultural stimulation

- Diversity in property values
- Inequities in the legal system
- Lack of community connectedness
- Cultural heterogeneity
- Inequities in access to health care
- High number of non-English speakers and non-English media
- High degree of mobility
- Inequities in the educational system
- Large complex educational systems

# The Urban Context of Schools

Urban schools in large measure reflect the characteristics of the environment in which they are located. The status of urban public education has become a topic of wide-ranging scrutiny in recent years (Blanchett, Mumford & Beachum, 2005; Council of Great City Schools, 1999; Gallay & Flanagan, 2000; Gordon, 2003; Howard, 2003; Hunter & Donahoo, 2003; Kolodny, 2001; Noguera, 2003; Rice & Roellke, 2003; Snipes & Casserly, 2004: U.S. Department of Education, National Center for Education Statistics, 2005). It is evident that there are significant issues faced by public schools in urban areas that are qualitatively different than those confronting schools in rural or suburban contexts. Olsen & Jerald (1998), in reviewing a number of indicators provide an important framework for examining the context and inherent challenges of urban education:

- *The Achievement Gap.* Urban youth are less likely to receive a post secondary degree and are more likely to drop out of high school compared to rural and suburban youth. In addition, they are less likely to meet the minimum standards on national tests and less likely to complete high school in four years. Significantly, urban youth often enter college or the work force unprepared to succeed at competent levels which places them in a precarious situation for attaining meaningful work.

- *Concentrated Poverty.* Concentrated poverty is a major urban phenomenon. Urban students are more than twice as likely to attend high-poverty schools. Concentrated poverty heightens the probability that school-children will lack access to regular medical care, live in a household headed by a single mother, become a victim of crime, have a parent who never finished high school, become pregnant, and drop out of school.

- *The Teaching Challenge.* Urban school districts face major challenges hiring teachers and filling teacher vacancies. Significantly, urban schools are far more likely to hire unlicensed or under qualified teachers. In many instances, urban school systems can not meet the salaries or working conditions that are offered by suburban districts which contributes to a high rate of teacher turnover.

- *School Climate.* On average, urban students attend bigger schools than nonurban students. The climate in urban schools is more often than not characterized by teacher reports that weapons and physical conflicts among students are a problem. Significant student absenteeism and tardiness are often associated with urban school climate. Likewise, a lack of parent involvement is often a characteristic of urban schools.

- *Access to Resources.* The share of public resources for funding urban schools is often a major challenge. Nationally, urban districts spend less per student than do nonurban districts. This lack of resources is often seen in aging and crumbling school facilities where students with a lack of books and supplies attempt to learn. Urban schools are also often lagging behind in access to educational technology so crucial to the contemporary learning process. Significantly, funding problems in urban schools are often exacerbated by financial mismanagement on the part of educational leaders.

- *Politics and Governance.* Urban school districts are, in most instances, large bureaucratic institutions that are fueled by highly-charged political realities. These realities include the ever-growing influence of key political stakeholders on the educational process. Mayors, city council members, school board members, union officials and in some cases, state officials can be counted among these major stakeholders. The political realities of urban schools are exacerbated by central administrations that are highly bureaucratic, grossly mismanaged and increasingly inefficient when it comes to educational governance. Within the morass of politics and governance are superintendents, who on average, serve less than three years as chief executives of urban school systems.

The inherent educational inequities within the urban context present formidable challenges to the psychosocial development of many young people. There is a serious stifling of achievement, aspiration and pride on the part of many of youth in urban school systems throughout the country. It is important to emphasize that while there are many urban schools and school systems that are finding ways to successfully educate young people, the data generally suggest that frustration, underachievement, and ultimate failure comprise the educational reality for scores of students within the urban educational context (Council of great City Schools, 1999).

# School Counseling in the Urban Environment

Given the contextual factors that characterize urban schools and their impact on student development, it is important to consider the nature of professional school counseling in this environment. Urban school counselors must support young people as they explore options, make choices and prepare for life after high school against a backdrop of the challenges that confront the school systems in which they work.

The overarching issue confronting urban school counselors is pervasive academic failure (Olsen & Jerald, 1998; U.S. Department of Education, National Center for Education Statistics, 2005). In their attempts to address this issue, counselors often must confront complex factors that significantly undermine the ability of many young people to achieve academic success in urban schools. They also must deal with structural dynamics that greatly impinge upon their professional roles.

Implementing a counseling program in urban schools is often hampered by chronic student absenteeism, family instability, high levels of student transience, and increasing school and community violence. Additionally, urban school counselors are faced with major challenges associated with increasing cultural diversity in schools. Counseling interventions are greatly impacted by language issues and value differences that come with the cultural diversity that characterizes many urban schools (Lee, 2005).

Urban school counseling is further complicated by major structural challenges to programming. These include: ever-increasing work loads, meager resources, minimal professional development, unionization, expanding bureaucratic interference or indifference, and high rates of administrative turnover.

As if these issues and challenges were not enough, urban school counselors must also contend with the contemporary demands placed upon schools for greater accountability. In an era of legislative initiatives such as *No Child Left Behind* (2001), urban school counselors, as do their rural and suburban counterparts, find themselves under significant public pressure to ensure that all students achieve to high academic standards.

## Urban School Counseling Competencies

It is evident that school counseling in urban areas brings with it significant challenges. Counselors who work in urban educational environments must be prepared to confront serious impediments to student development. Counseling in urban schools, therefore, implies a set of competencies on the part of professionals that will enable them to effectively address the personal, interpersonal and structural challenges that tend to stifle academic success for scores of young people. These competencies are underscored by a major movement underway to transform the nature of professional school counseling.

## School Counseling Reform: The Foundation of Urban School Counselor Competency

Within the last decade, professional school counseling has undergone a transformation. School counselors have been challenged to achieve new professional goals and assume new and more proactive roles (American School Counselor Association, 2003; Education Trust, 2000; Erford, House & Martin, 2003). Professional school counselors are being called upon to be visible leaders in national educational reform movements and central to the mission of schools (House & Hayes, 2002; Martin, 2002). The work of a school counselor in this transformational effort is predicated on the principles of access, equity and social justice. These principles reflect a commitment to ensuring that all children regardless, of race/ethnicity or socioeconomic status, have the opportunity to achieve to their fullest potential.

School counselors are now challenged to assume roles that reflect a commitment to these principles. Accordingly, they are being asked to shift from an individual focus to a systemic focus in their work. Rather than work in isolation with individual student problems, professional school counselors are being asked to team and collaborate with other educational stakeholders and work at a macro level to bring about systemic change (Lee, 2001; Simcox, Nuijens & Lee, in press). In addition, they are being called upon to move beyond a primary focus on school counseling activities to more extensive involvement as leaders in both the school and community (Erford, House & Martin, 2003). Finally, in an era of greater educational accountability, professional school counselors are being called upon to demonstrate with data that their efforts make a difference in the lives of the students with whom they work (Dahir & Stone, 2003).

## Competencies for the Transformed Urban School Counselor

Within the context of this national reform initiative, the following represent a set of important competencies for professional school counselors in urban educational environments. These competencies reflect the knowledge set, skills and attitudes/beliefs needed to promote student academic, career and personal-social development given the realities of contemporary urban schools.

1. *Cultural Competence.* Urban school counselors must be culturally competent (Holcomb-McCoy, 2004; Lee, 2001). They should possess the awareness, knowledge and skills to intervene in responsive and appropriate ways into the lives of the increasingly culturally diverse student population that characterizes the urban school setting. The foundation of cultural competency should be multicultural literacy on the part of urban school counselors. To be multiculturally literate is to possess basic information needed to negotiate the diverse interconnected global society of the 21$^{st}$ century. Multicultural literacy goes beyond competency to embracing a way of life that encourages maximum exposure to and understanding of the realities of multiculturalism. Ways to promote multicultural literacy include: gaining knowledge of ethnic variations in history, traveling (both nationally and internationally), reading a variety of newspapers, being open to new cultural experiences, reading literature from diverse cultures, working toward religious/spiritual tolerance, and learning a new language (Lee, in press).

2. *Counseling Skills that Promote Empowerment.* Urban school counselors must have individual and group counseling skills that are grounded in the concept of empowerment. Empowerment is a developmental process whereby people who are powerless or marginalized in some fashion become aware of how power affects their lives. They then develop the skills for gaining reasonable control over their lives that they use to help themselves and others in their community (McWhirter, 1994).

Given the personal and structural challenges that often confront young people in urban schools, counselors should be able to move beyond traditional counseling practice when promoting academic, career and personal-social development. They should have the skills to engage in programmed intervention that facilitates a process in which young people become empowered to proactively address urban challenges that impede their overall educational success. As part of the empowerment process, counselors should be able to promote the development of posi-

*Joe Wittmer, Ph.D. and Mary Ann Clark, Ph.D.*

tive attitudes toward academic achievement, as well as foster academic competency among students (Eschenauer & Chen-Hayes, 2005).

Counseling for empowerment should also involve the ability to promote positive self-identity and cultural awareness in young people. This is necessitated by the failure identity fostered in many youth as a result of their experiences with educational processes that have been negatively impacted by the challenges facing urban schools (Lee, 2001).

An empowerment perspective on counseling also includes skill to promote individual and collective awareness among young people about how their ultimate academic, career and personal-social success is linked to the potential betterment of their communities. As students become empowered, counselors should be able to help them to channel their interest and potential into helping empower their families and communities.

As counselors work to help urban youth become empowered, they should possess the ability to promote important noncognitive factors that have been found to be predictive of future educational success for young people from marginalized or oppressed backgrounds (Sedlacek, 2004; Tracey & Sedlacek, 1985). It is imperative that individual or group counseling with students in urban schools focus on:

- *Helping students to develop a positive self-concept*: Counselors should be able to assist students in demonstrating confidence, strength of character, determination, and independence in all of their activities.

- *Helping students appraise themselves realistically*: Counselors should be able to help students recognize and accept their academic strengths and deficiencies and help them to work hard at self-development to broaden their individuality.

- *Helping students to learn how to understand and handle systemic racism*: Counselors should help students learn how to assess the effects of systemic racism on their lives and development. Students should be assisted in learning strategies to effectively negotiate racism and other systemic barriers to their educational and social progress.

- *Helping students to engage in long-range planning*: Counseling interventions should focus on helping students learn how to defer immediate gratification and learn to establish long-term goals

- *Helping students to find a strong support person/ network*: Counselors should be able to assist students in finding and taking advantage of a strong support person or network of people. Such a connection could be an individual or a group that a student can turn to in a crisis or for encouragement.

- *Helping students engage in successful leadership experiences*: Counselors can assist students to find ways to demonstrate leadership in any area of interest or expertise in their school or community.

- *Helping students to find ways to engage in community service*: Counselors should encourage students to become actively involved in service activities within their communities, thus helping them to contribute to solutions to problems.

- *Helping students acquire or refine knowledge in or about a field*: Counselors should work with students to help them develop or increase their knowledge base in any field of interest to them. Increasing interest and involvement can increase motivation.

3. *Systemic Perspective.* Urban school counselors must adopt a systemic perspective with respect to their helping roles and functions. Rather than focus exclusively on the etiology of problems originating with students, the urban systems in which young people develop and function must also become a target for programmed intervention (Cox & Lee, in press). Adopting a systemic perspective demands that counselors develop an understanding of important urban systems and how they interact to affect student development. These include: the educational system, the family system, the political system, the criminal justice system, and the social welfare system.

4. *Advocacy Skills.* Adopting a systemic perspective suggests advocacy. Urban school counselors must be advocates for their students. In this role, counselors intervene in social systems on behalf of students in ways designed to eliminate barriers to academic success (Bailey, Getch & Chen-Hayes, 2003; Cox & Lee, in press; Lee, 2001). As advocates, urban school counselors are systemic change agents, working to impact urban social systems in ways that will ultimately benefit the students with whom they work (Bemak & Chung, 2005).

5. *Collaboration.* Urban school counselors must be able to collaborate with key educational stakeholders to promote student development (Bryan, 2005; Bryan & Holcomb-McCoy, 2004; Cox & Lee, in press; Simcox,

Nuijens & Lee, in press). They should be able to collaborate, for example, with urban families to help them become empowered as a proactive force in the educational success of children. Such collaboration should be based on important considerations about urban family life. Counselors must be sensitive to the economic and social realties of many urban families and meet them where they are with respect to such things as language proficiency and cultural customs.

In addition, urban school counselors must collaborate with community stakeholders to advance the educational interests of students. Counselors should be able to form alliances within the business, religious, and political sectors of urban communities to promote education. They should be able to broker such alliances so that community resources can be channeled to support both counseling and teaching initiatives. An example of this might be collaborating with community stakeholders and actively supporting their efforts to develop supplemental academic support programs (e.g., tutoring programs) in neighborhood religious institutions, community centers, and other areas of social activity.

Urban school counselors should also collaborate with educational stakeholders within the school setting. In particular, they should collaborate with teachers and administrators on ways to increase their educational effectiveness given the social and structural challenges with which educators are often confronted. School counselors should facilitate faculty development initiatives that focus on increasing awareness of the urban systemic factors that impinge upon student development or that introduce innovative methods for promoting students success in this environment.

6. *Leadership.* Urban school counselors must be leaders in their schools and within the larger community (Bemak, 2000: Cox & Lee, in press). They are in a pivotal position to assist in the development of new educational initiatives that promote student development and can also be active participants on leadership teams within their respective schools and in the school district. Urban school counselors can be influential in the development of new educational policies and procedures from the board of education to the school building level.

Likewise, urban school counselors must be politically and socially active leaders in the community at large. By seeking leadership positions within strategic community organizations and institutions they can positively impact the quality of life for young people and their families. Such strategic leadership can directly influence important community political decisions and policy initiatives that have a connection to the quality of education for students as well as the welfare of their families (Lee, 2005).

7. *Proactive Use of Data.* School counselors in urban settings must have the skills to develop and maintain comprehensive data-driven programs (Eschenauer & Chen-Hayes, 2005). It is essential that they be proficient in accessing, analyzing, interpreting and presenting data related to various aspects of student development which can be used as the basis for program direction. Urban school counselors must be able to make data driven decisions about effective student interventions and use it as an advocacy tool to challenge behavior, funding patterns, programs and policies that have traditionally prevented maximum achievement for all students within the urban context of schools. Given the challenges of urban education, school counselors are in a pivotal position to use data to point out inequities within the urban educational context and advocate for systemic change.

Additionally, data must be used to underscore counselor accountability. In the politically charged atmosphere of many urban school systems, where resource allocation and job insecurity is an on-going challenge, school counselors must use data in a manner that graphically demonstrates their effectiveness in promoting student achievement. It is vital given the pervasive challenges to academic success in many urban school systems that school counselors be proficient in using data to effectively answer the question, *how has student achievement increased as a result of what I do?*

# The Challenge of Urban School Counseling Competencies

While it may be argued that these competencies are important for school counselors in all settings, the pervasive failure and wasted potential of scores of young people that characterize much of the urban educational landscape underscore the importance and urgency of this skill set for counseling in urban schools. These competencies imply a rejection of many long-standing traditions characteristic of professional school counseling. They require school counselors who work in urban school settings to transcend the traditional boundaries of school counseling practice. The competencies challenge urban school counselors to "think outside the box" and take risks in their efforts to address the complex issues that confront them and the students with whom they work. In developing these competencies counselors must be willing to commit themselves to understanding the complexities of the urban environment and how they directly affect young people. Having a deep commitment to empowering and affirming urban youth through their individual, group, and collaborative interventions with students is essential. Innovative leadership and collaboration with school and community stakeholders can provide the impetus for educational success for urban students.

## Conclusion

Counseling in urban schools is significantly different from school counseling in other settings. This chapter has provided direction for effective school counseling in an urban environment. It is based on the important notion that professional school counselors in this setting must possess the knowledge, skills and attitudes to effectively address profound and often unique social and structural impediments to educational success for urban youth. The future of these young people and urban America demands no less.

## References

American School Counselor Association. (2003). The ASCA national model: A framework for school counseling programs. Alexandria, VA: Author

Bailey, D.F., Getch, Y.Q., & Chen-Hayes, S. (2003). Professional school counselors as social and academic advocates. In B.T. Erford (Ed.), *Transforming the school counseling profession* (pp. 411-434). Upper Saddle River, NJ: Merrill Prentice Hall.

Bemak, F. (2000). Transforming the role of the counselor to provide leadership in educational reform through collaboration. *Professional School Counseling, 3,* 323-331.

Bemak, F., & Chung, R. (2005). Advocacy as a critical role for urban school counselors: Working toward equity and social justice. *Professional School Counseling, 8,* 196-202.

Blanchett, W., Mumford, V., & Beachum, F. (2005). Urban school failure and disproportionality in a post-Brown era. *Remedial & Special Education, 26,* 70-81.

Bryan, J. (2005). Fostering educational resilience and achievement in urban schools through school-family-community partnerships. *Professional School Counseling, 8,* 219 - 227

Bryan, J., & Holcomb-McCoy, C. (2004). School counselors' perceptions of their involvement in school-family-community partnerships. *Professional School Counseling, 7,* 162-171.

Council of Great City Schools (1999). *Closing the achievement gap in urban schools: A survey of academic progress and promising practices in the great city schools, Preliminary report.* Retrieved January 3, 2006 from http://www.cgcs.org/taskforce/achievegap3.html

Cox, A.A., & Lee, C.C. (in press). Challenging educational inequities: school counselors as agents of social justice. In C.C. Lee (Ed.). *Counseling for social justice.* Austin TX: Pro-Ed.

Dahir, C., & Stone, C. (2003). Accountability: A M.E.A.S.U.R.E. of the impact school counselors have on student achievement. *Professional School Counseling, 6,* 214-221.

Education Trust. (2000). *National initiative for transforming school counseling summer academy for counselor educators proceedings.* Washington, DC: Author.

Erford, B.T., House, R., & Martin, P. (2003). Transforming the school counseling profession. In B.T. Erford (Ed.), *Transforming the school counseling profession* (pp. 1-20). Upper Saddle River, NJ: Merrill Prentice Hall.

Eschenauer, R., & Chen-Hayes, S.F. (2005). The transformative individual school counseling model: An accountability model for urban school counselors. *Professional School Counseling, 8,* 244-248.

Gallay, L.S., & Flanagan, C.A. (2000). The well-being of children in a changing economy: Time for a new social contract in America. In R.D. Taylor & M.C. Wang (Eds.), *Resilience across contexts: Work, family, culture, and community (pp. 3-34).* Mahwah, NJ: Erlbaum.

Gordon, E.W. (2003). Urban education. *Teachers College Record, 105,* 189-209.

Holcomb-McCoy, C. (2004). Assessing the multicultural competence of school counselors: A checklist. *Professional School Counseling, 7,* 178-186.

House, R.M., & Hayes, R.L. (2002). School counselors: Becoming key players in school reform. *Professional School Counseling, 5,* 249-256.

Howard, T.C. (2003). Who receives the short end of the shortage? Implications of the U.S. teacher shortage on urban schools. *Journal of Curriculum & Supervision, 18,* 142-160.

Hunter, R.C., & Donahoo, S. (2003). The nature of urban school politics after Brown: The need for new political knowledge, leadership, and organizational skills. *Education and Urban Society, 36,* 3-15.

Kolodny, K.A. (2001). Inequalities in the overlooked associations in urban educational collaborations. *The Urban Review, 33,* 151-178.

Lee, C.C. (2001). Culturally responsive school counselors and programs: Addressing the needs of all students. *Professional School Counseling, 4,* 257-261.

Lee, C.C. (2005). Urban school counseling: Context, characteristics, and competencies. *Professional School Counseling, 8,* 184-188.

Lee, C.C. (in press). Social justice: A counselor call to action. In C.C. Lee (Ed.). *Counseling for social justice.* Austin TX: Pro-Ed.

McWhirter, E.H. (1994). *Counseling for empowerment.* Alexandria, VA: American Counseling Association.

Martin, P.J. (2002). Transforming school counseling: A national perspective. *Theory Into Practice, 41,* 148-154.

Noguera, P. (2003). *City schools and the American dream: reclaiming the promise of public education.* New York: Teachers College Press.

Olson, L., & Jerald, C.D. (1998). *Quality counts 98': The urban picture.* Retrieved January 3, 2006, from http://www.edweek.org/reports/qc98/challenges.htm

Rice, J.K., & Roellke, C. (2003). Urban school finance: Increased standards and accountability in uncertain economic times. *School Business Affairs, 69,* 30-33.

Sedlacek, W. E. (2004). *Beyond the big test: Noncognitive assessment in higher education.* San Francisco: Jossey-Bass.

Simcox, A.G., Nuijens, K.L, & Lee, C.C. (in press). School counselors and school psychologists: Collaborative partners in promoting culturally competent schools. *Professional School Counselor.*

Snipes, J.C., & Casserly, M.D. (2004). Urban school systems and education reform: Key lessons from a case study of large urban school systems. *Journal of Education for Students Placed At-risk, 9,* 127-141.

Tracey, T.J., & Sedlacek, W.E. (1985). The relationship of noncognitive variables to academic success: A longitudinal comparison by race. *Journal of College Student Personnel, 26,* 405-410.

U.S. Bureau of the Census (2002). *Census 2000 urban and rural classification.* Retrieved January 5, 2006, from http://www.census.gov/geo/www/ua/ua_2k.html

U.S. Bureau of the Census (2005). *Annual population estimates 2000-2005.* Retrieved January 5, 2006, from http://www.census.gov/popest/estimates.php

U.S. Department of Education (2001). *No child left behind act of 2001 (H.R.1).* Washington, DC: U.S. Department of Education.

U.S. Department of Education, National Center for Education Statistics (2005). *The condition of education 2005* (Report No. 2005-094). Washington, DC: Government Printing office.

# Chapter 25

# The Transformed School Counselor: A Collaboration and Teaming Specialist

by
**Laura Pedersen**

*Laura Pedersen, Ph.D., is the Director of the School Counseling Program in the Graduate School of Education and Counseling at Lewis & Clark College. She has had extensive school counseling experience in both stateside and international schools.*

## New Perspectives on School Counseling

As the new millennium approached, several forces were in play that necessitated a reconceptualization of school counseling's philosophy and mission. The profession was in a period of flux, hampered by rising caseloads for practitioners, increasing marginalization based on new accountability and standards based reform for public education, and a poor public image. At the same time, more students appeared to be left behind in the quest for educational opportunities and for a wide range of educational and employment opportunities at the post-secondary level. It was clearly time for an in-depth examination of how well school counselors were doing their jobs in serving students, and how they were being perceived in the overall academic mission of K-12 public schools.

Spurred by the efforts of the DeWitt-Wallace Reader's Digest Foundation, the movement to redefine essential functions of school counselors found voice. In partnership with the American School Counselor Association (ASCA) and the Education Trust, Dewitt-Wallace Reader's Digest Foundation funded approved Universities as they defined and worked at integrating a new set of beliefs about what school counselors could and should be doing in the schools (The Education Trust, 1997). These beliefs were founded on several key principles: all students need access to the best possible educational opportunities, but particularly those students who have traditionally been underserved or at risk of failure; school counseling must be intimately connected with the overall academic mission of the schools rather than

being seen as a peripheral service that was designed to help students feel better about themselves; and, school counselors need to take a leadership role in their schools if they are to be effective advocates and equity agents.

While reconceptualizing an entire profession is admittedly a daunting task, the initiation of a philosophical framework, supported by grant money for examination and implementation, permitted a collaborative effort between foundations, universities, school districts and state education departments (The Education Trust, 1997). This collaborative network set the groundwork for an energizing, exciting process of vision, creativity, and teamwork. In many essential ways, the process modeled what school counselors are now being asked to do in their daily practice.

The ASCA National Model provided an important framework for defining the new role of school counselors. The National Model lays out the three components of service delivery for children in schools: all children should be exposed to a comprehensive, development school counseling program that addresses the domains of academic, personal/social, and career development (American School Counselor Association, 2005). In addition, these three domains need to be directly tied to academic achievement and opportunities for all children. School counseling programs should be customized to a school or community setting based on data, and also need to be supported by data which demonstrates that the school counseling program contributes to the learning of students.

The Transforming School Counseling Initiative (TSCI), administered by and housed within the Education Trust, provided an in-depth exploration of what it could look like if school counselors became integral in social advocacy, assuring equity of access to services, and support for student success that is inclusive of all members of the community (National Center for Transforming School Counseling, 2003). School counselors must be seen as those who empower students to envision a successful future, and as those who provide the tools to help them get there. In order to accomplish these huge tasks in a standards-based school climate, school counselors must embrace data as the means to create relevant services and to celebrate the results of those services (Martin, 2002).

One of the essential functions addressed in both the ASCA National Model and the TSCI is the need for school counselors to be change agents in their schools and in their communities (Perusse, Goodenough, Donegan, & Jones, 2004). This can only be accomplished if school counselors see themselves as collaborators and teaming specialists. All members in the school community must be mobilized and united in efforts to help students learn, and in overcoming barriers to academic achievement. School counselors are the development and relationship specialists in schools (Myrick, 2003), but they also have specific skills in communication, mediation, problem solving, and goal setting. They are ideally placed to help diverse members of school communities work together to define issues, collect data, design and implement a response, and assess results. In this way, the school counselor can have great effect on the learning environment for all students, while serving as a resource for stakeholders who are committed to a shared vision for change.

# New Visions for School Counseling

Several organizations have been instrumental in re-thinking the needs of students and the roles of school counselors in K-12 settings, and in the training of school counselors at the university level. These institutions have worked in concert, combining efforts without duplicating them, and have developed a refined vision for how schools can better serve children. These institutions are the American School Counselor Association, the DeWitt Wallace Reader's Digest Foundation and The Transforming School Counseling Initiative, and finally, the National Transforming School Counseling Office of the Education Trust.

# The American School Counselor Association

The American School Counselor Association (ASCA) has a long tradition of support and professional development for practitioners, advocacy for the profession, and definition of professional identity and roles for school counselors. The groundbreaking work they performed in the late 1990s and into the 2000s is indicative of an association that is responsive to changing needs of the profession, and of changing social mores.

Traditional models of school counseling focused on the emotional needs of children in schools. Much of a school counselor's time was spent providing responsive services to children in crisis, often in the form of individual or small group counseling. Unfortunately, this led to a common perception that school counselors were not closely aligned with the academic mission of the schools. Concerns about individual counseling in the schools centered around the facts that it is not efficient given the caseloads of counselors, that there is a lack of outcome research about the effectiveness of individual counseling in the schools, and that individual counseling is generally not focused on essential issues of equity and access to educational opportunities (Eschenauer & Chen-Hayes, 2005). School counselors have often been trained within the context of counselor education programs that focus on mental health and individual counseling skills, rather that focusing primarily on school-based interventions and interactions.

A change in emphasis to one that addresses developmental concerns and processes for all children, particularly lessons and group work that support student learning, seemed essential for school counselors to be able to define and defend their work (Dahir, Sheldon & Valiga, 1998). ASCA led the way in creating standards that reflect the needs of students, schools, and communities.

# The Education Trust

The Education Trust is a nonprofit organization dedicated to closing the achievement gap between majority status students and those of color or economic privation. The focus of The Education Trust's work is K-16 public education in our country, but the organization took an early leadership role in transforming school counseling to better serve the needs of all students, with substantial assistance from the DeWitt-Wallace Reader's Digest Fund and MetLife Foundation.

In analyzing the achievement gap, these organizations came to the conclusion that school counselors are well positioned to take a leadership role in closing the achievement gap (National Center for Transforming School Counseling, 2003). The traditional roles of school counselors, focusing on mental health and self-esteem issues in the school setting, were no longer functioning in a way that reflected the overall mission of schools. As such, groups of students were being left behind in the quest for academic success and post secondary options, and school counselors were increasingly being seen as marginal, nonessential staff members.

It was a crystallizing moment: school counseling could be redefined to promote equity and achievement, and school counselors can make use of their unique skill sets to work systemically within the school community (House & Hayes, 2002). No longer could school counselors place a major emphasis on individual counseling with students who were having mental health or adjustment problems, they need to enlist the assistance of all school personnel in assuring that underserved students are being identified, systemic influences are examined and addressed, and all students have equal access to high standards and expectations in the learning process.

The essential ideals behind the transforming movement are those of equity and social justice. All students have the right to experience high quality educational opportunities and the right to graduate from high school with a wide range of post secondary opportunities, including college. In order to achieve these ambitious but attainable goals, changes in the school counseling profession needed to be sweeping. Today's transformed school counselors are being trained to focus on leadership, teaming, and organizational change (DeVoss & Andrews, 2006). They are being trained to use data to evaluate school needs but also to use data to assess the effectiveness of their own programs and interventions. Decisions must be made based on facts, not intuition, and results must be empirically validated rather than based on anecdotal information. If school counselors are to be integral, essential members of their communities, they must be able to tie their mission to the academic mission of their schools, and they must demonstrate accountability as do all other members of the school community.

There are five essential skills that the Transforming School Counseling Initiative has identified for school counselors to master and implement in our current educational environment. Those skills are teaming and collaboration, leadership, assessment and uses of data to bring about change, advocacy, and counseling and coordination (Musheno & Talbert, 2002). The ASCA national model, with its emphasis on Academic, Personal/Social, and Career development domains, points the way to redefining school counselors as the staff members who remain experts in child development and relationship issues, but who work differently in terms of ensuring opportunities for all students, rather than providing specialized services to the few (ASCA, 2005).

While these essential shifts in philosophy and practice are extremely challenging, they hold the promise of hope for future generations of students. It is imperative that children of all backgrounds have access to the best possible education and that children of all backgrounds be held to high standards and supported in their academic efforts and dreams of the future.

# Collaboration and Teaming: Essential Mechanisms for Change

The demands of educational settings, with their high student/counselor ratios, create a need for school counselors to approach their work from a teamwork perspective. To adequately meet the needs of students, all school-based personnel must be involved in a comprehensive, developmental school counseling program. Skills in teaming and collaboration allow school counselors to create groups of adults working towards a common goal on behalf of students. This creates an atmosphere in which change, energy, and shared accountability foster a greater sense of community among professionals (Stone & Dahir, 2006). The perspective of a transformed school counselor is one that looks for systemic change, and as such, collaboration and teaming create common language, stronger relationships, and a renewed focus on improving academic achievement.

While collaboration and teaming are similar concepts, there are distinct differences in the rationale and goals for the two processes. Both embrace the need for adults to work together towards common goals with different members of the partnership bringing different perspectives. In both types of groups, there is shared responsibility for outcomes and in both groups there is a need for evaluation and follow-up. Collaboration, however, focuses on creating relationships between members as they come together to address a problem, while teaming emphasizes task completion. Thus, teaming may or may not be collaborative. In the schools, teaming is a group of professionals working together to provide effective educational programs and services, while collaboration often focuses on system-wide problems or brings together people from more diverse stakeholder groups.

Nicki Thomas, an outstanding school counselor in a high-needs elementary school in a rural Oregon town, relies on teaming and collaboration to meet the many academic, personal/social, and career needs of her students. She and a high school counselor have teamed to create mentoring relationships between elementary and high school students, with the outcome fostering academic development and school engagement. The elementary and high school students co-author children's books. These books are bound by a local printing press and copies are donated to the local libraries. Nicki also has formed a long-term collaborative relationship with several community organizations to implement a Lunch Buddy program. Community volunteers are enlisted to come to campus and have lunch with a student who has been identified by school staff members as needing mentoring or adult support. The advertisements for volunteers run throughout the year in local newspapers and on radio stations. Nicki uses the resources of the community in creative ways in order to help her students be successful in school.

One essential requirement for both types of groups is the need to examine data in order to define the problem. Data must be used to define the problem, to express the scope or severity of the problem, and to evaluate the effectiveness of the teaming or collaborative efforts after the intervention or response (Dahir & Stone, 2003). In an outcome based school counseling environment, the data will tell the story.

## Collaboration

Collaboration is a process by which people with different perspectives on a problem create and implement solutions that go beyond their own limited ideas of what is possible. It is the essence of systemic change in the school community because it is based on direct interaction between equal partners who all have a stake in outcomes (Center for Applied Research and Educational Improvement, 2001). The motivation for working outside one's own frame of reference is the fact that collaboration is a voluntary process, it includes shared decision-making, and a common goal defines the problem solving process.

Collaboration efforts need to be data driven. In order to understand the scope of the problem, and thus provide motivation for action, it is important to examine and disaggregate data. Both commitment to the search for a solution and commitment to specific goals arise naturally from the information that defines the problem. There are many types of data that can be examined, and the process does not need to be overly demanding or time intensive. Some of the most useful data can be accessed immediately from records that schools keep on a daily, monthly, or yearly basis. Data that can be explored include graduation rates, dropout rates, failure rates in specific classes, attendance, percentages of racial/ethnic/SES groups in AP or other advanced classes, incidents of bullying, referrals, or other disciplinary data.

Marsha Setzer, a new school counselor in a large suburban high school, disaggregated data on a group of students who had been identified by teachers as disengaged in school and therefore at risk for dropping out. She examined the data on these students by age, gender, GPA, and special services received and then formed a committee with diverse representation to address the concerns. These types of data can delineate student groups or subpopulations whose needs are not being met in the schools or who face special barriers in their educational journey. These issues are all significant ones and the above list is far from definitive. However, the impetus for action is clear as is the need for the responses to be team efforts. All of these concerns are too large for one person to have a significant impact upon, yet groups of people from differing constituencies within the school can identify and work towards systemic interventions that serve all of our children.

Brian Penney, a third-year school counselor at a large, urban middle school in Oregon, was concerned that the disciplinary process at his school might not be the best one to meet the needs of his students. He read about a child-centered approach that appeared to be having empirically supported results and discussed the issue with his building administrator. A committee to address the disciplinary problems was created with members from school staff, administration, and parents. The result of the committee work is a three-year roll out of the new discipline system which includes meetings with other schools that are implementing the new model. It also includes meetings with families and community members on how the program can be supported and reinforced outside of the school building and weekly meetings with school administrators, school counselors, and classroom teachers. The program is in the second year of the roll out process, but data shows that discipline referrals have been significantly lowered in Brian's school.

Collaborative relationships have additional benefits for school communities. They create a common language within the school and a better understanding of the issues which can impact student learning (DeVoss & Andrews, 2006). They can also develop networks of services for children which out last the issue that inspired the collaborative efforts. The process of collaboration can also improve communication and commitment throughout the school based on the fact that key stakeholders are united in common purpose. "Effective collaboration may look different at each school, but it relies on many of the same strategies: focusing on student data and work; reflecting on and changing classroom practices; applying research, and honing teamwork skills" (Northwest Regional Education Laboratory, 2005, p. 6). No specific plan that worked in one setting will necessarily work in others. It is important to have the collaborative team reflect the school community. Instead of including just those who are visible and prone to volunteering, look for opposing viewpoints and those whose voices are not being heard. Effective interventions need divergent perspectives and need the buy-in of community members. Having a collaborative group that truly mirrors the community is the most effective way to accomplish the desired end.

Collaboration presents challenges for all involved.

*"Collaboration is not for the faint of heart; it involves risk, relationship building, personal interaction skills that are above the norm. A spirit of cooperation, leadership ability, mediation skills, a thorough understanding of the nature and function of schools, likeableness, the ability to think on your feet, flexibility, a willingness to compromise, confidence, and an attitude and sincere belief that you can and will make a difference regardless of the attestations of the naysayers"* (Stone & Dahir, 2006, p. 184).

The process of creating collaborative relationships and bringing people together to work on common goals requires that school counselors step out of their traditional roles in order to address broad concerns in their communities. The power of systemic change, and the results which transform the lives of students, make these efforts well worth it. The synergy created through these relationships can change the world for children.

## Teaming

Teaming is a more specific and time-limited process than is collaboration. Teaming focuses on bringing together school stakeholders to address one specific issue. A team will be formed in response to a defined problem in educational programs or services. The team will disband after solutions have identified, implemented, and evaluated.

Nicki Thomas, the previously mentioned elementary school counselor in a rural, high-needs school, formed a team to address the large number of impoverished students whose basic physical needs were going unmet. She organized a "Giving Tree" which marshaled the resources of community volunteers and school personnel to purchase and distribute gifts to families once a year. Another example of a teaming issue might be examination of why large numbers of ninth grade students are failing Algebra. Teaming is based on shared leadership responsibilities, common purpose, mission, and goals, and accountability of all members (DeVoss & Andrews, 2006). Teaming must also include careful attention to group processes within the team, efficiency of time management and effectiveness of the teaming efforts. Shared resources, shared responsibility, and shared accountability for outcomes are all hallmarks of the teaming process.

The types of data to examine in teaming are equivalent to the data utilized in the collaborative process: test scores; enrollment in advanced courses; graduation rates; attendance, G.P.A. and class ranks; discipline referrals; retention rates; special education referrals; and dropout rates. The teaming process looks at these issues as defining problems that can be solved. Collaboration takes a broader look at how the school system can be adapted to better meet the needs of all students.

It is important to keep in mind that change is not a linear process. It is quite common for successes to be followed by small setbacks, or by periods of stasis (Center for Applied Research and Educational Improvement, 2001). The team should remain committed to the final goal, and should remain flexible in terms of assessing results and disbanding. Follow up is essential to determining long-term viability of a solution, and of the change process. Final evaluation should take place after the end of the active problem-solving stages, and can include celebration, re-evaluation, and identification of subsequent steps for change. Lasting change is most often achieved when the change process is seen as a series of steps that include planning, acting, revising, planning, acting, and continuing until the desired results have been attained, measured, and shared.

## Potential Roadblocks to Teaming and Collaboration

Teaming and collaboration are not inherently integrated into the cultures of most schools. Some of the roadblocks can appear at least daunting, and perhaps even prohibitive. Typical barriers include the physical isolation inherent in the structure of schools, school cultures of independence and autonomy or self-reliance, and the lack of resources such as time, space, and materials.

American schools are structured in such a way that personnel generally work in their own rooms, with their distinct schedules for the day, and with their own groups of students. It is quite possible for teachers in most schools to get through the day with minimal interaction with peers. Teachers value autonomy, but that very autonomy often ensures that they remain focused on their students, their lesson plans, and their observable student outcomes. Asking advice or sharing concerns can be seen as admissions of failure. Giving teachers and other staff members opportunities for meaningful interaction around how their daily practice is serving students can be an extremely motivational intervention. The sense of support and common purpose is very empowering.

Beyond the cultural deterrents to teaming and collaboration are the practical issues around resources (Northwest Regional Educational Laboratory, 2005). Time, especially, is an extremely valuable and scarce resource in our schools. Common periods during the day when school personnel might have flexible time for meetings can be very difficult to identify. With work loads often approaching the overwhelming mark for teachers and other staff members, it is difficult to identify times to meet, and difficult for personnel to give up preparation and planning time. Creativity is often required in scheduling team meetings, and might include times before or after school, common lunch or planning periods, or time during professional development experiences or faculty meetings. School leaders have to value collaboration and to believe in the power of teaming in their communities. The support of building administrators is essential in creating pockets of time where staff, parents, and community members might gather. While difficult, this is not impossible. In other countries, notably in many European and Asian countries, school schedules are arranged so that up to 10 hours a week is available for teachers to plan together, observe each other's practice, and work on common issues of assessment and student outcomes (Northwest Regional Educational Laboratory, 2005). The very issue of common planning time is an example of a potential collaborative systemic intervention in many schools.

Barriers to teaming and collaborating in our schools should be identified and considered in every planning process. The barriers, cultural and practical, differ from school to school. Any plan that does not include careful consideration of these roadblocks is destined to fail. These problems are not insurmountable however, and the results in terms of student achievement and community building justify the efforts. There must be a recognized need to motivate the collaboration, a commitment of the time and energy to develop relationships, clearly defined common goals, and supportive key players such as administrators in order for these approaches to succeed (Stone & Dahir, 2006). School counselors who serve as leaders in their schools and advocates for the success of students, however, will find that collaboration and teaming are essential tools for creating schools where all students can thrive.

# Steps for Teaming and Collaborating

## Problem Identification

Problem identification is the heart of teaming. Adequate time and attention must be given to this process if team members are going to share a common goal, language, and commitment to participation. It is imperative that the problem be described in terms of outcomes for students: what are they not receiving, learning, applying, or achieving? The problem should be delineated through the use of data. This makes the problem concrete and also generates more support for action from stakeholders. During the problem identification process, an examination of possible contributing factors adds clarity and helps point the way for the future action plan. These contributing factors also allow for consideration of both the benefits and the potential costs of bringing about change. Who will be better off, and who might not be, if your team addresses the problem?

## Identify and Recruit Team Members

It is important to Identify teaming partners next. They should be a mirror of your community in terms of representing diverse constituencies. Ideally, teachers, parents, students, and community members should all be brought to the table. It is also advisable to include diverse opinions on the problem: those who are eager to see change and those who might not be convinced of the need. This provides an opportunity to understand and plan for resistance as well as to persuade those in opposition that the plan is important.

While time and space are often difficult factors, a little creativity goes a long way. Requesting information on preferred times and availability when first contacting potential team members can save a great deal of time later. It might be necessary to look for additional members if one or two have demanding schedules rather than wait weeks to get everyone together. However, always make sure that people who can't participate this time know that they will be invited to join in future projects. It is also important that you have a time line before requesting participation of potential team members. Asking busy individuals to commit to three meetings with one possible follow up gathering is much more likely to achieve success than an open-ended or vague invitation to participate.

The time and space for meeting might require creativity and flexibility. It could be before or after school on campus, or it might be an evening meeting in the library, coffee shop, or a private home. Confidentiality must be considered if a meeting takes place in a public venue. These factors can make or break a team and it is essential that participants feel that their time is being respected and that their needs are being considered in the planning process.

## Objectives and Action Plan

The objective defined should be based on data—how will you know that things are different for students in your school? The statement of objectives or desired results should be clear, observable and measurable. It might be necessary in the early stages of teaming to collect additional data or disaggregate data differently based on the team's requests and needs. This remains essential in defining and supporting the change process.

The action plan should have well-delineated responsibilities and steps. It is important to maintain a focus on shared responsibility among team members for objectives, action and results (Rhode Island School Counselor Association, 2005). The creation of a time frame is also vital at this point. A teaming effort must have an end date with the possibility of revision and additional action steps if the objective has not been met. The design of the action plan must include consideration of possible sources of resistance and plans for circumventing that resistance. What are potential stumbling blocks and how will team members react when they are encountered?

All members should play a role in implementation whether it is an active role or a support or advisory function. If a team is to be effective, all must share the work and the rewards, just as all must believe that the outcome will be worth the effort. The team should reassemble after implementation to share results and outcomes, revise the action plan and set a new timetable for implementation if needed, and to decide how to publicize the results. The celebration of positive change is all too often overlooked once the results have been achieved. It is important for the school community should be informed of the progress. This creates a climate where solutions can be generated collaboratively and additional members of the community can be made aware of opportunities for teaming and problem solving.

It is clear that in the new millennium, the world is a very different place. It is also clear that schools reflect an increasingly diverse and complex society and that the degree of societal change is happening at an ever increasing pace. School counselors as collaborative and teaming specialists are in a pivotal position as catalysts for important and positive changes for our students; changes that include access and opportunities for a bright future for students and for our society.

## Figure 25.1
## Planning your Team

### Participants

| Who | What<br>(Role or Title) | Why<br>(Contributions) | Outcome<br>(Desired Results) | Contact<br>Information |
|---|---|---|---|---|
|  |  |  |  |  |
|  |  |  |  |  |
|  |  |  |  |  |
|  |  |  |  |  |
|  |  |  |  |  |
|  |  |  |  |  |

## Figure 25.2
## Action Plan

| Objective: |
|---|
| Data Utilized: |

| Action Steps | Begin Date | End Date | Person<br>Responsible | Resources<br>Needed |
|---|---|---|---|---|
|  |  |  |  |  |
|  |  |  |  |  |
|  |  |  |  |  |
|  |  |  |  |  |

# References

American School Counselor Association. (2005). *The ASCA national model: A framework for school counseling programs*. Alexandria, VA: Author.

Campbell, C.A., & Dahir, C.A. (1997). *Sharing the vision: National standards for school counseling programs*. Alexandria, VA: Author.

Center for Applied Research and Educational Improvement, Technical Report 01-6(2001). *Partnerships as a vehicle for change*. University of Minnesota, MN: Author. Retrieved October 31, 2005 from http://education.umn.edu/CAREI/Reports/

Center for Applied Research and Educational Improvement, Technical Report 02-3(2002). *Implementing a vision for change in schools: Creating a cadre of advocates for student success*. University of Minnesota, MN: Author. Retrieved October 31, 2005 from http://education.umn.edu/CAREI/Reports/

Dahir, C.A., Sheldon, C.B., & Valiga, M.J. (1998). *Vision into action: Implementing the national standards for school counseling programs*. Alexandria, VA: American School Counselor Association.

Dahir, C.A., & Stone, C.B. (2003). Accountability: A M.E.A.S.U.R.E. of the impact school counselors have on student achievement. *Professional School Counseling, 6,* 214-22.

DeVoss, J.A., & Andrews, M.F. (2006). *School counselors as educational leaders*. New York: Lahaska Press/Houghton Mifflin.

Education Trust, The. (1997). *The national guidance and counseling reform program*. Washington, DC: Author.

Eschenauer, R., & Chen-Hayes, S.F. (2005). The transformative individual school counseling model: An accountability model for urban school counselors. *Professional School Counselor, 8,* 244-48.

House, R.M., & Sears, S.J. (2002). Preparing school counselors to be leaders and advocates: A critical need in the new millennium. *Theory into Practice, 41,* 154-62.

House, R.M., & Hayes, R.L. (2002). School counselors: Becoming key players in school reform. *Professional School Counselor, 5,* 249-56.

Martin, P.J. (2002). Transforming school counseling: A national perspective. *Theory into Practice, 41,* 148-53.

Musheno S., & Talbert, M. (2002). The transformed school counselor in action. *Theory into Practice, 41, 186-91.*

Myrick, R.D. (2003). *Developmental guidance and counseling: A practical approach* (4th ed.). Minneapolis, MN: Educational Media.

National Center for Transforming School Counseling, The Education Trust (June 2003). Retrieved November 11, 2005 from http://www2.edtrust.org/edtrust/Transforming+School+Counseling/counseling+background

National Center for Transforming School Counseling, The Education Trust (June 2003). Retrieved November 11, 2005 from http://www2.edtrust.org/edtrust/Transforming+School+Counseling/mission+statement

Northwest Regional Educational Laboratory. (2005). Exorcising the "Lone Ranger." *Northwest Education, 11,* 6.

Perusse, R., Goodenough, G.E., Donegan, J., & Jones, C. (2004). Perceptions of school counselors and school principals about the national standards for school counseling programs and the transforming school counseling initiative. *Professional School Counseling, 7,* 152-61.

Rhode Island School Counselor Association. (2005). Retrieved November 10, 2005 from www.rischoolcounselor.org

Stone, C.B., & Dahir, C.A. (2006). *The transformed school counselor.* New York, NY: Lahaska Press/Houghton Mifflin.

# Chapter 26

# Teaching Children to Respect and Care for Others: A Character Education Program to Support Academic Achievement

**by Mary Ann Clark and Joe Wittmer**

*This chapter briefly describes the rationale and implementation of a Character Education program developed by the authors in Wittmer, J. & Clark, M.A. (2002), Teaching children to respect and care for others, and Wittmer, J. & Clark, M.A. (2002), Teaching children to respect and care for others: The instructor's guide.*

Since the inception of *A Nation at Risk* (1983), there has been heated debate concerning the goals and outcomes of American public education. Reform initiatives have taken place in almost every school and community, yet there continues to be a debate about what is working and what is not. The *No Child Left Behind Act* (2001), although controversial, has redefined the federal role in K-12 education and is designed to help close the achievement gap between disadvantaged and minority students and their peers.

Statistics concerning at risk youth, increasing violence and criminal activity, and an increasing gap between the "haves and have nots" have become important political and economic issues with regard to the educational well being of our country. Furthermore, there has been an increase in the diversity of students in our schools with regard to race, ethnicity, and socioeconomic status. Much pressure has been placed on students and educators at all levels to raise academic standards, both with regard to achievement test scores as well as increased credit and more rigorous coursework requirements for graduation from high school (Quaglia, 2000).

Experts agree that establishing meaningful connections between teachers and the students in their classrooms, as well as among the students themselves, is essential for the mission of education to be successful. Many educators assert that too much instructional time is taken up with classroom management issues including the lack of positive communication between teacher and student(s) (Dodd, 2000). They are recognizing that when schools attend to students' social and emotional skills, the academic achievement of children increases, the incidence of problem behaviors decreases, and the quality of the relationships surrounding each child improves (Cummings & Haggerty, 1997; Elias, Zins, Weissberg, Frey, Greenberg, Haynes, Kessler, Schwab-Stone, & Shriver, 1997). An increasing research base suggests that teachers' relationships with students contribute to their social and cognitive development through instilling motivation to learn, addressing their need to belong, and by serving a regulatory function for the development of emotional, behavioral, and academic skills (Davis, Davis & Smith, 2003).

A school's climate can be a positive influence on or a significant barrier to learning and achievement for students, and includes the quality of interactions among students and adults and the level of safety, respect and comfort they feel (Pasi, 2001). One of the most important aspects of a positive school climate is its daily emphasis on respect, specifically as modeled by adults to students (Wittmer & Clark, 2002a). Many schools do include a character education component in their curricula, and many more are looking for effective programs to enhance learning and achievement.

A caring, respectful classroom environment can provide an atmosphere more conducive to, and encouraging of, learning and achievement (Dodd, 2000; Elias, Bruene, Butler, Blum, & Schuyler, 1997; Zins, Bloodworth, Weissberg, & Walberg, 2004). A cooperative environment can have substantial effects on the cooperative behavior of the students, increasing feelings of empathy for others, reducing intergroup tensions and antisocial behavior, improving moral judgment, and building positive feelings toward others including those of other ethnic groups (Zins et al., 2004). A positive climate affects student achievement and fosters problem-solving skills (Cohen, 1999; Pasi, 2001). Students and educators in a school with a positive school climate take pride in identifying and solving problems (Payne, Conroy & Racine, 1998). By creating nurturing environments, teachers encourage children to want to come to school, thus improving attendance and motivation to learn (Glasser, 1997; Kohn, 1996). Research findings have indicated that the affective climate of the classroom can predict social as well as academic outcomes including empathy (Battistch, Solomon, Watson, & Schaps, 1997), help-seeking, (Ryan & Pintrich, 2001) and intrinsic motivation for school and reading comprehension (Battistch et al., 1997). The perception of teacher support and school belonging predicted increased academic self-efficacy, positive school affect, and academic achievement (Roeser, Midgley, & Urdan, 1996).

## Emotional Intelligence

The concept of emotional intelligence is an important one. As educators, many of us know students who have possessed high intelligence and academic skills, but who have had social and emotional problems that have kept them from achieving their potential. On the other hand, we can each think of instances where students may have had average academic skills and abilities, but were successful in getting along with others and in pursuing educational and career goals. In fact, the vast majority of people who lose their jobs do so because they can not get along with the other people with whom they work, rather than lacking the skills to do the job. Goleman (1998) cites numerous studies that point to the importance of the five emotional intelligence areas; self-awareness, self-regulation, motivation, empathy, and social skills. He writes that it is the hidden ingredient in star performance in leadership as well as every level of an organization, and that emotional intelligence is multiplicative rather than additive to cognitive ability.

These concepts certainly apply to young students as they develop their academic and social repertoire of skills. Emotional awareness, in which people can recognize and link their feelings with behavior and performance as well as their values and goals, is a major competency. Additionally, having "people" skills and being able to collaborate, is especially important in today's changing world (Goleman, 1998). With increased globalization and diversity of populations, learning to respect and embrace differences as well as commonalities has become an essential nuance of emotional intelligence and effective functioning in society. Such skills can be taught and modeled in a character education program. These programs have been recognized as being an essential part of many school curricula and indeed, are mandated by some states.

## Changing Times

With major worldwide changes regarding work, gender roles, family structure, and cultural diversity, many traditional functions in the upbringing of children have been increasingly transferred to schools, transforming the role of educators. Furthermore, the growth of the media, marketing, and the internet have expanded the worldwide exposure of children to outside influences resulting in parents sharing their role in the character formation of their children with factors which give them less control (Elkind, 2001). Research and common sense tell us that the influence of caring adults who are positive role models is a major factor in children's healthy development and academic success.

## Creating Relationships

The Carnegie Commission has strongly urged school administrators at all levels, but particularly at the elementary level, to develop comprehensive programs focusing on teaching students the communication and other pro-social skills necessary to get along with others successfully. When these skills are in place, there tend to be fewer discipline problems and the classroom/school climate is more conducive to higher academic achievement and lower drop out rates. Creating a classroom climate of respect and collaboration where everyone has a responsibility to learn and help others learn is essential (Dodd, 2000; Pasi, 2001). "Raising Healthy Children", a social and emotional learning project, found that students become better mood managers when they learn concrete ways to handle their emotions and can increase their repertoire of appropriate responses until such responses become almost automatic (Cummings & Haggerty, 1997).

Making "deposits" into an "account" that are the basis of relationships, such as understanding, kindness, courtesy, clarification, and feedback are the first step to creating relationships with students and adults as well as in student to student relationships (Clark, 2005; Covey, 1989, Covey, 1998, Myrick, 2003; Payne, 1998).

## School Climate

The issue of positive school culture or climate has received substantial attention as an identified attribute of "effective" schools. Research reveals that certain internal conditions are typical in schools that have higher student achievement levels. These differences in outcomes appear to be systematically related to variations in the schools' climate, culture or ethos and their "quality" as social systems. Positive school climate has been linked to learning, and there is an increasing amount of research on the impact of classroom climate on academic achievement (Zins et al., 2004).

The school counselor, serving as a consultant and collaborator with teachers, can be in a pivotal position to teach and model communication skills to both teachers and their students. Both counselors and teachers can teach and model for children how to convey caring and respect for one another in the classroom. Going a step further, counselors and counselor educators can conduct training in these skills for classroom teachers so that communication skills will become a natural part of the teaching repertoire. Such skills taught in a proactive, organized program that is part of the daily curriculum can generalize to students' everyday lives resulting in more positive interactions with others (Wittmer & Clark, 2002a).

## Teaching Children to Respect and Care for Others: The Lessons

This chapter describes a training program (Wittmer & Clark, 2002ab) in which school counselors can train teachers and interns to model and teach basic social communication skills in their classrooms to their students. By being student-centered as they work with children, teachers and school counselors can create a caring classroom environment which is conducive to academic achievement and positive social interaction.

The purpose of the communications skills training is to provide a framework and accompanying activities for school counselors, teachers and interns to teach and model caring, empathy, respect and understanding of students with their peers in the classroom. To create and foster a caring climate in a classroom and in a school, both relationship and facilitative communication skills are necessary. Although these may come more naturally to some people than to others, they can be taught to and modeled for students.

The relationship skills include caring, acceptance, respect, empathy, trust, understanding, and helping. The facilitative communication skills, which are taught to teachers by the school counselors, and by teachers to their students, include teaching acceptance, attentive listening, asking appropriate questions, summarizing and simplifying what others have to say, following feelings, giving and receiving facilitative feedback, and responsible decision-making. A validation program is introduced, whereby students partner up weekly and publicly share positive and true attributes about their partner for the week, thus building cohesion. These skills are the means by which positive relationships can be initiated and nurtured.

Furthermore, specific communication skills that are taught, modeled, and practiced can be linked with corresponding relationship skills. For example, attentive listening can teach respect, following feelings can teach and model empathy, and summarizing/simplifying and asking appropriate questions can teach understanding and interest. Giving and receiving facilitative feedback can foster trust in one another, while responsible decision making can teach and model helping oneself and others. Put together, these related skills can create a caring and respectful classroom environment which can, in turn, provide an atmosphere that promotes learning and achievement (Wittmer & Clark, 2002ab).

The training takes place at a time convenient for the school staff, usually during planned in-service training time in nine 90 minute sessions. It is desirable to hold the training sessions on a weekly basis if possible so as to ensure continuity and to build cohesion and commitment among the staff being trained. The format for the classroom implementation of the program after training has been completed involves several components that take place during each school week.

## Structure of the Program

Wednesday C.A.R.E. (Caring, Acceptance, Respect and Empathy) time

This session is held for 20-30 minutes a week and is a structured classroom activity with the purpose of teaching and modeling the communication skills mentioned earlier. Each week will have a specific focus. C.A.R.E. time is the heart of the program and is devoted to actual instruction of the specific skills that are designated to be taught each week. The day of the week can be adjusted to meet the needs of the individual school.

## Monday Morning Circle of Caring and Sharing

The teacher holds this session in the classroom each Monday morning for 10-15 minutes. It is a structured session, in which students are invited to engage in a sharing go-around to talk about something important to them that happened the previous week. This is a time when teachers and their students can practice and apply the techniques, facilitative responses and special activities that they have learned in the lesson presented the previous week.

One way to get the circle started in the beginning is to ask such questions as: "Tell us about the pet(s) you have or someone you know has." "We'd like to hear about your favorite ____". Or, "Tell us about something exciting that happened on the way to school one day this week." Go-arounds are conducted but a ground rule is that students can pass if they wish. They may be given another opportunity to respond at a later time but are not pressured to do so. Building trust and cohesion is one of the goals of the Monday Morning Circle of Sharing and Caring time. Holding this session early in the week can reinforce skills that have been learned previously and can start the week on a positive note.

## Weekly Student Meeters and Greeters Program

Each classroom will appoint two meeters and greeters for the week. They arrive ten minutes early each morning and are to meet and address each student by name along with a smile and a handshake as they enter the classroom. All students will have the opportunity during the school year to serve as meeters and greeters.

## Weekly Theme

A theme for the week is presented at the end of each C.A.R.E. lesson and teachers are encouraged to reinforce the theme by placing displays on bulletin boards, using signs or posters, and asking students to share examples of how they have practiced the theme during the week.

## Every Friday Validation (EFV)

EFV is a designated time in which each student is paired with another child on a weekly basis for the purpose of getting to know one another individually and to learn to appreciate and acknowledge the attributes each possess. Each pair validates each other in front of the class by saying something specifically positive and true about the other having had the week to think about it and plan a written validation to present. Each student will eventually be paired up with every other student in the class to validate one another.

## The Training Sessions: Teaching the Skills to Teachers

A series of nine sessions is optimal for training teachers to implement the communications skills program in an elementary school. These sessions are devoted to specific skills as well as to group discussions and practice. Each subsequent session begins with a brief review of the previous lesson with an opportunity for teachers to give feedback about its implementation (Wittmer & Clark, 2002b).

### Lesson one: Interpersonal Relationships within the Classroom

The first training session consists of introductions and an explanation of the program, its purpose, and goals. The importance of teaching and modeling interpersonal relationships in the classroom is emphasized and the components of the program introduced and described with examples. The concept of teachers as classroom facilitators who find effective ways to use themselves, their talents, and their surroundings to assist students in their personal, social and academic development is emphasized. The significance of the teacher-student relationship in learning and in character development is stressed.

### Lesson Two: Validation

This lesson introduces the concept of Validation, a partnership program whereby students find the good in one another and have the opportunity to reach out to one another in caring, sincere, respectful ways. Thus, each week, students honor one another in front of the class by sharing a written validation that they have prepared during the week which reflects positive and true things about their partners. This plan is an evolving, optimistic reinforcement for student growth and kindness. Each child is paired with another for a week for the purpose of getting to know each other individually and to learn to appreciate and acknowledge the positive attributes that each possesses. Verbalizing these discoveries in front of their classmates at the end of the week is powerful for the student sharing the feedback and for the recipient as well as the rest of the class who is listening. Be the end of the term, all students will have had the opportunity to be paired with the other students in the class. The teacher participates in the validation process as well.

### Lession Three: Teaching Acceptance through Classroom Connections

This lesson helps teachers and interns focus on two basic responses with students that can help in leading classroom discussions. The "connecting" response involves the building of class cohesion by linking students' cognitive as well as affective responses through teacher observations and comments. Connecting statements accentuate relationships among students by pairing information, similarities and differences. Finding similarities among students, especially if they differ from one another by race, gender, or other characteristics can help with bonding in the classroom so that caring, compassion, and respect become the norm. Simple acknowledging is a second response that involves giving closure to a student's statement or idea by recognizing and affirming a contribution to a discussion. For example, "Thank you for sharing" acknowledges a student's idea and also allows a teacher to move on to another student or a next step in a lesson.

### Lesson Four: Teaching Interest and Respect by Attentive Listening

Effective listening is an essential skill in today's world; and although it is recognized as being extremely important, it is not a skill that is usually taught. It is a skill that can be demonstrated and modeled as a part of the classroom repertoire. Most children want to be listened to, and many in today's world compete for attention among each other and the adults in their world. Being attended to and having an opportunity to talk about a matter that is important to us fulfills a basic human need; that we are important to someone and that we matter. Listening for interest and understanding will help build bonds between students and adults, and will facilitate the building of respect and caring. We can build up our "chips in the relationship bank account" (Covey, 1998; Myrick, 2003) meaning that more open patterns of communication are established.

The principles of good listening behaviors and learning to listen for feelings as well as to respond appropriately verbally as well as nonverbally are summarized and practiced in the training session. These skills can teach children to show respect and empathy for others.

### Lesson Five: Showing Interest in Others by Asking Appropriate Questions

In this lesson, the concept of asking "inviting" and "non-inviting" questions is introduced. The art and skill of questioning has often been thought of as a central part of the teaching process. However, asking questions can become a dominating part of a classroom, and specifically, questions that ask "why" can often put students on the defensive. Effective questions which invite a student to share thoughts, feelings and ideas are open-ended and start with what, how, when or where. These questions reveal interest in the student as a person and encourage students to further develop their responses. In contrast, a "non-inviting" or closed question may be one that just asks for a yes or no response or a shrug of the shoulders. The inviting questions show our interest in and respect for the student as a person and what is being said at the moment. This lesson introduces activities that can be used to help students identify and practice asking inviting questions. These skills can teach and model interest and in one another.

### Lesson Six: Teaching Understanding by Summarizing and Simplifying

Any response that is an attempt to acknowledge the content of what a person has said, or to identify the most significant ideas or themes can be termed a summarizing or simplifying response. This skill is an important one in developing academic skills as well as positive relationships within the classroom. Teachers can demonstrate to children how to use their own words to pick out the main ideas of what someone is saying. Being able to restate, reframe, or simplify what has been said can help focus a conversation. It is also a skill that students are asked to use often in reading comprehension as well as most other academic subjects. And, by helping students summarize what others are saying, we are teaching them another way to show their understanding of a situation or event which can contribute to a caring, respectful classroom environment. Being able to summarize and simplify issues requires attentive listening, a previously taught skill. Practice activities that model summarizing and simplifying can be introduced to a class and practiced in pairs or smaller groups.

## Lesson Seven: Teaching Empathy by Following Feelings

Research indicates that certain types of verbal responses tend to be perceived as empathic, caring, warm, respectful, and student-centered. Educators who use these kinds of responses have a higher probability of creating a classroom atmosphere that is more receptive to student interaction and learning. Using such responses shows interest in others and helps build cohesion, leading to a more caring, respectful school atmosphere. Empathic or "following feelings" responses involve identifying with a person's emotions and perceptions and showing intentional focus on the person who is talking, adult or child. Following feelings involves going beyond words to discover feelings and to acknowledge them. Making such a response is to capture the essence of what another person is feeling and to affirm those feelings. Although this process may seem to take time, it can also create an atmosphere in the classroom so that time is not wasted with disciplinary problems. Furthermore, empathy for others fosters critical and creative thinking and reasoning and can broaden one's perception and range of emotional experiences. Caring increases connection, reaching out, and altruistic behaviors. Goleman (1998) considers empathy to be the most socially desirable of personality traits. This training session helps teachers aid students in developing a feeling word vocabulary and in responding to the feelings of others. Activities are presented that invite students to recognize various nuances of feelings and to provide support for others.

## Lesson Eight: Teaching Students to Build Trust by Using Facilitative Feedback

Students of all ages are interested in knowing more about what others think and feel about them and where they stand with one another. They can learn a model for giving and receiving feedback which can help them think about their relationships and actions and give them a means by which they can organize their thoughts and verbal messages to others. In this lesson, students are taught a model of giving feedback that has three parts. The components of a feedback message include stating the other person's specific behavior that is to be addressed, telling how the person's behavior makes you feel, and what these feelings make you want to do. This approach helps students focus on a person's behavior rather than the person, avoiding name calling and criticism. Feedback messages can be complimentary or confrontive. The first, is a positive message, while the second may focus on a behavior that is not desirable. Students are taught that the timing of a feedback message is important and that it should be specific to be most effective. Activities are provided that can help students try out and become more comfortable with complimenting and confronting others.

## Lesson Nine: Caring about Consequences in Decision Making

As students mature, they are expected to become increasingly responsible for their educational and personal decisions. Decision making is an important life skill that will be used continually over the life span. Although the range of issues confronting children can be vast and vary in intensity, they can be taught a model that will help them organize their thoughts and feelings about decisions they may need to make. They can also use such a model to listen to and potentially help their peers to problem solve which shows concern for others and contributes to a more caring and respectful classroom and school.

It should be emphasized to students that not making a decision when one is called for can also have consequences. One way to help students think about outcomes is to discuss "rights and responsibilities." It seems that many students as well as adults in our society are concerned with their rights. Discussing the corresponding responsibilities and potential consequences of actions may help young people see that rights should be earned and are accompanied by responsibilities, to oneself and others.

Following is a five step guide that can be taught to students and can be used as a model in the classroom for problem solving and decision making.

1. What is the problem (or concern or situation)?
2. What have you tried so far in attempting to solve the problem?
3. What would you like to have happen?
4. What other possibilities could you try?
5. What is your next step?

It is important in step five to have students commit to a tangible plan with a time frame in mind. And, when students use this decision making model, they can be encouraged to include the other skills they have learned previously, such as summarizing and simplifying, and following feelings.

# Conclusion

The social skills of emotional intelligence are becoming increasingly recognized as essential competencies in today's complex world and can be taught and practiced in a character education program such as the one described in this chapter. Establishing bonds and connections among teachers and their students in the classroom is an important step to helping students develop the repertoire of skills they need to be successful in their academic lives as well as to develop into good citizens who care about others and the world outside their individual domains. Understanding and respecting oneself and others is the key to embracing diversity and differences and ultimately to a more satisfying and productive life, individually and collectively. These attributes enhance the quality of life for individuals as well as for families, communities, and institutions. Teaching these social skills to young students and modeling them in the classroom can build important human connections and provide life long skills that will create more interpersonal and external harmony in the world.

# References

Battistich, V., Solomon, D., Watson, M., & Schaps, E. (1997). Caring school communities. *Educational Psychologist, 32,* 137-151.

Clark, M.A. (2003). Training school interns to teach elementary students to respect and care for others. *The Journal of Humanistic Counseling, Education and Development, (42),* 91-106.

Clark, M.A. (2005). Building connections, communication, and character in classrooms. *ASCA School Counselor. 42*(3), 8-13.

Cohen, J. (Ed.). (1999). *Educating minds and hearts: Social emotional learning and the passage into adolescence.* New York: Teachers College Press.

Covey, S. (1998). *The seven habits of highly effective teens.* New York: Simon and Schuster.

Covey, S. R. (1989). *The seven habits of highly effective people: Powerful lessons in personal change.* New York: Simon and Schuster.

Cummings, C., & Haverty, K.P. (1997). Raising healthy children. *Educational Leadership, 54* (8), 28-31.

Davis, H., Davis, S., & Smith, T. (April, 2003). Middle school students' perceptions of classroom climate: The role of perceived organization and rule clarity in predicting relationship quality, motivation, and achievement. Paper presented as part of a Symposium on School Atmosphere, Motivation and Achievement at the Biennial meeting of the *Society for Research in Child Development,* Tampa, Florida.

Dodd, A. (2000). Making schools safe for all students: Why schools need to teach more than the 3 R's. *NASSP Bulletin, 84,* 614, 25-31.

Elias, M., Bruene-Butler, L., Blum, L., & Schuyler, T. (1997). How to launch a social and emotional learning program. *Educational Leadership, 54,* (8), 15-20.

Elias, M., Zins, J., Weissberg, P., Frey, K., Greenberg, M., Haynes, N., Kessler, R., Schwab-Stone, M., & Shriver, T. (1997). *Promoting social and emotional learning: Guidelines for educators.* Alexandria, VA: Association for Supervision and Curriculum Development.

Elkind, D. (2001). The cosmopolitan school. *Educational Leadership,* 12-17.

Glasser, W. (1997). A new look at school failure and school success. *Phi Delta Kappan, 78,* 597-602.

Goleman, D. (1998). *Working with emotional intelligence.* New York: Bantam Books.

Kohn, A. (1996). What to look for in a classroom. *Educational Leadership, 54,* 54-55.

Myrick, R.D. (2003). *Developmental guidance and counseling: A practical approach* (4th ed). Minneapolis, MN: Educational Media Corporation.

National Commission on Excellence in Education. (1983). *A nation at risk: The imperative of educational reform.* Washington, DC: U.S. Government Printing Office.

No child left behind act of 2001 (H.R. 1). Retrieved July 6, 2006, from http://www.ed.gov/nclb/.

Pasi, R.J. (2001). A climate for achievement. *Principal Leadership, 2,* (4), 17-20.

Payne, R. (1998). *Poverty: A framework for understanding and working with students and adults from poverty.* Baytown, TX: RFT Publishing.

Payne, M.J., Conroy, S., & Racine, L. (1998). Creating positive school climates. *Middle School Journal, 30,* (2), 65-67.

Quaglia, R.J. (2000). Making an impact on student aspirations: A positive approach to school violence. *NASSP Bulletin, 84,* 614, 56-60.

Roeser, R.W., Midgley, C., & Urdan, T.C. (1996). Perceptions of school psychological environment and early adolescents' psychological and behavioral functioning in school: The mediating role of goals and belonging. *Journal of Educational Psychology, 88,* 408-422.

Ryan, A.M., & Patrick, H. (2001). The classroom social environment and changes in adolescents' motivation and engagement during middle school. *American Educational Research Journal, 28,* 460.

Wittmer, J., & Clark, M.A. (2002a). *Teaching children to respect and care for others.* Minneapolis, MN: Educational Media Corporation.

Wittmer, J., & Clark, M.A. (2002b). *Teaching children to respect and care for others. Instructor's guide.* Minneapolis, MN: Educational Media Corporation.

Zins, J.E., Bloodworth, M.R., Weissberg, R.P., & Walberg, H.J. (2004). The scientific base linking social and emotional learning to school success. In *Building academic success on social and emotional learning: What does the research say?* New York: Teacher's College, Columbia University.

# Chapter 27

# Reaching Out:
# Involving Parents and Community Members in the School Counseling Program

**by Nancy S. Perry**

---

*Nancy S. Perry, M.S., NCC, NCSC, is the retired Executive Director of the American School Counselor Association, Alexandria, Virgina. She has been a teacher, counselor, and state supervisor of guidance.*

## Introduction

School counselors serve a unique position in the education of our young people in that they are charged with serving both the individual student and the environment in which they function. That means, to be truly effective, counselors must reach beyond the school milieu to the families and community which shape the lives of children. Children, especially in their formative years, live within the powerful force of family and community influence. The child and his or her environment are interconnected. The effective school counselor realizes that he or she must understand the *entire* system if the whole child is to be best served. Since developmental school counselors are dedicated to the development of the whole child, they must reach beyond the walls of the school building and actively involve and interact with the families and community.

In this chapter, interactions with parents and families are addressed, and strategies to effectively involve the parents and community in the comprehensive, developmental school counseling program are suggested.

## Involving Parents and Families

Without a doubt, parents are the strongest influence in a child's life. Researchers report that parental involvement in a child's education transmits the importance of education to the child, thus enhancing self-esteem and academic achievement. Therefore, it is imperative that parents be actively involved in the school in positive ways which will help them better understand the schooling process.

Every educator knows that the parents most actively involved in their children's education are those whose children are most actively involved in the educational process. Open Houses at school always bring out the parents whose children are doing well. These parents eagerly attend parent-teacher conferences, lead the parent/teacher groups, and volunteer to assist in many ways. This group of parents needs to be nurtured and provided with opportunities to show their support and to extend in-school learning at home. These parents thrive on outside speakers, literature on child development, and information about their children's in-school activities. It is especially important that school counselors explain the guidance curriculum to them in detail as most parents have not experienced such a program themselves. Unfortunately, in many schools parents are not actively involved in their child's education. Ideas for involving the "resistant" parent are provided later in this chapter.

## Orientation to the School Counseling Program

The one common characteristic of past school counseling programs has been the inconsistency from one school to the next. Every parent in your school may have had a different guidance experience. In 2003, The American School Counselor Association (ASCA) took a huge stride forward in publishing *The ASCA National Model: A Framework for School Counseling Programs.* This model professionalized school counseling and ensured greater consistency in delivery of services across the nation. Adherence to this model assures parents (and the school community) that your program is backed by research and experience. However, most parents, used to the constellation of services model, will not be familiar with the program approach to school counseling. Therefore, it is important that an orientation to the school counseling program be offered for parents whose children are new to the school. Such a program should include a rationale, objectives, and strategies for involving parents in the program. For example, at the orientation, parents may be requested to complete a short questionnaire to help the counselor in understanding the concerns parents may have with their children about the guidance program. Using the results of this needs assessment, the counselor may decide to form parent support groups around certain issues; invite experts to address major issues listed; provide reading lists or other resources on those issues; or take the issues to the Guidance Program Advisory Council to determine how the needs expressed by the parents can best be met. It is important to have materials used in the guidance curriculum available for parental review at all times. Invite participation and involvement in the program. Most complaints concerning the guidance curriculum come from lack of understanding or information on the part of the parents. Use the opportunity of an orientation meeting with new students' parents to open new avenues of communication.

## Guidance Curriculum

Most parents have never experienced affective education. In fact, many may even be concerned about the word "affective." Consider your use of words carefully as unfamiliarity of their usage may trigger negative reactions. Even such terms as "Magic Circle" can bring out fears of voodoo or brain-washing. Some counselors have used terms such as "Learning for Life," or "Responsibility Curriculum" to describe their classroom efforts. These labels seem to be better understood by parents. It is important that parents be aware of each guidance unit, especially at the elementary level. A rule of thumb might be that the younger the child, the more parents need to be involved and informed. Do not assume that just because a program has been in place for five years that it will automatically be accepted. Keep in mind that a school's parental audience is constantly changing.

Parents can be valuable assets to a developmental guidance curriculum, especially when counselors "empower" them to extend the lessons into the home. For example, if one is teaching primary age children about the world of work, together, children and their parents might list the jobs in their home—cooking, cleaning, nurturing, and so forth—and who the particular workers are in the home performing these tasks. The activity will help children develop an appreciation of their home, an understanding of responsibility, and possibly an appreciation of gender equity issues. When teaching effective communication skills to early adolescents, ask for the cooperation of the parents in practicing the skills at home. Invite the parents to a session where they, too, can learn what their children are learning in large group guidance. Parental inclusion or involvement may produce benefits well be-

yond the teaching of a skill. For example, as eighth graders are beginning to think about educational decisions and careers, have them interview a parent about his or her career pathway from the earliest job up to the present one. Most children think that their parents are doing now what they have always done. In other words, look for opportunities to extend the learning at home in every guidance lesson taught. One middle school guidance department invites the parents of each eighth grader (written invitations) to sit in on an educational planning session regarding high school that a counselor plans to have with their child. This is a routine part of their guidance program and has come to be expected by the eighth graders and their parents alike.

## Barriers to Parental Involvement

As noted above, the parents most likely to attend school functions are those least likely to need to be there. They are the parents who demonstrate, in other ways, involvement in their child's education. The parents of the neediest children are often the most difficult to involve in the school. Do not assume that this means that they do not care. Most parents want their children to succeed. However, some parents find it extremely difficult to actually enter the school for many different reasons. It may be due to their own negative experiences in school, or perhaps they are fearful of doing the wrong thing or embarrassing their children. School events might not be scheduled at convenient times when these parents are available and have access to transportation to and from the school. The school building itself might be too intimidating. Plan meetings at places where your target parents feel comfortable – the library, church, community center, or even the grocery store. Most businesses have some kind of meeting room that they would be happy to use for school meetings, especially at off-hours. There may also be cultural or lifestyle barriers to involvement in school activities. If faced with particularly resistant parents, the best strategy may be to practice empathy at the basic level—the counselor puts him/herself into their shoes and acts accordingly!

Some parents are uneasy in large groups. Therefore, opportunities for small group or individual interaction may be the most successful alternative. As a former junior high counselor, I invited every parent of a seventh grader to come to school for coffee in a small group, not to exceed the size needed to accommodate the parents of eight children. I talked about adolescent development, what to expect, and how the school counseling program could help them and their children to master and survive those developmental tasks. I used this opportunity to become acquainted with the parents, to help them know me, and to hear their concerns. It opened communication pathways that still exist sixteen years later as some now call me about their grandchildren! It also garnered the support needed for a comprehensive, developmental school counseling program.

Time spent with parents at this point will pay future dividends. Sending a letter of invitation home may not be enough. Offer a variety of times—morning, afternoon, and evening—to meet, create a comfortable environment, offer light refreshments—food is a wonderful socializer, and provide baby-sitting if at all possible. The writer paid junior high aged students to baby-sit their younger siblings at the school. Follow up the letters of invitation with phone calls when a response is not received. It is wise to state within the letter that the counselor will be calling if no response is given. Receiving such a letter from their child's school counselor *motivates* parents to respond. Be careful not to forget the non-custodial parent in families of divorce. Unless the courts have stated otherwise, both parents should have equal access to and participation in their child's education (see Remley, Chapter 31 ). Let the parents decide if they want to attend together or separately, but encourage both to be in attendance.

High school counselors may invite parents by class (freshman, sophomore, junior, senior) or by homeroom (depending on class size) to spend an evening using the career resources of the Guidance Office. Have several "stations," such as the computer, video, career books and brochures, and interest surveys set up for parent use. Parents are especially impressed by computerized career information systems and will encourage their children to use the resources if they understand them through their own personal use. Use any method available to get them "hooked" into the guidance program. Small group gatherings for parents provide the foundation for future involvement. And, this writer has found that most are simply waiting for an "invitation" to get involved—ask and they'll show up!

## Parenting Education

Many school counselors understand the importance of parenting education but feel overwhelmed at the thought of providing it. One of the most successful methods of offering parenting education is through the adult education program already offered within the school system. There are several excellent syllabi offered commercially or one may develop and construct his or her own program. Convince the school district to provide scholarships for parents unable to afford the small fee. It is especially important to encourage parents of "at-risk" children to attend as a way of working with the counselor and the school to help their child. A more subtle form of parenting education is forming support groups for parents of children who are involved in a counseling group in school. For example, if a target group of children has difficulty with conflict management, form a small group at school to teach conflict resolution skills and then ask their parents to form a group with the counselor to learn the same skills so that they may reinforce them at home. Many parents have difficulty with conflict at home and will welcome the opportunity to work on the issue. It may also give the child an opportunity to get positive attention at home.

Empowering the parents to help their child may be the most important role of a school counselor. And, any effort at parenting education should have the ultimate goal of *empowering* parents in their child-rearing roles. Thus, ample opportunity for open discussion and flexibility to meet emerging needs should be built into the program. Parenting education must be non-judgmental and built on enrichment of skills and growth rather than remediation for failures. It is not a time to "stamp out" their mistakes as parents. The needs of both the parent and the child need to be considered with the focus on the future. Parenting education, especially in families with young children, can truly make a difference in the child's life. It takes counselor time, but it is well worth the effort!

## Parent Volunteers

School counselors, like teachers, can often use a helping hand. Parental volunteers may offer on-going assistance or respond to a "one-shot" appearance. Besides the usual field trip chaperones and cookie making duties, counselors may use such volunteers in more creative ways within the guidance program. However, a word of caution is in order since much of what school counselors do is in the realm of confidential information. Particular care must be taken with who gains access to student records. The Family Education Rights and Privacy Act (FERPA) is very clear about who may view and have access to student records (see Remley, Chapter 31). It may be better not to give such responsibilities to volunteers. However, under any circumstances, parent volunteers should understand that "What's said here, stays here." As the school counselor, one has an obligation to protect the privacy of his or her students.

Parents are particularly helpful in career development activities. They may share their expertise or experiences with classes or help facilitate the use of computer-assisted career or college exploration and information giving activities. You may call on a parent for expertise in designing a computer program to fit your needs, or to provide job shadowing experiences for a student. Many working parents want to assist but cannot obligate themselves to regular volunteerism. Solicit information early in the school year about special skills or talents that parents are willing to share. Give away as much of your job as is ethically possible and responsible. You will always have more than you can handle. Work yourself out of a job when and where appropriate by utilizing parents and others in your developmental counseling program.

# Newsletters

Regular letters or notices to parents and the schools' community can build support for your school counseling program and bring about needed involvement in the program. With common access to the Internet now, it is so much easier to communicate with parents. Either post your messages on the school site or, with permission of participants, send your messages directly to the homes via e-mail. Using a database, messages can be customized for specific populations. At the high school level, a calendar of college and employer visits, important testing deadlines, and informative workshops can keep parents and community members informed. At the elementary level, information about guidance units in process will keep parents aware. However, the newsletter also offers opportunities to educate. Write articles about issues that concern parents such as "Signs of Substance Abuse," "Motivating the Underachiever," "Understanding the Shy Child," "Communicating With Your Teenager," and so forth. Share resources such as magazine articles or books that provide effective hints for everyday problems—bibliotherapy works with parents! Present child-raising issues and ask for strategies to handle them from the parent readers. For example, many parents are concerned about the TV-watching habits of their children. One creative mother said that she allowed her children to watch anything they wanted. However, they had to write a short review of every program watched. This certainly led to more discriminating viewing on the part of the children and simultaneously enhanced their writing skills.

The written word is a powerful tool and an inexpensive way to involve parents in your school guidance program. Know the type of parents whose children attend your school—poor, wealthy, culturally different, and so forth, and develop the guidance newsletter accordingly. If your school has a large Hispanic population, for example, ask for a parent volunteer to translate the newsletter into Spanish. This will acknowledge the diversity of the school's population, reveal that you value diversity, and help you to reach *all* parents.

# Advisory Council

As noted several times in this book, a Guidance Advisory Council is your official link to the needs and wishes of the community. This council usually consists of representatives of those populations which you serve. Typical membership might include teachers, administrators, special service providers (nurse, social worker, school psychologist, etc.), parents, community official, business/industry representatives, a law enforcement official, clergy, and a school board member. Middle and secondary levels may also want to include student members. The role of the Advisory Council is to make recommendations, in an advisory capacity, for guidance programming based on perceived student needs and available resources. Time and patience are required to educate the Advisory Council as to the purposes and scope of a comprehensive school counseling program, but the political support, public relations, and procurement of resources that may result from such widespread community support provide the incentives to make it work.

# School Board

You work for the School Board, School Committee, or whatever your governing body is within your specific school system. Ultimately, on the recommendations of administrators, they can make or break your program. Therefore, it is in your best interest to assure that they are well-informed and supportive of your school guidance program. Such communication should be on-going in the form of interesting newsletters delineating the activities of your program, minutes of Advisory Council meetings, and so forth. Keep administrators informed. However, most boards want hard data documenting that what counselors are doing is the best use of school time and available resources.

Accountability is important, both quantitative and qualitative. One strategy to deliver numbers is to keep a daily record of activities. This can be done easily by setting up a data-base on the computer and filling in the blanks at the end of each day. This might include the number of students seen in classroom guidance, small groups, individual counseling, peer advisors, consultation with parents, teachers, administrators, committee meetings, and so forth. At the end of a period, month or quarter, total the numbers and report them to your principal with copies to the superintendent and school board. Even you will probably be surprised at the number of student contacts you have made. Generally speaking, providing others in authority with such "head counts" pays off in the long run. However, we must also assure our public that we perform "quality" work through supplying the community with "hard," supportive data.

Qualitatively, one of the easiest and most effective strategies this writer has observed was by a practicing K-8 counselor who conducts classroom guidance at all grade levels. At the end of each guidance lesson, she asks the students to list three things they have learned that day and then she writes them on the board (and keeps them for later). Since this is done every time, even the five year olds know that they must listen to learn. This also allows the counselor time to reinforce any important learnings and to correct any misunderstandings. At the end of a unit, the counselor reports to the Board, and others via the newsletter, what the purpose of the unit was and what the children said they learned. It is very impressive to have the children's own words giving value to their learning experiences. These can also be shared with your principal, school board, and so forth.

School Board members often wonder aloud if the money spent to send educators to conferences or workshops is a good use of dwindling financial resources. Continuing professional development is important but counselors seldom convey that message to those who make the decisions. Therefore, it is important that counselors let them know what benefit they derive from participating in such activities. One sure-fire method is a simple thank-you note to the Board for allowing the counselor time and/or financial support to attend a conference. The counselor might include a reference to a session that was of particular value in helping him or her to be a better, more effective counselor. Let the Board know the professional impact this conference had and ultimately, its value to the students in the school. Another strategy is to write an article for the school/guidance newsletter, or do an in-service for others sharing one's newly acquired knowledge. These are tangible benefits to an employer and future insurance that one will be able to continue his or her professional development.

Arrange to periodically update the School Board on the counseling program with numbers, stories, and future needs. As an example, you might talk about the number of teenage pregnancies you have dealt with in the past quarter, the resolution of issues involved, and the trend toward increasing numbers. Then, when presenting a proposal for a new program to meet this need, they will be better prepared to listen and support your request. Their approval is your job guarantee.

## Community

Schools are generally community-based and community supported. People often make choices of where to live based on the reputation of schools. School budgets are the major topic of conversation every spring. Community members who do not have children in school are also often the most vocal and least informed. Therefore, it is important to let the public know what you are doing and why their support is valued. Service organizations such as the Kiwanis or Lion's Clubs, church fellowships, town councils, and others are usually eager to learn what is happening locally. Let them know you are available and plan to be on their program as a speaker at a time when you are *not* making a request for something. Then, when you do need their support, they will be more willing to listen. When provided the opportunity, talk about what the major issues facing young people today are and relate the issues to your school counseling program. *Don't be afraid to blow your own horn.* If you're doing good things, don't be modest about them. How else will they learn about your accomplishments?

Such groups can also be a resource when needed for special programs in your school. Mentoring is a meaningful way to involve community members in your program. Intergenerational bonds can be formed when children adopt a grandparent from a nursing home or vice versa. Contacts for job shadowing and career days can also be found in such organizations. Don't be afraid to ask, or assume that someone is too busy to help the children in your school. People want to be proud of their schools and their community. Give them the opportunity to get involved.

## School Counselors as Change Agents

It is generally accepted that school counselors serve as change agents for individual students, faculty and others. They work with students and others to bring about a desired or agreed upon outcome. This usually means some kind of behavior or performance change in the individual. Although school counselors interact with specific individuals to bring about internal change, they are also concerned with the environment in which their students operate. That environment may be defined as the collective perceptions of those who work and learn there. The environment can be described as good, poor, relaxed, restrictive, creative, or any variety of adjectives. A term often used to describe this set of perceptions is "school climate." Just as the system itself is affected by the external forces acting upon it, the members of the system—students, staff, parents community—are affected by what occurs around them in the internal environment. Counselors know that physical and psychological safety and comfort are important to the learning process. Therefore, the counselor's task to help students become better learners means that he or she must be as concerned with the school climate as with the other forces that impact on the individual. The motivation and behavior of students are directly related to the environment in which they operate. The question is not *whether* the school counselor should act as a change agent for the school climate, but *how* the school counselor can make a positive difference in the school's climate. Counselors serve as the "catalysts" for making school climates more conducive to learning.

Some counselors may feel that they are not in a power position to effect change in the school environment. However, as a school counselor, you are uniquely positioned to "see the big picture." You hear from students, parents, teachers, members of the community, and administrators, and, not being a part of the authority hierarchy, you are more likely to hear honest feelings and perceptions. And, the more favorably this population perceives the climate in which they interact, the easier your job will be to effect change in the individual. For example, if the school staff feel that they are treated as professionals, they will be more willing to take that extra step to accomplish the goals of the individual student or the school. If parents feel that the school staff really cares about the welfare of their children, they will be more open to listening and cooperating with recommendations made on behalf of their children. The same can be said regarding other members of the community. A positive and healthy school climate is the key for individual change and improvement.

In a counseling relationship, the counselor usually assesses the problem, determines the desired change or outcome with the client, and then works on strategies/interventions to effect the change. The same process is appropriate in effecting change in a system. The problem is identified, the desired outcome is determined and the strategies for effecting the change are considered. The principal difference for the school counselor is that the strategies may need to be delegated to those who have the *power* to make the change. For example, assigned seats in the junior high cafeteria during lunch may be an effective management technique but such a practice is depriving the emerging adolescents of one of the few opportunities to satisfy their need to socialize with friends of their choice. Therefore, as the human development specialist in the school, use your facilitative skills in bringing this concern to the attention of your principal.

Raising the awareness level of the administration and other staff as to the developmental needs of the students can be a valuable consideration in establishing a positive school climate. Effective counselors meet with the top administrator regularly to discuss climate issues and provide in-service for the staff on relevant topics affecting the school's climate (e.g., conducting a multicultural communication workshop). There are many other ways to effect change. One counselor, frustrated by the resistance of teachers in allowing students to participate in small group counseling, formed a support group for teachers. As the teachers recognized the value of the small growth group experience in their lives, they were more willing to support such involvement for their students. School counselors can be advocates for change by reaching out to parent groups, service clubs, and businesses, and seeking their support for programs that will enhance the overall learning environment. Of course, as noted earlier, a knowledgeable school board may be the strongest ally for supporting and initiating change in a school.

School counselors are change agents, individually and systemically. Their knowledge of human development and relationships can be invaluable in garnering the support of others to create the kind of school climate that nurtures learning.

## Summary

The current reform movements are centering more and more on the need to provide community services within the school and making the school the center of the community. The educational community is finally realizing that it cannot fragment a child's life by separating their physical, emotional/social, and cognitive development into small, convenient niches. As human development specialists, school counselors must reach out to "parents as partners." They must work together in the best interest of the child. School counselors need to involve parents, educators, and community members in their developmental guidance program if it is to be truly responsive to the needs of all students. Comprehensive, developmental school counseling programs lead the way for educational reform. It is up to the counselors to let others know what services they provide and how they positively affect students' growth and abilities to learn.

# Figure 27.1
# Tips for Parent Conferences

School counselors are frequently asked to participate in parent-teacher conferences. This list of helpful tips, which appeared in *The ASCA Counselor*, will enhance your work with parents.

**Do....**

- Arrange for an uninterrupted private session.
- Be as friendly and relaxed as possible.
- Explain that the child's behavior and school performance are the result of many variables.
- Describe the performance of students as precisely as possible.
- Emphasize the child's strengths and assets leading to realistic suggestions for improvements.
- Provide time to ask questions and encourage interruptions.
- Ask for parents' help and cooperation.
- Gain insights into parents' attitude toward child.
- Listen to what parents have to say without showing alarm, disgust, or disapproval.
- Encourage children to attend; Include them in the problem solving process.

**Don't....**

- Dwell on the inadequacies, such as intelligence, and so forth.
- Sit behind a desk.
- Answer questions in reference to administration or school policies unless you are absolutely accurate.
- Assume full responsibility for the child's education. Do stress the parents' role.
- Use misleading technical terms (parents will seldom ask for explanations).
- Discuss other teachers, students, or administration unless positive.
- Argue with parents.
- Criticize parents' effectiveness, even subtly.
- Assume parents want advice.
- Forget how you would feel as a parent. (Fox, R. *The ASCA Counselor*, ASCA, Alexandria, VA, December, 1991).

# Figure 27.2
# Food for Thought: PR for Parent Involvement

The following appeared in *The ASCA Counselor* (1992), and provided some excellent strategies for involving parents in school programs.

*The recent dramatic increase in parent involvement and citizen interest in Maine's public schools puzzled some folks. But the statewide grocery chain was not surprised because they had recently tucked one of the brightly colored brochures called "Your schools won't make the grade without YOU," into every shopper's grocery bag. The brochure, developed by the Maine State Board of Education, was full of ideas for all to get involved in the schools. More than 200,000 brochures made their way into Maine homes and response was immediately gratifying.*

*Counselors in several Maine schools have had offers from brochure-inspired volunteers to assist with their work and requests from business and civic leaders offering career awareness activities. The following points to parents were taken from the Maine brochure:*

**To Parents: Your Schools Won't Make the Grade Without You**

Get involved. If you believe that education is important, if you care about children, if you care about the future of Maine, get involved in your schools. You can make a difference.

## In Schools

- Volunteer as a classroom assistant, as a tutor, as a library aide; share a hobby or skill; show slides from a trip; serve as a resource for local history
- Be an audience for children
- Attend school events
- Get to know a teacher or administrator
- Be a mentor or a special friend to a child
- Attend parent conferences
- Request parenting classes and discussion groups

## At Home

- Show your children that you care about their education
- Provide books and a place for studying
- Make reading a family activity
- Establish high expectations for children
- Show an interest in your child's progress
- Discuss schoolwork with children
- Establish rules and let children know what they are
- Be consistent in discipline matters
- Monitor television time
- Observe routines for meals, bedtime, and homework
- Provide good nutrition and health care
- Continue your own education
- Learn about appropriate toys and activities for your child's age level
- Help children learn to make decisions
- Give children time to play
- Limit the number of hours your child can work in after school jobs

## At Work

- Invite a class to visit the workplace
- Share information about your occupation with students
- Develop company policy encouraging parents to attend school conferences and activities
- Release employees to volunteer in the schools
- Talk with educators about the curriculum needed for success in your job
- Give a child his or her first job
- Stay in touch with student employee needs
- Limit the number of hours students can work in after school jobs
- Be a mentor
- Donate toward scholarships, books, equipment, class trips
- Offer internships to teachers and students

## In the Community

- Join PTA/PTO or get one started
- Serve on an advisory council or a study committee
- Attend School Board meetings
- Run for the School Board
- Vote on school related issues
- Learn more about the schools in your town

## You Want to Help but You Don't Have Much Time

- Get your service club or organization to make supporting schools a priority
- Take a teacher to lunch
- Make a donation
- Write a thank you note to a teacher or school administrator
- Vote in federal, state, local elections

You can make a world of difference and a difference in our world by becoming actively involved in your schools. (Adapted from *The ASCA Counselor*, December, 1992).

# Section VII

# Accountability, Public Relations, Ethical and Legal Issues, Technology, and School Counselor Professionalism

Being accountable within the developmental counseling program has been a central theme throughout this book. In Chapter 28, Dr. John Schmidt advocates that school counselors *must* assume the leadership role in designing and conducting evaluation procedures as it concerns the counseling program. He writes: *As a school counselor, you have responsibility for evaluating your program, reporting the results, and suggesting changes to address the findings of the evaluation process. Without an accountability process, you run the risk of failing to address the needs and expectations of the students, parents, and teachers you serve. In doing so, you threaten the program's value and jeopardize your reputation as a significant and essential member of the school team. Comprehensive school counseling programs are essential to today's schools, and adequate program accountability and accurate counselor performance appraisal verify the importance of these services.*

Dr. Schmidt presents several easy to understand and use evaluation procedures, techniques, and processes that contribute to a counselor's ability to be accountable.

In Chapter 29, Dr. Harry Daniels and Mr. William Goodman, present a step-by-step process that school counselors can use to document their counseling services. They address the importance of documenting service delivery and provide examples of strategies for doing so. They stress the shift in emphasis as espoused by the ASCA National Model to using data to plan school counseling programs. By disaggregating data, counselors can pinpoint specific needs of groups of students, and can use the data to provide a rationale for interventions tailored to student needs.

Selling, promoting, and marketing the developmental counseling program is essential to its survival and a deliberate, planned public relations program is needed. In Chapter 30, we present such a structured PR approach along with the strategies and techniques to ensure the successful promotion of a K-12 counseling program. Several unique, "workable" PR ideas and concepts suggested by others are also presented at the end of the chapter.

Drs. Theodore Remley and Mary Hermann (Chapter 31) address the ethical and legal issues facing school counselors today. They indicate that professional counselors in all settings increasingly are finding the legal and ethical issues they face to be complex and challenging. Although problems related to the law and ethical standards may be difficult for counselors in various agencies, school counselors are regularly confronted with the most difficult issues on a daily basis, especially as they are working with minors and their parents.

Remley and Hermann state: *There are two basic reasons why school counselors have substantial problems addressing legal and ethical issues. First, K-12 school counselors offer services most often to minors and the law and professional ethical standards are inadequate regarding a practical resolution of the competing interests of children and the adults who are responsible for their welfare. In addition, despite the fact that dual relationships are prohibited in counseling, counselors in schools have multiple roles and interact with a variety of individuals who demand their professional services.*

They provide some excellent guidelines for the school counselor facing an ethical or legal problem.

In the next chapter, Dr. Tom Clawson, Susan Eubanks, and Kristi McCaskill, in writing about the school counselor and the importance of appropriate credentialing, state: *As the profession continues to evolve, counselors must demonstrate to the public that they recognize the value in meeting increasingly high standards and continuing to develop professionally. School counselors can best reaffirm their professional identity and protect their role within schools through certification.* The authors aptly define several, sometimes confusing, credentialing terms, discuss the importance of appropriate credentialing for school counselors, and discuss several credentialing concerns facing the school counselor.

Dr. Russell Sabella (Chapter 33) does an excellent job in writing about the impact that the ever changing world of technology continues to play in school counseling. It is essential that professional school counselors adapt to new ways of interfacing with technology in promoting the goals and objectives of their work.

Chapter (34) by Dr. Beverly O'Bryant concerns the development of the school counselor's professional image. Dr. O'Bryant, a long-time proponent of school counselor professionalism, offers some excellent tips (and a "quiz") to school counselors desiring to enhance their professional images.

Section VII concludes with a chapter by ASCA President, Dr. Carolyn Stone, on current challenges, issues and trends in our changing profession.

*Joe Wittmer and Mary Ann Clark*

# Chapter 28

# Counselor Accountability: Justifying Your Time and Measuring Your Worth

by
John J. Schmidt

*Dr. John J. (Jack) Schmidt is professor emeritus of counselor education at East Carolina University and Executive Director of the International Alliance for Invitational Education. A school counselor and counselor educator for more than 35 years, Dr. Schmidt is the author of numerous articles and several books, including **Counseling in Schools, A Survival Guide for the Elementary/Middle School Counseling,** and **Social and Cultural Foundations of Counseling and Human Services.***

## Introduction

As noted throughout this book, comprehensive programs enable school counselors to offer a wide range of services and activities to students, parents, and teachers. One challenge that counselors face in determining which services to provide and how much time to devote to specific activities is in designing procedures for assessing priorities, monitoring the use of time, and evaluating the effects of their services. These are processes that contribute to a counselor's ability to be accountable. In this chapter, you will learn about accountability processes and how they assist you as a school counselor in setting program goals, linking goals to specific services, and measuring how well you meet objectives. The emphasis given to accountability by the American School Counselor Association through its National Standards (Dahir, 2001) and the ASCA National Model (2005), as well as other perspectives on comprehensive school counseling programs (Gysbers & Henderson, 2006; Myrick 2003; Schmidt, 2003), is given practical meaning with the examples and illustrations in this chapter.

The importance of accountability in school counseling emerged in the 1970s and 1980s, and continues today as an essential element of comprehensive school counseling programs (Gysbers, 2004; Myrick, 2003; Schmidt, 2003). The same national events and legislative actions that encouraged the identification and evaluation of effective schools have fueled discussion about how important it is for counselors "to demonstrate clearly *what* they do and *how well* they do it" (Schmidt, 2003, p. 241). Some counselors are hesitant to design and implement accountability processes. In part, this is because they are so busy performing important functions, that so little time is available to evaluate how effectively they deliver services. Also, school counseling relationships and services are so varied, and at times so personal, that it is difficult to assess counselor's effectiveness or measure the broad impact of a comprehensive program of services. Nevertheless, successful school counselors accept responsibility for identifying the important services of their programs and evaluating the effectiveness of those services. This stance is imperative if we expect school counseling to continue as a credible profession and as an essential component of educational programs.

As a practicing school counselor, you share this responsibility. Your willingness to identify your role in the school, account for the time you allot to specific activities, and measure whether or not these services make a difference in the lives of students, parents, and teachers adds to the efficacy of the profession.

## Accountability Processes

A counselor's accountability begins with an assessment of needs of students, parents, and teachers who are being served by the school counseling program. The importance of needs assessment was addressed earlier in this book (Chapter 2). It is from this assessment that school counselors, administrators, and advisory committees make decisions about program goals, learning objectives, and specific services. At the same time, they assign responsibilities for delivering these services. As seen in the descriptions of the ASCA National Model and other comprehensive school counseling programs throughout this book, many people—counselors, teachers, and others—have a variety of responsibilities to fulfill for a comprehensive, developmental program to be successful. In addition to needs assessment, accountability includes the assessment of activities, surveys of students, parents, and teachers, self-rating scales by counselors, performance appraisal of counselors by supervisors and principals, and time management procedures (Schmidt, 2003, 2004). In this chapter you will learn about these procedures by focusing on two aspects of accountability: program evaluation and counselor effectiveness. Each of these has specific purpose within the broad arena of counselor accountability.

## Purpose of Evaluation

The processes that you create to evaluate your school counseling program and to measure your effectiveness as a counselor have four major purposes. First, data-driven comprehensive programs verify that the services offered are most needed in helping students achieve in school. Second, evaluation processes are used to gather evidence to support your position as a counselor in the school and make a case for comprehensive school counseling services. Third, adequate evaluations enable you to participate in research that advances the counseling profession. Lastly, when you develop and implement reasonable methods of accountability, you gather data about your performance with which to enhance your professional development.

There are countless methods of evaluation to create, adopt, and adapt. The methods you choose can focus on either a single purpose or address several. Before you decide which evaluative methods to adopt in your program, some general guidelines are worth considering.

## Evaluation Guidelines

1. Everyone involved in a school counseling program has a role in the evaluation process. In comprehensive, developmental programs, students, parents, and teachers, should all partake and contribute to the evaluation process. It may be that the evaluation methods you design would not include all these groups for every service you assess, but generally you seek participation from everyone who uses services in the program. In addition, you want to receive information and feedback from your principal, counseling supervisor, and yourself about the progress of your program and the success of particular services.

2. The goals and objectives of your school counseling program must be clearly defined with consensus among those who participate in and benefit from the program. As noted in previous chapters, a clear description of your program goals and objectives helps students, parents, teachers, and administrators understand your unique role in the school. In addition, it enables them (your publics) to assess accurately the effectiveness with which you implement services to reach those goals and objectives.

3. Program evaluation is most beneficial when the methods and procedures used to gather data emphasize positive aspects of your services. In other words, you want to plan methods of evaluation that focus on the benefits of counseling and consulting services. While it is helpful to discover weaknesses and deficiencies and to correct these defects, it is more important to determine whether or not the services you provide have met program goals and satisfied the populations you serve.

4. The instruments and processes you develop to gather data about the counseling and consulting services you deliver should generate valid measures of what you do and how well you meet program goals and objectives. It serves little purpose to develop instruments and processes that do not reliably show how you spend your time and whether or not your services effectively help others. That is, such instruments and processes should be locally appropriate.

5. Guard your time carefully, and be cautious about creating accountability procedures and methods of assessment that consume too much time to administer, or an inordinate amount of time to score. Because time is such a precious commodity for counselors, teachers, and others who work in school settings, it should not be squandered needlessly. You want to design clear and efficient procedures

because accountability methods that are cumbersome, time-consuming, and confusing overwhelm us and detract from the primary services for which we are responsible. Streamline your evaluation procedures to use as little time as possible, while simultaneously generating useful results.

6. Program evaluation is a continuous process developed and executed throughout the year to illustrate the importance of comprehensive counseling services and to identify your role as a school counselor. For this reason, evaluation processes are an ongoing aspect of a comprehensive program and not simply a temporary response to administrative requests or public outcries for accountability.

7. Evaluation of school counselors, by definition, enables the school to demonstrate that the services of a comprehensive school counseling program advance the mission of the school to educate all students and to provide them equal opportunity to learn. In this sense, evaluation of counselors should be more than simply noting the strength and weaknesses of performance or gathering data to take personnel action. Counselor performance appraisal should be an additional avenue within which to explore the relationship between program goals and the services offered. In sum, your annual evaluation is another means of examining whether or not you have achieved program goals that help the school towards its ultimate mission. For this reason, it is essential that you accept responsibility for gathering some of the data and information used in your performance appraisal each year.

8. All evaluation is predicated on the belief that action is forthcoming. Planning, developing, and implementing accountability procedures without hope of follow-through and appropriate action is a senseless and needless waste of time. Part of your responsibility as a counselor is to decide how to use the results of your program evaluation and the assessment of your own effectiveness. What program changes are indicated? What services should receive more emphasis? Which aspects of your program should be adjusted to satisfy needs of students, parents, and teachers? Questions such as these are addressed and appropriate action is taken as an integral part of the evaluation process.

The preceding guidelines, generated and adapted from various sources (Atkinson, Furlong, & Janoff, 1979; Fairchild, 1986; Krumboltz, 1974; Schmidt, 2003, 2004; Stronge & Helm, 1991), illustrate the importance of developing a clear plan and purpose for accountability processes. They are a framework to guide you in this planning process. In the remaining sections of this chapter you will learn about specific procedures to use in program evaluation and for measuring your own effectiveness as a school counselor. I begin with aspects of program evaluation.

## Program Evaluation

There are countless ways that counselors and their supervisors design and carry out program evaluation. In this section, you will read about strategies to help you, the school counselor, focus on what you do, whether or not you reach identified goals, and the degrees to which students, parents, and teachers are satisfied with the services you deliver. As noted in earlier chapters, program planning and organizing consist of the identification of specific goals to address various aspects of student development. These goals include personal adjustment, academic achievement, career development, and social skills learning, among others. As a counselor who leads the school in the selection of these goals, you have responsibility to assess whether or not these objectives are achieved during the year.

### Goal Achievement

The goals you set for your school counseling program evolve from an analysis of the annual needs assessment done with students, parents, and teachers. They also reflect local school system objectives established by the administration and state initiatives planned by state boards of education, state departments of education, and state legislatures. In addition, they may reflect national goals and standards put forth by the American School Counselor Association. In most instances, the procedures for evaluating whether or not these goals are met rests with the individual school counselor.

Some goals relate to specific information, skills, or tasks to be learned by students. For example, a goal in a middle school might indicate: *all eighth grade students will learn about the requirements for high school graduation.* Evaluation of this type of goal requires that you design particular processes and instruments that will indicate whether or not students know and understand what courses they need to take in high school and other requirements related to graduation. Such processes might include a survey of students asking them about high school requirements or an assessment of how efficient these students are in responding to preregistration for ninth grade classes. Figure 28.1 illustrates a survey used by a middle school counselor to follow up presentations conducted regarding high school graduation requirements. Analysis of students' responses to this questionnaire enables the counselor to report how well this learning goal was met by students after hearing the presentation (Figure 28.1).

Sometimes the goals you select for your counseling program relate to specific services. As an example, if several parents express an interest in learning more about preadolescent behavior and development, you might set a goal to plan and present educational programs for parents of middle school students. To meet this goal you might design and implement parent education seminars throughout the year. Evaluation of this goal could consist simply of counting the number of sessions held and the number of parents who attended these meetings. While this type of evaluation does not reflect the *quality* of your presentation, it does indicate how you spent your time meeting this goal and the number of people who attended. These kinds of assessments are important to show people where and how you allot your time, the types of services you deliver to address identified goals, and the number of students, parents, and teachers (a head count) you served in the process of meeting these goals; all aspects of being accountable. Without these types of quantitative summaries, people may not understand the multitude of services you offer in a comprehensive school counseling program, the time you spend in delivering these services, and the proportion of the school population that benefits from these helping relationships. By offering these types of data, you demonstrate the breadth of your program and the range of issues addressed by your services. At the same time, you analyze your use of time, and assess where to make adjustments so that your efficiency increases. Sometimes school systems ask counselors to complete a monthly report of activities they use in their programs. If this is true in your school system, a monthly report form is probably available. If not, you may want to design a form of your own so that you can assess and report on the services you deliver. Figure 28.2 illustrates a sample monthly report form for an elementary school counselor. You can adapt this form to fit your particular situation (Figure 28.2).

While processes and reports that account for time and assess broad program goals are essential in establishing your identity and monitoring efficient use of your time, they do not adequately speak to the issue of counselor effectiveness. In planning accountability processes, it is equally important to examine how well particular services meet intended goals. To do so, you will want to assess the outcome of the services and activities in your school counseling program. It is especially important to assess student outcomes of the counseling services and other activities you design and deliver.

## Student Outcomes

Throughout this book, you have read that a comprehensive school counseling program assists students with a myriad of learning problems, developmental issues, career concerns, academic concerns, information gathering, behavioral adjustment, and other goals. When you as the school counselor plan and deliver services to help particular students reach specific goals, it is imperative to evaluate whether or not these students succeed. For example, if you organize group counseling sessions to assist students with peer relationships, it is important that you establish some evaluative process to determine whether the students have improved their interactions with others and enhanced their peer relationships. Without such assessment, no one can say that this service has been beneficial to the students.

There are several methods of measuring student outcomes, and some methods are more practical for school counselors to use than others. Here I will briefly describe four procedures for measuring student outcomes. The first method uses prepared standards issued by the local school, district-wide school system, or state board of education. For example, a predetermined standard might state: *Over half of all the students will achieve an attendance rate of 95% for the school year.* If a school counselor planned services to address students' attendance during the year, the counselor could measure success by compiling the absentee rates of participating students and comparing the results to this prearranged standard. Much data exists in schools to measure student progress and increasingly easy to use technology makes such comparisons less difficult and time-consuming.

Another method of measuring student outcomes uses a "control group" or "waiting group" procedure. In this procedure, the counselor establishes one group of students who will receive services first while a second group waits to receive the same services later. Data are collected on both groups at the beginning of the program and then again after the first group finishes. The counselor examines the results to determine if there are any changes in the first group and if any differences exist between the first group and the second group. If differences are found, the counselor then provides the same service to the second group and again measures any changes after the students participate in the program. When you design this type of evaluation and find that changes do occur, you establish a reasonable level of certainty that the service has had a beneficial impact on students. By evaluating activities in this way, you make a stronger claim regarding the value of counseling and consulting services in the school program.

A third type of outcome evaluation asks students to assess their participation in particular services or activities, or requests parents and teachers to provide feedback about changes they have observed among students who have participated in a specific program. This method often employs the use of checklists, rating scales, and surveys to gather data from students, parents, and teachers. As with other types of self-assessment instruments and processes, reliability and validity are essential conditions for drawing accurate conclusions (Schmidt, 2003). You can design your own school appropriate instruments or use ones designed and validated by others. In either case, you want to be comfortable with the reliability of the forms you choose to use. Figure 28.3 illustrates a sample questionnaire designed by a counselor to assess students' reactions to participation in group counseling sessions (Figure 28.3).

One type of outcome assessment that is useful to school counselors is to conduct a study using a pretest and post-test comparison. This type of evaluation can be used with individual cases or with groups of students. To begin, you gather data about the individual student or group regarding the specific problem or concern to be addressed. For example, if you were beginning to work with a student who was fighting much of the time at school, you might first ask the teacher to collect baseline data to assess the frequency of fighting. Once these data were collected, you would begin an intervention such as individual counseling. After several counseling sessions in which you and the student focused on the use of fighting to solve differences, and also explored alternative forms of problem solving, you would again ask the teacher to gather data for the same length of time that the baseline data were collected. A comparison of the "before counseling" data with "post counseling" data would enable you, the student, and the teacher to note any improvement in behavior and any use of alternative strategies for resolving differences.

Sometimes, counselors demonstrate sufficient success with student outcomes, yet struggle to prove themselves to their teaching colleagues, administrators, parents, or the community at large. In part, this lack of approval may come from the uncertainty people have about the counselor's role in the school, and this, in turn, results in indecision about the value of counseling services. For this reason, it is important that, in addition to goal attainment, and student outcomes, counselors also seek input from students, parents, teachers, and administrators about their satisfaction with services.

## Consumer Satisfaction

Comprehensive school counseling programs include a wide range of services for students, parents, and teachers. In a sense, as noted throughout this book, these three groups are the primary consumers served in a school counseling program. As such, another method of accountability is to gather information from these three groups and summarize their opinions about the services they have received. In contrast to some of the *empirical* measures proposed earlier for assessing goal achievement and student outcomes, consumer satisfaction consists in large part of *perceptual* measures gathered through informal interviews or more formal surveys with students, parents, and teachers (Myrick, 2003; Schmidt, 2003).

Given the diverse and expanded services counselors offer in a comprehensive school counseling program, it is unrealistic to conceive evaluative procedures that empirically assess the level of attainment for all program goals or the degree of effectiveness for every service provided. Some measures of goal achievement and student outcomes are necessary to demonstrate the value of particular counseling and consulting processes. However, if you spend all your time designing and implementing these types of evaluations, you will find little time to actually offer the services of your comprehensive program. Therefore, the methods you choose for assessing consumer perceptions about your program complement the empirical measures you use.

When you design surveys for students, parents, and teachers, it is important to make them clear, understandable, and easy to complete. Think of questionnaires you have received in the past and recall your reactions to them. If they seemed too intimidating or too long, you probably ignored them. In most instances, people discard surveys that appear threatening or are time-consuming to answer. For this reason, it is essential to design surveys that are brief and "user friendly." At the same time, it may be helpful to design instruments that can be efficiently scored and tallied with computer technology.

The first step in developing questionnaires to evaluate your counseling services is to decide *what* you want to know. In a comprehensive school counseling program it may be impossible for you to assess every aspect each year. Therefore, you might focus on different components of the program each year, and design different instruments depending on the focus you choose. For example, you might decide to assess student, parent, and teachers' opinions about group counseling services. If so, the instruments you create would contain similar items about group counseling to which all three groups would respond. Figures 28.4, 28.5, and 28.6 illustrate sample questionnaires for students, parents, and teachers with an emphasis on group counseling services.

You will notice from these sample surveys for students, parents, and teachers that they contain some parallel items. By designing surveys in this way, you are able to check perceptions across all three populations about similar issues related to student development. For example, on the sample surveys illustrated here, the counselor assesses how the students, parents, and teachers perceive adherence to confidentiality. (See items 7, 11, and 5 on the respective questionnaires.)

Differences in levels of satisfaction across these three groups will help a counselor plan strategies to explain the importance of maintaining confidences in counselor-student relationships. At the same time, this information will help the school counselor identify groups that may need to have more feedback about ongoing counseling services than they are currently receiving. Of course, sharing of information must be done in a way that maintains confidentiality when appropriate to do so.

One final note about designing and using survey questionnaires in program accountability is appropriate here. Depending on the size of your school populations, it may not be necessary to have every student, parent, or teacher complete a questionnaire. Sample groups of students and parents may be sufficient to give you an overall picture of consumer satisfaction and program effectiveness. In sampling your populations be careful to randomly select participants, thereby avoiding a biased and inaccurate view of your program. For most school counseling programs, I advise selecting a sample of students and parents, but recommend including *all teachers* in these types of surveys. The exact size of your sample will be influenced in part by the methods available to you for tallying the results. If you have access to electronic or computer scoring systems, larger samples are more feasible.

In this section I have offered different methods of program evaluation for your consideration. Assessing program goals, measuring student outcomes, and evaluating consumer satisfaction are ways of gathering data to enable you, the counselor, to take stock of your program, account for your time, and determine whether the direction you have chosen meets the needs and expectations of the groups you serve. How you *use* these results is as important as the processes you design for collecting data. Program evaluation is incomplete if the results obtained are not shared with the people who benefit from the program, and with the administrators who make decisions about hiring counselors and expanding school counseling services. In addition, the evaluation is incomplete if changes are indicated by the results, but not incorporated into the program. In being accountable, part of your responsibility is to use these results in an appropriate manner.

# Reporting Results

To determine how you will use the *results* of various program evaluation procedures it is best to begin with the *purposes* for which you designed and implemented the evaluation. Earlier in this chapter I identified four major purposes for evaluation: (1) to use data in supporting specific services and verifying their efficiency. (2) to support your position as counselor in a comprehensive school counseling program; (3) to provide research about effective services that advances the school counseling profession; and (4) to examine areas of skill development, knowledge, and understanding that will expand and enhance your professional development. The methods you choose to report the findings of your ongoing and annual evaluations can support each of these goals. For example, by posting the summary of each monthly report (see Figure 28.2) in the front office near the teachers' mail boxes or in the faculty lounge on the bulletin board, you show your colleagues where your time is being spent; who is doing what and how effectively! By sharing this information with teachers, non-teaching staff and administrators you remove all mystery about what goes on in the counseling program, and you verify that the services being offered are ones that address the *important* goals set by the school. This will assist you and your program's reputation, both in and outside the teachers' lounge.

By the same token, a summary of students and parents' evaluations demonstrates how they perceive the counseling program and what services they believe to be most important. These reports allow you, the counselor, to take control of your program by making decisions that reflect the needs and desires of students, parents, and teachers whom you serve. In this way, you avoid the pitfall of serving only a single group, or restricting your program to a narrowly defined mission. By sharing these types of evaluation reports, "counselors take control of *who* they are and *what* services they should offer in helping students reach their educational, personal, and career goals" (Schmidt, 2003, p. 250). At the same time, when you share these results, you inform others of the perceptions of all the groups who are being served by the school counseling program.

Sometimes the results you report will not show a positive reaction to services in the program. Sharing these negative findings can be as powerful as reporting positive results, particularly when you demonstrate an acceptance of these perceptions and illustrate plans for change. Counselors who demonstrate a willingness to listen to other points of view and make appropriate adjustments in their programs win many allies and cultivate strong support for their services.

Evaluations that demonstrate the effectiveness of particular counseling and consulting services contribute to the identification and authenticity of the school counseling profession. Avenues by which you can share these types of results include columns in your school and town newspapers, a counselor's website, articles in your state counselor's newsletter, research publications in state and national journals, and reports for your local school board about effective services. All of these reporting processes help to identify and clarify the counselor's role in school and demonstrate the efficacy of comprehensive counseling services.

Lastly, the types of evaluation procedures encouraged in this chapter enable you to examine skills and areas of knowledge in which you excel in addition to ones for which you need additional training or other technical assistance. School counseling, as with many other professions, is an emerging field of study. The issues that students, parents, teachers and administrators face today may not be the same issues they will confront in the future. For this reason, effective counselors continuously assess their knowledge and skills, and seek avenues to enhance their professional development. By sharing evaluation results with your principal and supervisor, you gather ammunition to make a case for assistance and support from the school or school

system. This support might come in the form of financial assistance to pay for graduate course work or registration at a counselor's workshop. Similarly, it might come in the form of paid leave to attend classes or participate in a national symposium. However, unless you can demonstrate this need with hard data, the chances of obtaining such assistance are probably remote.

In some instances, your annual evaluations may provide support for an external assessment of your school counseling program (Schmidt, 2003; Vacc, Rhyne-Winkler, & Poidevant, 1993). An external assessment would provide the funds and technical assistance to bring outside experts to your school to evaluate the counseling program. An external assessment offers the opportunity for a broader perspective that reflects statewide, national, and international trends and issues. It also guards against a parochial posture that limits your internal "evaluations to restricted and repetitious views of *what should be*" (Schmidt, 2003, p. 251). When financial assistance for an external view is not feasible, developing a peer auditing model is another option. In this process, you would ask a fellow counselor (or counselors) from another school to visit your program, assess its scope and effectiveness, and write a report of the findings. If a number of counselors expressed interest in this type of evaluative process, the outcome could provide an excellent avenue for sharing successful ideas and strategies for all involved.

All the evaluation procedures advocated here have the potential to strengthen your role and position in the school as a professional counselor. In addition to these procedures there is one other aspect of accountability that needs to be addressed, and it is counselor evaluation, which is sometimes referred to as counselor performance appraisal (Schmidt, 2004; Stronge & Helm, 1991).

# Counselor Performance Appraisal

Public attention on accountability in schools has included an additional focus on the performance appraisal and evaluation of professional staff. School counselors have been included in this process, but only in the last few years have we seen a distinction between the evaluation processes used with teachers and those designed especially for counselors (Schmidt, 2003, 2004). When planning your own performance appraisal as a school counselor, you might consider the following guidelines:

1. Instruments used to rate a school counselor's performance should reflect the functions for which counselors are hired, and the goals for which programs are designed. Instruments designed to evaluate teacher or administrator performance, therefore, are probably not suitable for counselor evaluation.

2. An instrument that is used to rate a school counselor's performance should reflect the major functions outlined in the literature of the counseling profession. Generally, these functions, as noted in previous chapters, include descriptions of individual and group counseling services, consulting services with parents, teachers, and other professionals, group consultation and instructional services (e.g., classroom guidance, parent education, and teacher in-service), student appraisal and assessment, ethical and legal practices, and program development and coordination. Good standards and fair practices prescribe that you be evaluated according to the actual assignment and expectations of your school counseling position.

3. The person who gathers and interprets data by which a rating is determined for any given practice or function should be highly trained and competent in that particular skill area. The purpose of a performance appraisal system is defeated if the person responsible for assessment does not have adequate knowledge and competence in the areas being evaluated. Since most school principals are not trained counselors, this raises a significant dilemma. The challenge for you, your principal, and your school system is to identify methods and procedures for you to receive appropriate supervision and accurate performance appraisal for the job you do in the school.

4. The major purpose for performance appraisal is to help counselors identify strengths and weaknesses in order to make sound decisions about professional development and program improvement. The least important reason to evaluate a counselor is for personnel action, but sometimes this is unavoid-

able. For this reason, you want to become familiar with the evaluation guidelines and procedures of your school system, and be aware of your rights and responsibilities as outlined in personnel policies.

5. The methods used to gather data for performance appraisal with counselors should be determined at the beginning of the evaluation cycle. Counseling services offer a unique challenge in performance appraisal processes. Due to the confidential nature of many relationships formed by counselors, direct observation may not be an option for the evaluator. As a counselor, you can take charge of this decision by suggesting alternative methods of evaluation for you and your supervisor to use. Such alternatives might include interviews, audio or video taping, simulations, or results of surveys with students, parents, and teachers (Schmidt, 2003, 2004). Observations are appropriate for some services, such as classroom guidance, but you want to have a range of methods available due to the diverse nature of services offered in a comprehensive school counseling program.

The preceding guidelines set the stage for developing an appropriate, fair and accurate performance appraisal system. If your school system has a clear performance appraisal process, you will want to become familiar with the policies and procedures that are involved. If your school does not have a clear process you may want to establish one with your principal and supervisor. The following steps are offered as suggestions for establishing a clear process.

# Performance Appraisal Process

One of the first goals to accomplish in setting up a performance appraisal process is for you, your supervisor, and principal to agree on the purpose of evaluation. As stated earlier, this purpose is primarily to assist you in your professional development. A second goal is to establish a collaborative relationship with your evaluator (either the principal or supervisor) in which you both accept responsibility for gathering data to use in the performance appraisal process. Following an agreement on these two points, you proceed to design steps for the evaluation. Briefly, these steps might include:

1. An initial conference in the beginning of the year to discuss the major functions and practices to be evaluated during the year. Because school counselors provide such a wide array of services, it may not be realistic to assess all these functions equally in a single year. In which case, you and the evaluator might agree to focus on particular functions one year and save other functions for the next evaluation cycle. In this conference, you would also agree on how data would be gathered and who would be responsible for the different types of data needed in the evaluation. Next, a schedule for gathering data and holding formative conferences during the year would be established.

2. Formative conferences would be held between you and your evaluator periodically during the year. At these conferences, data on particular functions would be shared and an assessment would result. If weaknesses are noted, the evaluator offers suggestions about ways to address these deficiencies. At this time, discussion about technical and financial support to take courses, attend seminars, or participate in professional conferences takes place.

3. At the end of the year, you and the evaluator would meet in a summative conference to review the evaluations performed, assess the progress made, and discuss an annual performance appraisal. As noted earlier, the instrument used for this process should reflect the expectations of a comprehensive school counseling program as presented in professional literature. With your annual performance appraisal complete, you can then begin to formulate professional goals and a plan of action for your further professional development.

A related aspect of performance appraisal is self-assessment by the counselor. The counselor's perspective adds another dimension to the evaluation process. By creating a self-assessment process and tying it to your annual evaluation, the goals and plans you make for professional development become personalized and thereby more attainable.

## Self-Assessment

When you perform a self-assessment, you are the first to identify and recognize your own strengths and weaknesses. In this way, you identify skills and knowledge to share with colleagues, while at the same time you note areas for further development and improvement. An accurate self-assessment is an appropriate initial step to your annual performance appraisal be-

cause it enables you to gather evidence of competent practices to share with your principal or supervisor. In this manner, you become a collaborator in the performance appraisal process, advocating a credible and valid relationship that will assist you in your own professional development.

A starting point in your self-assessment is to write your professional goals for the year. By writing down your objectives, you make a personal commitment to see that these goals are targeted during the school year. To help you determine what goals are most important, it is useful to design a self-assessment instrument about you and your school counseling program. Figure 28.7 illustrates a sample assessment form designed by a counselor who is preparing for a new school year. This sample form attempts to evaluate the balance of services in the school counseling program and examine aspects of the program the counselor may want to adjust. An assessment form such as this one is easy to create, or you can use forms published by counseling associations and other organizations.

A final way that you can be actively involved in your self-assessment and annual performance appraisal is to document your work and achievements by compiling a counselor's portfolio (Rhyne-Winkler & Wooten, 1996). By gathering evidence to place in a portfolio under each of the major functions expected of you, each year you take control and responsibility for your annual evaluation.

## Summary

In this chapter, I have explored various issues and ideas related to counselor accountability. The position taken here advocates that school counselors assume a leadership role in designing and conducting evaluation procedures. As a school counselor, you have responsibility for evaluating your program, reporting the results, and suggesting changes to address the findings of the evaluation process. Without an accountability process, you run the risk of failing to address the needs and expectations of the students, parents, teachers, and administrators you serve. In doing so, you threaten the program's value and jeopardize your reputation as a significant member of the school team. Comprehensive school counseling programs are essential to today's schools, and adequate program accountability and accurate counselor performance appraisal verify the importance of these services.

# Figure 28.1
# Middle School Survey of a High School Presentation

**Students:** Please answer the following questions about the presentation you just heard regarding high school graduation requirements. Your responses will help the counseling department and teachers plan future programs to help students prepare for high school. Thank you for your help.

1. How many total credits are required for high school graduation in this state? _____

2. Write down the number of credits that are required in each subject area for high school graduation:

   English            _____

   Mathematics        _____

   Social Studies     _____

   Science            _____

   Vocational Educ.   _____

   Physical Educ.     _____

   Foreign Lang.      _____

   Electives          _____

3. What are the exams you have to pass to qualify for a high school diploma in this state? _____
   _____

4. What science classes are required for high school graduation? _____
   _____

5. What mathematics courses are required? _____
   _____

6. For which ninth grade classes do you plan to preregister? _____
   _____

# Figure 28.2
# Elementary Counselor's Monthly Report Form

Month:_____

1. Number of individual counseling sessions          _____

2. Number of group counseling sessions          _____

3. Number of students served in group counseling sessions          _____

4. Number of group guidance sessions          _____

5. Number of consultations with parents          _____

6. Number of consultations with teachers          _____

7. Number of parent education presentations          _____

8. Number of teacher in-service presentations          _____

9. Number of referrals to in-school programs          _____

10. Number of referrals to outside agencies          _____

11. Number of meetings attended          _____

12. Hours spent coordinating special events          _____
    (listed below)

_____

_____

_____

# Figure 28.3
# Student Evaluation of Group Counseling

**Students:** Thank you for participating in our group. Please give your responses to the following items so that I can plan other groups in the future. Do not put your name on the form. Return the form to the counselor's mail box in the office. Thank you.

**Circle your response for each statement.**

| | | | |
|---|---|---|---|
| 1. I enjoyed being in this group. | Yes | No | Unsure |
| 2. This group helped me learn new things about myself. | Yes | No | Unsure |
| 3. I have changed some behaviors as a result of being in this group. | Yes | No | Unsure |
| 4. I feel better about myself and my actions since being in this group. | Yes | No | Unsure |
| 5. The counselor was helpful in this group. | Yes | No | Unsure |
| 6. This counselor listened to me in this group. | Yes | No | Unsure |
| 7. I want to be in another group sometime. | Yes | No | Unsure |
| 8. I would recommend this type of group to my friends. | Yes | No | Unsure |

**Comments:**

# Figure 28.4
# Student Evaluation of a High School Counseling Program

**Instructions:** Please help your counselor(s) evaluate services of the school counseling program for this school year. Your answers will help the counselor(s) plan services for the coming year. Thank you for your assistance.

**Circle your responses for each question.**

1. Have you met with your counselor this year?                                              Yes       No    Unsure

2. Did you meet with your counselor individually?                                        Yes       No    Unsure

3. Did the counselor invite you to participate in group counseling this year?       Yes       No    Unsure

4. Was the counselor helpful in any way this year?                                         Yes       No    Unsure

5. Would you recommend the counselor to your friends if they needed to talk to someone?   Yes   No    Unsure

6. Did you participate in a group led by your counselor this year?                     Yes       No    Unsure

   If you participated in group counseling this year, please answer the remaining questions.

7. Was the group helpful to you?                                                             Yes       No    Unsure

8. Did the counselor keep information shared in group confidential?              Yes       No    Unsure

9. Did the counselor effectively lead the group?                                          Yes       No    Unsure

10. Do you believe the group was helpful to other students?                        Yes       No    Unsure

11. Would you recommend this type of group to other students?                  Yes       No    Unsure

**Comments:**

# Figure 28.5
# Parent Evaluation of a School Counseling Program

**Instructions:** Please complete this survey to help the counseling department plan future services in the school counseling program. Return the questionnaire to the school counseling office in the self-addressed envelope. Thank you for your help.

**Circle your response to each question.**

| | | | |
|---|---|---|---|
| 1. Do you know the counselor at your child's school? | Yes | No | Unsure |
| 2. Has the counselor met with your child this year? | Yes | No | Unsure |
| 3. In your opinion, has the counselor been helpful to your child at school? | Yes | No | Unsure |
| 4. Have you talked with your child's counselor? | Yes | No | Unsure |
| 5. Did the counselor help you in any way this year? | Yes | No | Unsure |
| 6. Would your recommend the counselor to other parents who needed assistance? | Yes | No | Unsure |
| 7. Was your child in a group with the counselor this year? | Yes | No | Unsure |

If your child was in a group with the counselor this year, please answer the following questions.

| | | | |
|---|---|---|---|
| 8. Did your child talk with you about being in the group? | Yes | No | Unsure |
| 9. Do you know the purpose of the group? | Yes | No | Unsure |
| 10. Was the group helpful to your child? | Yes | No | Unsure |
| 11. Did the counselor maintain confidentiality about information your child shared in group? | Yes | No | Unsure |
| 12. Do you think groups such as these are important services for students? | Yes | No | Unsure |

**Comments:**

*Joe Wittmer, Ph.D. and Mary Ann Clark, Ph.D.*

# Figure 28.6
# Teacher Evaluation of a School Counseling Program

**Instructions:** Please complete this survey to help the counseling office plan future services in the school counseling program. Return the questionnaire to the school counselor's mail box in the office. Thank you for your help.

**Circle your response to each question.**

1. Has the counselor met with any of your students this year?                                Yes      No     Unsure

2. In your opinion, has the counselor been helpful to your students?                         Yes      No     Unsure

3. Have you received feedback from the counselor?                                            Yes      No     Unsure

4. Does the counselor maintain confidences?                                                  Yes      No     Unsure

5. Did the counselor help you in any way this year?                                          Yes      No     Unsure

6. Would your recommend the counselor to students or parents who needed assistance?          Yes      No     Unsure

7. Were any of your students in a group with the counselor this year?                        Yes      No     Unsure

If any students were in a group with the counselor this year, please answer the following questions.

8. Do you know the purpose of the group?                                                     Yes      No     Unsure

9. Did the group schedule interfere with class instruction?                                  Yes      No     Unsure

10. Was the group helpful to your student(s)?                                                Yes      No     Unsure

11. Do you think groups such as these are important services for students?                   Yes      No     Unsure

**Comments:**

# Figure 28.7
# Counselor Self-Assessment Form

|  | Met | Partially Met | Not Met |
|---|---|---|---|
| 1. The counseling program consists of a wide range of services, including individual counseling, group counseling, parent consultations, teacher collaboration, referrals, large group guidance, parent education programs, and student appraisals. | ❏ | ❏ | ❏ |
| 2. The counselor spends sufficient time in individual relationships with students. | ❏ | ❏ | ❏ |
| 3. The counselor leads sufficient number of group counseling sessions with students. | ❏ | ❏ | ❏ |
| 4. The counselor plans classroom guidance activities with teachers. | ❏ | ❏ | ❏ |
| 5. The counselor develops a written plan for the program each year | ❏ | ❏ | ❏ |
| 6. An Advisory Committee assists the counselor with program planning. | ❏ | ❏ | ❏ |
| 7. The counselor spends limited time in clerical tasks, and these functions do not detract significantly from direct service to students, parents, and teachers. | ❏ | ❏ | ❏ |
| 8. The counselor spends a majority of time in crisis intervention. | ❏ | ❏ | ❏ |
| 9. The counselor is comfortable leading large group activities with students, parents, or teachers. | ❏ | ❏ | ❏ |
| 10. The counselor uses appropriate assessment procedures to make decisions about professional services for students. | ❏ | ❏ | ❏ |

**Comments:**

*Joe Wittmer, Ph.D. and Mary Ann Clark, Ph.D.*

# References

American School Counselor Association. (2005). *The ASCA national model: A framework for school counseling programs*. Alexandria, VA: Author.

Atkinson, D.R., Furlong, M., & Janoff, D.S. (1979). A four component model for proactive accountability in school counseling. *The School Counselor, 26,* 222-228.

Dahir, C.A. (2001). The national standards for school counseling programs: Development and implementation. *Professional School Counseling, 4,* 320-327.

Fairchild, T.N. (1986). Time analysis: Accountability tool for counselors. *The School Counselor, 34,* 36-43.

Gysbers, N.C. (2004). Comprehensive guidance and counseling programs: The evolution of accountability. *Professional School Counseling, 8,* 1-14.

Gysbers, N.C., & Henderson, P. (2006). *Developing and managing your school guidance and counseling program* (4th ed.). Alexandria, VA: American Counseling Association.

Krumboltz, J.D. (1974). An accountability model for counselors. *Personnel and Guidance Journal, 52,* 639-646.

Myrick, R.D. (2003). *Developmental guidance and counseling. A practical approach* (4th ed.). Minneapolis, MN: Educational Media Corporation.

Myrick, R.D. (2003). Accountability: Counselors count. *Professional School Counseling, 6,* 174-179.

Rhyne-Winkler, M.C., & Wooten, H.R. (1996). The school counselor portfolio: Professional development and accountability. *The School Counselor, 44,* 146-150.

Schmidt, J.J. (1990). Critical issues for school counselor performance appraisal and supervision. *The School Counselor, 38,* 86-94.

Schmidt, J.J. (2004). *A survival guide for the elementary/middle school counselor* (2nd ed.). San Francisco, CA: Jossey-Bass.

Schmidt, J.J. (2003). *Counseling in schools. Essential services and comprehensive programs* (4th ed.). Needham, MA: Allyn and Bacon.

Stronge, J.H., & Helm, V.M. (1991). *Evaluating professional support personnel in education*. Newbury Park, CA: SAGE Publications.

Vacc, N.A., 0 Rhyne-Winkler, M.C., Poidevant, J.M. (1993). Evaluation and accountability of counseling services: Possible implications for a midsize school district. *The School Counselor, 40,* 260-266.

# Chapter 29

# Documenting Counseling Services: Changing to Evidence-based Practices

**by**
**Harry Daniels and William J. Goodman**

*Harry Daniels, Ph.D., is Professor and Chair of the Counselor Education Department at the University of Florida. He has devoted his professional career to public education, serving as a classroom teacher, a high school counselor and as a counselor educator. He also has ten years of experience as a school board member.*

*William Goodman, Ed.S., is the Director of Guidance Services for the School Board of Alachua County in Gainesville, Florida, and a licensed mental health counselor. Prior to assuming his current position he developed and managed a highly successful developmental counseling program at one of the high schools in the district.*

We begin this chapter by pointing to an old adage that is attributed to the ancient Greek philosopher Heraclitus of Ephesus: Change is the only constant in life. We can be reasonably confident that Heraclitus was not thinking about school counseling programs when he uttered this aphorism; nonetheless, as we will describe below, it is clear that this truism pertains to the work of today's school counselor. School counselors have always had a responsibility for documenting *all* of the programs and services that are part of their counseling program. However, within the last decade the focus on documentation changed from a simple enumeration of services that were provided to different clientele to an assessment of the quality of the services (Studer, Oberman, & Womack, 2006). Now, in keeping with the mandates of the No Child Left Behind Act (NCLB, 2001), school counselors are expected to demonstrate that their interventions on the behalf of children contribute to the academic success of all their students.

The NCLB mandate creates a new set of expectations for school counselors. Previously it was enough for counselors to keep a record of who was seen and for what purposes, and to document the outcome of the meeting. In contrast, NCLB requires school districts to establish and maintain interactive databases that will allow for the quantitative analysis of student behavior. Further, districts are required to disaggregate and analyze the data for the purpose of identifying where gaps in student learning exist. Finally, districts are expected to use the evidence found in the results of their analyses to document adequate yearly progress in academic achievement, or to develop and introduce new programs that will close the existing gaps. In short, NCLB calls for districts to used evidence-based strategies to monitor student performance and introduce change into the schools.

It is important to note that evidence-based decision making is not a new idea for school counselors. Indeed, it is one of the cornerstones of the ASCA National Model: A Framework for School Counseling Programs (2005) as well as a major principle of the Education Trust's Transforming School Counseling Initiative (2005). Evidence-based counseling is closely tied to the idea of professional accountability, that is, "being responsible for one's actions ... and documenting effectiveness through measures of professional activity outcomes" (Loesch & Ritchie, 2005, p.2). In order to fulfill this responsibility, counselors will need to use both enumerative and evidence-based strategies to document their work. In the remainder of this chapter we provide descriptive examples of both strategies.

# Enumerative Strategies

A step-by-step method for documenting the delivery of school counseling programs and services was provided by Daniels and Daniels (2000). This structured format identified four factors that school counselors need to consider when they develop a system for documenting counseling services: (1) Structure; (2) Techniques; (3) Easy to use forms; and (4) Procedures. Considered together, the first letter of each of these issues provides an acronym (**STEP**) that can be used to remember the critical issues to attend to in the process of documenting counseling services. A brief discussion of each issue follows.

**Structure**. During a single year a school counselor will be involved in literally hundreds of professional contacts that pertain to the students with whom they work. These contacts may be with the students themselves with their parents, teachers, administrators and/or friends. The contacts with students may be made directly in one-on-one sessions, or in small or large group counseling, or they may be made through more indirect means such as telephone calls or e-mail. Given the variety of ways that counselors connect with students, it is essential to determine what needs to be documented and by whom. We believe that the decision about what needs to be documented is informed by two primary factors: the counselor's position description and the local standards and expectations. Because local standards and expectations will vary widely from place to place, we will emphasize the counselor's position description.

School counselors have a responsibility for documenting *all* of the programs and services that are part of their counseling program including, but not limited to, any assistance provided to students, parents, teachers and administrators, or contacts with appropriate state agencies or court officials. The prospect of documenting almost everything they do can be overwhelming for most counselors. Indeed, the task of documenting the delivery of counseling programs and services can be arduous and time consuming. Yet, as many experienced school counselors know, the benefits of providing documentation will far outweigh the costs of doing so, particularly in instances when a counselor's course of action is questioned by a third party. Moreover, we believe the task of documenting program and service delivery can be structured in such a way as to make the process almost second nature. One example of such a structure is presented in Figure 29.1. It provides a summary of the types of counseling interventions for which documentation is recommended. Identified in the summary are four different types of information, each of which is linked to a critical issue that counselors need to consider as they begin to organize their documentation efforts. Framed as questions, the critical issues are:

- Who is the client?
- What is the nature of the counseling intervention and/or contact?
- What information about the intervention/contact is critical and needs to be documented?
- Who is (are) the potential beneficiary (ies) of the documentation?

(Readers interested in obtaining a more detailed description of this structure are encouraged to read "Documenting Counseling Services: A Step by Step Method" in *Managing your K-12 School Counseling Program: Developmental Strategies,* (Daniels & Daniels, 2000).

**Techniques**. Documenting counseling interventions and/or contacts is an essential component of every school counselor's job. Despite its importance, there is no single best technique for counselors to use in fulfilling this responsibility. Most counselors' first experience in documenting their activities occurs during their supervised field experiences in their graduate programs. Then, with additional experience and experimentation with different strategies for keeping accurate records, counselors adopt a strategy that works for them. You are encouraged to experiment with different ways to record your efforts, but we also want to provide some general guidelines that may prove helpful.

1. Keep counseling records in such a way that they will both benefit clients and assist you in being a more effective practitioner. Good records enable counselors to reconstruct the student's participation in all aspects of the counseling program and to demonstrate that the services provided were consistent with accepted practice. Additionally, the retention of accurate and thorough client records will be the best counter to *any* assertion of professional negligence.

2. When writing your notes, use behavioral, objective language Your written words will be the only record of any contact you have with a client, and it is important that you emphasize clarity and precision in all that you write. Insofar as possible avoid using adjectives! It is vital that your notes are clear and precise—using adjectives adds to the subjectivity of the record.

3. Know what information is required to be included in client records by state statute and take pains to provide it. Although different states have different requirements about what is to be included in an intervention record, most will include the following elements:

- Basic information such as the client's name, dates of contact, types of service provided;

- A summary of the client's presenting concerns, what transpired in the session, any comments the client made regarding sensitive matters (i.e., abuse and/or neglect, threats of violence, etc.), and a record of the client's progress;

- Records of contacts with significant others in the client's life, including telephone contacts, e-mail messages, and face-to-face conversations.

4. Document client participation whenever appropriate, perhaps including the client's signature.

5. Retain records for as long as there is a need for them. There is no general record retention rule, but know whether your school district has such a policy. Then, maintain as accurate and complete a client record as possible during the period of time established by the retention policy.

6. Assume any of your records may someday be read in open court with you and your client present along with newspaper, radio and television reporters.

**Easy to Use Forms**. We have discovered that it is easier to keep accurate and up-to-date records if we use pre-designed forms to record our contacts and activities. In general, forms should be developed to suit the purposes and needs of a particular counselor, school, or district. Readers interested in seeing specific examples of forms that we have developed may do so by turning to "Documenting Counseling Services: A Step by Step Method" in *Managing your K-12 School Counseling Program: Developmental Strategies* (Daniels & Daniels, 2000). We encourage you to use and/or modify the forms as needed to fit your own purposes. That is, redesign each as appropriate to make it locally relevant.

**Procedures**. The single most important factor to consider in terms of procedures for documenting counseling services is timeliness. The word *timely* is a directive to record information immediately! Notes about contact with clients should be made as soon as possible after the end of the session, presentation, or other contact. Waiting even one day can blur one's memory and thus, the accuracy of the record. Having a supply of the forms described above on hand – either on one's desktop or in a desk drawer – will allow school counselors to make a record of any session before going on to the next one. It only takes a few minutes, and it is good practice.

# Evidence-based Strategies

As noted above, NCLB law mandates that school districts adopt evidenced-based strategies for monitoring student achievement and insuring that all children will succeed in school. In this section we provide a description on one school district's response to this mandate and illustrate how school counselors use the system to monitor the quality of their programs.

The district Student Services department in Alachua County, Florida has developed a student data-based system to address the needs of students for various guidance and counseling services. The system provides instant access to student data, and allows for the disaggregation of data, monitoring of student progress, acquisition of new data, and dissemination of student information to improve services and better meet the educational needs of students. Information from the system can be downloaded in a variety of formats including EXCEL, comma delimited, pdf, and html. The system provides users with both real time and historical data in the following areas:

- Demographic Information: student name, social security number, date of birth, home address and telephone number, race/ethnicity, and gender information.

- Academic Information: grade point average, course credit information, test assessment information, graduation option, and enrollment in dual enrollment & advanced placement class information.

- Attendance Information: Excused & unexcused absences, and the number of times students are tardy to school.

- Discipline Information: Number of discipline referrals, number of suspensions and days suspended.

- Disability & Language Barrier Information: Exceptional Student Education, Section 504, home & spoken language, and English as a Second Language (ESOL) information.

- Economic Information: Free or reduced lunch status, public assistance, homeless and displaced student information.

- Health Information: Codes for various health disorders, warnings, restrictions and mediation information.

The district student database system also allows counselors to collect new information through online surveys. At the present time there are two surveys in use. A Senior Survey that provides us with information about each senior's post secondary educational and career plans, financial aid needs, and student-parent contact information (e.g. cell phone numbers & email addresses), and a Career Interest Survey that provides us with information about student interests in specific careers and career pathways, as well as, the student-parent contact information mentioned above. Information from these surveys is merged with other information in the database to create online reports that can be used to improve academic and career advisement services for middle and high school students.

All student information in the system can be downloaded into EXCEL where it can be filtered and sorted to create lists that assist with service delivery. The system also contains a Student Profile Page that contains up-to-date individual student information in a scroll down form that can be viewed from a desktop or laptop computer, or downloaded as a pdf document for use in conferences with students, parents, and teachers, such as child study teams. Another feature of the system is its Academic History Page, which contains information from each student's most recent grade report, as well as academic grades and course credits earned over the previous four years.

Counselors use the information in the student database system to identify students for a variety of services. These services include prevention and early intervention, academic and/or career advisement, financial aid counseling, and locating community health services to name a few. Students who are at risk because of attendance, disciplinary problems, academic grades, poor test scores on required reading and mathematics examinations, credit deficiencies, health, or language problems can be identified immediately. The system is also a valuable tool for identifying students whose educational credentials and/or school behaviors (e.g. attendance, discipline) indicate that they are strong candidates for alternative curricular programs and educational training options. Because the data can be disaggregated, underrepresented and overrepresented populations of students can also be identified and actions undertaken to correct these inequities in the service delivery system.

Having easy access to accurate student information allows school counselors (and other student services personnel) to zero in on specific individual and school-related needs and problems, and plan services directed toward specific outcomes. It also allows school counselors to monitor the progress of individual students, groups of students (small groups or classroom cohorts) and the entire school toward specific goals.

Each school in the district has now developed a Student Services Plan based on an evidenced-based educational needs analysis of their school. These plans are also tied to critical indicators of school success (e.g. attendance, discipline, promotion, graduation and post secondary placement rates) that contribute to Florida schools' evaluations. The plans are continuously monitored and revised as needed by school counselors and others on the student services team. Some the areas being addressed in our Student Services Plans include:

- Increasing enrollment of African American students in Advanced Placement courses.

- Increasing the number and percentage of seniors who receive Bright Futures (state awarded tuition) scholarships.

- Increasing the number of high achieving seniors from low SES family backgrounds who complete a Free Application for Federal Student Aid (FAFSA) form.

- Increasing the number and percentage of students who are meeting the FCAT testing requirements for promotion and graduation (e.g. a score of 300 or above) at all grade levels tested – grades 3 through 12.

- Increasing enrollment in career and technical education programs that lead to careers with a high employment outlook for all students, but particularly for students on free or reduced lunch & underrepresented groups.

- Identifying student interests in specific career areas (e.g. building construction, health care, information technology) and partnering with local employers to provide direct, real-life, hands-on experiences that make school and class work more relevant.

- Decreasing barriers to learning by monitoring student attendance, discipline and suspension rates for our most at risk students.

The district is redesigning and developing intelligent forms and spreadsheets, as well, to reduce the time spent by school counselors doing paperwork that can be better managed by advances in technology. The intent is to free up counselor time for more direct, appropriate, and measurable services to students and parents.

## Concluding Remarks

Documenting counseling services has been, and continues to be a critical responsibility for counselors, but the nature of the task has changed. Although school counselors may want to continue to enumerate the variety of services that they have provided for all of their clientele, the passage of the NCLB law requires us to do more. That is, we must engage in evidenced–based practices like the one described above. Adopting evidence–based practices may seem burdensome at first, but we are convinced that it will prove to be a benefit for you and your counseling program. Documenting services and providing evidence of results is a major transformation of the role of the school counselor in contributing to success for all students, as called for by stakeholders, professional ethics, and federal legislation such as NCLB. As shown by a growing body of literature that describes evidence-based procedures that counselors can use to demonstrate the success of their programs (Cary & Dimmitt, 2006; McDougal & Smith, 2006; Ware & Galassi, 2006), our future as a profession seems very bright.

## References

American School Counselor Association. (2005). *The ASCA national model: A framework for school counseling programs* (2nd ed). Alexandria, VA: Author.

Cary, J.C., & Dimmitt, C. (2006). Resources for school counselors and counselor educators: The center for school counseling outcome research. *Professional School Counseling, 9*, 416-420.

Daniels, M.H., & Daniels, D.K. (2000). Documenting counseling services: A step by step method. In J. Wittmer (Ed.), *Managing your school counseling program: K-12 developmental strategies.* Minneapolis: Educational Media Corporation.

Education Trust. (2005). *National center for transforming school counseling at the education trust.* Retrieved July 18, 2005, from http:www2.edtrust.org/EdTrust/Transforming+School+Counseling/main

Loesch, L. C. & Ritchie, M. H. (2005). *The accountable school counselor.* Austin, TX: Pro-Ed.

McDougal, D., & Smith, D. (2006). Recent innovations in small-n designs for research and practice in professional school counseling. *Professional School Counseling, 9*, 392-400.

No child left behind act of 2001, Pub.L.No.107-110 (2001).

Studer, J.R., Oberman, A.H., & Womack, R. H. (2006). Producing evidence to show counseling effectiveness in the schools. *Professional School Counseling, 9*, 385-391.

Ware, W.B., & Galassi, J.P. (2006). Using correlational and prediction data to enhance student achievement in k-12 schools: A practical application for school counselors. *Professional School Counseling, 9*, 344-356.

# Figure 29.1
## Summary of the Types of Counseling Interventions for which Documentation is Recommended

| Client | Intervention/Contact | Critical Information | Potential Beneficiaries |
|--------|---------------------|---------------------|------------------------|
| Students | Individual Counseling | Student's Name | Client |
| | | Date | Counselor |
| | | Purpose | Parents |
| | | Summary | School Staff |
| | | Outcome | Court |
| | Group counseling | Participants' names | Clients |
| | | Date | Counselor |
| | | Purpose/Topic | Parents |
| | | Summary | School Staff |
| | | Outcome | Court |
| | Classroom guidance | Class/Teacher's name | Students |
| | | Class list | Counselor |
| | | Date/Time | Parents |
| | | Purpose/Topic | School Staff |
| | | Summary | |
| | Telephone contact | Student's Name | Client |
| | | Date/Time | Counselor |
| | | Purpose/Topic | Parents |
| | | Summary | School Staff |
| | | Outcome | Court |
| | E-mail contact | Student's Name | Client |
| | | Date/Time | Counselor |
| | | Purpose/Topic | Parents |
| | | Summary | School Staff |
| | | Outcome | Court |
| | Letter | Contents of letter | Client |
| | | | Counselor |
| | | | Parents |
| | | | School Staff |
| | | | Court |

## Figure 29.1 (cont.)
## Summary of the Types of Counseling Interventions
## for which Documentation is Recommended

| Client | Intervention/Contact | Critical Information | Potential Beneficiaries |
|---|---|---|---|
| Parents | Individual consultation | Parent's Name | Student |
| | | Date/Time | Parents |
| | | Purpose/Topic | Counselor |
| | | Summary | School Staff |
| | | Outcome | Court |
| | Telephone contact | Parent's Name | Student |
| | | Date/Time | Parents |
| | | Purpose/Topic | Counselor |
| | | Summary | School Staff |
| | | Outcome | Court |
| | E-mail contact | Parent's Name | Student |
| | | Date/Time | Parents |
| | | Purpose/Topic | Counselor |
| | | Summary | School Staff |
| | | Outcome | Court |
| | Workshops | Purpose/Topic | Parents |
| | | Date/Time | Students |
| | | Participants | Counselor |
| | | Summary | School Staff |
| | Large group presentations | Purpose/Topic | Parents |
| | | Date/Time | Students |
| | | Organization | Counselor |
| | | Summary | School Staff |
| | Letter | | |

*Joe Wittmer, Ph.D. and Mary Ann Clark, Ph.D.*

## Figure 29.1 (cont.)
## Summary of the Types of Counseling Interventions
## for which Documentation is Recommended

| Client | Intervention/Contact | Critical Information | Potential Beneficiaries |
|---|---|---|---|
| School Staff | Individual consultation<br>Teachers<br>Administrators<br>Resource officers<br>Other | Contact's name<br>Student's name<br>Date/Time<br>Purpose<br>Summary | School Staff<br>Students<br>Counselor<br>Parents |
| | Workshops/Inservice | Purpose/Topic<br>Date/Time<br>Participants<br>Summary | School Staff<br>Students<br>Counselor<br>Parents |
| | Staffings<br>IEP Staffings<br>Disciplinary Staffings | Student's name Participants' names<br>Date<br>Purpose<br>Summary<br>Outcome | Students<br>School Staff<br>Counselor<br>Parents |
| Community | Referrals to other professionals<br>Counselors<br>Psychologists<br>Physicians<br>Other | Student's name<br>Referral's name<br>Date<br>Purpose<br>Summary<br>Outcome | Students<br>Parents<br>Counselor |
| | Referrals to agencies | Student's name<br>Referral's name<br>Date Purpose<br>Summary<br>Outcome | Students<br>Parents<br>Counselor |
| | Presentations | Purpose/Topic<br>Date/Time<br>Organization<br>Summary | Parents<br>Students<br>Counselor<br>School Staff |
| Court | Mandated reporting<br>Abuse/Neglect<br>Violence/Suicide | Student's name<br>Referral's name<br>Date<br>Purpose<br>Summary<br>Outcome | Students<br>Counselor<br>Community |

# Chapter 30

## Promoting a K-12 Developmental Guidance Program

**by**
**Joe Wittmer and Mary Ann Clark**

## Introduction

Selling, promoting, and marketing a comprehensive, developmental counseling program to students, professional colleagues, and parents is not an easy task, nor one to be taken for granted. It is essential to the survival of the program and a structured, deliberate, and planned, public relations (*PR—performance recognized*) approach is needed. The strategies and techniques presented in this chapter have been used to help promote developmental guidance at all grade levels; they can be adapted to coincide with any school level (elementary, middle, high).

Cialdini (2000) outlined several stages that individuals attempting to successfully sell, promote, market, or otherwise persuade others to use a product, a service, or a program, should follow. Among these are:

**Identification**—To recognize what is being "sold" and promoted to whom and why. The program (product) is then promoted within the target population (students, teachers, administrators, and parents) through the use of newsletters, logos, slogans, success stories, and other types of appropriate promotional activities.

**Legitimacy**—A legitimate product (i.e., a developmental counseling program) has credibility which has been established. Several strategies can be employed including the testimony of experts and the visible participation of supporters and consumers of the product (program).

**Participation**—Cialdini defines this as that phase when even the previously uncommitted individuals begin to show support and begin participating in the program. In the case of school counseling, this means all publics—administrators, parents, teachers, students, and so forth.

**Accountability**—A program (i.e., the counseling program) that has been successfully sold will have lived up to promises previously made and produces tangible results. That is, who is delivering what services to whom and how effective is the specific service being provided?

These four stages are briefly presented below concerning each target population deemed important to "sell" on a comprehensive counseling program: *administrators, teachers, parents,* and *students.* Several ideas and suggestions are listed, but are not intended to be all inclusive. It is suggested that counselors select from among those most appropriate and applicable to their particular school and publics.

## Administration

As stated in the beginning of this book, it is imperative that the school administration be sold on the need for a developmental school counseling program in order for it to be successful. And, as also noted, it is the job of the school counselor to "sell" the program to his or her administrators. Optimally, school counselors and administrators are partners in promoting "their" comprehensive, developmental school counseling program which serves all students. When school counselors and administrators work closely together and set common goals for the school, all stakeholders will benefit!

### Identification

First and foremost, it is important to describe (in writing) the comprehensive developmental counseling program in concert with . The following components are essential.

- Develop and implement a school counseling curriculum for *everyone* in the school.

- Make individual, small and large group counseling potentially available to all students in the school.

- Plan and organize a system of parental involvement in the program.

- Organize and implement a peer helper/peer mediation program.

- Provide consultation and coordination of direct and indirect guidance services to parents, faculty, and community agencies.

An important aspect of the identification of the program is the visibility and teamwork approach shown by school counselors. Counselors can write a regular press release for the principal's newsletter describing important components of the counseling program. The newsletter may be sent home or it may be posted on the school's website. It may be that counselors may have their own section of a school's website that is geared towards counseling goals, objectives and activities.

## Legitimacy

Establish the genuine credibility of the counseling program to the administration. This cannot be accomplished through words alone; the administration must see action-oriented results. Assist them in understanding a developmental counseling program. Your credibility with the administration is best established if you:

- Recognize the movement away from reactive counseling to the preventive, proactive, developmental approach: work at the image of becoming a facilitator of educational success across the school's entire curriculum.

- Watch for increasing opportunities to serve as a consultant, working with individual groups of teachers concerning classroom management, dealing effectively with special problem students, behavioral techniques, motivation, and so forth.

- Demonstrate your effectiveness as a program planner. A legitimate, effective planner possesses three general planning skills: needs assessment, program design, and program evaluation/accountability.

- Work at continually convincing the administration that you are using your special skills to make *their* job easier as a school administrator; that you are a vital member of the educational team, not just an auxiliary service provider!

- Work on enhancing the counselor-administrator partnership necessary for successful comprehensive school counseling programs.

## Participation

Administrative support will grow for a school developmental counseling program if you:

- Learn and use the art of positive influence and persuasion.

- Offer to help lead in-service teacher and other staff development programs (agree to serve on the in-service staff development committee for your school).

- Request time to make announcements or reports in faculty meetings, at PTA meetings, and so forth.

- Report back when you attend any in-service, professional development meetings. Make copies of your notes from these meetings for distribution to others in the school who might benefit. Write a memo to the administrators apprising them of what you learned and how you will apply it. Offer in-service training for others on what you learned at the meeting/convention.

- Keep a *regular, weekly* appointment time with your administrator. Listen! Your principal probably has very few people to confide in; as the counselor, become that person.

- Present an administrator(s) with a certificate or plaque recognizing his or her accomplishments and contributions to the guidance program when appropriate. Let them know they are appreciated.

- If your school does not currently have a developmental guidance program, talk with the principal about working into an authentic, developmental program "one step at a time." Do not ask for too much too soon. Take your gains where you can.

- At the beginning of the school year, ask your head administrator to help you set three priority goals for the academic year, then together plan a program to meet these goals. And, let the administration periodically know of your progress toward meeting these goals. These goals can be part of the school improvement committee's goals.

- Remember that what happens in your counseling program is everybody's business, and the more sensitive the staff (especially administrators) become to the counseling related needs of students, the more successful the school counseling program will be.

## Accountability

An ongoing, continuous evaluation system is imperative. Reveal, in writing, the results of your program. Gather "hard" data and present it to the administration periodically. This can best be accomplished by:

- Providing a weekly schedule of services—a weekly, semester-long, and yearly calendar for the administration and others in the school.

- Regularly advise the administration of program accomplishments through monthly reports. Don't burden them with long, drawn out reports—keep them brief and to the point; "just the facts."

- Invite your principal to sit in on a large group counseling unit in a classroom, or present it to him or her on video; show off some of your accomplishments.

- Place your program, goals, objectives, plans for implementation, materials, and accountability procedures on paper. Give copies to the administration and revise as often as necessary.

- Keeping your principal informed at all times (i.e., regarding any media coverage forthcoming, etc.) about everything you deem important. Ideally, work together on program planning and media coverage.

# Teachers

As noted throughout this book, teachers play a vital role in a developmental school counseling program. They are the ones who know students best, probably better than any other adult in the school. Thus, they are in a prime position to notice changes in students' behaviors and refer them for counseling, special assistance, and so forth. It is essential that open communication exist between counselors and teachers if the developmental school counseling program is to be successful.

## Identification

Inform the teachers of the types of services the counseling department has to offer to assist them as they work with students on a day to day basis. This can be accomplished best if you:

- Let them know you are available to them. Pencil in "flexible" or "teacher consultation" time on your calendar and share it with all teachers. And, "be there" for them when needed.

- Send them memos describing groups and other developmental services that can, or are, being provided to assist with target students. Request they nominate students for certain small groups that you lead on specific themes that have been identified as being needed to meet student needs..

- Develop a structure for meeting substitute teachers and develop a short handout for their use that details services you can offer them.

- Form a list of possible in-service activities for teachers and then set up some programs for which they might volunteer (i.e., Character Education,, Embracing Diversity in the Classroom, School Success Skills for Students). Develop a resource list of readings, websites, and activities that are relevant to their concerns.

## Legitimacy

Establish the credibility of the guidance program to teachers. Some suggestions include:

- Work with the administration to give incentives to teachers to attend in-service training where you discuss your developmental program, the goals, objectives, and so forth.

- A teacher appreciation day might be held stressing the benefits of a developmental guidance and counseling program and how it benefits all students and teachers.

- Share with teachers student success stories that are non-confidential in nature.

## Participation

Work at gaining the support of teachers who are not yet committed to the program. This can be best accomplished by:

- Having teachers fill out personal needs assessments and provide them with the results—what services do they "expect" and "desire" from the guidance department?

- Holding a session (consider a breakfast meeting or after school social) to discuss the results of the needs assessments and ask teachers for ways to meet these needs.

- Getting teachers to utilize peer facilitators where appropriate.

- Ask reluctant teachers which "special" academically oriented large group classroom activities they would like to see implemented (i.e., study skills, note taking, paying attention in class, asking appropriate questions, etc.).

- Send "Thank-u-Grams" to teachers who have provided you with assistance, who have helped a student in a "special" way, and so forth.

- Hold annual orientation meetings with new teachers concerning the counseling program. Develop a structure to assign a "buddy" to each new teacher in your school.

## Accountability

Demonstrate the value of your developmental counseling program through evaluative methods. Ask for the teachers' evaluation of you and the overall program at least once a year by having:

- Teachers complete evaluative forms that focus on the various specific components of the developmental counseling program of which they are aware. You may have district level forms that are used as part of the school improvement program.

- Share your results with teachers and administrators. How have students changed as a result of your intervention(s)? You may be able to present data such as discipline referrals, absences, and grades. Perceptual data, that is teachers' perceptions of changes that students have made in their classrooms as a result of your interventions, are also important. Such data could include behavior, attentiveness, peer relationships and attitudes.

## Parents

As noted throughout this book, it is important and essential that parents become involved in the developmental counseling program. Parents play a vital role in effective developmental programs. Parental involvement is also vitally important to the success of their own child. Parents who understand the goals and objectives of the counseling department are more likely to become involved and to assist in meeting these goals in a variety of ways.

### Identification

Increase the awareness of your developmental counseling program to the parents whose offspring are enrolled in your school. By doing this, parents learn who you are, what you do, and how this helps their own child, as well as others in the school. This can be accomplished by:

- Developing a brochure that describes you, your job, and your developmental program. This should include a brief written philosophy, goals, and objectives of your developmental counseling program. Then, send it home to the parents. Many schools now have websites that post this kind of information as well.

- Inviting parents to an orientation open house at the beginning of each year.

- Sending home a periodic calendar of events concerning the counseling program.

- Sending home a certificate of achievement/improvement when their child successfully completes a group, individual work project, and so forth.

- Attending and participating in PTA meetings where you describe the counseling program in detail or are a featured speaker on a specific topic of interest to parents.

- Make phone calls to the homes of each new student by the end of their first week at your school. A letter of welcome to the home of the new parents is always appreciated.

### Legitimacy

Parents must be convinced that the counseling program is sound and helpful to their *own* child.

- Present a slide show or video/DVD of successful program activities at the PTA meeting or other meetings where parents are invited.

- Have students who have successfully used your services speak with parents at the beginning of the year, perhaps a panel of students at the PTA meeting. The Advisory Committee could also be a helpful resource in explaining their role and in soliciting parental input.

## Participation

As parents learn to know you better, what you do, and the successes you've had, they will be much more willing to participate in your counseling program. Some suggestions for increasing parental participation in the program are as follows:

- Conduct a needs assessment of parents on an annual basis. District or accreditation data may be collected which could also be used.

- Provide each parent with a calendar that lists program activities for each month.

- Solicit parents as volunteers (i.e., for career week, college night, as tutors, helpers for special projects, etc.).

- Invite parents to sit in on an educational and/or career counseling/planning session with you and their child. Involve them in a student led conference as described in chapter 19.

- Establish a counseling website for parents.

## Accountability

Parents will want to see the results of your program.

- At the end of the year, send each parent a questionnaire on the efficiency and effectiveness of the guidance department and its program. And at the end of the questionnaire, ask for volunteers to serve on a special guidance committee to help decide goals for the following year and for their suggestions concerning the guidance program.

## Students

Students need to know the goals and objectives of your program, what you do and can do for them. If they do not know the counselors, or what services are provided by the counseling office, the program will not be effective. Develop the program in such a manner so that each student in school knows who the counselors are and what services they have to offer. Students are your primary concern; your main *consumers*!

## Identification

Use different methods to identify who you are and what you do. Give the students an opportunity to match a face with a name. Be creative!

- Visit each classroom early in the year, make a brief presentation, and distribute information (a student-oriented brochure) regarding the role and function of the counseling department.

- Begin a special Counseling Department section in the school newspaper (i.e,. perhaps a "Dear Abby" type column).

- Be visible: keep in touch with what students are doing; be in attendance at athletic events, and so forth.

- Use bulletin boards to provide information on what is offered to students through the counseling department, as well as upcoming events, appointment forms, groups that are being formed, and so forth.

- Involve students in publicity campaigns, especially the student council, peer helpers, and so forth.

- Have a *Counseling Services Week* at your school. Involve the students in planning the week. ASCA sponsors a "National School Counseling Week" which highlights and recognizes the importance of school counselors and their special contributions. Ideas and accompanying materials are available from ASCA for local implementation (See www.schoolcounselor.org)

## Legitimacy

Continually demonstrate that the developmental counseling program is credible and is there for the basic purpose of meeting the *needs* and *concerns* of *all* students. Legitimacy can be gained and maintained by:

- Having students who have utilized your program's services tell other students about their experiences (i.e., at a student assembly, via closed circuit TV, written surveys, etc.).

- Advertising small groups such as "Peer Facilitators," "New To School Student Groups," "Your Changing Family," and so forth, by using available school media, bulletin boards, and the school website. Closed circuit television announcements are also a good way to publicize this information.

## Participation

The primary goal is to get all students interested and involved in the developmental counseling program. This can best be accomplished by:

- Utilizing positive peer pressure.

- Distributing questionnaires in the classrooms, including needs assessment surveys, possible topics of interest to them, setting up a counseling department suggestion box, and so forth.

- Establish a positive atmosphere in the counseling department and make access easy for the students.

- Increase student awareness of current events and forthcoming counseling related activities. This will increase their involvement.

## Accountability

Continually update and work on your image with the students by being accountable. Have them assist you in deciding whether what you are doing is effective, and make revisions where necessary.

- Find out what students know about your guidance services through questionnaires.

- Publish results of evaluations in the school paper, through announcements, newsletters or the school website. Then, follow-up with information concerning *changes* that have, or will be made, as a result of the student evaluations.

- Keep a "real" open door policy.

- Be accessible to students. Develop a system as to how you can be reached when out of the office. Many counselors keep a schedule posted on their door.

- Encourage self-referrals and referrals from concerned students regarding their friends who they think need to see you ("Care-Grams").

- Develop a "buddy system" for new students and provide them with a "You are Here" map of your school.

- Be part of a committee that visits hospitalized students and sends cards, as appropriate.

## Summary

A public relations program needs to be an ongoing part of the developmental counseling program. To gain the support from your publics it is imperative that you inform them of what you are doing, and how effectively. Basically, school counselors need to promote themselves and their program, or their importance in the academic, personal/social, and career successes of students will not become known. Good public relations are an excellent way to gain and strengthen the support and encouragement of everyone. Though it will take much time and creative energy, developing and implementing a good public relations program can help you and your counseling program immeasurably.

Dozens of additional creative PR ideas are presented in Figure 30.1 (Ayes & Buchan, 1992). As a practicing counselor, review the list given and check off those you think appropriate for you and your school. Then, ask the question; how does my PR program rate? Does it measure up? Answering the questions provided in Figure 30.2 in the affirmative would be a good indication of just how good your current PR program is and may suggest some needed changes.

## References

Ayes, Z., & Buchan, B.A. (1992). School counselors exploring human potential: Set sail with PR. *The ASCA Counselor*, p. 7.

Cialdini, R.B. (2000). *Influence science and practice* (4th ed.). Glenview, IL: Scott Foresman.

## Figure 30.1
## School Counselors Exploring Human Potential: Set Sail with PR

### Publicity

- Posters
- Flyers
- Awards
- Public service announcements
- Information about scholarships
- Booths at school fair
- Radio and television announcements
- Newspaper articles
- Brochures
- Community events
- Invite legislators to speak
- Cable TV programs
- School/District websites

### Professional Services

- Advisory committees
- Advisor for school clubs
- PTA/PTO presentations
- Conduct workshops
- Institute a teacher swap shop within district and neighbor districts
- Coordination of school activities or events
- Newsletter
- Public speaking
- Consultation with parents, teachers, administrators, and community agencies

### Student Activities and Events

- Celebrate National School Counseling Week
- Assemblies
- Career fair contests (essay, art, song writing, poetry, brainstorming, and so forth.)
- Peer helper program
- College Fair Step-up Day
- Initiate International Pen-Pal Club
- Create a Holiday (i.e., Crazy Hat Day, Stress Reduction Day)
- Student involvement in National Career Development Month activities
- Incorporate student ideas into professional services
- Orientation programs
- Career Inventions project

### Visual Displays

- Bulletin boards
- Calendars
- T-shirts
- Bumper stickers
- Mugs
- Buttons
- Videos
- Banners
- Wall signs
- Lapel pins
- Calling cards
- Tote bags with school counselor message
- Displays in the hall
- Wallet-size cards with emergency numbers on them
- Order specialty logo items through ASCA
- Posters
- Bookmarks

(Adapted from Ayes, Z. & Buchan, B.A., *The School Counselor*, February, 1992).

# Figure 30.2
## Self-Evaluation Inventory for a School Guidance Public Relations Program

| | YES | NO |
|---|---|---|

1. Have you worked with the sponsor of your school newspaper and discussed *regular* coverage of guidance news?  ❏ ❏

2. Do you know the person at your local newspaper/radio/TV station you should contact for a story? Have you recently developed a Public Service Announcement (PSA)?  ❏ ❏

3. Do you have an orientation program for incoming kindergarten, sixth or seventh, ninth or tenth graders? Did you evaluate it and share the findings?  ❏ ❏

4. Do you have an orientation program for new students? (Ones who transfer in after school begins.) Did you evaluate it and show the results?  ❏ ❏

5. Have you developed a brochure or a website link to explain your guidance program to students, parents, teachers, administrators and others?  ❏ ❏

6. Do you make a presentation concerning the guidance program at one school board meeting each year?  ❏ ❏

7. Do you have a minimum of three articles or feature stories about the guidance program in the local newspaper each year?  ❏ ❏

8. Do you have written plans or guides for a public relations plan for your program?  ❏ ❏

9. Do you have news from the guidance department in each issue of the school newspaper?  ❏ ❏

10. Do you give a minimum of three speeches each year to local, civic, and service organizations?  ❏ ❏

11. Do you make a minimum of three annual presentations concerning guidance programs at your school faculty meetings?  ❏ ❏

12. Do you make reports about the guidance program at one or more administrative staff meetings annually?  ❏ ❏

# Chapter 31

# Legal and Ethical Issues in School Counseling

**by**
**Theodore P. Remley, Jr. and Mary A. Hermann**

---

*Theodore P. Remley, Jr., J.D., Ph.D., is a Professor of Counseling at Old Dominion University In Norfolk, Virginia. He has served as a school counselor and a university counselor educator. In addition, he has maintained private practices in both counseling and law.*

*Mary A. Hermann, J.D., Ph.D., is an Assistant Professor of Counseling at Virginia Commonwealth University in Richmond. She is both an attorney and university counselor educator and has had experience as a school teacher and school counselor.*

## Introduction

Professional counselors in all settings increasingly are finding the legal and ethical issues they face to be complex and challenging (Corey, Corey, & Callanan, 2007). Although problems related to the law and ethical standards may be difficult for counselors in community mental health agencies, rehabilitation facilities, universities, or private practices, school counselors are regularly confronted with the most difficult issues on a daily basis (Culbreth, Scarborough, Banks-Johnson, & Solomon, 2005; Hermann, 2002).

There are two basic reasons why school counselors have substantial problems addressing legal and ethical issues. First, K-12 school counselors offer services most often to minors and the law and professional ethical standards are inadequate regarding a practical resolution of the competing interests of children and the adults who are responsible for their welfare (Lawrence & Kurpius, 2000). In some cases, law and ethics appear to be conflict (Rowley & MacDonald, 2001). In addition, despite the fact that dual relationships are discouraged in counseling (Herlihy & Corey, 1992), counselors in schools have multiple roles (counselor, educator, colleague, and parent substitute) and interact with a variety of individuals who demand their professional services (students, parents, guardians, other interested adults, teachers, and administrators). Legal and ethical standards that strongly discourage dual relationships with clients cause continuing headaches and hardships for school counselors, as some dual relationships are unavoidable.

## Minors as Clients

As a school counselor, you will primarily be counseling and otherwise serving children below the age of 18, the age of legal majority in the United States. Until individuals are 18, they are legally under the control and care of their parents or court appointed guardians. Minors have only in the last few decades been recognized as having a legal status that extends beyond the rights of their parents (Wrightsman, 1997).

While the ethical standards for counselors inform you that you have primary responsibilities to your clients, the law clearly implies that, until your clients reach the age of 18, parents are the individuals to whom you are *legally* responsible. As a result, even though you have personal counseling relationships with minors, their parents or guardians have legal authority and control over those relationships. School counselors know that, in most cases, there is much to be gained from involving parents in the lives of their children (Davis & Lambie, 2005). On the other hand, when parents and their children are in conflict with each others, counselors sometimes find themselves unsure of how to proceed.

A good practice rule to follow when counseling students is to assume that your professional responsibilities are to your minor clients. On the other hand, if parents or legal guardians become involved in the counseling process, you must acknowledge that they have authority over minors. They, therefore, are legally in charge of the counseling relationship and you must defer to their rights.

Because counseling is a part of the general educational experience in schools, parental permission for students to receive counseling services is not required by law. Many school principals or school districts have enacted policies that do require parental permission before counselors enter into counseling relationships with minors. Such policies are based on the preference of administrators or board members and are not legally required. Thus, it is extremely important that you become familiar with the policies in your specific school system.

In the event, however, parents insist that counseling or guidance services within a school environment be discontinued, they *probably* have a legal right to have their wishes followed because such services are not a required part of the school curriculum. If you ever plan to ignore the demands of parents requesting that you stop counseling their child, it is strongly suggested that you obtain the support of your direct supervisor before doing so, since you may violate the parents' legal rights. That is, the legal rights, in this case, belong with the parents.

Our legal system is based on a strong belief that individual and family privacy should not be violated by others, particularly those who are public employees. Generally, parents have complete control and authority over their children, unless it is determined by formal means that parents are harming their children in some way. As a school counselor, it is important that you remember the legal rights of parents and guardians concerning their children, even when it may seem to you that the interests of children are not being best served. Simply stated, poor or inappropriate judgment (in your opinion) on the part of parents generally does not diminish their legal rights over their minor offspring.

## Consultation with Attorneys

School counselors are sometimes reluctant to seek the advice of attorneys when they are faced with a legal problem. All schools have attorneys available to advise them. The best way to access your school's attorney is to ask your supervisor to arrange for you to consult with your school's lawyer. You may be required to submit your question in writing, but school officials should be willing to provide you with legal advice when it is requested. Don't hesitate, seek legal advice when needed.

In the event you ask for legal advice, and your school does not comply, it is suggested that you document your request in writing. A written document will protect you later if it turns out legal advice could have prevented a problem. In this litigious day and age, you must also protect yourself.

## Confidentiality

Graduate students in counseling have little trouble understanding the rule that they *must* keep *secret* information they learn in counseling relationships. And, most students have little or no problem grasping the importance of such a requirement. What causes problems for graduate students and counselors is that there are many *exceptions* to confidentiality and that most of the problems that occur when you begin practicing school counseling center around the *exceptions*, not the rule itself. Confidentiality issues are particularly troublesome for school counselors because most of their clients are minors. Issues such as teen pregnancy, drug abuse, and suicide are causing school counselors to become more vulnerable to legal action. (Davis & Ritchie, 1993). The student on student violence that is prevalent in our schools is also complicating the confidential relationship between student and counselor and increasing the legal vulnerability of school counselors.

A major exception to the rule that counselors must keep secret what is told to them by clients occurs when counselors determine that their clients are a *danger to themselves or others*. If you arrive at the professional judgment that a client is a danger to self or others, you *must* take whatever steps are necessary to prevent harm. Often, the prohibition against telling others information you have learned in a counseling session must be compromised when you are taking steps to prevent harm. Counselors can be held accountable for an ethical violation or legal malpractice if clients they are serving harm themselves or others and it can be shown that the counselors *knew*, or *should have known*, that the clients were a danger to themselves or others.

For example, if a school counselor knew or should have known that a student was at risk for suicide and the child commits suicide, the counselor can be held legally liable. In recent years, school counselors have been sued and found negligent for not responding to suicidal threats made by students. Courts have found that even if the risk of the student actually committing suicide is remote, the possibility may be enough to establish a duty to contact the student's parents.

A counselor could be held liable if the counselor knew or should have known that a student was a danger to others and didn't take steps to prevent the harm. The Fifth Circuit Court of Appeals has stated that the "epidemic of violence in American public schools is a relatively new phenomenon, but one which has already generated considerable caselaw." *Johnson v. Dallas Independent School District*, 38 F.3d 198 (5th Cir. 1994). Counselors and other school personnel have a legal obligation to exercise reasonable care to protect students from foreseeable harm. *Eisel v. Board of Education,* 597 A.2d 447 (Md. 1991). In 1999, the United States Supreme Court noted that state courts routinely uphold claims alleging that schools have been negligent in failing to protect their students from the violent acts of their peers. *Davis v. Monroe County Board of Education,* 119 S.Ct. 1661 (1999).

Yet, counselors are only required to act like reasonable professionals. In determining what is reasonable, courts have found that school counselors are accountable for the degree of care that would be utilized by other professionals with similar education and experience. *Wyke v. Polk County School Board,* 129 F.3d 560 (11th Cir. 1997). You cannot anticipate acts of random violence and are not required by law to do so. Only failure to exercise reasonable care exposes counselors to liability.

When clients request that you give information obtained in a counseling session to a third party, you may do so, and in most circumstances, it would be inappropriate not to comply. In the case of minors, parents or guardians must grant permission to transfer confidential information to another individual.

A major exception to the confidentiality requirement occurs when a parent or legal guardian demands to know the contents of counseling sessions that have transpired with their children (Zingaro, 1983). If parents inquire about your sessions with their child, *always* ask the child if he/she they would object to your relating the contents of your sessions to the parents. Children are often less concerned about their privacy than are adults.

In the event children object, or you feel it would not be in the best interests of children you are counseling for their parents to be informed of the contents of counseling sessions, you certainly should try to convince the parents to trust you to tell them anything they need to know. You should explain to the parents why confidentiality is important in a counseling relationship and assure them you will involve them to the fullest possible extent in their children's lives. Conducting a joint session with parents and their children might satisfy the parents' concerns. However, always clear this with your client prior to conducting such joint sessions.

As a school counselor, it is doubtful you would be held in violation of any ethical or legal standards if you told parents information you obtained from counseling sessions with their children. However, there may be instances in which you might decide that you should not give parents the information they are demanding. You should realize that you could be violating the legal rights of the parents. Historically, courts have protected parental rights (Isaacs & Stone, 1999).

A legal and ethical exception to confidentiality exists when a *court* formally *orders* you to disclose information obtained in a counseling relationship. A subpoena, however, is *not a court order* to disclose information and an attorney's advice must be sought when you are presented with a subpoena. That is, do not produce any records simply because you receive a subpoena until you have been advised to do so by an attorney. However, you must comply with court orders and you cannot be held legally or ethically accountable for breaching confidentiality if you are following the formal instructions of a judge.

Some of the other exceptions to confidentiality include the following situations: 1) you are receiving clinical supervision of your work as a counselor; 2) your secretary has access to confidential information; 3) you are consulting with a colleague or expert regarding a difficult case; and/or 4) you are consulting your employer or an attorney regarding a questionable circumstance.

As a school counselor, you may often be asked by a teacher or administrator to reveal personal information about the students or families you are counseling. An important question to consider in deciding whether the person asking has an "educational" need to know. In other words, does he or she need to know the information in order to provide appropriate educational services for the student? Will providing such information enhance the student's learning? Certainly, students and parents have a right to know if a counselor relates personal information about them to another school professional.

School counselors are increasingly using the Internet in providing counseling services (Layne & Hohenshil, 2005). The ACA *Code of Ethics* (2005) contains specific guidelines regarding confidentiality for counselors who use the Internet. However, Heinlen, Welfel, Richmond, and Rak (2003) and Shaw and Shaw (2006) found that counselors who provide online counseling services often do not comply with these ethical standards. In a study with surprising results, Reese, Conoley, and Brossart (2006) discovered that clients who had received counseling services over the telephone were more likely to indicate they would again seek counseling services than clients who had received counseling services face-to-face.

Confidentiality is an *ethical* obligation that you owe to clients. You can be held *legally* accountable, however, for any harm that occurs to clients because you *did not* keep information confidential (see Figure 31.1).

# Privileged Communication

A different, but similar, concept is privileged communication. Communication between two individuals is legally privileged if a statute exists in your state that specifically grants it. If privilege exists, a judge *cannot* require that confidential information be disclosed. If legal privilege does not exist, judges *always* can order counselors to disclose information obtained in counseling relationships.

In order for school counselors to have privilege with their clients, a state statute must specify that privilege exists between school counselors and students (Glosoff, Herlihy, & Spence, 2000). If a school counselor is a licensed, certified, or registered professional counselor, it is possible that privilege may exist based on that credential. An excellent reason for school counselors to become licensed, certified, or registered professional counselors is to qualify for "privilege" with their clients. Certification by a state department of education or by a national credentialing board (i.e., NBCC) does not extend privilege to the clients of school counselors.

# Counseling Records

School counselors must be concerned about two types of records—*administrative* and *clinical*. Administrative records include cumulative folders and other records concerning students that are available to other school personnel. Clinical records are case notes that are kept to refresh the counselor's memory and to document important events regarding a counseling relationship with a student.

As a school counselor, it is important that you read and understand the provisions of the Family Educational Rights and Privacy Act of 1974, also known as FERPA or the Buckley Amendment (Walker & Larrabee, 1985). Essentially this federal law requires that schools receiving federal funds provide access to all school records to parents of students under the age of 18 and to students themselves once they reach 18. In addition, the amendment requires that *no student records* be released to third parties without the express written consent of parents of minor students or the written consent of adult students.

One exception to the requirement that students or their parents have access to school records is that records kept in the *sole* possession of the maker do not have to be shown to students or parents. Counselor clinical records, or case notes, would come under this exception if you do not show them to anyone else. You should be cautioned, however, that just because students or parents do not have access to your clinical records under FERPA or the Buckley

Amendment, they might gain access through a court ordered or subpoena or the records might be obtained through other legal processes.

You should keep any administrative or clinical records you need as a counselor in order to do a good job. Merlone (2005) surveyed school counselors and found that they are attempting to keep records according to guidelines they have learned from professional materials and workshops, but that they are unsure of whether they are keeping records in an appropriate manner. There is not only one way to keep clinical counseling records. There are a number of formats available for school counselors to consider (Cameron & turtle-song, 2002). It is important that you record enough information to refresh or jog your memory, and to document events that take place that demonstrate you have performed your responsibilities in an appropriate and professional manner based on *standards of practice*. In court, experts might be asked to review your records and make a judgment concerning whether you followed "standards of practice." You should not be concerned that students or parents may eventually see the records you are keeping. In fact, it is recommended that you *write each record as if it might someday be given out in court as public information with you, TV cameras, your student client, his or her parents, and others present!*

The same principles that apply to confidentiality and privileged communication apply to student records as well. Even if the relationship between you and the students you counsel is privileged by state or federal statute, there are circumstances under which you might be forced to reveal clinical records you have kept. For example, students *themselves* may subpoena records you have kept regarding sessions with them.

Keeping secret records does not protect them from a subpoena. Most subpoenas that seek records ask for *all* records kept under *all* circumstances in any location. You could be asked, following the taking of an oath, if there are any records related to the case being litigated. Records must be kept in secure locations, but there is no reason to keep records in secret places.

If you receive a subpoena requesting your records, tell your supervisor and consult the school's attorney as soon as possible. Do not automatically comply with the subpoena and do not panic. You could violate your client's legal rights if you turn over records in response to a non-court ordered subpoena without first protesting the subpoena in court.

Never destroy records you think might be subpoenaed at a later date. You could be guilty of a serious crime if you destroy evidence. In a school setting, you should destroy your clinical records on a regular schedule. For example, it might be wise to destroy clinical records at the beginning of each school year for students who are not presently attending the school. Inform your supervisor of your plan and procedure for destroying records and then act accordingly. In addition, check to see if your school system or state has a policy concerning records. It is *unwise* to keep records forever because they could be accidentally seen by others. However, if you regularly destroy most records, you should keep particular records for extended periods of time if the records document actions you took that would prove you acted responsibly in difficult situations. Check your local and or state regulations concerning the length of time (if any) that records should be kept.

# Interaction with Families

School counselors must face many difficult legal and ethical problems related to family situations due to the fact that family life has become more complex (Sprinthall, Hall, & Gerler, 1992) and school aged youth have become more socially isolated (Hazler & Denham, 2002). As noted, most school students are minors, they are under the control of either parents or legal guardians. And, as mentioned previously, you must acknowledge the rights of parents and guardians and you have a legal obligation to interact with them.

## Custody Cases

One of the more difficult areas is divorce and child custody. Parents who are going through the divorce process often seek to involve school counselors to assist them in obtaining custody of their children. That is, parents might ask you to agree to testify on their behalf at custody hearings. However, you should *never* agree to take sides in a custody struggle, no matter how strongly you may feel that one parent is *superior* to the other (Remley, 1991).

There are several challenges that occur if you become involved as a witness at a child custody hearing. First, you lose your objectivity and effectiveness as the child's counselor and second, you run the risk of the accusation of being a biased expert witness by the opposing attorney. In addition, you become an advocate rather than an impartial helper and you will probably have difficulty responding to your other job responsibilities because of the time and energy such involvement demands.

It is recommended that you refuse to testify willingly in custody hearings. Of course, you may be subpoenaed and forced to participate. If you receive a subpoena, immediately ask your supervisor to arrange for you to speak with your school's attorney. It would be in your best interest to inform the attorney that you would rather not be involved in custody hearings and then follow the attorney's advice. In the event you do appear as a witness at a custody hearing, it is strongly recommended that you *never* give an opinion (unless ordered to do so by the judge) and that you restrict your testimony to *factual* information only regarding the parents and the child in question.

Once a court order has been issued involving custody, it is important to realize that most legal rights regarding the child have not been compromised for the noncustodial parent. In most states, noncustodial parents are entitled to many of the same rights that the custodial parent has, except that the custodial parent has the right to the physical possession of the child. Check with your supervisor concerning the existing policies regarding noncustodial parents in your state or school. Obtain a copy of the policy manual, if available, and become familiar with it.

When noncustodial parents demand records, visits, or even the right to remove their children from the school, the matter should be *referred* to school administrators. As a school counselor, you generally should not have to make decisions regarding the rights of noncustodial parents without administrative or legal assistance.

## Non-Legal Parents, Guardians, and so forth

Stepparents, grandparents, and non-married partners of parents cause problems for school counselors. Legally, these individuals have no control over children you counsel, unless there are specific court orders giving them these rights. On the other hand, such people often are intimately involved with children and perform many parenting functions. You should be aware that individuals who are not parents or legal guardians *cannot waive* the rights of children or families of the children you serve. Obtaining written consent of a parent or legal guardian to interact with an adult who is in a child's life is one possible way to involve a non-parent or non-guardian without risking violation of another person's rights. Administrators *should* be consulted and their directions should be followed when questions arise concerning the involvement of stepparents, grandparents, and non-married partners of parents.

# Laws and Child Abuse

Almost all political jurisdictions in the United States (all states, the District of Columbia, and territories) require that school counselors report to authorities cases of *suspected* child abuse. If child abuse is suspected and a report is not made, in most situations, you can be found guilty of committing a crime. In addition, statutes protect those who make reports from being sued by individuals who are suspected of child abuse. In a recent study, Bryant and Milsom (2005) found that school counselors report an average of four cases of suspected child abuse a year.

Laws requiring that reports of suspected child abuse be made were passed because legislators were concerned that children were being harmed by those who were supposed to be taking care of them. And additionally, because these abused children had no recourse. Our society has decided that it is better to make a report of a *suspicion* of abuse that later proves to be false, than it is to hesitate in reporting simply because you are not absolutely certain that abuse has taken place.

Although the ethical standards of counselors prohibit you from revealing information you receive as a result of a counseling relationship, statutes that require reporting of suspected child abuse are an exception to this requirement.

## Statutes in Your Jurisdiction

As a school counselor, you *must* read the exact words of the statute in your jurisdiction that controls the reporting of suspected child abuse cases. Become *completely* familiar with all the details of the statute. It will pay off in the long run. You can find the statute by going to the Internet site for your state government. Stautes are also available in the state code books in most local public libraries or in college or university libraries. Obtain a copy for your files. The exact words of the statute are very important because they vary so much from jurisdiction to jurisdiction. In some statutes, reports must be made directly by the person who suspects the abuse; in others, those who suspect abuse have fulfilled their legal obligations if a report is made to their *direct* supervisor in their work setting. In some laws, reports of abuse inflicted by *anyone* must be made; while in others, only abuse inflicted by a parent or guardian must be reported (and the person making the report is only protected if the report is made against a parent or guardian). In most statutes, the length of time that has passed since the abuse occurred is not mentioned (Smith, 1990); while in others, the language specifically states that abuse that occurred at any point in time must be reported. Some laws have defined *emotional abuse*, but the wording varies. As mentioned, the wording of statutes varies greatly and each word can be important

as you attempt to comply with legal requirements as to when and how you report suspected child abuse situations. Again, it will be in your best interest to obtain a copy of your states' statutes and that you become familiar with the reporting policies in your school or district.

## Professional Judgment and Suspected Abuse

The first difficult tasks regarding suspected child abuse cases is to make a professional judgment whether abuse might have occurred. Ferris and Linville (1985) and Lambie (2005) have offered some guidelines regarding abuse determinations. You do not have to be certain, you only must, in your professional judgment, have a legitimate suspicion. Exercising professional judgment means that you have to take into account all of the facts concerning this particular case and make an evaluation based on the knowledge and experience you have had as a counselor. Counselors must take cultural differences into account when making a determination as to whether child abuse may have occurred (Fontes, 2002). From an ethical perspective, it is wise to consult with colleagues and experts when you are unsure. However, consultation is not required under child abuse reporting statutes. After you have carefully reviewed a situation, if you have any indication at all that child abuse might have occurred, you must make a report in the manner that is required by statute.

You may be tempted to not make a report even when you do suspect that a child has been abused. You may feel that it would cause more harm than good for a report to be made. If you do not understand the process that occurs after a report is made or are frustrated with the response of social services agencies, you should schedule a meeting with case workers who investigate reports of suspected child abuse cases (Wilder, 1991). If you *fail* to make a report and abuse is later discovered, along with the fact that you knew about it, you could be found guilty of a crime.

If it does not violate school policies, it is important that you remain involved in child abuse investigations, to the extent possible, so that you can continue to be of help to students and their parents. Filing a report of suspected child abuse fulfills your legal obligations, but your ethical responsibilities require that you continue to offer the best professional services available to the students and families you serve (Alessi & Ballard, 2001; Horton, Johnson, Roundy, & Williams, 1990). However, again, become familiar with your school and school system's policies. Some school administrations forbid counselors' continued involvement in a case if that counselor was the individual reporting the suspected abuse.

## Supervision

School counselors have ethical and legal obligations related to supervising others (Herlihy, Gray, & McCollum, 2002; Page, Pietrzak, & Sutton, 2001). Individuals you might supervise include graduate program practicum students or interns, other full-time counselors who are employed in your department, clerical employees, and peer helpers in your school (Studer, 2005).

Since supervision implies control over the person being supervised, it is possible that you could be held ethically or legally responsible for the improper acts of others. A supervisor generally must ensure that people being supervised are performing their duties in an appropriate manner. You need to train those you supervise and check their work. Of course, you cannot observe or direct everything completed by those under your supervision. You are expected to maintain the amount of control over your supervisee that a *reasonable* counselor would exercise in a similar situation.

In the event you learn that someone you are supervising is involved in any activities that violate school policies or procedures, ethical standards of the counseling profession, or laws, you must take whatever steps are necessary to correct the situation. If you look the other way or ignore violations of policies or procedures, you personally could be held accountable for harm that results.

Requiring graduate students or employees you are supervising to buy professional liability insurance for themselves does not protect you from being sued if they harm someone. Although professional liability insurance is a good idea for any person who renders professional services, it protects the individual who purchases the insurance, not the supervisor. Generally, professional liability insurance will cover you, however, if you are sued for the act or omission of a supervisee.

School counselors sometimes are given responsibility for supervising an employee, but are not given evaluation or dismissal power over the individual. If you find that an employee under your supervision is acting inappropriately, but you do not have the authority to correct the person, it is vital that you put your supervisor on notice of the problem and request that he or she take whatever action is necessary to ensure that the employee is acting ethically and legally.

## Counselors as Employees

Employers have the right to demand that employees do what they are told. If an employee refuses to follow an employer's directive, the employee can be accused of insubordination, which is legal cause for dismissal. As long as the demands of your employer or supervisor are legal, you are required to comply.

School counselors have the responsibility of knowing all rules and regulations within the environment in which they work. It is important for you to follow the policies of your school, district, and state. If you find rules, regulations, or policies that are objectionable, you should work toward getting them changed, but must adhere to them in the interim.

### A Written Job Description

For your own protection, you should have an accurate and complete job description that you and your employer have agreed constitutes your responsibilities. *Written* job descriptions signed by both you and your supervisor are preferable. You can ask for a written job description if one does not exist. Job descriptions developed within your school must conform to district or state job descriptions, which generally are rather broad.

A good job description lists all duties you regularly perform and does not include any activities for which you are not responsible. It is detailed enough that an outsider could understand your job, but does not include so many specifics that you are given little or no flexibility in accomplishing your objectives.

### Ethical Violations and Employment

School counselors may find that they are being forced by their employers to do things that they feel violate the *Ethical Standards* (2005) of the American Counseling Association (ACA) or the *Ethical Standards for School Counselors* (2005) promulgated by the American School Counselor Association (Figure 31.2). If you find yourself in such a situation and refuse to follow your employer's directives, you could find yourself being fired for insubordination. If you challenged your dismissal, you would have to prove that what you were being asked to do violated the standards of your profession and that your employer's demands were therefore unreasonable. Because the burden would be on you to prove your employer's unreasonableness, and that would be difficult, you have a better chance of correcting a situation if you use *persuasion* and *education*, rather than confrontation. You might offer to your employer the professional literature which supports your position that whatever you are being asked to do is unethical. You also could ask the American Counseling Association or the American School Counselor Association ethics committees (assuming you are a member) to provide you formal rulings related to the questionable activity. Most employers are respectful of professional ethical standards and will yield if they can be convinced that a particular activity or act constitutes a violation of those standards.

## Private Practice and the School Counselor

School counselors sometimes open part-time private practices. It is important that any private practice activities in which you become involved are within legal and ethical standards.

In many states, you must have a state license as a professional mental health counselor in order to open a private practice. Licenses are issued by state regulatory boards.

A private practice is a business, and you must have a business license to operate in most political jurisdictions. Business licenses are available in town halls, city halls, or county court houses. Local political entities issue business licenses to collect local taxes on the income of businesses. If you fail to purchase a business license, you could be found guilty of a crime and perhaps even tax evasion.

Ethical standards require that you not accept clients in your private practice who have a relationship to your school. You must use your own judgment, given your particular circumstances, but it is possible that you should not accept private practice clients who are connected to your school district in any way. Some school districts have policies concerning private practice on the part of their counselor employees. It would be in your best interest to know about and adhere to such an existing policy. For example, one Florida school board does not permit its school counselor employees to conduct private practice within the boundaries of their particular county.

## Personal Liability

All professionals should purchase professional liability insurance, and school counselors are no exception. Although the chance of school counselors being sued for negligence or malpractice still is quite low, as counselors become more visible and accepted as mental health professionals in our society, the number of cases is increasing dramatically.

School counselors sometimes are under the mistaken impression that if their school is covered by professional liability insurance, then they are protected as well. Policies that cover schools will defend the *school* and pay off any judgments against the school related to malpractice cases. In defending a school, attorneys for the school usually work closely with individuals who are also named in a suit and give the appearance that they are attorneys for the individuals as well. In reality, the best interests of the *school* and the *counselor* in question may not be the same. Anytime you are individually named in a lawsuit (which usually is the case if a counselor is involved), you need to have your own professional liability insurance which will provide you with your own personal lawyer who has only *your* best interests in mind.

Professional liability insurance sometimes is an automatic benefit for school counselors who belong to unions. It can be purchased from the American Counseling Association, but is available only to members.

# Facing Ethical and Legal Problems: Some Guidelines

Listed below are some general guidelines for dealing with ethical and legal dilemmas as they arise:

- Know and follow the ethical standards of the American Counseling Association and the American School Counselor Association. The ethical practice recommendations given in Figure 31.3 will also prove helpful.

- Always consult with colleagues and experts when you are unsure. Since the standards for ethics and law relate to generally accepted practices, consultation that leads to a consensus of opinion can be very important if decisions you make are later challenged.

- Always ask for a legal opinion or a personal consultation with the school's attorney when you are facing a difficult legal problem.

- Document any actions you take that can prove that you have acted in a professional and appropriate manner.

- Turn over to administrators difficult situations that are not within your power to resolve.

- Read the current professional literature related to law and ethics to ensure that you understand the issues and have the latest advice.

- Attend professional seminars and programs related to legal and ethical issues in counseling.

- Be sure you have your own professional liability insurance policy.

# Figure 31.1
# Exceptions to Confidentiality and Privileged Communication

1. Client is a danger to self or others.
2. Client requests release of information.
3. A court orders release of information.
4. Systematic clinical supervision of the counselor.
5. Clerical assistants who process information and papers.
6. Client care team members.
7. Legal and clinical consultation.
8. Clinical supervision.
9. Clients raise the issue of their mental health in a lawsuit.
10. A third party is present in the room.
11. Group counseling.
12. Family counseling.
13. Clients are below the age of 18.
14. Counselors must defend themselves against a complaint regarding their services.

# Figure 31.2
# Ethical Practice Recommendations

## School counselors should:

- Act in the best interests of their clients at all times. Act in good faith and in the absence of malice.

- Inform clients of possible limitations on the counseling relationship prior to beginning the relationship.

- Increase awareness of personal values, attitudes, and beliefs; and refer when personal characteristics hinder effectiveness.

- Function within the boundaries of personal competence. Be aware of personal skill levels and limitations.

- Be able to fully explain why they did what they did. A theoretical rationale should undergird counseling strategies and interventions.

- Encourage family involvement, where possible, when working with minors in sensitive areas which might be controversial.

- Follow written job descriptions. Be sure that what they are doing is defined as an appropriate function in their setting.

- Read and adhere to the ethical standards of their profession. Keep copies of the ethical standards on hand, review them periodically and act accordingly.

- Consult with other professionals (colleagues, supervisors, counselor educators, ethics committees, etc.). Have a readily accessible support network of professionals.

- Join appropriate professional associations. Read association publications and participate in professional development opportunities.

- Stay up-to-date with laws and current court rulings, particularly those pertaining to counseling with minors.

- Consult with a knowledgeable attorney, when necessary. In questionable cases, seek legal advice prior to initiating actions (*The ASCA Counselor*, December, 1991).

# Figure 31.3
# American School Counselor Association
# Ethical Standards for School Counselors

## (Revised 2004)

## Preamble

The American School Counselor Association (ASCA) is a professional organization whose members are certified/licensed in school counseling with unique qualifications and skills to address the academic, personal/social and career development needs of all students.

Professional school counselors are advocates, leaders, collaborators and consultants who create opportunities for equity in access and success in educational opportunities by connecting their programs to the mission of schools and subscribing to the following tenets of professional responsibility:

- Each person has the right to be respected, be treated with dignity and have access to a comprehensive school counseling program that advocates for and affirms all students from diverse populations regardless of ethnic/racial status, age, economic status, special needs, English as a second language or other language group, immigration status, sexual orientation, gender, gender identity/expression, family type, religious/spiritual identity and appearance.

- Each person has the right to receive the information and support needed to move toward self-direction and self-development and affirmation within one's group identities, with special care being given to students who have historically not received adequate educational services: students of color, low socio-economic students, students with disabilities and students with nondominant language backgrounds.

- Each person has the right to understand the full magnitude and meaning of his/her educational choices and how those choices will affect future opportunities.

- Each person has the right to privacy and thereby the right to expect the counselor-student relationship to comply with all laws, policies and ethical standards pertaining to confidentiality in the school setting.

In this document, ASCA specifies the principles of ethical behavior necessary to maintain the high standards of integrity, leadership and professionalism among its members. The Ethical Standards for School Counselors were developed to clarify the nature of ethical responsibilities held in common by school counseling professionals.

The purposes of this document are to:

- Serve as a guide for the ethical practices of all professional school counselors regardless of level, area, population served or membership in this professional association;

- Provide self-appraisal and peer evaluations regarding counselor responsibilities to students, parents/guardians, colleagues and professional associates, schools, communities and the counseling profession; and

- Inform those served by the school counselor of acceptable counselor practices and expected professional behavior.

### A.1. Responsibilities to Students

The professional school counselor:

a. Has a primary obligation to the student, who is to be treated with respect as a unique individual.

b. Is concerned with the educational, academic, career, personal and social needs and encourages the maximum development of every student.

c. Respects the student's values and beliefs and does not impose the counselor's personal values.

d. Is knowledgeable of laws, regulations and policies relating to students and strives to protect and inform students regarding their rights.

### A.2. Confidentiality

The professional school counselor:

a. Informs students of the purposes, goals, techniques and rules of procedure under which they may receive counseling at or before the time when the counseling relationship is entered. Disclosure notice includes the limits of confidentiality such as the possible necessity for consulting with other professionals, privileged communication, and legal or authoritative restraints. The meaning and limits of confidentiality are defined in developmentally appropriate terms to students.

b. Keeps information confidential unless disclosure is required to prevent clear and imminent danger to the student or others or when legal requirements demand that confidential information be revealed.

Counselors will consult with appropriate professionals when in doubt as to the validity of an exception.

*Joe Wittmer, Ph.D. and Mary Ann Clark, Ph.D.*

c. In absence of state legislation expressly forbidding disclosure, considers the ethical responsibility to provide information to an identified third party who, by his/her relationship with the student, is at a high risk of contracting a disease that is commonly known to be communicable and fatal. Disclosure requires satisfaction of all of the following conditions:

- Student identifies partner or the partner is highly identifiable
- Counselor recommends the student notify partner and refrain from further high-risk behavior
- Student refuses
- Counselor informs the student of the intent to notify the partner
- Counselor seeks legal consultation as to the legalities of informing the partner

d. Requests of the court that disclosure not be required when the release of confidential information may potentially harm a student or the counseling relationship.

e. Protects the confidentiality of students' records and releases personal data in accordance with prescribed laws and school policies. Student information stored and transmitted electronically is treated with the same care as traditional student records.

f. Protects the confidentiality of information received in the counseling relationship as specified by federal and state laws, written policies and applicable ethical standards. Such information is only to be revealed to others with the informed consent of the student, consistent with the counselor's ethical obligation.

g. Recognizes his/her primary obligation for confidentiality is to the student but balances that obligation with an understanding of the legal and inherent rights of parents/guardians to be the guiding voice in their children's lives.

## A.3. Counseling Plans

The professional school counselor:

a. Provides students with a comprehensive school counseling program that includes a strong emphasis on working jointly with all students to develop academic and career goals.

b. Advocates for counseling plans supporting students right to choose from the wide array of options when they leave secondary education.

Such plans will be regularly reviewed to update students regarding critical information they need to make informed decisions.

## A.4. Dual Relationships

The professional school counselor:

a. Avoids dual relationships that might impair his/her objectivity and increase the risk of harm to the student (*e.g.*, counseling one's family members, close friends or associates). If a dual relationship is unavoidable, the counselor is responsible for taking action to eliminate or reduce the potential for harm. Such safeguards might include informed consent, consultation, supervision and documentation.

b. Avoids dual relationships with school personnel that might infringe on the integrity of the counselor/student relationship

## A.5. Appropriate Referrals

The professional school counselor:

a. Makes referrals when necessary or appropriate to outside resources. Appropriate referrals may necessitate informing both parents/guardians and students of applicable resources and making proper plans for transitions with minimal interruption of services.

Students retain the right to discontinue the counseling relationship at any time.

## A.6. Group Work

The professional school counselor:

a. Screens prospective group members and maintains an awareness of participants' needs and goals in relation to the goals of the group.

The counselor takes reasonable precautions to protect members from physical and psychological harm resulting from interaction within the group.

b. Notifies parents/guardians and staff of group participation if the counselor deems it appropriate and if consistent with school board policy or practice.

c. Establishes clear expectations in the group setting and clearly states that confidentiality in group counseling cannot be guaranteed. Given the developmental and chronological ages of minors in schools, the counselor recognizes the tenuous nature of confidentiality for minors renders some topics inappropriate for group work in a school setting.

d. Follows up with group members and documents proceedings as appropriate.

### A.7. Danger to Self or Others

The professional school counselor:

a. Informs parents/guardians or appropriate authorities when the student's condition indicates a clear and imminent danger to the student or others. This is to be done after careful deliberation and, where possible, after consultation with other counseling professionals.

b. Will attempt to minimize threat to a student and may choose to 1) inform the student of actions to be taken, 2) involve the student in a three-way communication with parents/guardians when breaching confidentiality or 3) allow the student to have input as to how and to whom the breach will be made.

### A.8. Student Records

The professional school counselor:

a. Maintains and secures records necessary for rendering professional services to the student as required by laws, regulations, institutional procedures and confidentiality guidelines.

b. Keeps sole-possession records separate from students' educational records in keeping with state laws.

c. Recognizes the limits of sole-possession records and understands these records are a memory aid for the creator and in absence of privilege communication may be subpoenaed and may become educational records when they 1) are shared with others in verbal or written form, 2) include information other than professional opinion or personal observations and/or 3) are made accessible to others.

d. Establishes a reasonable timeline for purging sole-possession records or case notes. Suggested guidelines include shredding sole possession records when the student transitions to the next level, transfers to another school or graduates. Careful discretion and deliberation should be applied before destroying sole-possession records that may be needed by a court of law such as notes on child abuse, suicide, sexual harassment or violence.

### A.9. Evaluation, Assessment and Interpretation

The professional school counselor:

a. Adheres to all professional standards regarding selecting, administering and interpreting assessment measures and only utilizes assessment measures that are within the scope of practice for school counselors.

b. Seeks specialized training regarding the use of electronically based testing programs in administering, scoring and interpreting that may differ from that required in more traditional assessments.

c. Considers confidentiality issues when utilizing evaluative or assessment instruments and electronically based programs.

d. Provides interpretation of the nature, purposes, results and potential impact of assessment/evaluation measures in language the student(s) can understand.

e. Monitors the use of assessment results and interpretations, and takes reasonable steps to prevent others from misusing the information.

f. Uses caution when utilizing assessment techniques, making evaluations and interpreting the performance of populations not represented in the norm group on which an instrument is standardized.

g. Assesses the effectiveness of his/her program in having an impact on students' academic, career and personal/social development through accountability measures especially examining efforts to close achievement, opportunity and attainment gaps.

### A.10. Technology

The professional school counselor:

a. Promotes the benefits of and clarifies the limitations of various appropriate technological applications. The counselor promotes technological applications (1) that are appropriate for the student's individual needs, (2) that the student understands how to use and (3) for which follow-up counseling assistance is provided.

b. Advocates for equal access to technology for all students, especially those historically underserved.

c. Takes appropriate and reasonable measures for maintaining confidentiality of student information and educational records stored or transmitted over electronic media including although not limited to fax, electronic mail and instant messaging.

d. While working with students on a computer or similar technology, takes reasonable and appropriate measures to protect students from objectionable and/or harmful online material.

e. Who is engaged in the delivery of services involving technologies such as the telephone, videoconferencing and the Internet takes responsible steps to protect students and others from harm.

### A.11.    Student Peer Support Program

The professional school counselor:

Has unique responsibilities when working with student-assistance programs. The school counselor is responsible for the welfare of students participating in peer-to-peer programs under his/her direction.

## B. RESPONSIBILITIES TO PARENTS/ GUARDIANS

### B.1. Parent Rights and Responsibilities

The professional school counselor:

a. Respects the rights and responsibilities of parents/guardians for their children and endeavors to establish, as appropriate, a collaborative relationship with parents/guardians to facilitate the student's maximum development.

b. Adheres to laws, local guidelines and ethical standards of practice when assisting parents/guardians experiencing family difficulties that interfere with the student's effectiveness and welfare.

c. Respects the confidentiality of parents/guardians.

d. Is sensitive to diversity among families and recognizes that all parents/guardians, custodial and noncustodial, are vested with certain rights and responsibilities for the welfare of their children by virtue of their role and according to law.

### B.2. Parents/Guardians and Confidentiality

The professional school counselor:

a. Informs parents/guardians of the counselor's role with emphasis on the confidential nature of the counseling relationship between the counselor and student.

b. Recognizes that working with minors in a school setting may require counselors to collaborate with students' parents/guardians.

c. Provides parents/guardians with accurate, comprehensive and relevant information in an objective and caring manner, as is appropriate and consistent with ethical responsibilities to the student.

d. Makes reasonable efforts to honor the wishes of parents/guardians concerning information regarding the student, and in cases of divorce or separation exercises a good-faith effort to keep both parents informed with regard to critical information with the exception of a court order.

## C. RESPONSIBILITIES TO COLLEAGUES AND PROFESSIONAL ASSOCIATES

### C.1. Professional Relationships

The professional school counselor:

a. Establishes and maintains professional relationships with faculty, staff and administration to facilitate an optimum counseling program.

b. Treats colleagues with professional respect, courtesy and fairness.

The qualifications, views and findings of colleagues are represented to accurately reflect the image of competent professionals.

c. Is aware of and utilizes related professionals, organizations and other resources to whom the student may be referred.

### C.2. Sharing Information with Other Professionals

The professional school counselor:

a. Promotes awareness and adherence to appropriate guidelines regarding confidentiality, the distinction between public and private information and staff consultation.

b. Provides professional personnel with accurate, objective, concise and meaningful data necessary to adequately evaluate, counsel and assist the student.

c. If a student is receiving services from another counselor or other mental health professional, the counselor, with student and/or parent/guardian consent, will inform the other professional and develop clear agreements to avoid confusion and conflict for the student.

d. Is knowledgeable about release of information and parental rights in sharing information.

## D. RESPONSIBILITIES TO THE SCHOOL AND COMMUNITY

### D.1. Responsibilities to the School

The professional school counselor:

a. Supports and protects the educational program against any infringement not in students' best interest.

b. Informs appropriate officials in accordance with school policy of conditions that may be potentially disruptive or damaging to the school's mission, personnel and property while honoring the confidentiality between the student and counselor.

c. Is knowledgeable and supportive of the school's mission and connects his/her program to the school's mission.

d. Delineates and promotes the counselor's role and function in meeting the needs of those served. Counselors will notify appropriate officials of conditions that may limit or curtail their effectiveness in providing programs and services.

e. Accepts employment only for positions for which he/she is qualified by education, training, supervised experience, state and national professional credentials and appropriate professional experience.

f. Advocates that administrators hire only qualified and competent individuals for professional counseling positions.

g. Assists in developing: (1) curricular and environmental conditions appropriate for the school and community, (2) educational procedures and programs to meet students' developmental needs and (3) a systematic evaluation process for comprehensive, developmental, standards-based school counseling programs, services and personnel.

The counselor is guided by the findings of the evaluation data in planning programs and services.

### D.2. Responsibility to the Community

The professional school counselor:

a. Collaborates with agencies, organizations and individuals in the community in the best interest of students and without regard to personal reward or remuneration.

b. Extends his/her influence and opportunity to deliver a comprehensive school counseling program to all students by collaborating with community resources for student success.

## E. RESPONSIBILITIES TO SELF

### E.1. Professional Competence

The professional school counselor:

a. Functions within the boundaries of individual professional competence and accepts responsibility for the consequences of his/her actions.

b. Monitors personal well-being and effectiveness and does not participate in any activity that may lead to inadequate professional services or harm to a student.

c. Strives through personal initiative to maintain professional competence including technological literacy and to keep abreast of professional information. Professional and personal growth are ongoing throughout the counselor's career.

### E.2. Diversity

The professional school counselor:

a. Affirms the diversity of students, staff and families.

b. Expands and develops awareness of his/her own attitudes and beliefs affecting cultural values and biases and strives to attain cultural competence.

c. Possesses knowledge and understanding about how oppression, racism, discrimination and stereotyping affects her/him personally and professionally.

d. Acquires educational, consultation and training experiences to improve awareness, knowledge, skills and effectiveness in working with diverse populations: ethnic/racial status, age, economic status, special needs, ESL or ELL, immigration status, sexual orientation, gender, gender identity/expression, family type, religious/spiritual identity and appearance.

## F. RESPONSIBILITIES TO THE PROFESSION

### F.1. Professionalism

The professional school counselor:

a. Accepts the policies and procedures for handling ethical violations as a result of maintaining membership in the American School Counselor Association.

b. Conducts herself/himself in such a manner as to advance individual ethical practice and the profession.

c. Conducts appropriate research and report findings in a manner consistent with acceptable educational and psychological research practices. The counselor advocates for the protection of the individual student's identity when using data for research or program planning.

**d.** Adheres to ethical standards of the profession, other official policy statements, such as ASCA's position statements, role statement and the ASCA National Model, and relevant statutes established by federal, state and local governments, and when these are in conflict works responsibly for change.

**e.** Clearly distinguishes between statements and actions made as a private individual and those made as a representative of the school counseling profession.

**f.** Does not use his/her professional position to recruit or gain clients, consultees for his/her private practice or to seek and receive unjustified personal gains, unfair advantage, inappropriate relationships or unearned goods or services.

### F.2. Contribution to the Profession

The professional school counselor:

**a.** Actively participates in local, state and national associations fostering the development and improvement of school counseling.

**b.** Contributes to the development of the profession through the sharing of skills, ideas and expertise with colleagues.

**c.** Provides support and mentoring to novice professionals.

## G. MAINTENANCE OF STANDARDS

Ethical behavior among professional school counselors, association members and nonmembers, is expected at all times. When there exists serious doubt as to the ethical behavior of colleagues or if counselors are forced to work in situations or abide by policies that do not reflect the standards as outlined in these Ethical Standards for School Counselors, the counselor is obligated to take appropriate action to rectify the condition. The following procedure may serve as a guide:

**1.** The counselor should consult confidentially with a professional colleague to discuss the nature of a complaint to see if the professional colleague views the situation as an ethical violation.

**2.** When feasible, the counselor should directly approach the colleague whose behavior is in question to discuss the complaint and seek resolution.

**3.** If resolution is not forthcoming at the personal level, the counselor shall utilize the channels established within the school, school district, the state school counseling association and ASCA's Ethics Committee.

**4.** If the matter still remains unresolved, referral for review and appropriate action should be made to the Ethics Committees in the following sequence:

- state school counselor association
- American School Counselor Association

**5.** The ASCA Ethics Committee is responsible for:

- educating and consulting with the membership regarding ethical standards
- periodically reviewing and recommending changes in code
- receiving and processing questions to clarify the application of such standards; Questions must be submitted in writing to the ASCA Ethics chair.
- handling complaints of alleged violations of the ethical standards.

At the national level, complaints should be submitted in writing to the ASCA Ethics Committee, c/o the Executive Director, American School Counselor Association, 1101 King St., Suite 625, Alexandria, VA 22314.

## References

Alessi, H.D., & Ballard, M.B. (2001). Memory development in children: Implications for children as witnesses in situations of possible abuse. *Journal of Counseling and Development, 79,* 398-404.

American Counseling Association. (2005). *Ethical standards.* Alexandria, VA: Author.

American School Counselor Association. (2004). *Ethical standards for school counselors.* Alexandria, VA: ASCA Press.

Bryant, J., & Milsom, A. (2005). Child abuse reporting by school counselors. *Professional School Counseling, 9,* 63-71.

Cameron, S., & turtle-song, i. (2002). Learning to write case notes using the SOAP format. *Journal of Counseling and Development, 80,* 286-292.

Corey, G., Corey, M.S., & Callanan, P. (2007). *Issues and ethics in the helping professions* (7th ed.). Pacific Grove, CA: Brooks/Cole.

Culbreth, J.R., Scarborough, J.L., Banks-Johnson, A., & Solomon, S. (2005). Role stress among practicing school counselors. *Counselor Education and Supervision, 45,* 58-71.

Davis, K., & Lambie, G.W. (2005). Family engagement: A collaborative, systemic approach for middle school counselors. *Professional School Counseling, 9,* 144-151.

Davis, T., & Ritchie, M. (1993). Confidentiality and the school counselor: A challenge for the 1990s. *The School Counselor, 41,* 23-30.

Ferris, P.A., & Linville, M.E. (1985). The child's rights: Whose responsibility? *Elementary School Guidance & Counseling, 19,* 172-180.

Fontes, L.A. (2002). Child discipline and physical abuse in immigrant Latino families: Reducing violence and misunderstandings. *Journal of Counseling and Development, 80,* 31-40.

Glosoff, H.L., Herlihy, B., & Spence, E.B. (2000). Privileged communication in the counselor-client relationship. *Journal of Counseling and Development, 78,* 454-462.

Hazler, R.J., & Denham, S.A. (2002). Social isolation of youth at risk: Conceptualizations and practical implications. *Journal of Counseling and Development, 80,* 403-409.

Heinlen, K.T., Welfel, E.R., Richmond, E.N., & Rak, C.F. (2003). The scope of webcounseling: A survey of services and compliance with NBCC standards for the ethical practice of webcounseling. *Journal of Counseling and Development, 81,* 61-69.

Herlihy, B., & Corey, G. (1992). *Dual relationships in counseling.* Alexandria, VA: American Counseling Association.

Herlihy, B., Gray, N., & McCollum, V. (2002). Legal and ethical issues in school counselor supervision. *Professional School Counseling, 6,* 55-60.

Hermann. M.A. (2002). A study of legal issues encountered by school counselors and perceptions of their preparedness to respond to legal challenges. *Professional School Counseling, 6,* 12-19.

Horton, A.L., Johnson, B.L., Roundy, L.M., & Williams, D. (1990). *The incest perpetrator: A family member no one wants to treat.* Newbury Park, CA: Sage Publications.

Isaacs, M.L., & Stone, C. (1999). School counselors and confidentiality: Factors affecting professional choices. *Professional School Counseling, 2,* 258-266.

Lambie, G.W. (2005). Child abuse and neglect: A practical guide for professional school counselors. *Professional School Counseling, 8,* 249-258.

Lawrence, G., & Kurpius, S. E. R. (2000). Legal and ethical issues involved when counseling minors in nonschool settings. *Journal of Counseling and Development, 78,* 130-136.

Layne, C.M., & Hohenshil, T.H. (2005). High tech counseling: Revisited. *Journal of Counseling and Development, 83,* 222-226.

Merlone, L. (2005). Record keeping and the school counselor. *Professional School Counseling, 8,* 372-376.

Page, B.J., Pietrzak, D.R., & Sutton, J.M., Jr. (2001). National survey of school counselor supervision. *Counselor Education and Supervision, 41,* 142-150.

Reese, R.J., Conoley, C.W., & Brossart, D.F. (2006). The attractiveness of telephone counseling: An empirical investigation of client perceptions. *Journal of Counseling and Development, 84,* 54-60.

Remley, T.P., Jr. (1991 ). *Preparing for court appearances.* Alexandria, VA. American Counseling Association.

Rowley, W.J., & MacDonald, D. (2001). Counseling and the law: A cross-cultural perspective. *Journal of Counseling and Development, 79,* 422-429.

Shaw, H.E., & Shaw, S.F. (2006). Critical ethical issues in online counseling: Assessing current practices with an ethical intent list. *Journal of Counseling and Development, 84,* 41-53.

Smith, K.M. (1990). A counselor goes to court. In B. Herlihy & L.B. Golden, *AACD ethical standards casebook* (4th ed.). Alexandria, VA: American Counseling Association.

Sprinthall, N.A., Hall, J.S., & Gerler, E.R., Jr. (1992). Peer counseling for middle school students experiencing family divorce: A deliberate psychological education model. *Elementary School Guidance and Counseling, 26,* 279-294.

Studer, J.R. (2005). Supervising school counselors-in-training: A guide for field supervisors. *Professional School Counseling, 8,* 353-359.

Walker, M.M., & Larrabee, M.J. (1985). Ethics and school records. *Elementary School Guidance and Counseling, 19,* 210-216.

Wilder, P. (1991). A counselor's contribution to the child abuse referral network. *The School Counselor, 38,* 203-214.

Wrightsman, L.W. (1997). *Psychology and the legal system.* Pacific Grove, CA: Brooks/Cole.

Zingaro, J.C. (1983). Confidentiality: To tell or not to tell. *Elementary School Guidance and Counseling, 17,* 261 - 267.

# Chapter 32

# The School Counselor and Credentialing

by

**Thomas Clawson, Susan Eubanks, and Kristi McCaskill**

*Thomas W. Clawson, Ed.D., NCC, NCSC, is the President and CEO of the National Board for Certified Counselors, Inc. (NBCC®). Dr. Clawson is a former school counselor, a private practitioner, and a counselor educator. A past chair of the National Commission for Certifying Agencies and a past president of the National Organization for Competency Assurance, Dr. Clawson is currently is a board member of The Center for Quality Assurance in International Education.*

*Susan H. Eubanks, M.Ed., NCC, NCSC is Executive Vice-President of NBCC. Ms. Eubanks, a former elementary school counselor, is a past Elementary Vice-President of the American School Counselor Association and also a past-president for the National Organization for Competency Assurance.*

*Kristi McCaskill, M.Ed., NCC, NCSC is the Counseling Advocacy Coordinator at NBCC. Ms. McCaskill is a former middle school counselor and has served as Central Region Representative for the North Carolina School Counselor Association.*

## Introduction

Twenty percent of professional counselors specialize in school counseling. School counselors have played a vital, decisive role in the chronology of state counselor regulation. The professional school counseling movement has given tremendous support to the "appropriately credentialed" practicing counselor through the years.

The first credentialed counselors were school counselors regulated by state departments of education as guidance counselors or guidance teachers. Since they functioned in a milieu of teachers and other educators, school counselors were originally required to have teaching cer-

tificates in a cognitive subject area, as well as possess an additional endorsement in school counseling. In the early 1970s, some states began removing the cognitive subject area certification and experience requirement for school counselors. This began the process of formally recognizing school counseling as a profession separate from teaching. A few states continue to require teacher certification prior to being hired as a school counselor.

Professional school counselors have been instrumental in helping private practice counselors gain statutory recognition. Almost all of the original licensure advocacy committees in states seeking counselor licensure legislation have included school counselors. In some cases, particularly in the early '80s, school counselors chaired and constituted a majority of these committees. Historically, school counselors' motivation regarding credentialing has been, and remains, exemplary.

School counselors assist private practitioners in seeking state legislation because:

- First, while most practice in a school setting, licensure offers school counselors the option of private practice, allowing for a second income, a retirement income, or professional development.

- Second, school counselors accept and understand credentialing as they have a prior familiarity with regulation through their states' educational system. School counselors recognize the value of professional collaboration with qualified private practitioners. Referral and consultation with private practitioners is often necessary to assist and remediate issues facing troubled youth.

- Their longer credentialing history resulted in a clearer professional path for school counselors than for their counterparts in mental health and substance abuse counseling during the early years (1976-1990) of the counselor licensure movement. Counselor education programs often focused on developing the skills and knowledge necessary to provide effective counseling services; therefore graduates had little practical knowledge about how to develop their professional careers. School counselors, on the other hand, had familiarity with state department of education regulations because they know they must become state licensed or certified to practice in a school. The American School Counselor Association (ASCA) actively promotes professionalization through credentialing. The ASCA National Model (2005) has been a major component in the development of current counselor credentialing programs. ASCA presidents from the late 1980s through today have vigorously espoused the role of the school counselor as a professional member of our educational and mental health teams, as well as the need for individual credentialing. Professionalism is a theme of the current ASCA movement, and credentialing is one of the essential avenues to reach this goal.

- Third, school counselors are active in professionalization movements and understand that private practice credentialing elevates all professional counselors through increased public recognition. Any enrichment for the whole profession also enhances the specialty practices of that profession.

- Fourth, school counselors recognize that actively supporting the professionalization of private practitioners is best for the profession of counseling. School counselors consult with private practice and agency counselors valuing their service with students. Supporting their efforts towards professionalization grows naturally from this relationship.

A real "maze" exists today in the credentialing realm and some brief definitions might be helpful.

# Definition of Terms

**License:** Permission granted by a state government allowing practice of a trade by an individual meeting professional criteria. While most states designate teaching and school counseling as a *certificate or endorsement,* that educational credential is probably a *license* in the strictest of terms.

**Certification:** Usually a voluntary credential granted by a private agency or government to denote professional status. Again, the use of the term "certification" in education is confusing. National certifications (discussed later) are voluntary, while state educational certificates are mandatory to hold school counselor positions.

**Registration:** Of the three types of credentials for individuals, registry is the least restrictive. Registry can range from formal submission of a portfolio including training, experience and examination to simple listing of names, addresses and areas of expertise.

**Endorsement:** Some state boards of education still require a school counselor to hold a teaching license (or certificate) and then go on to endorse specific areas of competence. Endorsements vary from state to state. Some endorse a teaching certificate for K-12 or K-6/6-12 or as a Guidance Counselor, School Counselor or Pupil Personnel Specialist. Training required for endorsements varies widely across states.

**Accreditation:** Official agency approval of an academic institution's degree program. In counseling, the Council for the Accreditation of Counseling and Related Educational Programs (CACREP) has approved 198 (CACREP, 2005) institutions with counselor education programs meeting high standards of quality, length, supervision, and curriculum.

School Counseling programs existing in institutions of higher education can seek CACREP accreditation and often are among the most comprehensive master's level counselor preparation programs.

## State Credentialing

State credentialing, sometimes referred to as licensure, protects the public and assures parents, teachers, and students that school counselors meet the minimum requirements of education, experience, and adhere to a code of ethics. In any field, professionals often utilize credentialing as a means of professional enhancement and as a means to obtain prestige; however, state credentialing is primarily designed for the protection of the public. Counselors are often frustrated with state regulatory agencies' inability to work with individual differences in the training. The state board of education, in turn, responds that their mission is not to protect or enhance the practice of counseling, but conversely, to protect clients from malpractice.

The presence of clear credentialing standards enhances the professionalism of school counseling. State credentialing serves the profession in a variety of ways. As minimum standards for school counselors have increased, the quality of practice has improved. State credentialing also promotes identifiable titles and qualifications making it easier for the public to understand the professional school counselor role. State credentialing provides professional protection when salary negotiations in school systems ignore special services. Role definition is more easily argued when a tradition of credentialing is evident thus allowing school counselors to make persuasive arguments for salary equity. Administrators in school systems who hire unqualified school counselors risk the loss of accreditation and open themselves to scrutiny, as well as to legal action against such hiring practices.

State credentialing also provides a measure of security by requiring school counselors to follow established ethical standards. Codes of ethics delineate appropriate conduct for practice as well as provide a method of defense against baseless or false charges. In the majority of ethics charges brought against National Certified Counselors (NCCs) over a 23 year period (1982-2005), proper practice was validated. In short, the ethical codes that protect the public can also protect the school counselor's reputation. School counselors have a very low rate of ethics charges when compared with all other mental health professionals.

Most state credentialing boards mandate school counselors to obtain a set number of continuing education units. School counselors have a wealth of options for continued professional growth as the fields of education and counseling have long maintained that current training is an ongoing necessity. Most school districts provide in-service training and/or support for attending workshops and seminars. An additional advantage for school counselors is that with an estimated 90,000 school counselors in the United States (*American School Counselor Association*, 2005), state and national credentialing systems require hundreds of thousands of continuing education hours. In many systems, school counselors are trained to provide much of this continuing education to their peers. This opportunity creates yet another source of career development for school counselors.

## National Credentialing

Dynamically evolving since 1958, school counseling continues to redefine itself. As mentioned above, state credentialing serves the profession; however, professionals in school counseling must also monitor the profession from a national perspective. Leaving identity related decisions to multiple state legislatures will erode and could eventually weaken or eliminate school counseling as a profession. National credentialing standards establish a framework for legislators to reference when creating or revising regulatory guidelines. Beyond providing an important ingredient towards maintaining the status quo, national certification continually upgrades minimum requirements. National standards for school counselors must originate in the counseling profession and continue the profession as an area of specialization. There was a time when administrators alone defined the role of school counselors. That relic remains, but the trend is towards counselors defining their new roles—not as clerical help for administrators or as specialized teachers—but as developmental experts serving as the primary coordinators of professional teams.

Counselor educators contribute to the development of school counselor programs and professional identity. A 2004 study reveals that over 490 educational institutions offer master's degrees in counseling (Clawson, 2004). Program accreditation, like individual certification, is another way to ensure continuing and recognized standards. Counselor education accreditation agencies consist of two organizations: the Council for Accreditation of Counseling and Related Educational Programs (CACREP) and the Commission on Rehabilitation Education (CORE). Both groups primarily consist of counselor educators who set training standards; however, only CACREP recognizes school counseling as an individual program of study. Even unaccredited programs tend to subscribe to the common core of training required of recognized schools. In conjunction with accreditation, certification establishes commonality for these 490 divergent programs. Counselor education accreditation agencies and national certification are important elements contributing to the definition of school counseling. These cornerstones are supported by counselors, academic institutions, and professional counseling organizations like the American Counseling Association (ACA). Since national boards solicit experts from academia, upgraded national certification requirements should be incorporated into master's degree programs.

ACA, ASCA, and NBCC began developing national school counselor certification requirements in 1989-90. The resulting certification, the National Certified School Counselor (NCSC) credential was established for the purposes of:

- **Promoting** school counselors' professional identity, visibility and accountability on a national level,

- **Identifying** to the counseling profession and the public those counselors who have met national professional school counseling standards,

- **Advancing** cooperation between school systems, professional organizations and other credentialing and professional development agencies,

- **Encouraging** professional growth and development of school counselors (NBCC, 1992).

The NCSC recognizes accomplished school counselors and attests to their educational background, knowledge, skills, and competencies. Those holding this important credential demonstrate a willingness to voluntarily challenge themselves through a rigorous process including an assessment, peer review, and continuing education requirements. The NCSC credential is an advanced specialty of the National Certified Counselor (NCC) general practice credential created by NBCC. To become certified as NCSCs, applicants must document that they have acquired a minimum of three years of supervised school counseling experience. They must also pass NBCC's National Certified School Counselor Examination (NCSCE) which assesses knowledge of both school counseling and general counseling and the ability to respond to clinical scenarios under pressure. As a part of the process, applicants must also document 100 hours of school counseling supervision, obtain two professional endorsements, and complete a professional practice statement. In addition to establishing minimum training and experience standards for school counselors, NBCC requires continuing education and adherence to NBCC's Code of Ethics. The ethical standards set forth by NBCC contribute to client protection, as well as providing needed answers to complicated questions of ethical practice. Ethical standards protect the profession and clients. At the conclusion of each five-year certification period, NCCs must have completed 100 hours of continuing education, and for NCSCs, 25 of those hours must be specific to school counseling.

While NBCC offers a combination application process for candidates to apply for both the NCC and the NCSC concurrently, applicants still must meet the requirements for both credentials. Applications and information are available on NBCC's web site at www.nbcc.org. Certificants who complete this process state that the NCSC enhances their self-esteem and sense of professionalism.

National certification also helps in establishing reciprocal agreements between states. There are many stated education department reciprocal agreements, but they vary from year to year as individual states continue to upgrade requirements. Several states accept the NCSC as an alternative entry for state school counselor credentialing. NBCC plans to propose that state boards of education adopt the NCSC as an "alternative" method to gain state school counselor endorsement. Under this proposal, each state's unique requirements would remain the same, but for those holding the NCSC, the state requirements would be considered to have been met. If all states adopt such a plan, a de facto reciprocity would exist. Thus, as noted, the NCSC has added greatly to school counseling as a whole and, hopefully, will be considered essential to current and aspiring school counselors.

## Identity Crisis

After working for years to establish an identity separate from the teaching profession, school counseling now faces an identity crisis. This crisis fundamentally results from a recent and different motivation for seeking national certification. The NCSC, the established credentialing path, identified school counseling as a specialty within the counseling profession. Prior to the establishment of a school counselor credential by the National Board for Professional Teaching Standards (NBPTS), school counselors obtained a voluntary national credential for the purpose of demonstrating professionalism. In 2003, NBPTS expanded its "National Board Certified Teacher" credential to include school counselors. This new national credential aligned school counseling with the teaching profession. With the NBPTS credential, financial gain became a primary motivation.

The NBPTS credential for school counselors replicates its teacher certification process. While this provides an opportunity for some to enjoy the financial recognition awarded to teachers with this certification, counseling organizations have expressed concerns. NBPTS fails to recognize the fundamental differences between the two professions. Despite the fact that a master's degree is the entry level educational requirement for the counseling profession, NBPTS requires only a bachelor's degree. The education and training of school counselors clearly differentiates the two professions. Like other school professionals, such as school nurses and school psychologists, school counselors play integral roles in education by utilizing training and skills to provide specific services. Today, most school counselors do not enter the school counseling profession through teaching. Highly effective school counselors recognize the importance of retaining their unique identity.

As more states employ the NBPTS certification to financially recognize counselors, NCSCs have started communicating with their legislators to also recognize their credential. In 1999, the Mississippi legislature passed a law entitling all Mississippi school counselors who are NCSC certified to a $6,000.00 yearly pay supplement. This figure matches the original award given NBPTS credentialed teachers in that state. In 2001, Louisiana also passed legislation recognizing NCSCs practicing in their public school systems. Currently, recognition for NCSCs in several other states is pending. To explore this issue check the NBCC web site <www.nbcc.org>.

## Other Factors Influencing Certification

No discussion is complete without a discussion of other influencing factors:

- At the individual level, test anxiety is one of the largest deterrents to national certification. Packaged study guides are available to help counselors review for tests and provide some relief for test anxiety.

- Some school counselors consider voluntary certification superfluous; however, electing to continue professional growth through voluntary certification strengthens the profession.

- As noted, there are approximately 90,000 school counselors in the United States. In 2005, over 18,000 are members of ASCA (ASCA, 2005), and even more are members of their respective state school counselor associations. The members and leaders of these organizations are the driving force behind progress and change. Those who do not participate in their professional associations and do not choose to hold national certification obstruct the profession's advancement.

- With the advent of the ASCA National Model, school counselors have a vehicle to assist in professional definition. Unfortunately, financial constraints play a decisive role in the employment of and compensation for school counselors. Some school systems utilize outside agencies, often with unqualified personnel, for supplemental services.

- Recent national legislation has strongly influenced the current direction of the school counseling profession. Chief among these is No Child Left Behind. Another legislative factor is funding for national credentialing organizations.

## Summary

Credentialing for school counselors is a permanent part of our lives. School counselors now have various alternatives such as: whether to work in public schools, to work in private schools, to work in a private practice; and whether to voluntarily become nationally certified and by which credentialing organization. In 1980, state board of education mandates represented the only avenue for credentialing. As the profession continues to evolve, counselors must demonstrate to the public that they recognize the value in meeting increasingly high standards and continuing to develop professionally. School counselors can best reaffirm their professional identity and protect their role within schools through certification.

## References

American School Counselor Association. (2005). *The ASCA national model: A framework for school counseling programs* (2nd ed). Alexandria, Va: Author.

Clawson, T., Henderson, D., Schweiger, W. (2004). *Counselor Preparation: Programs, Faculty Trends. New York, New York,* Brunner Routledge.

CACREP (2005). Directory of CACREP Accredited Programs, http://www.cacrep.org/directory.html.

## Figure 32.1
## National Certified School Counselor (NCSC)

Created in 1990, through the joint efforts of the American Counseling Association (ACA), the American School Counselor Association (ASCA), and the National Board for Certified Counselors (NBCC), the National Certified School Counselor (NCSC):

- Ensures a National Standard for School Counselors
- Promotes Professional Identity
- Recognizes the Accomplished School Counselor
- Encourages Professional Growth

To become certified as NCSCs, counselors must:

- Be identified as National Certified Counselors (NCCs), the premiere general practice credential for professional counselors.
- Hold a master's degree with specific coursework and field experience in the field of school counseling.
- Document they have acquired a minimum of three years of supervised school counseling experience.
- Pass NBCC's National Certified School Counselor Examination (NCSCE), an assessment of a school counselor's counseling knowledge and ability to respond under pressure to clinical scenarios
- Document 100 hours of in person supervision, obtain two professional endorsements, and complete a self assessment.

(While NBCC offers a combination application process where candidates can apply for both the NCC and the NCSC at the same time, applicants must still meet the requirements for both credentials. Fees, deadline information and applications are available on NBCC's web site at www.nbcc.org.)

**National Board for Certified Counselors (NBCC®)**
**3 Terrace Way, Suite D**
**Greensboro, North Carolina 27403-3660**

**www.nbcc.org**

# Chapter 33

# School Counseling and Technology

by
**Russell A. Sabella**

*Dr. Russell A. Sabella, Ph.D., is Professor of Counseling in the College of Education, Florida Gulf Coast University. His concentration of research, training, and publication includes counseling technology, comprehensive school counseling programs, peer helper programs and training, sexual harassment risk reduction, and solution focused brief counseling. Dr. Sabella is author of various articles in journals, magazines, and newsletters, as well as the author of several books. He conducts a variety of workshops and training sessions on technology, consultation, and sexual harassment issues. He can be reached at rsabella@fgcu.edu.*

The march of human progress has been marked by milestones in science and technology. Gutenberg's creation of moveable type in the 15th century laid the foundation for universal literacy. Watts's invention of the steam engine in the 18th century launched the Industrial Revolution. The inventiveness of Bell and Marconi in the 19th and 20th centuries - creating the telephone and radio - helped bring a global village into being. The United States and the world are now in the midst of an economic and social revolution every bit as sweeping as any that has gone before: computers and information technologies are transforming nearly every aspect of American life. They are changing the way Americans work and play, increasing productivity, and creating entirely new ways of doing things. Every major U.S. industry has begun to rely heavily on computers and telecommunications to do its work (Getting America's Students Ready for the 21st Century, 1996; Tyler & Sabella, 2004). Relentlessly, technology continues to underpin our fastest growing industries and high-wage jobs, provides the tools needed to compete in every business today, and drives growth in every major industrialized nation.

One tool in particular that is changing the fabric of how we interact, work, and conduct business is the Internet. Consider that the Internet, which connected 2,000 computers in 1985, 100 million in 1997, and now connects an estimated 973 million computers (Internet World Stats, 2005) is continuing to double in size every year. And, in addition to growing in terms of people accessing the Internet, it is growing in terms of the types of services provided over the network. Satellite and wireless systems now provide users with "anytime, anywhere" communications. Directory and search services help users locate important resources on the Internet. Electronic mail and network servers manage and store critical information. Authentication and electronic payment services handle more and more of the Nation's commerce. Building blocks for new applications have been developed such as digital signatures, secure transactions, modeling and simulations software, shared virtual environments for collaboration, tools for discovering and retrieving information, and speech recognition. Computers and the Internet provide access to a wealth of information on countless topics contributed by people throughout the world. On the Net, counselors have access to a wide variety of services: electronic mail, file transfer, vast information resources, interest group membership, interactive collaboration, multimedia displays, and more.

Progressively powerful computers, software, and expanding networks are rapidly changing traditional school counseling approaches and standards of performance as well. Although no one is truly certain if or when the exponential growth of technology will taper, it is well recognized that we are immersed in a new age of information, communication, and collaboration. For better or worse, computers are changing the ways in which we conduct our work, interact, and especially make decisions. Counseling professionals must adapt to new ways of interfacing with technology and the people that use them in a way that promotes the goals and objectives of their work (Sabella, 2003). According to McClure (1996), no aspect of society or economy can function effectively and compete without such tools. Information and networking technologies are now essential tools for manipulating ideas and images and for communicating effectively with others – an important component of the counselor's job. In the 21st century, our ability to harness the power and promise of leading-edge advances in technology will determine, in large measure, our national prosperity, security, and global influence, and with them the standard of living and quality of life for all. School counselors that decide to "opt out" of information technology would be working with students who perceive them to live in a world that no longer exists.

This chapter provides a practical overview of the current practice and potential for using high-tech tools in our work. To better conceptualize the extremely broad topic of technology, I have developed a categorization scheme which can help you manage how you think about and implement technology (Sabella, 2003). Technology can help counselors in one or more of four areas:

1. *Information/Resource*: In the form of words, graphics, video, and even three-dimension virtual environments, the Web remains a dynamic and rapidly growing library of information and knowledge.

2. *Communication/Collaboration*: Chat rooms, bulletin boards, virtual classroom environments, video conferencing, online conferences, electronic meeting services, e-mail – the web is now a place where people connect, exchange information, and make shared decisions.

3. *Interactive/Productivity tools*: The maturing of software and web based programming has launched a new and unforseen level of available tools off the shelves and on the Net. These high-tech tools can help counselors build and create anything ranging from a personalized business card to a set of personalized website links. Interactive tools help counselors to process data and manipulate information such as calculating a GPA or the rate of inflation, convert text to speech, create a graph, or even determine the interactive effects of popular prescription drugs.

4. *Delivery of services*: Most controversial, yet growing in popularity, is how counselors use the web to meet with clients and deliver counseling services in an online or "virtual" environment.

In fact, technologically literate counselors use an array of technologies in two or more of the above areas to most effectively and efficiently accomplish their goals.

## The Case for Counselor Technological Literacy

Imagine the frustration of suddenly living in a new country where you cannot effectively and efficiently communicate or interact with others, you are not able to decipher road signs, or navigate basic living tasks because you are unfamiliar with the country's language and customs. Children watch you in amazement and find it difficult to believe that you live in such a place without these basic capabilities. Increasingly so, such might be the experience in any developed country, especially here in the U.S., for counselors who do not have a basic level of technological literacy. For now, some people still take refuge by being able to live their lives in a relatively low-tech manner although this lifestyle is becoming more difficult every day. Americans understand the rapid progress in the development and integration of technology through every day experience and have thus embraced technological literacy as the "new basic" for today's world, along with reading, writing, and arithmetic.

Today's children find it difficult to imagine a life as we lived it not so long ago - without compact discs, high powered computers, and palm-sized appliances such as cell phones and personal digital assistants. It is likely that our future counselors, now in grade school and even college, will not hesitate to integrate high-tech tools in their work. They will merely continue along an already well established path of learning to use and apply new technologies as they become available, probably assisted by the technologies themselves. The majority of today's counselors grew up learning and practicing counseling in a very different environment. We used index cards instead of spreadsheets; typewriters instead of word processors; reference books instead of online journals and the web; overheads in lieu of multimedia presentations; and we waited until class to communicate with the professor and our classmates instead of sending e-mails or conversing in chat rooms.

Many of today's counselors acknowledge the usefulness of computers and the need for keeping up with the rapidly changing times, yet remain frozen in the fear generated by an unknown frontier. "I feel intimidated by computers," has been a common comment by counselors, who even after training, sometimes revert to more traditional procedures. The customary statements, "My kids know more about computers than I do" and "I'm not a technical person" suggest that although counselors may be interested or even intrigued, they frequently feel awkward and uneasy with computers and their operations (Myrick & Sabella, 1995). My own experience, luckily, is that once such counselors are exposed and begin to truly learn how to use technology in their work, they quickly become excited and adept. Many of my older students at the university who are forced to learn high-tech tools in my

*Joe Wittmer, Ph.D. and Mary Ann Clark, Ph.D.*

courses often tell me that they receive many kudos from their own children who perceive their moms or dads to be "more with it." Their more highly technologically literate friends and partners share in their delight and also get excited about new shared interests. And the students themselves bask in the pride they take in working with contemporary tools.

According to Sabella (2003), counselors who took an early interest and continued to gradually follow technology's progression have probably accumulated relatively high levels of technology literacy at a manageable pace. Veterans to the Net, for instance, may find themselves only having to keep pace with incremental changes, new additions, and creative ways for harnessing the Net's power to more effectively and efficiently do their jobs. For those whom have more recently taken an interest, or force themselves to be exposed to technology because of trends or new standards, becoming technologically literate may be perceived to be a burdensome venture. The good news, however, is that you can effectively start today. The road to technology literacy does not necessarily have a beginning and an end, but like an intricate system of highways and side roads, can be accessed from many on-ramps. Today's software is more user-friendly and more highly automated than ever before. Beginning a course of self-study and formal training will better assure more enjoyable travel for the road ahead. Before you know it, you will be traveling along side others whom have laid many more miles behind them on the information superhighway. And sooner, rather than later, you will be staking and claiming your property on this vast electronic terrain.

## What exactly is technological literacy?

Many people have written on the subject of technological literacy. Hayden (1989), after a literature review, takes the position that technological literacy is having knowledge and abilities to select and apply appropriate technologies in a given context. While not revealing the source of his thoughts, Steffens (1986, p. 117-118) claims that technological literacy involves knowledge and comprehension of technology and its uses; skills, including tool skills as well as evaluation skills; and, attitudes about new technologies and their application. This insight is similar to that of Owen and Heywood (1986) who say there are three components to technological literacy: the technology of making things; the technology of organization; and, the technology of using information. Applying a Delphi technique to opinions expressed by experts, Croft (1991) evolved a panel of characteristics of a technologically literate student. Those are: abilities to make decisions about technology; possession of basic literacy skills required to solve technology problems; ability to make wise decisions

about uses of technology; ability to apply knowledge, tools and skills for the benefit of society; and, ability to describe the basic technology systems of society (Waetjen, 1993).

A theme among various attempts to define technological literacy is that technology has evolved to become a powerful medium - not only a set of high-tech tools. If technology functioned merely as a set of tools, as the pervasive mechanical, user-in-control view of technology holds, the problem of advancing technological literacy would not be so challenging. A few more required courses or conference training sessions, and more specialists to teach them, could simply be added. But technology has become more than a set of devices to be picked up and used when a person decides he or she needs them. It has become a required medium that mediates experience in most aspects of peoples' lives (Fanning, 1994). Broadly speaking, technological literacy, then, can be described as the intellectual processes, abilities and dispositions needed for individuals to understand the link between technology, themselves and society in general. Technological literacy is concerned with developing one's awareness of how technology is related to the broader social system, and how technological systems cannot be fully separated from the political, cultural and economic frameworks which shape them (Saskatchewan Education, 2002). These definitions, together with one provided by the International Technology Education Association (2000) have provided the foundation for a definition of counselor technological literacy developed by Tyler and Sabella (2004):

> The intellectual processes, abilities and dispositions needed for counselors to understand the link among technology, themselves, their clients, and a diverse society so that they may extend human abilities to satisfy human needs and wants for themselves and others.

This means that counselors who have adequate levels of technological literacy are able to:

- understand the nature and role of technology, in both their personal and professional lives;

- understand how technological systems are designed, used, and controlled;

- value the benefits and assess the risks associated with technology;

- respond rationally to ethical dilemmas caused by technology;

- assess the effectiveness of technological solutions;

- feel comfortable learning about and using systems and tools of technology in the home, in leisure activities, and in the workplace; and

- critically examine and question technological progress and innovation.

---

## How are Counselors Already Using Technology in their Work?

Counselors whom have used computers to assist them in their work have done so in many areas such as computer-assisted live supervision (Froehle, 1984; Neukrug, 1991); discussions of counseling issues with other counselors (Rust, 1995); supervision (Myrick & Sabella, 1995); advocacy (Stone & Turba, 1999); counselor training (Cairo & Kanner, 1984); school counseling program promotion (Sabella & Booker, 2003); as part of counselor interventions with children (D'Andrea, 1995; Glover, 1995; Shulman, Sweeney, & Gerler, 1995) and counseling simulations (Sharf & Lucas, 1993). Probably the most extensive use of computers in counseling so far has been in the area of career development and guidance (e.g., Bobek, Robbins, Gore, Harris-Bowlsbey, Lapan, Dahir, & Jensen, 2005; Chapman & Katz, 1983; Friery & Nelson, 2004; Haring-Hidore, 1984; Harris, 1972; Katz & Shatkin, 1983; Kivlighan, Johnston, Hogan, & Mauer, 1994; Pyle, 1984). Career counselors need to amass and process a great deal of information about various careers, the career decision-making process, and a diversity of client personal and professional characteristics. Computers do a splendid job of compiling such data and helping individuals select the best fit among working environments, required aptitudes, interests, values, and other human qualities.

In May of 2005, I conducted an informal survey among the over 18,000 subscribers to my School Counselor.com eNewsletter (which focuses on advancing tech-literacy among counselors) about how they currently use technology in their work (Sabella, 2005). I was pleased to receive 49 responses that included descriptions of a variety of innovative and creative ways that school counselors were using technology to help them manage, deliver, or otherwise support their counseling programs. The range of responses included using technology to connect mentors and students; developing databases to manage student information not included in the districts database system; conducting online surveys; chart data; automate forms; translate documents from one language to another; maintain student services websites; conduct career development activities; communicate with parents and other stake holders; and develop television and other multimedia broadcasts.

In general, computers and the Internet can be especially helpful in a variety of ways including as technologies for information and resource retrieval, communication, collaboration, productivity (interactive tools), and intervention delivery.

## Technologies for Information & Resource Retrieval

The Internet could be described as the world's largest library and the availability of counseling-related bibliographies, abstracts, full-text journal articles, lectures, research projects, and funding sources is currently a "mouse click" away from your desktop. Counseling organizations, associations and individual professionals are creating websites every day and access to authoritative information on specialized topics is current, convenient, and almost limitless (Jackson & Davidson, 1998). Following are descriptions of various sources of information and resources that school counselors would probably find useful:

### The World Wide Web

The World Wide Web was continues to be mostly used as a source of rich, diverse, and highly current information in the form of text, graphics, sounds, video, and some animation. Although, the Web has evolved into an environment that contains tools and functions which could easily cut across all four areas of technology previously mentioned (information/resource, communication/collaboration; interactive tools, intervention delivery). The key to effectively and efficiently using what the Web makes available is finding specific sites or pages that can best help you. Basically, there are four methods to do this (in order of increased sophistication):

1. *Know the URL.* Each site on the Web has its own unique, case-sensitive, electronic address called a Universal Resource Locator (URL) that points a computer to the Web page's location. Users who discover a useful site might communicate to others, probably via electronic mail, the page's URL. Once known, a user can simply enter the URL into his or her Web browser and go directly to the intended site. Once at the site, a counselor can then place an electronic "bookmark" that will allow him or her to point and click on a description of the site without ever again having to recall the URL. This form of finding information on the Web is quickest and easiest.

2. *Surf the Web.* A second method for finding information is to rely on the hypertext feature of the Web and "jump" from page to page using related links. Moving from one link to another is affectionately known as "surfing the Web." As a counselor surfs the Web, he or she might bookmark and essentially create his or her own compilation of valuable Websites. The advantage of surfing the Web is that it gives the user control over what sites are deemed valuable. The disadvantage is that such a search is less than systematic and can be very time consuming.

3. *Directories.* Third, you might consult an Internet directory which categorizes websites into various hierarchies of information: a vast collection of categories and sub-categories, some created by people and others created by computers. By browsing the directory, you can have in front of you a pretty good (although not complete) listing of all the sites that cover a particular subject. For instance, check out the Yahoo! Guidance and Counseling Directory at http://dir.yahoo.com/Education/K_12/Guidance_Counseling/ or the Google Counseling and Guidance directory at http://www.google.com/Top/Reference/Education/K_through_12/Counseling_and_Guidance/.

4. *Search Engines.* A search engine is a program designed to help find information stored on a computer system such as the World Wide Web, or a personal computer. The search engine allows one to ask for content meeting specific criteria (typically those containing a given word or phrase) and retrieves a list of references that match those criteria. Search engines use regularly updated indexes to operate quickly and efficiently. Without further qualification, search engine usually refers to a Web search engine, which searches for information on the public Web. Other kinds of search engine are enterprise search engines, which search on intranets, personal search engines which search individual personal computers, and mobile search engines. Some search engines also mine data available in newsgroups, large databases, or open directories like DMOZ.org. Unlike Web directories, which are maintained by human editors, search engines operate algorithmically (Search Engines, 2005). Using unique search terms and search conditions can narrow the results from hundreds of thousands of possible sites to a more manageable number in a matter of seconds. Literally hundreds of search engines exist although several popular ones stand out and include http://www.google.com, http://www.yahoo.com, http://www.lycos.com, http://www.dogpile.com, http://www.excite.com, http://www.alltheweb.com, http://search.msn.com/, http://a9.com/, and http://www.av.com.

It seems there is no topic that cannot be entered into a search engine that will not result in at least a few sites being found. For many topics, the number of sites runs into the thousands or tens of thousands. And, the availability and popularity of electronic books or e-books which can be instantly downloaded is steadily increasing. Like so much in technology, this creates challenge as well as opportunity. The challenge lies in sorting through the available information to find that which is of high quality and targets your particular needs. Many counselors, while technologically capable, may not have the skills necessary to evaluate a site or the information provided. Lacking any sort of review or oversight, anyone can put any information they choose on the web. With basic technology skills (or the money to purchase assistance) a site can be created that looks quite polished. Without adequate knowledge and skills to evaluate sites, counselors may be drawn to sites that appear professional and are easy to understand, rather than sites that contain accurate and current information which may be slightly more difficult to understand and navigate. School counselors can save a great deal of time and increase their productivity by advancing their expertise in searching and navigating the web (e.g., see http://www.schoolcounselor.com/cd/). Also, familiarizing yourself with criteria for evaluating any web site or page (e.g., see http://www.schoolcounselor.com/website-evaluation.htm) will help you become a smart consumer of web based information/resources.

## Full-Text Electronic Databases

The number of journal, magazine, and newspaper titles available online has grown rapidly in recent years. Many databases are only accessible by paying a fee although, often, schools and local universities provide free access to anyone while on campus. Some databases are designed for individual users and are more reasonably priced. Finally, other full-text databases have been provided for free as a government service or by the incredible generosity of individuals and organizations. Following are examples:

## Larger and More Expensive Databases Typically Subscribed to by Institutions

1. CollegeSource® Online features over 33,550 college catalogs in complete cover-to-cover original page format including 2-year, 4-year, graduate, and professional schools. http://www.collegesource.org/

2. Congressional Universe is a web-based indexing and abstracting service for Congressional committee publications, including hearings (testimony), committee prints, reports, documents, and public laws. It also includes the full text and status of bills, selected testimony, regulations, and two periodicals, National Journal and Congress Daily. Additional features include Member directories and campaign contributions and a guide to creating citations. The publisher, Congressional Information Service, is an affiliate of LEXIS-NEXIS, so much of the full text is identical to material found in the LEXIS on-line data base. https://web.lexis-nexis.com/congcomp/

3. EBSCO Information Services provides information access and management solutions through print and electronic journal subscription services, research database development and production, online access to more than 150 databases and thousands of e-journals, and e-commerce book procurement. EBSCO has served the library and business communities for more than 60 years. http://www.ebscohost.com/

4. IngentaConnect allows subscribers to search over 19 million articles, chapters, reports and more. http://www.ingentaconnect.com/

5. LexisNexis® provides authoritative legal, news, public records and business information; including tax and regulatory publications in online, print or CD-ROM formats. http://www.lexisnexis.com/

6. Online Computer Library Center (OCLC) is a non-profit, membership, library computer service and research organization dedicated to the public purposes of furthering access to the world's information and reducing information costs. http://www.oclc.org

7. Ovid is a Platform-independent access to bibliographic and live full text databases for academic, biomedical and scientific research. http://www.ovid.com/

8. ProQuest® online information service provides access to thousands of current periodicals and newspapers, many updated daily and containing full-text articles from 1986. Deep backfiles of archival material are also expanding daily as they digitize 5.5 billion pages from their distinguished microfilm collection. http://www.proquest.com/

9. ReferenceUSA contains more than 12 million U.S. businesses; 102 million U.S. residents; 683,000 U.S. health care providers; 1 million Canadian businesses; and 11 million Canadian residents. http://reference.infousa.com/

## Inexpensive Full-Text

For those that do not have access to expensive full-text databases provided by schools or other institutions, HighBeam Library Research (http://www.highbeam.com/library/) has an extensive archive of more than 35 million documents from over 3,000 sources — a vast collection of articles from leading publications, updated daily and going back as far as 20 years. As of this writing, a monthly subscription is $19.95 or $99.95 for an annual subscription.

Another example of an inexpensive full-text database ($11.95 per month) is the Encyclopedia Britannica online (http://www.britannica.com/) which includes the complete encyclopedia as well as other resources such as dictionary, thesaurus, and newsletters.

## Free full-text

Following are examples of various full-text resources which are freely available online:

1. National Center for Research in Vocational Education (NCRVE) is the nation's largest center engaged in research, development, dissemination and outreach in work-related education, and is funded by the Office of Vocational and Adult Education of the U.S. Department of Education. The Center's mission is to strengthen school-based and work-based learning to prepare all individuals for lasting and rewarding employment, further education, and lifelong learning. http://vocserve.berkeley.edu/fulltext.html

2. Maintained by an individual, this page links to websites containing full-text state constitutions, statutes (called codes or compiled laws in some states), legislation (bills, amendments and similar documents) and session laws (bills that have become laws). http://www.prairienet.org/~scruffy/f.htm

3. The Education Resources Information Center (ERIC), sponsored by the Institute of Education Sciences (IES) of the U.S. Department of Education, produces the world's premier database of journal and non-journal education literature. The ERIC online system provides the public with a centralized ERIC Web site for searching the ERIC bibliographic database of more than 1.1 million citations going back to 1966. More than 107,000 full-text non-journal documents (issued 1993-2004), previously available through fee-based services only, are now available for free. ERIC is moving forward with its modernization program, and has begun adding materials to the database. http://www.eric.ed.gov/

4. A list of free (29 titles at the time of this writing) free full-text journals on the Web and maintained by the Lesley College Library are located at http://www.lesley.edu/faculty/kholmes/libguides/cpfulltext.html

5. The Journal of Technology Education provides a forum for scholarly discussion on topics relating to technology education. Manuscripts should focus on technology education research, philosophy, and theory. In addition, the Journal publishes book reviews, editorials, guest articles, comprehensive literature reviews, and reactions to previously published articles. http://scholar.lib.vt.edu/ejournals/JTE/

6. The Journal of Technology in Counseling publishes articles on all aspects of practice, theory, research and professionalism related to the use of technology in counselor training and counseling practice. The Journal accepts manuscripts that respond to the full scope of technology interests of its readers. The Journal recognizes that modern technology has surpassed

traditional ways of presenting information to readers by encompassing learning methods that go beyond the two-dimensional page. Authors are encouraged to use the full range of available web resources when submitting manuscripts including hyperlinks to other web resources, audio, graphics, video clips and video-streaming. http://jtc.colstate.edu/

7. FindArticles. Search millions of articles from leading academic, industry and general interest publications. http://www.findarticles.com/

8. Technology Horizons in Education (T.H.E.) is a free magazine for educators dedicated to technology solutions in education. http://www.thejournal.com/

9. Edutopia Magazine gives practical, hands-on insight into what works, what's on the horizon, and who is shaping the changing future of education. http://www.edutopia.org/

# Technologies for Communication/ Collaboration

Over the Net, counselors can communicate and collaborate with students, teachers, administrators, parents, other counselors, and community members with continually greater convenience and efficiency. While you are reading this, thousands of school counselors enjoy the convenience of corresponding and consulting with each other via e-mail, listservs, bulletin boards, chatrooms, instant messaging, and more.

Collaboration is a process by which people work together on an intellectual, academic, or practical endeavor. In the past, that has meant in person, by letter, or on the telephone. Electronic collaboration, on the other hand, connects individuals electronically via the Internet using tools such as e-mail, or through access to sites on the World Wide Web. This Internet-based work allows collaborators to communicate anytime, from anywhere to any place. People from different parts of a building, state, country, or continent can exchange information, collaborate on shared documents and ideas, study together, or reflect on their own practices.

Most counselors are used to short-term professional development seminars and workshops that provide finite information. Electronic collaboration —because it can be done at any time, from anywhere—allows for a sustained effort where participants can propose, try out, refine, and shape ideas themselves. The potential to communicate with others from all over the world provides a pool of

resources and professional companions that counselors might not find within their own school walls. It can also provide them with a sense of belonging, a sense of identity within a larger community. Using high tech tools to collaborate, counselors actively and interactively contribute to exploring innovative ideas. With electronic collaboration, the adage "two heads are better than one" could just as well be "two hundred heads are better than one." One person's provocative question can lead to many creative, exciting solutions. By sharing what they know with others, participants advance their own knowledge and the collaborative community's knowledge.

## E-Mail

One can hardly be effective without the use of e-mail in business, industry, or in education. Beyond day-to-day internal communications, e-mail offers counselors the same kind of advantage that it offers those involved with distance learning education – it forms the basis of a network that conveniently connects counselors and others (e.g., supervisors, community members, parents, and students) individually and in groups (Myrick & Sabella, 1995). The advantages of electronic mail have contributed to its pervasiveness and popularity and include:

- the convenience of corresponding at any time of the day or night;
- being able to think through a communication before making it;
- not having to rely on a mutual time to communicate as one would with a phone conversation;
- saving money in long distance charges when having to make only brief comments;
- instantaneously communicating the same message to multiple people on a distribution list;
- diminished inhibitions that face-to-face conversation may present;
- that, whereas spoken words must remain in memory and are sometimes lost in a quick exchange, written e-mail messages can be reviewed; and
- large files, especially documents, can be instantly sent to others via e-mail which can save precious time and money as compared to printing and shipping the document via traditional postal carriers.

However, anyone who uses e-mail as a staple form of communication, can readily tell you about the disadvantages of e-mail communication which would include that:

- for some, typing can be slow and tedious;

- the absence of nonverbal communication such as gestures, facial expression, or tone of voice can sometimes lead to mistaken interpretations of an e-mail message;

- although relatively very secure, sending an e-mail over the Net is sometimes like sending a postcard through the mail – others whom desire to do so might intercept and read an e-mail. Therefore, issues of confidentiality and privacy are central to communicating sensitive information;

- if not careful, counselors can receive too many e-mail messages which may lead to time and organizational management challenges. In this sense, counselors must be smart consumers of information and determine how much one reads, digests, discards, and to which messages one should respond.

Many school counselors take the opportunity to participate in an electronic network that enables participants to share professional ideas and information. It offers counselors a unique and valuable opportunity for supervision and consultation. For example, Myrick & Sabella (1995) write about how they used e-mail as a supplement to practicum and internship supervision which they called cybervision. In this case, the student counselors, during group supervision, first learned how to access the Internet through computers in their schools or with their own personal computers and modems at home. They could also access the system through computer stations at various locations on campus. Each person had his or her own e-mail address, which was known to the supervisor and other group supervision members. Using e-mail, a student-counselor could send written messages to a supervisor asking for information or describing a case. When appropriate, the case was forwarded to other group members for their interest and reactions. The group supervision members discussed the best way to send an e-mail case. It would include (a) a brief description of the counselee; (b) the presenting problem, including the referral source; c) the observed behaviors related to the problem or concern; (d) the counselor interventions to that point; and (e) any concerns or questions that were evolving. The authors concluded that e-mail supervision supplements the traditional modes of face-to-face meetings, telephone conferences, and fax transmissions. An ongoing group experience, it can take place in remote and diverse locations. Although the common once-a-week group meeting has its own value, group members felt that they were always within reach of assistance or encouragement. They felt closer to one another, and e-mail created a special bond that also enabled them to be more open about their situations.

## List Servers

List servers are programs that allow an administrator to create lists of e-mail addresses and attach them to a single e-mail address (called the listserv address). All messages that are e-mailed to the listserv are distributed, again via e-mail, to all subscribers, sometimes by a "moderator" who reads them first (in a "moderated list") or more typically in an automated manner (or "unmoderated list"). Some list servers require an administrator to add people to the list. In others, anyone who wishes can automatically subscribe (or unsubscribe) by either sending an e-mail message to the program which resides on a server or by completing an online form. List server programs can provide some security by allowing only authorized users to post to the list or by using a moderator to approve messages before they are posted to the list. Counselors can also set up their listserv to act more like a mailing list for those who simply want to receive reminders, newsletters, or announcements. This is called a post-only listserv. Creators (or "owners") of these listservs are usually the only people who can send an e-mail via the listserv. Any one else who tries is humbly and automatically rejected. Try subscribing to two different types of listservs, a post only newsletter listserv and a full fledged discussion listserv, respectively. The Scout Report is the flagship publication of the Internet Scout Project. Published every Friday both on the web and by e-mail, it provides a fast, convenient way to stay informed of valuable resources on the Internet. The report is developed by a team of professional librarians and subject matter experts who select, research, and annotate each resource. Visit http://scout.wisc.edu/mailman/listinfo/scout-report, and complete the form. Next, you will be sent an e-mail requesting confirmation to prevent others from gratuitously subscribing you (this is called a double opt-in list). Second, the International Counselor Network (ICN) is a network for counselors working in all specialty areas. Topics range widely, including such issues as self-esteem, multicultural issues, program development, career planning, play theory, professional issues and more. Complete the online form at http://listserv.utk.edu/cgi-bin/wa?SUBED1=icn&A=1 and you will once again receive an e-mail with instructions for how to confirm your identity.

List servers are an efficient way of sending e-mail to large and/or specific groups and are ideal for disseminating timely information, such as announcements of conferences, pointers to new websites of interest, and descriptions of print resources. Anyone on the list can be a source of information. List servers are well-suited to groups of users who regularly use e-mail and who need to receive information in a timely way. They are less effective for extended or lengthy discussions, because participants may not be able to remember all the previous entries when they respond to a particular item. Another disadvantage is that mailing list servers can be inconvenient for recipients, filling their e-mail in-boxes when they're busy with other things. Two of the most commonly used mailing list server programs are Majordomo (http://www.greatcircle.com/majordomo/) and Listserv ("(http://www.lsoft.com)." http://www.lsoft.com).

There are primarily two methods for learning about available listservs of interest. First and most popular, a specific listserv of interest may be announced in relevant professional or related publications such as journals, magazines, newsletters, or newspapers. Second, you may seek for listservs of interest by conducting a basic web search using keywords such as "counseling listserv" which should take you to web pages that describe the listserv and provide instructions for subscribing. Remember, however, not all listservs are open to the public, some are private and require administrative approval. Creating your own listserv is not always easy although definitely doable. The best thing to do is work with your school's technology people to see if they can do it for you. Or, you can use a free online mail list service such as http://www.coollist.com. Otherwise, read up on how to do this yourself by visiting web pages such as http://www.librarysupportstaff.com/4creategroup.html and http://lists.gurus.com/creating.html.

## Chat Room

E-mail is a great way to communicate electronically although this method suffers from the lack of real-time interaction between one person and with others whom he/she would like to communicate. Historically, real-time communication has occurred either in face-to-face conversation or over the telephone. The use of chat software, especially over the Internet, makes it possible to electronically converse in real time. Following the metaphor for which this technology is named, imagine yourself entering a room in which you can converse with other users you will find there. You can see on screen what each user is typing into the conversation, and when you type something, the other users in the room can see your message as well.

Chat environments have progressed from simple text-based interactions to full blown graphical user interfaces (GUIs). Today's chatrooms allow users to personalize their communications by posting their photos or a close facsimile (sometimes a computer generated likeness) next to their text communications. Other programs also allow for sending to members of the chatroom audio files that contain music, sound effects, or the users own recorded voice. One of the most popular chat clients (not be confused with the clients with whom we work, software that resides on our computer and act as the recipients of server programs are also called clients) is a program called

mIRC available for download at most shareware sites or directly at http://www.mirc.com/. However, many chats are now conducted over the Web which eliminates the need to download any software. Simply visit the site, choose your chat community, log in, and begin chatting (e.g., see http://chat.msn.com or http://chat.yahoo.com). You should know that, like anything else on the Net, some chatrooms are not intended for the easily offended. Not all, but many of the rooms are "R" to "X" rated because they contain inappropriate and/or pornographic communications including text, sound, and sometimes graphics. Also, users of chatroom can easily maintain anonymity and, even worse, pose as someone they are not. To create a chat room for your very own special gathering, you could use a free online service such as http://www.chatzy.com/ or http://chatshack.net/. Or, if you have a website, you can insert some coding that will allow you to house your own chat environment (e.g., see http://www.parachat.com/basic/createhtml.html).

## Instant Messaging

Instant messaging (IM) requires the use of a client program that hooks up an instant messaging service and, similar to chat rooms, conversations are then able to happen in realtime. What IM has that chat rooms do not have are extra abilities such as a presence information feature, indicating whether people on one's list of contacts are currently online and available to chat. This may be called a "Buddy List". Other features include voice and video transfer, file transfer, the ability to play games with other users, and application sharing (such as working together in real time on a spreadsheet or document). Popular instant messaging services on the public Internet include Qnext (http://www.qnext.com/), MSN Messenger (http://messenger.msn.com/), AOL Instant Messenger (http://www.aim.com/), Yahoo! Messenger (http://messenger.yahoo.com/), Google Talk (http://www.google.com/talk/), Jabber (http://www.jabber.org/) and ICQ (http://www.icq.com/). These services owe many ideas to an older (and still popular) online chat medium known as Internet Relay Chat (IRC) (Instant Messaging, 2005).

## WebBoards

One drawback of e-mail, listservs, and even instant messaging is that they organize discussions chronologically. This type of organization is fine for many short discussions or written materials, but most discussions aren't linear and well-organized. One comment can generate ideas on many different tangents. In this case, you may want to organize the discussion by topic. But that doesn't always work well; what if one message in a discussion has ideas that relate to several different parts of the discussion? Topic-oriented and threaded discussion systems, oftentimes called Bulletin Board Systems or WebBoards, attempt to respond to this problem by keeping an archive and allowing different ways of organizing the discussion. Because of the creative, inventive, and nonlinear nature of human conversation, it's difficult to develop an ideal method of organizing records of conversation. The information in a threaded discussion system is organized and displayed hierarchically, so you can see how the messages are related. Each posting (or "article") in a threaded discussion has a topic or subject. Users can comment on the topic, see what others have to say about it, and reply to questions or other people's comments. All of the comments, replies, and discussions on a single topic are collectively called a "thread." The difference between topic oriented and threaded discussions is a matter of format and organization. Usually messages in topic oriented discussions are listed chronologically on a single topic page, messages in threaded discussions are organized in an outline format with replies indented and listed directly under the message to which they are a reply (Koufman-Frederick, et al., 1999). As a member benefit, the American School Counselor Association provides various bulletin boards (e.g., organized by grade level) to facilitate communication and collaboration among its members.

## Blogs

You've probably heard the term blog more than once, most likely used on television or print news media. However, you may still not exactly understand what a blog is. According to the Webopedia (Blog, 2005), a blog, short for "web log," is a web page that serves as a publicly accessible personal journal for an individual. Typically updated on a daily basis, blogs often reflect the personality of the author. Google owned Blogger.com describes a blog as, "A blog is a personal diary. A daily pulpit. A collaborative space. A political soapbox. A breaking-news outlet. A collection of links. Your own private thoughts. Memos to the world." Creating a blog is simple and free. It only takes a few minutes by entering your name, e-mail address and a few other pieces of (usually personal) information. You select "the look" (template) for your blog from a set of standard options, click a few buttons, and another blog has been added to the "blogosphere." Once the blog is set up, you can post text, links, audio, video, and more to your hearts delight. From your computer or cell phone, you can say or show anything and everything. With a bit of know-how, you can even syndicate to other blogs and websites. Syndication is a process by which the latest content from a blog, or from any other web page, can be made available for re-publication in another website or in some other application. And millions of people (including children) are doing it.

As compared to dynamic websites, blogs feature several unique characteristics (How Blogs Work, 2005) such as:

- A blog is normally a single page of entries. There may be archives of older entries, but the "main page" of a blog is all anyone really cares about.

- A blog is organized in reverse-chronological order, from most recent entry to least recent.

- A blog is normally public — the whole world can see it.

- The entries in a blog usually come from a single author.

- The entries in a blog are usually stream-of-consciousness. There is no particular order to them. For example, the blogger sees a good link, he or she can throw it in his or her blog. The tools that most bloggers use make it incredibly easy to add entries to a blog any time they feel like it.

- A typical blog has a main page and nothing else. On the main page, there is a set of entries. Each entry is a little text blurb that may contain embedded links out to other sites, news stories, etc. When the author adds a new entry, it goes at the top, pushing all the older entries down. This blog also has a right sidebar that contains additional permanent links to other sites and stories. The author might update the sidebar weekly or monthly.

The technology that allows individuals to write one's own blog is so relatively simple and inexpensive that it is no surprise that blogs have proliferated the Web as fast as they have. Any counselor can create a basic blog for free, and most of these toolsets have additional features available for a price. Here are just a few of the services available.

- Blogger is a free, automated weblog publishing platform in one easy to use website. http://www.blogger.com/

- bBlog is a powerful, elegant personal publishing system written in PHP and released as free, Open Source software under the GPL. It is a flexible but simple way to blog that works for blogging beginners, and can grow into a more advanced user's needs. http://www.bblog.com/

- Xanga is a community of online diaries and journals. http://www.xanga.com/

- TypePad is similar to blogger, another blogging service although this one has a minimal cost. http://www.sixapart.com/typepad/

- LiveJournal is free although users can choose to upgrade their accounts for extra features. http://www.livejournal.com/

- Moveable Type is another popular web publishing platform. http://www.sixapart.com/movabletype/
- MySpace.com is actually a hybrid site that allows people to post their personal interests, write blogs, put up video and set up ways to communicate with their friends. http://www.myspace.com/

Consumers of blogs, in this case, our stake holders, have several ways that they can learn about new updates or additions to your blogs. First, they can periodically visit your blog and look for any updates which is easy to do since entries are listed in chronological order. Second, if your blog allows it, they can sign up to receive e-mail notification of any new information. Or third, you can subscribe to the blog if the blog host offers RSS (Real Simple Syndication) feed capability. In this case, you simply copy the website address of the feed into a feed reader or aggregator (e.g., see http://blogspace.com/rss/readers). Anytime the blog is updated, you automatically receive a copy of it right in your reader.

## Podcasting

Podcasting, in its basic form, is creating audio files (most commonly in MP3 format) and making them available online in a way that allows users to automatically download the files for listening at their convenience (i.e., subscribing to the podcast). After subscribing to the podcast, future "broadcasts" automatically download to your computer, which can then be transferred easily to a handheld such as a Palm OS Handheld, a Pocket PC, or an iPod - hence, the name Podcast. In essence, anyone with a computer, Internet access, free software, and a microphone can turn their computer into a personal studio and produce their very own radio show/program [see Valesky and Sabella (2005) for a more detailed description of how this technology works].

Podcasting is clearly in its infancy although shows great potential for disseminating information in a timely and efficient manner. The potential of podcasting stems from several advantages to using this relatively new medium. For one, it's cheap. Podcasting requires no more hardware or software than a typical computer user has. Second, the MP3 files and accompanying text which are served over the World Wide Web are supported among virtually all operating systems (i.e., podcasting works across many platforms). As a result, these types of files have become quite pervasive. Third, given the difficulties and intricacies of using computer technology sometimes, podcasting is surprisingly simple to do. Only three steps are required (create the MP3 file, upload the file, and update your RSS feed) to broadcast any content you would like. Fourth, podcasting further removes barriers of space,

pace, and time by allowing the consumer to download and listen to broadcasts at his or her convenience (sort of like the Tivo® of radio). And, the consumer may listen to a broadcast using various devices such as computers, MP3 players, CD players (after burning the files to a CD), personal digital assistants (PDA's), Bluetooth or USB enabled call our radios, and eventually cell phones. Finally, I have found that podcasting is just plain fun.

Several disadvantages that accompany podcasting do exist, some of which are related to the use of any technology:

1. Podcasting is still in its early stages of development and so finding those that are valuable and meaningful to you may be somewhat difficult. Relatedly, although the number of podcasts is growing in leaps and bounds, many are personal and amateurish which will probably not be useful to you other than for entertainment purposes.

2. Like everything else on the Web, podcasts are not regulated. Pornographers, bigots, bullies, and others have also discovered podcasts as a powerful method for disseminating information. This information is currently limited to audio although video podcasts or v-casts are already in development. Anyone who has the knowledge, including children, can easily access a range of smut or obscene matter.

3. Technology, computers, and the Internet seem to have become a ubiquitous component of life in the United States, yet there still exists a digital divide among the "haves" and the "have-nots." High speed Internet connections, computers, MP3 players, microphones, etc. do cost money which may prevent the economically disadvantaged from benefitting from this promising emerging technology.

4. Lastly, the development of podcasting emphasizes once again the importance of media literacy among youth and adults alike. Evaluating, choosing, and using information presents challenges that, if not managed, can leave us unbalanced, unfocused, and in a state of deterioration.

The potential for how podcasts can become a useful tool for mass communication in the school counseling profession is only beginning. For instance, school counselors can share best practices with each other, essentially having access to "on-demand professional development." Consider the motivational effects of students developing their own podcasts. Students could create a series of podcasts specifically for their parents that describe their learning experiences and inform them of school activities. Busy parents could listen to the podcasts on their commute to work. Imagine a peer helper model where K-12 students develop a podcast series to which other students listen and learn more about how to advance their competencies in key guidance and counseling areas delineated by the ASCA National Model (ASCA, 2005).

## Internet Conferencing

With the increased proliferation of high speed Internet access, more powerful computers, and the need to work on a more global scale comes an increasing popularity in the use of Internet conferencing technology. These programs or services provide users with multi-point data conferencing, text chat, audio/video chat, whiteboard, file transfer, as well as application sharing. The Internet conferencing environment is similar to a live conference which allows a presenter to speak, present multimedia slides, conduct polls, allow for questions and answers, share handouts (in the form of files), point to websites, and share other visuals from his or her computer. In most cases, participants can also interact among themselves via a simultaneous phone conference. The cost of these programs range from free to 39¢ per minute per participant. Following are a few of the more popular online conferencing tools:

- Microsoft NetMeeting (http://www.microsoft.com/windows/netmeeting/).
- Microsoft Office Live Meeting (http://www.microsoft.com/office/rtc/livemeeting/)
- GoToMeeting (http://www.gotomeeting.com)
- WebEx (http://www.webex.com/)
- Macromedia Breeze (http://www.macromedia.com/software/breeze/)

## Social Networking

In addition to professional development, counselors who attend conferences report that "networking" with others is another reason why they attend these meetings. Face to face networking provides counselors with new ideas, opportunities for partnering and collaborating, support, and usually inspiration. Until now, these networks were primarily designed for use among adults for both professional and personal fulfillment. For business and industry, social networks connects buyers and sellers, employers and prospects, and otherwise facilitates the sharing of business opportunities and contacts. For example, sites such as http://openBC.com, http://spoke.com, http://ryze.com, and http://zerodegrees.com help a user to set up their own Internet space to store contacts, invite others to join his/her own network, and ultimately search across the extended network for individuals and organizations that can help the user achieve his/her business, career and/or personal goals.

These networks can grow very quickly and be quite effective at making important business contacts. For example, on the Spoke Web site, a user completes a simple personal profile (e.g name, title, company, contact information) and then clicks a button marked "build network." A program is then downloaded from the Spoke website that mines the user's Outlook e-mail and contact database for information about who he/she knows and how frequently he/she maintains contact with them. In a few minutes, the user's new, online "Spoke book'" is populated not only with the hundreds or thousands of contacts he/she had manually entered into his/her Outlook contacts list, but also with everyone she/he had ever exchanged e-mail with from that e-mail account. Spoke also rates the strength of these relationships based on how often and how recently the user e-mailed with each person, as well as whether he/she was the only recipient of a message or was simply part of a larger distribution list.

Social networking technologies can help counselors network all year around, perhaps as a supplement to live networking. For instance, one of the most popular social networking services is MySpace (http://myspace.com). At MySpace, a counselor can create a private community and share photos, journals, e-mails, classifieds, music, start/join interest groups, blog, discuss issues, and share events with a growing network of mutual colleagues and/or friends. Other similar social networks of interest include Friendster (http://www.friendster.com/), LinkedIn (http://www.linkedin.com/), Xanga (http://www.xanga.com), Yahoo! 360° (http://360.yahoo.com), and Facebook (http://www.facebook.com/).

## Social Bookmarking

Social bookmarking is an online process that allows users to save and categorize a personal (or professional) collection of bookmarks or favorites and share them with others. Users may also take bookmarks saved by others and add them to their own collection, as well as to subscribe to the lists of others. This means that we can use our collective judgement to "pool" what we deem as valuable websites. One social bookmarking site, del.icio.us (http://del.icio.us), has become very popular because of its ease of use, tagging abilities (i.e., one can sort bookmarks using different tags or categories), and sharing features.

# Technologies as Interactive Tools

The types of interactive tools that professionals are most typically interested are those that help us to be more productive. Most counselors would agree that they perceive themselves as having to meet increasing work loads with either the same or reduced resources – that is, they are having to "do more with less." Thus, the common cry among counselors, "How can I provide quality services and programs (i.e., continue to be effective) for my students in a more efficient manner?" High-tech interactive tools allow us to input certain data which is processed or manipulated and then returned to us in a more meaningful or valuable format. Word processing, data processing (e.g., spreadsheets and data bases), desktop publishing, audio/video editing, calculators, web browsers, multimedia development, etc. are all examples of interactive tools. Tools usually come from software which we download or purchase and run on our computers or other electronic devices, or they can be run on the Internet. In addition to the readily available productivity suites (e.g., Microsoft Office), following are descriptions of selected interactive tools that the school counselor would find helpful:

## Data and Accountability

School counselors are responsible for knowing and keeping track of all sorts of information such as student records, student contacts, parent conferences, case notes, counseling schedules, accountability data, list of tasks, and sometimes grades. Without the help of technology, counselors may feel overwhelmed, unorganized, or lost as a result of the sheer quantity of information. Consequently, effectiveness and motivation could suffer. Yet, measuring outcomes or using the current research to help inform school counselors of the nature of their efforts is an important task for ensuring the viability of a school counseling program. Technology can make the process more efficient, accurate, and automated.

Database and spreadsheet programs are designed and intended to help users store, organize, and retrieve data. This function can be especially helpful as counselors feel the effects of the "information age." In addition to managing information, database programs can also be used to facilitate decision making. For instance, Sabella (1996) wrote about how school counselors can use a database program to use existing data collected by his/her school to identify and assign students to small groups for counseling. Using a database program for small group assignment is especially helpful when group membership is contingent on traits such as age, race, and sex (e.g., balancing groups by race and sex while perhaps keeping age uniform). The key to this procedure lies in how the data are identified, sorted (also known as indexed), and processed.

Current database and spreadsheet programs allow counselors to collect data and conduct basic analyses such as monitoring changes in student test scores or attendance rates throughout the year. Once a data query is initially set up and run, all a counselor needs to do next time is press a button which conducts the same procedure over any data set. The savings in time over the long run can be quite significant. Relatedly, database/spreadsheet programs do a very good job of seamlessly integrating with word processors and other programs so that a counselor can then glean any data from a spreadsheet, for instance, and insert it in appropriate places in a counseling report. Sabella (1996) gave several examples of how school counselors use the integration of database and word processing programs to collect, process, and use data in various documents:

- In consultation with the Dean of Students and the district database person, a counselor obtained a file containing a list of students who had not been referred for discipline problems that year. It was requested that the list be sorted by home room teachers, who were also included in the data file. The Dean and the counselor created an award on the computer and merged the names of each student on the award. The certificates printed in the same order that they appeared in the file—by home room teacher. After each certificate printed, all that had to be done was deposit them in the home room teachers' mailboxes, which were also in alphabetical order. This process required 30 minutes to set up and 90 minutes to print the approximately 600 awards. A nearby student assistant was responsible for refilling the printer with paper when it ran out.

- A counselor who conducted an outdoor adventure field trip at the beginning of each semester asked her district office to send her a file with the names, lunch numbers, last semester grade point averages (GPAs), and home room teachers for all students at her school. She also asked that the list be sorted by GPA, race, and sex. The counselor was then able to identify students with the lowest GPAs and print out a list balanced by race and sex. Then, she merged a list of names with lunch numbers to give to the cafeteria staff who provided lunches for the trip. Using the data and her word processor, the counselor was also able to generate certificates, permission letters, and a list of participants that would be used for gathering post intervention data. At the end of the year, she had the district office provide GPAs for the same students so that she could compare them against GPA's at the beginning of the year.

- For an annual career day, an elementary school counselor maintained a database of speakers and other participants. He merged this information into standard invitations, confirmations, brochures, and thank-you letters.

- Another counselor used the merge capability of her word processor while working closely with a program designed for students who were not successful in the regular classroom environment. These students were self-contained with only 15 other students and a teacher with advanced training. The counselor worked with the students, their parents or guardians, and juvenile case workers. She maintained information about each student in a database file to help her manage each case. She then used these files to complete already formatted reports for the juvenile justice department, drop-out prevention office, district office, and parents. All she had to do was indicate to the computer which report she wanted to complete and for which child or group of children. The computer and printer did the rest.

- Using a spreadsheet program, a counselor maintained an activity log which included time spent in various categories of activities (e.g., consulting with parents, individual counseling, large group guidance, peer helper training, and professional development to name a few). With one click of the mouse each quarter, he could print out a report which he provided to his principal compete with textual descriptions and bar graphs.

In addition to off-the-shelf software, customized software for counselors is becoming increasingly available. For instance:

- EZANALYZE is a computer program designed to enhance the capabilities of Microsoft Excel™ by adding "point and click" functionality for analyzing data and creating graphs. It works on both Macs and PC's. http://www.ezanalyze.com/

- SCAATAP provides school counselors a quick and easy way to record activities and create daily, weekly, monthly, quarterly, and annual reports. The data generated by these reports will provide the "process" accountability that administrators and policy-makers desire. The reports will help answer the question "What do school counselors do?" http://www.scaatap.com/

- TheraScribe® 4.0 Counseling Record Management Software eliminates hours of time-consuming paperwork. You can quickly enter all the necessary information about a client including personal, diagnostic, treatment plans, medical information and much more. http://www.4ulr.com/products/counseling/thera-scribesoftware.html

- CounselingSurveys.org is a not-for-profit web site created to promote quantitative research in the Counseling profession by sponsoring electronic surveys free of charge for researchers and practitioners. (This site does not offer services to the general public.) http://www.counselingsurveys.org/.

## Multimedia

One popular technology tool for persuasive communication is multimedia presentation (MMP) software. A multimedia presentation (MMP) is created by a computer program and incorporates a series of projected images called slides. Slides may incorporate animated text, graphics, pictures, audio and video clips, graphs, tables – and any other electronic representations – in an integrated series (Sabella, 1998). Effective comprehensive school counseling programs/services include a diversity of stake holders, which include students, principals, teachers, staff, parents, community members, and others. Helping stake holders to advance their knowledge and understanding about your work and how they may become involved can be a tough task. A method which is highly expedient and yet effective is needed. Technology such as multimedia presentations is one tool that can effectively and efficiently proliferate a message about your work among many important people. Also as important, multimedia software may be a feasible answer to the question, "How can I provide others training that will help them better cope and succeed in realizing developmental milestones?"

Specifically, coupled with the power of the Internet, using multimedia software can help counselors:

1. Communicate a message that is rich with sound, animation, clip art, photos, graphs, data, and other elements;

2. Provide information that is highly up-to-date and easily accessed anytime of day or night;

3. Present to others without having to be present at a conference or meeting. This advantage has the benefit of also being quite cost and time effective;

4. Tailor information to each specific audience without building a new presentation from scratch. Existing MMPs can be altered and saved under a new name;

5. Collaborate with others more efficiently by enhancing the democratic process; and

6. Communicate to others that they are knowledgeable and capable of using desirable technology skills which can respectably be modeled for the clients they serve. In this case, the medium is the message.

Perhaps the most important use of electronic tools for communicating with important others is the ability to shift time and location. No longer are counselors required to be present for collaborating and communicating with others. A multimedia presentation can be stored on various devices to accommodate a wide variety of recipients' needs. Using the Internet to share presentations allows counselors to literally cultivate the message across a global audience within a matter of seconds. Once a presentation arrives, target audience members can access and view the presentation at their own convenience and at their own pace. Because today's multimedia software allows the counselor to easily include narration and timed slide transitions, an audience member can listen to and learn from a presentation, almost as if the counselor were present. And, if the recipient chooses, he or she may study the information as frequently as desired, pass along the information to others, or respond to the counselor for further inquiry or feedback.

How might counselors use multimedia presentations in their work? Sabella & Booker (2003) wrote specifically about counselors have and could use MMPs to enhance the impact of their work:

1. Counselors can enhance multicultural competencies by sharing rich MMP with others around the world. For example, D'Andrea (1995) wrote about several activities which include music, art, food, and photos that can foster both multicultural appreciation and technological literacy among elementary school students;

2. Scan in the work of clients, such as art projects, and share with appropriate others (e.g., faculty, parents, other consulting counselors);

3. Create a MMP that describes the counselor's work so that others such as teachers, administrators, parents, and community members may better understand and increase their involvement for facilitating client progress.

4. MMPs can also offer suggestions for how others may choose to support the school, refer clients, and otherwise contribute needed resources.

5. Similar to distance learning, MMPs can be used as professional/personal development delivery systems to help others learn important skills, knowledge, and attitudes to do their part in the client's progress (e.g., academic, personal, social, and career achievements); and

6. School counselors can (a) conduct a very large group guidance for all students at the same time. After a MMP is created, it can be transferred to video and then shown on the school's television network. For classes that have computers, the counselor can use the Internet to conduct a live chat about the topic. For classes that do not have a computer, the counselor can follow up that day and conduct live discussions; (b) provide teachers-as-advisors with a MMP to use with students thus insuring that they are presenting consistent and accurate information to students; and c) provide peer helpers (e.g., peer mediators) MMPs for learning relevant helping skills and attitudes as part of a homework assignment.

## Personal Information Managers

Personal information managers (PIMs) are a type of software application designed to help users organize random bits of information. Although the category is fuzzy, most PIMs enable you to enter various kinds of textual notes – reminders, lists, dates – and to link these bits of information together in useful ways. Many PIMs also include calendar, scheduling, and calculator programs. The usefulness of this type of software lies in it's ability to integrate data and provide feedback in the form of potential scheduling conflicts and event reminders. Microsoft Outlook, one of the most "mature" PIMs, allows users to integrate e-mail, calendars, coordination of meetings, notes, alerts, and much more. Several online PIM's such as My Yahoo! (http://my.yahoo.com/) and MSN Hotmail (http://www.hotmail.com) allow you to automatically import events that others manage (e.g., educational programming on television) as well as information from other PIMs such as Microsoft Outlook. Finally, your personal information can be synchronized with other portable devices such as your cell phone, handheld computer, or Ipod which makes access to the data highly convenient.

# Technologies for Intervention Delivery

When you think of conducting counseling with your students, you probably envision you and your client(s) in your office, in the classroom, or perhaps even on a "walk and talk." However, others may also have a mental image of a counselor who sits in front of the computer and conducts counseling over the Internet.

Webcounseling is the attempt to provide counseling services in an Internet environment. The environment may include connecting with your clients via e-mail, chatrooms, instant messenger, or Internet video conferencing. The practice of webcounseling, also referred to as cybercounseling, cybertherapy, e-therapy, e-counseling, and online counseling to name a few, began slowly although is rapidly finding popularity among both counselors and clients. Among counseling professionals, webcounseling has created somewhat of a debate about the utility and effectiveness of this new medium and whether "cybercounseling" even really exists. Moreover, those involved in traditional counseling ethical and legal issues are wondering how such matters relate to the Internet environment.

Some counselors would say that defining the nature and practice of webcounseling is futile and misleading. Counselors and others in this camp believe that webcounseling is a term which leads people to erroneously believe that the work of professional counselors can effectively and appropriately be conducted in an electronic or "virtual" environment such as the Internet. They argue that, although noteworthy attempts are currently in progress, empirically supported counseling theories and techniques have not yet been adequately tested in the virtual environment. Thus, we cannot confidently assume current approaches have the same effect or, even worse, do not have unanticipated negative effects for online clients. This group further argues that these online services cannot be considered counseling unless and until they can be demonstrated to be effective. Similarly, an important question has remained unanswered: Is counseling in cyberspace so different from traditional face-to-face counseling that it requires special training and certification?

Many counselors wonder if the therapeutic alliance can reliably be established without ever working with the client in person. Even if the counseling relationship could be developed in cyberspace, they wonder if the online personality with whom you are working is the same as the "real world" personality of the client. Finally, it is unknown if potential growth or progress made during online sessions will generalize to life in the real world as we would expect to happen in face-to-face counseling. Counselors who view cybercounseling as more of a potential than an existing counseling modality may be optimistic about how developing technology can help counselors do their work in alternative environments and media. However, for now, they caution us that traditional or face-to-face counseling is not well understood by the general public, notwithstanding its much longer history and exposure via public relations, and that discussing webcounseling as if it exists stands to confuse the practice of counseling even more. This group wants the public to understand the difference between the special relationship a counselor and client share, as compared to the relationships established in other related helping activities such as advising, mentoring, coaching, and teaching. These counselors argue that "cybercounselors" who believe they are counseling in cyberspace are more accurately providing cyberadvice, cybercoaching, cybermentoring, and distance learning. While each of these is important and valuable, none are adequate substitutes for professional counseling.

Other counselors have adopted a more "middle of the road" belief about cybercounseling. They espouse that cybercounseling is not counseling per se but an effective means to supplement live counseling sessions. They believe that technology has not yet developed tools to effectively create an environment that can substitute for a live setting although tools do exist to help counselors (and clients) be more effective and efficient in meeting their goals. Such counselors may indeed call themselves cybercounselors or e-therapists, for instance, but only insofar as it describes their use of computer and Internet technologies as a part of their face-to-face work with clients. These counselors affirm the role that technology plays throughout the process of counseling, including collaboration and communication, and continue to explore how such tools can enhance the probability of successful live interaction (Tyler and Sabella, 2004).

On the other side of the continuum reside counselors and researchers who view the web as a new delivery and management system for doing the work of professional counseling. These cybercounselors celebrate the latest tools provided by computers and networking technologies as providing the means to work with clients whom, without these tools, they could never connect. With some adaptations, they posit that they can effectively use their counseling knowledge and skills to provide counseling services in cyberspace.

Many future possibilities and potential problems in the delivery of counseling services exists. Following is an overview of each:

## Possibilities

- *Delivery of counseling services*: Walz (1996) noted that the information highway "allows counselors to overcome problems of distance and time to offer opportunities for networking and interacting not otherwise available" (p. 417). In addition, counseling over the Net may be a useful medium for those with physical disabilities whom may find even a short distance a significant obstacle. And yet for others whom are reticent in meeting with a counselor and/or self-disclosing, the Net may prove to be an interactive lubricant which may very well foster the counseling process.

- *Delivery of information resources*: The Internet is a convenient and quick way to deliver important information. In cybercounseling, information might be in the form of homework assignment between sessions or bibliocounseling. Also, electronic file transfer of client records, including intake data, case notes (Casey, Bloom, & Moan, 1994), assessment reports, and selected key audio and video recordings of client sessions, could be used as preparation for individual supervision, group supervision, case conferences, and research (Sampson, Kolodinsky, and Greeno, 1997).

- *Assessment and evaluation*: Access to a wide variety of assessment, instructional, and information resources, in formats appropriate in a wide variety of ethnic, gender, and age contexts (Sampson, 1990; Sampson & Krumboltz, 1991), could be accomplished via Web and FTP sites.

- *Communications*: Especially via e-mail, counselors and clients can exchange messages throughout the counseling process. Messages may inform both counselor and client of pertinent changes or progress. E-mail can provide an excellent forum for answering simple questions, providing social support, or to schedule actual or virtual meeting times.

- *Marriage and family counseling*: If face-to-face interaction is not possible on a regular basis, marriage counseling might be delivered via video conferencing, in which each couple and the counselor (or counselors) are in different geographic locations. After independent use of multimedia based computer-assisted instruction on communication skills, spouses could use video conferencing to complete assigned homework (e.g., communication exercises) (Sampson, et al., 1997).

- *Supervision*: Anecdotal evidence has shown that e-mail is an enhancing tool in the process of counselor supervision and consultation, It provides an immediate and ongoing channel of communication between and among as many people as chosen (Myrick & Sabella, 1995).

## Potential Problems

- *Confidentiality*: Although encryption and security methods have become highly sophisticated, unauthorized access to online communications remains a possibility without attention to security measures. Counselors whom practice on the Net must ethically and legally protect their clients, their profession, and themselves by using all known and reasonable security measures.

- *Computer competency*: Both the counselor and client must be adequately computer literate for the computer/network environment to be a viable interactive medium. From typing skills to electronic data transfer, both the counselor and client must be able to effectively harness the power and function of both hardware and software. Similar to face-to-face counseling, counselors must not attempt to perform services outside the limitations of their competence.

- *Location-specific factors*: A potential lack of appreciation on the part of geographically remote counselors of location-specific conditions, events, and cultural issues that affect clients may limit counselor credibility or lead to inappropriate counseling interventions. For example, a geographically remote counselor may be unaware of traumatic recent local events that are exacerbating a client's reaction to work and family stressors. It may also be possible that differences in local or regional cultural norms between the client's and counselor's community could lead a counselor to misinterpret the thoughts, feelings, or behavior of the client. Counselors need to prepare for counseling a client in a remote location by becoming familiar with recent local events and local cultural norms. If a counselor encounters an unanticipated reaction on the part of the client, the counselor needs to proceed slowly, clarifying client perceptions of their thoughts, feelings, and behavior (Sampson, et al., 1997).

- *Equity*: Does the cost of Internet access introduce yet another obstacle for obtaining counseling? Does cybercounseling further alienate potential clients whom might have the greatest need for counseling? Even when given access to the Net, could a client competently engage cybercounseling without possibly having ever had a computer experience? Webcounseling seems to exacerbate equity issues already confronting live counseling.

- *Credentialing*: How will certification and licensure laws apply to the Internet as state and national borders are crossed electronically? Will counselors be required to be credentialed in all states and countries where clients are located? Could cybercounseling actually be the impetus for a national credential recognized by all states? Will we need to move towards global credentialing? Who will monitor service complaints out-of-state or internationally?

- *High Tech v. High Touch*: How can counselors foster the development of trusting, caring, and genuine working relationships in cyberspace? Until video transmission over the Web makes telecounseling a reality, cybercounseling relies on a process devoid of nonverbal or extraverbal behavior. Even if we were able to conduct real-time counseling over the Net via video, can this medium help us to communicate so as to foster the counseling core conditions? Further, Lago (1996) poses a key question: "Do the existing theories of psychotherapy continue to apply, or do we need a new theory of e-mail therapy? (p. 289)"' He then takes Rogers' (1957) work on the necessary and sufficient conditions for therapeutic change as his starting-point and lists the computer-mediated therapist competencies as: the ability to establish contact, the ability to establish relationship, the ability to communicate accurately with minimal loss or distortion, the ability to demonstrate understanding and frame empathic responses, and the capacity and resources to provide appropriate and supportive information. This proposal begs the question as to whether such relationship conditions as outlined by Rogers can be successfully transmitted and received via contemporary computer-mediated telecommunications media.

- *Impersonation*: A famous cartoon circulated over the Net depicts a dog sitting in front of a computer. The caption says, "The nice thing about the Internet is that nobody knows you're a dog." Experienced Internet users can relate to the humor in this cartoon because they know that there are many people who hide behind the Net's veil of anonymity to communicate messages they ordinarily would not communicate in real life. Messages that convey unpopular sentiments and would ordinarily be met with castigation. Others rely on anonymity provided by the Net to play out fantasies or practical jokes. Who is your cyberclient, really? Does your client depict himself/herself as an adult and is actually a minor? Has the client disguised their gender, race, or other personal distinctions that may threaten the validity or integrity of your efforts.

- *Ethics*: How do current ethical statements for counselors apply or adapt to situations encountered online? For the most part, counselors can make the leap into cyberspace and use current ethical guidelines to conduct themselves in an ethical fashion. However, problems exist. The future will inevitably see a change in what it means to be ethical as we learn the exact nature of counseling online.

## The Ethics of WebCounseling

In 1995, the NBCC Board of Directors appointed a webcounseling Task Force to examine the practice of online counseling and to assess the possible existence of any regulatory issues NBCC might need to address. The task force established a listserv composed of more than 20 individuals who had specific knowledge, expertise, skills and opinions regarding the practice of what is herein referred to as webcounseling. Soon it became apparent that counseling had a diverse presence on the Internet, from websites that simply promoted a counselor's home or office practice, to sites that provided information about counseling and others which actually claimed to offer therapeutic interventions either as an adjunct to face-to-face counseling or as a stand alone service. Some sites were poorly constructed, poorly edited and poorly presented. Others were run by anonymous individuals, individuals with no credentials or fraudulent credentials, and some sites were operated by individuals with appropriate credentials and years of professional experience. However these credentials were all based on education and experience gained in face-to-face counseling, and the relevance of these credentials to the practice of webcounseling is unknown. No one knew if the lack of visual input made a difference in the outcome of the counseling process. No one knew about the legality of counseling across state or national boundaries. No one knew if there was any relevant research in any field of communication which could shed light on these questions (Bloom, 1998). As a result of the Task Force's work, a set of standards, the *Standards for the Ethical Practice of Webcounseling,* were developed and are now included online at http://www.nbcc.org/.

# Ethical and Legal Use of Technology

Computer and networking technologies such as the Internet provide vast power, especially as a medium for communication, collaboration, and as an intervention delivery. Internet users enjoy the freedom of conducting all kinds of transactions, including counseling, over the Net. With this freedom, however, comes an important responsibility to use computers, and especially the Internet, in a manner which is safe, secure, ethical, and contributes to the overall welfare of all involved. Counselors should dedicate themselves to becoming aware of the dangers involved in using computers and the Internet. For instance, Sabella (2003) wrote about counseling related issues that computer and Internet technology have spawned and includes: Internet addiction, equitable access, pornography, online sexual harassment, security, and safety. With increased awareness, counselors can more effectively make decisions about their computing and online behavior. In addition, Tyler and Sabella (2004) dedicated a chapter in their book, *Using Technology to Improve Counseling Practice: A Primer for the 21st Century*, about the legal and ethical issues involved in counseling technology. They reviewed precautions for protecting confidentiality such as using encryption methods for communication, file passwords, and electronic file shredders. The authors also included tips for keeping one's personal computer secure from threats such as spyware and viruses which could compromise sensitive information.

# The Future of School Counseling and Technology

Technology poses either opportunities or threats to the development of our work as school counselors and to our profession, depending upon how it is used. Focusing on the parts that are helpful and avoiding those which are not can be a difficult task because of the vastness and morphological nature of technology. As part of ongoing professional development, school counselors are wise to stay informed of new technological developments and how they are being applied to our work. Technologies currently under development and becoming more pervasive (and thus usually less expensive) merit special attention:

1. Digital cameras allow for counselors to take pictures and instantly use them in a variety of ways. Some are posting photos of evidence of their work on counseling websites or electronic portfolios as a matter of public relations and accountability. Others are using digital cameras, both video and still, to help clients capture and describe "their world" in the form of electronic collages or journals which are then used in the counseling process.

2. Voice recognition software allows for humans and machines to interact in more meaningful ways than ever before considered. Counselors can dictate their words into various applications as well as issue computer voice commands that will further increase efficiency and effectiveness.

3. As bandwidth (the capacity of copper and fiberoptic wires to move data) increases, we will see the proliferation of Internet videoconferencing and online full-length videos which will further enhance efforts in communication, collaboration, consultation, distance education, and intervention delivery. Websites will become more dynamic, offering virtual three dimensional worlds. In addition, wireless high speed access to the Internet throughout the country is becoming a reality.

4. Computer scientists are making rapid gains in developing what is known as natural language so that computers can better "understand" human questions or commands and more appropriately respond.

5. Massive data warehouses and mining applications will provide educators with an early warning alert system to better help identify students who perform outside of expectations. These systems will also help counselors to maintain sophisticated student profiles and design customized guidance lessons, perhaps even electronically deliver those lessons.

6. Computers are breaking capacity and speed barriers every day. As they become faster, smaller, and are able to store more data, computers will help us to perform and manage tasks with unprecedented proficiency.

7. The rapidly advancing gaming technology (e.g., Xbox, Playstation) will advance how counselors can create and deliver "virtual reality" experiences as part of guidance and counseling interventions.

8. Social networking technologies will help school counselors share, collaborate, and support each other in all aspects of the profession.

The experience and world views of our clients and stake holders have been profoundly impacted by the rapid evolution of computer technologies. We sit at the edge of an electronic frontier without knowing for certain what lies ahead. The journey, with its extraordinary potentials and realistic pitfalls, is exciting and oftentimes frightening. Careful and purposeful practice, however, can help us to stay connected and competent amidst chaotic transition. This chapter sought to provide readers with an introduction and overview of technology and its special meaning to school counselors. As an agent of change and advocacy, it is your job now to explore how technology best works for you so that you may work best for your clients.

In summary, no counseling professional is immune from the significant impact technology has made on how we practice, communicate, manage, and measure the outcomes of our work. In addition, technology is also changing the types of counseling issues presented by our clients within the various systems in which they live and work (e.g., family, peer, society). The message is clear: Opting out of technological literacy and implementation in today's high-tech world reduces effectiveness and efficiency while increasing the risk of unethically practicing beyond one's competency. On the other hand, counselors who march along with the progress of high-tech tools and electronic media stand to enjoy the benefits and temper the potential dangers that prevail. Technological literacy and implementation is not merely a response to a problem, but an important and life-long part of professional development and training. For better or worse, the availability of various technologies and how we apply them will continue to change. Changes will be pleasant or unpleasant, in large part determined by our familiarity and abilities to adapt.

# References

American School Counselor Association. (2005). *The ASCA national model: A framework for school counseling programs* (2nd ed.). Alexandria, VA: Author.

Blog. (Retrieved December 11, 2005). Webopedia. [Online]. Available: http://www.webopedia.com/TERM/b/blog.html.

Bloom, J. W. (1998). The ethical practice of webcounseling. *British Journal of Guidance and Counselling, 26*(1), p. 53-59.

Cairo, P.C., & Kanner, M.S. (1984). Investigating the effects of computerized approaches to counselor training. *Counselor Education and Supervision, 24*, 212-221.

Casey, J.A., Bloom, J.W., & Moan, E.R. (1994). Use of technology in counselor supervision. In L. D. Borders (Ed.), *Counseling supervision*. Greensboro: University of North Carolina, ERIC Clearinghouse on Counseling and Student Services. (ERIC Document Reproduction Service No. ED 372 357)

Chapman, W., & Katz, M.R. (1983). Career information systems in the secondary schools: A survey and assessment. *Vocational Guidance Quarterly, 32*, 165-177.

Croft, V. (1991). Technological literacy: Refined for the profession, applications for the classroom. Unpublished paper presented at the 1991 annual conference of the International Technology Education Association.

D'Andrea, M. (1995). Using computer technology to promote multicultural awareness among elementary school-age students. *Elementary School Guidance and Counseling, 30*(1), p. 45-55.

Fanning, J. M. (1994). Integrating academics and technology: Uncovering staff development needs. In J. Willis, B. Robin, & D. A. Willis (Eds.). *Technology and Teacher Education Annual, 1994,* (pp. 331-334). Washington, DC: Association for the Advancement of Computing in Education.

Friery, K., & Nelson, J.G. (2004). Using technology to develop a high school career awareness workshop: The REACH program. *TechTrends: Linking Research & Practice to Improve Learning, 48*(6), p. 40-42.

Froehle, T.C. (1984). Computer-assisted feedback in counseling supervision. *Counselor Education and Supervision, 24*, 168-175.

*Getting America's students ready for the 21st century: Meeting the technology literacy challenge*—June, 1996 [Online]. Available: http://www.netc.org//cdrom/tlc/pdf/tlc.pdf.

Glover, B.L. (1995). DINOS (drinking is not our solution): Using computer programs in middle school drug education. *Elementary School Guidance & Counseling, 30*, 55-62.

Haring-Hidore, M. (1984). In pursuit of students who do not use computers for career guidance. *Journal of Counseling and Development, 63*, 139-140.

Harris, J. (1972). *Computer-assisted guidance systems.* Washington, DC: National Vocational Guidance Association.

Hayden, M. (1989). What is technological literacy? *Bulletin of Science, Technology and Society, 119*, 220-233, STS press.

How blogs work. (Retrieved December 21, 2005). *Howstuffworks.* [Online]. Available: http://computer.howstuffworks.com/blog1.htm.

Instant messaging. (Retrieved December 20, 2005). *Wikipedia.* [Online]. Available: http://en.wikipedia.org/wiki/Instant_messaging.

Internet world stats. (November 21, 2005). *Internet usage statistics—the big picture: World internet users and population stats.* [Online]. Available: http://www.internetworldstats.com/stats.htm.

International Technology Education Association. (2000). Standards for technological literacy: Content for the study of technology. *International Technology Education Association.* [Online]. Available: http://www.iteaconnect.org/TAA/Publications/STL/STLMainPage.htm.

Jackson, M.L., & Davidson, C.T. (1998). The web we weave: Using the internet for counseling research; Part I. *Counseling Today, 39*(2).

Katz, M.R., & Shatkin, L. (1983). Characteristics of computer-assisted guidance. *The Counseling Psychologist, 11*(4), 15-31.

Kivlighan, D. M., Jr., Johnston, J. A., Hogan, R. S., & Mauer, E. (1994). Who benefits from computerized career counseling? *Journal of Counseling and Development, 72*, 289-292.

Koufman-Frederick, A., Lillie, M., Pattison-Gordon, L., Watt, D.L., & Carter, R. (1999). *Electronic collaboration: A practical guide for educators.* Providence, RI: The LAB at Brown University. [Online]. Available: http://www.alliance.brown.edu/pubs/collab/elec-collab.pdf.

Lago, C. (1996). Computer therapeutics. *Counselling, 7*, 287-289.

McClure, P.A. (1996, May/June). Technology plans and measurable outcomes. *Educom Review, 31*(3).

Myrick, R.D., & Sabella, R.A. (1995). Cyberspace: New place for counselor supervision. *Elementary School Guidance and Counseling, 30*(1), p. 35-44.

Neukrug, E.S. (1991). Computer-assisted live supervision in counselor skills training. *Counselor Education and Supervision, 31*, 132-138.

Owen, S., & Heywood, J. (1988). Transition technology in Ireland. *International Journal of Research in Design and Technology Education, 1*(1).

Pyle, K.R. (1984). Career counseling and computers: Where is the creativity? *Journal of Counseling and Development, 63*, 141-144.

Rogers, C.R. (1957). The necessary and sufficient conditions of therapeutic personality change. *Journal of Consulting Psychology, 21*, 95-103.

Rust, E.B. (1995). Applications of the international counselor network for elementary and middle school counseling. *Elementary School Guidance and Counseling, 30*, 16-25.

Sabella, R.A. (2005). *What are school counselors doing with technology?* [Online]. Available: http://www.schoolcounselor.com/pdf/counseling-technology-activities.pdf.

Sabella, R.A. (2003). *SchoolCounselor.com: A friendly and practical guide to the world wide web* (2nd ed.). Minneapolis, MN: Educational Media Corporation.

Sabella, R.A. (1998). Practical technology applications for peer helper programs and training. *Peer Facilitator Quarterly, 15*(2), 4-13.

Sabella, R.A. (1996). School counselors and computers: Specific time-saving tips. *Elementary School Guidance and Counseling, 31*(2), p. 83-96.

Sabella, R.A., & Booker, B. (2003). Using technology to promote your guidance and counseling program among stake holders. *Professional School Counseling, 6*(3), p. 206-213.

Sampson, J.P., Jr. (1990). Computer-assisted testing and the goals of counseling psychology. *The Counseling Psychologist, 18*, 227-239.

Sampson, J.P., Jr., & Krumboltz, J.D. (1991). Computer-assisted instruction: A missing link in counseling. *Journal of Counseling and Development, 69*, 395-397.

Sampson, J.P., Kolodinsky, R.W., & Greeno, B.P. (1997). Counseling on the information highway: Future possibilities and potential problems. *Journal of Counseling and Development, 75*(3), p. 203-213.

Saskatchewan Education. (2002). *Understanding the common essential learnings: A handbook for teachers.* Regina, SK: Saskatchewan Education.

Search Engines. (Retrieved December 19, 2005). *Wikipedia.* [Online]. Available: http://en.wikipedia.org/wiki/Search_engine.

Sharf, R.S., & Lucas, M. (1993). An assessment of a computerized simulation of counseling skills. *Counselor Education and Supervision, 32,* 254-266.

Shulman, H.A., Sweeney, B., & Gerler, E.R. (1995). A computer-assisted approach to preventing alcohol abuse: Implications for the middle school. *Elementary School Guidance and Counseling, 30,* 63-77.

Steffens, H. (1986). Issues in the preparation of teachers for teaching robotics in schools. In J. Heywood & P. Matthews (Eds.). *Technology, society, and the school curriculum.* Manchester, England: Roundthorn Publishing.

Stone, C., & Turba, R. (1999). School counselors using technology for advocacy. *The Journal of Technology in Counseling, 1* (1). [Online]. Available: http://jtc.colstate.edu/vol1_1/advocacy.htm.

Tyler, J.M., & Sabella, R.A. (2004). *Using technology to improve counseling practice: A primer for the 21st century.* Alexandria, VA: American Counseling Association.

Valesky, T., & Sabella, R.A. (2005). Podcasting in educational leadership and counseling. Paper presented at the Southern Regional Council on Educational Administration Conference (SRCEA), Atlanta, Georgia, October 27-30. [Online]. Available: http://coe.fgcu.edu/edleadership/podcasting.pdf.

Waetjen, W.B. (1993). Technological literacy reconsidered. *Journal of Technology Education, 4*(2). [Online]. Available: http://scholar.lib.vt.edu/ejournals/JTE/v4n2/waetjen.jte-v4n2.html.

Walz, G.R. (1996). Using the i-way for career development. In R. Feller & G. Walz (Eds.), *Optimizing life transitions in turbulent times: Exploring work, learning and careers.* Greensboro: University of North Carolina, ERIC Clearinghouse on Counseling and Student Services. p. 415-427.

# Chapter 34

# Maintaining Your Professional Image: A Report Card

by
Beverly O'Bryant

---

*Dr. Beverly J. O'Bryant is Assistant Provost for Graduate Studies and Research, Director of the Doctoral Program in Educational Leadership, Research Coordinator of the Minority Male Health Research Project and a professor with a dual appointment in the Graduate School of Education in both the Department of Counseling and the Department of Educational Studies and Leadership at Bowie State University. She is a licensed professional counselor, Chair of the Board of Health Information, Education and Practice Partners, Inc., and the President and CEO of Counseling and Training Systems Inc.*

## Introduction

A primary issue in our profession is the role of the counselor-as-person. Counseling professionals have long felt that this may be the most important aspect in effective counseling outcome. We ask our clients to face the truth about themselves; to look honestly at what they are and to choose how they want to change and grow. Should we as counselors not be willing to do the same? Should we not be willing to focus on counselor-as-person as well as on counselor-as-professional?

Growing personally and professionally contributes significantly to our success with student clients and others with whom we work. Keeping abreast of new and innovative changes in our profession enables us to serve our "publics" better; and, provides our student clients with a measure of confidence that their welfare is most important. Being ever mindful of our "professional image" provides indices of competence and professionalism. And, the individual commitment to attend to each of these areas provides a fairly good indicator of the overall well being of the discipline, and a prognostication of longevity relative to the profession's acceptance by its constituents.

How would you fare? Are you growing professionally and personally? Do you keep abreast of new and innovative changes? Are you attentive to your professional image among your various publics? Do you know who your many publics are? Are you committed to your own professional development? And, are you the type of counselor from whom you would seek help?

Our graduate counselor preparation programs require grounding in both theory and practice. Use of theory provides the framework and direction for the most effective practice. However, because the profession of counseling is constantly in a state of flux, it becomes incumbent of each professional counselor to remain conversant with the best and latest information.

Continued self-enhancement and professional growth is made easy today through the myriad of professional opportunities available. Professional school counselors will want to take advantage of them. Professional growth necessitates keeping in touch with other professionals and professional organizations, and with new concepts and new materials. Membership in ACA and ASCA provides a relationship with other counselors and information about what is happening nationwide. Maintaining current facts from the counseling journals keeps the proactive, developmental counselor abreast of the trends. Attending local, state, and national conferences opens doors to new ideas and exciting personal and professional contacts.

It is our duty (ethically) as professional school counselors to maintain and enhance our "professional image." And, staying in touch with developing, growing, innovative people in our profession can be fun and very rewarding. It can sometimes be a little disconcerting to learn how little we may know in comparison to some others in our profession, but it can also be very rewarding to learn that we know enough to contribute to the professional growth of others.

---

Throughout this book reference has been made to the counselor as a professional. There are chapters concerning your appropriate role and function, legal and ethical issues, effectively promoting your school counseling program, and so forth. All of these are topics of concern to the professional school counselor. However, none may be more important than a preceding chapter (32) by Dr. Tom Clawson and colleagues concerning credentialing and the school counselor. Are you appropriately credentialed? Are you a Nationally Certified Counselor (NCC)? A Nationally Certified School Counselor (NCSC)? If not, are you interested in becoming one? If yes, see Figure 32.1 and then write: *NBCC, 3-D Terrace Way, Greensboro, NC 27403* for an application. The appropriate credential identifies to our "publics" that we have met specific professional standards and most importantly, that we "cared" enough about them and ourselves to meet such standards.

What kind of a "professional image" report card would you issue concerning yourself at this time in your career? Would it be "Satisfactory" or "Unsatisfactory"? If you are a practicing school counselor, respond honestly to the following items as they pertain to you. If you are a school counselor-to-be, respond to the items as to how you would like to "grade" yourself two years following your graduation from a graduate level program in counselor education.

# Counselor's Report Card

**Use one of the following as your response to each item: below:**

S = Satisfactory Progress

N = Needs Improvement

U = Unsatisfactory Progress

**As a professional school counselor, I:**

S N U    1. conduct appropriate school counselor functions.

S N U    2. follow a written job description.

S N U    3. am a member and involved in ASCA.

S N U    4. attend and participate in my annual state counseling association meetings.

S N U    5. made a presentation (or submitted a proposal for consideration) at my state or national ASCA Conference this past year.

S N U    6. attended an in-service workshop, a conference, or took a non-required graduate course for my own personal growth during the past year (other than 4 above).

S N U    7. am familiar with the ASCA Ethical Standards and adhere to them.

S N U    8. conduct individual and group counseling only within my level of expertise.

S N U    9. subscribe to and read ASCA and state school related journals, newsletters, and so forth.

S N U    10. am up-to-date on State and Federal laws affecting my work as a school counselor.

S N U    11. read professional books.

S N U    12. am a member of ACA and attend the annual ACA conference.

S N U    13. have an attractive and inviting office.

S N U    14. have a pleasant yet efficient and professional, personal demeanor.

S N U    15. use my many talents to create a positive atmosphere in my school.

S N U    16. am a voluntary participating committee member as requested by others at my school and/or by state, regional, or national counseling organization representatives.

S N U    17. am actively involved in determining my own schedule as well as goals and directions for the school counseling program.

S N U  18. model mental and physical health.

S N U  19. hold membership and participate in local service clubs.

S N U  20. promote the image of the counseling profession.

S N U  21. take a stand as an advocate for my students.

S N U  22. carry professional liability insurance.

S N U  23. attend a conference and then share what I learned with colleagues.

S N U  24. exhibit pride in myself as a counselor.

S N U  25. speak with assurance, even when saying "I'm not sure about that, but I'll be glad to investigate it for you."

S N U  26. appear, in dress, and mannerisms revealing professionalism.

S N U  27. have the appropriate professional accessories: briefcase, business cards, and so forth.

S N U  28. take advantage of the home study programs offered by ACA and other reputable agencies.

S N U  29. network with counselors from other schools and school systems as often as possible.

S N U  30. am a National Certified Counselor (NCC)—a National Certified School Counselor (NCSC).

S N U  31. display my degrees, certifications, plaques and honors prominently on my office walls.

S N U  32. articulate the positive.

S N U  33. "write-up" some of the innovative in-the-field things I do for publication.

S N U  34. attend legislative hearings.

S N U  35. know my local, state, and national legislators.

S N U  36. am accountable.

S N U  37. participate in locally relevant research.

S N U  38. have written an article for a counseling journal or newsletter (very few writers to our journals are school counselors).

S N U  39. perceive myself as an up-to-date, growing "professional".

S N U  40. respect the confidentiality of the counseling relationship (and never "talk too much" in the teachers lounge).

S N U  41. make a clear distinction between my personal views and opinions and those I make as a representative of the school counseling profession (if different).

S N U  42. view my professional development as a continuing *must*.

S N U  43. strive to impact legislation and decisions affecting my profession: locally, statewide, and nationally.

S N U  44. am working at changing the perception, attitudes and systems that are working against our young people.

S N U  45. am an advocate of the school counseling profession.

What sort of a "report card" did you issue yourself? Do you "need improvement" in several areas? If yes, the best way to strengthen your weak areas, to "remain abreast," is to get involved professionally. The "involved" school counselor seldom burns out.

Now that you've finished reading this book you have been exposed to many, many excellent strategies and plans for use in effectively managing your school counseling program. How well do you manage your own personal and professional growth? As a counselor, developing a plan to effectively manage your own personal and professional growth may be more important than managing your school counseling program. Develop a plan and stay with it! However, it is true, the best laid plans will forever be "best laid" if not put into action. As you've read throughout this book, there is a lot (to say the least) going on in our profession! "Buy in!" It's your profession and your future.

A school counselor's continued professional development is not really a choice, it is imperative.

# Figure 34.1
# My Professional Development:
## A Self-Assessment Inventory By Joe Wittmer

**Directions:** Below are several current professional issues, questions, etc. which should be of concern to you as a professional school counselor or school counselor to be. Answer each item by checking "Met," "Partially Met", or "Not Met". A "Met" answer means you are convinced that you possess the skills and knowledge to fully meet the statement as written. Of course, if you are a student preparing to become a professional school counselor, you may not be able to respond appropriately to each item given below.

1. I am a member of the American Counseling Association, the American School Counselor Association, a national certified counselor (NCC) and a national certified school counselor (NCSC).

      Met _____       Partially Met _____       Not Met _____

2. I am prepared to work as a counselor in a diverse, multicultural school setting:

I have obtained formal instructions, practice and supervision on providing multicultural counseling to school aged student clients.

      Met _____       Partially Met _____       Not Met _____

3. Technology is/will be an integral part of my overall developmental school counseling program:

I am able to construct a web page, make power point presentations, etc. in support of my personal counseling and school counseling program activities.

      Met _____       Partially Met _____       Not Met _____

4. I remain updated (and have obtained the necessary skills) regarding current social issues that do, and/or will, impact my student clients, i.e. drug use, school violence, etc.:

I have obtained knowledge and skills regarding the current social issues facing my student clients.

      Met _____       Partially Met _____       Not Met _____

5. I remain abreast and understand the changes in careers and the labor market and how these currently affect my student clients/future student clients:

I have obtained knowledge about the impact of technology, diversity, and globalization on work/workers and apply (will apply) it as appropriate thorough out my school counseling program.

      Met _____       Partially Met _____       Not Met _____

*Joe Wittmer, Ph.D. and Mary Ann Clark, Ph.D.*

6. I have knowledge and skills in the latest assessment and diagnosis tools available to me as a school counselor:

I have the knowledge and skills in the latest assessment tools used in my school district as well as the skills to use with individual student clients to formulate a diagnosis as needed.

      Met _____           Partially Met _____           Not Met _____

7. I have a copy of the ACA, ASCA and NBCC Ethical Standards and conduct myself accordingly:

I have obtained formal instruction in ethical decision making and have a working knowledge of the current ASCA, NBC, and ACA Ethical Standards.

      Met _____           Partially Met _____           Not Met _____

8. I am aware of the referral sources in my community and know when to refer my student clients as needed.

      Met _____           Partially Met _____           Not Met _____

During the next year I will seek professional development in the following area(s):

_____

_____

_____

# Chapter 35

## School Counseling: Envisioning the Future

by
**Carolyn Stone, Ed.D.**

---

*Carolyn B. Stone, Ed.D., is a Professor in Counselor Education at the University of North Florida in Jacksonville, Florida. Dr. Stone spent 22 years with the Duval County public school system in Jacksonvillle as teacher, counselor, and Supervisor of Guidance. As a counselor educator, she has written numerous articles and books and has conducted workshops in the areas of legal and ethical issues for student services personnel as well as school counseling program development. She is currently serving as the president of the American School Counselor Association.*

The future and next chapter in the history of school counseling promises to be one of the most productive and exciting in our long and illustrious history. The compass guiding the actions of current and future school counselors points to work that supports students' learning with a data driven school counseling focus. Past and future, the lure and success of the school counseling profession has been and continues to be the promise of making a difference in the lives of hundreds of students. How many professionals can say with assurance, "Over the course of my career I will advantage thousands of lives?"

The future will see a continuation and growth of model state programs that align with the American School Counselor Association's (ASCA) model (ASCA, 2005). This model, acquired through the hard work of Trish Hatch and Judy Bowers, brought together the best and brightest work from the field into one place. The ASCA model is a compilation of many respected pioneers in our field: Pat Martin, Norm Gysbers, Bob Myrick, Curly Johnson, Carol Dahir, Chari Campbell and others. Pat Martin, of The Transforming School Counseling Initiative (TSCI) (Education Trust, n.d.), significantly influenced the most sweeping change in the school counseling profession of the 21st century with her work impacting the achievement gap through systemic change, leadership, advocacy, and collaboration. Started as a grant given by the DeWitt Wallace-

Readers Digest Foundation and managed by the Education Trust, the TSCI, along with the ASCA model of which TSCI is a significant part, brought the future hurtling full speed toward the school counselor's door. The Education Trust's TSCI movement sparked a lively and sometimes riotous debate about the focus and purpose of the school counseling profession. The decade's long discourse, brought forward by the principal investigators of TSCI under the tutelage of Patricia Martin, has turned into one of the most productive ten years of our history. TSCI caused us to rethink our roles and helped us form these core beliefs of 21st century school counseling:

- Act as a *counselor, advocate, leader, team member, and consultant* to maximize opportunities for students to succeed academically, emotionally, and socially.

- Strive to develop in K-12 students a *commitment to achievement* and to the realization of *ambitious goals* and to provide conditions that enable students to accomplish high aspirations.

- Help students understand the *potential of their lives* and to enhance K-12 students' *capacity to make academic and career decisions* by providing students with programs which enable them to analyze their perceptions, attitudes, and feelings in relationship to decision-making.

- Become a *leader* and steward of *equity and excellence efforts* and be able to use data to recognize *institutional and environmental barriers* impeding students ability to realize their full academic potential and to be equipped to take the lead in remedying these inequalities.

- Provide all students with *academic/career advising* to help them form values and attitudes about the significance of education to their future economic success and their quality of life.

- Become *managers of resources* and partnership builders- enlisting the support of parents, agencies, and community members (Stone, 1996).

Equity and access are the watchwords for our profession. Believing and following the tenet that each and every student is entitled to an equitable and quality educational experience and acting on this belief defines our actions. The ASCA Model, revised in 2005 (ASCA, 2005), the ASCA Ethical Codes and Standards of Practice, revised in 2004 (ASCA, 2004), and the Education Trust's TSCI work (Education Trust, n.d.), require that practicing school counselors behave as leaders and advocates, identifying and rectifying school based practices that inhibit the success of individuals and groups of students. School counselors of the 21st century use data to determine who is being left out of the success picture in schools and along with other stakeholders develop strategies to support all students to be successful learners. School counselors, like every educator, are accountable for student success and have a responsibility to contribute significantly to systemic change.

## Defining Who We Are

The school counseling profession, moving away from the traditional view of school counseling to transformed practice, respects the bold past but recognizes that in order to advantage students we must embrace a "new vision" school counseling approach. Future school counseling programs are building on the great work that has been done in the past with time-on-task and results based data and moving in the direction of impact data. The former question in school counseling (answered in part by survey and time-on-tasks data) is, "What do school counselors do?" The new question that defines school counseling present and future is, "How are students impacted academically because they have a school counselor (Education Trust, 1997)?"

More than 20 years ago, Inbody (1984) identified six basic premises that were critical to the future of school counseling (p. 216-217).

1. What the school counseling profession does today will have an impact on the quality of the field of school counseling and educational environments in which school counselors and students must live.

2. Scientific methods of researching school counseling can be used for anticipating the various futures school counselors could create unknowingly.

3. There is no longer just one future that awaits the school counseling profession, but many different possible futures, depending on what school counselors and their profession choose today.

4. School counselors assume a moral urgency in their responsibility to future generations of students and school counselors.

5. Technology continues to serve as a powerful tool for school counselors; however, school counselors are responsible for technology integration and use in the future in a way that may have been inconceivable twenty years ago.

Future school counselors will be the beneficiary of the discourse of the last ten years, having the preparation, skills, and voice to connect to the educational reform initiatives such as No Child Left Behind (U.S. Department of Education, 2001). Accountability governs educational reform and the 21st century school. School counselors are more frequently illustrating the influence and impact of their programs through the use of data. However, the profession continues to struggle with accountability. With the best of intentions, school counselors have not successfully documented that students have been more successful in schools as a result of their actions and interventions (Whiston and Sexton, 1998). Sharing accountability for student success with stakeholders is a driving force for transforming and re-framing the work of school counselors across the nation (ASCA, 2005; Gysbers and Henderson, 2006; Myrick, 2003; Stone and Dahir, 2004).

The 21st Century school counseling program will be data-driven to secure the counselor's position as a valued player in school improvement (Schmidt, 2003; Myrick, 2003; Stone and Dahir, 2004) but more importantly, data-driven school counseling advantages students in acquiring and applying life-long learning skills. Accountability means demonstrating that something worthwhile is happening. In a public school setting, this principle may be manifested in procedures used to show that taxpayers are getting their money's worth. In such situations, the counselors are challenged to develop evaluations of their efforts (Baker, 2000, p. 31)

## Skills Past, Present, and Future

Where lies the future of the school counseling profession? Have school counselors "become the academic conscience of the school, insuring that the school remains focused on student achievement and accepts responsibility for student outcomes" (Hart & Jacobi, 1992, p. 49) as suggested years ago? When school counselors embrace the ethical and moral obligation to reduce and eliminate the institutional and/or social barriers that may stand in the way of every student's academic, career, or personal-social development (Stone, 2005), they advance the moral dimensions of school to include a strong social justice agenda to "close the gap" especially for diverse populations of students who have been traditionally underserved or underrepresented. Leadership, advocacy, teaming and collaboration, data-driven decision making skills, and technology have become common practice (Ed Trust, 1997; ASCA, 2003, 2005) and integral to the vocabulary of school counselors nationwide.

## Achievement, Opportunity, and Information Gaps

Theobald suggested that we need to envision the society we really want and to 'create methods by which we can move from the present future into the conditional future that we choose' (Maples, 1984. p.xiii)." School counselors in the future, will increasingly partner with other educators to impact the achievement, opportunity, and information gaps. According to the College Board's National Task Force on Minority Achievement (1999) significant differences exist in grades, college-going rates, class rank, SAT scores, enrollment in AP classes, and the number of bachelor, professional and doctoral degrees earned. These gaps among student groups translate into reduced numbers of African-American, Latino and Native American students entering the labor force with the educational preparation necessary for well-paying professional careers (U.S. Department of Labor, 2004). This reality is alarming as the changing demographics mean that these groups will make up two-fifths of the school-age population by 2030 (U.S. Census Bureau, 2003). In our rapidly changing society these educational inequities will impact the overall economic picture of America.

| Past | Present | Future |
|---|---|---|
| 20th Century School Counseling: service driven | Transformed School Counseling: data driven and standards-based | Intentional and Purposeful School Counseling: aligned with the educational enterprise |
| Counseling | Counseling | Counseling |
| Consultation | Consultation | Consultation |
| Coordination | Coordination | Coordination |
| | Leadership | Leadership |
| | Advocacy | Advocacy |
| | Teaming and collaboration | Teaming and collaboration |
| | Use of data to inform practice | Use of data to inform practice |
| | Technology | Technology |
| | Assessment | Assessment |
| | | Accountability |
| | | Cultural mediation |
| | | Systemic change agent |
| | | Social change agent |

(adapted from Education Trust, 2001; Dahir, in press)

*Joe Wittmer, Ph.D. and Mary Ann Clark, Ph.D.*

## ASCA Standards and Model

Many factors influence these inequities in achievement among groups and some of these factors can be addressed by forward thinking school counselors who ferret out the opportunity gaps in their schools. Opportunity gaps are the differences between who gets a rigorous curriculum, the best teachers, resources to optimize learning, and a safe and respectful school climate (Education Trust, 2001). Katie Haycock, Founder of the Educational Trust, sums up the findings of her organizations work on the achievement gap, "We continue to give the have nots the least when they come to school" (2001).

No Child Left Behind (2001) legislation mandates educational accountability to close the opportunity gaps between student groups. School counselors' future roles must unmistakably promote equity by ensuring all students have access to a rigorous academic curriculum. "College Ready, Work Ready, No Difference" (Education Trust, 2001) requires that school counselors through their academic and career advising roles, contribute to closing the information gap and to helping all students' choose from a wide array of opportunities following high school graduation.

School counselors as leaders and advocates behave as change agents when the community and institutions' standards of behavior adversely stratify students' opportunities, then our ethical standards and codes give us a directive to act responsibly to try and change those policies and practices that impede student success (ASCA, 2004). The message here is to understand the prevailing written and unwritten standards of the community, school district, and individual work site and behave consistently within the parameters of those standards while working responsibly to change practice and policy that hurt students (ASCA, Standard F.1.d).

Across America school counselors are developing state specific models that align with the ASCA National Model with a solid accountability component to support school counselors to deliver data-driven school counseling. The school counseling program of the 21st Century aligns with the mission of schools (Myrick, 2003). The ASCA ethical standards and ASCA model help professionals develop a common language to describe their work and contributions to accountability (Myrick, 2003).

Cutting edge school counseling programs reinforce the importance of delivering a comprehensive, developmental, and results-based program that carefully considers local demographic needs and the political climate of the community.

When goals of comprehensive school counseling programs are aligned with the mission of the school, it is inevitable that student achievement will improve as a result of the efforts of school counselors (ASCA, 2005). Accountability links the work of school counselors to student success.

**Culture and Belief System.** Twenty first century school counselors develop a core belief system about student learning. Almost all educators espouse the belief that given the right conditions all children can achieve to high levels. School counselors will be the additional set of eyes and ears looking to see if this belief is translated into action in the school's programs and opportunities.

*There have been too many examples of academic success in the face of tremendous adversity to conclude that intelligence and ability are handed out sparingly or based on only genetic endowments, or that they cannot be affected by educational environments. These examples are powerful reminders that great potential exists in all students. What needs changing first are the attitudes, beliefs, and values with which teachers approach their students, and the conditions in schools to support the high-level learning of all students. (Nieto, 1999, p. 173).*

Jim MacGregor: Systemic Change Agent. Jim is a Florida High School counselor. His mantra is, "Not on my watch." This systemic change agent must surely be the father of data-driven school counselors. For over two decades he has been using data to advantage students and to drive the direction of his work. As Jim says, "Without data, I don't know where I am, I don't know where I am going, and I don't know if I ever got there." He is one determined school counselor that refuses to accept status quo as good enough for the students under his charge. His "not on my watch" mentality means that he will do what ever it takes to see that all his students receive solid career and academic advising in order to close the information gap. Jim developed a computer based four year plan that interfaced with students' identified career clusters. Using the career cluster as a guide, Jim's program informed students as to which mathematics and sciences they would need to match their career plans. Jim's efforts to help students see that they would have brighter futures if they would stretch and strive academically was made considerably easier when he tied course taking to a student's career goals. Their four year career plan became a living document, changing as the student's career cluster changed. Over the course of six years, Jim's advocacy resulted in a 40 percent increase in African-American students choosing higher level mathematics and science courses.

From 2004 to 2006, Jim considerably increased the number of students enrolled in Advanced Placement (AP) classes and increased the number of AP tests taken by 377 percent. Jim acts purposefully to connect students to their future opportunities, impact the instructional program and change the status quo of who will reach graduation with a wide range of paths from which to choose (Stone and Dahir, 2004).

# Supporting the Instructional Program

Good teaching matters! William Sanders and June Rivers (1996) studied thousand of student records in Tennessee. These researchers found that there was a difference of 50 percentile points as a result of teacher sequence after only three years. By looking at the individual student achievement histories of approximately 3 million records for Tennessee's entire grade 2-6 student population, these researchers had the unique opportunity to investigate the cumulative effects of teachers on student academic achievement over grade levels.

*The single most dominant factor affecting student academic gain is teacher effect. Groups of students with comparable abilities and initial achievement levels may have vastly different academic outcomes as a result of the sequence of teachers to which they are assigned. These analyses also suggest that the teacher effects are both additive and cumulative with little evidence of compensatory effects of more effective teachers in later grades. The residual effects of both very effective and ineffective teachers were measurable two years later, regardless of the effectiveness of teachers in later grades (Sanders and Rivers, 1996, p. 6).*

Future school counselors will consider it an imperative to impact the instructional program. The tough job of teaching will require that all educators under the schoolhouse roof, to include school counselors, support the instructional program and teachers' efforts. Understanding the school's curriculum offerings, the Special Education program, and all support systems in place for struggling students will become common activities in school.

# Conclusion

In the last decade the school counseling profession has reinvented itself. Since the late 1990's, school counselors have progressed from a traditional responsive service driven approach to a proactive and programmatic system that is inextricably integrated with the mission of schools. The ASCA National Standards (ASCA, 1997), the Transforming School Counseling Initiative (Education Trust, 1997), and the ASCA National Model (ASCA, 2005) have directed school counselors to respect the past, embrace the present, but forge a path to the future (Dahir, in press). The challenges facing students and 21st century schools have influenced the paradigms and practices that forward the profession and placed a renewed emphasis on student achievement and school counselor accountability. The future will be defined by intentional efforts and data-driven practice. Twenty-first century school counselors are in a powerful and pivotal position to effectively demonstrate how the complement of academic rigor and affective development is the formula to student success (Stone & Dahir, 2006). These new vision school counselors will embrace the critical part they play on the educational team and rise to the challenge to share in the responsibility to prepare students to meet the expectations of higher academic standards and become productive and contributing members of society. Counselor educators, practitioners, and future school counselor degree candidates have established a way of work as leaders, collaborators, advocates, and systemic change agents in concert with the dynamics of the educational landscape, the globalization of society and economics, and the plethora of diverse student needs (Stone & Dahir, 2006).

School counselors and counselor educators, by their beliefs and behaviors, can propel the profession to its rightful position as the fifth discipline. The future lies in the profession's ability to change with the times and come to consensus to promote paradigms and practices that will forward the profession. Rigor and relevance hold fast for school counselors as they do for faculty and administrators. School counselors must provide the leadership in the school of today and the future to ensure that human relationships are nurtured, diversity is valued, and every student receives equitable and quality education. This generation of school counselors is social justice advocates who ensure that academic, career, and interpersonal success is woven into the fabric of education for every student. Constituents and stakeholders need to see results; measures of success move well beyond one student at a time.

We have looked into the crystal ball and gazed on the faces of the future. We have struggled with the fears of the known and the unknown, and explored alternative methods of accessing students. We have embraced the preeminence of social justice to shape the path to the future, and accepted and understand that accountability is critical if we are to survive and thrive as a profession in the 21st century.

Where lies the future of school counseling? We invite you to shape it with us.

# References

American School Counselor Association. (2005). *The ASCA national model: A framework for school counseling programs*. Alexandria, VA: Author.

American School Counselor Association. (2004). *Ethical standards for school counselors*. Alexandria, VA: Author.

Baker, S.B. (2000). *School counseling for the 21st century* (3rd. ed.). Upper Saddle River, NJ: Merrill Prentice Hall.

The College Board. (1999). *College board's national task force on minority achievement*. College Entrance Examination Board.

Dahir, C. (Ed.). (2001*). Planning for life: A resource guide for counselors*. American School Counselor Association & the U.S. Army Recruiting Command. Fort Knox:, KY: American School Counselor Association & the U.S. Army Recruiting Command.

Dahir, C. (in press). School counseling for the 21st century: Where lies the future. *Journal of Counseling and Development*.

Education Trust. (2001). Achievement in America. Retreived January 11, 2005 from http://www2.edtrust.org/edtrust/

Education Trust. (1997, November). *Transforming school counseling: DeWitt Wallace-Reader's Digest grant* [Request for grant proposal]. Washington, DC: Author.

Education Trust. (n.d.) *Transforming school counseling initiative*. Retrieved January 25, 2005, from http://www2.edtrust.org/EdTrust/Transforming+School+Counseling/Counseling+tsci.htm

Gysbers, N.C., & Henderson, P. (2006). *Developing and managing your school guidance program* (4th ed.). Alexandria, VA: American Counseling Association.

Hart, P.J., & Jacobi, M. (1992). *From gatekeeper to advocate: Transforming the role of the school counselor*. New York: College Entrance Examination Board.

Inbody, N.M. (1984). Futurism: Philosophy and procedures adapted to counseling. *The School Counselor, 31*, 215-222.

Maples, M.F. (1984). ASCA and AACD: Distinguished past, challenging present, hopeful future. *The School Counselor, 31*(4), 393-398.

Myrick, R.D. (2003). Accountability: Counselor count. *Professional School Counseling, 6*(3), 174-179.

Nieto, S. (1999). The light in their eyes: Creating multicultural learning communities. New York: Teachers College Press.

Sanders, W. L., & Rivers, J. C. (1996). *Cumulative and residual effects of teachers on future student academic achievement*. Knoxville, TN: University of Tennessee Value-Added Research and Assessment Center. Retrieved on June 6, 2006 from http://www.mccsc.edu/~curriculum/cumulative%20and%20residual%20effects%20of%20teachers.pdf.

Schmidt, J. (2003). *Counseling in schools: Essential services and comprehensive programs* (4th ed.). Boston: Allyn and Bacon.: Boston, MA.

Stone, C. (1996). Unpublished successful grant application for the Transforming School Counseling DeWitt-Wallace Grant.

Stone, C., & Dahir, C. (2004). *School counselor accountability: A measure of student success*. Upper Saddle Riber, NJ: Pearson Education.

Stone, C., & Dahir, C. (2006). *The transformed school counselor*. Boston and New York: Houghton Mifflin.

Stone, C. (2005). *School counseling principles: Legal and ethical issues*. Alexandria, VA.: American School Counselor Association.

Theobald, R. (1973). *Futures conditional*. Indianapolis: Bobbs-Merrill.

U.S. Census Bureau. (2003). *Population projections*. Washington, DC: U.S. Department of Education.

U.S. Department of Education. (2001). *The no child left behind act*. Washington, DC: Author.

U.S. Department of Labor. (2004). Occupational Outlook Quarterly. Spring 2004. Washington, DC: Author.

Whiston, S. C., & Sexton, T. L. (1998). A review of school counseling outcome research: Implications for practice. *Journal of Counseling and Development, 4*(76), 412-426.

# Some Concluding Thoughts

In these 35 chapters we and the contributing writers have described a comprehensive developmental K-12 school counseling program and have raised some important problems, concerns and issues that school counselors of today and the future will most surely encounter. Additionally, we've provided the school counselor with effective strategies to assist in planning and managing a K-12 developmental school counseling program.

If there is one fundamental theme that serves to tie together the wide array of issues, approaches, and challenges discussed in this book, it is that a school counseling program should serve *all* students in the school as well as *all* teachers, *all* administrators, and *all* parents; the school's entire public. With this theme in mind, in summary, we've written concerning the developmental school counselor's: 1) *goals and objectives* (What are you trying to accomplish? Are your goals in written form and shared with others?) 2) *role and function* (what are you doing to accomplish your goals? Have you "sold" your principal on developmental counseling? Is your role and function statement written and approved by the administration? How are you managing your time? Have you established priorities? Is your "calendar" available to everyone?) 3) *procedures, activities, and tasks needed to carry out your role* (How have you organized your time? Are you conducting individual and small group counseling? Large group guidance? Consulting? Coordinating appropriate programs? Do you have a peer program?) 4) *Are you being accountable?* (Are you "proving" your worth or just "doing good?" How are students different as a result of your program and intervention? With whom have you shared these results?) and, 5) *Are you effectively managing your personal and professional growth?* (What contributions are you making to the profession? Do you know, understand and adhere to ASCA's Ethical Standards? Do you stay abreast and updated through continuing education, reading, attending conventions, etc.?)

In a nutshell, these are the important aspects covered in this book. However, whether you use the strategies and advance and achieve the goals and objectives put forth in this book, will be up to you. That is, it does not depend on textbook writers, but on you; school counselors of the present and of the future.

We close this volume with the conviction that those school counselors and others committed to the "developmental" approach to school counseling will welcome the challenges raised, the approaches discussed, and the strategies provided within this book. We appreciate your interest in the book and wish you well!

*Mary Ann Clark and Joe Wittmer*

# Index

## A